D0077525

# LEGAL ANALYSIS AND WRITING

## An Active-Learning Approach

*Editorial Advisors*

**Rachel E. Barkow**
*Segal Family Professor of Regulatory Law and Policy*
*Faculty Director, Center on the Administration of Criminal Law*
*New York University School of Law*

**Erwin Chemerinsky**
*Dean and Jesse H. Choper Distinguished Professor of Law*
*University of California, Berkeley School of Law*

**Richard A. Epstein**
*Laurence A. Tisch Professor of Law*
*New York University School of Law*
*Peter and Kirsten Bedford Senior Fellow*
*The Hoover Institution*
*Senior Lecturer in Law*
*The University of Chicago*

**Ronald J. Gilson**
*Charles J. Meyers Professor of Law and Business*
*Stanford University*
*Marc and Eva Stern Professor of Law and Business*
*Columbia Law School*

**James E. Krier**
*Earl Warren DeLano Professor of Law Emeritus*
*The University of Michigan Law School*

**Tracey L. Meares**
*Walton Hale Hamilton Professor of Law*
*Director, The Justice Collaboratory*
*Yale Law School*

**Richard K. Neumann, Jr.**
*Alexander Bickel Professor of Law*
*Maurice A. Deane School of Law at Hofstra University*

**Robert H. Sitkoff**
*John L. Gray Professor of Law*
*Harvard Law School*

**David Alan Sklansky**
*Stanley Morrison Professor of Law*
*Faculty Co-Director, Stanford Criminal Justice Center*
*Stanford Law School*

ASPEN COURSEBOOK SERIES

# LEGAL ANALYSIS AND WRITING

## An Active-Learning Approach

**Danielle M. Shelton**
*Professor of Law*
*Drake University Law School*

**Karen L. Wallace**
*Professor of Law Librarianship*
*Drake University Law School*

**Melissa H. Weresh**
*Dwight D. Opperman Distinguished Professor of Law*
*Drake University Law School*

Copyright © 2021 CCH Incorporated. All Rights Reserved.

Published by Wolters Kluwer in New York.

Wolters Kluwer Legal & Regulatory U.S. serves customers worldwide with CCH, Aspen Publishers, and Kluwer Law International products. (www.WKLegaledu.com)

No part of this publication may be reproduced or transmitted in any form or by any means, electronic or mechanical, including photocopy, recording, or utilized by any information storage or retrieval system, without written permission from the publisher. For information about permissions or to request permissions online, visit us at www.WKLegaledu. com, or a written request may be faxed to our permissions department at 212-771-0803.

Cover image: LightField Studio/Shutterstock

To contact Customer Service, e-mail customer.service@wolterskluwer. com, call 1-800-234-1660, fax 1-800-901-9075, or mail correspondence to:

Wolters Kluwer
Attn: Order Department
PO Box 990
Frederick, MD 21705


Printed in the United States of America.

1 2 3 4 5 6 7 8 9 0

ISBN 978-1-5438-1306-7

Library of Congress Cataloging-in-Publication Data

Names: Shelton, Danielle M., 1970- author. | Wallace, Karen L., author. |
    Weresh, Melissa H., author.
Title: Legal analysis and writing : an active-learning approach / Danielle
    M. Shelton, Karen L. Wallace, Melissa H. Weresh.
Description: New York : Wolters Kluwer, 2020. | Includes bibliographi-
    cal references and index. | Summary: "Legal writing coursebook for
    strategic legal analysis for first semester law school"-- Provided by
    publisher.
Identifiers: LCCN 2020017598 | ISBN 9781543813067 (paperback) |
    ISBN 9781543823394 (ebook)
Subjects: LCSH: Legal composition. | Law--United States--Interpretation
    and construction.
Classification: LCC KF250 .S525 2020 | DDC 808.06/634--dc23
LC record available at https://lccn.loc.gov/2020017598

SUSTAINABLE FORESTRY INITIATIVE — Certified Sourcing
www.sfiprogram.org
SFI-01051

## About Wolters Kluwer Legal & Regulatory U.S.

Wolters Kluwer Legal & Regulatory U.S. delivers expert content and solutions in the areas of law, corporate compliance, health compliance, reimbursement, and legal education. Its practical solutions help customers successfully navigate the demands of a changing environment to drive their daily activities, enhance decision quality and inspire confident outcomes.

Serving customers worldwide, its legal and regulatory portfolio includes products under the Aspen Publishers, CCH Incorporated, Kluwer Law International, ftwilliam.com and MediRegs names. They are regarded as exceptional and trusted resources for general legal and practice-specific knowledge, compliance and risk management, dynamic workflow solutions, and expert commentary.

*To my parents, Steve and Diane Shelton,*
*for everything and then some.*
—DMS

*With gratitude to those who listened along*
*the way. Barb, Cathy, Dave, Marc,*
*Rebecca, Tammy, Xander, and Zach,*
*I'm looking at you.*
—KLW

*To MASH, for listening, and to Duncan,*
*for walking me home.*
—MHW

# Summary of Contents

*Contents*                                                    xiii
*Preface*                                                     xxiii
*Acknowledgments*                                             xxv

## ▦ MODULE I

## THE BIG PICTURE                                              1

1. Introduction to Legal Analysis and Communication          3
2. Reading, Thinking, and Writing Like a Lawyer              15
3. Predictive Legal Analysis                                 47
4. The Structure of a Predictive Legal Memorandum            55
5. The Process of Drafting a Predictive Legal Memorandum     73

## ▧ MODULE II

## FOUNDATIONS OF LEGAL ANALYSIS                               81

### PART I
### INTRODUCTION TO LEGAL RULES                                83

6. Overview of Legal Rules                                   85
7. Working with Rules                                        95
8. Working with Cases to Determine the Rule of Law           107

### PART II
### TYPES OF LEGAL REASONING                                   133

9. Overview of Types of Legal Reasoning                      135
10. Rule-Based Reasoning                                     141
11. Analogical Reasoning                                     147
12. Policy-Based Reasoning                                   155

## ▨ MODULE III

## FOUNDATIONS OF LEGAL COMMUNICATION:
## Drafting a Legal Discussion with a Single Authority        159

### PART I
### PRE-DRAFTING ANALYSIS USING A SINGLE
### AUTHORITY                                                  161

13. The Process of Pre-Drafting Analysis                     163
14. Large-Scale Organization of the Discussion               175

PART II
**DRAFTING THE DISCUSSION USING A SINGLE AUTHORITY**                                                183

15. From Pre-Drafting to Drafting: Outlining the
    Components of a Single Authority Legal Discussion       185
16. Drafting the Roadmaps                                   195
17. Drafting the Rule Explanation                           205
18. Drafting the Rule Application                           217

**MODULE IV**

**THE NEXT LEVEL:**
**Legal Analysis and Drafting a Legal Discussion**
**Using Multiple Authorities**                              235

PART I
**LEGAL ANALYSIS AND PRE-DRAFTING ANALYSIS USING MULTIPLE AUTHORITIES**                           237

19. Making the Transition: The Components
    of a Multiple Authorities Legal Discussion              239
20. Integrating Multiple Authorities into the Rule:
    Synthesized Rules of Law                                251
21. Sorting and Selecting Authorities                       265
22. The Process of Pre-Drafting with Multiple Authorities   283

PART II
**DRAFTING THE DISCUSSION USING MULTIPLE AUTHORITIES**                                    295

23. Organizing and Outlining a Discussion
    with Multiple Authorities                               297
24. Drafting the Roadmaps with Multiple Authorities         313
25. Drafting the Rule Explanation with Multiple Authorities 319
26. Drafting the Rule Application with Multiple Authorities  331

**MODULE V**

**COMPLETING THE LEGAL MEMORANDUM:**
**Additional Components, Finishing Touches,**
**and Variations**                                          345

27. Additional Memo Considerations: Question Presented,
    Short Answer, Statement of Facts, Internal Discussion
    Headings, and Conclusion                                347
28. Revising, Editing, and Proofreading Your Legal
    Memorandum                                              359
29. Writing Using a Lawyer's Language and Style             371
30. Email Communication                                     381

31. Drafting Talking Points for Your Legal Memorandum          393
32. From Predictive to Persuasive Writing          397

APPENDIX A
**Sample Memos Using Single Case Authority**          403

APPENDIX B
**Sample Memos Using Multiple Case Authorities**          415

APPENDIX C
**Checklists for Memo Writing**          431

APPENDIX D
**Answers to Check In Exercises**          441

APPENDIX E
***U.S. v. Purcell* (modified)**          473

APPENDIX F
**Sources of Law**          483

APPENDIX G
**Glossary of Terms and Concepts**          485

*Index*          489

# Contents

*Preface*                                                            xxiii
*Acknowledgments*                                                     xxv

## ▦ MODULE I

## THE BIG PICTURE                                                      1

CHAPTER 1

### Introduction to Legal Analysis and Communication                   3

Welcome to law school!                                                  3
How we organized this book for you                                      5
Terminology used throughout the book                                    8

CHAPTER 2

### Reading, Thinking, and Writing Like a Lawyer                       15

  I.  How a Lawyer Reads                           16
    A.  Reading Full Cases Versus Case Excerpts    16
    B.  Editorial Enhancements in Full Cases        17
  II.  How a Lawyer Thinks                          40
  III.  Putting It Together: A Lawyer Begins to Write    44

CHAPTER 3

### Predictive Legal Analysis                                         47

  I.  Understanding Predictive Legal Analysis       47
  II.  How Analogical Reasoning Helps Lawyers
      Use Prior Cases to Make Legal Predictions    48
  III.  Using Guiding Factors to Reason by Analogy  49
  IV.  Using Predictive Analysis to Solve Client Problems    51
  V.  Inductive and Deductive Analysis              53

CHAPTER 4

### The Structure of a Predictive Legal Memorandum                    55

  I.  Sample Predictive Memo                        55
  II.  Key Features of a Predictive Memo            62
  III.  Organization of a Memo                      65

CHAPTER 5

### The Process of Drafting a Predictive
### Legal Memorandum                                                   73

  I.  Steps for Writing a Predictive Memo          73
  II.  The Importance of Pre-Drafting               76

⬡ MODULE II

## FOUNDATIONS OF LEGAL ANALYSIS          81

PART I
## INTRODUCTION TO LEGAL RULES          83

CHAPTER 6
### Overview of Legal Rules          85
I. What Are the Sources of Law?          86
II. Which Sources of Law Are Binding?          87
III. The Importance of Understanding the Sources of
Law and Which Are Binding          89
IV. The Role of Cases in Discerning the Rule of Law          89
V. Discerning Emergent Legal Rules from Multiple Cases          93

CHAPTER 7
### Working with Rules          95
I. The Three Key Features of Legal Rules          95
A. What Are the Rule's Conditions? Elements
Versus Factors          95
B. How Do the Rule's Conditions Relate to One Another?          98
C. What Is the Result of the Rule?          100
II. Outlining the Rule          100
A. Variation in Outlining Rules: Some Rules Are
Trickier Than Others          102
B. The Purpose of Outlining the Legal Rule          103
III. Putting It All Together: How Lawyers Approach Rules          104
IV. Revisiting Elements Versus Factors          105

CHAPTER 8
### Working with Cases to Determine the Rule of Law          107
I. In General: How Lawyers Use Cases to
Determine the Rule of Law          107
II. Specific Ways that Courts Interpret Rules          110
A. Interpreting the Existing Legal Rule Through
Standards and Definitions          110
B. Interpreting the Existing Legal Rule with Guiding Factors          113
1. What Are Guiding Factors?          113
2. Implicit Versus Explicit Guiding Factors          115
3. Why Are Guiding Factors Important?          121
4. Discretion in Labeling Implicit Guiding Factors          121
C. Interpreting the Existing Legal Rule by Showing
How the Conditions of the Rule Fit Together          122
III. Putting It All Together: Examining How a Court
Processes the Rule for a Given Condition          124
A. Using a Case to Find Law-Centered Interpretations
and Discern a Fact-Based Holding          124

B.  Using the Information Obtained from a Case to Outline
    the Emergent Rule                                    128
IV. Expert Tips for Working with Guiding Factors         129
    A.  Testing Your Guiding Factors                     130
    B.  Labeling Your Guiding Factors                    130

PART II
**TYPES OF LEGAL REASONING**                             **133**

CHAPTER 9
**Overview of Types of Legal Reasoning**                 **135**
  I.  Rule-Based Reasoning                               135
 II.  Analogical Reasoning                               136
III.  Policy-Based Reasoning                             138

CHAPTER 10
**Rule-Based Reasoning**                                 **141**
  I.  Overview of Rule-Based Reasoning                   141
 II.  Key Features of Rule-Based Reasoning               143

CHAPTER 11
**Analogical Reasoning**                                 **147**
  I.  Making Comparisons in Analogical Reasoning         147
 II.  Characteristics of Effective Analogical Arguments  151
III.  Combining Different Types of Reasoning             152

CHAPTER 12
**Policy-Based Reasoning**                               **155**
  I.  Introduction to Policy-Based Reasoning             155
 II.  How Do Lawyers Develop Arguments That Use
      Policy-Based Reasoning?                            157
III.  Why Is Policy-Based Reasoning Less Powerful Than
      Rule-Based Reasoning and Analogical Reasoning?     158

MODULE III

**FOUNDATIONS OF LEGAL COMMUNICATION:**
**Drafting a Legal Discussion with a Single Authority**  159

PART I
**PRE-DRAFTING ANALYSIS USING A SINGLE**
**AUTHORITY**                                            161

CHAPTER 13
**The Process of Pre-Drafting Analysis**                 **163**
  I.  Gathering Content Before Drafting                  163
      A.  Memo Content as It Appears in the Drafted Discussion  164
      B.  Obtaining the Discussion Section Ingredients   166
 II.  Worksheet Approach to Gathering Content            167

CHAPTER 14
**Large-Scale Organization of the Discussion**                     175
   I.  Discussion Organization                             175
  II.  The Global Roadmap Framework                        178

PART II
**DRAFTING THE DISCUSSION USING A SINGLE
AUTHORITY**                                                        183

CHAPTER 15
**From Pre-Drafting to Drafting: Outlining
the Components of a Single Authority Legal Discussion**            185
   I.  Discussion Paragraph Templates                      185
  II.  Moving from Templates to Annotated Outline of the Memo  188
 III.  Putting It Together: Annotated Discussion            191

CHAPTER 16
**Drafting the Roadmaps**                                          195
   I.  Global Roadmaps                                     195
  II.  Issue Roadmaps                                      199

CHAPTER 17
**Drafting the Rule Explanation**                                  205
   I.  Rule Explanation in Context: The Bridge Between
      the Issue Roadmap and the Rule Application
      Section for an Issue                             205
  II.  The Template with Ingredients for a Rule
      Explanation Paragraph                            208
     A.  Starting the Rule Explanation Paragraph:
         The Framing Sentence                         208
     B.  The Other Ingredients of a Rule Explanation Paragraph  210
 III.  Variations in Rule Explanation: Multiple Rule
      Explanation Paragraphs Using the Same Authority  212

CHAPTER 18
**Drafting the Rule Application**                                  217
   I.  Content of the Arguments                            218
     A.  What Arguments Are Included in Your Rule Application?  218
     B.  How Are Arguments Conveyed? The Basic Formula
        for a Rule Application Paragraph               219
     C.  Weaving Facts with the Rule                     220
     D.  How Many Rule Application Paragraphs?            221
  II.  Organizing the Arguments                            221
 III.  Presenting the Arguments: Stylistic Options          227
 IV.  Drafting Effective Analogical Arguments              228
  V.  The Relationship Between Rule Explanation and Rule
      Application: Impact on Organization              232
 VI.  The Role of Rule-Based Arguments in Your Rule
      Application: Using Rule-Based Arguments in
      Conjunction with Analogical Arguments            233

⌗ MODULE IV

## THE NEXT LEVEL:
### Legal Analysis and Drafting a Legal Discussion Using Multiple Authorities                                   235

PART I
## LEGAL ANALYSIS AND PRE-DRAFTING ANALYSIS USING MULTIPLE AUTHORITIES             237

CHAPTER 19
### Making the Transition: The Components of a Multiple Authorities Legal Discussion          239
  I. What Is the Same?                                           239
 II. What Is Different?                                          241

CHAPTER 20
### Integrating Multiple Authorities into the Rule: Synthesized Rules of Law                              251
  I. What Is a Synthesized Rule of Law?                          251
 II. The Process of Synthesis: How Lawyers Use
     Cases to Synthesize the Legal Rule                          252
     A. The Basics of Rule Synthesis                             252
     B. Different Types of Synthesis: Ways in Which an
        Additional Authority May Process the Existing Rule       255
        1. A Case Can Simply Confirm the Existing Rule
           and Add Little or No New Information                  255
        2. A Case May Modify the Existing Rule, Most
           Often by Changing or Refining the Guiding Factors     256
     C. Synthesis of Guiding Factors in a Non-Legal Context      256
     D. Synthesis of Guiding Factors in the Legal Context        258
     E. Synthesis When Cases Seem Inconsistent                   262

CHAPTER 21
### Sorting and Selecting Authorities                            265
  I. For What Purposes Do Lawyers Select Cases?                  265
     A. Selecting Cases That Provide the Rule of Law             266
        1. Selecting Cases to Discern the Global Rule of Law     267
        2. Selecting Cases to Discern the Rule of Law
           for a Condition                                       269
     B. Selecting Factually Similar Cases                        271
        1. How Do Lawyers Determine Which Cases
           Are Factually Similar?                                272
        2. Selecting at Least One "Factually Similar"
           Case for Each Position                                275
        3. Plugging Gaps When Selecting Factually Similar Cases  276
        4. Takeaways for Selecting Factually Similar Cases       277

II.  Other General Considerations When Selecting Cases      278
     A.  The Date of the Authority                          278
     B.  The Level of Court of the Authority                278
     C.  The Thoroughness of the Authority's Decision
         and Reasoning                                      279
III. Looking Ahead                                          281

CHAPTER 22
**The Process of Pre-Drafting with Multiple Authorities**   283
  I.  How Is Pre-Drafting Generally Different with
      Multiple Authorities?                                 283
 II.  Reconsidering the Foundational Checklist for Pre-Drafting   285
III.  Worksheet Approach to Gathering Content with
      Multiple Authorities                                  286

PART II
**DRAFTING THE DISCUSSION USING MULTIPLE
AUTHORITIES**                                               295

CHAPTER 23
**Organizing and Outlining a Discussion with Multiple
Authorities**                                               297
  I.  In General: How Multiple Authorities Affect
      the Outline of Your Discussion                        297
 II.  The Large-Scale Organization of a Discussion
      Using Multiple Authorities                            298
      A.  Review: Large-Scale Organization with a Single Authority   298
      B.  Large-Scale Organization with Multiple Authorities   300
III.  Small-Scale Organization: Focusing on
      the Organization of Each Issue Segment of Your Discussion   301
      A.  Issue Roadmap Changes                             301
      B.  Rule Explanation Changes                          305
          1.  Organizing Your Rule Explanation Section
              with Multiple Authorities: Two Approaches     305
          2.  Deciding Which Approach to Use                307
      C.  Rule Application Changes                          308
          1.  Changes to the Organization of the Rule
              Application Section                           308
          2.  Changes to the Content of the Rule
              Application Section                           309
IV.  Putting It Together: A Sample Outline for a
     Discussion with Multiple Authorities                   310
 V.  Using Visual Maps to Assist with Organization
     of Your Discussion                                     312

CHAPTER 24
**Drafting the Roadmaps with Multiple Authorities**         313
  I.  In General: What's the Same and What's Different in
      Roadmap Paragraphs for Memos with Multiple Authorities?   313

II.  Global Roadmap Integrating Multiple Authorities          314
III. Issue Roadmap with Multiple Authorities          316

CHAPTER 25
**Drafting the Rule Explanation with Multiple Authorities**  319
  I.  In General: What's the Same and What's Different in
      Rule Explanation Paragraphs for Memos with
      Multiple Authorities?          319
 II.  Drafting a Rule Explanation Using Multiple Authorities  320
      A.  The Importance of Framing Sentences with
          Multiple Authorities          321
      B.  Using Transitions Between Rule Explanation Paragraphs  322
      C.  Using Signals to Include Additional Supporting
          Cases in the Rule Explanation Section          323
III.  Challenges in Drafting Rule Explanation Sections
      Using Multiple Authorities          324
      A.  Avoiding the Parade of Cases          325
      B.  Unique Challenges When Using the Guiding
          Factors Approach          326
      C.  Unique Challenges When Using the Organizing
          by the Cases Approach          328
IV.   Putting It Together: A Checklist for Your Rule
      Explanation Section When Using Multiple Authorities  329

CHAPTER 26
**Drafting the Rule Application with Multiple Authorities**  331
  I.  In General: What's the Same and What's Different
      in Rule Application Paragraphs for Memos with
      Multiple Authorities?          331
 II.  Drafting a Rule Application Section Using Multiple
      Authorities          332
      A.  Changes in the Organization and Overall Content
          of the Rule Application Section          332
      B.  Components of a Rule Application Section
          Using Multiple Authorities          334
          1.  Breaking It Down: Why Are These Arguments Effective?  336
          2.  Organizing Arguments Under Party/Position Approach  338
      C.  Other Considerations When Drafting Rule Application
          Paragraphs          341
          1.  Use Transitions Between Your Rule Application
              Paragraphs          341
          2.  Provide the Foundation for Your Rule Application
              Section with an Effective Rule Explanation Section  341
          3.  Explain the Relevance of the Analogy or Distinction  342
          4.  Consider Starting with a Rule-Based Argument
              Before Making Analogical Arguments          342

## ✖ MODULE V

## COMPLETING THE LEGAL MEMORANDUM:
## Additional Components, Finishing Touches, and
## Variations                                                    345

### CHAPTER 27
### Additional Memo Considerations: Question Presented, Short Answer, Statement of Facts, Internal Discussion Headings, and Conclusion          347

I. Memo Heading                                                  348
II. Substantive Memo Sections Beyond the Discussion              348
   A. Question Presented                          348
   B. Short Answer                                350
   C. Statement of Facts                          351
   D. Headings                                    354
   E. Conclusion                                  356

### CHAPTER 28
### Revising, Editing, and Proofreading Your Legal Memorandum          359

I. Revising Your Legal Memorandum                                360
   A. Revision Checklist Questions                360
   B. Techniques for Revising                     362
II. Editing Your Memo                                            363
   A. Editing Checklist Questions                 363
   B. Editing Techniques                          366
III. Proofreading Your Memo                                      368

### CHAPTER 29
### Writing Using a Lawyer's Language and Style          371

I. Introduction to the Language of the Law                       371
II. Introduction to Legal Writing Style                          372
III. Quoting and Paraphrasing in Legal Writing                   374
   A. When Must You Use Quotation Marks?          375
   B. When Is Paraphrasing Better than Quoting?   375
IV. Tips for Effective Writing in General                        377

### CHAPTER 30
### Email Communication          381

I. Unique Challenges of Professional Email Communication         381
   A. Challenges of Email as a Medium             381
   B. Strategies to Address These Challenges      382
      1. Pay Attention to Tone     382
      2. Craft a Helpful Subject Line          383
      3. Include a Signature Line and Legal Disclaimer          384
      4. Consider Content and Organization          384

     5. Ensure Readability 385
     6. Review Before Hitting "Send" 385
  II. Drafting Emails That Convey Legal Analysis 385
  III. Additional Email Tips 389
    A. Professionalism 389
    B. Style 389
    C. Recipients 390
    D. Automated Features 390
    E. Other Forms of Communication 391

CHAPTER 31
**Drafting Talking Points for Your Legal Memorandum** 393
  I. Guidelines for Developing Talking Points 393
  II. Talking Points in Action: Talking Points for the Warrantless
    Bomb Search Fourth Amendment Memorandum 395

CHAPTER 32
**From Predictive to Persuasive Writing** 397
  I. What Is the Same? 398
  II. What Is Different? 398

APPENDIX A
**Sample Memos Using Single Case Authority** 403

APPENDIX B
**Sample Memos Using Multiple Case Authorities** 415

APPENDIX C
**Checklists for Memo Writing** 431

APPENDIX D
**Answers to Check In Exercises** 441

APPENDIX E
**U.S. v. Purcell (modified)** 473

APPENDIX F
**Sources of Law** 483

APPENDIX G
**Glossary of Terms and Concepts** 485

*Index* 489

# Preface

This textbook introduces you to the rigors of legal analysis and professional legal writing. Because legal writing requires an in-depth understanding of legal analysis, you will spend considerable time learning how lawyers analyze and apply legal rules before learning how to draft your legal analysis. Just as a scientist could not write about the thermodynamic qualities of nickel without first learning about and analyzing that subject, a lawyer cannot write about a particular legal question until she has learned about the relevant law and its application.

Several things are noteworthy about this book. First, this book provides all the content you need to learn legal writing. It need not be supplemented by classroom lecture. This allows time in class to be spent practicing and refining knowledge and skills, rather than learning basic concepts. Second, and related to that, we have filled this book with explanations and examples. Both play an important role in helping you understand the concepts. Theory alone is rarely sufficient to provide a practical understanding of concepts. On the other hand, examples alone fail to communicate underlying principles. Knowing this, we have included both. Finally, we have included ample opportunities to test your understanding of the material and to practice the skills. These opportunities include Study Guide Questions and Check In exercises.

Legal analysis and writing are no doubt challenging. You are entering a profession in which high standards exist both for writing and for thinking critically. A student who engages with this book will be rewarded with not only a solid understanding of legal writing but also a solid understanding of how lawyers think. So, consider this challenge an opportunity. We look forward to your success.

# Acknowledgments

The authors thank research assistant Ashle Bray for her excellent work on this textbook. She created fabulous illustrations, helped us view the textbook through a student's eyes, and was an all-around utility player. We cannot thank her enough for her many contributions to this project.

Likewise, we thank administrative assistant Debbie Booth, who cheerfully sought images, turned scrawls into diagrams, and provided other administrative support throughout this project. We also are indebted to Dean Jerry Anderson and Associate Dean Andrew Jurs for their support of this project.

Finally, we thank all of you—our readers—for engaging with this textbook. We have written it with you in mind.

# LEGAL ANALYSIS AND WRITING

## An Active-Learning Approach

# The Big Picture

This module introduces (1) a type of legal analysis known as predictive, or objective, analysis, and (2) the most common legal document that memorializes that analysis: the predictive, inter-office memorandum. In contrast to persuasive writing, predictive writing attempts to provide an unbiased explanation of the most likely application of the law to a particular situation, noting and evaluating arguments on all sides of the issue, rather than promoting a preferred outcome.

### CHAPTER 1

# Introduction to Legal Analysis and Communication

This chapter provides a brief overview of predictive legal analysis and the skills you will be learning in this course. We will describe the organization of the book and explain how, in conjunction with the rest of your course, the book is intended to facilitate your learning. Finally, we will define key concepts related to predictive legal analysis.

## Study Guide Questions for Chapter 1

1. How is learning legal analysis and communication like riding a bicycle?
2. What are some foundational concepts that will be important to legal analysis and communication? Which concepts seem the clearest at this point? Which concepts are unclear? What questions do you have about unclear concepts that might help you clarify them?
3. What is the process of looping, and how will it facilitate your understanding of the material addressed in this text?
4. What is the difference between an "element" and a "factor?"
5. What is an initial ethical consideration you should be aware of when deciding whether to represent a potential client?

## Welcome to law school!

During the next several years you will be learning about many different areas of law. Much of that law will remain unchanged as you embark on your life as a practicing attorney, while some of it may change dramatically, particularly in areas like environmental law or cyber law. Fortunately, law school will prepare you for both situations. You will learn current legal rules and principles. You will also learn how to find, analyze, and apply the underlying legal authorities, enabling you to monitor, and perhaps even help shape, developing areas of law. What you learn in this course will apply to all that you do in law school and beyond. Legal analysis and communication are skills you will use in your legal writing course, on your casebook course exams, on the bar examination, and in your representation of clients.

Lawyers do not study the law in a vacuum. Instead, lawyers read the law with a purpose in mind—to solve client problems. When we read statutes and cases, we keep our clients' facts in mind. Consequently, our understanding of a client's problem will inform how we read and use the law. So, in this course, we will address legal analysis and communication in a client-focused context. Rather than writing a legal analysis of a particular area of law, like products liability, we will write a memo *applying* the law of products liability to a client problem, perhaps one involving a defective lawnmower. We will examine products liability laws that apply to the client's problem so we can make arguments (and, ultimately, a prediction) about the client's ability to recover for damages associated with the defective lawnmower.

In this course you will learn how to memorialize that predictive analysis in what is commonly referred to as a predictive, or objective, memorandum. We call this predictive, because it is the lawyer's job to initially analyze the client's situation from a neutral perspective, considering the arguments that each party might make and the efficacy of those arguments. It is only by engaging in that predictive analysis that the lawyer can advise the client, with candor, as to the viability of the client's legal situation.

In order to identify and analyze possible legal issues, you will master concepts like stare decisis, precedent, and hierarchy of authority. You will also develop skills such as analogical and predictive reasoning, rule processing and synthesis, and communication of analysis. That's a lot to learn in a single semester, but you've mastered complex skills in the past. The enthusiasm, perseverance, and patience that helped you obtain new skills before will also help you in this course. When you acquired those non-legal skills, you probably had someone who cheered you on and gave you practical tips along the way. We'll be doing that in this book as you learn new legal skills. You'll see boxes alongside the text throughout this book that, collectively, we call **bicycle boxes**.

 **GEARING UP: Like Riding a Bike**

Learning the legal skills of analysis and communication is going to be like learning to ride a bike. There are a lot of ways to prepare to ride a bike—having someone hold on to your bike, using training wheels, or watching others ride bikes. No matter how much you prepare, though, you'll learn the most about riding a bicycle by getting on the bike, balancing the best you can, and getting as far as you can before you fall.

The more willing you are to get up on the bike and try, the sooner you'll learn how to keep your balance. So, as you use this book, we're going to give you a lot of opportunities to try out your bike, fall off, make adjustments, and try again. And as with riding a bicycle, if you embrace learning from your mistakes, you'll be headed down the road, wind at your back, before you know it.

Many people remember when they learned to ride a bicycle, so we will use that experience to highlight best practices to overcome the natural struggles that come with learning any new skill, including legal analysis and communication. (If bike riding does not resonate with you, please substitute another skill you have developed in the past.) The first type of bicycle box is called **Gearing Up**. This box helps prepare you to learn about a particular concept or skill. This preparation may take the form of previewing what is to come, introducing you to a concept in relation to other concepts with which you already are familiar, or revealing the underlying mechanics of a legal writing competency. You switch gears on a bike more fluidly when you are aware of the terrain ahead and understand how different gears work; similarly, you learn better when you preview upcoming material and are aware of different strategies for mastering skills and concepts. The second type of bicycle box is called **Rules of the Road** and will alert you to ethical and professional considerations associated with legal writing. The third type of bicycle box is called **Crash Warnings** and will warn you about common pitfalls you may encounter in your first semester as a legal analyst and communicator. The last type of bicycle box is called **Equipping Yourself**. Although this is not a research text, research and writing often go hand-in-hand; this box type provides research and citation strategies that will assist you in your writing. A bicycle ride is much smoother when you have, and can use, appropriate equipment (things like a properly sized bicycle, a helmet, lights, etc.). Similarly, familiarity with research tools and techniques, as well as standard citation practices, will enable you to more efficiently and effectively find the relevant legal authorities that you will apply in your writing.

## How we organized this book for you

This text is designed to introduce new concepts and materials **prior** to class, freeing class time for deeper learning activities, such as quizzes, application exercises, and discussions. Research supports this active-learning approach; we most effectively learn new skills—and legal analysis and writing are indeed new skills—through practicing those skills, not by passively sitting through a lecture. You've likely noticed the conversational tone of this book. In part, that's because we conceive of this text as one component of a learning partnership that also includes your classmates, your professors, and, most importantly, you. Together, we will be working toward the goal of your mastery of legal writing concepts and skills.

To that end, we have structured your learning in five main sections, or modules. Each module is broken down into chapters that begin with study guide questions for you to review and keep in mind as you read the chapter. This will help focus your reading. Then, when you finish reading each chapter, we recommend you return to these questions to make sure you can answer them. This will help ensure you have established the foundation necessary to engage in the in-class activities.

In addition to the bicycle-themed boxes described above, you will also encounter two additional types of recurring content: **Concept in Action** and **Check In**. Concepts in Action illustrate particular concepts (rule structures, components of material in a legal decision or in a case brief, etc.), often with explanatory information. Each Check In provides an opportunity to test your understanding of concepts and skills that have just been presented. These Check Ins may take the form of questions to review and answer or exercises that allow you to practice the skill you read about in the chapter. Answers to the Check Ins are located in Appendix D. Both opportunities will help you understand and retain the basic concepts just covered.

You will notice that many chapters contain illustrations of the skills you will be learning. These illustrations are linked to several hypothetical client fact patterns. The two most complex hypotheticals involve one of the following issues: (1) tortious interference with business expectancy (wrongful outside interference between parties who have a prospective business relationship), or (2) search and seizure. In addition, we will repeatedly return to several simpler scenarios to demonstrate concepts and skills. These include issues such as assault with a dangerous weapon, licensing dangerous dogs, and determining what "unlawful entry" means in a burglary statute. The hypotheticals we think you might want to revisit as you progress through the book are marked with a centered title.

You'll get the most out of this book if you use all the resources your professor assigns. The point of all of these resources and avenues of learning is not to overwhelm you. Rather, it is to enable you to come to

---

 **CRASH WARNING: Learn from the Struggle**

Law school assembles some of the best and the brightest from a variety of academic and professional backgrounds. Many law students experience academic struggle for the first time in law school. It's tempting to write off the struggle as an indication that either you or your professors are "doing it wrong."

In truth, deep learning requires struggle. Just as falling off a bike and occasionally even crashing are part of learning the bike-riding skill, falling off and the occasional crash are part of learning legal skills. Don't obsess over bumps in the road, but don't ignore them. Instead, recognize the missteps as a natural part of the educational process and learn from them.

If you are not sure what went wrong, where it went wrong, or why it went wrong, check in with your professors, who can help you correct course.

class prepared to engage in higher-level thinking, having already thoroughly worked through the fundamental concepts on your own. You will find that much of law school is self-taught. This does not mean that your professors and class time are not valuable. It means that you have to put in more work before class, and after class, than you are likely accustomed to doing.

While this out-of-class preparation will be important for all of your law school classes, let's look more carefully at what it means for this course. As noted earlier, legal writing classes blend content mastery with skill development. Learning how to identify, understand, and apply legal rules requires a firm comprehension of certain foundational concepts.

To help you master these new concepts, we will use a strategy called **looping**. This means we will introduce concepts and terminology and then revisit them in greater depth in later chapters. The repeated exposure to key ideas and the progression from initial presentation to more intense discussion is intended to improve learning. It should help you store these concepts in long-term memory so you can retrieve them when you need them—even long after you've finished this course. It will also help you to readily apply them to novel situations. You may have noticed that in the introduction to this module we briefly described predictive analysis, only to explain it in more detail in this chapter. That is looping.

At the same time that you're mastering these essential ideas, you'll start developing your legal writing skills. This process will also employ looping. You will practice different legal writing techniques in increasing depth throughout the semester. You will learn the building blocks of legal analysis that will eventually enable you to write memos and other legal documents—and that will also help you craft solid exam answers.

This progression emphasizes knowledge acquisition at the start of the semester. Then, as you build a strong conceptual foundation, the focus of your learning will become skill development. Consequently, you will find that most of your reading will be assigned near the start of the term, when you will have narrower writing exercises. Later the balance will change. You will have fewer pages to read but more expansive writing assignments. In order for you to succeed, each phase requires both active classroom participation and focused effort beyond the classroom. To underscore this point, much of your learning will occur in your preparation for each class session, as well as through follow-up assignments. To set your expectations further, here is a broad overview of the way the course material is organized into the five modules of the book.

**Module I** gives you the context for the skills lawyers need to address client problems and outlines how the related tasks take shape in the form of predictive memoranda.

**Module II** addresses Foundations of Legal Analysis. In this section, you will learn about types of legal rules and types of legal reasoning.

**Module III** turns to Foundations of Legal Communication, where you will learn about the components of a legal memo, large-scale organization, and small-scale organization.

**Module IV** loops back around to the legal analysis introduced in Modules I-III and delves deeper by introducing synthesis of multiple authorities and drafting a legal memo with multiple authorities.

Finally, **Module V** puts the foundational concepts discussed above together with questions presented, short answers, and facts so you can draft a full memo. In addition, we discuss the purpose of and some techniques for revising, editing, and proofreading your memo. We also include some skills closely related to memo writing, such as drafting emails containing your legal analysis and crafting talking points for orally communicating your legal analysis.

## Terminology used throughout the book

As noted, we will employ a looping process for complicated skills and concepts. These will be introduced at a general level, with greater instruction, illustration, and application appearing later in the text. This section provides basic definitions for some of these foundational concepts. As you progress through the text and review these concepts in greater detail, you may want to return to these general descriptions to solidify your understanding. To facilitate that process, you will find an alphabetically organized glossary in Appendix G that provides definitions for these and other terms. All terms included in the glossary are presented in bold italics in the textbook where they are first substantively discussed. In addition, every chapter begins with a study question about your understanding of the terminology. You may wish to annotate the glossary in the appendix or create your own glossary to help you master these concepts.

 **GEARING UP: Learning Is a Process**

You likely will not fully understand all of these concepts now, and that's okay.

Remember that this section of the chapter just provides an introduction to some very complex material. Your understanding of these ideas and their application will deepen as you repeatedly encounter—and use—them.

**Predictive analysis:** Before a lawyer can persuade a jury or a judge, she evaluates her client's case by attempting to predict the result. The evaluation is neutral, requiring the lawyer to analyze the law objectively from both parties' perspectives. The dual viewpoints are called either *analysis* and *counter-analysis* or *argument* and *counter-argument*. Both sets of terms simply indicate that you consider the arguments one party will likely advance (analysis or argument) and then the arguments the other party will likely advance (counter-analysis or counter-argument). Together, the process of neutrally exploring both parties' positions is called *predictive analysis*, also referred to as objective analysis. Predictive analysis is the foundation for all other lawyering skills. All predictive analysis is based on the law, either enacted law or common law.

**Predictive writing and persuasive writing:** The lawyer memorializes her predictive analysis in *predictive writing*. Predictive writing may take the form of a memorandum or email to a colleague or supervisor. It may also take the form of an advice letter to a client. Predictive writing sets forth the objective analysis of the law, enabling the reader to make informed decisions about how best to go forward in the case. In contrast, *persuasive writing* aims to convince someone, typically the court, to adopt your client's position. Persuasive writing still builds on predictive analysis, but rather than neutrally presenting both parties' positions, persuasive writing advances your client's arguments, addressing counter-arguments strategically to diminish their impact.

**Enacted law:** *Enacted law* is a set of rules passed by a governmental body to apply broadly to all citizens in the future. The enacted law with which you are probably most familiar is the body of statutes passed by the legislative branch of government, such as a public law passed by Congress that becomes part of the *United States Code*. Legislatures use specific structure and language to achieve their result. Therefore, when you work with enacted law, the legislature intends for you to adhere to the exact language of the law as stated by the statute.

**Common law:** *Common law* is a set of rules developed by a court to apply (1) specifically to the parties whose dispute the court is currently resolving and (2) broadly to all citizens in the future. These rules are found in court opinions, also called judicial decisions or case law. Because a court's primary concern is the parties whose dispute is before the court, the court does not necessarily labor over the language of an opinion in the same way a legislature labors over statutory language.

**Existing legal rule of law:** Both enacted law and common law may serve as the starting point for predictive analysis. We refer to this starting point as the *existing legal rule of law*. One of the earliest steps in predictive analysis is identifying the existing legal rule that applies to the client's situation. An existing legal rule may be explicitly or implicitly stated. You may find it in enacted law or common law.

Once you have identified the existing legal rule that applies, you will break this rule down into: (1) the result of the rule; (2) the conditions that must be assessed in order for the court to determine if the result will occur; and (3) a structure that identifies how the conditions relate to one another to determine whether the result will occur.

- **Result:** The *result* of the rule is simply what follows if the court concludes the client's claim or charge is established in accordance with the rule's conditions.
- **Conditions:** The *conditions* considered to determine the applicability of a rule may relate to one another in several ways: (1) they may **all** be required for the result to occur (i.e., they are mandatory), (2) the court might **weigh** the conditions against one another, or (3) the conditions might be *disjunctive*, representing a choice between mutually exclusive options. Below are the two most common rule structures: the elements test and the factors test.
  - **Elements:** When the result requires **all** conditions to be met, the conditions are *elements*. Elements work like a checklist. If you can check off all the elements, then the result occurs. If you cannot check off one or more elements, the result will not occur.
  - **Factors:** When the result of the existing legal rule is triggered by **weighing** conditions rather than checking them off, those conditions are *factors*. Factors work like items to be weighed, like fruit on a scale. The rule will identify factors to consider, and the result may be triggered by (1) an equal amount of each factor or (2) different amounts of each factor, with some weighing more heavily than others. Sometimes all factors are essential, and each factor needs to be weighed; other times factors are discretionary, meaning that each factor may not need to be considered.

**Emergent legal rule:** It is not uncommon for a legal rule to require clarification. Legal doctrine evolves over time, in part as judges refine earlier principles (*process the legal rule*) when applying them to new disputes. We call this clarification to an existing legal rule the *emergent rule*. The law develops through this continuous process of emergent rules becoming the new existing rules.

**Issues and non-issues:** For any legal test, the lawyer must determine whether the conditions, whether elements or factors, are contested. If the condition is not subject to dispute and thus is clearly satisfied, it is considered a *non-issue*. Where a condition is contested, meaning each side has a viable argument as to whether it is satisfied, it is considered an *issue*. Whether a condition is an issue or not depends on the particular client situation.

**Global rule versus rule for the condition (or issue rule):** Once you have identified the rule and broken it down into its components (i.e., its result, its condition(s), and the relationship between the conditions), you have the *global rule*. However, the precise meaning of the rule, particularly of the conditions, is often opaque. Over time, as a court applies a rule to a specific dispute, it refines the rule by providing *gloss*—detail that more fully explains what is important in interpreting or applying the rule. In particular, as courts interpret and apply a rule, our understanding of the meaning of each condition expands. This expanded understanding of each condition can be conceptualized as the *rule for the condition* or the issue rule. Collectively, the rule comprises the global rule and the rules for the conditions.

**Law-centered interpretations and fact-based holdings:** There are two main frameworks by which courts provide *gloss*: (1) law-centered interpretations, and (2) fact-based holdings. *Law-centered interpretations* explicitly explain the rule without relying on the case facts. These are the two most common examples:

- **Definitions:** *Definitions* explain the meaning of the condition at issue.
- **Standards:** *Standards* can take more than one form; broadly, they provide some type of additional information about how a court does—or does not—evaluate a condition. In contrast to definitions, standards often appear as an articulation of a weight, or measurement, that guides the court's analysis.

In contrast, *fact-based holdings* reveal additional information about the court's interpretation of the rule by looking at how the rule was applied to the facts of the case. Lawyers must identify what specific facts mattered in the court's analysis and how they affected the application of the rule.

**Guiding factors:** *Guiding factors* are developed from fact-based holdings. They further explain what the court will consider when evaluating a specific condition; they might also reveal how the court will prioritize different elements or factors. Although guiding factors may be explicit, more often lawyers must use the key facts from a case (or a series of cases) to craft implicit guiding factors. These guiding factors operate as bases upon which the lawyer can compare the specific facts of a judicial opinion to the facts of the client's case.

## CONCEPT IN ACTION: Understanding Rules of Law

We will address rules of law in much more detail in later chapters, but let's take a non-legal example as an illustration. Assume the following rule:

If you are not home by curfew, you will be grounded.

The rule can be broken down into a condition—not being home by curfew—and a result—being grounded. However, the precise meaning of this rule may evolve as different situations arise that challenge it. Perhaps the parents/guardians have defined "being home" as being inside the home, not sitting in a car in the driveway. You now have a definition for "being home." In another instance, imagine the result is not triggered if the teen is late because of a flat tire, and the teen called the parent to let her know what was happening. Now our understanding of the condition is enhanced. Specifically, we understand the condition has implicit considerations that guide it (guiding factors), namely, (1) the reason for lateness, and (2) whether the teen provided notice regarding lateness. Finally, assume that, in one instance, the teen was going to be late because the driver had to make an unanticipated stop. The teen did not call and was therefore grounded. This could be characterized as a standard: when the teen has the ability to notify the parents/guardians and fails to do so, the result (grounding) occurs.[1]

**Synthesized legal rules:** A collection of emergent rules may lead to a synthesized legal rule. *Synthesized legal rules* derive from multiple cases in which the rule is not stated explicitly.

**Legal reasoning:** Rules are applied to facts primarily using three types of reasoning: rule-based, analogical, and policy-based. The simplest is *rule-based reasoning.* This form of argumentation relies upon the language and principles of the rule. It is a basic logical syllogism, like the classic one involving Socrates: All men are mortal. Socrates is a man. Therefore, Socrates is mortal. The more complex form of reasoning is *analogical reasoning*, in which a lawyer makes an analogy between a situation that has already been resolved by a court in a published opinion and a new situation posed by a client. The better the analogy, the more likely the client's result will mirror the one in the court opinion. Finally, *policy-based reasoning* invokes the justification for the law when it was created to show that the same justification compels a particular result in your client's case. So, for example, you may argue that a statute was enacted primarily to promote public safety and that similar safety concerns are at issue in your case. You would therefore further assert that, when resolving your case, the statute should be interpreted in the manner that best promotes public safety.

**Legal memorandum:** A *predictive legal memorandum* is one of the more common forms of predictive writing. The audience for a legal memorandum is a law-trained reader. The tone is predictive rather than persuasive. It contains five sections: Header, Question(s) Presented, Short Answer(s), Statement of Facts, and Discussion.

---

1. The authors independently explored this example and then learned of its similarity to an example Charles Calleros uses in LAW SCHOOL EXAMS: PREPARING AND WRITING TO WIN (2d ed. 2013). Calleros also uses many other non-legal examples throughout his book, so you might want to check it out if you find this approach helpful.

**Large-scale organization:** *Large-scale organization* refers to the expected progression of information in a Discussion section of a legal memorandum. Lawyers have many ways of describing this organization. You have probably already heard it described as *IRAC* (issue, rule, application, conclusion). Another way of describing it is *CREAC* (conclusion, rule, explanation, application, conclusion). Regardless of the acronym or description, the resulting Discussion is the same. You can think of large-scale organization as the way you think about driving directions. To get from point *A* to point *B,* one person may describe it in four steps while someone else may describe it in five steps. The route is the same, however, as is the end point.

**Roadmap paragraphs:** These paragraphs are intended to orient the reader to the material that follows. A broad roadmap paragraph known as the *global roadmap paragraph* appears at the beginning of the Discussion to orient the reader to that entire section. There may also be more focused roadmap paragraphs to orient the reader to each analytical section of the memo, where disputed elements or factors are discussed in rule explanation and rule application sections. This type of paragraph is known as an *issue roadmap paragraph*.

**Rule explanation paragraphs:** In IRAC, the *R* refers to a statement of the rule as well as an example of how a court has applied the rule. In CREAC, the *R* refers to the rule and the *E* refers to rule explanation. A *rule explanation paragraph* begins with a rule, states the facts of the case in which the rule was applied, and summarizes the court's rationale and holding using the rule.

**Rule application paragraphs:** In both IRAC and CREAC, *A* refers to the rule application. The content of a *rule application paragraph* will vary depending on whether you are using rule-based, analogical, or policy-based reasoning. Because the most common type of reasoning you'll use is analogical reasoning, we'll describe the rule application paragraphs in terms of analogical reasoning. You will apply the law to the facts by showing either (1) the similarities between the facts of the cases in the rule explanation paragraphs and the facts of your client's situation, or (2) distinctions from the facts of the cases in the rule explanation paragraphs and the facts of your client's situation.

At this point, we recommend that you return to the study guide questions at the start of the chapter that helped frame your reading. Try to answer them in your own words without re-reading

 **RULES OF THE ROAD: Rules of Professional Conduct**

When you are admitted to the bar, your conduct will be regulated by rules of professional conduct. All states, as well as D.C., Guam, and the Northern Mariana Islands, have adopted some form of the Model Rules of Professional Conduct, which were prepared by the American Bar Association. You need to be familiar with these rules, both in terms of their content and, more importantly, how they inform your practice. In this text, we will address rules associated with client representation, legal research, legal analysis, and legal communication.

the text. Then check your knowledge. Now that you have some foundational concepts under your belt, we turn our attention in the next chapters to learning some of the discipline-specific skills used to engage in predictive analysis.

### CHAPTER 2

# Reading, Thinking, and Writing Like a Lawyer

This chapter focuses on the unique way that lawyers read and process the law. As noted in Chapter 1, lawyers read the law to solve client problems. In this chapter, we will look at examples of how a lawyer actively reads and takes notes on a full case, as opposed to how a law student reads an edited version in a casebook. We will also examine how this client-focused approach to the law forms a critical component of the pre-drafting stage of the writing process.

## Study Guide Questions for Chapter 2

1. What is the law student's objective when reading cases in a doctrinal casebook? What active reading strategies facilitate that objective?
2. What is the law student or lawyer's objective when reading cases to engage in predictive or persuasive analysis? What active reading strategies facilitate that objective?
3. What types of considerations inform the way lawyers approach a text?
4. What are the components of a case brief?
5. What discipline-specific qualities characterize how lawyers consume and analyze legal information?
6. What are some ethical considerations that guide written communications with clients?
7. What new terms were introduced in this chapter? How do these terms relate to your existing understanding of predictive memo writing? Did your understanding of any other terms change as a result of reading this chapter?

Now that you have selected law as your career path, you have undoubtedly been told that you will need to learn to "think like a lawyer." The authors of this book recall that admonition as well, and not necessarily fondly. Admission to law school indicates that a student has been academically successful and can "think" effectively. It can be disconcerting to hear that you will need to think in a new way. It might help to realize that you are not completely abandoning your established way of thinking, reading, and writing. Certainly, some of the skills you have developed scrutinizing texts, organizing your thoughts, and clearly communicating will still apply. However, you will need to further hone and adjust these skills as you learn the specific ways that lawyers process and organize information. You will become adept at consuming legal information, which includes content, style, and organization unique to the discipline. This chapter is thus designed to introduce you to the discipline-specific ways in which lawyers read, think, and write, focusing on one fundamental source of law: the judicial opinion.

# I. How a Lawyer Reads

Reading cases is a fundamental lawyering skill. Below, we first discuss the mindset with which lawyers read cases. We then use an annotated case to illustrate how lawyers employ active reading strategies when reviewing cases.

## A. Reading Full Cases Versus Case Excerpts

Lawyers do a tremendous amount of reading, and when they consume legal information, they do so with a specific context and objective in mind. Typically, they seek to synthesize legal principles to determine how those principles might impact a client's situation. In other words, lawyers do not usually read cases simply to better understand an area of law in the abstract. Rather, they want to know what that case means for their client; the client situation provides the lens through which lawyers determine the relevance of a case. Furthermore, because many cases address multiple legal issues, this client lens helps the lawyer determine which part(s) of the case apply.

This client-centered reading stands in marked contrast to the way law students read excerpted cases in casebooks. In your casebook courses, you will read cases that have been carefully *edited* to focus your attention on some aspect of doctrinal law. In your contracts casebook, for example, you may have a lengthy section on the concept of "offer." The cases that appear in that section likely address other contractual issues as well, but the excerpts presented in the casebook focus solely on some nuanced aspect of what "offer" means in the context of the doctrinal area of contract law. As you read that series of cases, your objective will be to actively synthesize the relationship between the cases to develop principles of "offer" in the context of the law of contracts. You will therefore have an active focus on how the cases relate to one another as you read. In other words, you are not reading each case in isolation; rather, you are reading selections from a series of cases with the objective of understanding how they work together to present and further develop legal principles. (Remember the Chapter 1 discussion of how legal rules often become more nuanced as courts apply them to new disputes.)

In contrast, in your legal writing class, you will be reading *unedited* cases. You will be asked to evaluate those cases in light of a particular client's situation. For example, your focus may be on whether your client has a viable claim for intentional infliction of emotional distress. The cases you consider in evaluating her claim may address myriad other claims, but your focus in reading those cases will be solely on the court's analysis of intentional infliction of emotional distress.

## B. Editorial Enhancements in Full Cases

Lawyers often access cases through a service like Lexis or Westlaw (or the print reporters from these publishers) rather than obtaining opinions directly from the court. The commercial publishers add features, known as "editorial enhancements," to the opinion to help the reader better understand and navigate the case. Among these publisher-added enhancements, you may find a brief synopsis of the opinion, a list of the court's *holdings*, and *headnotes*, which identify the legal issues the case discusses and flag the locations in the opinion where this discussion occurs.

The savvy case reader makes use of these editorial enhancements while remembering they are not part of the official case opinion. In other words, they are not the words of the court. In practice, this means that when these features are available, you will use them as a preview of what you will expect to find in the opinion itself. This will help you focus your reading. Later, when you cite the case to support your legal analysis, you will be sure to reference and cite the text of the opinion, rather than any editorial enhancements. In Westlaw or Lexis, the opinion appears under the section heading "Opinion."

### ⊞ CONCEPT IN ACTION: Reading a Case Through a Client Lens

Here we introduce the hypothetical Assault with a Fitbit. Then we will use this client context to illustrate how a law-trained reader might actively read a case.

#### Assault with a Fitbit

Jeffers Peterson works for Ricochet, Inc., which markets handball equipment. Another Ricochet employee, James Peevey, works in the PR department. During the annual holiday party, the company sponsored a handball tournament. James, who is not athletic, initially declined to participate. Under intense pressure from his supervisor to participate, James relented and began a game of handball with Jeffers, who is a former college basketball star. During the game, which occurred on a court that was centrally located at the party venue and was viewed by the entire party, Jeffers played aggressively and easily won the game against James. Jeffers was enraged that James had represented the company so poorly. As James approached Jeffers and reached out his hand, presumably to congratulate him on his win, Jeffers slapped James across the face, cutting his cheek with a Fitbit activity tracker Jeffers wore around his wrist. Embarrassed and bleeding, James drove directly to the local police precinct to press charges. Jeffers was charged with assault with a dangerous weapon for the slap.

Sofía Currier is a new associate who represents Jeffers. Sofía researches cases that discuss assault with a dangerous weapon and finds *Com. v. Hermione H.*, a case in which the victim was injured after being punched by someone wearing rings. Below are Sofía's thoughts as she considers the applicability of this case in light of Jeffers's potential criminal liability.

(As you read this case, you might notice that it is quite short. Indeed this opinion is shorter than most published cases. The Massachusetts court rule under which the order was published provides for both an abridged judicial process and a court opinion written primarily for the parties that may not completely discuss the case facts or court's rationale.)

## *Com. v. Hermione H.*
68 Mass. App. Ct. 1106, 861 N.E.2d 809 (2007)

### MEMORANDUM AND ORDER PURSUANT TO RULE 1:28

This looks like an overview of what is to come in the case. ——— On appeal from adjudications of delinquency, the juvenile maintains that (1) the Commonwealth presented insufficient evidence to establish an assault and battery by means of a dangerous weapon; and (2) the adjudication of delinquency on the charge of assault and battery is duplicative of that of assault and battery by means of a dangerous weapon. We affirm the adjudication of delinquency on the charge of assault and battery by means of a dangerous weapon for substantially the reasons set forth in the Commonwealth's brief at pages eleven through twenty-one. We agree, and the Commonwealth concedes, that the adjudication of delinquency on the charge of assault and battery is duplicative of that of assault and battery by means of a dangerous weapon because the jury were not instructed that separate acts were required. *See Commonwealth v. Howze*, 58 Mass. App. Ct. 147, 149–150 (2003).

A statement of the defendant's arguments. ———The juvenile does not contest that the evidence was sufficient to prove that she punched the victim in the face with a closed fist, thereby committing an assault and battery. She maintains, however, that the Commonwealth offered insufficient evidence to prove that the rings on her fingers were dangerous weapons as used, an essential element of the greater offense of assault and battery by means of a dangerous weapon. *See Commonwealth v. Appleby*, 380 Mass. 296, 305 (1980),

cert. denied, 464 U.S. 941 (1983). We disagree. We cannot say as — The court's initial holding on
matter of law that the rings used by the juvenile in these circumstances    the matter.
were not capable of causing serious bodily harm. *See Commonwealth v.
Rossi*, 19 Mass. App. Ct. 257, 261 (1985).

Rings are objects that are not dangerous per se, but become dan- — The court begins its discussion
gerous weapons when they are "used in a dangerous fashion." *See*    on the case at hand. This is
*Commonwealth v. Appleby*, supra at 304. "[T]he essential question, when    important so I need to start
an object [such as a ring]... is alleged to be a dangerous weapon'...    reading more carefully at this
[is] 'whether the object, as used by the [juvenile], is capable of pro-    point.
ducing serious bodily harm.'" *Commonwealth v. Mercado*, 24 Mass. App.    In this paragraph the court
Ct. 391, 397 (1987), quoting from *Commonwealth v. Marrero*, 19 Mass.    seems to provide gloss about
App. Ct. 921, 922 (1984). "Resolution of these questions is invari-    the issue rule of law. Very
ably for the fact finder... and involves not only consideration of any    helpful in terms of definitions
evidence as to the nature and specific features of the object but also    and standards. Then, the
attention to the circumstances surrounding the assault and the use of    end of the paragraph tells
the object, and the manner in which it was handled or controlled."    me about potential guiding
*Commonwealth v. Marrero*, supra.    factors.

It is not required that the perpetrator intend to use the instrumen- — The court is further explaining
tality as a dangerous weapon. *See Commonwealth v. Appleby*, 380 Mass.    the rule through its
at 308; *Commonwealth v. Tevlin*, 433 Mass. 305, 313 (2001).    application. Read carefully in
order to further develop the
legal test for this condition,
including possible guiding
factors.

Possible standard: intent
is not required but may be
considered? This is a little
confusing to me—how does
intent come into play for this
condition? I need to see if that
becomes clearer as I continue
reading.

Application: Intended use. Like
this defendant, Jeffers may
not have intended to use the
Fitbit as a dangerous weapon.

"[O]rdinarily innocuous items can be considered dangerous weap- — Another standard: "innocuous
ons when used in an improper and dangerous manner." *Commonwealth*    items can be considered
*v. Sexton*, 425 Mass. 146, 149 (1997), and see cases cited. What is    dangerous." Plus, possible
required is that the item as used be capable of causing the requisite    guiding factor—the way the
degree of bodily harm. *See Commonwealth v. Lord*, 55 Mass. App. Ct.    item is used.
265, 269 n.7 (2002) (described variously as "great bodily harm," "seri-    Another possible guiding
ous bodily harm" and "bodily harm, that 'endangers another's safety"    factor—what the item is
[citations omitted]). "The law need not wait until the instrument actu-    capable of.
ally does cause serious bodily harm in order to classify the weapon as    I am thinking about these
dangerous." *Commonwealth v. Appleby*, supra at 307.    guiding factors in relation to
my client. Like the ring on this
defendant's hand, the Fitbit
on Jeffers's wrist was used
improperly. It was also capable
of causing injury to James.

This is likely to be favorable to
the government.

Possible guiding factor—victim's injuries. Like the victim here, James also suffered injury to his face, namely a cut to the cheek causing him to bleed.

—— Viewed in the light most favorable to the Commonwealth, the victim's testimony that the juvenile punched her with a ring-clad fist, the victim's hospital records, and photographs of the victim's injuries were sufficient to permit the jury to conclude that the rings worn by the juvenile, as used, were dangerous weapons, *see Commonwealth v. Roman*, 43 Mass. App. Ct. 733, 736 (1997) (use of dangerous weapon may be inferred from victim's injuries), S.C., 427 Mass. 1006 (1998), and that the juvenile had committed an assault and battery by means of a dan-

This is also likely to be favorable to the government.

The *Appleby* case is cited several times. Look at this case later to see how it compares to our client's facts.

—gerous weapon. *See Commonwealth v. Appleby*, supra; *Commonwealth v. Tevlin,* 433 Mass. at 311, and cases cited. Greater specificity in description of the rings used by the juvenile is not required. *See Commonwealth v. Zawatsky*, 41 Mass. App. Ct. 392, 398–399 (1996); *Commonwealth v. Charles*, 57 Mass. App. Ct. 595, 599 (2003).

Final holding of the case. ——The adjudication of delinquency on the charge of assault and battery by means of a dangerous weapon is affirmed; the adjudication of delinquency on the charge of assault and battery is vacated and the complaint dismissed.

So ordered.

This example illustrates that Sofía read this case not only to understand how and why the court arrived at the ruling it did, but also with an eye toward how the rule and its application in that prior case may impact the resolution of Jeffers's legal situation. In legal writing class, and later in practice, you will similarly read cases with a *client-centered* focus.

### More Practice Reading a Case: The Smell Shoppe Hypothetical

Now let's look at case reading in a slightly more complex context. In the example below, assume that you represent Gene Arnold, a business owner who is concerned that his competitor is improperly interfering with Arnold's customer relationships. (We will provide more detail later on this hypothetical, called The Smell Shoppe Hypothetical after the name of Arnold's business.) You plan to assert a claim for the tort of "interference with business expectancy" and are reading this case to better understand the law for that particular claim. Once again, the annotations reflect what you might be thinking as you read this case through the lens of your client's situation.

You will notice that this case includes information that is not pertinent to the claim you are researching. For instance, the case includes lengthy discussions of other claims not at issue in your client's case, as well as lengthy information about the procedural posture of the case that is also unimportant to your claim. Thus, although this case is, at first glance, lengthy, a law-trained reader quickly realizes that she can skim large portions of it. Over time you will become more proficient at reading unedited cases both effectively and efficiently, identifying portions that at first glance seem important but are ultimately irrelevant.

## Chicago's Pizza, Inc., Chicago's Best, Inc., and Flovig, Inc., Plaintiffs–Appellants
### v.
## Chicago's Pizza Franchise Limited USA, f/k/a Pizza USA, Inc., and Irfanullah Muhammed, Defendants–Appellees

384 Ill.App.3d 849, 893 N.E.2d 981, 323 Ill.Dec. 507

No. 1-07-0679

Decided: Aug. 7, 2008. Rehearing Denied: Sept. 8, 2008. Appeal denied: Jan. 28, 2009.

**Summary:** Pizza chain alleged competing chain used its name, misleading the public and filed claims for tortious interference with business expectancy and violations of Deceptive Trade Practices Act and Consumer Fraud Act. Judge Barbara Disko presided over bench trial and court entered judgment for competitor; pizza chain appealed.

*I will remember that these initial sections are editorial enhancements and use them to get a sense of what the opinion says and focus my reading of the opinion itself. With that in mind, this summary indicates that the case discusses multiple claims; the portion concerning TIBE likely is useful. To the extent that I know I am not dealing with a claim relating to the Deceptive Trade Practices Act or the Consumer Fraud Act, I can expect that there will be portions of the case that I can skim/ignore, as they will not be relevant to my client issue.*

**Holdings:** The Appellate Court held that:

1. With regard to the tortious interference with business expectancy claim:

a. pizza chain had reasonable expectancy of maintaining and entering into business relationships with existing and new customers who contemplated a business relationship with the chain

*To the extent that my client's issue involves TIBE, this helps me determine, right away, that reasonable expectancy and contemplation of a business relationship are important considerations.*

b. competitor's name and advertising campaign suggested knowledge of expectancy.

*I will want to consider how competitor's knowledge of expectancy is shown in a TIBE claim.*

c. competitor intentionally and unjustifiably prevented pizza chain's realization of doing business with specific customers of pizza chain;

*I will want to consider how to establish whether the competitor intentionally and unjustifiably prevented a realization of doing business.*

d. pizza chain did not meet burden of establishing, with reasonable certainty, damages as a result of competitor's efforts to mislead the public;

*I will want to determine whether proof of damages is essential to my TIBE claim.*

*This underscores the impression I got from the summary that there will be parts of the case not relevant to my client matter.*

———— 2. With regard to the Deceptive Trade Practices Act claim:

a. competitor's trade practices created a likelihood of confusion or misunderstanding.

b. competitor willfully engaged in a deceptive trade practice, entitling pizza chain to reasonable attorney fees; and

*This also underscores the impression I got from the summary that there will be parts of the case not relevant to my client matter.*

———— 3. Pizza chain did not prove actual damages, and thus had no private cause of action under the Consumer Fraud Act.

Affirmed in part, reversed in part, and remanded.

## OPINION

*Okay. This is where the opinion itself begins.*

———— JUSTICE MURPHY delivered the opinion of the court:

Plaintiffs, Chicago's Pizza, Inc., Chicago's Best, Inc., and Flovig, Inc., filed a complaint against defendants, Chicago's Pizza Franchise Limited and Irfanullah Muhammed, alleging that defendants used the Chicago's Pizza name to mislead consumers, benefit from plaintiffs' investment in the Chicago's Pizza name, and divert sales from plaintiffs' restaurants to defendants'. After a bench trial, the trial court found that plaintiffs did not meet their burden of proving that defendants' actions caused plaintiffs to lose revenue.

## I. BACKGROUND

*I will skim the facts, but not begin to write extensive notes on what is important. I will need to first carefully review the court's analysis of the TIBE claim so that I can determine what material is essential from this lengthy description of the establishments, their customers, and the procedural history.*

————

Martin Flores and his wife opened their first Chicago's Pizza restaurant in 1991. By 2002, they had three Chicago's Pizza locations in Chicago: 3114 North Lincoln Avenue, 3006 North Sheffield, and 1919 West Montrose. From 2002 until 2006, Muhammed ran an unaffiliated Chicago's Pizza pizzeria, with its sole location at 5062 North Sheridan Road. Although Muhammed had only one store, his ads listed multiple "locations," some of which corresponded with plaintiffs' locations. The ads also described worldwide locations and claimed that defendants' restaurant had been in existence since 1970, even though Muhammed did not open the restaurant until 2002.

Certain of plaintiffs' restaurants were called Chicago's Pizza, while others went by Chicago's Pizza & Pasta. Plaintiffs' logo was a red oval with the word "Chicago's" written inside, with either "Pizza" and "Pizza & Pasta" under the oval. Defendants' logo was a red, white, and blue pizza with "Chicago's Pizza" written in the bottom, blue portion and "Pizzeria" written in green in the middle.

Plaintiffs filed a 10-count complaint alleging that defendants used the Chicago's Pizza name in an effort to mislead the public into thinking that it was a franchised business affiliated with plaintiffs. Plaintiff Chicago's Pizza, Inc., the Lincoln Avenue location, alleged tortious interference with business expectancy and violations of the Uniform Deceptive Trade Practices Act (Deceptive Trade Practices Act)

(815 ILCS 510/1 *et seq.* (West 2004)) and the Consumer Fraud and Deceptive Business Practices Act (Consumer Fraud Act) (815 ILCS 505/1 *etseq.* (West 2004)). Chicago's Best, the Montrose Avenue location, and Flovig, the Sheffield Avenue location, alleged violations of the Deceptive Trade Practices Act against both defendants.

In 2006, the case proceeded to trial, where the following evidence was presented.

### A. Martin and Patricia Flores

Martin Flores testified that he owns four locations of Chicago's Pizza: North Lincoln, North Sheffield, West Montrose, and West Irving Park. At the time of trial, the Irving Park location had just been opened, and his West Wilson store relocated to Montrose two years before. The Lincoln store opened in 2001.

Chicago's Pizza was incorporated in 1992 and started as a two-person operation. Sales increased every year, and at the time of the trial, the business had 160 employees. However, at the end of 2002 or 2003, Flores saw a decrease in sales, especially in the Wrigley Field area. Until that time, other competitors opened in the area, but they did not affect his business. He believed that the decrease in business was a result of the opening of a Chicago's Pizza on Sheridan Road, which was not affiliated with his restaurants. He received hundreds of complaints from customers about the quality of the Sheridan restaurant's food.

Furthermore, in February and March 2006, people began complaining that plaintiff was fraudulently charging their credit cards; however, plaintiffs did not charge their credit cards, and the alleged customers were not in plaintiffs' computer system.

Plaintiffs' tax records showed that gross sales for the Lincoln location was $1.9 million for the 2000 tax year; $2.3 million for 2001; $2,078,765 for 2002; $1.8 million for 2003; and $2,296,000 for 2004. During the time frame when he noticed a decrease in sales, he increased his advertising to recover some of the customers he had lost. Sales increased when defendants' restaurant closed in 2006.

In 2000, Flores changed the name of the restaurant on his menus and the Internet to Chicago's Pizza & Pasta. When he opened his first full-service restaurant on Lincoln in 2001, the name on the sign was Chicago's Pizza & Pasta. The signs at the Wilson and Sheffield locations have always been Chicago's Pizza, and the sign on Montrose was Chicago's Pizza & Pasta beginning in 2003.

Patricia Flores, Martin's niece, testified that until the year before, she worked at the Chicago's Pizza location on Montrose. At one point, a customer presented a coupon for what purported to be Chicago's Pizza, which listed one phone number for "downtown area, Lincoln area" and "Lincoln Park, Sheffield area" and another number for "Wilson area,

—— It is helpful that the court has labeled facts relating to both the plaintiff and defendant. This will enable me to get back to these sections once I know what facts are important to the TIBE analysis.

Montrose location" and "Rogers Park, Sheridan area." Patricia testified that this coupon was not for plaintiffs' Chicago Pizza. After receiving additional complaints, she called the phone number that the customer gave her for a Chicago's Pizza located on Sheridan. Patricia asked the person who answered the phone whether the restaurant was affiliated with the Chicago's Pizza on Montrose, and he said yes.

Patricia testified that when the Montrose store was opened in 2002, the sign placed outside said Chicago's Pizza & Pasta, as did the menus. However, they always answered the phone "Chicago Pizza."

### B. Defendant Irfanullah Muhammed

Irfanullah Muhammed testified that he bought the goodwill of an existing pizzeria named Paisan's Pizza for $87,000 and changed the name. He did not examine the books and records for the business before purchasing it, and his only experience with the pizza business was observing his friend's pizza business in Japan for three or four months.

At the time he incorporated his business in 2002, Muhammed told the State that he would be doing business under the name Chicago Pizza Inn U.S.A. However, he never opened a business named Chicago Pizza Inn U.S.A. When he opened his business under the name Chicago's Pizza, he did not look in the phone book to determine whether any other businesses were already using that name. For a short time in 2004 the business was dissolved for failure to pay the franchise fee, but he continued to run it. When he reincorporated in 2004, he learned that he could not use the name Pizza U.S.A. and instead tried to use the name Chicago Pizza & Pasta. He ultimately closed the business in February or March 2006.

Defendants' ads had either a "circle R" next to "Chicago's Pizza," as if it were registered, or the "TM" designation. Muhammed never obtained a registration; he abandoned his application with the United State Patent and Trademark Office.

Although defendants only had one location, on Sheridan Road, their ads included multiple "locations," with different phone numbers for each. For example, defendants' phone book ad and one of their menus[1] showed locations for Lincoln/Sheffield, Downtown/Loop, Montrose/Wilson, and Lakefront/Sheridan/Loyola, and urged customers to "call for your nearest location." In a Yellow Book coupon, defendants listed one phone number for "Downtown Area, Lincoln Area, Lincoln Park, Sheffield Area" and a second number for "Wilson Area, Montrose Location, Rogers Park, Sheridan Area." Another ad had six phone numbers for different areas that were not labeled "locations": Lincoln Park, Sheffield area, Montrose/Wilson, Downtown, UIC & Loop, and Sheridan & Loyola. Muhammed testified that his ads had different

---

1. Two other menus included in the record do not list the multiple "locations."

phone numbers for different "locations" to avoid overwhelming one phone line and so that the order could be assigned to drivers who delivered in particular areas. He denied that he was trying to create the impression that his restaurant had multiple locations.

Several of defendants' ads or menus listed worldwide locations, including Dubai, Frankfurt, Rome, and New York. Muhammed admitted that these locations did not exist, but he wanted to open franchises in New York and Tokyo. His friend was going to open a location in San Francisco and his brother was going to open one in Washington, D.C.

Certain ads or menus also made reference to "Established 1970" and "Since 1970" or provided, "Thanks to all Wonderful Customers for their Continued Support towards the Prosperity of Chicago's Pizza Since 1970." As Muhammed did not open the restaurant until 2002, the restaurant was not established in 1970. He testified that the year 1970 refers to when a restaurant called Strawberry Pizza, located in Japan, began using a particular crust recipe.

Certain ads also state that defendants' restaurant is open until 5 a.m. Muhammed testified that the restaurant's closing time was 5 a.m. but was changed to 3 a.m. During the time when a 5 a.m. closing time was advertised, sometimes he closed earlier.

Muhammed testified that he first learned of plaintiffs' restaurants after this lawsuit was filed. In response, he put up a sign visible to both the public and the employees that answered the phone saying that the restaurant was not affiliated with any other locations or companies. Employees answered the phone "Chicago's Pizza Sheridan," and he instructed them that if any customers asked about Chicago's Pizza & Pasta, "tell them to call different numbers."

Muhammed testified that plaintiffs' and defendants' restaurants carry different items. For example, Muhammed testified that his pizzeria did not carry 40% of the appetizers listed on plaintiffs' menu, and he did not sell any of plaintiffs' salads, chicken dishes, wraps, or gourmet sandwiches. They sold different desserts, and defendants carried Pepsi products, while plaintiffs carried Coke products. In addition, halal food, which plaintiffs do not sell, constituted 20 to 30% of defendants' gross sales.

Muhammed testified that after this litigation ends, he plans to reopen his business under the name "Chicago's Pizza."

### C. Customers

#### 1. *Wolf Stern*

Wolf Stern testified that he ordered pizzas about once a month from plaintiffs' Lincoln Avenue location. In December 2003, he decided to order a pizza and looked in the Yellow Pages for the Chicago's Pizza on Lincoln Avenue. When he could not find it, he called the Chicago's Pizza on Sheridan and asked for the phone number of the Lincoln

—— Hmm, it is interesting that in the factual background, the court pays so much attention to the customers. This suggests to me that this is essential in a TIBE claim. Once I have a better idea of the relevance of customer facts, I will need to circle back around to the client to ascertain additional facts about his customers.

Avenue location. The person Stern spoke to asked him for his address and said they could deliver from the Sheridan location, so Stern placed an order. Stern's understanding was that he was ordering from an affiliate of the Chicago's Pizza on Lincoln. When the pizza did not arrive within the agreed-upon period of time, Stern called the location two or three times and was told that the driver was right around the corner. He had to wait almost two hours for the delivery to arrive, and the pizza he bought was "terrible." Stern called the store again to express his dissatisfaction, and the man he talked to offered him a discount on his next order, which would be placed in the computer system and honored at all of their locations, including Lincoln Avenue.

In 2004, Stern met Martin Flores when Flores threw a party for their sons' baseball team at Chicago's Pizza. Flores told him about issues he was having with another store with a similar name, and Stern explained the problem he had in December 2003. In the meantime, Stern had stopped ordering from Chicago's Pizza and had told his friends of his negative experience. After speaking to Flores, Stern again began patronizing the Chicago's Pizza on Lincoln Avenue.

### 2. Travis Cohen

Travis Cohen testified that for two years until February 2006, he ordered pizza from the Sheffield location of Chicago's Pizza at least once a week. In February 2006, he looked in the phone book, which had multiple locations for Chicago's Pizza. Because he knew that Sheffield turned into Sheridan, he thought that the Sheridan location was the same as the Sheffield location. Therefore, he ordered a pizza from the Sheridan location. He testified that Chicago's Pizza charged his debit card $22.12 for this order, but another charge for $55 appeared on his account two days later. Cohen called the Sheridan location regarding the extra charge and was advised to call Maria, the area manager for Chicago's Pizza. Cohen called Maria at the number that the person at the Sheridan location gave him and discovered that the two locations were not affiliated. Cohen filed a police report and filed a grievance with his bank. After this incident, he is ordering pizzas again from the Sheffield location.

### 3. Anthony Poole

Anthony Poole testified that in February 2005, he saw an ad for Chicago's Pizza and called the number listed to order a pizza. He had ordered from the Montrose and Wilson locations of Chicago's Pizza at least 12 times. When the pizza arrived, the quality was different, but he assumed there was a new person in plaintiffs' kitchen. A few weeks later, he ordered another pizza by using the phone number from the same ad. He asked the employee on the phone whether this was the location on Wilson, and the employee responded that it was. When the pizza arrived, the packaging and aroma were different from normal, so he asked the deliveryman what location it came from. The deliveryman said the Chicago's Pizza on Sheridan. Poole told him to take the pizza back and called the Sheridan location. He spoke to the same person as before and questioned him on the discrepancy between locations. The employee responded that he told Poole earlier that they deliver to the Wilson area, not that the location was on Wilson Avenue. After this incident, he is ordering pizzas again from the Montrose and Wilson locations.

#### 4. *Joseph Bitterman*

Joseph Bitterman testified that he was a customer of the Chicago's Pizza on Sheffield beginning in late 2004. In July 2005, he looked in the phone book and saw an ad for Chicago's Pizza, with different phone numbers for each of its four locations: Lincoln/Sheffield, Downtown/ Loop, Montrose/Wilson, and Lakefront/Sheridan/Loyola. The ad listed a toll-free number to call "for your nearest location" and represented that the pizzerias were open until 5 a.m. Bitterman called the Sheffield location believing he was calling the Chicago's Pizza he had done business with on Lincoln and Sheffield. The food he received was "disgusting to say the least," but when he called the store at 4 a.m. to complain, it was closed. The following day, he returned the food to the Chicago's Pizza on Sheffield, from which he thought he had ordered, but did not believe the employees when they told him that they had not made the sandwich. He disparaged the store to 20 or 30 people before he learned that he had ordered from a Chicago's Pizza on Sheridan.

#### 5. *Judith Levine*

Judith Levine testified that she has been patronizing the Wilson and Montrose locations of plaintiffs' Chicago's Pizza for 15 years. In April 2005, she clipped a Yellow Book coupon for Chicago's Pizza with three phone numbers—one for "Lincoln Park and Sheffield areas," one for "Wilson and Montrose areas," and a third for "Sheridan and Broadway areas." She believed that the coupon was for plaintiffs' restaurants, since it had the same name and the locations listed on the coupon were similar to plaintiffs' locations, so she attempted to use it at plaintiffs' Montrose location. Plaintiffs' Montrose location informed her that the coupon was not theirs but still honored it.

#### 6. *Mary DeArmond*

Mary DeArmond testified that she was referred to the Chicago's Pizza on Montrose. In the summer of 2005, her friend searched in his cell phone for the nearest Chicago's Pizza. A number of Chicago's Pizza locations came up, but her friend called the location on Sheridan because it was the closest to his house. Her friend placed an order, and when she went to pick it up, she asked whether the restaurant was affiliated with the Chicago's Pizza on Montrose. The employee said that it was. Since then, she has not ordered from the Sheridan location, but she has ordered from the Montrose location several times.

### D. Accountant Sam Remer

Sam Remer, an accountant, testified that he was retained by Martin Flores to determine whether defendants' actions damaged plaintiffs' business and the amount of lost revenue. He reviewed Chicago's Pizza, Inc.'s (the Lincoln location) tax returns for 2000 through 2004 and spoke to Martin Flores, his assistant, and his accountant. Remer did not review any other financial records of plaintiffs'. He concluded that the Lincoln location's sales declined in 2002 and 2003 but increased somewhat in 2004. He estimated that lost sales for 2002 and 2003 were $830,000 and its lost profits were $500,000. The carry-out and delivery portions of the business sustained the majority of the losses. Flores told him that a number of delivery drivers had to be laid off.

Although the Lincoln Avenue dining room opened in 2001, Remer testified that Martin Flores told him that it did not open until 2002. Believing that the Lincoln Avenue's dining room was an extra source of income in 2002 that the business did not have in 2001, Remer added $250,000 to the difference between the numbers for 2001 and 2002. Therefore, of the $830,000 he estimated in lost sales for those two years, $250,000 was attributable to the dining room income that he believed plaintiffs had in 2002 but not in 2001. Remer agreed that if there was a dining room operating in 2001, his numbers "would have to be changed." Remer testified that before he learned that the dining room revenue needed to be added to the damages calculation, he had concluded that plaintiffs' lost sales "appeared to be minimal."

Remer opined that defendants' actions caused these losses. Based on his research, the depositions of Muhammed, his brother, and a driver, Remer concluded that there was a concerted effort to cause confusion between the two establishments.

Defendants' tax return for 2002 showed sales of $30,000 a year, or approximately $100 a day. Remer discounted the tax return, however, because it contradicted the deposition testimony of Muhammed, his brother, and a driver, who stated that the daily sales were between $2,000 and $4,000 a day. He also identified mathematical errors in the return and stated that the gross profit ratio was understated. No employees were shown on the tax returns for 2002 and 2003; apparently defendants' employees were paid in cash. Defendants' business records were not provided to Remer, who considered the tax returns to be fraudulent.

Remer did not know the geographic area that plaintiffs' Lincoln Avenue store delivered to, nor did he know how many other businesses had a pizza delivery business within the same area. He discounted other area businesses' contribution to any decrease in plaintiffs' sales based on what Martin Flores told him. He also relied on *Pizza Today Magazine's* conclusion that national pizza consumption had not changed much in the last 15 years.

### E. Trial Court's Decision

At the close of plaintiffs' case, defendants moved for a directed finding, which the trial court denied. The trial resumed; defendants did not call any witnesses but did present exhibits. The trial court found that Muhammed was not truthful in his advertising, including his use of the trademark designation and his claims of being established in 1970 and having restaurants in foreign countries; however, the trial court "fails to see how this false advertisement hurt Plaintiff's business." Furthermore, although Martin Flores testified that his business was injured because defendants had "such an inferior product," "if Muhammed had a better product, he may have been more serious competition. Bad pizza will not survive in Chicago; there is too much competition. Flores apparently does have a very good product and have very loyal customers at each of his restaurants. However, in the very competitive food business, he could lose them for any number of reasons." The trial court concluded that plaintiffs failed to meet their burden of proving that defendants interfered with the business in such a manner as to cause lost revenue. Therefore, it found for defendants on all counts.

— Well, this certainly looks like it is essential to establish a loss in business/revenue in order to prevail. However, at this point, I do not have enough context to determine how this issue of lost business/revenue relates to the TIBE analysis.

Plaintiffs' motion for new trial was denied, and this appeal followed.

## II. ANALYSIS

### A. Manifest Weight of the Evidence

The standard of review in a bench trial is whether the judgment is against the manifest weight of the evidence. *Dargis v. Paradise Park, Inc.,* 354 Ill.App.3d 171, 177, 289 Ill.Dec. 420, 819 N.E.2d 1220 (2004). A reviewing court will not substitute its judgment for that of the trial court in a bench trial unless the judgment is against the manifest weight of the evidence. *First Baptist Church of Lombard v. Toll Highway Authority,* 301 Ill.App.3d 533, 542, 234 Ill.Dec. 878, 703 N.E.2d 978 (1998). "A judgment is against the manifest weight of the evidence only when the opposite conclusion is apparent or when findings appear to be unreasonable, arbitrary, or not based on evidence." *Judgment Services Corp. v. Sullivan,* 321 Ill.App.3d 151, 154, 254 Ill.Dec. 70, 746 N.E.2d 827 (2001).

— This section appears to relate to the appellate standard of review. Because we have not yet pursued a claim, it is not relevant to my analysis, and I can skim.

As the trier of fact, the trial judge was in a superior position to judge the credibility of the witnesses and determine the weight to be given to their testimony. *Buckner v. Causey,* 311 Ill.App.3d 139, 144, 243 Ill.Dec. 786, 724 N.E.2d 95 (1999). When contradictory testimony that could support conflicting conclusions is given at a bench trial, an appellate court will not disturb the trial court's factual findings based on that testimony unless a contrary finding is clearly apparent. *Buckner,* 311 Ill. App.3d at 144, 243 Ill.Dec. 786, 724 N.E.2d 95.

### 1. *Denial of directed finding*

Plaintiffs first contend that the trial court erred by entering judgment in favor of defendants when it denied their motion for directed finding pursuant to section 2-1110 of the Code of Civil Procedure (735 ILCS 5/2-1110 (West 2004)) and defendants did not present any evidence during their case. Defendants argue that the evidentiary record before the trial court at the time of the motion for directed finding was not the same as the record before the court after trial because at the close of trial, the court considered all of the evidence, "including the testimony of Defendants' witnesses, Defendants' exhibits, and the written findings of fact and conclusions of law presented by both parties." As plaintiffs point out, defendants did not present any witnesses, and the exhibits they submitted duplicated plaintiffs' trial exhibits, with the exception of defendants' exhibits 7, 8,[2] and 9, which were substantially similar but not the same.

Plaintiffs cite *Geske v. Geske,* 343 Ill.App.3d 881, 279 Ill.Dec. 26, 799 N.E.2d 829 (2003), in support of their argument. In *Geske,* at the close of the plaintiff's case, the defendant presented a motion for directed finding, which the trial court denied. The defendant rested without presenting any evidence, and the trial court found for the defendant. On the first appeal the court found in an unpublished order pursuant to Supreme Court Rule 23 (166 Ill.2d R. 23) that the trial court erred by entering judgment in the defendant's favor because when the defendant rested without offering any additional evidence, the initial determination that the plaintiff had satisfied his required burden of proof was unchallenged. *Geske,* 343 Ill.App.3d at 883, 279 Ill.Dec. 26, 799 N.E.2d 829. On remand, the trial court, citing its previous application of an incorrect standard, denied the plaintiff's motion for entry of judgment in her favor and ruled in favor of the defendant. On a second appeal, the court affirmed the trial court's decision to reopen the motion and correct its prior ruling. *Geske,* 343 Ill.App.3d at 885, 279 Ill.Dec. 26, 799 N.E.2d 829.

Unlike the defendant in *Geske,* who did not present *any* evidence, defendants here submitted their trial exhibits, even if most were the same as plaintiffs'. Therefore, the trial court's initial determination that plaintiffs satisfied their burden of proof was not "unchallenged," as it was in *Geske.* See *Geske,* 343 Ill.App.3d at 883, 279 Ill.Dec. 26, 799 N.E.2d 829. Furthermore, defendants' exhibits 7 and 9, while similar to plaintiffs' exhibits, are not identical to them. Although plaintiffs claim that defendants' exhibit 8 duplicates their exhibits,

Again, this section seems to relate to a procedural challenge, so I can skim, but I should do so with an eye toward any assertion about the sufficiency of evidence related to the TIBE claim.

---

2. While plaintiffs argue that defendants' exhibit 8 corresponds to plaintiffs' exhibits 4 and 5, exhibit 8 is missing from the record.

that exhibit is missing from the record, and the omission must be construed against plaintiffs. *Foutch v. O'Bryant,* 99 Ill.2d 389, 392, 76 Ill.Dec. 823, 459 N.E.2d 958 (1984) (an appellant has the burden of presenting a sufficiently complete record of proceedings at the trial court level to support a claim of error, and a reviewing court will resolve any doubts arising from the incompleteness of the record against the appellant).

*Bruss v. Klein,* 210 Ill.App.3d 72, 154 Ill.Dec. 683, 568 N.E.2d 904 (1991), is instructive. In *Bruss,* the defendants presented a motion for directed finding at the close of the plaintiff's case, which the trial court denied. The defendants called one witness to the stand, and following the trial, the trial court entered judgment for the defendants. On appeal, the plaintiff argued that the trial court's ruling in favor of the defendants was against the manifest weight of the evidence because by denying the motion for directed finding, the trial court found that he met his burden of proof. The court noted that, in ruling on a defendant's motion for directed finding, a trial court must first determine whether the plaintiff made out a *prima facie* case. *Bruss,* 210 Ill.App.3d at 77–78, 154 Ill.Dec. 683, 568 N.E.2d 904, citing *Kokinis v. Kotrich,* 81 Ill.2d 151, 155, 40 Ill.Dec. 812, 407 N.E.2d 43 (1980). If a *prima facie* case exists, then the trial judge must consider all the evidence, pass on the credibility of witnesses, draw reasonable inferences from the testimony, and consider the weight and quality of the evidence. *Bruss,* 210 Ill.App.3d at 78, 154 Ill.Dec. 683, 568 N.E.2d 904. If the weighing process results in the negation of some of the evidence necessary to the plaintiff's *prima facie* case, the court should grant the defendant's motion and dismiss the action. *Bruss,* 210 Ill.App.3d at 78, 154 Ill.Dec. 683, 568 N.E.2d 904.

> This really just seems to relate to the sufficiency, rather than content, of the evidence.

"We do not agree with plaintiff's argument, however, that the court's ruling in the motion for a directed finding must be considered a determination that plaintiff's testimony was credible and that his case was thus proved, precluding a judgment for defendants at the conclusion of the trial." *Bruss,* 210 Ill.App.3d at 78, 154 Ill.Dec. 683, 568 N.E.2d 904. The court noted that if a defendant's motion is denied, the court should continue as if the motion had not been made and proceed with trial. *Bruss,* 210 Ill.App.3d at 78, 154 Ill.Dec. 683, 568 N.E.2d 904, citing *Kokinis,* 81 Ill.2d at 155, 40 Ill.Dec. 812, 407 N.E.2d 43. "The fact that the trial court did not grant either of defendants' motions does not mean that the court could not rule for defendants at the conclusion of the trial, even based on a ground raised in the motions." *Bruss,* 210 Ill.App.3d at 78, 154 Ill.Dec. 683, 568 N.E.2d 904.

Therefore, we find that the trial court's denial of the motion for directed finding did not cause its final judgment to be against the manifest weight of the evidence.

*2. Tortious interference with business expectancy*

Here is my issue. I need to pay attention to the rule of law, its issues/conditions, and the facts that support the court's determination on each issue.

Plaintiffs also contend that the trial court's finding that Chicago's Pizza, Inc. failed to prove tortious interference with business expectancy was against the manifest weight of the evidence. This tort recognizes that a person's business relationships constitute a property interest and, as such, are entitled to protection from unjustified tampering by another. *Miller v. Lockport Realty Group, Inc.,* 377 Ill.App.3d 369, 373, 315 Ill.Dec. 945, 878 N.E.2d 171 (2007). The elements of the tort of intentional interference with a business expectancy include (1) a reasonable expectancy of entering into a valid business relationship; (2) the defendant's knowledge of the expectancy; (3) the defendant's intentional and unjustified interference that prevents the realization of the business expectancy; and (4) damages resulting from the interference. *Mannion v. Stallings & Company, Inc.,* 204 Ill.App.3d 179, 188, 149 Ill.Dec. 438, 561 N.E.2d 1134 (1990). A cause of action for intentional interference with a business expectancy need not be based on an enforceable contract that is interfered with; rather, it is the interference with the relationship that creates the actionable tort. *Lusher v. Becker Brothers, Inc.,* 155 Ill.App.3d 866, 869–70, 108 Ill. Dec. 748, 509 N.E.2d 444 (1987).

This seems to be important language. It seems to be some sort of standard, or basis for the TIBE law. To the extent that it emphasizes a business owner's interest, I want to make note of how it might weigh in favor of my client.

Ah, ha—the test! This is helpful, and the court even reinforces that it is an elements test. In other words, I will have to show (on Arnold's behalf) that all four conditions are satisfied.

This also seems important. It seems to be a standard of some sort that applies to the entire test, reinforcing that the plaintiff's interest is in the relationship with customers rather than in some right bestowed by contract.

Here is the analysis of the first issue. I will likely want to go back to the factual discussion of these customers at some point.

Plaintiffs first argue that they proved a reasonable expectancy of maintaining and entering into business relationships with existing and new customers. Specifically, they had a reasonable expectancy of maintaining business relationships with Stern, Poole, Cohen, and other customers deceived by defendants, and of entering into a new business relationship with DeArmond.

The trial court found that while Flores apparently had a good product and loyal customers, "in the very competitive food business, he could lose any of them for any number of reasons." Similarly, defendants, citing *Intervisual Communications, Inc. v. Volkert,* 975 F.Supp. 1092 (N.D.Ill.1997), argue that offering proof of a past customer relationship is not sufficient to prove a reasonable expectation of a future business relationship. In *Intervisual,* the court stated that the first element requires the plaintiff to "specifically identify [third] parties who actually contemplated entering into a business relationship with him." *Intervisual,* 975 F.Supp. at 1103. If a plaintiff were not required to specifically identify parties who actually contemplated entering into a business relationship with him, "'liability under a theory of tortious interference with prospective business expectancies would be virtually without limit and impossible to calculate.'" *Intervisual,* 975 F.Supp. at 1103, quoting *Celex Group, Inc. v. Executive Gallery,* 877 F.Supp. 1114, 1125–26 n. 19 (N.D.Ill.1995).

Both this sentence and the subsequent sentence are critical to understanding this first issue. It looks like I will have to identify specific customers with whom Arnold had a relationship. In other words, it will not be sufficient to identify potential customers.

It is clear that Wolf Stern contemplated a business relationship with plaintiffs, as he called defendants' store and asked for the phone number of the Lincoln Avenue location. The person Stern spoke to asked for his address and said they could deliver from the "Sheridan location." When he ordered from defendants, he believed he was doing business with plaintiffs. Jason [sic] Bitterman also ordered from defendants, believing he was doing business with the Chicago's Pizza on Lincoln and Sheffield. Furthermore, this court has previously ruled that "the opportunity to obtain customers is an expectancy protected by the tort of interference with a business expectancy." *Downers Grove Volkswagen, Inc. v. Wigglesworth Imports, Inc.,* 190 Ill.App.3d 524, 529, 137 Ill.Dec. 409, 546 N.E.2d 33 (1989), citing *North Broadway Motors, Inc. v. Fiat Motors of North America, Inc.,* 622 F.Supp. 466, 469 (N.D.Ill.1984). See also Restatement (Second) of Torts §766B, Comment *c*, at 22 (1979) (one type of protected relation is "interference with a continuing business or other customary relationship not amounting to a formal contract").

> Now I am getting somewhere. It looks like I can show that a customer contemplated a business relationship with my client by showing that the customer made calls or inquiries attempting to do business with my client. These facts will likely be useful to me in comparing Arnold's situation. I will likely want to try to generalize these specific facts into a basis upon which I can compare what happened to Arnold. Also, it looks like the plaintiff prevailed at the trial court level on this issue (and these facts), and that the appellate court is not overturning that finding.

Second, the name of defendants' restaurant and their advertising campaign suggest the defendants' knowledge of the expectancy. Also, defendants deceived customers Stern, DeArmond, Poole, and Cohen into thinking they were an affiliate of plaintiffs'.

> Again, these seem to be essential facts—a similarity in the business names, and intentional deception as to the business identity by the defendant. Once again, the court seems to be reiterating the factual basis on which the trial court concluded that the defendant had knowledge of the plaintiff's business expectancy.

Plaintiffs contend that they satisfied the third element, the defendant's intentional and unjustified interference that prevents the realization of the business expectancy. To prevail, it is insufficient for a plaintiff to merely show that the defendant interfered with a business expectancy. Rather, "[t]he element of 'purposeful' or 'intentional' interference refers to some impropriety committed by the defendant in interfering with the plaintiff's expectancy." *Romanek v. Connelly,* 324 Ill.App.3d 393, 406, 257 Ill.Dec. 436, 753 N.E.2d 1062 (2001); Restatement (Second) of Torts §766B, Comment *a*, at 20 (1979). Plaintiffs must prove that defendants acted "intentionally with the aim of injuring" plaintiffs' expectancy. *Romanek,* 324 Ill.App.3d at 406, 257 Ill.Dec. 436, 753 N.E.2d 1062. While "one may not simply sue any competitor who lures away customers, * * * the privilege of competition is not available to those who use wrongful means to interfere." *Downers Grove Volkswagen,* 190 Ill.App.3d at 528, 137 Ill. Dec. 409, 546 N.E.2d 33.

> This is helpful. It explains that interference alone is insufficient and that the plaintiff must show intentional or purposeful interference. This will be useful to me in showing how the court evaluates this element/issue.

Plaintiffs argue that defendants intentionally and unjustifiably prevented plaintiffs' realization of doing business with Stern, DeArmond, Poole, and Cohen by allowing them to place orders with defendants and then lying to Poole and DeArmond about the affiliation. While the trial court found that defendants used a distinctive logo on their

It looks like the court is disagreeing with the trial court's determination that customers were simply mistaken. Here, the court seems to conclude that the representations made by the defendants were misleading and therefore intentional, finding that the plaintiff satisfied this element.

— advertising, we disagree with their argument that Bitterman and Cohen simply mistook defendants' ad for plaintiffs'. Defendants' ads represented that they had numerous locations when they only had one. Two of the four locations (Downtown/Loop, Lakefront/Sheridan/Loyola) described in several of defendants' ads did not match plaintiffs'; however, two others (Lincoln/Sheffield, Montrose/Wilson) corresponded with plaintiffs' Lincoln, Sheffield, and Montrose stores.

The fourth element is damages resulting from the interference. *Mannion,* 204 Ill.App.3d at 188, 149 Ill.Dec. 438, 561 N.E.2d 1134. "Although the amount of an award of lost profits need not be proven with absolute certainty, the plaintiff bears the burden of proving such damages with reasonable certainty." *SK Hand Tool Corp. v. Dresser Industries, Inc.,* 284 Ill.App.3d 417, 426–27, 219 Ill.Dec. 833, 672 N.E.2d 341 (1996). Plaintiffs contend that they suffered damages because defendants diverted four specific orders, and Stern refused to do his usual weekly business with plaintiffs for one year. They also cite Remer's testimony that plaintiffs' lost sales for 2002 and 2003 exceeded $730,000 and their lost profits were $500,000. Significantly plaintiffs do not challenge any of the trial court's specific findings as to

OK, it looks like the trial court ruled in favor of the defendants on the issue of damages. I will need to determine what facts this court evaluates and what determination it reaches on this issue.

— damages. The trial court concluded that plaintiffs did not meet their burden of proving that defendants interfered with their business in such a manner to cause them to lose revenue.

These paragraphs seem to evaluate how diverted orders can demonstrate damages. These facts (value of diverted orders) will provide a useful comparison as I analyze Arnold's position on damages.

So here it looks like some of the customers did not divert orders, and in fact returned to the plaintiff.

— Regarding the diversion of specific orders, as the trial court found, each witness testified that he or she returned to ordering from plaintiffs. Furthermore, the only customer to testify as to defendants' actions during 2002 and 2003, the time when plaintiffs alleged, and their expert testified to, diminished sales, was Stern.

I will have to further consider whether the court is suggesting a way in which a plaintiff could demonstrate lost revenue.

Furthermore, the trial court rejected Remer's testimony because he did not conduct an independent investigation as to changes in the industry, the area of the city, or of people's eating habits at the time of the alleged decline in revenue. In addition, Remer accepted Flores's explanation as to lost revenues. While Remer testified that defendants' records were inaccurate and that his gross sales must have been $800,000 a year, the trial court doubted whether defendants earned that much if the food was as bad as plaintiffs' witnesses testified it was.

In addition, Remer's initial figures were based on erroneous assumption that the Lincoln dining room did not open until 2002, when in fact it opened in 2001. Remer agreed that if there was a dining room operating in 2001, his numbers "would have to be changed," but he did not testify as to what that change would be. He also testified that before he learned that the dining room revenue needed to be added to the damages calculation, he had concluded that plaintiffs' lost sales "appeared to be minimal." We find that the trial court's conclusion as to damages was not against the manifest weight of the evidence.

Therefore, we conclude that plaintiffs failed to demonstrate that the trial court's findings as to tortious interference with business expectancy were against the manifest weight of the evidence.

*So, I can conclude that the appellate court upheld the trial court's determination on the plaintiffs' failure to show damages. The facts cited by the appellate court—and lack thereof—might be useful to me in determining how my client could develop the appropriate evidence to support a finding of damages.*

### 3. *Deceptive Trade Practices Act*

*Since this is not a legal issue I intend to pursue, I can simply skim. I know it is always helpful to skim, rather than ignore, just in case the court makes reference to anything that might be useful to my TIBE claim.*

Plaintiffs argue that they are entitled to injunctive relief and attorney fees because defendants violated the Deceptive Trade Practices Act. The purpose of the Deceptive Trade Practices Act is to prohibit unfair competition, and it is primarily directed toward acts that unreasonably interfere with another's conduct of his or her business. *Phillips v. Cox,* 261 Ill. App.3d 78, 81, 198 Ill.Dec. 338, 632 N.E.2d 668 (1994). "Unfair competition is a broader concept than trademark infringement and depends upon likelihood of confusion as to the source of plaintiff's goods when the whole product, rather than just the service mark, is considered." *Thompson v. Spring–Green Lawn Care Corp.,*126 Ill.App.3d 99, 113, 81 Ill. Dec. 202, 466 N.E.2d 1004 (1984); *Phillips,* 261 Ill.App.3d at 81, 198 Ill.Dec. 338, 632 N.E.2d 668. A plaintiff may be granted relief under the theory of unfair competition regardless of whether his product or service is in direct competition with the defendant's product or service. *Thompson,* 126 Ill.App.3d at 113, 81 Ill.Dec. 202, 466 N.E.2d 1004.

In relevant part, section 2 of the Deceptive Trade Practices Act provides:

"A person engages in a deceptive trade practice when, in the course of his or her business, vocation, or occupation, the person:

(1) passes off goods or services as those of another;

(2) causes likelihood of confusion or of misunderstanding as to the source, sponsorship, approval, or certification of goods or services;

(3) causes likelihood of confusion or of misunderstanding as to affiliation, connection, or association with or certification by another;

(4) uses deceptive representations or designations of geographic origin in connection with goods and services;

(5) represents that goods or services have sponsorship, approval, characteristics, ingredients, uses, benefits, or quantities that they do not have or that a person has a sponsorship, approval, status, affiliation, or connection that he or she does not have;

\* \* \*

(8) disparages the goods, services, or business of another by false or misleading representation of fact;

(9) advertises goods with intent not to sell them as advertised;

\* \* \*

(12) engages in any other conduct which similarly creates a likelihood of confusion or misunderstanding."

815 ILCS 510/2(a) (West 2004). In order to prevail under section 2, "a plaintiff need not prove \* \* \* actual confusion or misunderstanding." 815 ILCS 510/2(b)(West 2004).

The trial court found that plaintiffs did not prove that defendants' conduct caused their lost revenue, a finding that we concluded is not against the manifest weight of the evidence. However, the Deceptive Trade Practices Act does not require proof of "monetary damages, loss of profit, or intent to deceive" to merit injunctive relief. 815 ILCS 510/3 (West 2004). In fact, plaintiffs cannot seek damages under the Deceptive Trade Practices Act. *Empire Home Services,* 274 Ill.App.3d at 671, 210 Ill.Dec. 657, 653 N.E.2d 852; *Greenberg v. United Airlines,* 206 Ill.App.3d 40, 46, 150 Ill.Dec. 904, 563 N.E.2d 1031 (1990). Rather, a "person likely to be damaged by a deceptive trade practice of another may be granted injunctive relief upon terms that the court considers reasonable." 815 ILCS 510/3 (West 2004); *Greenberg,* 206 Ill.App.3d at 47, 150 Ill.Dec. 904, 563 N.E.2d 1031. See *Disc Jockey Referral Network, Ltd. v. Ameritech Publishing of Illinois,* 230 Ill.App.3d 908, 915, 172 Ill.Dec. 725, 596 N.E.2d 4 (1992) ("Private suits for injunctive relief may be brought in situations where one competitor is harmed or may be harmed by the unfair trade practices of another"). In *Bingham v. Inter–Track Partners,* 234 Ill.App.3d 615, 621, 175 Ill.Dec. 447, 600 N.E.2d 70 (1992), the court held that "injunctive relief is warranted when a party's trade practice creates a likelihood of confusion or misunderstanding."

Defendants argue that they did not "pass off" their goods and services as those of plaintiffs because the words "Chicago's Pizza" are generic and descriptive of the parties' location and goods. They also point out that they prominently display their distinctive logo on their advertising, menus, and telephone book listings.

We disagree with defendants and conclude that plaintiffs demonstrated that defendants' trade practices created a likelihood of confusion or misunderstanding. Specifically, defendants' trade practices

(1) cause the likelihood of confusion or of misunderstanding as to the source, sponsorship, approval, or certification of goods and services, in violation of subsection 2(a)(2); (2) cause the likelihood of confusion or of misunderstanding as to affiliation, connection, or association with or certification by another, in violation of subsection 2(a)(3); and (3) use deceptive representations or designations of geographic origin in connection with goods and services, in violation of subsection 2(a)(4). See *Multiut Corp. v. Draiman,* 359 Ill.App.3d 527, 537, 295 Ill.Dec. 818, 834 N.E.2d 43 (2005). Defendants have also engaged in "any other conduct which similarly creates a likelihood of confusion or misunderstanding," in violation of subsection 2(a) (12). 815 ILCS 510/2(a)(12) (West 2004).

In addition to the similar name, defendants' menus, coupons, and ads falsely advertised numerous locations, even though they only had one. The ads urged customers to "call for your nearest location" and had different numbers for the different "locations." These phone numbers corresponded to each of the phony locations, so defendants appeared to have locations in different parts of the city. Two of defendants' "locations" (Lincoln/Sheffield, Montrose/Wilson) corresponded to plaintiffs' locations on Lincoln, Sheffield, and Montrose/Wilson. Adding to the confusion, many of the ads and coupons that touted multiple "locations" did not have defendants' own address on them.

While defendants blame the customers for their own alleged "mistakes," it was defendants' ads that caused their confusion. Indeed, plaintiffs proved not only a *likelihood* of confusion or misunderstanding as a result of defendants' ads and coupons, as required by the Deceptive Trade Practices Act, but also *actual* confusion by customers. See *Thompson,* 126 Ill.App.3d at 113, 81 Ill.Dec. 202, 466 N.E.2d 1004. For example, Anthony Poole, an established customer of plaintiffs', testified that defendants' employee told him he was ordering from the Wilson "location," when plaintiffs, not defendants, had a restaurant on Wilson. Similarly, Wolf Stern, also a regular customer of plaintiffs', called defendants because he wanted the phone number for the Lincoln Avenue location. Stern specifically testified that when he ordered a pizza, he believed he was doing business with an affiliate of plaintiffs'. When he called defendants to complain about the poor quality of the food, an employee offered him a discount, which would be good at the Lincoln Avenue "location," even though plaintiffs, not defendants, had a restaurant on Lincoln Avenue. Mary DeArmond also testified that one of defendants' employees told her that their restaurant was affiliated with the Chicago's Pizza on Montrose.

Similarly, Joseph Bitterman saw an ad for Chicago's Pizza with different phone numbers for different locations. Bitterman called the number for the Sheffield "location" believing he was calling plaintiffs' restaurant on Sheffield and placed an order. Judith Levine, a customer of plaintiffs' for 15 years, believed that defendants' coupon, which listed three "locations," was for plaintiffs' restaurants until she attempted to use it. Finally, Patricia Flores testified that she called a phone number on one of defendants' ads and was advised that it was affiliated with the Chicago's Pizza on Montrose. Martin and Patricia Flores also testified that they received a number of customer complaints regarding defendants' products, even though they were not plaintiffs'.

In *Phillips,* the plaintiffs bought the defendant's sign-making business, which included both real and personal property and the right to use the name "David Cox Signs." Six years later, the defendant opened a sign-making business next door to the plaintiffs and named his business "David R. Cox d/b/a Sign Design and Construction." The plaintiffs filed a complaint for injunctive relief, claiming that the defendant diverted the plaintiffs' customers, thereby depriving them of sales and revenue. The complaint was dismissed. On appeal, the court applied the "broad language" of subsection 2(12) of the Deceptive Trade Practices Act and noted that any conduct that creates a likelihood of consumer confusion or misunderstanding is potentially actionable under subsection 2(12), even if the conduct is not specifically covered by other sections of the act. *Phillips,* 261 Ill.App.3d at 81–82, 198 Ill. Dec. 338, 632 N.E.2d 668. The court held that the plaintiff alleged facts sufficient to state a cause of action because (1) the defendant located his sign-making business next door to the plaintiffs' business, (2) both parties were engaged in the same type of business, and (3) the defendant was operating his business under a name that is "very similar" to the name used by the plaintiffs. *Phillips,* 261 Ill.App.3d at 83, 198 Ill.Dec. 338, 632 N.E.2d 668.

Similarly, in *Empire Home Services,* the plaintiff's advertising emphasized a telephone number, 588–2300, which generated more than 1,000 responses a day. The defendant began using the phone number 588–3200, and when some potential Empire customers mistakenly phoned the defendant, told the customers that they reached Empire, or a company "just like Empire." The defendant referred the customers to Carpet America, which contacted the caller and claimed to be Empire, using a sales presentation and purchase orders similar to Empire's. The court ruled that the complaint stated a claim under subsections 2(1), (2), and (3) of the Deceptive Trade Practices Act. *Empire Home Services,* 274 Ill.App.3d at 670, 210 Ill.Dec. 657, 653 N.E.2d 852.

While *Phillips* and *Empire* involved the sufficiency of complaints rather than the sufficiency of the proof at trial, they demonstrate the type of conduct that this court has found violative of the Deceptive Trade Practices Act. Defendants used a similar name, and their ads advertised numerous locations, some of which corresponded to plaintiffs' locations on Lincoln, Sheffield, and Montrose/Wilson. In light of the evidence of defendants' ads, menus, and coupons, and the potential for customer confusion, we find that plaintiffs demonstrated that defendants violated section 2 of the Deceptive Trade Practices Act. Furthermore, although defendants' restaurant is currently closed, Muhammed testified that after this litigation ends, he plans to reopen his business... under the name "Chicago's Pizza," thus perpetuating the potential for confusion. Therefore, we find that plaintiffs are entitled to injunctive relief. 815 ILCS 510/3 (West 2004); *Empire Home Services,* 274 Ill.App.3d at 671, 210 Ill.Dec. 657, 653 N.E.2d 852; *Greenberg,* 206 Ill.App.3d at 46, 150 Ill.Dec. 904, 563 N.E.2d 1031.

In addition, costs or attorney fees may be assessed against a defendant "only if the court finds that he has wilfully engaged in a deceptive trade practice." 815 ILCS 510/3 (West 2004). "Willful" is defined as "voluntary and intentional, but not necessarily malicious." Black's Law Dictionary 1630 (8th ed. 2004). Muhammed denied knowing about plaintiffs' restaurants until this lawsuit was filed in 2003. Even assuming that to be the case, the uncontroverted customer testimony was that defendants continued to mislead consumers about their association with plaintiffs' restaurants after the complaint was filed. Therefore, we find because defendants "wilfully engaged in a deceptive trade practice," plaintiffs are entitled to reasonable attorney fees.

### 4. *Consumer Fraud Act*

Plaintiff Chicago's Pizza, Inc., also alleged a violation of the Consumer Fraud Act. Section 2 of the Consumer Fraud Act provides that the use of any practice described in section 2 of the Deceptive Trade Practices Act also constitutes a violation of the Consumer Fraud Act. 815 ILCS 505/2 (West 2004). While plaintiffs are entitled to injunctive relief under the Deceptive Trade Practices Act, the same does not apply for Chicago's Pizza, Inc.'s claim for violation of the Consumer Fraud Act.

Section 10a(c) of the Consumer Fraud Act provides that "in any action brought by a person under this Section, the Court may grant injunctive relief where appropriate." 815 ILCS 505/10a(c) (West 2004). We have previously held that the "Consumer Fraud Act provides a private cause of action only where a plaintiff can show that he suffered damage as a result of unlawful conduct proscribed by the statute." *Smith v. Prime Cable of Chicago,* 276 Ill.App.3d 843, 859, 213 Ill.Dec. 304, 658 N.E.2d 1325 (1995). Although "a *violation* of the Consumer Fraud Act may occur in the absence of damages, a *private cause of action* does not arise absent a showing of both a violation and resultant damages." (Emphasis in original.) *Tarin v. Pellonari,* 253 Ill.App.3d 542, 554, 192 Ill.Dec. 584, 625 N.E.2d 739 (1993). We find that Chicago's Pizza, Inc.'s failure to prove actual damages, as described above, precludes damages or injunctive relief under the Consumer Fraud Act.

— Since this is not a legal issue I intend to pursue, I can simply skim. I know it is always helpful to skim, rather than ignore, just in case the court makes reference to anything that might be useful to my TIBE claim.

Since this is not a legal issue I
intend to pursue, I can simply
skim. I know it is always
helpful to skim, rather than
ignore, just in case the court
makes reference to anything
that might be useful to my
TIBE claim, especially insofar
as it relates to damages.
Having skimmed this section,
however, I can conclude
that it is the analysis of a
procedural challenge to
the evidence, rather than a
substantive one.

## B. Discovery

Finally, plaintiffs contend that the trial court precluded them from engaging in complete discovery concerning defendants' financial and business records and the identity of their customers. A trial court has great latitude in ruling on discovery matters. *Mutlu v. State Farm Fire & Casualty Co.*, 337 Ill.App.3d 420, 434, 271 Ill.Dec. 757, 785 N.E.2d 951 (2003). A trial court's rulings on such matters will not be disturbed absent a manifest abuse of discretion. *Mutlu,* 337 Ill.App.3d at 434, 271 Ill.Dec. 757, 785 N.E.2d 951.

Plaintiffs argue that the trial court erred when it denied them access to defendants' "financial and business records" and computer-based customer lists. Plaintiffs do not, however, cite to pages of the record for their requests or the trial court's denial. Indeed, it is unclear what requests plaintiffs are referring to. Therefore, we consider this argument waived. 210 Ill.2d R. 341(h)(7); *Feret v. Schillerstrom,* 363 Ill. App.3d 534, 541, 300 Ill.Dec. 449, 844 N.E.2d 447 (2006).

## III. CONCLUSION

Plaintiffs have failed to demonstrate that the trial court's findings as to their claims for tortious interference and consumer fraud are against the manifest weight of the evidence. However, we find that plaintiffs are entitled to injunctive relief and attorney fees pursuant to the Deceptive Trade Practices Act. Therefore, we reverse in part and remand for entry of injunctive relief and a determination as to reasonable attorney fees.

Affirmed in part and reversed in part; cause remanded.

CAMPBELL and O'BRIEN, JJ., concur.

We will now turn to the topic of "thinking like a lawyer," which is similarly informed by a client focus and engagement with the text.

## II.  How a Lawyer Thinks

As the prior section illustrates, lawyers engage in active reading. They read legal information with a purpose in mind, typically to synthesize cases to discern legal principles and often to use those principles to determine how they might apply to a client's situation. This client context informs how a lawyer reads, determining the information the lawyer is seeking and consequently dictating where he focuses attention and where he skims. Legal analysis therefore not only informs **what** the lawyer does with legal content when he reads it, but also **how** he actually consumes the legal information. The lawyer is actively searching for different types of content: material related to the rule of law that governs the situation; facts in *precedent* cases that were relevant to the court's determination of the legal issues; and ways in which those precedent facts might be argued to be analogous to or distinguishable from his client's facts.

It is for this reason that law-trained readers "brief" cases as they read them—either explicitly as notes for class when students are in law school, or implicitly in practice, as lawyers read cases with certain components in mind. Below is the framework for a "case brief," which is simply the term law students use to refer to the conventional notes they take as they read cases in preparation for class.

## ⊞ CONCEPT IN ACTION: Case Brief

## Case Brief for *Com. v. Hermione H.*, 68 Mass. App. Ct. 1106, 861 N.E.2d 809 (2007)

*Citation*: The case citation will help you obtain the full text of the case and is important if you intend to cite the case in a written document. The citation also gives useful information, such as which court decided the case and the date of the opinion. The identity of the issuing court provides information about the precedential value of the case, and the date of the decision puts the case in historical perspective.

### *COM. V. HERMIONE H.*, 68 MASS. APP. CT. 1106, 861 N.E.2D 809 (2007)

*Facts*: Keep the facts as simple and concise as possible. Refer to the parties with descriptive terms (e.g., seller, landlord, plaintiff) and include only legally relevant facts. A relevant fact is one that influenced the court's decision. Do not include irrelevant names, dates, or details.

**Defendant hit the victim in the face with a closed fist while wearing rings**

*Procedure*: Include the following:

*Who is suing whom for what?* Most published cases represent an appellate decision. This means the case has already been heard and decided at the trial level, typically with a jury assessing witness credibility and other evidence to determine the facts of the case, then applying the relevant law to these facts; this law is communicated to the jury in the form of jury instructions. The *appellant* is the complaining party on appeal, and the *appellee*, the respondent. Appellate courts primarily hear cases where the lower court may have made an error. Typically, the contention will relate to an error of *substantive law* (e.g., torts, contracts), or an error of *procedural law*.

*What is the legal claim?* You want to understand the original legal *claim* at the trial court level, as well as the specific legal claim on appeal. In the case of an appeal relating to an issue of substantive law, these may be the same (e.g., whether a legally binding offer was made, or whether the defendant owed the plaintiff a duty). In the case of an error relating to an issue of procedural law, the issues at trial and on appeal may be vastly different. To have a good understanding of the case, you want to be familiar with, and able to distinguish between, each legal claim.

*How did the lower court rule?* This portion of the brief should describe, in simple terms, how the case progressed to the current appeal.

> Defendant was adjudicated delinquent. Namely, the trial court adjudicated the defendant delinquent on the *charge* of assault and battery by means of a dangerous weapon. It also adjudicated the defendant delinquent on the charge of assault and battery.

> The defendant appealed both findings. As to the latter finding, the appeals court reversed because, as the State acknowledged on appeal, that general delinquency charge was duplicative.

> As to the finding of delinquency for assault and battery by means of a dangerous weapon, the defendant appealed, arguing that the evidence was not sufficient to show that the assault and battery was "by means of a dangerous weapon."

*Issue*: This can be the most difficult portion of the brief, because frequently there are multiple issues on appeal. And, among those issues, some are factual issues, some are procedural issues, and some are issues involving questions of law. A good first step is to focus on the issue or issues of significance to your client's situation. Ask yourself: "What does the appellant [the party that lost in the lower court and is now appealing] argue the trial court did wrong? What grounds has the appellant offered to persuade the appellate court to correct the error?" From that answer, construct the issue statement. The issue statement is typically framed as a question that can be answered either "yes" or "no." Generally, you want to state the issue in the broadest terms that can be *reasonably* used as precedent for future cases.

> Did the trial court properly find that the defendant's rings constituted a "dangerous weapon"?[1]

*Rule of Law*: What is the legal rule that the court applied to the conflict facts?

> In determining whether the ring is a dangerous weapon, the court will consider "whether the object, as used by the [defendant], is capable of producing serious bodily harm."

---

1. Note that lawyers sometimes present the issue not as a question but as a "whether" statement, such as "Whether the trial court properly found that the defendant's rings constituted a 'dangerous weapon.'" Either way is acceptable, and because a case brief is primarily for your own use, you should adopt whichever style resonates with you.

*Holding*: The ***holding*** is the court's answer to the issue presented. It may be a rephrasing of the issue statement from a question into a declarative statement. Alternatively, you may state the holding as a simple response to the issue. The level of detail you provide when stating the holding will depend on the level of specificity with which you stated the issue. The more broadly you stated the issue, the more detail you will need to provide in the holding statement, and vice versa. The holding is also known as the ruling of the case.

> **Yes.** [This alone might be acceptable where the issue is stated with sufficient specificity, but because the issue above is stated broadly more detail is warranted]. **The evidence was sufficient to conclude that the rings as used were a dangerous weapon.**

*Analysis*: The analysis portion of the brief is a summary of the specific legal reasons given by the court in support of its decision. Include all legal reasons, as well as other reasons the court noted, such as social, moral, or political justifications. You should also include the *reasoning* set forth in *concurring* and *dissenting* opinions.

> **"Resolution of these questions is invariably for the fact finder... and involves not only consideration of any evidence as to the nature and specific features of the object but also attention to the circumstances surrounding the assault and the use of the object, and the manner in which it was handled or controlled."**

> **"It is not required that the perpetrator intend to use the instrumentality as a dangerous weapon."**

> **"'[O]rdinarily innocuous items can be considered dangerous weapons when used in an improper and dangerous manner.' ... What is required is that the item as used be capable of causing the requisite degree of bodily harm."**

> **"[T]he victim's testimony that the juvenile punched her with a ring-clad fist, the victim's hospital records, and photographs of the victim's injuries were sufficient to permit the jury to conclude that the rings worn by the juvenile, as used, were dangerous weapons."**

*Disposition*: Describe the full *disposition* of the case. Include whether the ruling was in favor of the appellant or the appellee and note any relief granted. Note whether the case was affirmed in whole or in part, reversed in whole or in part, or remanded (meaning it was sent back to the lower court for further action).

> The adjudication of delinquency on the charge of assault and battery by means of a dangerous weapon is affirmed; the adjudication of delinquency on the charge of assault and battery is vacated and the complaint dismissed.

**CRASH WARNING: Skim First to Focus Your Case Brief**

Students who are new to the process of case briefing often make the mistake of drafting the facts section of the case brief as they read the case. This is inefficient because the case brief should reflect the key facts upon which the court based its ruling. However, most cases include a lengthy facts section, which likely includes background information that may not be particularly relevant to the court's determination of the legal issue. Experienced lawyers know that it is typically more efficient and effective to first skim the entire case, getting context for how the court ruled, and why. Only with that context can the lawyer discern what facts were most relevant to the court's resolution of the issue. This process of reading actively and with a purpose illustrates how lawyers read cases differently from readers outside of the profession.

## III. Putting It Together: A Lawyer Begins to Write

The discipline-specific ways in which lawyers read (consume) and evaluate (analyze) legal information should be a bit clearer at this point. Note that these activities are a critical portion of the writing process. Any kind of research-based writing requires some degree of preliminary work before you actually begin drafting a document. The components of this *pre-drafting process* vary somewhat from discipline to discipline, but they typically include research and analysis, clarifying your topic, identifying and carefully reading relevant sources, and beginning to formulate your ideas. In some disciplines, it is possible to give only superficial attention to the pre-drafting process, simply circling back to research and analysis as needed to complete the project. In contrast, for professional legal writing, this is an ineffective—and ill-advised—strategy.

The pre-drafting stage is particularly important in legal writing because a firm grasp of the applicable legal rule is essential to writing a reliable and useful document, regardless of document type. In Chapter 5, we present a multi-step writing process, and many of these steps relate to pre-drafting analysis. It may seem cumbersome at first to complete so much preliminary work before you even start the first draft of your final product. However, by carefully attending to each step of the pre-drafting process, you will be well prepared to begin drafting when it is time to do so, and you will help ensure that you fulfill your duty to provide useful and competent advice to your client. While attention to the pre-drafting process makes the drafting process more efficient, the writing process frequently remains recursive, such that you will move between drafting and pre-drafting. Nonetheless, like most skills, as you become more practiced, these steps will become easier.

**RULES OF THE ROAD: Ethical Rules Regarding Memo Preparation**

A *predictive memorandum* (also called objective or interoffice memorandum) is an informal document used by lawyers to memorialize their analysis of a legal issue. Because memoranda are informal and typically not disseminated outside the lawyer's practice, they are not subject to direct regulation by ethical rules. Memoranda are frequently prepared at the beginning of representation to determine whether a client should proceed with a legal matter. Memoranda are also prepared during the representation of a client to determine how to proceed with a claim or issue. Because they provide a written record of the lawyer's analysis, they establish the basis for the lawyer's advice. They therefore invoke the lawyer's obligation of counseling and advising. Moreover, predictive memoranda may form the basis for documents a lawyer later prepares for court—documents that are subject to direct regulation.

Ethical rules that impact memo preparation include (1) the obligation to be competent in representation, (2) the obligation to communicate adequately and candidly with the client, and (3) the obligation to advise the client. With regard to (1) competence, the ABA Model Rules and rules adopted in most jurisdictions require a lawyer to have or obtain the requisite knowledge to represent the client. This requires the lawyer to be able to properly identify the client's legal issue, which is not always straightforward, and to be able to determine key facts and relevant law related to that issue. Ethical obligations associated with (2) communications also require the lawyer to keep the client apprised of developments in legal matters and to communicate candidly, even in the face of news that will be upsetting or disappointing to the client. When (3) advising the client, the lawyer will present proposed courses of action. Ultimately, the client has the decision-making authority to choose how to proceed. The lawyer must adequately explain the legal situation and proposed actions to the client so that the client understands the advantages and disadvantages of each recommendation.

After helping you establish your pre-drafting skills, we will walk you through the deductive framework in which legal analysis is communicated. We will primarily describe how this framework applies in a predictive memorandum; however, regardless of the particular vehicle used for communicating your analysis, predictive analysis always begins with general legal principles then moves to specific application to client facts.

### CHAPTER 3

# Predictive Legal Analysis

In Chapter 1 we briefly touched on predictive legal analysis—the type of objective, neutral analysis a lawyer engages in when assessing the merits of a client's situation in order to predict the likely result. This chapter explores predictive analysis in more detail. We will discuss how a lawyer employs an inductive (proceeding from specific to broad) analytical framework at the pre-drafting stage of writing a predictive memo, versus using a deductive (proceeding from broad to specific) framework when communicating the legal analysis in the memo. In addition, we will describe how lawyers reason by analogy, crafting guiding factors to help them compare their client's facts to facts from precedent cases.

---

### Study Guide Questions for Chapter 3

1. How is predictive legal analysis different from persuasive legal analysis?
2. Can lawyers be sanctioned if their predictions are not accurate? Under what circumstances?
3. What is the process of analogical reasoning?
4. Describe the analytical framework used to engage in pre-drafting predictive analysis.

How does that analytical framework differ from that employed to communicate legal analysis in writing?

5. What new terms were introduced in this chapter? How do these terms relate to your existing understanding of predictive memo writing? Did your understanding of any other terms change as a result of reading this chapter?

---

## I. Understanding Predictive Legal Analysis

This semester you will focus on predictive legal analysis. This simply refers to the process a lawyer uses to analyze relevant prior cases and apply those cases to the client's situation in order to predict a result. As we emphasized in Chapter 1, this type of analysis is objective, or neutral. *Predictive analysis* requires the lawyer to evaluate the situation from the perspective of both parties to assess the relative merits of each party's position in order to predict the likely result. *Predictive writing* captures that neutral analysis. The counterpart to predictive writing is *persuasive writing*. The latter includes documents filed with the court or presented to adversaries in which the lawyer makes arguments. The purpose of persuasive writing is to advocate, not to predict. Even so, predictive analysis underlies persuasion because the writer must be aware of the strengths and weaknesses of arguments on both sides of the issue (i.e., *arguments* and *counter-arguments*).

How is predictive writing used in the practice of law? Clients rely on lawyers to analyze legal situations and to help them determine a course of action. A predictive legal analysis explains the legal issue and examines how and why a court would likely resolve it. For example, a client considering opening a bar may come to a lawyer to inquire about her potential exposure under state dram shop law (the law that governs liability for bars that serve alcohol to patrons who later cause harm while under the influence).

The client is not asking the lawyer to craft the best arguments as to why her bar should never be held liable. The client instead wants to hear "the good, the bad, and the ugly," meaning all sides of the analysis. Only when fully informed of how, when, and why her bar might be held liable can she decide whether to open the bar and, if so, what measures to put in place to minimize the bar's exposure to liability.

New law students are often understandably reluctant to predict how a court will apply the law. They worry that their lack of experience precludes them from making an accurate *prediction*. Your confidence in your predictions will increase over time, but for now you should keep in mind that the analysis that leads up to your bottom-line prediction constitutes the most critical part of the memo.

Predicting how a court might decide a legal matter requires a lawyer to accurately identify the legal issue posed by the client's facts, to research applicable law, to identify and understand the applicable rule of law, and to then apply that law to the client facts. We will examine each of these activities in more detail in later chapters; here we focus briefly on the process of applying prior cases to the client's current situation. More specifically, we will introduce *analogical reasoning*, which is the process of comparing the facts in judicial opinions to the facts of a client's case.

## II.  How Analogical Reasoning Helps Lawyers Use Prior Cases to Make Legal Predictions

Much of predictive analysis entails identifying arguments about how a court is likely to rule based upon how it has ruled in the past. This type of analysis is called analogical reasoning. As you are likely aware, the concept of *stare decisis*, literally "to stand by things decided," means that similar situations must result in similar decisions. Thus, in analogical reasoning, a lawyer makes arguments based upon similarities and differences between her client's situation and prior cases.

For example, assume a court decides that a riding lawnmower is a "motor vehicle" in the context of a statute. If a later factual situation involves a riding lawnmower, the lawyer can be confident the court will determine that the lawnmower is a motor vehicle under the same statute. This concept therefore promotes consistency and fairness. The tricky part of legal analysis, however, is that facts tend to differ, ever so slightly, such that it is often unclear how similar facts are. What if your client's situation does not involve a riding lawnmower, but a motorized scooter? A lawyer for one side would argue that the motorized scooter is a motor vehicle because it is similar to the riding lawnmower. A lawyer for the other side would argue that the motorized scooter is unlike a riding lawnmower and is therefore not a motor vehicle.

How, specifically, do lawyers make these comparisons? What makes a motorized scooter like or unlike a riding lawnmower? Lawyers compare distinct fact patterns on the basis of legally significant considerations used by courts in prior cases. These considerations, which we refer to as *guiding factors*, operate as the bases upon which a lawyer can meaningfully compare the specific facts of a judicial opinion to the facts of the client's case.

## III.  Using Guiding Factors to Reason by Analogy

To understand how lawyers use guiding factors to reason by analogy, let's consider a non-legal example. Compare an apple to an orange. How are they similar? How are they different? You might first note that they are both small, round fruits. After identifying the specific similarities, you can frame each similarity as a generalized basis of comparison: size, shape, and type of food. These generalized bases of comparison are known as "guiding factors."

Apples and oranges are different, however, in other ways. Apples are most often red, and oranges are, well, orange. An orange must be peeled in order to eat it, while an apple does not need to be peeled in order to be eaten. From these specific differences, you can decide that two guiding factors upon which apples and oranges differ are "color" and "manner of consumption."

If we were asked to predict how a court would rule on similarity, we would have to make comparisons on the basis of all of these guiding factors: size, shape, type of food, color, and manner of consumption.

Because some guiding factors show similarities between an apple and an orange, while others illustrate differences, we would need to learn which guiding factors are most significant to the decision maker. If the guiding factor of shape is not important at all, but the manner of consumption is critical, apples and oranges will likely be found to be different. On the other hand, if size and shape are the most important considerations, the two fruits will likely be deemed similar.

We will be using similar bases of comparison in predictive legal analysis. Recall your reading in Chapter 1. There you learned that legal rules function like tests—certain *conditions* have to be met for a *result* to occur. Sometimes *all* of the conditions must be satisfied for the result to occur. This type of test is called an "elements test," and the conditions are therefore referred to as *elements*. If the conditions are *discretionary*, that means they do not all need to be satisfied; instead, they are considerations to be weighed when making a decision. In this case, the conditions are called *factors,* and the test is called a "factors test."

Whether elements or factors, conditions tend to be somewhat vague, requiring lawyers to seek additional information to determine the fuller meaning and limits of a condition. Lawyers do that by using prior cases that have interpreted and applied that condition. Doing this helps the lawyer better understand what a court considers when determining if that condition is met. Sometimes these guiding factors are explicit. For instance, imagine a prior case that states: "In determining whether a food is a good picnic food, the court considers the size, type of food, and manner of consumption." Although the condition—whether a food is a good picnic food—is vague and subjective, we know the court explicitly considers three guiding factors in making its determination. These guiding factors provide the lawyer with a way to evaluate if a certain food satisfies the condition of being a good picnic food.

More often than not, however, a case does not provide explicit guiding factors. Instead, we typically have to cull the pertinent information from the case ourselves in order to make inferences about what is guiding the court. That process, which entails identifying and articulating implicit guiding factors, can be difficult. It is an *inductive* analytical process that involves taking the specific facts that matter to a court and generalizing those facts into a category. This is what we did in the fruit example above: we took specific facts (red, orange, round, necessity of peeling) and generalized those facts into categories (colors, shape, manner of consumption). Those categories are indeed implicit guiding factors. We follow this same process—making generalizations from specific facts—to identify implicit guiding factors in legal contexts. Chapter 8 further explores both explicit and implicit guiding factors.

**GEARING UP: Identifying Guiding Factors Is a Flexible Process**

Identifying guiding factors starts with a somewhat formulaic approach; you identify facts that matter to the court, group them together into categories that matter to the court, and apply those categories to your case. However, this basic process allows for a great deal of discretion and creativity. Legal analysis requires you to think criti- cally about the law, and part of that process involves noticing gray areas. As we continue to explore guiding factors, you will see that you can shape reasonable, yet beneficial, interpretations of the law within those gray areas, in part based upon the way that you group and label these guiding factors.

## IV. Using Predictive Analysis to Solve Client Problems

Legal analysis requires the attorney to locate the applicable rule of law and then break it down into its conditions. Then, the lawyer must determine whether each condition, whether factor or element, is *contested*, meaning each side has a viable argument as to whether it is satisfied. Where a condition is contested, it is considered an *issue*. If the condition is clearly satisfied, such that it cannot reasonably be contested, it is considered a *non-issue*.

### Dangerous Dog Hypothetical

Let's take a brief example. Imagine the City of Bakerville enacted an ordinance that states: "All dangerous dogs must be licensed." A new client, Gianna, comes to you because she has a pit bull named LuLu, and the city has given notice that LuLu must be licensed. How do you advise Gianna? What is your prediction?

Let's look at the process. Once you have located the rule of law, you need to analyze the rule itself: What is the result? What are the conditions? How do the conditions relate to one another? Here the legal result is the obligation to license. One condition is that the animal must be a dog. Another condition is that the animal is dangerous.

Because the client's animal is a pit bull, it would not be contested that the animal is, in fact, a dog. Thus, the condition that the animal must be a dog would be a non-issue. However, the condition of whether the animal is dangerous almost certainly would be contested. Unlike whether an animal is a dog, the notion of whether an animal is "dangerous" is highly subjective and subject to debate. In other words, it is an issue.

Because the ordinance does not define "dangerous," a significant part of your predictive analysis would consist of locating factually similar cases in which the ordinance has been applied in the past. You might, for example, find a case in which a German Shepherd was deemed dangerous because her breed was considered aggressive and she had bitten people on two different occasions. You might also find a case in which an Akita was held not to be dangerous when she had no history of biting, even though her breed was associated with protective, and possibly aggressive, tendencies. On the basis of these cases, you might construct guiding factors for the condition of "dangerous" so that you could compare your client's dog to the dogs in the prior cases.

| CONDITION | FACTS | GUIDING FACTOR |
|---|---|---|
| Dangerous | German Shepherd; Akita | Aggressive breed |
| | Two instances of biting; no biting | History of biting |

 **Rules of the Road: Ethically Addressing Uncertainty in the Law**

A lawyer has an obligation to research and know the law. However, where the law is unsettled or where reasonable minds could differ on the meaning of the law, the doctrine of judgmental immunity protects a lawyer from liability for mere errors. As one court explained:

Other jurisdictions considering this question have concluded that an attorney who acts in good faith and with an honest belief that his or her actions are well founded in the law and in the best interests of his or her client is not answerable for a mere error of judgment or for a mistake in a point of law which has not been settled by the court of last resort in his or her state and on which reasonable doubt may be entertained by well-informed lawyers. *Collins v. Wanner*, 382 P.2d 105 (Okla.1963). "A lawyer would need a crystal ball, along with his library, to be able to guarantee that no judge, anytime, anywhere, would disagree with his judgment or evaluation of a situation." *Denzer v. Rouse*, 48 Wis.2d 528, 534, 180 N.W.2d 521, 525 (1970), *overruled on other grounds, Hansen v. A.H.*

*Robins, Inc.,* 113 Wis.2d 550, 335 N.W.2d 578 (1983). We agree.

*Baker v. Fabian, Thielen & Thielen*, 254 Neb. 697, 705, 578 N.W.2d 446, 451–52 (1998).

Even though a lawyer might not be liable for malpractice when giving advice in an area where the law is unsettled or otherwise unclear, the lawyer still has the obligation to *explain* that uncertainty to the client so that the client is able to make decisions accordingly. As another court explains:

The decision to settle a controversy is the client's…. If a client is to meaningfully make that decision, he or she needs to have the information necessary to assess the risks and benefits of either settling or proceeding to trial…. [Thus] the doctrine of judgmental immunity does not apply to an attorney's failure to *inform* a client of unsettled legal issues relevant to a settlement.

*Wood v. McGrath, N., Mullin & Kratz, P.C.*, 589 N.W.2d 103, 106, 108 (1999) (emphasis added).

You would make your prediction by analyzing how your client's case is similar to and how it is different from these two prior cases. In other words, you will be making predictions as to how similar or dissimilar your client's facts are to the facts of precedent cases. You will be making those comparisons on the basis of legally significant considerations: the guiding factors that relate to the condition of "dangerous." While this may seem daunting, know that you are capable of making these predictions. Further, be aware that in making predictions you are not guaranteeing the result, nor should you use language with the client that might suggest that you are.

## V.  Inductive and Deductive Analysis

As will be explained in more detail in Modules II and III, a lawyer uses *inductive reasoning* to engage in pre-drafting predictive analysis, taking her analysis of specific cases and using those examples to frame general principles. When she communicates that analysis in writing, she will employ a *deductive framework*, beginning with general principles and moving to specific comparisons. That distinction can be visualized as follows:

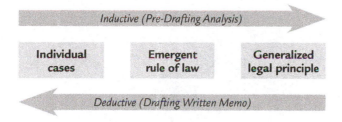

### CHAPTER 4

# The Structure of a Predictive Legal Memorandum

At this point, you have gained familiarity with the predictive writing process that shapes how lawyers read, write, and think. In this chapter, we will first look at an example of a predictive memo. Then we will deconstruct that memo, considering its features and organizational components. Evaluating this final product will help you understand your target and will provide a framework for the steps of the memo writing process, which we will explore starting in Chapter 5. Because legal writing is first and foremost legal analysis, you will not actually begin drafting your memo until Chapter 15. Up until that point, you will be engaging in a rigorous legal analysis and pre-drafting process that will provide the foundation for drafting your memo.

---

### Study Guide Questions for Chapter 4

1. How does evaluating the end product (the predictive memo) help you understand the process of writing a memo?
2. What are some key *features* of a predictive memo?
3. What are the main *sections* of a predictive memo? What does each section achieve?
4. What are the primary purposes of a global roadmap paragraph? What are the primary purposes of an issue roadmap paragraph?
5. What new terms were introduced in this chapter? How do these terms relate to your existing understanding of predictive memo writing? Did your understanding of any other terms change as a result of reading this chapter?

---

## I. Sample Predictive Memo

This section provides a complete sample predictive memo to preview the type of product you will be writing. Additionally, it provides more detail on our tortious interference with business expectancy hypothetical: The Smell Shoppe. As is typical of a predictive memo, this example has five sections: a *Header*, a *Question Presented*, a *Short Answer*, a *Statement of Facts*, and a *Discussion*. As you read the memo, what else do you note about its form and content?

## MEMORANDUM

To:     Senior Partner
From:   Junior Associate
Re:     Arnold Matter: Whether Mr. Arnold Can Prove Tortious
        Interference with Business Expectancy
Date:   August 17, 2020

### QUESTION PRESENTED

Under Illinois law, is a defendant liable for tortious interference with business expectancy when it created a competing business with a logo similar to that of the plaintiff's business, yet indicated that it was not affiliated with the plaintiff's business during a phone call inquiry, and when it created an online website with printed coupons stating, "Come See Us at Our New Location," but when that coupon only listed the defendant's one true business location?[1]

### SHORT ANSWER

No, it is not likely that Mr. Green will be liable for tortious interference with business expectancy. Because Mr. Arnold can demonstrate a specific contemplation from his customers and can demonstrate that the customers expressed their belief that they were doing business with his store, it is likely that the court will find that he possessed a reasonable expectancy of entering into a valid business relationship. However, because Mr. Green was not dishonest with customers when he received a phone call regarding the affiliation, it is unlikely that the court will find that it was Mr. Green's intentional and unjustified interference that prevented the realization of business expectancy.

### STATEMENT OF FACTS

This is a case involving an allegation of tortious interference with business expectancy on behalf of Gene Arnold against Carl Green. Both parties operate candle businesses in the Chicago area.

Gene Arnold opened his first candle and scents store, called The Smell Shoppe, in 2010 in Chicago, Illinois. He incorporated in 2011. His candles and wax scents became popular and well known for the variety of scents offered, the potency of scents, and how long they lasted. He also offers his candles at reasonable prices and is kind to his customers. He was so successful that by 2015 he had opened two additional shops, one in Elgin, Illinois, and another in DeKalb, Illinois. They both bore the name "The Smell Shoppe" with a corresponding logo, which was an outline of an orange

---

1. Note that this is a very detailed question presented, resulting in a long sentence. Depending upon your reader (professor, advisor, supervisor), you may include far less factual detail.

candlestick with a red fire on top. Mr. Arnold has had a steady rise in sales since the birth of The Smell Shoppe and has contributed to two competitors going out of business during his eight years of scent making. His sales are especially high during the winter holiday season, when customers buy candles for gift giving. One of Mr. Arnold's competitors that was forced out of business was "Candles, Etc.," a shop that was owned by Carl Green. That business closed in 2014.

Mr. Green later decided to try his hand at a candle business again. On January 1, 2016, he opened his store that he called "Smell Shop" in Chicago, Illinois. He created a business logo of an outline of a blue, unlit candle sitting in a candleholder. Mr. Green's candles were cheaply made, as he was probably still suffering from the effects of his first closed business. In effort to quickly rebuild capital, he charged double the price and posted "buy one, get one half off" coupons for Smell Shop to make the prices seem like a good deal. He created a website at smellshop.com where people could access these coupons as well as view the candle options.

Meanwhile, Mr. Arnold started to notice a significant decline in his sales in the Chicago store towards the middle of 2017. He became extremely concerned when he noticed a marked decline in his holiday sales. This was particularly unusual for Mr. Arnold, as this was the most profitable time of the year. He began hearing from people in the community that his candles "just weren't what they used to be." He would hear complaints that the potency was weak and that the candles were burning down too quickly. Customers also did not appreciate the increase in price, especially considering the decrease in quality coupled with a notable decline in customer service. They complained that the owner "didn't seem to know anything about the candles he was selling." They also complained that he acted "put off by having to answer their questions." They informed Mr. Arnold that they would not be coming back. All of this came as a shock to Mr. Arnold, and he struggled to make sense of these complaints. Nothing in his business practices had changed—he was still offering the same high-quality candles and still providing great customer service.

Desperate to win back customers, he therefore tried to offer better deals in an attempt to lure in more customers over the holiday season. Mr. Arnold also informed these complaining customers that he hadn't opened a new store and that he was not sure what they were referencing. In response, at least four customers replied that they were, of course, talking about the new location in Chicago. They said that the owner of that location told them the Chicago shop was the newest location and was affiliated with the Elgin and DeKalb stores. Mr. Arnold remained perplexed about what these angry customers meant and simply tried to pacify them with better deals and great customer service.

In early 2018, things got stranger: Mr. Arnold's staff started receiving customers arriving with "buy one, get one half off" coupons that he had never seen before. His staff noticed the coupons had been printed from a website called smellshop.com. The coupons further read, "Come See Us at Our Newest Location," with only Mr. Green's shop's address listed. Mr. Arnold was puzzled by this, as he didn't have an online presence, nor had he opened a new location at the address listed. Mr. Arnold instructed one of his employees to investigate this website. The employee did so and found the brand to be very similar to what Mr. Arnold had been using all these years, with a similar name and logo. After doing some digging, Mr. Arnold found out that the owner was Mr. Green. Mr. Arnold recognized him as the former owner of Candles, Etc., one of the businesses that shut down back in 2014 after Mr. Arnold started seeing great success in his candle-making business. Curious, Mr. Arnold's wife called the number listed on the website. She inquired of the person answering whether the shop was connected to "The Smell Shoppe" locations in Elgin, Illinois, and DeKalb, Illinois. The person answering hesitated and then replied, "No, ma'am, we just have the one location in Chicago," and then abruptly hung up.

Mr. Arnold now understands the true source of his customers' confusion and unhappiness. He is concerned about the impact this has had on his business. On the basis of these facts, Mr. Arnold would like to file a claim of tortious interference with business expectancy against Mr. Green.

### DISCUSSION

Mr. Gene Arnold will likely be unsuccessful in his tortious interference with business expectancy claim against Mr. Green. In order to successfully prevail in this claim, Mr. Arnold will need to prove four elements: "(1) [the plaintiff's] reasonable expectancy of entering into a valid business relationship; (2) the defendant's knowledge of the expectancy; (3) the defendant's intentional and unjustified interference that prevents the realization of business expectancy; and (4) damages resulting from the interference." *Chicago's Pizza, Inc. v. Chicago's Pizza Franchise Ltd., USA*, 893 N.E.2d 981, 993 (Ill. App. Ct. 2008). As per the instruction of the senior partner, this memo will not discuss whether Mr. Green knew of Mr. Arnold's expectancy, nor will it discuss whether Mr. Arnold suffered damages as a result of the interference. Instead, this memo will only discuss whether Mr. Arnold possessed a reasonable expectancy of entering into a valid business relationship and whether it was Mr. Green's intentional and unjustified interference that prevented the realization of business expectancy. Notwithstanding the likelihood that Mr. Arnold will be successful in showing that he possessed a reasonable expectancy of entering into a valid business relationship, he will likely fail in his claim. This is because Mr. Green was not dishonest with customers and therefore Mr. Arnold will be unable to show that Mr. Green intentionally and unjustifiably interfered with the realization of business expectancy.

### 1. Whether Arnold Possessed a Reasonable Expectancy of Entering into a Business Relationship

The court will first consider whether Mr. Arnold possessed a reasonable expectancy of entering into a valid business relationship. *Id.* In assessing whether Mr. Arnold possessed this expectancy, the court will consider the specific contemplation of customers and the customers' belief that they were doing business with Mr. Arnold. *Id.* at 993-94. A plaintiff will be found to have possessed a reasonable expectancy of entering into a valid business relationship when it can be demonstrated that specific customers called the defendant's store with the belief that they were doing business with the plaintiff. *Id.* at 994. Because Mr. Arnold spoke to several people regarding their experiences while shopping at Mr. Green's candle store who expressed the belief that they were shopping at Mr. Arnold's store, he will likely prevail on this element.

When customers demonstrate specific contemplation of doing business with the plaintiff and they express the belief that they are doing business with the plaintiff, the plaintiff will be successful in showing a reasonable expectancy of entering into a valid business relationship. *Id.* at 993-94. In *Chicago's Pizza*, the court stated that it was clear that the testifying customers contemplated a business relationship with the plaintiff. *Id.* at 993. In particular, one customer stated he had called the defendant's store believing it was one of the plaintiff's four locations and he asked for the phone number to another location of the plaintiff's restaurant so that it could deliver to him. *Id.* Another customer testified that he did believe that he was ordering from the plaintiff when in fact he was ordering from the defendant. *Id.* at 993-94. Moreover, the court noted the fact that the first testifying customer proceeded to then order from the defendant after being told that the location he had called was able to deliver to him. *Id.* Because the plaintiff successfully demonstrated a specific contemplation from the customers and because the customers expressed belief that they were doing business with the plaintiff, the court found the plaintiff had established a reasonable expectancy of business relationship. *Id.*

It is likely that Mr. Arnold will be able to show that he possessed a reasonable expectancy of entering into a valid business relationship. Like the plaintiff's customers in *Chicago's Pizza*, the customers in Mr. Arnold's situation contemplated specific business relationships with him. *See id.* Mr. Arnold will argue that, like the testimony of the customers in *Chicago's Pizza*, he also has customers who can testify to their specific contemplation in conducting business with him. *See id.* Namely, Mr. Arnold himself will testify that he began hearing people in the community express concerns about his candles, including telling him that the candles "just weren't what they used to be." This is similar to the testimony of the customers in *Chicago's Pizza* who expressed that they clearly believed they were doing business with the plaintiff. *Id.* Indeed, in Mr. Arnold's case, the customers' contemplation that they were doing business with him is even stronger, insofar as the customers specifically complained that his candles were weak in potency and were burning down too quickly, notwithstanding the fact that he had not made any changes to his candle-making practices. The dissatisfied community members may also be called to testify to their specific contemplation of conducting business with Mr. Arnold's candle shop, similar to the testimony of the customers in *Chicago's Pizza*. *See id.*

In addition, Mr. Arnold will assert that customers in fact believed they were doing business with him, not Mr. Green. As with the convincing testimony of the customers in *Chicago's Pizza*, Mr. Arnold can use the testimony of his customers to illustrate their belief that they were in fact doing business with him when they purchased their candles with the confidence that they would be strongly scented and long-lasting, just as Mr. Arnold's candles had proven to be. *See id.*

Alternatively, Mr. Green will argue that Mr. Arnold did not have a reasonable expectancy of a business relationship. He will argue that unlike the defendant in *Chicago's Pizza*, he did not receive phone calls from customers who directly indicated that they believed they were doing business with Mr. Arnold. *See id.* He may further distinguish his situation from that of *Chicago's Pizza* by showing that he did not process the order from a customer who conveyed that she believed she was purchasing from Mr. Arnold. *See id.* Additionally, Mr. Green may argue that if other customers believed they were conducting business with Mr. Arnold's business, he was not made aware of this misapprehension. Notwithstanding Green's assertions, it is likely that Mr. Arnold will prevail on this element because he will be able to show that his customers specifically contemplated doing business with him and believed that they were in fact doing business with him.

### 2. Whether Green's Intentional and Unjustified Interference Prevented the Business Expectancy

Next, the court will consider whether it was Mr. Green's intentional and unjustified interference that prevented Arnold's realization of a business expectancy. *Id.* at 994. In assessing this element, the court will consider the defendant's conduct in allowing customers to place orders under a mistaken belief, the defendant's truthfulness to the customers regarding an affiliation with the plaintiff's business, and the content of any of the defendant's advertisements. *Id.* at 994. A plaintiff will be successful in demonstrating that it was the defendant's intentional and unjustified interference that prevented the realization of business expectancy when the defendant allows customers to place orders with its business while being dishonest with the customers when they inquire about an affiliation with the plaintiff's store. *Id.* Further, a plaintiff can demonstrate interference with an expectation of a business relationship when the defendant represents an affiliation with the plaintiff through advertising materials. *Id.* Because Mr. Green was not dishonest when he received a phone call regarding an affiliation with Arnold's business, and because his website's printable coupons only listed one location to shop from, it is unlikely that Mr. Arnold will prevail on this element.

When a defendant allows customers to place orders with its business while being dishonest with them about an affiliation with the plaintiff's store, and uses that false affiliation to advertise its store, the plaintiff will be successful in showing that it was the defendant's intentional and unjustified interference that prevented the realization of business expectancy. *Id.* In *Chicago's Pizza*, the defendant prevented the plaintiff from realizing business by permitting customers to place orders with the defendant's store and being dishonest with them about an affiliation with the plaintiff's business. *Id.* Furthermore, the court specifically rejected an argument presented by the defendant that the customers simply mistook the defendant's store for the plaintiff's. *Id.* The court pointed out that the defendant's advertisements listed multiple locations when in fact there was only one. *Id.* More specifically, the court emphasized the fact that the advertisements listed the corresponding address of the plaintiff's store. *Id.* Because the plaintiff was able to demonstrate that the defendant allowed the customers to proceed with sales while being dishonest with those customers regarding an affiliation with the plaintiff, and because the defendant listed the plaintiff's locations on its advertisements, the court ruled in favor of the plaintiff on this element. *Id.*

It is unlikely that Mr. Arnold will be able to show that it was Mr. Green's intentional and unjustified interference that prevented the realization of business expectancy. Mr. Arnold may argue that, like the defendant's conduct in *Chicago's Pizza*, Mr. Green allowed customers to proceed with their purchases after learning that the customers believed they were doing business with Mr. Arnold. *See id.* Specifically, Mr. Arnold can demonstrate that Mr. Green permitted customers' sales after those customers were misled to believe that they were shopping at the newest location of the stores affiliated with Arnold's existing stores. Second, Mr. Arnold can argue that like the defendants in *Chicago's Pizza*, Mr. Green proceeded to place advertisements that further cemented customers' belief that there was an affiliation between the two parties. *See id.* Namely, Mr. Arnold will point to the fact that Mr. Green placed advertisements in the form of a website with similar branding and printable coupons that used the phrase "our newest location," strongly implying there was more than one location.

In contrast, Mr. Green will assert that he did not intentionally or unjustifiably interfere with Mr. Arnold's business. He will argue that, unlike the defendant in *Chicago's Pizza* who actively misled customers, Mr. Green was not dishonest. *See id.* In fact, when someone called Green's store inquiring about the affiliation with the other stores, he was honest and informed the caller that there was no affiliation with Arnold's stores. *See id.* He will further distinguish his advertising situation from that of the one in *Chicago's Pizza* by stating that his coupons did not expressly provide multiple locations like the misleading material at issue in *Chicago's Pizza*, and instead identified only the one true location of his store. *See id.* Green may also argue that the court should narrowly construe what actions are "unlawful and unjustifiable interference," particularly when the defendant's actions are commercial speech. A defendant's right to advertise in the way it deems most effective would be stifled if the plaintiff's argument were accepted. Notwithstanding Mr. Arnold's arguments, it is unlikely that he will prevail on this element because Mr. Green was not dishonest when he received a phone call regarding the affiliation and the website's printable coupons only listed one location.

Thus, Mr. Arnold likely will not succeed in his tortious interference with business expectancy claim against Mr. Green. Despite Mr. Arnold's success in proving that he possessed a reasonable expectancy of entering into a valid business relationship, he will likely fail to prove that it was Mr. Green's intentional and unjustified interference that prevented the realization of business expectancy.

## II. Key Features of a Predictive Memo

Having read the above memo, what are some things you notice about its form and content? Here is a list of the key features of a predictive memo.

- It covers a precise, client-centered topic. The memo is based around the client's particular legal situation. Note that the memo did not set out to explain any and all aspects of tortious interference with business; it set out to provide a prediction for one particular client. So, it is client-focused.
- The information moves from general principles to specific application of those principles: as discussed in Chapter 3, this is a deductive framework (general to specific). In a predictive memo, the Discussion starts with a statement of the applicable legal rule; it then gives an example of how the rule has been used by courts before, and follows with an application of that rule to the client's situation.
- The law is applied from both the perspective of the client and the perspective of the opposing party. In other words, it presents both analysis and counter-analysis. To thoroughly assess the strength of the client's argument, you also need to evaluate the strength of the opposition's argument. As in a game of chess, the best players think through their opponent's moves just as carefully as they think through their own.
- It comes full circle. It both starts and ends with the big picture: the overall legal question and the overall prediction.

---

⊠ **CHECK IN: Assessing the Features of a Predictive Memo**

Read through the following memo. When you have finished, go through the above checklist of Key Features of a Predictive Memo. With which of these features does it comply? On which features does it fall short? (Hint: It does fall short.) When it falls short, how did that affect your understanding of and/or confidence in the memo?

### MEMORANDUM

To:　　　Senior Partner
From:　　Junior Associate
Re:　　　Tortious Interference with Business Expectancy
Date:　　August 17, 2020

---

### QUESTION PRESENTED

Under Illinois law, is a defendant liable for tortious interference with business expectancy when it created a competing business that looked exactly like the former business and misled customers as to whether it was a different business?

### SHORT ANSWER

No, it is not likely that the defendant will be liable for tortious interference with business expectancy. The court will find that he possessed a reasonable expectancy of entering into a valid business relationship but will not find that he was intentional.

### STATEMENT OF FACTS

Gene Arnold opened his first candle and scents store, called The Smell Shoppe, in 2010 in Chicago, Illinois. One of Mr. Arnold's competitors that closed for business was called Candles, Etc. and was owned by Carl Green. He closed for business in 2014.

Last year, Mr. Green decided to try his hand at candle making again. On January 1, 2016, he opened his store that he called "Smell Shop" in Chicago, Illinois. Mr. Arnold started to notice a significant decline in his sales in the Chicago store towards the middle of the 2017. He became extremely concerned when he noticed a special decline in his holiday sales. This was particularly unusual to Mr. Arnold, as this was the most profitable time of the year. He began hearing from people in the community that his candles "just weren't what they used to be."

In early 2018, Mr. Arnold's staff started receiving customers arriving with "buy one, get one half off" coupons that his staff noticed had been printed from a website called smellshop.com. The coupons further read, "Come See Us at Our Newest Location," with only Mr. Green's shop's address listed below. Mr. Arnold was puzzled by this, as he didn't have an online presence, nor had he opened a new location at the address listed. Mr. Arnold instructed one of his employees to investigate this website. After doing some digging, Mr. Arnold found out that the owner was Mr. Green.

### DISCUSSION

This memo addresses whether the defendant's unjustified interference caused the loss of a business relationship and whether the plaintiff had a reasonable expectancy of entering into a valid business relationship.

The court will first consider whether Mr. Arnold possessed a reasonable expectancy of entering into a valid business relationship. *Chicago's Pizza, Inc. v. Chicago's Pizza Franchise Ltd., USA,* 893 N.E.2d 981, 993 (Ill. App. Ct. 2008). In assessing whether Mr. Arnold possessed this expectancy, the court will consider the facts and circumstances of the case, including the facts that Mr. Arnold spoke to several people regarding their experiences while shopping at Mr. Green's candle store who expressed apparent beliefs that it was Mr. Arnold's store they had been shopping at, so he will likely prevail on this element.

In *Chicago's Pizza*, the court addressed this question. The court wrote that it was clear that the testifying customers contemplated a business relationship with the plaintiff; one stated he had called the defendant's store believing it was one of the plaintiff's four locations and asked for the phone number to the plaintiff's restaurant that could deliver to him, and the other customer testified that he did believe that he was ordering from the plaintiff while in fact he was ordering from the defendant. *Id.* at 993-94. Moreover, the court pointed to the fact that the first testifying customer proceeded to then order from the defendant after being told the location he had called was able to deliver to him. *Id.*

Like the plaintiff's customers in *Chicago's Pizza*, the customers in Mr. Arnold's situation contemplated specific business relationships with him. *See id.* Mr. Arnold will argue that like *Chicago's Pizza*, he also will be able to have customers testify to their specific contemplation in conducting business with him. *See id.* Namely, Mr. Arnold will testify to the fact that he began hearing people in the community express concerns about his candles, as they were telling him that they "just weren't what they used to be." Indeed, he heard further complaints that his candles were weak in potency and were burning down too quickly, notwithstanding the fact that he had not made any changes to his candle-making practices. The dissatisfied community members may also be called to testify to their specific contemplation of conducting business with Mr. Arnold's candle shop. Likewise, Mr. Arnold can use their testimony to draw out their belief that they were in fact doing business with him when they purchased their candles with the confidence that they would be strongly scented and long-lasting, as Mr. Arnold's candles had proven to be.

Mr. Green may argue that unlike the defendant in *Chicago's Pizza*, he did not receive phone calls directly indicating that they believed they were doing business with the plaintiff. *See id.*

Next, the court will consider whether it was Mr. Green's intentional and unjustified interference that prevented the realization of business expectancy. *Id.* at 993. It is unlikely that Mr. Arnold will be able to show that it was Mr. Green's intentional and unjustified interference that prevented the realization of business expectancy. Mr. Arnold may argue that, like *Chicago's Pizza*, Mr. Green allowed customers to proceed with their purchases after learning that they believed they were doing business with Mr. Arnold. *See id.* Specifically, Mr. Arnold can demonstrate that the defendant permitted sales after customers were misled to believe that they were shopping at the newest location of the stores affiliated with the Elgin and DeKalb stores. Second, Mr. Arnold can argue that, like the defendants in *Chicago's Pizza*, Mr. Green proceeded to place advertisements that led customers to believe there was an affiliation between the two parties. *See id.* Namely, Mr. Arnold will point to the fact that Mr. Green placed advertisements in the form of a website with similar branding and printable coupons that used the phrase "our newest location," implying there was more than one location.

Alternatively, Mr. Green will argue that his conduct wasn't like the conduct of the defendant in *Chicago's Pizza*. The court will probably agree with this. Despite Mr. Arnold's success in proving that he possessed a reasonable expectancy of entering into a valid business relationship, he will likely fail to prove that it was Mr. Green's intentional and unjustified interference that prevented the realization of business expectancy.

## III. Organization of a Memo

All effective memos contain the previously noted key features: (1) focuses on the client's situation; (2) proceeds in a deductive manner, explaining the applicable law before applying it to the client's situation; (3) applies the law from the perspective of both parties (i.e., provides both analysis and counter-analysis); and (4) begins and ends with the precise legal question posed by the client facts and a global prediction as to its likely resolution. These features are the hallmarks of clear and effective predictive writing. Throughout this text, we will refer back to these features as we address the various steps in the memo writing process. For example, when we discuss sorting and selecting factually similar cases to use for comparative purposes, we will note how and where the selected cases fit within the memo's deductive approach.

In addition, legal memos have standard organizational components. These include dividing the content into the five sections noted above: the Header, a Question Presented, a Short Answer, a Statement of Facts, and the Discussion. Organizational components also include the use of certain paragraph types: a *global roadmap* that announces the *global rule* with its conditions; one or more *issue roadmaps* that introduce the reader to the analysis of a condition (element or factor); *rule explanation* paragraphs that explain how the condition has been analyzed in prior cases; and *rule application* paragraphs that include arguments from both parties' perspective in order to predict how a court might decide our client's claim or charge.

### ⊞ CONCEPT IN ACTION: Annotated Predictive Memo

Below is an annotated example of the sample memo with which we began this chapter. Each memo section and special paragraph type is identified in the margin. For now, you need not memorize or have more than a superficial understanding of each organizational component. The purpose of this marked-up example is to expose you to the components, each of which will be explored in great detail in Module III.

**MEMORANDUM**

This is referred to as the
"heading" for the memo. The
heading "MEMORANDUM"
designates the document as
a predictive memo. It also
shows to whom the memo
is directed and from whom
the memo comes, includes
a subject line with the client
matter and the legal question
addressed, and includes
the date the memo was
completed.

To:      Senior Partner
From:   Junior Associate
Re:      Arnold Matter: Whether Mr. Arnold Can Prove Tortious Interference
          with Business Expectancy
Date:    August 17, 2020

**QUESTION PRESENTED**

The "Question Presented"
may also be referred to as the
"Issue." This memo employs
the "Under/Does/When"
format discussed in Chapter
27. This format results in a
question that identifies the
source of law, announces the
precise legal question, and
identifies key facts from the
client's situation that give rise
to the legal tension.

Under Illinois law, is a defendant liable for tortious interference with business expectancy when it created a competing business with a logo similar to that of the plaintiff's business, yet indicated that it was not affiliated with the plaintiff's business during a phone call inquiry, and when it created an online website with printed coupons stating, "Come See Us at Our New Location," but when that coupon only listed the defendant's one true business location?

**SHORT ANSWER**

The "Short Answer" section
of the memo ideally
accomplishes three objectives:
(1) it answers the legal
question, (2) it alludes to the
law applicable to the client's
situation, and (3) it justifies
the prediction with key facts
from the client's situation.

No, it is not likely that Mr. Green will be liable for tortious interference with business expectancy. Because Mr. Arnold can demonstrate a specific contemplation from his customers and can demonstrate that the customers expressed their belief that they were doing business with his store, it is likely that the court will find that he possessed a reasonable expectancy of entering into a valid business relationship. However, because Mr. Green was not dishonest with customers when he received a phone call regarding the affiliation, it is unlikely that the court will find that it was Mr. Green's intentional and unjustified interference that prevented the realization of business expectancy.

**STATEMENT OF FACTS**

The "Statement of Facts"
section memorializes the
facts that the author of the
memo relied on to frame the
analysis. It demonstrates
what the writer knew at
the time the prediction was
made, which is significant
because if a new fact later
comes to light, it may change
the prediction.

This is a case involving an allegation of tortious interference with business expectancy on behalf of Gene Arnold against Carl Green. Both parties operate candle businesses in the Chicago area.

Gene Arnold opened his first candle and scents store, called The Smell Shoppe, in 2010 in Chicago, Illinois. He incorporated in 2011. His candles and wax scents became popular and well known for the variety of scents offered, the potency of scents, and how long they lasted. He also offers his candles at reasonable prices and is kind to his customers. He was so successful that by 2015 he had opened two additional shops, one in Elgin, Illinois, and another in DeKalb, Illinois. They both bore the name "The Smell Shoppe" with a corresponding logo, which was an outline of an orange candlestick with a red fire on top. Mr. Arnold has had a steady rise in sales since the birth of The Smell Shoppe and has contributed to two competitors going out of business during his eight years of scent making. His sales are especially high during the winter holiday season, when customers buy candles for gift giving. One of Mr. Arnold's competitors that was forced out of business was "Candles, Etc.," a shop that was owned by Carl Green. That business closed in 2014.

Mr. Green later decided to try his hand at a candle business again. On January 1, 2016, he opened his store that he called "Smell Shop" in Chicago, Illinois. He created a business logo of an outline of a blue, unlit candle sitting in a candleholder. Mr. Green's candles were cheaply made, as he was probably still suffering from the effects of his first closed business. In effort to quickly rebuild capital, he charged double the price and posted "buy one, get one half off" coupons for Smell Shop to make the prices seem like a good deal. He created a website at smellshop.com where people could access these coupons as well as view the candle options.

Meanwhile, Mr. Arnold started to notice a significant decline in his sales in the Chicago store towards the middle of 2017. He became extremely concerned when he noticed a marked decline in his holiday sales. This was particularly unusual for Mr. Arnold, as this was the most profitable time of the year. He began hearing from people in the community that his candles "just weren't what they used to be." He would hear complaints that the potency was weak and that the candles were burning down too quickly. Customers also did not appreciate the increase in price, especially considering the decrease in quality coupled with a notable decline in customer service. They complained that the owner "didn't seem to know anything about the candles he was selling." They also complained that he acted "put off by having to answer their questions." They informed Mr. Arnold that they would not be coming back. All of this came as a shock to Mr. Arnold, and he struggled to make sense of these complaints. Nothing in his business practices had changed—he was still offering the same high-quality candles and still providing great customer service.

Desperate to win back customers, he therefore tried to offer better deals in an attempt to lure in more customers over the holiday season. Mr. Arnold also informed these complaining customers that he hadn't opened a new store and that he was not sure what they were referencing. In response, at least four customers replied that they were, of course, talking about the new location in Chicago. They said that the owner of that location told them the Chicago shop was the newest location and was affiliated with the Elgin and DeKalb stores. Mr. Arnold remained perplexed about what these angry customers meant and simply tried to pacify them with better deals and great customer service.

In early 2018, things got stranger: Mr. Arnold's staff started receiving customers arriving with "buy one, get one half off" coupons that he had never seen before. His staff noticed the coupons had been printed from a website called smellshop.com. The coupons further read, "Come See Us at Our Newest Location," with only Mr. Green's shop's address listed. Mr. Arnold was puzzled by this, as he didn't have an online presence, nor had he opened a new location at the address listed. Mr. Arnold instructed one of his employees to investigate this website. The employee did so and found the brand to be very similar to what Mr. Arnold had been using all these years, with a similar name and logo. After doing some digging, Mr. Arnold found out that the owner was Mr. Green. Mr. Arnold recognized him as the former owner of Candles, Etc., one of the businesses that shut down back in 2014 after Mr. Arnold started seeing great success in his candle-making business. Curious, Mr. Arnold's wife called the number listed on the website. She inquired of the person answering whether the shop was connected to "The Smell Shoppe" locations in Elgin, Illinois and DeKalb, Illinois. The person answering hesitated and then replied, "No, ma'am, we just have the one location in Chicago," and then abruptly hung up.

Mr. Arnold now understands the true source of his customers' confusion and unhappiness. He is concerned about the impact this has had on his business. On the basis of these facts, Mr. Arnold would like to file a claim of tortious interference with business expectancy against Mr. Green.

## DISCUSSION

The Discussion section is the most important part of the memo. This is where the writer identifies the key law and applies it to the client's situation. Note that the Discussion proceeds in a deductive manner, from a more general explanation of the law to a more specific application.

Mr. Gene Arnold will likely be unsuccessful in his tortious interference with business expectancy claim against Mr. Green. In order to successfully prevail in this claim, Mr. Arnold will need to prove four elements: "(1) [the plaintiff's] reasonable expectancy of entering into a valid business relationship; (2) the defendant's knowledge of the expectancy; (3) the defendant's intentional and unjustified interference that prevents the realization of business expectancy; and (4) damages resulting from the interference." *Chicago's Pizza, Inc. v. Chicago's Pizza Franchise Ltd.*, USA, 893 N.E.2d 981, 993 (Ill. App. Ct. 2008). As per the instruction of the senior partner, this memo will not discuss whether Mr. Green knew of Mr. Arnold's expectancy, nor will it discuss whether Mr. Arnold suffered damages as a result of the interference. Instead, this memo will only discuss whether Mr. Arnold possessed a reasonable expectancy of entering into a valid business relationship and whether it was Mr. Green's intentional and unjustified interference that prevented the realization of business expectancy. Notwithstanding the likelihood that Mr. Arnold will be successful in showing that he possessed a reasonable expectancy of entering into a valid business relationship, he will likely fail in his claim. This is because Mr. Green was not dishonest with customers and therefore Mr. Arnold will be unable to show that Mr. Green intentionally and unjustifiably interfered with the realization of business expectancy.

This is the *global roadmap* paragraph. It alerts the reader to the global prediction as to the resolution of the client's claim or charge; announces the global rule of law, including its conditions; alerts the reader to any non-issues; confirms for the reader what conditions are at issue and addressed in the memo; and reiterates the global prediction, supporting that prediction with a few, key facts.

### 1. Whether Arnold Possessed a Reasonable Expectancy of Entering into a Business Relationship

This paragraph is known as an *issue roadmap* paragraph. It is another roadmap paragraph, but it lays the groundwork for a more limited portion of the memo—the discussion of an arguable issue/condition of the rule. The key components of the issue roadmap paragraph include the following: (1) the announcement of the specific issue/condition that will be analyzed following this roadmap paragraph; (2) guiding factors or standards

The court will first consider whether Mr. Arnold possessed a reasonable expectancy of entering into a valid business relationship. *Id.* In assessing whether Mr. Arnold possessed this expectancy, the court will consider the specific contemplation of customers and the customers' belief that they were doing business with Mr. Arnold. *Id.* at 993-94. A plaintiff will be found to have possessed a reasonable expectancy of entering into a valid business relationship when it can be demonstrated that specific customers called the defendant's store with the belief that they were doing business with the plaintiff. *Id.* at 994. Because Mr. Arnold spoke to several people regarding their experiences while shopping at Mr. Green's candle store who expressed the belief that they were shopping at Mr. Arnold's store, he will likely prevail on this element.

When customers demonstrate specific contemplation of doing business with the plaintiff and they express the belief that they are doing business with the plaintiff, the plaintiff will be successful in showing a reasonable expectancy of entering into a valid business relationship. *Id.* at 993-94. In *Chicago's Pizza*, the court stated that it was clear that the testifying customers contemplated a business relationship with the plaintiff. *Id.* at 993. In particular, one customer stated he had called the defendant's store believing it was one of the plaintiff's four locations and he asked for the phone number to another location of the plaintiff's restaurant so that it could deliver to him. *Id.* Another customer testified that he did believe that he was ordering from the plaintiff when in fact he was ordering from the defendant. *Id.* at 993-94. Moreover, the court noted the fact that the first testifying customer proceeded to then order from the defendant after being told that the location he had called was able to deliver to him. *Id.* Because the plaintiff successfully demonstrated a specific contemplation from the customers and because the customers expressed belief that they were doing business with the plaintiff, the court found the plaintiff had established a reasonable expectancy of business relationship. *Id.*

It is likely that Mr. Arnold will be able to show that he possessed a reasonable expectancy of entering into a valid business relationship. Like the plaintiff's customers in *Chicago's Pizza*, the customers in Mr. Arnold's situation contemplated specific business relationships with him. *See id.* Mr. Arnold will argue that, like the testimony of the customers in *Chicago's Pizza*, he also has customers who can testify to their specific contemplation in conducting business with him. *See id.* Namely, Mr. Arnold himself will testify that he began hearing people in the community express concerns about his candles, including telling him that the candles "just weren't what they used to be." This is similar to the testimony of the customers in *Chicago's Pizza* who expressed that they clearly believed they were doing business with the plaintiff. *Id.* Indeed, in Mr. Arnold's case, the customers' contemplation that they were doing business with him is even stronger, insofar as the customers specifically complained that his candles were weak in potency and were burning down too quickly, notwithstanding the fact that he had not made any changes to his candle-making practices. The dissatisfied community members may also be called to testify to their specific contemplation of conducting business with Mr. Arnold's candle shop, similar to the testimony of the customers in *Chicago's Pizza*. *See id.*

In addition, Mr. Arnold will assert that customers in fact believed they were doing business with him, not Mr. Green. As with the convincing testimony of the customers in *Chicago's Pizza*, Mr. Arnold can use the testimony of his customers to illustrate their belief that they were in fact doing business with him when they purchased their candles with the confidence that they would be strongly scented and long-lasting, just as Mr. Arnold's candles had proven to be. *See id.*

Alternatively, Mr. Green will argue that Mr. Arnold did not have a reasonable expectancy of a business relationship. He will argue that unlike the defendant in *Chicago's Pizza*, he did not receive phone calls from customers who directly indicated that they believed they were doing business

---

that direct the court's analysis of this issue/condition; (3) "rule proof" to satisfy the skepticism of the law-trained reader; and (4) a prediction as to the resolution of this issue/ condition.

This paragraph is known as the *rule explanation*. Here the writer will go into more detail about the facts, holding, and rationale of prior cases to create a foundation for the application that will follow. The key components of rule explanation are (1) a framing sentence that provides direction for the reader; (2) a discussion of key facts from the prior cases that relate solely to the issue/condition discussed in this analytical portion of the memo; and (3) the holding and rationale of the prior cases as they relate to the issue/condition discussed in this analytical portion of the memo.

These two paragraphs are known as *rule application*. Here the writer is comparing the relevant case facts from the precedent cases to the facts of the client's case. Note that these comparisons are being made on the basis of legally significant considerations: namely, those rule components the writer articulated in the issue roadmap paragraph. Key components of rule application include the following: (1) analysis and counter-analysis relevant to the issue/condition addressed in this analytical portion of the memo; (2) a prediction as to the court's determination of the issue/condition at issue in this analytical portion (or *issue segment*) of the memo.

with Mr. Arnold. *See id.* He may further distinguish his situation from that of *Chicago's Pizza* by showing that he did not process the order from a customer who conveyed that she believed she was purchasing from Mr. Arnold. *See id.* Additionally, Mr. Green may argue that if other customers believed they were conducting business with Mr. Arnold's business, he was not made aware of this misapprehension. Notwithstanding Green's assertions, it is likely that Mr. Arnold will prevail on this element because he will be able to show that his customers specifically contemplated doing business with him and believed that they were in fact doing business with him.

## 2. Whether Green's Intentional and Unjustified Interference Prevented the Business Expectancy

This is the second issue roadmap paragraph, announcing the analytical framework for the second issue.

——— Next, the court will consider whether it was Mr. Green's intentional and unjustified interference that prevented Arnold's realization of a business expectancy. *Id.* at 994. In assessing this element, the court will consider the defendant's conduct in allowing customers to place orders under a mistaken belief, the defendant's truthfulness to the customers regarding an affiliation with the plaintiff's business, and the content of any of the defendant's advertisements. *Id.* at 994. A plaintiff will be successful in demonstrating that it was the defendant's intentional and unjustified interference that prevented the realization of business expectancy when the defendant allows customers to place orders with its business while being dishonest with the customers when they inquire about an affiliation with the plaintiff's store. *Id.* Further, a plaintiff can demonstrate interference with an expectation of a business relationship when the defendant represents an affiliation with the plaintiff through advertising materials. *Id.* Because Mr. Green was not dishonest when he received a phone call regarding an affiliation with Arnold's business, and because his website's printable coupons only listed one location to shop from, it is unlikely that Mr. Arnold will prevail on this element.

This is the rule explanation for the second issue.

——— When a defendant allows customers to place orders with its business while being dishonest with them about an affiliation with the plaintiff's store, and uses that false affiliation to advertise its store, the plaintiff will be successful in showing that it was the defendant's intentional and unjustified interference that prevented the realization of business expectancy. *Id.* In *Chicago's Pizza*, the defendant prevented the plaintiff from realizing business by permitting customers to place orders with the defendant's store and being dishonest with them about an affiliation with the plaintiff's business. *Id.* Furthermore, the court specifically rejected an argument presented by the defendant that the customers simply mistook the defendant's store for the plaintiff's. *Id.* The court pointed out that the defendant's advertisements listed multiple locations when in fact there was only one. *Id.* More specifically, the court emphasized the fact that the advertisements listed the corresponding address of the plaintiff's store. *Id.* Because the plaintiff was able to demonstrate that the defendant allowed the customers to proceed with sales while being dishonest with those customers regarding an affiliation with the plaintiff, and because the defendant listed the plaintiff's locations on its advertisements, the court ruled in favor of the plaintiff on this element. *Id.*

It is unlikely that Mr. Arnold will be able to show that it was Mr. Green's intentional and unjustified interference that prevented the realization of business expectancy. Mr. Arnold may argue that, like the defendant's conduct in *Chicago's Pizza*, Mr. Green allowed customers to proceed with their purchases after learning that the customers believed they were doing business with Mr. Arnold. *See id.* Specifically, Mr. Arnold can demonstrate that Mr. Green permitted customers' sales after those customers were misled to believe that they were shopping at the newest location of the stores affiliated with Arnold's existing stores. Second, Mr. Arnold can argue that, like the defendants in *Chicago's Pizza*, Mr. Green proceeded to place advertisements that further cemented customers' belief that there was an affiliation between the two parties. *See id.* Namely, Mr. Arnold will point to the fact that Mr. Green placed advertisements in the form of a website with similar branding and printable coupons that used the phrase "our newest location," strongly implying there was more than one location.

*This is the rule application for the second issue. Note that the writer not only concludes the analysis of the second issue, but below also provides a global prediction as to the resolution of the entire claim—whether the claim will be successful.*

In contrast, Mr. Green will assert that he did not intentionally or unjustifiably interfere with Mr. Arnold's business. He will argue that, unlike the defendant in *Chicago's Pizza* who actively misled customers, Mr. Green was not dishonest. *See id.* In fact, when someone called Green's store inquiring about the affiliation with the other stores, he was honest and informed the caller that there was no affiliation with Arnold's stores. *See id.* He will further distinguish his advertising situation from that of the one in *Chicago's Pizza* by stating that his coupons did not expressly provide multiple locations like the misleading material at issue in *Chicago's Pizza*, and instead identified only the one true location of his store. *See id.* Green may also argue that the court should narrowly construe what actions are "unlawful and unjustifiable interference," particularly when the defendant's actions are commercial speech. A defendant's right to advertise in the way it deems most effective would be stifled if the plaintiff's argument were accepted. Notwithstanding Mr. Arnold's arguments, it is unlikely that he will prevail on this element because Mr. Green was not dishonest when he received a phone call regarding the affiliation and the website's printable coupons only listed one location.

Thus, Mr. Arnold likely will not succeed in his tortious interference with business expectancy claim against Mr. Green. Despite Mr. Arnold's success in proving that he possessed a reasonable expectancy of entering into a valid business relationship, he will likely fail to prove that it was Mr. Green's intentional and unjustified interference that prevented the realization of business expectancy.

*This is the conclusion paragraph. It reiterates the global prediction as to the resolution of the claim or charge, and then reiterates the issue prediction.*

## EQUIPPING YOURSELF: Memo Dates

The date the author completes the memo is a standard part of the memo heading. In Chapter 27, we will discuss how lawyers might return to an older memo for guidance in a different client matter. As you know, the law changes over time. This makes it particularly important to identify in each memo you write the date of the legal rules you discuss and the predictions you reach.

### CHAPTER 5

# The Process of Drafting a Predictive Legal Memorandum

Chapter 4 presented a sample predictive legal memorandum and described its features and organizational components. This approach should have provided you with a more concrete idea of what you will be writing. Now that you have a sense of where you are going, we will dissect how to get there. In this chapter, you will see the steps in the writing process, both the pre-drafting stage and the drafting stage, which resulted in the sample memo you reviewed in Chapter 4.

---

### Study Guide Questions for Chapter 5

1. What are the main steps in drafting a predictive memo?

2. How does viewing the end product, the predictive memo, help you better understand the steps in the writing process?

3. Why is pre-drafting analysis an important step to take before beginning to draft a predictive legal memo?

4. What is the difference between inductive and deductive analysis? When does each type of analysis occur during the process of writing a predictive memo?

5. How is the memo-writing process different from other writing projects you have worked on?

6. What new terms were introduced in this chapter? How do these terms relate to your existing understanding of predictive memo writing? Did your understanding of any other terms change as a result of reading this chapter?

---

## I. Steps for Writing a Predictive Memo

The steps for writing an effective predictive memo are explained below. As you can see from the description of the steps, the process is not entirely linear. You may have to circle back to prior steps as your analysis becomes more nuanced. Also, note that the steps below reflect the work a lawyer would do in preparing a comprehensive, multi-case memo. In contrast, in Modules I through III, your focus will be on a predictive memo using a single authority. Nonetheless, this overview should provide you with the context for the type of legal analysis we will build toward addressing in Module IV.

**Step 1. Understand your client's factual situation:** Your client will likely come to you and tell you a story about what has happened to the client or what the client wants. Because you, as the lawyer, know more about the law, you may have to ask questions to further develop the facts that are likely to be relevant to the legal issue.

**Step 2. Determine the legal question:** The legal question is the claim or charge. For example, "Is this intentional infliction of emotional distress, or is it instead libel?"

**Step 3. Determine the applicable (global) rule of law:** Once the lawyer has determined the question, she must locate the applicable rule of law. The existing legal rule may be from an enacted source, like a statute or constitution, or it may be a common law rule from a case. In reading cases that apply the existing legal rule, you may develop an emergent legal rule. In some cases, you may have to synthesize a rule of law from multiple cases. (This means that as you select cases and learn more about the rule of law in step 4, you might return to this step.)

**Step 4. Determine the conditions for the rule and assess which conditions are at issue:** From the applicable rule of law, determine the conditions for that rule. Every rule will contain conditions, which are the elements or factors that must be assessed in order for the court to determine if the result will occur. For each condition, assess whether it is contested in the client's situation and thus at issue. As you undertake this step, you may expand your understanding of each condition. This expanded understanding can be conceptualized as the *rule for the condition*. Together with the global rule, this constitutes the rule of law.

**Step 5. Select cases that are analogous:** At this point, the lawyer has identified a number of cases related to the relevant legal issue(s) in order to determine the rule of law. With the rule in mind, the lawyer will begin reviewing these cases to find those that can be compared and contrasted with the client's situation. Analogous fact patterns are *comparable*—this means they may involve different facts, but facts that can be compared on the basis of legally significant characteristics. Lawyers evaluate the relevance of a case issue by issue. For instance, one case may only apply to a single element or factor, while another case applies to multiple conditions that are at issue. Similarly, some cases might support one side of the legal case, while others support the other side. A lawyer will take notes that clearly indicate how each case pertains to her client's situation and then select the cases that she believes will be most useful when formulating arguments for both sides.

**Step 6. Analyze and develop arguments as to the likely application of the rule of law to your client's situation:** Once the lawyer has selected cases relevant to the client's situation, she will begin to develop arguments, again issue by issue, both for and against her client's position. She will consider how she can favorably draw similarities to cases that are beneficial to her client's position and distinguish cases that are not beneficial to her client's position. Then she will develop counter-analysis, crafting case similarities and distinctions on behalf of the opposing party. Identifying the best potential arguments that both sides can make will help the lawyer not only predict a likely outcome for each issue, but also reach a global prediction in response to the legal question.

**Step 7. Determine whether additional research is necessary to further develop the analysis of an element or factor:** In some instances, as the lawyer begins to develop arguments, she recognizes the need for additional research to fill gaps related to a particular element or factor. In this instance, she will research further, focusing on that specific aspect of the rule of law, rather than conducting more of the comprehensive research she completed earlier. This is another way in which research and analysis are, at times, recursive processes.

**Step 8. Outline the Discussion section of your memo:** Having engaged in the pre-drafting, analytical steps, the lawyer is now in a position to develop an annotated outline of the Discussion. The rule of law, including the conditions at issue, will form the framework for the Discussion section. The initial paragraph of the Discussion, the global roadmap paragraph, will announce the global rule of law and identify the conditions (elements or factors) that are at issue and that will be addressed in the memo. For each condition, there will be an analytical section (which we refer to as an *issue segment*) comprised of an issue roadmap paragraph followed by rule explanation and then rule application paragraphs that consider the rule of law for the issue/condition. The lawyer can annotate the outline with the relevant authorities.

**Step 9. Draft the Discussion section of your memo:** Armed with an annotated outline, the drafting process becomes much more focused and streamlined.

**Step 10. Revise and edit the Discussion section of your memo:** As the saying goes, "there is no good writing, there is only good re-writing." Chapter 28 examines the process for revising and editing your Discussion.

**Step 11. Draft and edit the remaining sections of your memo:** The sections of your memo other than the Discussion—the Header, the Question Presented, Short Answer, and Statement of Facts—are addressed in Chapter 27.

**Step 12. Proofread your entire memo:** Proofreading adds the final touch to your memorandum, ensuring it is polished. Chapter 28 identifies critical proofreading steps.

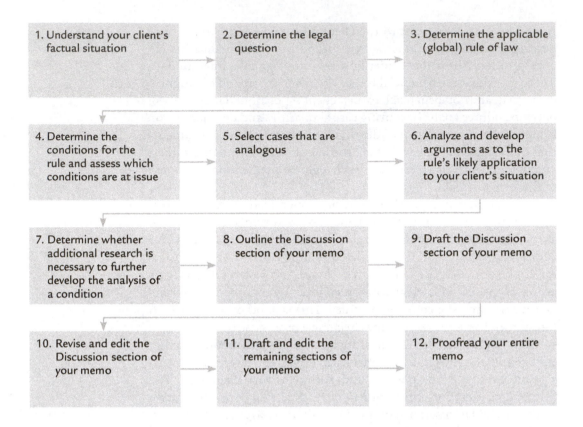

## II. The Importance of Pre-Drafting

Notice that it is not until step 8 that we outline the memo, and then in step 9 that we begin writing the memo. Why does the drafting—*writing*—occur so late in the process if the written document is the ultimate work product? Because, in order to draft, or even outline, an effective predictive memo, we first must thoroughly and methodically analyze the legal question. That pre-drafting analysis necessarily precedes the written communication.

For instance, consider steps 1 and 2 of the process: understand your client's factual situation and determine the legal question. Combined, these steps help establish the purpose and scope of your work—foundational considerations. If you do not pay adequate attention to this work, or forget about it as the process continues, you risk writing an otherwise fabulous analysis with the fatal flaw of addressing the wrong issues.

In steps 3 through 7, you identify and analyze relevant authorities. This portion of the pre-drafting process is inductive, meaning you are reading specific cases to derive a more general rule. Inductive analysis can be messy and complicated—you are superimposing structure on lots of details. Therefore, approaching this work methodically can facilitate the challenge of distilling an array of cases into an overarching principle.

This extensive pre-drafting process may be quite different from the process you have employed with other writing projects in the past. For example, you may have done some research and reading, written a brief outline, and then jumped into drafting. However, unlike some other kinds of writing, legal writing employs a structure driven by the rule of law. Thus, a thorough grasp of the rule of law is essential before drafting. That rule of law, in fact, forms the basis for your memo outline (step 8).

Note that the chapters in this book roughly follow the order of these steps. From Module I through Module III, Part I, we address pre-drafting analysis with a single authority. This corresponds with steps 1 through 6. Then in Module III, Part II, we start drafting that analysis in written form, going from outlining to drafting as set forth in steps 8 and 9. (Befitting the recursive nature of writing, the gaps addressed in step 7 might become evident at either the pre-drafting or the drafting stage.) In Module IV, we begin the process of drafting with multiple authorities, so we will resume this process with additional authorities in tow, completing steps 1 through 9. Finally, in Module V we include techniques for revising, editing, and proofreading your memo, thus completing the final steps of memo writing, steps 11 and 12.

## CRASH WARNING: Pre-Drafting Is Not Optional

We cannot emphasize enough the importance of thorough pre-drafting. You simply must take the time to superimpose structure on the law before you can articulate clear, generalized legal principles. The more time and attention you give to pre-drafting, the more efficient and effective you will be in drafting the memo. In contrast, if you rush the pre-drafting stage, you will not be well situated to draft an effective memo.

## EQUIPPING YOURSELF: Categorizing a Legal Problem

Effective legal writing rests on accurate legal research. Just as writing requires preparatory work, so, too, does legal research. Analyzing your research needs to identify the legal problem as clearly as possible will suggest logical starting points for your research as well as help you focus your efforts. Such an analysis includes answering questions like:

• How can you categorize this research need? Does it involve civil or criminal law? Is it substantive or procedural? What specific topical area is involved (e.g., torts, labor and employment, environmental law)?

• Is this likely to be a matter of federal, state, or local law?

• How much do you already know about the area of law? Particularly if it is new to you, you might want to start with a descriptive secondary source rather than jumping straight into the law itself.

• What type of legal authority is likely to apply? Common law? A specific type of enacted law (constitution, statute, regulation, e.g.)?

**CHECK IN: Identifying Memo-Writing Steps and Categorizing Legal Problems**

Read the Warrantless Bomb Search hypothetical below. (Note that this hypothetical is the basis for a single authority memo in Appendix A and a multiple authority memo in Appendix B.) You will then be asked to match specific tasks with the steps of the memo-writing process and to categorize this legal problem.

### Warrantless Bomb Search Hypothetical

On December 30, 2018, FBI agents from the Cincinnati field office descended on the fenced-in lot of Van Zanda Trucking outside Woodlawn, Kentucky. The agents searched a shipping container sitting on the lot. Inside the container, agents discovered bricks of marijuana and cocaine. The FBI discovery led to the arrest of Theodore "Double T" Van Zanda, a notorious Woodlawn mobster and owner of the trucking company. A grand jury indicted Van Zanda on narcotics trafficking charges, and he is currently in detention awaiting trial.

According to the FBI special agent in-charge ("SAIC"), FBI agents organized the raid immediately after receiving a tip from a trustworthy informant. The informant told agents the container held a shipment of volatile explosives that Van Zanda had ordered for a "hit" on Dalton "Torpedo" Anderson—a fellow mobster suspected of skimming money from the organization's illicit gambling revenues. The informant did not know exactly when the "hit" would happen, but he said the explosives were already prepped by a bomb maker and merely needed to be rigged to Anderson's motorcycle to be effective. The agents were also aware, from prior experiences, that nongovernment explosive materials are generally unstable and thus subject to spontaneous and unintentional detonation, especially when there is nearby movement.

In addition to the tip, agents were notified before arriving at Van Zanda Trucking that according to the FBI's intelligence files, Van Zanda's DNA was lifted from a trigger device used in the infamous bombing of the DeBoom Social Club, although he was inexplicably acquitted of arson and murder charges in that case.

The SAIC said when agents arrived on the lot, an FBI bomb-sniffing dog, Scooter, immediately "hit" on the shipping container. Immediately before searching the container, agents cleared all employees out of the nearby Van Zanda headquarters and put on specialized blast suits. Though they did not find a bomb, the SAIC said the canine's FBI handlers are confident Scooter would not "hit" on the shipping container unless explosives were present or had recently been stored there. Scooter was not trained to detect drugs, such that the drugs would have no effect on Scooter.

The SAIC further explained that, upon arriving on the lot, agents made contact with a man known only as "The Earl." Agents found him standing outside the container and spoke to him for ten minutes before beginning the search. The Earl explained he was renting the container from Double T and had used it to store a collection of vintage guitars. But a month before the search the two men had argued, and Van Zanda had ordered The Earl to stay off the property. At that time, The Earl moved his entire collection—except for three guitars—back into his home. He was on the lot that day to retrieve his remaining three guitars. Agents asked The Earl for permission to search the container, and he answered that it was "OK." The Earl then volunteered to open the container for the agents using his key. The agents did not ask, and do not know, why The Earl still had a key if he had been ordered to stay off the property. They also did not ask, and do not know, whether The Earl had paid rent for the month following his falling out with Van Zanda.

Upon opening the container, the agents found three guitars left by The Earl and tools used by Van Zanda Trucking mechanics, in addition to the bricks of marijuana and cocaine. The agents have told the SAIC that they believed there was a strong likelihood of a risk from a bomb in the container at the time they conducted the search and that they will testify accordingly.

The FBI agents who conducted the search of the shipping container did not have a search warrant. Van Zanda's elite team of defense lawyers have focused on this fact and filed a motion to suppress to keep the marijuana and cocaine from being introduced by prosecutors as evidence at trial. His legal team contends that the evidence of drugs must be suppressed because the agents did not have a search warrant. A successful motion to suppress the marijuana and cocaine would destroy the government's case against Van Zanda.

---

**Check In: Part 1**

Below is a list of work you might conduct if tasked with writing a predictive memo related to the Warrantless Bomb Search hypothetical. Assign the appropriate writing process step number to each of the lettered actions listed below. Note any actions that should not be included as part of the writing process, as well as any steps that are missing.

A. Develop likely arguments that our client, the U.S. government, will make.

B. Identify the emergent legal rule related to the permissibility of evidence acquired through a warrantless search.

C. Find cases from the Sixth Circuit that are factually similar.
D. Find cases from neighboring circuits that are factually similar.
E. Create an outline of the memo from which you can then identify the emergent legal rule.
F. Develop a keen understanding of the factual situation.
G. Develop arguments that the potential defendant, Van Zanda, may make.

**Check In: Part 2**
Try to answer the questions listed in the Equipping Yourself: Categorizing a Legal Problem box above in relation to the Warrantless Bomb Search hypothetical.

 **RULES OF THE ROAD: Determining the Client Issue**

One of the fundamental ethical obligations a lawyer has is to be able to determine a client's legal issue. Because ethical rules can vary somewhat by jurisdiction, let's assume we are writing a predictive memorandum in Alabama. Thus, we look to the Alabama Rules of Professional Conduct. The rule on Competence, 1.1, provides, "Some important legal skills, such as the analysis of precedent, the evaluation of evidence, and legal drafting, are required in all legal problems. Perhaps the most fundamental legal skill consists of determining what kind of legal problems a situation may involve, a skill that necessarily transcends any particular specialized knowledge." While all these skills are integral to preparing a legal memorandum, the skill of determining the client's legal issue necessarily comes first and provides the foundation for the rest of the lawyer's work.

Note that although the language quoted above comes from the Alabama Rules of Professional Conduct, many states share similar language because, as noted in Chapter 1, all states have adopted some version of the American Bar Association's Model Rules of Professional Conduct. Nonetheless, as with any kind of uniform law or model code, the ethical rules only become applicable upon adoption in a particular jurisdiction, and their impact may differ from jurisdiction to jurisdiction. Moreover, each jurisdiction may change the ABA model rules, including altering language, deleting model provisions, or adding new provisions. As such, be sure to directly consult the rules of professional conduct in your own jurisdiction to read the rule.

# Foundations of Legal Analysis

In Module I, you learned the big picture of legal analysis and writing. In this module, we're going to loop back around and delve more deeply into the concepts you learned in Module I.

Recall that, at its core, legal analysis entails applying the pertinent legal rule to your client's factual situation. So, to analyze whether a client is likely to be convicted of burglary, you must apply the legal rule for burglary to that client's factual situation. That process of applying the legal rule to the facts is what lawyers refer to as making arguments. In predictive writing, we must make arguments from each party's perspective.

But before we can make an argument, we first have to identify the applicable legal rule. Accordingly, Part I of this module (Chapters 6 through 8) focuses on how to discern the applicable legal rule for a given claim or charge.

Part II of this module (Chapters 9 through 12) takes us to the next step in legal analysis. Having discerned the applicable legal rule, you will then apply the rule to the unique facts and circumstances of your client's claim or charge. Lawyers apply the rule of law to unique facts by employing various methods of legal reasoning. Part II addresses the three main types of legal reasoning.

# Introduction to Legal Rules

We begin with an introduction to legal rules (Chapter 6). Next, we discuss types of legal rules and how lawyers work with and break down legal rules (Chapter 7). Finally, we examine how cases change our understanding of rules within our system of stare decisis (Chapter 8).

### CHAPTER 6

# Overview of Legal Rules

Legal rules provide the foundation for legal analysis. This chapter explores the sources of law that provide these rules, the importance of determining which sources of law are binding in your client's situation, and the role of cases in discerning legal rules.

---

## Study Guide Questions for Chapter 6

1. What are the two main sources of law?
2. What are the criteria by which a lawyer determines whether a source of law is binding for his legal question?
3. What does it mean for a court to "process" a legal rule, creating an emergent legal rule? Generally speaking, how are cases helpful in determining the rule of law?
4. What is the difference between an emergent rule and an existing rule?
5. What new terms were introduced in this chapter? How do these terms relate to your existing understanding of predictive memo writing? Did your understanding of any other terms change as a result of reading this chapter?

---

Recall that discerning the rule of law that applies to your client's situation forms a critical early step in your legal analysis. The reason is straightforward: until a lawyer understands the applicable law, she cannot possibly know what conditions must be analyzed in order to apply that law to her client's situation. Thus, once we identify our client's legal claim or charge, we next must research and understand the relevant rule of law.

> Issue
>
> **Rule of Law [MODULE II, PART I]**
>
> Application to Client Situation [MODULE II, PART II]
>
> Prediction

At first glance, finding the rule of law, or legal rule, may seem like a straightforward task: you just need to "look it up." Yet, it is not that simple. First, there is no single place to "look up" a legal rule. Legal rules arise from different sources and change over time.

Moreover, whatever their source—whether *common law* or *enacted law*, as further explained below—legal rules are subject to interpretation by courts in judicial decisions. Take, for example, the charge of assault with a dangerous weapon, discussed in Chapter 2. There, the existing legal rule did not define the term "dangerous weapon." A case in which the court had to interpret and apply that rule further defined that term, holding that any instrument used in a dangerous manner can be a dangerous weapon. That emergent legal rule—that a dangerous instrument is an instrument used in a dangerous manner—became the applicable rule in all subsequent cases.

This chapter first explains the two main sources of law that lawyers use when discerning the rule of law. Next, the chapter introduces three broad types of rules of law that can arise from these legal authorities. In Appendix F, the chart "Where Does Law Come From, and Which Law Applies?" summarizes some of these essential concepts.

## I.  What Are the Sources of Law?

Legal rules can arise from either the common law or enacted law. Common law is law created by courts in judicial opinions. Enacted law is law created by a nonjudicial entity, most notably legislatures, and primarily consists of constitutions, statutes, rules, and regulations.

In the past, most U.S. law originated from the common law. As novel legal issues came before them, courts had little choice but to create the law. Courts did so on a case-by-case basis as they confronted different claims and charges. However, in recent decades, more and more laws have been enacted. Most notably, criminal laws generally are enacted law.

Legislatures pass statutes not only to address novel legal issues but also to change common law with which they disagree. Because legislatures, unlike courts, can enact comprehensive law to address a variety of circumstances, enacted laws tend to be more comprehensive than common law. The legislature's purpose is to pass a law that will cover possible situations that might arise. Courts, on the other hand, cannot pass legislation, but instead can only address the individual case before them. As a result, common law rules tend to start out more simplistic and then develop into more sophisticated rules over time.

 **CHECK IN: Sources of Law**

While visiting a friend in West Dakota, David has been arrested for operating a vehicle while intoxicated. What sources of law do you likely need to consult and why?

**EQUIPPING YOURSELF: Finding and Reading Statutes**

A statutory code provides topical access to all current statutes for a given jurisdiction (e.g., federal United States law or the laws of a certain state). Codes are divided into various divisions, often called (from broadest to most narrow) titles, subtitles, chapters, and sections. Each title covers a particular subject, e.g., *taxation,* which is then divided into narrower aspects of the topic, e.g., *income tax.* Often, the most efficient approach to locating relevant content in a code is to look up concepts in the index, which will identify the code sections that discuss these concepts. Because legislatures attempt to pass comprehensive laws, it is critical to read statutes as a whole and in context. Each word of the statute can be important to discerning its meaning. Likewise, the meaning of a single code section will often depend on its place in the entire statutory scheme—the division (e.g., title, subtitle, and chapter) in which the section appears. For instance, the start of a chapter might provide a section with definitions that apply throughout that chapter. Because the exact wording of the statute can be critical, do not paraphrase statutes in your notes, and use quotation marks to indicate the material is taken verbatim from the source. Later in the chapter, we discuss a statutory rule on burglary; note its use of quotation marks.

## II. Which Sources of Law Are Binding?

Not every legal authority on a topic will be binding in your client's case. For example, in the above Check In, you are asked to determine the rule of law for operating while intoxicated in West Dakota. In that instance, only sources of law from West Dakota (whether enacted or common law) are binding law. Law from other states would not be binding law for that charge.

### Mandatory Versus Persuasive Law

Lawyers refer to laws as either binding (also known as *mandatory*) or *persuasive.* Courts must follow binding law under principles of stare decisis, but courts do not have to follow law that is merely persuasive. They can take guidance from persuasive law, but they are not required to do so. Usually a court will not consider persuasive law (i.e., law from other jurisdictions) unless there is no binding law in the jurisdiction.

### Federal, State, and Local Law

Because law exists at the federal, state, and local levels, that distinction is also important in determining what law is binding in a case. If a case considers a state law question (e.g., "What constitutes intoxicated driving in West Dakota?"), then the state sources of law will be binding and will govern. On the other hand, if a case considers a federal law question (e.g., "Were Defendant's Fourth Amendment rights violated?"), then federal sources of law are binding.

### Hierarchy of Law Within Federal or State System

Finding the source of law can get even more complicated than that. In addition to the basic filter of state versus federal, a lawyer also must consider where in the *hierarchy* of that jurisdiction the source of law arises. State and federal courts are multi-tiered, usually with a trial court, an intermediate appellate court, and the highest appellate court. In the federal system, the initial trial court is called a federal district court, the first appellate level is called the federal court of appeals, and the final appellate level is the U.S. Supreme Court. The higher the court, the more authoritative its opinion over lower courts. There are 13 federal courts of appeals: 12 circuits that each cover a different geographic area of the United States and the Court of Appeals for the Federal Circuit, which hears cases based on subject matter, not geography.

Diagram 6-1. Structure of the U.S. Court System

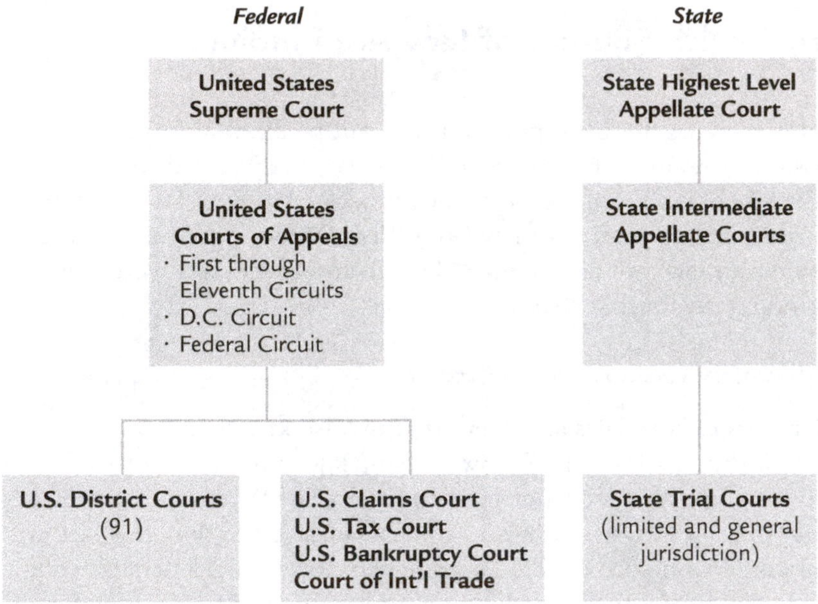

| *Federal* | | *State* |
|---|---|---|
| **United States Supreme Court** | | **State Highest Level Appellate Court** |
| **United States Courts of Appeals** · First through Eleventh Circuits · D.C. Circuit · Federal Circuit | | **State Intermediate Appellate Courts** |
| **U.S. District Courts** (91) | **U.S. Claims Court U.S. Tax Court U.S. Bankruptcy Court Court of Int'l Trade** | **State Trial Courts** (limited and general jurisdiction) |

What bearing does the hierarchy of the court systems have on which sources of law are binding? As it turns out, a great deal.

If a client question regarding whether the police violated the client's Fourth Amendment rights in a police search arose in Portland, Oregon, the binding sources of law would be the Fourth Amendment and cases interpreting the Fourth Amendment decided in the District of Oregon, the Ninth Circuit Court of Appeals, and the U.S. Supreme

Court. But if that client question instead arose in a case in El Paso, Texas, the binding sources of law would be the Fourth Amendment and cases interpreting the Fourth Amendment decided in the Western District of Texas, the Fifth Circuit Court of Appeals, and the U.S. Supreme Court. In the latter example, cases from any circuit other than the Fifth Circuit would be persuasive, but not binding.

## III. The Importance of Understanding the Sources of Law and Which Are Binding

In order to provide appropriate legal advice to the client to help him with his claim or charge, it is critical that the lawyer discern the applicable rule of law. That requires the lawyer to locate and consider multiple sources of law, which together will comprise the applicable rule of law. A lawyer who advised his client about a statute but failed to consider the cases that interpreted that statute would be of little use to that client. He would be applying an incomplete rule of law. Similarly, a client who wondered if a search of his home violated his Fourth Amendment rights would be ill-served by a lawyer who simply read the text of the Fourth Amendment while ignoring the multitude of cases that interpret that text in determining what constitutes an unlawful search.

 **CRASH WARNING: Don't *Just* Read the Case**

When considering the court's evolving interpretation of an enacted law, be sure to read that enacted law. You need to be familiar with the text of the enacted law in order to have the context for its interpretation and application in cases.

## IV. The Role of Cases in Discerning the Rule of Law

### Dangerous Dog Hypothetical

Recall from Chapter 3 your client Gianna, who owns a beloved pit bull, LuLu. One day, Gianna received an alarming notice from the city telling her that LuLu must be licensed as a "dangerous dog." "What does this mean?," Gianna wonders. "How does the city decide a dog is dangerous?" She asks you to advise her on this matter.

You start by carefully reviewing the city ordinance—an enacted law providing the requirement to license dangerous dogs. But that cannot be your only source of information. The ordinance did not define the term "dangerous" or provide any other guidance as to what makes a dog dangerous. As is typical, you need to research whether there are cases in which that enacted law has been interpreted and applied by courts.

You found two applicable opinions, one involving a German Shepherd that was determined to be dangerous and one involving an Akita that was not deemed dangerous. It is only with the benefit of the enacted law as well as the cases interpreting and applying that enacted law that you will have a grasp of the applicable legal rule. Chapter 8 of this module explains the specific ways in which cases *process the rule of law*, thus clarifying its meaning. For now, simply know that the law changes over time, and one primary way it changes is through evolving case law.

Generally speaking, whether a rule originates from enacted law or common law, that rule changes as cases apply and interpret it. When that happens, the rule evolves: the *existing legal rule* is replaced by the rule that emerges from that given case, called the *emergent legal rule*.

**Diagram 6-2**

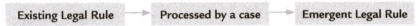

Consider our Warrantless Bomb Search hypothetical, in which we are assessing the legality of an FBI search of a shipping container. The enacted source of law, the Fourth Amendment, provides: "The right of the people to be secure in their persons, houses, papers, and effects, against unreasonable searches and seizures, shall not be violated." However, as noted above, the Fourth Amendment has been interpreted by thousands of judicial decisions. Each decision results in an emergent legal rule, which is evolved from the existing legal rule that the court started with in that case. Even though the text of the Fourth Amendment itself does not change, the understanding of its meaning does. We cannot understand the Fourth Amendment without also considering related judicial opinions. The rule of law changes and evolves as it is interpreted by different courts over time. This is stare decisis in action.

### Burglary Statute Hypothetical

Let's look at the concept of existing and emergent rules in the context of a burglary statute. Imagine your state legislature passed a law defining the crime of burglary that enumerated three elements:

> "A person commits burglary if he:
> a. Unlawfully enters;
> b. A building or structure;
> c. With the intent to commit a crime while inside the building or structure."

At the time it is passed, that enacted law is the existing legal rule. In due time, however, a defendant charged with burglary will challenge the meaning of that existing legal rule, thus requiring a court to interpret it.

What if, for example, in *State v. Smith*, a defendant challenges the element of "unlawful entry," arguing that his actions did not constitute unlawful entry? The existing legal rule does not define the term. As such, the court has to decide the meaning of that element. A court might do so by determining that entry was unlawful even if the defendant did not physically force himself into the building or structure. The court might further note that unlawfulness is judged by an objective standard of what a reasonable person would think.

The court's interpretation and application of the existing legal rule produces an emergent legal rule. The emergent legal rule adds to the existing legal rule by providing useful and defining information about what "unlawful entry" means.

In a subsequent case, a court will take the emergent legal rule from *State v. Smith* as its starting point when interpreting the statute. It will not go back to the rule that existed before that case. That is because once the existing legal rule is changed, it would not make sense to turn back the clock and apply the "old" existing legal rule. **The emergent legal rule is now the existing legal rule.**

Did you notice that the overall conditions for the rule did not change based on *State v. Smith*? Burglary still requires the same three elements. Even so, the burglary rule has changed because we now know more about what constitutes "unlawful entry."

When you think of a rule, you can think of it having two layers: the *global rule* and, beneath that, the *rule for each condition*. The global rule is the overall rule; it states what conditions are necessary for the result to occur. The rule for a condition is a subset of the global rule; it provides the rule for that particular condition, helping us to understand the meaning of the condition and to assess its applicability to our client's situation. Together, the global rule and the rules for each of the global rule's conditions comprise the rule. Thus, for the burglary example described above, the emergent burglary rule would look like this:

Diagram 6-3

A person commits burglary if he:

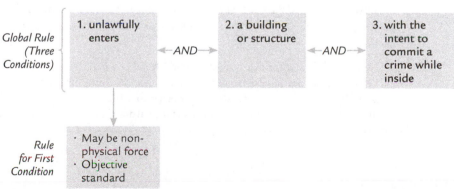

Note that we do not have information about the rule for the remaining two conditions, simply because we have not yet located cases that processed the rule for those conditions. Once we do, the burglary rule will once again evolve to include the rules for those conditions.

Note, too, that sometimes the emergent legal rule changes the existing global rule, not just the existing rule for the condition. For instance, the court may create an exception that modifies or deletes a condition, or it may adopt an additional condition. Therefore, lawyers must carefully read cases, paying close attention to how the court interpreted and applied the existing legal rule and considering how this changes the previously existing legal rule and its conditions.

---

 **CHECK IN: Existing and Emergent Legal Rules**

### Assault with a Fitbit Hypothetical

Recall from Chapter 2 Sofía's client, Jeffers Peterson, who was charged with assault with a dangerous weapon when, after a sporting match, he slapped someone across the face while wearing a Fitbit. The discussion in Chapter 2 pertained to the element of what constitutes a "dangerous weapon."

Now assume that Sofía wants to know if her client may be able to successfully defend himself by showing that the person he allegedly assaulted gave "implied consent" to the assault. Sofía found a Massachusetts case on point, *State v. Bird*, that discusses the implied consent defense in relation to assaults that occur in the context of sporting events. The case states:

> It is well-established that consent may operate as a defense to many crimes, and in the context of consensual sporting events, the doctrine of implied consent has particular application. Participants in sporting events are deemed to have consented to the physical contact and even possibly bodily harm that is part of their sport.

In an effort to better understand the implied consent defense, Sofía looks for additional authority. She finds the case of *State v. Johnson* in which the court held that the defendant did not commit assault because the alleged victim, who was his opponent in a racquetball game, gave "implied consent" to the alleged assault. In so holding, the court stated:

> Here, the defendant indisputably injured Mr. Jabar when the ball the defendant hit slammed into Mr. Jabar's cheek, crushing his cheekbone. While Mr. Jabar contends that in order to inflict such a serious injury the defendant must have hit the ball harder than was reason-

able in the context of the racquetball match, we think that is precisely the point of racquetball—to hit the ball hard and fast. That it hit Mr. Jabar's face is truly unfortunate but that is contact that Mr. Jabar implicitly agreed to when he participated in the racquetball game.

What was the existing legal rule of law that the court applied in *State v. Bird*? What is the emergent legal rule of law that comes out of *State v. Johnson*? Which rule would Sofía use to make arguments and prediction on behalf of her client? Why?

## V. Discerning Emergent Legal Rules from Multiple Cases

When there are multiple cases, a lawyer has to discern the legal rule by combining a series of "emergent legal rules" from these cases, creating a *synthesized legal rule*. We will consider synthesized legal rules beginning in Module IV. For now, our analysis will focus only on discerning an emergent legal rule from a single case, rather than discerning the synthesized legal rule from multiple cases.

Initially limiting our consideration to only a single emergent legal rule instead of a synthesized legal rule will allow us to more easily learn the foundations of legal analysis and the parts of a legal memo. Later, when we apply the synthesized legal rule, you will see that doing so is structurally very similar to working with an emergent legal rule from a single authority. However, the process of discerning the synthesized rule is a little more complicated because synthesized legal rules tend to be more detailed and complex.

This discussion of how rules originate and evolve demonstrates that discerning the legal rule is not as simple as just "looking it up." Rather, we have to find the existing legal rule and then find cases that interpret and apply that existing legal rule, creating emergent legal rules. After that, we have to combine, or synthesize, the cases' interpretations of the existing legal rule into a single rule. And when the initial rule arises from enacted law, we also have to consider whether amendments to that law may have affected the validity of the interpretive court cases.

Diagram 6-4

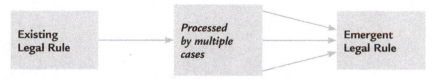

The next chapters in this section will explore in detail existing legal rules (Chapter 7) and emergent legal rules (Chapter 8). You will not only learn more about what these types of rules are, you will also work through examples so that you can identify and outline an existing legal rule as well as create an emergent legal rule from a case.

### CHAPTER 7

# Working with Rules

As you learned in Module I, rules can be likened to tests. In order for the result of the rule to occur, certain conditions must be satisfied. As a legal analyst, you need to understand the relationship between the conditions. Are all conditions required for the result to occur? Or will the court simply consider the conditions, without requiring any of them in particular? In this chapter, we will further explore rule structures and the importance of identifying the type of legal test in order to responsibly predict the resolution of the client's situation. We will also discuss how to outline rules in order to assist your legal analysis.

---

### Study Guide Questions for Chapter 7

1. How are elements different from factors?
2. What is a mandatory condition? What is a discretionary condition? How are they different?
3. What is the "result" of a legal rule?
4. Why is it important to outline legal rules?
5. What new terms were introduced in this chapter? How do these terms relate to your existing understanding of predictive memo writing? Did your understanding of any other terms change as a result of reading this chapter?

---

## I. The Three Key Features of Legal Rules

All legal rules have three components: (1) the conditions that must be satisfied in order for the result to occur; (2) a structure that identifies how the conditions relate to one another to determine whether the result will occur; and (3) a result that follows if the conditions are satisfied. Each of these features is discussed below.

### A. What Are the Rule's Conditions? Elements Versus Factors

All legal rules consist of certain conditions. Conditions may be either elements or factors. An item that *must* be proven to satisfy the rule is referred to as an *element*. An item that *is considered but not required* is referred to as a *factor*.

## Burglary Statute Hypothetical

The burglary rule discussed in Chapter 6 is an example of an *elements test*.

"A person commits burglary if he:
  a. Unlawfully enters;
  b. A building or structure;
  c. With the intent to commit a crime while inside the building or structure."

Each of these three conditions is an element. Each element must be proven. If one or more elements are not proven, then burglary has not been proven. You can think of elements as items in a true/false checklist; each and every item must be checked off as true in order for the test to be satisfied.

On the other hand, a rule in which the conditions are considerations, but not requirements, is called a *factors test*. Factors are not deemed true (satisfied) or false (not satisfied) in the same way as elements. Rather, the court considers and weighs each factor in determining whether the overall rule is satisfied. Just as you can think of an elements test as a checklist, you can think of a factors test as a scale. Ultimately, there needs to be enough of the factors—either in quantity or quality—to tip the scale toward satisfying or not satisfying the rule. How you arrive at "enough" depends on the particular factors test and the facts of the legal situation.

Rules that encompass a factors test tend to be flexible and far less exacting than rules that contain elements. Usually a single factor is not dispositive either way but will be considered along with other factors. A rule can be satisfied even if a party is weak in terms of some factors, so long as the party's position is strong in terms of other (more or more important) factors. Moreover, in some factors tests, the court may balance one set of factors against another set of factors.

 **CONCEPT IN ACTION: Factors Test for a Legal Rule**

### Physical Custody Rule Hypothetical

Let's look at an example of how the court might apply a factors test using the statutory legal rule for physical custody of a child:

"In determining the physical custody arrangement for a child, the court should consider the following factors:
  a. The child's age;
  b. Each parent's ability and willingness to support the child;

    c. The living accommodations in each parent's home;

    d. The ability of each parent to ensure a safe, stable, and loving environment;

    e. The impact of the custody decision on a child's educational, medical, and emotional needs;

    f. Past instances of neglect, abuse, or violence by either or both parents;

    g. The distance between the homes of the parents; and

    h. Any other factors the court deems significant."

Under the physical custody rule, each and every factor listed is not required; they are simply items that should all be considered. Further, when considering the various factors, the court is not asking whether that factor is "satisfied" or not. Instead, it is evaluating the facts that are relevant under that factor and weighing that factor against other factors.

The factor of "living accommodations in each parent's home" illustrates how courts analyze factors, as opposed to elements. "Living accommodations in each parent's home" cannot be "satisfied" or characterized as true or false. Rather, that factor directs the court's attention to consider the living accommodations of each parent. For example, the court might note that one parent owns a home whereas the other parent resides in a rental. The court will weigh that factor, along with the other factors, to decide what physical custody arrangements are in the child's best interests.

Although factors are separately enumerated, they ultimately are considered in relation to one another and through the lens of the specific dispute before the court. For instance, if considering "living accommodations" in isolation, the court might view home ownership as more stable, and therefore, preferable to renting. However, if that house is in disrepair and far from the child's current school while the well-maintained rental is in the child's current neighborhood, the scales would likely start tipping toward the renter.

This also means that one factor may not always be more important than another, yet it could be given more weight under certain circumstances. For example, take the factor in the child custody rule regarding "the child's age." If the child is very young, the court may decide that the child's age is the most critical factor and will be the most heavily weighted. That may lead the court to award one parent sole physical custody, even though both parents possess a strong ability to provide a good environment and the parents' homes are near each other. In a different case, a court might decide that although there was some neglect by one parent in the past, overall, the factors suggest that a joint physical custody arrangement is appropriate. As you can see, the court has a great deal of flexibility and discretion when evaluating and applying factors.

**CHECK IN: Elements and Factors**

Do you think rules in criminal law are likely to contain elements or factors? Why? What about laws governing contracts? What about laws governing child custody and other family law matters? Why?

## B. How Do the Rule's Conditions Relate to One Another?

Once you have identified whether a rule's conditions are elements or factors, your next task is to determine how those conditions relate to one another. While the relationship between conditions can be quite varied, a threshold matter you should consider is whether the conditions are *mandatory* or *discretionary*.

Generally speaking, rules with elements as conditions tend to be mandatory (sometimes referred to as "cumulative"), meaning that all of the elements **must** be satisfied. In fact, the use of the word "must" is the clearest indication that the rule's conditions are mandatory. In contrast, rules with factors as conditions tend to be discretionary, meaning that not all the factors necessarily must be considered in any given case, let alone satisfied. The absence of the word "must" is one indication of discretionary conditions; the rule might instead use another modal verb, such as "may" or "considers" or "weighs," to signal a discretionary condition. The above examples of the burglary rule (mandatory elements) and the physical custody rule (discretionary factors) exemplify these rule types.

However, not all rules fit easily into these two typical rule types. Rather, there are variations that flow from these two basic types of rules. Below are five of the most common ways that a rule's conditions may relate to one another. Knowing these prevalent rule types can help you identify—and better understand—the type of rule governing your legal issue.

1. The **mandatory elements test**. This is the most common kind of elements rule, where all listed elements must be satisfied to trigger the result.

   *Sample Rule:* In order be successful in a claim for common law fraud, the complaining party must show that the speaker made a material representation; the representation was false; when the representation was made, the speaker knew it was false or made it recklessly; the speaker made the representation with the intent that the other party should act upon it; the party acted in reliance on the representation; and the party thereby suffered injury.

2. The **either/or elements test**. For this rule, the result is triggered if either (or both) of the given conditions are satisfied.

   *Sample Rule:* To prove that a defendant is liable for the emotional distress of a plaintiff, the plaintiff must show that the defendant's conduct was intentional *or* reckless.

3. The **discretionary factors test**. This is the most common type of factors rule, where the court weighs several factors to determine if the overall rule has been satisfied.

   *Sample Rule:* To determine whether an individual is an employee or an independent contractor, the court shall consider the following factors as relevant: how much control the alleged employer exercised over the individual, the degree to which the services rendered by the individual are an integral part of the alleged employer's business, the degree to which the alleged employer determines the individual's opportunity for profit and loss, the permanency of the relationship, and the skill required in the claimed independent operation.

4. The **balancing test**. In this test, the court weighs competing factors against each other.

   *Sample Rule:* In determining whether an in-person hearing for the license suspension will be allowed, the hearing officer will consider the need for a hearing due to the inadequacy of the written record versus the likely time and expense of a hearing.

5. The **rule with an exception test**. This rule provides an exception to an otherwise applicable rule. That is, even if the conditions that generally trigger a certain result exist, if other conditions exist (the exceptions), the result will not occur.

   *Sample Rule:* The government must possess a warrant before conducting a search unless there is consent to search or there are exigent circumstances.

As you can see from the above examples, the words "and" and "or" provide critical information about whether all or only one of the conditions is needed. Likewise, the words "unless" and "except" also provide critical guidance about how the conditions relate to one another. When you are analyzing a rule, you should look for these words, as well as words like "must" or "may," in order to understand the rule.

## C. What Is the Result of the Rule?

Legal rules exist to clarify the law and make outcomes more predictable. In other words, we want to know what will happen. This notion of "what will happen" is referred to as the "result." It is what follows when the legal test is applied in a given case. In the burglary statute above, if the elements are satisfied, the result is that the defendant will be found to have committed burglary. In the custody rule above, after considering and weighing the various factors, the court decides on the desired result: the child's physical custody arrangements.

As you may have noticed, the result is generally fairly obvious. So, when determining what result follows from a legal rule, do not overthink it. You can think of the result as the "duh" component of the rule. For example, what happens if all of the elements of the burglary rule are proven? Duh, the defendant commits burglary. Or what happens after the judge considers and weighs all the factors for joint custody? Duh, the judge makes a determination regarding joint custody.

## II. Outlining the Rule

After you have identified the legal rule and determined its conditions, how those conditions relate to one another, and its result, it is time to outline the rule. An outline sets forth the rule, including breaking it down into its components.

For example, the common law fraud rule set forth above as an example of a mandatory elements test would be outlined as follows:

> In order to be successful in a claim for common law fraud, the complaining party must show:
> 1. that the speaker made a material representation,
> 2. the representation was false,
> 3. when the representation was made, the speaker knew it was false or made it recklessly,
> 4. the speaker made the representation with the intent that the other party should act upon it,
> 5. the party acted in reliance on the representation, and
> 6. the party thereby suffered injury.

This rule breaks down in a straightforward manner, with the outline closely following the language of the rule. The outline reinforces that this is a "mandatory elements test."

Let's look at how the other types of rules set forth above would be outlined.

### Outline for Either/Or Elements Test

In order to prove that a defendant is liable for the emotional distress of a plaintiff, the plaintiff must show that:
1. the conduct was intentional *or*
2. the conduct was reckless.

This outline, while closely following the language of the rule, makes clear that both prongs are not required (i.e., the plaintiff must only prove *x* or *y*). This outline makes clear that the "either/or" distinction is critical. It is easier to prove one element than both. Strategically, knowing that only one element has to be proven enables the lawyer to think about which element may better fit the facts of her case.

### Outline for Discretionary Factors Test

To determine whether an individual is an employee or an independent contractor, the court shall consider the following factors as relevant:
1. how much control the alleged employer exercised over the individual,
2. the degree to which the services rendered by the individual are an integral part of the alleged employer's business,
3. the degree to which the alleged employer determines the individual's opportunity for profit and loss,
4. the permanency of the relationship, and
5. the skill required in the claimed independent operation.

This outline, with the "factors as relevant" language, makes clear that the lawyer should consider both the *relevance* of each factor and its *relative weight*. The outline thus underscores that each factor may not be relevant under the circumstances. The lawyer should first evaluate whether the factor is relevant; then, if it is relevant, the lawyer will assess its importance relative to other factors.

### Outline for Balancing Test

An in-person hearing for the license suspension is allowed if the hearing officer determines:
a. the need for a hearing based upon the inadequacy of the written record *outweighs*
b. the likely time and expense of a hearing.

Again, this outline underscores the nature of the test, requiring the lawyer to *balance* the factors against each other.

***Outline for Rule with an Exception Test***

The government must possess a warrant before conducting a search unless at least one of the following exceptions exists:
1. There is consent to search.
2. There are exigent circumstances.

Once again, by outlining the rule, the lawyer's need to examine each exception is made clear, focusing her attention and the subsequent written analysis on each of the listed exceptions.

## A. Variation in Outlining Rules: Some Rules Are Trickier Than Others

In the above examples, the rules are largely broken down in a way that closely mirrors the rule's exact language. Note, however, that sometimes the outline for a rule does not closely mirror the rule, but instead reorganizes the components, reflecting the precise meaning of the rule's text without directly echoing its exact wording.

For example, assume a state law provides:

"A casino operator must take all reasonable steps to ensure that self-excluded patrons are not permitted to be on the casino premises, regardless of whether the patron is engaging in gambling games. This also applies to patrons who have been banned under casino policies. Self-excluded patrons are permitted on the non-gaming premises of a casino, such as a dining establishment or golf course."

The outline for this rule would ***not*** be:

1. A casino operator
2. must take all reasonable steps
3. to ensure that self-excluded patrons are not permitted to be on the casino premises, regardless of whether the patron is engaging in gambling games.
4. This also applies to patrons who have been banned under casino policies.
5. Self-excluded patrons are permitted on the non-gaming premises of a casino, such as a dining establishment or golf course.

That outline does not clarify the rule's requirements, nor does it help organize our legal analysis.

Rather, the outline for this rule would be:

> Casino operators must take all reasonable steps to ensure that:
> 1. Patrons who are either self-excluded or banned
> 2. Are not permitted on the casino's gaming premises.

Notice that to create the outline, the lawyer had to reorganize the components of the statutory rule in order to create a coherent rule that clearly sets forth the test. And it is only with this organizational strategy that the lawyer will be able to evaluate the conditions of the rule, how they relate to each other, and how they might satisfy the rule in order for the lawyer to predict whether the result is likely to occur. In other words, outlining the rule provides a clearer understanding of the rule structure: a prerequisite to making a sound legal prediction. We emphasize the importance of this pre-drafting step in the next section.

## B. The Purpose of Outlining the Legal Rule

As illustrated above, there are three main reasons why lawyers outline a legal rule.

**First, outlining the rule forces you to focus on all components of the rule and not overlook anything.** When you outline the rule, it forces you not only to identify the components of a rule but also to determine how those components relate to one another. This process also helps ensure that no component of the rule is overlooked.

**Second, your outline of the rule imposes structure on your legal analysis.** The rule outline guides your legal analysis by clarifying the conditions and their relationship to one another. Likewise, you can also begin to think about what facts may be significant to the key legal issues.

**Finally, your outline of the rule provides structure for your legal memorandum.** The rule outline eventually will serve as the *large-scale organization* for your legal memorandum.

---

 **CHECK IN: Rule Type and Outline**

Consider the following legal rule that governs on-street parking: "Unless deemed safe or a parking turn-out is provided, on-street parking is prohibited."

> What type of rule is this? How would you outline this rule? Looking ahead, how do you think you would organize a memo that applies this rule to a client's situation?

## III. Putting It All Together: How Lawyers Approach Rules

At this point, we have considered many aspects of existing rules. Let's consider how these different aspects fit together in order to better understand how to tackle a given legal rule.

**Step One: What is the existing rule?** This step requires you to figure out the source of the rule, be it enacted law or common law.

**Step Two: What are the rule's conditions, and how do those conditions relate to one another?** A rule generally will fall into one of the five tests described above. Regardless of whether it does, however, every rule you encounter can be analyzed through the lens of whether its conditions are elements or factors and how those conditions relate to one another.

**Step Three: What result follows from the rule?** As noted above, the result is generally obvious. Don't overthink it.

**Step Four: What is the outline of the rule?** The final step is to outline the rule. Doing so not only helps ensure that you have not missed anything, it also shows you how the parts of the rule fit together. Your outline of a rule has the added benefit of providing the structure for your analysis and for your legal memorandum.

 **CONCEPT IN ACTION: Tackling the Legal Rule**

### Dangerous Dog Hypothetical

Recall that your client recently was notified that the City has determined that her beloved dog is a dangerous dog and must be licensed. Your first task? You must determine the legal rule governing whether a dog must be licensed. You locate the relevant ordinance that reads: "All dangerous dogs must be licensed."

It is time to go through the four-step process described above.

**Step One: What is the existing rule?**
The ordinance itself is the existing rule. It is enacted law.

**Step Two: What are the rule's conditions, and how do the conditions relate to one another?**
There are two conditions: the animal must be a dog, and the dog must be dangerous. The phrase "must be" signals that these are requirements and thus elements, not factors. In other words, both conditions (elements) must be satisfied for the result to be triggered.

**Step Three: What result follows from the rule?**
The result is that the animal "must be licensed." Note that this was our inquiry: whether our client's dog had to be licensed.

**Step Four: What is the outline of the rule?**
An animal must be licensed if:
1. It is a dog; and
2. It is dangerous.

Note the three benefits that come from this outline of the rule. First, we understand the rule's conditions and how they fit together. Second, we have made sure we have not overlooked any part of the rule. While it is unlikely the lawyer would have missed that one element is whether the animal is "dangerous," she may have neglected to spell out the element of "whether the animal is a dog" and instead taken that as a "given" and therefore a non-issue. That oversight would not be problematic in most cases because whether the animal is a dog usually will be a non-issue. However, that oversight would be problematic in a case in which that element is at issue, say in a case in which the animal is a wolf hybrid or part coyote. In such cases, it becomes clear that the element of "dog" is indeed an element that needs to be separated out and analyzed.

Finally, we now have an organizational structure for our analysis in our legal memorandum; assuming both conditions are at issue, one part of the memo will address the issue of whether the animal is a dog and a separate part will address the other element of whether the animal is dangerous. These will be the two arguable issues in the memo and will be addressed in separate analytical sections, which we call "issue segments."

# IV. Revisiting Elements Versus Factors

The dichotomous nature of elements (either true/satisfied or false/not satisfied) may make these conditions appear much more straightforward than factors. However, determining whether an element has been satisfied also often involves nuanced analysis. Even something as seemingly black and white as whether a person "must be over the age of 18" may have some gray area. What if the person is 18 but, due to intellectual disability, has a mental age of 10? Is that element still automatically satisfied, or might the court consider the person's mental age as well as his chronological age?

Due to these kinds of complexities, courts often use *guiding factors* to help assess whether an element has been satisfied. Like the factors in a factors test, these guiding factors are considerations, not requirements. The use of guiding factors to establish whether an element has been satisfied does not change the rule test to a factors test. It remains an elements test because the result requires the satisfaction of that mandatory element. It simply means that the mandatory element can only be understood by discerning and weighing the guiding factors that guide the court's analysis about whether that element has indeed been satisfied.

Take the example from the burglary rule of the element of "unlawfully enters." There likely is no *bright-line* test for what it means to unlawfully enter. There is instead a gray area, which consists of circumstances the court considers in determining whether a given entry was unlawful. For example, did the defendant have permission? Did the defendant use physical force? Did the defendant engage in deception to gain entry? Those gray-area considerations are the guiding factors that help a court determine whether an element has been satisfied.

In contrast, elements are never a component of a factors test. For instance, in considering the factor of a "parent's ability and willingness to support the child," a court would not assert that one requirement (i.e., element) is that the parent must be gainfully employed. If that were the case, that matter would not be stated as a factor to begin with. Unlike an element, a factor is inherently something that the court *considers* rather than something that is *satisfied*.

---

 **GEARING UP: Explicit Versus Implicit Guiding Factors**

In the next chapter, we will further discuss how lawyers can identify guiding factors from cases. Sometimes a court explicitly states guiding factors, but more often than not guiding factors are implicit. Either way, guiding factors tell us the categories of information on which the court will focus.

### CHAPTER 8

# Working with Cases to Determine the Rule of Law

In Chapter 7 we discussed the three components of legal rules, the primary types of legal rules, and the process of outlining a legal rule. In this chapter, we consider how lawyers rely upon and use cases in determining what the legal rule is. Specifically, this chapter analyzes the ways in which cases "process"—meaning interpret and apply—existing rules of law, thereby changing and adding to our understanding of the rule.

---

### Study Guide Questions for Chapter 8

1. How is an emergent legal rule different from the existing legal rule?
2. What is the difference between a law-centered interpretation and a fact-based holding?
3. What are the ways that a case can process and interpret an existing legal rule?
4. What role do factors play in rules?
5. Why are factors important and useful in legal analysis?
6. What new terms were introduced in this chapter? How do these terms relate to your existing understanding of predictive memo writing? Did your understanding of any other terms change as a result of reading this chapter?

---

## I. In General: How Lawyers Use Cases to Determine the Rule of Law

Recall that determining the rule of law is a process. Because the law changes over time, a lawyer can rarely look to a single source to determine the rule of law for a given issue. Under our system of stare decisis, as courts interpret and apply an existing legal rule, the law changes. The emergent legal rule that results from a case replaces the previously existing legal rule. The court's explanation of how the rule applies to a given conflict sheds light on how it will apply to future conflicts.

Cases process an existing legal rule in two primary ways. First, cases can provide *law-centered interpretations*. A law-centered interpretation is language in a case in which the court explicitly discusses the rule. For example, imagine a court opinion included the sentence, "A dangerous dog is one that poses a threat to the community." By directly defining what "dangerous" means in this rule, the court provides a law-centered interpretation. Note that law-centered interpretations are not dependent on the facts of the case before the court.

In addition, cases provide *fact-based holdings*. A fact-based holding reveals what facts were important to the court in reaching its holding. Typically, fact-based holdings are implicit in a case; the court does not directly announce its fact-based holding. Thus, in order to determine the fact-based holding, the lawyer considers how the court applied the rule to the specific facts before it. An example of a fact-based holding would be "When a dog has sharp teeth and has bitten two people on two occasions, courts hold the dog is dangerous." The court's application of the rule enhances our understanding of the legal rule itself. Beyond helping us understand the result in that case, it also indicates what types of facts the court considers when applying that rule.

 ### CONCEPT IN ACTION: Law-Centered Interpretations and Fact-Based Holdings

#### Federal Wiretap Statute Hypothetical

Let's consider these two concepts using the federal wiretap statute.[1] Assume you represent a defendant for whom you are trying to get wiretapped evidence suppressed. You locate the statute that requires wiretapped evidence that has not been immediately sealed to be suppressed. However, the statute contains an exception that allows the use of such evidence if the government proves it has a satisfactory explanation for the delay in sealing.

In an effort to better understand this rule, and in particular whether the court in your case will find that the exception exists, you locate two cases. The first case, *Liberte*, states that a "satisfactory explanation is one which proves that the government acted with 'reasonable care' in safeguarding the evidence." This is an example of a law-centered interpretation. The court is interpreting what a "satisfactory explanation" means.

---

1. When working with a statute, you want to look at its exact language as well as the interpretive cases. However, to more clearly illustrate the concepts in the book, we have taken some liberties with our description of this very lengthy statute and therefore with the cases interpreting it. For our purposes, you can assume the statute reads: "The recording of the contents of any wire, oral, or electronic communication under this subsection shall be done in such a way as will protect the recording from editing or other alterations. The use or disclosure of the contents of any wire, oral, or electronic communication or evidence derived therefrom requires that such recordings be sealed immediately or a satisfactory explanation for the sealing delay be provided."

In addition, the court in *Liberte* applied that rule. It held that the government had not acted with reasonable care where the investigator "forgot" to seal the evidence, causing a 42-hour delay. This is an example of a fact-based holding.

The other case you found, *Thornton,* also applied the rule. It held that the government demonstrated reasonable care when the sealing was delayed by 18 hours because the government had to translate the tapes, a task made more difficult by equipment failure and limited personnel. This, too, is an example of a fact-based holding.[2]

Diagram 8-1

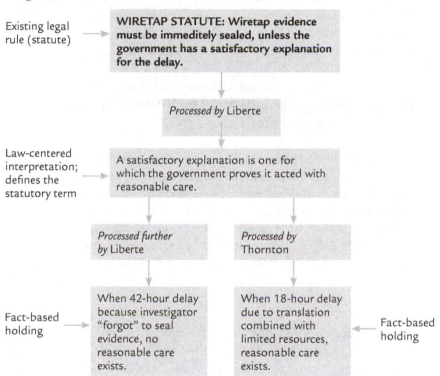

As this wiretap example shows, a case's interpretation of the rule through both law-centered interpretations and fact-based holdings results in a more detailed, clearer rule. We refer to this as the "emergent legal rule." The emergent legal rule is simply the existing legal rule as processed by a case. From that point on, the emergent rule becomes the new existing legal rule. It will be used as the starting point in the next case.

---

2. The Federal Wiretap hypothetical originated with Professor Robin Slocum. The authors have modified and expanded on the concept she introduced.

## II. Specific Ways that Courts Interpret Rules

Courts interpret rules in numerous ways based upon a case's law-centered interpretations and fact-based holdings. There are three main ways in which a case processes a rule: (1) by providing standards and definitions; (2) by providing explicit or implicit guiding factors; and (3) by showing how the conditions of the rule relate to one another. Note that these are not exclusive. There are other ways a case could process a rule. A case could, for example, modify the global rule of law by replacing an existing rule with a drastically different rule. However, because of stare decisis, such instances of a case altering a rule's fundamental meaning are few and far between. More typically, a case will process the existing rule in one or more of these three primary ways. Each is further described in the following sections.

### A. Interpreting the Existing Legal Rule Through Standards and Definitions

Courts may interpret a legal rule by providing *definitions* (the meaning of the condition at issue) and *standards* (further information about the way the court does—or does not—assess a condition, such as setting forth the weight that the court employs in evaluating the condition). These law-centered interpretations are explicit statements by the court that provide information that helps us understand the rule. Unlike guiding factors, which we discuss below, definitions and standards do not provide categories of what the court considers. Thus, they do not themselves form a basis upon which lawyers would make analogical arguments.

**Definitions.** Definitions often encompass the issue as a whole, providing insight into the meaning of the condition at issue. Definitions tend to be more conceptual than tangible. Take, for example, the wiretap rule described above. There, the court defined the statutory term of "satisfactory explanation." It stated: "A satisfactory explanation is one which proves that the government acted with 'reasonable care' in safeguarding the evidence." That information helps define that term, but it still leaves room for interpretation. Thus, we continued to dig into the meaning of 'reasonable care,' studying the types of facts that were important to the court in its consideration of that issue.

**Standards.** Like definitions, standards provide insight into a rule's meaning. Standards, however, tend to be more directive and thus more specific than definitions. Unlike guiding factors (which are merely considerations), standards may tell us a certain thing that the court requires for an issue (e.g., a court stating that "A satisfactory explanation must be proven under an objective standard, not a subjective standard" or "A satisfactory explanation must be presented with reasonable specificity"). Or a standard may indicate certain things the court does **not** consider for that issue (e.g., "In determining what constitutes a satisfactory explanation, the court will not consider reasons related to a government worker's inexperience or lack of training"). A standard may also tell us how strictly (or liberally) a court interprets a condition (e.g., "A 'satisfactory explanation' is a demanding standard, and the government faces a high burden to prove that one exists. Such a demanding standard is necessary to ensure that the wiretap statute's purpose is upheld, and that the exception does not swallow the rule").

In addition, a standard may present a bright-line requirement (as opposed to a mere consideration) under the rule for that issue/condition (e.g., "A satisfactory explanation may not be used as a reason for a delay if such reason has previously been used by the government more than six months prior even if that reason still exists").

As you may have noticed from the above examples, definitions and standards can convey the *policy behind the rule*, meaning the purpose or the reason behind the rule. Take, for example, the standard set forth above:

> A "satisfactory explanation" is a demanding standard, and the government faces a high burden to prove that one exists. Such a demanding standard is necessary to ensure that the wiretap statute's purpose is upheld, and that the exception does not swallow the rule.

That standard helpfully conveys the policy behind the rule. That background information about the rule's purpose helps us better understand the rule's meaning. That, in turn, helps us tailor our arguments so that a court will find them compelling.

 **CONCEPT IN ACTION: How Definitions and Standards Become Part of the Legal Rule**

### Burglary Statute Hypothetical

Consider the element of "unlawful entry" in the burglary statute. As discussed in Chapter 7, no bright-line rule exists as to what constitutes "unlawful entry." So, although we know that entry must be unlawful, we don't know exactly what that means. What is unlawful? Your idea of what is/should be unlawful may well differ from mine, and ultimately, what is important is how the court interprets that term. That is where standards and definitions (and guiding factors, as discussed below) come into play.

Imagine that in looking for cases to better understand the rule we found a case in which the court stated that entry through an open door without permission constituted "unlawful entry." That case has helped define unlawful entry, indicating that it does not require the use of physical force. Note that this definition does not tell us what is affirmatively required to show unlawful entry. It tells us what is **not** required. This still helps; knowing what is not required under the law tells us that certain arguments will not be effective. Under this precedent, for example, a lawyer would be unable to make a convincing argument that unlawful entry has not occurred simply because an entry was not physically forced.

In addition, the case might go on to state that "unlawful entry must be proven beyond a reasonable doubt" and that "unlawful entry is judged by an objective standard of what a reasonable person would think, not based on the defendant's subjective beliefs." Both examples provide us with the court's standards for "unlawful entry." Like all standards they provide us with specific information about the rule's contours.

Based upon these definitions and standards, this rule emerges for the first element:

> Defendant commits burglary if he:
> 1. "Unlawfully enters." Unlawful entry must be proven beyond a reasonable doubt. Unlawful entry does not require the use of physical force, and it is judged under the objective, not subjective, standard of what a "reasonable person" would think.

Even with the benefit of these definitions and standards, we still lack sufficient direction about what constitutes "unlawful entry" to engage in predictive legal analysis because we do not specifically know the categories of facts that a court will consider and use to make comparisons. For that information, we turn to guiding factors.

 **CRASH WARNING: Don't Fixate on the Difference Between Definitions and Standards**

If you are struggling with the difference between definitions and standards, know that it is not critical that you distinguish one from the other. Rather, it is simply important that, when reading a case, you recognize both as providing useful information about the rule. These two categories—definitions and standards—help to ensure that you identify and extract both types of information, to the extent available, from a case.

## B.  Interpreting the Existing Legal Rule with Guiding Factors

As the above discussion demonstrates, definitions and standards enhance our understanding of the rule. However, neither definitions nor standards tell us, specifically, the categories of facts that a court will consider and use for comparisons. That is where guiding factors come in. Guiding factors are critical because they are the categories on which lawyers make arguments. Let's look at what guiding factors are and how to discern them from a case.

*Guiding factors* provide additional guidance as to what categories of facts the court actually considers in deciding the issue. For example, the standard referenced in the wiretap rule provides that a "satisfactory explanation must be proven under an objective standard, not a subjective standard." Although helpful, that information, in and of itself, lacks a tangible basis on which we can evaluate facts. Most notably, we still have no idea what, specifically, the court considers under this objective standard. Is it whether the length of the delay was objectively reasonable? Is it whether the cause of the delay was objectively reasonable? Is it whether the government's belief that the evidence actually had been sealed was objectively reasonable? We simply cannot tell from the standard alone. Guiding factors provide this missing information, telling us what categories of facts, specifically, the court will consider.

Guiding factors play a crucial role in breaking down the rule in more detail and providing a tangible means of evaluating the significance of facts under the rule for the issue. The following sections discuss guiding factors at length, beginning with an in-depth look at what they are and then addressing the distinction between implicit guiding factors (discerned by the lawyer's inferences based upon the court's fact-based holding) versus explicit guiding factors (expressly stated in a case in a law-centered interpretation). We then discuss the importance of guiding factors to legal analysis.

### 1.  What Are Guiding Factors?

#### The Smell Shoppe Hypothetical

For any condition, guiding factors can provide another layer in the rule interpretation structure, helping us better understand and evaluate elements and factors. Guiding factors help us break down an element or factor into the components the court will examine. Take, for example, The Smell Shoppe hypothetical. We know that to establish that the defendant committed the tort of interference with business expectancy, one of the elements that the plaintiff must prove is that the defendant "intentionally and unjustifiably interfered" with the plaintiff's business expectancy. But what, in particular, will the court consider in determining whether such interference was "intentional and unjustifiable?"

Guiding factors help answer this question. In the *Chicago's Pizza* case, reprinted in Chapter 2 and cited in the initial memo in Chapter 4, the court interpreted and applied the element of whether the interference was "intentional and unjustifiable." From that case, the lawyer discerned that the rule for this element included three guiding factors, and was stated as follows: "In determining whether the interference was intentional and unreasonable, courts consider (1) the defendant's conduct in allowing customers to place orders under a mistaken belief, (2) the defendant's truthfulness to the customers regarding an affiliation with the plaintiff's business, and (3) the content of any of the defendant's advertisements." By making the condition more tangible, these guiding factors help the lawyer focus on what considerations will matter to the court. The lawyer eventually will make arguments about how the element is or is not satisfied using these guiding factors as the basis for those arguments.

Diagram 8-2

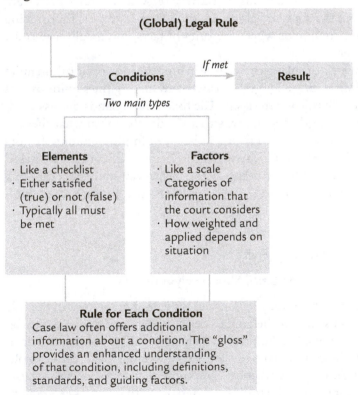

## 2. Implicit Versus Explicit Guiding Factors

Sometimes guiding factors are explicitly stated in a case, but more often than not they are only implied. When guiding factors are **explicit** it means they are directly stated by the court in a law-centered interpretation, and when they are **implicit** it means they are implied by the court through its fact-based holding. Let's look first at these more common, implied considerations—implicit guiding factors—then turn to explicit guiding factors before concluding this section by discussing how factors improve legal analysis.

### a. What Are Implicit Guiding Factors?

A guiding factor can be thought of as a generalized category for a set of related facts. If you saw that the court found it was significant to its holding in one case that there was a banana, and then in a later case found it significant to its holding that there was an apple, you could infer that one implicit guiding factor for the court's determination is "whether there is a fruit." The specific facts that were significant to the courts' holdings—the existence of a banana in one and of an apple in the other—both indicate a general category, or guiding factor, of "whether there is a fruit."

### Curfew Hypothetical

We all recognize implicit guiding factors in our everyday lives. Imagine that a father tells his teenage child that he must be home "at a reasonable time," but does not give a specific curfew time. The teen may attempt to figure out what his dad means by a "reasonable time" by looking to past instances in which his arrival time home was deemed reasonable or unreasonable. The teen would then extrapolate what considerations are important to his dad from those past examples.

For example, the teen might recall these past instances:

- A time when he got home at midnight on a school night, and his dad was upset.
- A time when he got home at midnight on a Saturday night, and his dad was not upset.
- A time when he got home at 1 a.m. after prom, and his dad made no fuss.
- A time when he got home at 1 a.m. after hanging out with friends, and his dad was livid.

From these past examples, the teen might conclude that, in deciding what constitutes a "reasonable time," his dad considers whether it is a school night and whether there is a special occasion. Those two considerations are what we refer to as implicit guiding factors—they direct us to the considerations that help determine whether a certain requirement is satisfied or not. Without these implicit guiding factors in mind, it would be difficult for the teen to figure out what a "reasonable time" means to his dad.

In the legal context, the same process helps us identify implicit guiding factors. Namely, determining guiding factors starts with identifying legally significant facts and assessing why those facts are legally significant. From there, we can determine a generalized category that accounts for those facts. This requires us to reason inductively, going from specific to general. For example, if there is an apple in a case and the court talks about it being a food product, we might infer that the category is "type of food." If instead there is an apple in a case in which the court emphasizes its red color, we might infer that the category is "color."

Why do we bother to categorize specific facts into guiding factors? Because the guiding factors provide categories through which we can make comparisons between the facts of our client's case and the facts of a prior case. For example, if a guiding factor is "type of food," we can now analogize the fact that the item in question in our case, a banana, is similar to the apple in the prior case because they are both fruits. In other words, once we know what guiding factors matter to the court, we know which facts from our client's case are important.

### Burglary Statute Hypothetical

Let's look at the process of inferring factors in the context of the burglary statute. In particular, to determine what constitutes "unlawful entry" under the burglary test, we necessarily turn to case precedent. Recall that we located a case in which the court held that a person who entered through an open door without permission engaged in "unlawful entry." Based upon that, we processed the first element of the burglary rule to further define "unlawful entry," as "not requiring the use of physical force." We also processed the rule to include two standards: "Unlawful entry must be proven beyond a reasonable doubt" and "Unlawful entry is judged an objective standard of what a reasonable person would think, not based on the defendant's subjective beliefs."

We still need more specific information to understand this element so we can make the rule for this element more tangible. Clearly, it is not just the absence of force or the fact that the court applied an objective standard that made the court decide entry in this example was unlawful—that would be nonsensical. We want to know why the court reached the holding it did. In other words, what facts did the court consider significant in reaching its holding? Again, we want to turn to guiding factors.

To discern the guiding factors, we look for language in the case in which the court discusses the facts that were significant to its holding on an issue, and we pay close attention to that language. Thus, as we read the case, we would note the following helpful language:

> Yet we know the defendant had no relationship with the owner of the home. We also know that the door was only slightly ajar and that no signage or other indicia suggested that the home was open to the public. And, of course, homes normally are not open to the public.

Although this language tells us what facts were important to the court in this case, it does not explicitly announce the guiding factors the court considers. Thus, we have to infer those guiding factors from the court's fact-based holding. That fact-based holding is simply what the court held and why it reached that holding, i.e., the key facts upon which that holding was based. Based upon the above language, we are able to state the fact-based holding as follows: "Entry is unlawful when there is no relationship between the owner and the defendant and when there is no signage to suggest the home is open to the public, even though the door to the home is slightly ajar."

From that fact-based holding, a lawyer could use inductive reasoning to identify two implicit guiding factors a court should consider in deciding whether there was "lawful entry": (1) the history, if any, between the defendant and the homeowner; and (2) any visual indications regarding whether the home was open to the public.

The diagram below depicts this process of discerning the guiding factors from the fact-based holding. The key facts from the fact-based holding are listed in the first column and the second column shows the guiding factors inferred from those key facts. Notice that there is not a one-to-one correlation between the facts and implicit guiding factors. Often, you will need to cluster related facts together to discern an implicit guiding factor. You can see below how we have done that with the second guiding factor regarding visual indications.

Diagram 8-3

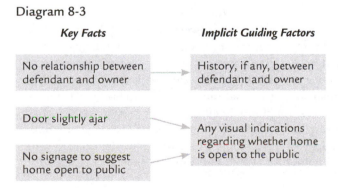

| Key Facts | Implicit Guiding Factors |
|---|---|
| No relationship between defendant and owner | History, if any, between defendant and owner |
| Door slightly ajar | Any visual indications regarding whether home is open to the public |
| No signage to suggest home open to public | |

Taken together, the definitions and implicit guiding factors provided in this case clarify the meaning of this condition. That new understanding of the rule for this condition is the emergent rule.

> Emergent Rule Outline for Condition of "Unlawfully Enters":
> Unlawful entry must be proven beyond a reasonable doubt. Unlawful entry does not require the use of physical force, and it is judged under the objective, not subjective, standard of what a "reasonable person" would think. **In determining whether entry is unlawful, the court considers: (1) the history, if any, between the defendant and the homeowner; and (2) any visual indications regarding whether the home was open to the public.**

With only one case, we do not have much data to help us discern the guiding factors. We made our best guess at identifying these guiding factors, ensuring they are consistent with the case. We could have labeled these implicit guiding factors differently, such as "whether the defendant was an invitee" or "whether a reasonable person would believe the structure or building was open to the public." It is difficult to pin down how broad or narrow a guiding factor should be with only one case to consider.

Notice, however, that we framed each of these plausible guiding factors as a category of consideration, not as a black-and-white requirement that either exists or does not exist. That is because guiding factors are merely considerations, not absolutes that are either satisfied or not satisfied. Thus, it would not be accurate to label the above-described guiding factors in the burglary example as "The defendant must demonstrate a history with the homeowner" or "There must be visual indications that the home was open to the public." These are simply not accurate given that the court did not state that either of these things was necessary; it simply stated that those facts, taken together, were sufficient to compel the result it reached.

---

 **GEARING UP: The Challenge of Inferring Guiding Factors**

What are we effectively doing when we infer guiding factors? First, we are assessing which facts were most important to a court's analysis of a condition and why those facts were significant. Then we are crafting a generalized basis for comparing those precedent facts to the facts of our client's situation. Because the court has not told us outright the rule that it applied for that condition, we have to extract the court's rule from its fact-based holding. When we discern implicit guiding factors, we are not creating the rule for that condition based on our own idea of what the rule should be. Instead, we are inferring the rule that the court implicitly applied for that condition. In effect, we are making explicit what the court made implicit. That type of inductive thinking (reasoning from specific to general) can be quite challenging.

**CHECK IN: How a Case Processes a Rule**

Recall the local ordinance that stated: "All dangerous dogs must be licensed." Recall further that that the rule broke down into two elements: (1) that the animal must be a dog; and (2) that the animal must be dangerous.

Read the following fictitious case in which this ordinance is at issue. As you read, consider how this case interprets and applies the "dangerous dog" ordinance. Specifically, what law-centered interpretations emerge from this case? What is the fact-based holding for the element at issue? What are the implicit guiding factors for that element? Outline the rule that emerges from this case, including the global rule and the rule for the element/condition at issue.

## *City of Bakerville v. Wilcox*
### 300 N.2d 334 (W.D. 1995)

Opinion by Parres, J. (writing for the majority).

We are asked in this appeal to interpret and apply the City of Bakerville's dangerous dog ordinance. *See* Bakerville Ordinance 2-115 ("All dangerous dogs must be licensed."). The district court concluded that the animal in question, Fido, must be licensed. After careful consideration, we affirm.

Last spring, the City became aware of two biting incidents involving Fido, a miniature schnauzer. In the first incident, Fido bit a seven-year-old child in his neighborhood. Less than a year later, Fido once again bit a child in his neighborhood—a four-year-old boy who was passing by Fido's house.

Fido's owners, appellants Tim and Lisa Wilcox, urge us to reverse the district court's holding that Fido is dangerous and must be licensed. (They do not challenge on appeal the Fido is a "dog" pursuant to the ordinance, and thus we do not address that part of the ordinance in this appeal.) They point out that Fido is a miniature schnauzer, which is not considered a dangerous breed. While acknowledging that Fido did bite two children, they argue that because neither child required medical care of any kind the dog cannot be deemed dangerous.

We note that the City bears the burden of proving by clear and convincing evidence that Fido is "dangerous." Despite this heavy burden, we conclude the City has satisfied it. In determining whether a dog is dangerous, our focus is on whether the dog poses a significant threat to the public. We think the City aptly demonstrated that Fido is dangerous. Fido bit two children. While the threat may be greater had those children required medical attention, the threat exists nonetheless. Fido's bite was not insignificant, as noted by the police report that detailed Fido's razor-sharp teeth. The fact that Fido is of a breed that is not typically considered to be threatening makes little difference to our analysis, given the facts before us. It is apparent to us from the record in this case that regardless of Fido's breed, he did indeed pose a threat.

For the foregoing reasons, we AFFIRM the judgment of the district court. Costs of this appeal are assessed to the appellants.

### b. What Are Explicit Guiding Factors?

In the burglary example, the guiding factors were implicit, meaning we had to do the work of discerning what guiding factors were implied based on the facts the court found legally significant. Sometimes, however, guiding factors are explicitly stated in a case. Typically, this happens only after several cases have already processed the rule, such that the court has a sound basis for explicitly stating the guiding factors. Note that while explicit and implicit guiding factors differ in terms of how the lawyer obtains them (directly from the case's language or by inference), both serve the same functional purpose.

Consider this excerpt from the Supreme Court of the United States (SCOTUS), in which the court addresses the legal rule for whether certain punitive damage awards are unreasonable:

> We instructed courts reviewing [the reasonableness of] punitive damages to consider three guideposts: (1) the degree of reprehensibility of the defendant's misconduct; (2) the disparity between the actual or potential harm suffered by the plaintiff and the punitive damages award; and (3) the difference between the punitive damages awarded by the jury and the civil penalties authorized or imposed in comparable cases.[3]

As noted, a court usually only arrives at an explicit guiding-factors test after many cases have already processed the rule, specifically the guiding factors. When the court makes explicit what it, over time, had implicitly been considering, those guiding factors are established as part of the legal rule. No longer does a lawyer have the discretion to discern his own set of implicit guiding factors. In the example above, the three explicit guiding factors that the Court considers in determining the reasonableness of a punitive damages award are now unquestionably part of the rule of law.

---

3. *State Farm Mut. Auto. Ins. Co. v. Campbell*, 538 U.S. 408, 418, 123 S. Ct. 1513, 1520, 155 L. Ed. 2d 585 (2003).

## 3. Why Are Guiding Factors Important?

Guiding factors help us understand the rule better so we can make more organized and effective arguments as well as more plausible predictions. As discussed, legal rules often include somewhat abstract concepts, like "unlawful entry." Guiding factors help shape those concepts by making them more tangible. By analyzing the court's past interpretation and application of the rule for "unlawful entry," we can discern what considerations are significant to the court and thus tailor our arguments in the next case around the guiding factors we have identified as significant.

The impact of guiding factors goes beyond simply breaking down and refining the rule of law for a condition as part of our pre-drafting analysis. Guiding factors also help us organize our analysis on behalf of our client. Specifically, in making arguments about whether a client's entry was lawful or not, a lawyer will structure her arguments around the guiding factors. By extension, she will organize the rule application section of her written analysis in accordance with those guiding factors.

What does this use of guiding factors suggest to you about the optimal number of guiding factors for a condition? Given that the guiding factors will serve as the basis on which you make arguments, you will want at least two. If you have only one, you have not helped your reader break down the condition. But how many is too many? While there is no hard-and-fast rule, usually you will want no more than four guiding factors. Any more than that can be overwhelming to the reader and interfere with the discussion's effectiveness. If you initially discern six guiding factors, pare them down to only four by combining one or more of them. For example, instead of guiding factors of "whether the defendant engaged in verbal abuse" and "whether the defendant engaged in physical abuse," if you needed to decrease the number of guiding factors these could be combined to a single guiding factor of "whether the defendant engaged in physical or verbal abuse."

## 4. Discretion in Labeling Implicit Guiding Factors

### Curfew Hypothetical

Implicit guiding factors can be articulated in a variety of ways. Consider the example of the teen's curfew, discussed earlier in this chapter. Recall that the parent in question told the child he must be home by a "reasonable time" but did not specify exactly what that meant. By looking at past instances, the child surmised that in deciding what constitutes a "reasonable time," his dad considers (1) whether it is a school night, and (2) whether there is a special occasion. In other words, these two considerations were the implicit guiding factors.

But the teen also could have labeled those guiding factors in other ways. Maybe instead of "whether there is a special occasion," he thought a narrower label would be appropriate, such as "whether there is a special occasion relating to school," or, perhaps, an even narrower label, such as "whether there is a school-sponsored event." Is one of these labels right and the others wrong? No, all are acceptable at this juncture.

Any of the labels is "correct" until proven otherwise by a later experience. If next week the teen's dad gets mad at him for coming home at 1:00 a.m. following an end-of-the-year celebration bonfire at his friend's house, that likely would constrain how he can label this guiding factor. The teen would now know that his dad does not consider all "special occasions," even those relating to school, as worthy of a later curfew; accordingly, he would use the narrowest label of "whether there is a school-sponsored event."

As advocates, part of our job is to use this flexibility to our advantage. If it helps our client to narrowly label a guiding factor, we should do so as long as that is consistent with the case holdings. On the other hand, if it helps our client to broadly label the guiding factor, we should do so, again, as long as the case law allows that discretion.

 **CRASH WARNING: The Lure of the Perfect Guiding Factor Label**

Students can sometimes fixate on finding precisely the right label for a guiding factor when, in fact, there often is no one right way to express implicit guiding factors. Rather than focusing on finding the "perfect" label for a guiding factor, instead ensure your label (1) fits the available information, and (2) when advocating, serves your client.

## C. Interpreting the Existing Legal Rule by Showing How the Conditions of the Rule Fit Together

Another way in which a case may process a legal rule is by discussing the relationship between the conditions of the test. This is particularly useful for a factors test when the existing legal rule does not set forth the relative weight and relationship between the factors. Recall the eight-factor statutory test for physical custody of a child we explored in Chapter 7. While helpful in focusing our legal analysis, that list did not rank or prioritize any of the factors, nor did it explain how the factors relate to one another.

To try to get additional insight into the interaction between the factors, we would turn to cases to seek information about how the court has applied these factors under different circumstances. We may find a case in which the court gives greater consideration to the factor of a child's educational needs when the child is older. Now we know something about the relationship between two of the factors ("the child's age" and "the impact of the custody decision on a child's education, medical, and emotional needs"). Likewise, a case that discussed the almost singular focus on the factor of "past instances of neglect, abuse, or violence by either or both parents" when there is a history of such behavior would suggest that when this factor arises, it tends to outweigh other factors.

Case analysis can also help us understand the interaction of different guiding factors. For example, under the burglary statute, we discerned two guiding factors the courts consider in determining the element of "unlawful entry": (1) the history, if any, between the defendant and the homeowner; and (2) any visual indications regarding whether the home was open to the public. If a case held that the second guiding factor is the most important one, we would know that we should emphasize that point. We could also feel confident arguing that this point outweighed the fact that our client may have been a social acquaintance of the defendant, a fact relating to the first guiding factor.

Sometimes a court will not just imply through its holding that a certain factor or guiding factor is more important than others; instead, it will explicitly note this aspect of the rule. Take, for example, this excerpt from a SCOTUS opinion in which the court explicitly states which guiding factor among three is the most important one when determining the reasonableness of a punitive damages award:

> [T]he most important indicium of the reasonableness of a punitive damages award is the degree of reprehensibility of the defendant's conduct.[4]

While it would be helpful to always have this sort of clarity about the relative weight of factors, this is decidedly not the norm. Instead, cases are usually less explicit about the relationship among guiding factors. While law students may initially dislike this ambiguous aspect of the law, many lawyers grow to appreciate it. This is because ambiguity in the legal rule provides flexibility for lawyers to ethically and credibly interpret the rule to the benefit of their clients.

---

4. *BMW of N. Am., Inc. v. Gore*, 517 U.S. 559, 575, 116 S. Ct. 1589, 1598, 134 L. Ed. 2d 809 (1996).

**RULES OF THE ROAD: Reasonable Interpretation of Judicial Opinions**

It may surprise you that the law from judicial opinions can be stated in a number of ways. While a characterization of a court's ruling does have a degree of flexibility, there is also a limit to that flexibility. Lawyers are prohibited from offering misleading information to the court, both about the law and about the client facts. And, while the ethical rules in most states do acknowledge that the law is sometimes unclear and typically not static,[5] an advocate must nonetheless remain within a reasonable zone of interpretation when articulating the breadth of a court opinion. If an advocate has stated the ruling more broadly or narrowly than can be substantiated by the case, she has exceeded that reasonable zone of interpretation and run afoul of her ethical obligation.

## III. Putting It All Together: Examining How a Court Processes the Rule for a Given Condition

Let's look at one more example of a case in which the court processes the legal rule for a given condition by providing both law-centered interpretations and a fact-based holding.

### A. Using a Case to Find Law-Centered Interpretations and Discern a Fact-Based Holding

#### Warrantless Bomb Search Hypothetical

Before we look at the case, recall our search warrant rule from the Warrantless Bomb Search hypothetical, which provides: "The government must possess a warrant before conducting a search unless there is consent to search or there are exigent circumstances." This begs the questions, "How is consent given?" and "What are exigent circumstances?"

---

5. *See, e.g.*, Iowa Rule of Professional Conduct 32: 3.1. Comment 1 to the rule on Meritorious Claims and Contentions provides:

> The advocate has a duty to use legal procedure for the fullest benefit of the client's cause, but also a duty not to abuse legal procedure. The law, both procedural and substantive, establishes the limits within which an advocate may proceed. However, the law is not always clear and never is static. Accordingly, in determining the proper scope of advocacy, account must be taken of the law's ambiguities and potential for change.

To answer those questions, lawyers look to cases that have applied that rule. Thus a lawyer seeking a better understanding of "whether consent was given" would search for a case in which a court examined whether consent was valid.

Assume that the lawyer finds the case of *United States v. Purcell*, 526 F.3d 953 (6th Cir. 2008).[6] She immediately deems the case helpful because it pertains to whether the government had authority to conduct a warrantless search in a similar situation. Based upon a careful reading of this case, the lawyer extracts useful law-centered interpretations and fact-based holdings in which the court processes the existing rule of law. As detailed below, she then uses those law-centered interpretations and fact-based holdings to provide a more detailed outline of the rule for "whether consent was given."

As you read through the case below, keep in mind the following questions. These questions help focus the lawyer's attention on what she hopes to learn from *Purcell*. Namely:

1. What law-centered interpretations of the rule does *Purcell* provide for this condition/element?
   - Does it provide any definitions?
   - Does it provide any standards?
   - Does it provide any *explicit* guiding factors?
2. What is the fact-based holding from *Purcell* on the condition/element? Namely:
   - How did the court hold on the issue of whether there was apparent authority to search?
   - Why did the court reach that holding; i.e., what facts led the court to that conclusion?
3. What *implicit* guiding factors might you discern based upon this fact-based holding?

In order to consent to a search, the person purporting to consent must possess either actual or apparent authority over the item or place to be searched. *United States v. Caldwell*, 518 F.3d 426, 429 (6th Cir.2008). Once an individual with actual or apparent authority consents to the search, "[t]he standard for measuring the scope of a suspect's consent under the Fourth Amendment is that of 'objective' reasonableness—what would the typical reasonable person have understood by the exchange between the officer and the suspect?"

The court starts by providing a definition of who can give consent. In other words, "consent to search" is defined as consent from someone with "actual or apparent authority." Assume we have been told to ignore whether there was actual authority and to focus only on the apparent authority prong.

The court tells us that the standard is an objective one; i.e., what would a reasonable person believe? This is a law-centered interpretation.

---

6. We have modified the *Purcell* opinion to some extent so that it more clearly illustrates the legal analysis and writing process. You should use the modified opinion, in Appendix E, for all exercises in this course that use *Purcell*.

The last sentence goes into the scope of the consent given. That is a law-centered interpretation, but one that we will ignore because our question focuses on whether there was apparent authority, not what the scope was of any assumed authority.

*Florida v. Jimeno,* 500 U.S. 248, 251, 111 S.Ct. 1801, 114 L.Ed.2d 297 (1991). Thus, when an officer receives consent, he is allowed to search only what is reasonably covered by the consent given; "[i]t is very likely unreasonable to think that a suspect, by consenting to the search of his trunk [of his car], has agreed to the breaking open of a locked briefcase within the trunk, but it is otherwise with respect to a closed paper bag." *Id.* at 251-52, 111 S.Ct. 1801.

\*\*\*

In this paragraph the court first explains that the consent element/condition can be satisfied in one of two ways: by showing actual authority or by showing apparent authority. That reinforces/confirms our understanding of this exception to the rule, which is an either/or test.

"We have held that even where third-party consent comes from an individual without actual authority over the property searched, there is no Fourth Amendment violation if the police conducted the search in good faith reliance on the third-party's *apparent authority* to authorize the search through her consent." *Morgan,* 435 F.3d 660, 663 (6th Cir.2006) (finding apparent authority where a wife claimed to have authority to access to her husband's computer).

Here the court provides us with a standard for the apparent authority condition; i.e., an objective standard based on information known to officer at the moment of search. In other words, what would a reasonable officer believe?

The court is providing us with a definition of when third-party consent is valid. Namely, apparent authority for third-party consent is valid only if the officer reasonably believed the person giving consent possessed joint access or control over the property searched.

In investigating whether officers reasonably concluded an individual possessed apparent authority, the "determination of consent ... must 'be judged against an objective standard: would the facts available to the officer at the moment ... warrant a man of reasonable caution in the belief' that the consenting party had authority over the [property]?" *Illinois v. Rodriguez,* 497 U.S. 177, 188, 110 S.Ct. 2793, 111 L.Ed.2d 148 (1990) (second omission in original) (quoting *Terry v. Ohio,* 392 U.S. 1, 21-22, 88 S.Ct. 1868, 20 L.Ed.2d 889 (1968)). In the third-party consent context, this means the officer must have reasonably believed the person giving consent possessed joint access or control over the property searched.

This language—"in the case at hand"—signals the court's transition to the application of the legal rule; i.e., the court's analysis regarding whether in this case there was, in fact, apparent authority.

In the case at hand, when the agents began their search of the luggage in the hotel room, they had a good-faith basis to believe that Crist had joint access or control over the bags.

In the application, the court tells us why it ruled as it did. In other words, which facts were significant and why? We will read this section carefully in order to come up with the fact-based holding.

Crist asserted control over the duffel bag that yielded the marijuana and gave consent to search. She said the bag was hers. Her words, standing alone, indicate that she had the requisite access and control.

> This first part of the paragraph tells us that the court is focusing on what the person said. That indicates that an implicit guiding factor is "whether the person reasonably asserted access and control over the property."

Her statement made sense in light of the circumstances as she was able to access the bags, and her purse was sitting on top of the duffel bag.

> This last sentence seems to suggest another guiding factor. It is clear that in addition to the person's assertion of control, the context is important. Not clear, however, is the label to give that guiding factor.

However, further context was revealed during the search of this first bag that called into question Crist's asserted control over the bags. During the search of the first bag, the officer learned that it contained only men's clothing and no personal effects of Crist. A reasonable officer cannot ignore that information and must consider the assertion of control in light of the context that evolves. Here, that context created ambiguity and doubt regarding Crist's asserted control. Any otherwise apparent authority evaporated. *See Rodriguez*, 497 U.S. at 188, 110 S.Ct. 2793 ("Even when the invitation is accompanied by an explicit assertion that the person lives there, the surrounding circumstances could conceivably be such that a reasonable person would doubt its truth and not act upon it without further inquiry."); *Jenkins*, 92 F.3d at 437 ("Of course, if the consenter provides additional information, the context may change in such a manner that no reasonable officer would maintain the default assumption.").

> This paragraph provides more information about the second guiding factor. The contextual facts that are significant relate to whether the person's words made sense in light of other circumstances. Thus, the second guiding factor can be labeled as "whether the context confirms or creates ambiguity regarding the spoken assertion."

\*\*\*

Thus, we conclude that the discovery of the men's clothing in the duffel bag that Crist claimed was hers created ambiguity sufficient to erase any initial apparent authority. Thus, at the point the firearm was discovered, there was no valid consent. The firearm was discovered as part of an illegal search, and the district court did not err when it suppressed the firearm.

> Overall, the above paragraphs suggest the fact-based holding could be stated as: "Apparent authority does not exist when a person asserts control and authority over the searched bags, yet shortly thereafter the officers have reason to doubt the bags belong to her."

[*United States v. Purcell*, 526 F.3d 953, 962–65 (6th Cir. 2008) (modified).]

As you can see from reviewing the annotated excerpt, *Purcell* provides useful information about determining whether consent existed. That information includes both law-centered interpretations and fact-based holdings. Both types of information provide us with a much better understanding of the rule for whether consent exists.

**CHECK IN: Framing Fact-Based Holdings**

Recall that there is flexibility in how a fact-based holding is framed. Above we noted the fact-based holding for *Purcell* could be stated as:

> Apparent authority does not exist when a person asserts control and authority over the searched bags, yet shortly thereafter the officers have reason to doubt the bags belong to her.

Yet that is not the only possible way to frame that fact-based holding. For example, it could be framed more narrowly, such as:

> Apparent authority does not exist when a person asserts control and authority over property to which she has access, yet it becomes clear that the assertion is false.

This holding is narrower in the sense that it suggests the surrounding context needs to be directly disconfirming, not merely casting doubt. Why would a lawyer want to use this narrower version of the fact-based holding? Which party/position would that narrower characterization favor?

## B. Using the Information Obtained from a Case to Outline the Emergent Rule

After carefully reading *Purcell* in order to note its law-centered interpretations and discern its fact-based holding, the next objective is to outline that information. The rule that emerges from *Purcell* for the condition of whether consent to search exists is fairly detailed and complex, so you might find it helpful to first draw a diagram depicting the components of the rule (see Diagram 8-4).

With or without the aid of a diagram, your next step is outlining the rule that emerges for this element from *Purcell*. Your outline puts together all of the interpretations of the rule that you gleaned from both the law-centered interpretations and fact-based holdings for this condition in *Purcell*.

### Outline for Element/Condition of Whether There Was Consent to Search

- Consent to search the property must come from someone with "actual or apparent authority."
- Apparent authority is judged by an objective standard based on the information known to officer at moment of search.
- In the third-party context, the officer must have reasonably believed the person giving consent possessed joint access or control over the property searched.

Diagram 8-4

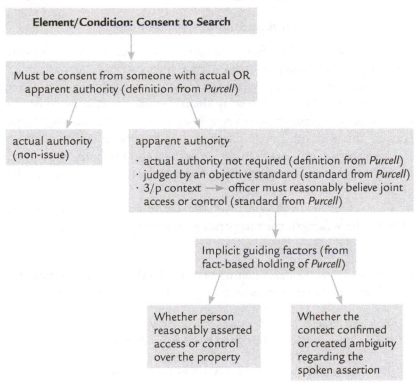

- In determining whether such apparent authority over the property searched existed, courts consider:
  1. whether the person reasonably asserted access and control over the property, and
  2. whether the context confirmed or created ambiguity regarding the spoken assertion.

Notice that the outline of the rule for this element/condition includes the definitions and standards followed by the guiding factors. You will need to include all of these components in order to convey to the reader the complete and accurate rule for this element/condition.

## IV. Expert Tips for Working with Guiding Factors

As noted above, students often struggle with assessing whether their implicit guiding factor is "right" and with determining what label to give an implicit guiding factor. This next section provides more practice and tips for working with guiding factors.

## A. Testing Your Guiding Factors

### Burglary Statute Hypothetical

Because implicit guiding factors are just that—implicit—you will never get absolute confirmation from a case that you have arrived at an "objectively correct" guiding factor. However, you can gain confidence in your guiding factors by testing them against the case by considering whether the guiding factors you developed match the relevant facts. Let's try this with our two implicit guiding factors for unlawful entry: (1) the history, if any, between the defendant and the homeowner; and (2) any visual indications regarding whether the home was open to the public.

First, carefully read the facts the court considered and assess whether these facts fit the categories we identified as guiding factors:

Matches with first factor of history between defendant and owner.
——— Yet we know the defendant had no relationship with the owner of the home such that permission could hardly have been implied.

Matches with second factor of visual indicators.
——— We also know that the door was only slightly ajar and that no signage or other indicia suggested that the home was open to the public.

Also matches with visual indicators.
——— And, of course, homes normally are not open to the public.

Next, consider whether one or more legally significant facts have no matching guiding factor. This example has no "stray" facts. However, if there were, that would tell us that we need to adjust our guiding factors by adding a guiding factor, making an existing guiding factor broader, or otherwise modifying our guiding factors to match all legally significant facts.

## B. Labeling Your Guiding Factors

Finding the precise label to give a guiding factor can also present a challenge. An effective label for a guiding factor should clearly indicate what that guiding factor means. If the writer had labeled the first guiding factor as "relevant history" rather than "the history, if any, between the defendant and the homeowner," the reader would not have had a clear idea what was meant by "relevant history." On the other hand, if the writer had labeled the guiding factor more narrowly as "whether the parties had a long-standing relationship," we would perhaps have had a misleading label. The case did not suggest that a relationship needs to be long-standing to suggest permission to enter.

Given that, we might even consider a label of "the history, if any, between the defendant and the homeowner *from which permission to enter might be inferred*" to be more effective than our original label. It is difficult to ascertain whether this would be too specific, given that we only have one case to consider. In Chapter 21, when we consider determining implicit guiding factors from multiple authorities, we will note that arriving at guiding factors generally becomes easier, not harder, when we have multiple authorities. Those additional authorities help us determine how broad or narrow the guiding factor should be, as well as further illuminating which facts are significant to the court and why.

 **EQUIPPING YOURSELF: Persuasive Authority**

The discussion in this chapter has revolved around how cases interpret and apply an existing legal rule and thus forever modify that rule. That discussion assumes that the cases interpreting the existing legal rule are binding authority in the jurisdiction in which the rule exists. (Remember the discussion in Chapter 6 of mandatory versus persuasive authority.) Occasionally, however, a lawyer is faced with an existing legal rule that has not been sufficiently interpreted by courts in that jurisdiction. Maybe that is because the rule is relatively new, or maybe it is only infrequently litigated. Whatever the reason, in such situations the lawyer may look to other jurisdictions for guidance on how a court might interpret certain aspects of the rule. Those cases from other jurisdictions are persuasive, not binding, authority.

# Types of Legal Reasoning

Part I of this module addressed how to determine the applicable legal rule and why this is so important. When a case has interpreted and applied an existing legal rule, the emergent legal rule from that case becomes the new existing legal rule and the rule of law we utilize in our legal analysis.

In Part II of this module we will focus on applying the rule of law to a set of facts. This should seem familiar. In order to discern the rule of law, we had to consider how a court in a previous case applied the law to particular facts. Now we start from an unresolved dispute: our client's situation. The "set of facts" is our client's situation, and we are now creating our own arguments, not just identifying a past application.

When lawyers apply the law to a client's situation, they identify the arguments each party will make about how the law applies to the facts. While such application may seem straightforward, it frequently is not. That is because, as we have seen in Chapter 8, rules of law contain ambiguity. Therefore, how that law applies to a novel set of facts is subject to differing views and arguments. Lawyers for opposing sides often do not agree on how the law applies to the unique facts of that case, and this enables lawyers to advocate for an application of the law that would benefit their client.

For example, a prosecutor may interpret the law for "unlawful entry" in an expansive way, arguing that the defendant unlawfully entered a property by using a key that he had not yet returned to the owner, despite a request to do so. The defense may argue the opposite: the fact that the defendant entered with a key that had been provided to him by the owner makes the entry lawful. Ultimately, a court would decide which argument prevails; for our purposes in the next several chapters, the focus is not so much on what a court will decide but more on what arguments can be made.

The arguments that lawyers make vary based on the particular nuances of the legal rule and the client's facts. However, they broadly fall into three different types of legal reasoning. We'll explore all three types in the remainder of this module, starting with an overview (Chapter 9), then delving into each type of legal reasoning in detail: rule-based reasoning (Chapter 10), analogical reasoning (Chapter 11), and policy-based reasoning (Chapter 12).

### CHAPTER 9

# Overview of Types of Legal Reasoning

**W**hen lawyers apply a legal rule to facts, they are engaging in *legal reasoning*. In this chapter, we consider the three main types of legal reasoning, which collectively form the basis of how lawyers make arguments.

---

### Study Guide Questions for Chapter 9

1. What are the three types of legal reasoning lawyers rely on in making arguments?
2. What types of legal reasoning rely upon case law?
3. How is the rule of law used in legal reasoning?
4. Which type of legal reasoning is most common? Why?

5. What new terms were introduced in this chapter? How do these terms relate to your existing understanding of predictive memo writing? Did your understanding of any other terms change as a result of reading this chapter?

---

Lawyers use three types of reasoning to make arguments:

- Rule-based reasoning
- Analogical reasoning
- Policy-based reasoning

In each of these types of reasoning, the lawyer applies the rule of law to the case facts. As you will learn in Chapter 18, in a predictive memo, this takes the form of providing and assessing the arguments each party will likely advance.

## I. Rule-Based Reasoning

In *rule-based reasoning*, the lawyer advocates for a result based on the application of the rule of law to the facts. It is the simplest form of legal reasoning. Typically, the argument is relatively straightforward and simply relies upon the language and principles of the rule.

A basic example of rule-based reasoning is:

> All dogs go to heaven. Fido is a dog. Therefore, Fido will go to heaven.

As this example demonstrates, rule-based reasoning takes the rule ("All dogs go to heaven") and applies it to the facts ("Fido is a dog"). The writer completes the argument by explicitly showing how the law applies to those facts ("Therefore, Fido will go to heaven").

Rule-based reasoning can also be more complex. Recall the tortious interference with business expectancy claim in The Smell Shoppe hypothetical. One element necessary to prove that claim is that the defendant must have engaged in "intentional and unjustified interference." The following example shows how a lawyer might use rule-based reasoning to argue that this element is satisfied.

 **CONCEPT IN ACTION: Rule-Based Reasoning**

Defendant's interference was intentional and unjustified. Defendant's advertisement referred to a "new location," when the defendant knew that this was in fact the only location. There can be no justification for an advertisement that refers to a "new location," when in fact it is the only location. Rather, the only purpose in including such language was to suggest that there were multiple locations, thus deliberately leading customers to infer the defendant's business was part of the plaintiff's chain.

Notice that rule-based reasoning neither references the facts of a precedent case nor makes comparisons to such facts. The precedent case facts, and how they may be similar to or different from the client's case facts, are not the basis for rule-based reasoning. Rather, this type of reasoning relies only on examining the rule of law and its underlying principles and then using a deductive approach to apply that rule to the client's facts.

## II. Analogical Reasoning

Analogical reasoning, the most common type of legal reasoning, consists of comparing the facts of a precedent to the facts of the client's case. The lawyer can reason that, because the facts are similar, they compel the same result, or, because the facts are distinguishable, they compel a different result. The lawyer must specifically show how the facts are similar or distinguishable.

A simple example of analogical reasoning is:

> Fido shares similar characteristics with the animal that went to heaven in *Lassie,* including fur, canine incisors, and a loving disposition.

Analogical arguments can be quite complex. In the tortious interference with business expectancy claim in The Smell Shoppe hypothetical, in the excerpt below the lawyer makes an analogical argument as to why the interference was intentional and unjustifiable.

 **CONCEPT IN ACTION: Analogical Reasoning**

The Plaintiff may argue that like the advertisements in *Chicago's Pizza,* the defendant's advertisements led customers to believe there was an affiliation between the defendant's restaurant and the plaintiff's. *See id.* Specifically, similar to the defendant in *Chicago's Pizza* that had included multiple locations on its coupons despite the fact that it only owned one location, the defendant here placed advertisements in the form of a website with similar branding and printable coupons. *See id.* The defendant went so far as to use the phrase "our newest location," implying, like the defendant in *Chicago's Pizza,* there was more than one location. *See id.*

The Defendant, on the other hand, may argue that his advertisements were unlike those in *Chicago's Pizza. See id.* The defendant's coupons did not contain multiple locations, or any inaccurate information, but rather provided only the one true location of his store. Stating a location is the "newest location" is factually true, unlike the multiple locations by the defendant in *Chicago's Pizza. See id.*

Both parties' arguments consist of reasoning by analogy. The plaintiff is arguing the circumstances of the case are similar to those of the precedent case and thus compel the same outcome. The defendant is arguing that the circumstances of the case are distinct from those of the precedent case and thus compel a different outcome. The plaintiff is making an *analogy*, and the defendant is drawing a *distinction*, both of which are forms of analogical reasoning.

Notice too that both parties are using the same case, *Chicago's Pizza,* to make their argument. That is common with analogical reasoning because some aspects of the precedent case are similar to the new case and some are dissimilar. It is a lawyer's job to emphasize certain facts and persuade the court that the cases are more alike than different or vice versa.

**RULES OF THE ROAD: Ethically Framing Legal Arguments**

As noted in the previous chapter, the latitude lawyers have in framing legal arguments is not without limits. Lawyers are obligated to be truthful and are prohibited from misleading the court as to the facts or law. Thus, lawyers cannot "stretch" their characterizations of the law beyond a reasonable zone of interpretation. The Hawai'i Rules of Professional Conduct explain the lawyer's duties in the context of argumentation as follows:

Legal argument based on a knowingly false representation of law constitutes dishonesty toward the tribunal. A lawyer is not required to make a disinterested exposition of the law, but must recognize the existence of pertinent legal authorities. Furthermore, as stated in paragraph (a)(3), an advocate has a duty to disclose directly adverse authority in the controlling jurisdiction which has not been disclosed by the opposing party. The underlying concept is that *legal argument is a discussion seeking to determine the legal premises properly applicable to the case.*

Hawai'i Rules of Professional Conduct 3.3, cmt. 3 (emphasis added).

You likely have already engaged in reasoning by analogy in your other law school courses. When you read a precedent case in your torts class and then discuss how a hypothetical conflict would be resolved under the emergent rule from that case, you are likely using analogical reasoning. Specifically, your class discussion consists of arguments as to why the hypothetical facts are similar to or different from the facts from the precedent. That is analogical reasoning. Because no two cases have entirely identical facts, quite often both sides can craft arguments using reasoning by analogy.

Reasoning by analogy is the most prevalent form of legal reasoning because the American legal system is a common law system. The law evolves from courts deciding cases and controversies, not in the abstract, but based upon their unique facts. Those facts are crucial to understanding the court's holding on a given issue. Thus, given the role of factually intensive case law in our legal system, it makes sense that reasoning by analogy is the primary tool lawyers use to make arguments.

## III.  Policy-Based Reasoning

The final type of legal reasoning is *policy-based reasoning*. Here, the lawyer argues that the court should resolve a conflict in favor of her client because doing so will also result in a desirable outcome for society, support a shared value, or, for enacted law, fulfill the intended objective. Policy reasoning typically is used less frequently than other types of reasoning because the system of stare decisis is based on following the existing precedent. To the extent that a rule of law advances important policy considerations, cases in that area should already reflect that policy, and lawyers should be able to incorporate the policy objectives through analogical reasoning. The converse is also typically true: if a policy is not already reflected in the precedent cases applying that rule, it is unlikely a later court will give much, if any, weight to that policy argument. The one caveat to this general principle is that social, moral, and political values and policies change over time, and the law then adapts to reflect these new policies.

It is not surprising, then, that when you review the sample memos and illustrations in this book, you will see very few examples of policy-based reasoning. The following is a simple example of policy-based reasoning:

> Fido should go to heaven. Heaven is intended for those who have lived good lives, and Fido has been an exceptionally loving and loyal dog.

Similarly, but with more complexity, a policy-based argument could be advanced in The Smell Shoppe hypothetical that "intentional and unlawful interference" should be narrowly and carefully applied in the context of a defendant's advertising given the liberties afforded by the First Amendment. While a precedent may not have advanced that argument, it nonetheless might be an argument that puts a "thumb on the scale" in favor of whatever result a lawyer is seeking.

 **CONCEPT IN ACTION: Policy-Based Reasoning**

The defendant may argue that the court should narrowly construe what actions are "unlawful and unjustifiable interference," particularly when the defendant's actions are commercial speech. A defendant's right to advertise in the way it deems most effective would be stifled if the plaintiff's argument were accepted.

 **CHECK IN: Legal Reasoning**

Now that you have labels for the three types of legal reasoning, can you find examples in your other courses of these types of legal reasoning used either in cases or during in-class discussions?

Why is it important to discern the legal rule before applying that rule? Put differently, would it be possible to reason by analogy without having a grasp of the legal rule? Why not?

# Rule-Based Reasoning

Chapter 9 introduced the three types of legal reasoning. This chapter explores rule-based reasoning in detail.

## Study Guide Questions for Chapter 10

1. What is rule-based reasoning?
2. Into what part of the legal memo do rule-based reasoning arguments fit?
3. In what way, if any, does rule-based reasoning rely upon the facts from a precedent?
4. Can different types of reasoning be used in conjunction with one another to develop an argument?
5. What new terms were introduced in this chapter? How do these terms relate to your existing understanding of predictive memo writing? Did your understanding of any other terms change as a result of reading this chapter?

## I. Overview of Rule-Based Reasoning

Rule-based reasoning is the most straightforward type of legal reasoning. The lawyer takes the existing rule and applies it to the specific case. In this deductive process, the attorney applies something general (the existing rule) to something specific (the facts of the client's case).

Although the existing rule has been gleaned from precedent cases, the *facts of the precedent cases* do not form the basis for this type of reasoning. That is, this type of reasoning does not rely on making comparisons between the precedent case and the client's case. Instead, rule-based reasoning is purely the logical and deductive application of the language or principle from the existing rule to the client's case.

Imagine a statute that authorizes a person to change their last name as part of their divorce:

> "As part of a divorce, a party has the right to have their last name restored to the party's last name as it existed before the marriage."

This rule is straightforward and clear. It is not nuanced in any way. As such, the law's application is also clear. In such situations, a rule-based argument is all that is needed. The party would simply argue:

> Ella Ramos almost certainly will be granted the requested name change. The statute expressly allows a person, as part of their divorce, to "have their last name restored to the... name as it existed before the marriage." Ella thus is clearly entitled to a name change under the statute. She falls under the statute's purview because she seeks the name change as part of her divorce. In addition, the change in name that she requests is expressly allowed under the statute. Specifically, she requests that her name be restored to "Helton," which was her "last name as it existed before the marriage."

An analogical argument is not only unnecessary, here it would needlessly muddle and belabor the argument. For example, consider whether adding the following sentence to the end of the paragraph above would be beneficial: "Thus, like the spouse in *Anderson* who was granted a name change back to her maiden name, here too Ella should be granted a name change because she too seeks to have her maiden name restored." Such a sentence would not be helpful. The analogical argument set forth in that sentence adds nothing to the reader's understanding of the rule's application and instead only wastes the reader's time.

Sometimes, however, a rule-based argument is helpful even when the rule's application is not self-evident. In such situations, a rule-based argument is not used as a substitute for an analogical argument but rather is used in conjunction with an analogical argument.

Recall the Warrantless Bomb Search hypothetical. From our discussion in Chapter 8, we've learned that:

- Consent to search is one exception to the warrant requirement.
- The person giving consent must possess either actual or apparent authority over the item or place to be searched.
- To prove apparent authority in third-party consent, the officer must have reasonably believed the person giving consent possessed joint access or control over the property searched.
- In determining whether such apparent authority over the property searched existed, courts consider: (1) whether the person reasonably asserted access and control over the property, and (2) whether the context confirmed or created ambiguity regarding the spoken assertion.

Now, let's look at an example of a rule-based argument using the above-described rule. In particular, the following example makes arguments about a specific part of the rule, namely the guiding factor of "whether the person reasonably asserted access and control over the property." As you can see, the writer starts with a rule-based argument. Then the writer next makes an analogical argument (i.e., in the sentence beginning, "Thus, similar to the situation in *Purcell*...").

> ⬚ **CONCEPT IN ACTION: Rule-Based Reasoning (Followed by Analogical Reasoning) from the Warrantless Bomb Search Scenario**
>
> The Earl reasonably asserted access and control over the shipping container. The Earl expressly asserted access and control when he told the agents he had a rental agreement to use the shipping container and that he stored various pieces from his guitar collection there. *See id.* Further, The Earl demonstrated that access and control over that shared space when he opened the shipping container for agents with his own key. *See id.* Thus, similar to the situation in *Purcell* in which the defendant's girlfriend had access to the bags, claimed the bags were hers, and had her purse on top of one of the bags, here too the agent was reasonable to believe, at least based upon the assertion alone, that authority existed. *Id.* at 957. The Earl's assertion of authority is even stronger than the girlfriend's in *Purcell* because The Earl's key leaves no doubt about his access to the property. *See id.*

In the rule-based argument, the Government applies the rule ("access and control") to the facts. No reference is made to the facts of the precedent case. In the analogical argument, the Government then compares those facts to the facts of a precedent. As this example illustrates, these two types of reasoning work well together to make the State's argument regarding the guiding factor of "access and control."

## II. Key Features of Rule-Based Reasoning

**Includes Factual Detail**: Notice that in rule-based reasoning, the lawyer describes the client's case facts in detail. This detail is critical for the argument to be effective. Without the benefit of specific facts, the reader has no basis to evaluate the validity of the rule-based argument.

**Explicitly Integrates Key Language About the Rule**: Rule-based reasoning expressly integrates the key language about the rule on which the argument is based. In the name change example above, that key language comes directly from the statute, i.e., the right to "have their last name restored to the party's last name as it existed before the marriage." Other times, such as in the excerpt from the Warrantless Bomb Search memo above, this key language still comes from the rule, but is not direct language in a statute or even a case.

**Explicitly Tethers the Facts to the Rule**: Facts alone do not equate with rule-based reasoning. The writer needs to integrate the rule being applied with those facts, explicitly showing how those facts satisfy the rule. In the above example, the writer has integrated the rule being addressed—the guiding factor of whether the person had access and control—along with the facts. Notably, the writer states: "Further, The Earl demonstrated that access and control over that shared space when he opened the shipping container for agents with his own key." The first part of that sentence integrates the rule ("access and control over shared space") and the latter part of the sentence tethers the specific client facts to that part of the rule.

If the lawyer had simply stated, "The Earl had a key to the shipping container," that would not have connected the dots for the reader. The reader would instead have been left to connect those dots himself by thinking, "Ah, a key, so if The Earl had a key then he probably had access and control." Although that may seem like an easy enough connection for the reader to have drawn on his own, making those connections is the lawyer's job, not the reader's. It is what differentiates making an argument from merely reciting facts. Indeed, in more complex arguments, it will not be obvious how certain facts do or do not connect with the principle set forth in the existing rule.

---

 **CHECK IN: Rule Mastery and Rule-Based Reasoning**

### Dog-Owner Liability Hypothetical

Imagine that your client, Sandra, has been sued by a neighbor who tripped and fell on her sidewalk. In his lawsuit, the neighbor claims that he sustained injuries caused by Sandra's dog. Specifically, the neighbor alleges he was walking on the sidewalk past Sandra's fenced yard, when Sandra's large Mastiff dog began barking wildly and lunging at the fence. The neighbor claims he was so startled by the dog's behavior that he tripped and fell on the sidewalk.

You have found the rule that addresses the owner's potential liability, and one condition of that rule is that the plaintiff *must prove* by clear and convincing evidence that the dog has engaged in threatening behavior. You also found a case that interprets that rule that says that in determining whether a dog has engaged in threatening behavior, courts consider the dog's overt actions and physical characteristics.

First, describe what type of global rule this is. Is the condition of whether a dog has engaged in threatening behavior an element or a factor? How do you know this?

Second, state the rule for the condition at issue. What are its components: definitions/standards/guiding factors?

Finally, using the rule for the condition that you have discerned, make one or more rule-based reasoning arguments. For example, what rule-based reasoning argument could the plaintiff/neighbor make regarding the dog's overt actions? What rule-based reasoning argument could the defendant/owner make about the dog's overt actions? Similarly, what rule-based reasoning arguments could each party make regarding the dog's physical characteristics?

# Analogical Reasoning

Chapter 9 introduced the three types of legal reasoning. This chapter explores analogical reasoning in more detail.

## Study Guide Questions for Chapter 11

1. What does it mean to reason by analogy?
2. How is analogical reasoning different from rule-based reasoning?
3. What role do guiding factors play in analogical reasoning?
4. How does a lawyer develop analogical arguments?
5. Into what part of the legal memo will analogical arguments go?
6. What new terms were introduced in this chapter? How do these terms relate to your existing understanding of predictive memo writing? Did your understanding of any other terms change as a result of reading this chapter?

## I. Making Comparisons in Analogical Reasoning

Analogical reasoning, the primary way in which lawyers reason, involves comparing your client's situation to precedent cases. Lawyers draw parallels and distinctions to show the reader how the client's situation is like, or unlike, a precedent case and should therefore result in either the same, or a different, outcome.

These comparisons are usually focused around the guiding factors for a given issue. (For a refresher on guiding factors, see Chapter 8.) Namely, for a given guiding factor, the lawyer argues that the facts of the client's situation are either significantly similar to or different from the facts of a precedent case.

You might wonder why lawyers so frequently use analogical reasoning. Analogical reasoning is powerful because the law is grounded in the principle of stare decisis. Thus, by making an analogical argument, a lawyer is telling the court the outcome it should reach in order to be consistent with prior decisions. That is indeed compelling.

Imagine your client, herself a lawyer, missed a deadline for filing an important brief. She says this happened because her office moved to a new space on the day of the deadline. On that day, and throughout the prior week, she had been consumed first with packing her files, equipment, and furnishings and then with ensuring they were successfully moved. She wants to know whether she will be excused from missing the deadline and allowed to file her brief late.

You locate a case, *Kramer v. Kostner*, in which the court states that the relevant test is whether "good cause" exists for not filing a brief on or before the deadline. In that case the court decided "good cause" did not exist because, although the lawyer had another large brief due on the same day, the lawyer had known for several weeks that the two briefs were due on the same day. The court thus reasoned that the lawyer could have either worked on the brief well in advance in order to meet the deadline or, alternatively, could have sought an extension of the deadline before it passed. The lawyer's failure to do either reflected inattention to the case and the deadline, not good cause.

What analogical arguments do you think might arise from the client's facts and the facts from the case precedent? One likely analogical argument (unfavorable to your client) would be:

> Like the lawyer in *Kramer v. Kostner* who missed the deadline when she had another brief due on the same day, here the lawyer's failure to meet the deadline reflects a similar lack of attention to the case and respect for the deadline. Namely, the lawyer here should have been aware that the deadline for the brief coincided with the date of her office move. Thus, like the lawyer in *Kramer* who for weeks knew that the two briefs were due on the same day and should have planned ahead, here, too, the lawyer could and should have planned ahead to avoid missing the deadline.

Can you think of an analogical argument that might favor your client by distinguishing the facts from the precedent? Perhaps you could argue:

> Unlike the lawyer in *Kramer v. Kostner* who for weeks knew that both briefs were due on the same deadline, here the lawyer could not similarly have anticipated that she would not be able to complete the brief by the deadline. The lawyer had not moved offices before and, as such, she did not anticipate the amount of time and chaos that the move would entail. So, although it is conceivable that she could have worked on the brief in advance of the deadline or could have sought an extension, the need for her to do so was not clear. Specifically, unlike *Kramer* where the lawyer was experienced in writing briefs and thus, had she been paying attention, would have known that the deadline was problematic, here the lawyer

was not aware of a looming problem. Thus, she could not be expected to act to avoid a problem of which she was unaware.

Because we are engaging in predictive analysis, we generated arguments for both the client and the opposing party. The opposing party's arguments are referred to as "counter-analysis," which simply means the arguments from the opposing party's perspective. When we eventually integrate these analogical arguments into the rule application for this issue in our memo, we will include both the client's arguments and the counter-analysis.

 **GEARING UP: Counter-Analysis in Persuasive Writing**

Predictive analysis requires that you evaluate a situation from the perspective of both parties. You create arguments for both sides—analysis and counter-analysis—with the objective of assessing the relative merits of each party's position in order to predict the likely result. In contrast, persuasive writing (which you will not focus on until the latter part of this course) focuses on the arguments that advance your client's position. Does this mean that you can ignore counter-analysis in your persuasive writing? Not at all. You will still need to be aware of the arguments the other side will likely make, and you will include responses to those counter-arguments.

### The Smell Shoppe Hypothetical

For a more complex example of analogical arguments, let's return to The Smell Shoppe hypothetical and the tortious interference with business expectancy claim. Recall that one element of this claim was whether the plaintiff had "a reasonable expectancy of entering into a valid business relationship." Specifically, the rule for that element is: "In determining whether the plaintiff had a reasonable expectancy of entering into a valid business relationship, the court considers: (1) the specific contemplation of customers, and (2) the customer's belief that they were doing business with the plaintiff."

To make analogical arguments, we start with the rule for the condition, which will almost always include guiding factors, as it does here. At this point in the pre-drafting analysis, we should already know what the guiding factors are as well as the facts from the prior case (*Chicago's Pizza*) that align with each guiding factor. We can therefore put those guiding factors into the first column of the chart below, accompanied by the relevant facts from the precedent in the second column.

Thus, the information in the first two columns in the chart below would already have been identified earlier when pre-drafting the rule. Now, at the pre-drafting stage for *application* of the rule, the lawyer uses those guiding factors as the basis for making analogies and distinctions.

| GUIDING FACTOR | FACTS FROM PRECEDENT | FACTS FROM CLIENT | ANALOGICAL ARGUMENT |
|---|---|---|---|
| F1: The specific contemplation of customers | Two testifying customers called the defendant's store intending to do business with the plaintiff's store | PLAINTIFF: Mr. Arnold began receiving complaints from people in the community about his candles; specifically, that they "just weren't what they used to be" even though he had not changed his practices | PLAINTIFF: Like the plaintiff's customers in *Chicago's Pizza*, the customers in Mr. Arnold's situation contemplated specific business relationships with him |
| F2: The customers' belief that they were doing business with the plaintiff | When both customers placed their orders, they thought they were placing them with the plaintiff's store; one inquired specifically as to which of the four locations would deliver to his home | PLAINTIFF: Customers complained to plaintiff about the candles purchased from defendant  DEFENDANT: Mr. Green indicates he did not receive phone calls directly indicating that the customers believed they were doing business with the plaintiff  Mr. Green did not process an order after learning the customer believed she was doing business with the plaintiff | PLAINTIFF: Like the plaintiff's customers in *Chicago's Pizza*, the customers in Mr. Arnold's situation believed that they were in fact doing business with Mr. Arnold  DEFENDANT: Mr. Green may argue that unlike the defendant in *Chicago's Pizza*, he did not receive phone calls from customers who directly indicated that they believed they were doing business with the plaintiff  Second analogical argument by defendant for this factor: Mr. Green may distinguish his situation from that of *Chicago's Pizza* by showing that he did not proceed to process an order after he learned that the customer believed she was purchasing from the plaintiff |

Looking ahead, how does this analogical argument fit into the legal memo? The paragraph below shows an excerpt from this memo that sets forth the counter-analysis for the second guiding factor. Note that the defendant makes two analogical arguments to show why his case is different from the precedent and therefore why his client's situation should not follow the same result as the precedent.

 **CONCEPT IN ACTION: Analogical Arguments**

Alternatively, Mr. Green will argue that Mr. Arnold ——First analogical argument by did not have a reasonable expectancy of a business        defendant for this factor. relationship. He will argue that unlike the defendant in *Chicago's Pizza*, he did not receive phone calls from customers who directly indicated that they believed they were doing business with Mr. Arnold. *See id.* He may further distinguish his situation ———Second analogical argument from that of *Chicago's Pizza* by showing that he        by defendant for this factor. did not process the order from a customer who conveyed that she believed she was purchasing from Mr. Arnold. *See id.* Additionally, Mr. Green may ———This last sentence is an argue that if other customers believed they were       example of rule-based conducting business with Mr. Arnold's business, he       reasoning, which was was not made aware of this misapprehension.             discussed in Chapter 10.

## II. Characteristics of Effective Analogical Arguments

Effective analogical arguments share three key features. First, they are based upon a particular part of the test, here one of the guiding factors, rather than making a global comparison between your case and a precedent. Global comparisons tend to be too general (e.g., "The client's case is unlike *Chicago's Pizza*.") and do not provide sufficient focus for the reader. The reader needs to know in what particular way the cases are similar or different.

Second, analogical arguments are factually detailed. To be effective, an analogy needs to persuade the reader that the facts truly are similar to or different from those in the precedent. This only can be accomplished if you explicitly make the comparison. Sometimes new legal writers will tell the reader that cases are similar but fail to actually make the factual comparison.

Imagine if in The Smell Shoppe hypothetical the writer stated: "The customers' beliefs that they were doing business with Mr. Arnold are unlike those in *Chicago's Pizza*." This tells us very little and does not meaningfully analogize the similarities. While it does provide the writer's ultimate prediction—that with regard to this factor the cases are distinguishable—it lacks the *factual basis* for that prediction. Only by providing the details—that no customers expressed such confusion in phone calls and that if confusion arose the defendant corrected it—can the reader assess the validity of the prediction, appreciating that these facts really are unlike those in *Chicago's Pizza*.

Third, analogical arguments keep the focus on the client's case, even though they are comparing it to a precedent. Notice that the focal point of the above excerpt is Mr. Green. The facts of *Chicago's Pizza* are included in order to make an argument for or against Mr. Green for this factor. It is easy to keep the focus on the client's case when you remind yourself that your purpose is to make arguments for the client's case, and that the precedent case is simply a tool that helps you fulfill that purpose.

---

 **CHECK IN: Making Analogical Arguments**

Recall the check-in problem from Chapter 10 in which Sandra was being sued by a neighbor for injuries he claims to have sustained when Sandra's dog barked and lunged at the fence. Further recall that one condition of the rule is that the plaintiff must prove by clear and convincing evidence the dog has engaged in threatening behavior and that in determining whether a dog has engaged in threatening behavior, courts consider the dog's overt actions toward the plaintiff and the dog's physical characteristics.

You have now located an additional case, *Davenport v. Dearfield*, in which the court held that a Great Dane that startled a neighbor who approached the house when the dog was sleeping on a front porch did not engage in threatening behavior.

What analogical arguments can you make on behalf of the client? What analogical arguments can you make on behalf of the neighbor? Which argument do you find most compelling, and why?

---

## III. Combining Different Types of Reasoning

In this chapter and Chapter 10, the examples from memos intentionally included more than one type of reasoning for a given argument. In the example in the Concept in Action box in this chapter, two analogical arguments are followed by a rule-based reasoning argument. In the prior chapter, the rule-based reasoning argument was followed by an analogical argument. A well-developed argument for an issue usually will entail more than one type of reasoning. In Chapter 18, when we consider actually drafting arguments in your memo, we will discuss this in more detail. For now, you need only keep in mind that these types of reasoning are not mutually exclusive and, in fact, often complement each other.

Although lawyers typically employ more than one type of reasoning to develop a legal argument, the order in which they use the reasoning varies. Sometimes an argument will flow better if rule-based reasoning is communicated first. Doing so will put the critical part of the rule and the essential facts from your client's case at the forefront. You can then build on that foundation by making analogical arguments. One benefit of this approach is that your analogical argument will be simplified, as you will not have to repeat your client's facts in making the analogy because you have just stated them.

On the other hand, if the facts are relatively limited, it can make sense to immediately jump into the analogical argument. An analogical argument tends to carry more weight than a rule-based argument because it is more closely tethered to what, specifically, the court has done in prior cases. And, under our system of stare decisis, what a court has done in the past is the best predictor of what it should do in the present case.

### CHAPTER 12

# Policy-Based Reasoning

Chapter 9 introduced the three types of legal reasoning. This chapter explores policy-based reasoning in more detail.

## Study Guide Questions for Chapter 12

1. What is policy-based reasoning?
2. How is policy-based reasoning different from rule-based reasoning and analogical reasoning?
3. How does a lawyer develop policy-based arguments?
4. Is policy-based reasoning as effective as analogical reasoning? Why or why not?
5. Into what part of the legal memo will policy-based reasoning arguments go?
6. What new terms were introduced in this chapter? How do these terms relate to your existing understanding of predictive memo writing? Did your understanding of any other terms change as a result of reading this chapter?

## I. Introduction to Policy-Based Reasoning

In addition to rule-based reasoning (Chapter 10) and analogical reasoning (Chapter 11), lawyers also engage in policy-based reasoning. While this type of reasoning is typically less powerful and thus less common than analogical reasoning, it nonetheless is a useful tool. In policy-based reasoning, the lawyer applies the rule's underlying policies (such as health, safety, protection of the environment, etc.) to the client's situation in order to make an argument.

Usually underlying policies come directly from a statute or prior judicial opinion that conveys the rule's purpose (for example, the preamble to a child abuse statute that reads: "The welfare and protection of this State's children is of utmost importance and is paramount to any other interests"). Other times the underlying policies are not policies espoused by the statute or even a prior judicial opinion but are general societal values that arguably would be advanced by a certain application of the rule (for example, that an overly broad interpretation of a particular condition would result in criminalizing relatively trivial behaviors).

How does a lawyer make an argument that uses the policy behind a rule? As illustrated below, often a lawyer does so by arguing that, based upon the rule's policy, the rule should apply, or that it should apply in a particular way. Likewise, a lawyer may use policy-based reasoning to argue that the rule's application should be limited or that the rule should not apply given the policy behind the rule.

 **CONCEPT IN ACTION: Policy-Based Reasoning**

The following memo excerpt relates to the Warrantless Bomb Search hypothetical discussed in earlier chapters. The end of the paragraph includes an example of policy-based reasoning. (You may notice that this excerpt also includes rule-based and analogical reasoning.)

First, the objective information available to the agents suggested an immediate and severe risk. A bomb prepared for rigging to a motorcycle presents a serious and immediate danger to the target of the explosion, any person who might be nearby, and law enforcement agents who attempt to defuse it. *Id.* at 961. Further, unlike the situation in *Purcell*, in which the information learned by the agents on site undermined the information contained in the tip, here the information learned by the agents on site corroborated the tip information. *See id.* When they arrived at the site, the agents knew that Van Zanda was previously connected to a mob bombing, and they also had received the informant's tip that the device was prepared for rigging to another gangster's motorcycle. Agents' concerns that a bomb was hidden inside the shipping container were then bolstered by Scooter the bomb-sniffing dog, who "hit" on the container. That corroboration of the tip and prior history is unlike the situation in *Purcell* in which the tip and prior history were not confirmed but instead were contradicted by what agents observed in the hotel room—only drug paraphernalia and the notable absence of any meth lab items. *See id.* Further the bomb posed an immediate risk even if the defendant had no intention of activating it—a bomb, especially a civilian one, is inherently unstable and can detonate accidentally. Faced with the credible evidence that there may be a bomb and that such bomb may explode, the risk of danger was high. *See id.* **Indeed, this is precisely the type of risk for which the exigent circumstances exception exists: Every minute that search is delayed due to having to obtain a warrant increases the likelihood that the bomb will detonate.**

Here is the policy-based argument. It comes after the rule-based and analogical arguments that precede it, confirming them. Indeed, that is typically where lawyers include a policy-based argument—after other arguments have been made. The policy-based argument clearly identifies the rule's purpose, thus reinforcing the arguments that precede it by showing that those other arguments support the intended policy.

The example above would be an even stronger argument if it cited to an authority that substantiates that this is indeed the policy behind this rule. Thus, if the writer has a case that conveys that policy behind the rule, she would want to cite to it; e.g., "*See Wilson*, 8 F.3d at 19 (noting that exigent circumstances exception is necessary so the feared harm does not occur while waiting for a warrant).

## II. How Do Lawyers Develop Arguments That Use Policy-Based Reasoning?

The lawyer must first identify the policy that underlies the particular law. Ideally this policy will stem from the rule itself or from a case that has interpreted and applied the rule. For example, a statute's legislative history may provide useful insight into the policy behind that statute. Likewise, a case may provide useful insight into a rule's purpose, such as language from a case that states that the rule of law is "premised on holding landowners responsible for hazards on their property."

Less ideally, an underlying policy will not be espoused by the rule itself or set forth in a case but instead will either be something the lawyer reasons must underlie the rule or a general societal value that the lawyer asserts would be furthered by a particular interpretation. For example, a lawyer might reason that fairness is a fundamental value and that a particular application of the rule is one that promotes fairness.

Regardless of the source of the policy, after the policy is identified, it is applied to the client's situation. The argument advocates for a certain result based upon that application. It may be that the rule application asserted by your adversary would not fulfill the rule's underlying policy. That therefore becomes a policy-based argument that supports your application of the rule. On the other hand, it may be that your application of the rule supports the underlying policy, thus bolstering your other arguments and confirming the wisdom of your rule application.

 **CHECK IN: Making Policy-Based Arguments**

Recall the check-in problem from Chapters 10 and 11 in which a neighbor sued a dog's owner for injuries he sustained when the dog barked and lunged at him. Further recall that one condition of the rule is that the plaintiff must prove the dog has engaged in threatening behavior and that in determining whether a dog has engaged in threatening behavior courts consider the dog's overt actions toward the plaintiff and the dog's physical characteristics.

> Now assume you have found a case that discusses the policy behind this rule of owner's liability. In that case, the court explains, "Dog owners must be held responsible for the aggressive acts of their dogs in order to provide an incentive for owners to control their dogs. At the same time, a dog's owner cannot control the reactions of other people to their dog, and as such should not be held responsible for a person's overreaction to natural dog behavior."
>
> Using the policies set forth above: (1) What policy-based arguments might the owner make? (2) What policy-based arguments might the neighbor-plaintiff make?

## III.  Why Is Policy-Based Reasoning Less Powerful Than Rule-Based Reasoning and Analogical Reasoning?

Both rule-based reasoning and analogical reasoning rely upon the rule itself, including its language and its components. These forms of reasoning are thus inescapable; the rule is what it is, even if that may be undesirable from a policy angle. Because policy-based reasoning often is more tangential to the rule itself, its use is typically limited to supporting these other forms of reasoning. In other words, a lawyer may urge a certain application of the rule to her client's situation based upon analogical reasoning, followed by a policy-based argument that shows the wisdom of that application. Or a lawyer's rule-based argument may be based upon a narrow interpretation of the rule that stems from the rule's policy.

# Foundations of Legal Communication: Drafting a Legal Discussion with a Single Authority

In this module we turn our attention to drafting a single authority predictive memorandum. In Part I (Chapters 13 and 14) we will engage in the pre-drafting analytical process lawyers typically employ to gather the information that will be included in the Discussion section of the predictive memorandum. Then, in Part II (Chapters 15 through 18), we focus on drafting the memo.

# Pre-Drafting Analysis Using a Single Authority

**B**efore you engage in drafting a legal memo, you need to marshal and begin to organize certain material. As noted in Chapter 5, you will draft the Discussion section of the memo before you draft other sections. For the Discussion, you will need to: (1) determine the global rule—its result, conditions, and how each condition relates to the others; (2) examine how each condition had been applied in a similar prior opinion—identifying the court's fact-based holding for that condition; and (3) determine the rule for each condition—its definitions, standards, and the guiding factors you discerned from the fact-based holding. In Part I of Module III, we will go through that pre-drafting process.

### CHAPTER 13

# The Process of Pre-Drafting Analysis

This chapter focuses on the steps lawyers routinely take to marshal information before they begin writing the legal analysis. It will identify the type of material you want to gather and organize before you begin drafting the Discussion section of your predictive memorandum. You will see that much of this material comes from the legal analysis you already undertook throughout Module II. In this chapter, we take the material we learned how to gather in Module II and consider the process of pre-drafting analysis in the context of the legal memorandum.

---

### Study Guide Questions for Chapter 13

1. What, generally, is the process of pre-drafting analysis?
2. What steps are involved in pre-drafting analysis?
3. What are the benefits of pre-drafting analysis?
4. What type of pre-drafting material might you cull directly from the legal authority? In contrast, what type of pre-drafting material might you have to process from the legal authority?
5. What new terms were introduced in this chapter? How do these terms relate to your existing understanding of predictive memo writing? Did your understanding of any other terms change as a result of reading this chapter?

---

## I. Gathering Content Before Drafting

Legal analysis can be complex, and the process of communicating that analysis in a straightforward and effective manner can therefore be quite demanding. It would be daunting to try to write legal analysis before you had a firm grasp of the law that governs your client's claim or charge, the conditions that have to be satisfied or assessed in order for the result to occur, how the courts generally evaluate each of the conditions, and how that evaluation can be compared to your client's situation. Therefore, lawyers typically collect and process this information before they begin to draft.

We can liken this process to baking—we gather all of our ingredients before we begin to combine them in the recipe. We need to know what those ingredients are and whether we have to do something with them before they are ready to go into the recipe. For example, if the recipe calls for softened butter, we would want to remove the butter from the refrigerator and let it come to room temperature before we use it in our recipe. We would also want to have all of the ingredients set out so that we can follow a thorough, precise process to ensure the recipe comes out properly.

So, too, with legal analysis. Continuing the baking analogy, there are essential "ingredients," or content, for each section of the Discussion. We'll look at these ingredients in two different ways. First, we will consider how the content will appear in the final product, which employs a deductive approach. Then, we will consider the general order in which you will gather the ingredients in your inductive, pre-drafting work.

## A. Memo Content as It Appears in the Drafted Discussion

Recall from Chapter 4 the components of the Discussion section of the predictive memorandum:

- Global Roadmap—A paragraph that announces the rule with its conditions;
- Issue Segment—A separate analytical segment for each issue, containing:
  - Issue Roadmap that introduces the reader to the analysis of a condition (element or factor);
  - Rule Explanation section for that issue that explains how the condition has been analyzed in prior cases;
  - Rule Application section for that issue that includes both arguments and counter-arguments in order to predict how a court might decide our client's claim or charge; and
- Global Conclusion

Each of these paragraphs has essential content. Below you will see the ingredients, or content, that belong in each section of the Discussion.

### Global Roadmap

1. A topic sentence that includes a global prediction as to the client's claim or charge.
2. The global rule of law, with its conditions and the relationship between the conditions clearly set forth, and with proper attribution.

3. An announcement of any non-issues, which are conditions that will not be addressed in the memo, ideally with a brief explanation as to why the conditions will not be addressed.
4. An announcement of the issues that will be addressed in the memo.
5. A global prediction, which is the prediction as to the resolution of the client's claim or charge, supported by key client facts related to that global prediction. A sentence or two should suffice, as this is simply the overall prediction and does not contain the separate issue predictions that will appear at the end of each issue roadmap.

### Issue Roadmaps

1. A topic sentence that announces the issue/condition that will be addressed in the issue roadmap.
2. The rule of law for the issue/condition: any definitions, standards, or guiding factors that are related to the court's analysis of the issue/condition.
3. The *rule proof*: the fact-based holding from the precedent, which provides "proof" of the rule.
4. A prediction of the resolution of that issue/condition, supported by key client facts related to that prediction.

### Rule Explanation Paragraphs

1. A framing sentence that illustrates how the guiding factors inform the court's analysis of the issue/condition.
2. Facts from the precedent case that are related to those guiding factors.
3. The court's holding on the issue/condition in light of those facts.
4. The court's reasoning; i.e., why it resolved the issue the way it did.

### Rule Application Paragraphs

1. Broken down by the components of the rule of law for the condition, most typically by guiding factors.
2. For each component:
   a. A topic or thesis sentence: An announcement of the aspect of the rule of law for the condition that will be addressed.
   b. One or more forms of legal reasoning to support arguments:
      i. Analogical arguments and counter-arguments, comparing and contrasting facts from the precedent case to the client's case;
      ii. Rule-based arguments and counter-arguments;
      iii. Policy-based arguments and counter-arguments.

    c. Ideally, each component of the issue rule of law should be addressed from each party's perspective.

3. At the end of rule application, an issue prediction: a prediction as to the court's resolution of that issue/condition.

### Global Conclusion

1. A global prediction as to the resolution of the client's claim or charge.
2. A reiteration of the issue prediction for each issue/condition.

## B. Obtaining the Discussion Section Ingredients

The order in which you ultimately present your content differs from the order in which you gather those ingredients. This is because your pre-drafting work requires an inductive approach to discern the law versus the deductive approach used to present it to your reader.

The following checklist provides the general order in which you gather your ingredients.

1. Identify the global rule of law that guides your client's claim or charge.
2. Break the global rule of law down into its result, conditions, and a structure for how the conditions relate to one another.
3. From those conditions, identify the issues and non-issues. Recall that non-issues are simply conditions that will not be addressed in the predictive memorandum because they have been satisfied on the basis of the facts, the parties have stipulated they have been satisfied, or you have been instructed to ignore them.
4. For each issue:
    a. Identify judicial decisions that apply the pertinent rule of law in an analogous factual situation.
    b. Identify the key facts from the judicial decision that guided the court's analysis of that issue.
    c. Discern the rule of law. (This will be the rule of law for the particular condition at issue.)
        i. Identify any standards or definitions for that condition.
        ii. Generalize the key facts from the judicial decision into guiding factors; these guiding factors will form the basis of analogical comparisons to your client's facts.
    d. On the basis of the guiding factors for that condition, compare the key facts of the judicial decision with the facts of your client's situation, making analogies and distinctions from both parties' perspectives.

e. Consider any additional rule-based and policy arguments and counter-arguments for that issue based on the rule of law and your client's situation.

Note that some of the material identified above comes from the legal authority, some of it comes from your client's factual situation, and some of it comes from your analysis. Further note that some of the material comes from the legal authority explicitly, while some may require you to process the court's analysis to identify implicit aspects of the rule of law. You might, for example, be able to pull the global rule of law directly from a judicial decision. You might also be able to quote a definition, standard, or guiding factor that the court provides in connection with its analysis of a particular issue.

In contrast, many times you must identify and label implicit guiding factors that direct the court's analysis of an issue/condition. As explained in Chapter 8, you do this by analyzing key facts that drove the court's prior decision on the resolution of an issue and then generalizing those facts into a guiding factor that provides the basis for comparing your client's facts to the facts of a legal decision. Clearly, gathering the material for your predictive memo is not as simple as reaching for the baking soda. This underscores why the process of pre-drafting analysis is critical to your ability to write a thorough and well-organized Discussion. In the next section, we will look at how you might use a worksheet to analyze and record this information when you are processing a single legal authority.

## II. Worksheet Approach to Gathering Content

In Module II, you learned many of the processes that are integral to pre-drafting your legal memorandum. For example, in Chapter 8 you learned how to discern the rule of law using the existing law and an additional authority, and in Chapters 9 through 12 you learned about the three types of arguments lawyers can make. The worksheet below gathers that information, and more, in the context of your client's particular claim or charge.

### The Smell Shoppe Hypothetical

Specifically, recall the facts from The Smell Shoppe hypothetical set out in Chapter 4. There, your client Mr. Arnold has come to you questioning whether he will be successful in a claim for tortious interference with business expectancy. The completed worksheet below demonstrates the way a lawyer might approach the pre-drafting process for that client's case. As you will learn in the next part of this module, this pre-drafting analysis greatly assists the lawyer in outlining the legal memorandum.

Note that before completing this worksheet, you had already located an applicable authority, *Chicago's Pizza*. You might even have already briefed the case. The worksheet will help you focus your analysis of the case on the client's factual situation and the arguable issues. As illustrated in Chapter 2, you will focus your case reading through the lens of Mr. Arnold's situation. Rather than wasting time culling case information related to claims or charges not at issue, you will concentrate on the conditions of the global rule of law that are at issue in your client's case. You will still need to identify the global rule of law for the claim or charge, but you would not spend a great deal of time evaluating issues/conditions that you will not be discussing in your memo.

## WORKSHEET: Pre-Drafting Using a Single Authority

### THE GLOBAL RULE, INCLUDING CONDITIONS/ISSUES

1. Based upon a single authority, what is the existing global rule of law? Outline it here. With only a single authority, the existing global rule of law will be the rule of law the court identifies as the starting point in its analysis. You will then arrive at the emergent global rule of law based on the court's processing of the rule within that case. Recall that the court's processing of the existing rule may change the rule itself (e.g., add or delete conditions). In most instances, though, the court's processing will simply confirm the conditions of the global rule.

   Authority: *Chicago's Pizza, Inc. v. Chicago's Pizza Franchise Ltd., USA*, 893 N.E.2d 981, 993 (Ill. App. Ct. 2008)

   EXISTING: *"The elements of the tort of intentional interference with a business expectancy include (1) a reasonable expectancy of entering into a valid business relationship; (2) the defendant's knowledge of the expectancy; (3) the defendant's intentional and unjustified interference that prevents the realization of the business expectancy; and (4) damages resulting from the interference."*

   a. Did your selected case provide any definitions or standards relevant to the global rule of law? List that information here.

   *The case does not provide any definitions or standards relevant to the global rule of law.*

   b. Did your selected case add or modify any conditions? List that information here.

   *The case did not add or modify any conditions relevant to the global rule of law.*

   c. Outline the emergent global rule of law.

   *The elements of the tort of intentional interference with a business expectancy include:*

   1. *[the plaintiff's] reasonable expectancy of entering into a valid business relationship;*

   2. *the defendant's knowledge of the expectancy;*

   3. *the defendant's intentional and unjustified interference that prevents the realization of the business expectancy; and*

   4. *damages resulting from the interference.*

   *Note: Chicago's Pizza* did not change the structure of the rule—it did not add or modify conditions, standards, or definitions. Therefore, the existing rule of law and the emergent rule of law are the same.

2. Determine which of these conditions are at issue.

   For each condition listed in the emergent global rule of law, determine if it is an issue or non-issue and why. Include that information in the table below. Depending on how many conditions you have, you may not need all of the rows below.

| CONDITION | ISSUE OR NON-ISSUE | WHY? |
|---|---|---|
| 1. Reasonable expectancy | Issue | Facts are contested |
| 2. Defendant's knowledge | Non-issue | Asked to ignore |
| 3. Intentional and unjustified interference | Issue | Facts are contested |
| 4. Damages | Non-Issue | Asked to ignore |

*Note:* As you consider *Chicago's Pizza*, note that you are reading it with Arnold's facts and the contested issues in mind. This client-focused reading helps you analyze the client's claim or charge.

**ANALYSIS OF ISSUE SEGMENT FOR ISSUE ONE**

1. List the first issue/condition here.

   Issue One: Whether the plaintiff had a reasonable expectancy of entering into a valid business relationship

2. Discern the rule of law for this issue/condition, using the following steps.

   a. For the first issue/condition, what is the court's fact-based holding in your selected authority? In answering this question, think about how the court applied the law regarding the issue to the facts.

      A plaintiff will be found to have possessed a reasonable expectancy of entering into a valid business relationship when specific customers called the defendant's store, and the customers expressed belief that they were doing business with the plaintiff.

   b. Identify any law-centered interpretations (definitions, standards, and/or explicit guiding factors) from your selected case.

      There are no explicit standards, definitions, or guiding factors related to this issue in the selected authority.

   c. What are the key case facts and related guiding factors from your selected authority? Specifically, complete the chart below:

| FACT | GUIDING FACTOR |
|---|---|
| Customers calling/ordering from the defendant's store, intending to do business with the plaintiff's store | The specific contemplation of customers |
| When customers placed their orders, they thought they were placing them with the plaintiff's store | The customers' expressed belief that they were doing business with the plaintiff |

   d. Using the information gathered from your selected case, provide the emergent rule of law for this condition, including standards, definitions, and/or guiding factors.

      A plaintiff will be successful in showing the first element exists if they can demonstrate that

      1. customers demonstrate specific contemplation of doing business with the plaintiff and

      2. the customers expressed belief that they were doing business with the plaintiff.

3. Determine what potential arguments are available for this condition.

   For each guiding factor for this condition, compare the facts of your client's case to the facts of your authority. Based on that comparison, you will make analogies and distinctions from the perspective of each party/position. Complete the table below. Note: The guiding factors and facts listed in the first two columns here are simply repeats of the two columns you've already completed above, with the first two columns flipped around.

| GUIDING FACTOR (INCLUDE WHY THIS GUIDING FACTOR IS IMPORTANT) | *CHICAGO'S PIZZA* FACTS | THE SMELL SHOPPE FACTS | COMPARISON |
|---|---|---|---|
| The specific contemplation of customers | Customers calling/ordering from the defendant's store, intending to do business with the plaintiff's store | Customers brought their concerns to Arnold's attention; candles "just weren't what they used to be" despite the fact that he had not changed the candle-making process | Both sets of customers demonstrated their intent/specific contemplation to purchase from the plaintiffs |
| The customers' belief that they were doing business with the plaintiff | When customers placed their orders, they thought they were placing them with the plaintiff's store; one inquired specifically as to which of the four locations would deliver to his home | Customers complained to plaintiff about the candles purchased from defendant<br><br>Mr. Green indicates he did not receive phone calls directly indicating that the customers believed they were doing business with the plaintiff<br><br>Mr. Green did not process an order after learning the customer believed she was doing business with the plaintiff | Both sets of customers appeared to believe they were purchasing from the plaintiff, while in fact purchasing from the defendant<br><br>Mr. Green will distinguish the situation with the one customer he turned away and suggest if others were under a false impression they were doing business with plaintiff, he did not know |

**ANALYSIS OF ISSUE SEGMENT FOR ISSUE TWO**

1. List the second issue/condition here.

    Issue Two: Whether the defendant's intentional and unjustified interference prevented the realization of business expectancy

2. Discern the rule of law for this issue/condition, using the following steps.

    a. For the second issue/condition, what is the court's fact-based holding in your selected authority? In answering this question, think about how the court applied the law regarding the issue to the facts.

    A plaintiff will be successful in demonstrating that it was the defendant's intentional and unjustified interference that prevented the realization of business expectancy when the defendant allows customers to place orders with its business while being dishonest with the customers when they inquire about an affiliation with the plaintiff's store. Further, a plaintiff can demonstrate interference with an expectation of a business relationship when the defendant represents an affiliation with the plaintiff through advertising materials.

b. Identify any law-centered interpretations (definitions, standards, and/or explicit guiding factors) from your selected case.

*There are no explicit standards, definitions, or guiding factors related to this issue in the selected authority.*

c. What are the key case facts and related guiding factors from your selected authority? Specifically, complete the chart below:

| FACT | GUIDING FACTOR |
|---|---|
| *Customers calling/ordering from the defendant's store, intending to do business with the plaintiff's store* | *The defendant's conduct in allowing customers to place orders under a mistaken belief* |
| *Defendant lied to customers regarding its affiliation with the plaintiff's stores* | *The defendant's truthfulness to the customers regarding an affiliation with the plaintiff's business* |
| *Defendant's advertisements represented that it had several locations, when in fact it just had the one* | *The content of the defendant's advertisements* |

d. Using the information gathered from your selected case, provide the emergent rule of law for this condition, including standards, definitions, and/or guiding factors.

*A plaintiff will be successful in showing the second element exists if*

1. *defendant allows customers to place orders at its business under a mistaken belief,*

2. *defendant is dishonest with customers when they inquire about an affiliation to the plaintiff's store, and*

3. *defendant is untruthful in advertisements.*

3. Determine what potential arguments are available for this condition.

For each guiding factor for this condition, compare the facts of your client's case to the facts of your authority. Based on that comparison, you will make analogies and distinctions from the perspective of each party/position. Complete the table below. Note: The guiding factors and facts listed in the first two columns here are simply repeats of the two columns you've already completed above, with the first two columns flipped around.

| GUIDING FACTOR (INCLUDE WHY THIS GUIDING FACTOR IS IMPORTANT) | *CHICAGO'S PIZZA* FACTS | THE SMELL SHOPPE FACTS | COMPARISON |
|---|---|---|---|
| The defendant's conduct in allowing customers to place orders under a mistaken belief | Customers calling/ ordering from the defendant's store, intending to do business with the plaintiff's store | Customers came to shop at Green's store possibly believing it was the "newest location"; Green allowed them to place orders | The plaintiff in *Chicago's Pizza* has a clearer argument for this factor. It might be a stretch to infer that Green allowed the customers to place orders after knowing for certain that the customers believed they were doing business with Arnold |
| The defendant's truthfulness to the customers regarding an affiliation with the plaintiff's business | Defendant lied to customers regarding its affiliation with the plaintiff's stores | Green was honest about his affiliation when he received the phone call inquiring | The defendant in *Chicago's Pizza* was explicitly untruthful, whereas Green was honest |
| The content of the defendant's advertisements | Defendant's advertisements represented that it had several locations, when in fact it just had the one | Green's ads had similar branding and coupons with the phrase "our newest location" | The defendant's ads in *Chicago's Pizza* listed multiple locations whereas Green listed just the one true location |

This worksheet should reinforce that, although time-consuming, the pre-drafting analysis process is helpful, if not essential, for writing a thorough and well-organized memorandum. Once you have taken the time to carefully analyze the precedent and have memorialized the information you will need to incorporate into the predictive memorandum, you will be well positioned to draft the memorandum clearly and efficiently.

### CHAPTER 14

# Large-Scale Organization of the Discussion

This chapter examines the large-scale framework of the Discussion section.

## Study Guide Questions for Chapter 14

1. What provides the framework, or organization, of the predictive memo?
2. What is CREAC? What is IRAC? How do these relate to the organization of a predictive memorandum?
3. In what ways does the predictive memo follow a deductive pattern?
4. How are the sections of the Discussion organized?
5. What new terms were introduced in this chapter? How do these terms relate to your existing understanding of predictive memo writing? Did your understanding of any other terms change as a result of reading this chapter?

## I. Discussion Organization

You will be preparing predictive memoranda to memorialize your evaluation of the client's legal question, including your analysis and prediction. Your reader for those documents will be law-trained—likely other lawyers with whom you work.

With regard to organizing the Discussion, you should be aware that law-trained readers have specific expectations about content and organization. In Chapter 13, you learned about the ingredients, or content, law-trained readers expect in each section of the Discussion, but you must also adhere to expectations about organization. In keeping with our cooking analogy, let's consider lasagna.

If you ordered lasagna at a restaurant and you received the following, you would be bewildered:

You can see all the ingredients, but they have not been baked into the presentation of lasagna you were expecting. You would also be confused if this was delivered:

Although the ingredients have now been combined into something reminiscent of lasagna, it appears to be a jumbled mess. On the other hand, there would be nothing jarring about receiving something like this:

Now that you have the ingredients you wanted in the order you expected, you can simply enjoy the lasagna.

So too with legal analysis. It is not sufficient to have the appropriate ingredients, or content; you must also put that content in the order that meets the expectations of the reader. Law-trained readers expect you to present the analysis deductively, from general to specific. You can imagine how confusing it would be to begin your analysis by discussing a case without first providing a roadmap. To help the reader understand their arguments, lawyers communicate their analysis by providing a global roadmap and by then following the large-scale organization that flows from that global roadmap. The global roadmap itself also follows a deductive approach. The framework comes first, then the detail. This approach is the opposite of what lawyers do in their pre-drafting analysis. At the pre-drafting stage, recall that lawyers use an inductive approach, going from specific to general.

Lawyers often use a mnemonic device to guide the organization of legal analysis, such as *CREAC, IRAC*, or a similar variation:

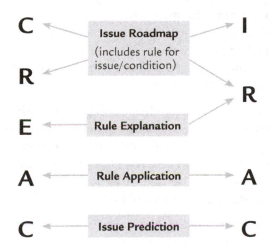

You can likely see how these mnemonic devices illustrate a deductive framework. Both begin broadly by identifying the issue or prediction of the likely outcome. The rule comes next, outlining for the reader the conditions that will follow. We then explain the law, giving the reader context for the application that follows. Finally, we complete our analysis with a conclusion that reiterates the global prediction—the court's likely resolution of the client's claim or charge.

Not surprisingly, legal writing employs this deductive framework. Specifically, as you will see below, each issue segment of your memo roughly comports with a CREAC/IRAC framework.

## II. The Global Roadmap Framework

The Discussion section of the memo begins with a global road-map paragraph. We will thoroughly address how to write those in Chapter 16, but you are already aware that one primary component of the global roadmap paragraph is the global rule of law. Why is that so important? Because the global rule of law pertinent to the client's claim or charge forms the large-scale organization of the Discussion that follows—the rule itself provides the outline for the Discussion. You will organize the Discussion around the issues implicated by the rule. Therefore, understanding the structure of the rule, including the conditions prompted by the rule and their relationship to one another, is an essential component of legal analysis.

### Burglary Statute Hypothetical

Take, for example, the statutory burglary rule we have discussed in earlier chapters:

> "A person commits burglary if he:
>      a. Unlawfully enters;
>      b. A building or structure;
>      c. With the intent to commit a crime while inside the building or structure."

In a predictive memo that addresses burglary, if all three conditions are at issue, we will have three issue segments, each consisting of an issue roadmap, rule explanation, and rule application. On the other hand, if there is no question that the place entered was a "building or structure," then we would have only two issue segments.

**Our large-scale organization will look like this:**

**Global roadmap**: Predicts the likely resolution of the client's claim or charge and sets forth the global rule of law, noting any non-issues. The reader will understand that burglary requires the satisfaction of three elements, all of which are at issue.

**Issue Segment 1 (unlawfully enters):**

**Issue Roadmap: Unlawful entry**. This paragraph will announce the issue; identify definitions, standards, and guiding factors related to the issue; provide rule proof for the guiding factors; and make a prediction as to the court's likely resolution of the issue of unlawful entry.

**Rule Explanation: Unlawful entry**. The rule explanation will illustrate how courts have analyzed unlawful entry in analogous cases, thereby helping us understand the meaning of the rule in practice.

**Rule Application: Unlawful entry.** The rule application will include arguments and counter-arguments, using all applicable forms of legal reasoning, including (1) analogical reasoning (arguments that compare and contrast the client's facts with facts from the precedent cases from both parties' perspectives), (2) rule-based reasoning, and (3) policy-based arguments. It will conclude with a prediction of the court's likely resolution of the issue of unlawful entry.

## Issue Segment 2 (a building or structure):

**Issue Roadmap: A building or structure.** This paragraph will transition to the second issue, reinforcing the relationship between the issues; e.g., "Next, the court will consider whether the defendant entered a building or structure." It will then identify definitions, standards, and guiding factors related to the issue; provide rule proof for the guiding factors; and make a prediction as to the court's likely resolution of the issue of "a building or structure."

**Rule Explanation: A building or structure.** The rule explanation will illustrate how courts have analyzed "a building or structure" in analogous cases, thereby helping us understand the meaning of the rule in practice.

**Rule Application: A building or structure.** The rule application will include arguments and counter-arguments, using all applicable forms of legal reasoning, including (1) analogical reasoning, (2) rule-based reasoning, and (3) policy-based arguments. It will conclude with a prediction of the court's likely resolution of the issue of "a building or structure."

## Issue Segment 3 (with the intent to commit a crime while inside the building or structure):

**Issue Roadmap: With the intent to commit a crime while inside the building or structure.** This paragraph will transition to the third issue, reinforcing the relationship between the issues; e.g., "Finally, the court will consider whether the defendant entered the area with the intent to commit a crime while inside." It will then identify definitions, standards, and guiding factors related to the issue; provide rule proof for the guiding factors; and make a prediction as to the court's likely resolution of the issue of "with the intent to commit a crime while inside the building or structure."

**Rule Explanation: With the intent to commit a crime while inside the building or structure**. The rule explanation will illustrate how courts have analyzed "with the intent to commit a crime while inside the building or structure" in analogous cases, thereby helping us understand the meaning of the rule in practice.

**Rule Application: With the intent to commit a crime while inside the building or structure.** The rule application will include arguments and counter-arguments, using all applicable forms of legal reasoning, including (1) analogical reasoning, (2) rule-based reasoning, and (3) policy-based arguments. It will conclude with a prediction of the court's likely resolution of the issue of "with the intent to commit a crime while inside the building or structure."

**Global Conclusion**: A prediction as to the court's likely resolution of the client's burglary charge and a reiteration of the court's likely resolution of each condition.

So, again, an important step in legal analysis is understanding the structure of the global rule, as the global rule forms the framework for the large-scale organization of the Discussion section of the memo.

The rigid structure of a legal memorandum may at times feel constraining. Yet we encourage you to consider the value that this rigid structure provides—namely, it ensures that you, as a novice legal writer, conform to the profession's time-tested expectations about how to analyze a legal question. Professional norms, such as IRAC for lawyers, benefit those who are new to the profession by setting explicit expectations. Indeed, one professor has described IRAC as a sort of "standard operating procedure" for the legal profession—it encompasses best practices, assures a minimum level of competency, and allows even those new to the law to structure complex analysis.[1] Thus, while the highly structured IRAC approach undoubtedly has some drawbacks, such as feeling overly mechanical and formal, its benefits greatly outweigh any weaknesses, especially for those new to the legal profession.

---

1. We credit Professor Andrew J. Turner with this helpful conceptualization of IRAC as a standard operating procedure.

### CONCEPT IN ACTION: How Does a Memo's Organization Mesh with IRAC/CREAC?

You may be wondering how, specifically, the IRAC/CREAC framework fits with the memo framework described above. The diagram below, which shows an issue segment, demonstrates how these frameworks roughly fit together.

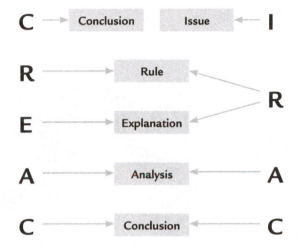

### CHECK IN: Large-Scale Organization

Map out the large-scale organization for the Discussion of a memo that involves the following global rule of law for the crime of grand larceny. Assume all conditions are issues.

To prove a defendant committed grand larceny, the State must prove: (1) The wrongful taking, obtaining, or withholding; (2) Of someone else's property; (3) With the intent to either deprive the owner of the property or enrich someone else.

### PART II

# Drafting the Discussion Using a Single Authority

In Part I, we completed our pre-drafting analysis to gather content for the Discussion section of the predictive memorandum. In Part II we will use that material to draft the Discussion for a single authority memo.

# From Pre-Drafting to Drafting: Outlining the Components of a Single Authority Legal Discussion

This chapter provides the bridge between the pre-drafting analysis process, where we culled the ingredients for the memo, and the drafting process, which starts by incorporating those ingredients into an outline. This chapter shows how, and where, the content from the pre-drafting process is incorporated into the Discussion section of the memo.

---

### Study Guide Questions for Chapter 15

1. What is the content for the global road-map paragraph?
2. What is the content for the issue road-map paragraph?
3. What is the content for rule explanation?
4. What is the content for rule application?
5. What new terms were introduced in this chapter? How do these terms relate to your existing understanding of predictive memo writing? Did your understanding of any other terms change as a result of reading this chapter?

---

## I. Discussion Paragraph Templates

Recall your reading in Chapter 4 where we addressed the components of the predictive memorandum. Here, we offer a *template* that illustrates how and where you incorporate pre-drafting material into some parts of the Discussion section of the memo.

A few words of caution before jumping into these templates: First, note that each of the bracketed prompts may require more than one sentence. For instance, you often may need to include several sentences for the template prompt for "[INSERT APPLICABLE GLOBAL RULE OF LAW, INCLUDING CONDITIONS.]."

Second, as will be discussed in the remainder of this chapter, the rule explanation section for an issue may be composed of more than one paragraph. In addition, the rule application section will almost always be composed of multiple paragraphs. With that said, each rule explanation paragraph will roughly follow the template set forth below, as will each rule application paragraph.

Finally, note that, notwithstanding the templates, writing a memo is rarely as straightforward as simply filling in the blanks. Much work goes into the development of the ingredients that you ultimately will insert into the template. And, because the content of the material to be included in the memo will become increasingly complex as additional authorities are added, these templates will not be strictly applicable to memos that incorporate multiple authorities, which are addressed in Module IV.

Despite their drawbacks, these templates serve a useful learning function. As you practice writing a memo in the simplified context of working with a single authority, the templates help you understand and ensure you include all required content. Consulting the templates helps you master the necessary components for each part of your arguments, as well as the expected order of those components.

### Global Roadmap

The client's claim will likely [INSERT GLOBAL PREDICTION]. In order to demonstrate the claim, the client must show [INSERT APPLICABLE GLOBAL RULE OF LAW, INCLUDING CONDITIONS]. [INSERT CITATION.] [INSERT ANY NON-ISSUES.] [INSERT ISSUES ADDRESSED IN THE MEMO.] Because [INSERT RESOLUTION OF ISSUE SUPPORTED BY RELEVANT CLIENT FACTS] and because [INSERT RESOLUTION OF ISSUE SUPPORTED BY RELEVANT CLIENT FACTS], [INSERT GLOBAL PREDICTION].

### For Issue One

Issue roadmap:

The first issue for the court to consider [INSERT FIRST ISSUE/ CONDITION]. To analyze this issue the court will consider [INSERT ISSUE/CONDITION RULE, INCLUDING DEFINITIONS, STANDARDS, AND GUIDING FACTORS]. [INSERT CITATION.] [INSERT RULE PROOF.] [INSERT CITATION.] The court will likely [INSERT PREDICTION AS TO THE RESOLUTION OF FIRST ISSUE SUPPORTED BY RELEVANT CLIENT FACTS].

## Rule explanation paragraph:

When [INSERT GUIDING FACTORS BEING ILLUSTRATED], [INSERT RESOLUTION OF ISSUE]. [INSERT CITATION.] [INSERT FACTS FROM PRECEDENT AUTHORITY RELEVANT TO ISSUE.] [INSERT CITATION.] [INSERT COURT'S RESOLUTION OF ISSUE] [INSERT COURT'S REASONING]. [INSERT CITATION.]

## Rule application paragraph:

[INSERT TOPIC SENTENCE INDICATING PARAGRAPH'S SCOPE.] [INSERT ARGUMENTS THAT SUPPORT THE TOPIC SENTENCE, INCLUDING RULE-BASED ARGUMENTS, ANALOGICAL ARGUMENTS, AND (WHERE APPLICABLE) POLICY ARGUMENTS.]

### *For Issue Two*

## Issue roadmap:

The second issue for the court to consider [INSERT SECOND ISSUE/ CONDITION]. To analyze this issue the court will consider [INSERT ISSUE/ CONDITION RULE, INCLUDING DEFINITIONS, STANDARDS, AND GUIDING FACTORS]. [INSERT CITATION.] [INSERT RULE PROOF.] [INSERT CITATION.] The court will likely [INSERT PREDICTION AS TO THE RESOLUTION OF SECOND ISSUE SUPPORTED BY RELEVANT CLIENT FACTS].

## Rule explanation paragraph:

When [INSERT GUIDING FACTORS BEING ILLUSTRATED], [INSERT RESOLUTION OF ISSUE]. [INSERT CITATION.] [INSERT FACTS FROM PRECEDENT AUTHORITY RELEVANT TO ISSUE.] [INSERT CITATION.] [INSERT COURT'S RESOLUTION OF ISSUE] [INSERT COURT'S REASONING]. [INSERT CITATION.]

## Rule application paragraph:

[INSERT TOPIC SENTENCE INDICATING PARAGRAPH'S SCOPE.] [INSERT ARGUMENTS THAT SUPPORT THE TOPIC SENTENCE, INCLUDING RULE-BASED ARGUMENTS, ANALOGICAL ARGUMENTS, AND (WHERE APPLICABLE) POLICY ARGUMENTS.]

**EQUIPPING YOURSELF: Legal Forms**

The templates provided here help the writer both structure the paragraphs in the memo's Discussion section and also ensure each paragraph includes all necessary ingredients in the order in which the reader expects them. For some different types of legal writing—litigation or transactional documents—you might be able to find another kind of template: legal forms. You can save time by using a legal form as a *starting* point when drafting court pleadings or a document like a contract. Forms can highlight the important facts and points of law that you need to provide and can help you determine the best format for presenting that information. Whenever using a form, or other kind of template, it is up to the lawyer to ensure she understands the client facts and the relevant law. Even with the benefit of a detailed legal form, you will still need to undertake the type of thoughtful pre-drafting analysis we have described in the earlier chapters of this book.

### *Global Conclusion*

[INSERT GLOBAL PREDICTION AS TO THE RESOLUTION OF THE CLIENT'S CLAIM OR CHARGE.] [INSERT A REITERATION OF THE ISSUE PREDICTION FOR EACH ISSUE/CONDITION.]

## II. Moving from Templates to Annotated Outline of the Memo

In Chapter 13 you used a worksheet approach to cull information from both the case and your client's factual situation. You also have a template for beginning to think about where the content from the worksheet will appear in the memo. You are now in a position to create the first draft of your Discussion section: an annotated outline.

### The Smell Shoppe Hypothetical

Taking The Smell Shoppe hypothetical, consider the following outline of the Discussion of the first issue. You may see that there is not a one-to-one correlation between the templates and the outline. (Remember the templates are just a tool to draw your attention to needed content and the expected order of material in a given paragraph.) The outline then shows you where source material will appear within the Discussion. Thus, as emphasized earlier in this chapter, even though we have provided templates that work in conjunction with an annotated outline, writing a memo is never as easy as filling in a blank.

---

## WORKSHEET: Discussion

### GLOBAL ROADMAP

Global Prediction: Arnold will not prevail

Global Rule of Law: The elements of the tort of intentional interference with a business expectancy include:

1. a reasonable expectancy of entering into a valid business relationship;

2. the defendant's knowledge of the expectancy;

3. the defendant's intentional and unjustified interference that prevents the realization of the business expectancy; and

4. damages resulting from the interference. Cite *Chicago's Pizza*

Non-Issues: Defendant's knowledge; Damages

Issues: Reasonable expectancy; Intentional and unjustified interference

Global Prediction: Because Green was not dishonest, Arnold will be unable to establish intentional and unjustified interference, and therefore the claim will fail.

### ISSUE 1

ISSUE ROADMAP

Issue/Condition to Note in Topic Sentence: Arnold's reasonable expectancy

Issue/Condition Rule of Law: In assessing whether Mr. Arnold possessed this expectancy, the court will consider the specific contemplation of customers and the customers' belief that they were doing business with Mr. Arnold.

Rule Proof: A plaintiff will be found to have possessed a reasonable expectancy of entering into a valid business relationship when specific customers called the defendant's store, and the customers expressed belief that they were doing business with the plaintiff.

Prediction: Arnold will prevail.

RULE EXPLANATION

Case facts from *Chicago's Pizza*, including the following: Customers calling/ordering from the defendant store, intending to do business with the plaintiff store; when customers placed their orders, they thought they were placing them with the plaintiff store.

Holding and Rationale from *Chicago's Pizza*: Held in favor of plaintiff because customers testified they thought they were dealing with the plaintiff.

RULE APPLICATION

Comparisons of the following facts on the basis of the identified guiding factors:

| GUIDING FACTOR (INCLUDE WHY THIS GUIDING FACTOR IS IMPORTANT) | *CHICAGO'S PIZZA* FACTS | THE SMELL SHOPPE FACTS | COMPARISON |
|---|---|---|---|
| The specific contemplation of customers | Customers calling/ordering from the defendant's store, intending to do business with the plaintiff's store | Customers brought their concerns to Arnold's attention; candles "just weren't what they used to be," despite the fact that he had not changed the candle-making process | Both sets of customers demonstrated their intent/specific contemplation to purchase from the plaintiff |
| The belief of customers that they were doing business with the plaintiff | When customers placed their orders, they thought they were placing them with the plaintiff's store; one inquired specifically as to which of the four locations would deliver to his home | Customers complained to plaintiff about the candles purchased from defendant<br><br>Mr. Green indicates he did not receive phone calls directly indicating that the customers believed they were doing business with the plaintiff<br><br>Mr. Green did not process an order after learning the customer believed she was doing business with the plaintiff | Both sets of customers appeared to believe they were purchasing from the plaintiff, while in fact purchasing from the defendant<br><br>Mr. Green will distinguish the situation with the one customer he turned away and suggest if others were under a false impression they were doing business with plaintiff, he did not know |

 **CHECK IN: Creating an Annotated Outline**

Using material from the worksheet above, create an annotated outline for the second issue in The Smell Shoppe hypothetical.

## III.  Putting It Together: Annotated Discussion

The following example annotates the Discussion section of The Smell Shoppe memo, addressing tortious interference with business expectancy. Note how the content of the memo corresponds with the pre-drafting analysis illustrated in Chapter 13.

### DISCUSSION

Mr. Gene Arnold will likely be unsuccessful in his tortious interference with business expectancy claim against Mr. Green. In order to successfully prevail in this claim, Mr. Arnold will need to prove four elements: "(1) [the plaintiff's] reasonable expectancy of entering into a valid business relationship; (2) the defendant's knowledge of the expectancy; (3) the defendant's intentional and unjustified interference that prevents the realization of business expectancy; and (4) damages resulting from the interference." *Chicago's Pizza, Inc. v. Chicago's Pizza Franchise Ltd.*, *USA*, 893 N.E.2d 981, 993 (Ill. App. Ct. 2008). As per the instruction of the senior partner, this memo will not discuss whether Mr. Green knew of Mr. Arnold's expectancy, nor will it discuss whether Mr. Arnold suffered damages as a result of the interference. Instead, this memo will only discuss whether Mr. Arnold possessed a reasonable expectancy of entering into a valid business relationship and whether it was Mr. Green's intentional and unjustified interference that prevented the realization of business expectancy. Notwithstanding the likelihood that Mr. Arnold will be successful in showing that he possessed a reasonable expectancy of entering into a valid business relationship, he will likely fail in his claim. This is because Mr. Green was not dishonest with customers and therefore Mr. Arnold will be unable to show that Mr. Green intentionally and unjustifiably interfered with the realization of business expectancy.

- **Global roadmap paragraph.** The first sentence provides a prediction. This is not a mystery, so there is no reason to keep the reader guessing as to the ultimate resolution of the claim or charge.
- The rule of law, with conditions clearly identified and with proper attribution.
- An identification of non-issues, with clarification as to why these will not be addressed.
- An identification of the issues addressed in the memo.
- A reiteration of the global prediction, now situated in predictions as to the resolution of each issue from the rule, justified by facts from the client's situation.

#### 1. Whether Arnold Possessed a Reasonable Expectancy of Entering into a Relationship

The court will first consider whether Mr. Arnold possessed a reasonable expectancy of entering into a valid business relationship. *Id.* In assessing whether Mr. Arnold possessed this expectancy, the court will consider the specific contemplation of customers and the customers' belief that they were doing business with Mr. Arnold. *Id.* 993-94. A plaintiff will be found to have possessed a reasonable expectancy of entering into a valid business relationship when it can be demonstrated that specific customers called the defendant's store with the belief that they were doing business with the plaintiff. *Id.* at 994. Because Mr. Arnold spoke to several people regarding their experiences while shopping at Mr. Green's candle store who expressed the belief that they were shopping at Mr. Arnold's store, he will likely prevail on this element.

- **First issue roadmap paragraph.** The issue roadmap begins by announcing the issue.
- These are the guiding factors for the issue, gleaned from the key facts of the precedent case.
- Rule proof: A fact-based holding from the precedent case to ground the guiding factors in specific facts from the precedent case.
- A prediction as to the resolution of the first issue, supported by facts from the client's situation.

**Rule explanation for the first
issue.** The rule explanation
begins with a framing
sentence that tethers the
guiding factors to the issue
and signals the content of the
rule explanation paragraph.
All of the sentences that follow
should flow from the framing
sentence.

Note that the writer included
the facts from the precedent
case that were relevant to the
resolution of the issue, as well
as the holding and rationale
on the issue.

This paragraph and the one
that follows are known as
**"Rule application."** Here,
the writer is comparing the
relevant case facts from the
precedent cases to the facts
of the client's case. Note that
these comparisons are being
made on the basis of legally
significant considerations—
namely, those guiding
factors or standards the
writer articulated in the issue
roadmap paragraph.

Key components of rule
application include the
following: (1) analysis and
counter-analysis relevant to
the issue/condition addressed
in this analytical portion of
the memo; (2) a prediction as
to the court's determination
of the issue/condition being
analyzed in this analytical
portion of the memo.

When customers demonstrate specific contemplation of doing business with the plaintiff and they express the belief that they are doing business with the plaintiff, the plaintiff will be successful in showing a reasonable expectancy of entering into a valid business relationship. *Id.* at 993-94. In *Chicago's Pizza*, the court stated that it was clear that the testifying customers contemplated a business relationship with the plaintiff. *Id.* at 993. In particular, one customer stated he had called the defendant's store believing it was one of the plaintiff's four locations and he asked for the phone number to another location of the plaintiff's restaurant so that it could deliver to him. *Id.* Another customer testified that he did believe that he was ordering from the plaintiff when in fact he was ordering from the defendant. *Id.* at 993-94. Moreover, the court noted the fact that the first testifying customer proceeded to then order from the defendant after being told that the location he had called was able to deliver to him. *Id.* Because the plaintiff successfully demonstrated a specific contemplation from the customers and because the customers expressed belief that they were doing business with the plaintiff, the court found the plaintiff had established a reasonable expectancy of business relationship. *Id.*

It is likely that Mr. Arnold will be able to show that he possessed a reasonable expectancy of entering into a valid business relationship. Like the plaintiff's customers in *Chicago's Pizza*, the customers in Mr. Arnold's situation contemplated specific business relationships with him. *See id.* Mr. Arnold will argue that, like the testimony of the customers in *Chicago's Pizza*, he also has customers who can testify to their specific contemplation in conducting business with him. *See id.* Namely, Mr. Arnold himself will testify that he began hearing people in the community express concerns about his candles, including telling him that the candles "just weren't what they used to be." This is similar to the testimony of the customers in *Chicago's Pizza* who expressed that they clearly believed they were doing business with the plaintiff. *Id.* Indeed, in Mr. Arnold's case, the customers' contemplation that they were doing business with him is even stronger, insofar as the customers specifically complained that his candles were weak in potency and were burning down too quickly, notwithstanding the fact that he had not made any changes to his candle-making practices. The dissatisfied community members may also be called to testify to their specific contemplation of conducting business with Mr. Arnold's candle shop, similar to the testimony of the customers in *Chicago's Pizza*. *See id.*

In addition, Mr. Arnold will assert that customers in fact believed they were doing business with him, not Mr. Green. As with the convincing testimony of the customers in *Chicago's Pizza*, Mr. Arnold can use the testimony of his customers to illustrate their belief that they were in fact doing business with him when they purchased their candles with the confidence that they would be strongly scented and long-lasting, just as Mr. Arnold's candles had proven to be. *See id.*

Alternatively, Mr. Green will argue that Mr. Arnold did not have a reasonable expectancy of a business relationship. He will argue that unlike the defendant in *Chicago's Pizza*, he did not receive phone calls from customers who directly indicated that they believed they were doing business with Mr. Arnold. *See id.* He may further distinguish his situation from that of

*Chicago's Pizza* by showing that he did not process the order from a customer who conveyed that she believed she was purchasing from Mr. Arnold. *See id.* Additionally, Mr. Green may argue that if other customers believed they were conducting business with Mr. Arnold's business, he was not made aware of this misapprehension. Notwithstanding Green's assertions, it is likely that Mr. Arnold will prevail on this element because he will be able to show that his customers specifically contemplated doing business with him and believed that they were in fact doing business with him.

### 2. Whether Green's Intentional and Unjustified Interference Prevented the Business Expectancy

Next, the court will consider whether it was Mr. Green's intentional and unjustified interference that prevented Arnold's realization of a business expectancy. *Id.* at 994. In assessing this element, the court will consider the defendant's conduct in allowing customers to place orders under a mistaken belief, the defendant's truthfulness to the customers regarding an affiliation with the plaintiff's business, and the content of any of the defendant's advertisements. *Id.* at 994. A plaintiff will be successful in demonstrating that it was the defendant's intentional and unjustified interference that prevented the realization of business expectancy when the defendant allows customers to place orders with its business while being dishonest with the customers when they inquire about an affiliation with the plaintiff's store. *Id.* Further, a plaintiff can demonstrate interference with an expectation of a business relationship when the defendant represents an affiliation with the plaintiff through advertising materials. *Id.* Because Mr. Green was not dishonest when he received a phone call regarding an affiliation with Arnold's business, and because his website's printable coupons only listed one location to shop from, it is unlikely that Mr. Arnold will prevail on this element.

When a defendant allows customers to place orders with its business while being dishonest with them about an affiliation with the plaintiff's store, and uses that false affiliation to advertise its store, the plaintiff will be successful in showing that it was the defendant's intentional and unjustified interference that prevented the realization of business expectancy. *Id.* In *Chicago's Pizza*, the defendant prevented the plaintiff from realizing business by permitting customers to place orders with the defendant's store and being dishonest with them about an affiliation with the plaintiff's business. *Id.* Furthermore, the court specifically rejected an argument presented by the defendant that the customers simply mistook the defendant's store for the plaintiff's. *Id.* The court pointed out that the defendant's advertisements listed multiple locations when in fact there was only one. *Id.* More specifically, the court emphasized the fact that the advertisements listed the corresponding address of the plaintiff's store. *Id.* Because the plaintiff was able to demonstrate that the defendant allowed the customers to proceed with sales while being dishonest with those customers regarding an affiliation with the plaintiff, and because the defendant listed the plaintiff's locations on its advertisements, the court ruled in favor of the plaintiff on this element. *Id.*

It is unlikely that Mr. Arnold will be able to show that it was Mr. Green's intentional and unjustified interference that prevented the realization of business expectancy. Mr. Arnold may argue that, like the defendant's

---

**Margin annotations:**

**Second issue roadmap paragraph.** These are the guiding factors that guide the court's analysis of the second issue.

**Rule proof: Fact-based holdings from the precedent case that ground the guiding factors in facts from the precedent case.**

A prediction, substantiated by facts from the client's situation.

**Rule explanation for the second issue.** Rule explanation begins with a framing sentence that tethers the guiding factors to the issue and frames the explanation that follows.

Rule explanation includes facts relevant to the second issue, together with the court's holding and rationale on the second issue.

**Rule application for the second issue.** Rule application begins with a prediction as to the court's likely resolution of the issue.

conduct in *Chicago's Pizza*, Mr. Green allowed customers to proceed with their purchases after learning that the customers believed they were doing business with Mr. Arnold. *See id*. Specifically, Mr. Arnold can demonstrate that Mr. Green permitted customers' sales after those customers were misled to believe that they were shopping at the newest location of the stores affiliated with Arnold's existing stores. Second, Mr. Arnold can argue that like the defendants in *Chicago's Pizza*, Mr. Green proceeded to place advertisements that further cemented customers' belief that there was an affiliation between the two parties. *See id*. Namely, Mr. Arnold will point to the fact that Mr. Green placed advertisements in the form of a website with similar branding and printable coupons that used the phrase "our newest location," strongly implying there was more than one location.

A helpful transition, signaling the counter-analysis/opposing party's position.

In contrast, Mr. Green will assert that he did not intentionally or unjustifiably interfere with Mr. Arnold's business. He will argue that, unlike the defendant in *Chicago's Pizza* who actively misled customers, Mr. Green was not dishonest. *See id*. In fact, when someone called Green's store inquiring about the affiliation with the other stores, he was honest and informed the caller that there was no affiliation with Arnold's stores. *See id*. He will further distinguish his advertising situation from that of the one in *Chicago's Pizza* by stating that his coupons did not expressly provide multiple locations like the misleading material at issue in *Chicago's Pizza*, and instead identified only the one true location of his store. *See id*. Green may also argue that the court should narrowly construe what actions are "unlawful and unjustifiable interference," particularly when the defendant's actions are commercial speech. A defendant's right to advertise in the way it deems most effective would be stifled if the plaintiff's argument were accepted. Notwithstanding Mr. Arnold's arguments, it is unlikely that he will prevail on this element because Mr. Green was not dishonest when he received a phone call regarding the affiliation and the website's printable coupons only listed one location.

The writer concludes the discussion with a global conclusion that predicts the overall resolution of the client's claim or charge, including a reiteration of the predictions about the issues.

Thus, Mr. Arnold likely will not succeed in his tortious interference with business expectancy claim against Mr. Green. Despite Mr. Arnold's success in proving that he possessed a reasonable expectancy of entering into a valid business relationship, he will likely fail to prove that it was Mr. Green's intentional and unjustified interference that prevented the realization of business expectancy.

### CHAPTER 16

# Drafting the Roadmaps

Now you understand how the rule of law forms the organizational structure of the predictive memo, where much of the content of the memo comes from, and how the memo content is organized during the pre-drafting process. With this understanding, we can turn our attention to drafting the roadmap paragraphs (Chapter 16), the rule explanation (Chapter 17), and the rule application (Chapter 18). As discussed in this chapter, the roadmap paragraphs orient the reader to material that follows in the Discussion.

---

**Study Guide Questions for Chapter 16**

1. What is a global roadmap paragraph? To what material does it orient the reader?
2. What is an issue roadmap paragraph? To what material does it orient the reader?
3. What is the difference between a global roadmap paragraph and an issue roadmap paragraph?
4. What is the content of a global roadmap paragraph?
5. What is the content of an issue roadmap paragraph?
6. What new terms were introduced in this chapter? How do these terms relate to your existing understanding of predictive memo writing? Did your understanding of any other terms change as a result of reading this chapter?

---

Roadmap paragraphs orient the reader to the material that follows. In the Discussion section you will be writing two types of roadmap paragraphs: global roadmaps and issue roadmaps. Each provides an overview that helps organize the more specific detail that follows. In addition, both types of roadmap paragraphs support the deductive framework of the memo. However, they differ in terms of their scope and the material to which they orient the reader, and they therefore necessarily differ in terms of content.

## I. Global Roadmaps

A global roadmap is the first paragraph of the Discussion. It orients the reader to the entire Discussion that follows. Lawyers like to have the bottom line up front, so the roadmap typically begins with a global prediction as to the court's likely resolution of the client's claim or charge. Further, the global roadmap includes the rule of law, which provides the organizational framework for the Discussion that follows. Law-trained readers will carefully track the conditions in the rule and will expect an analysis of each condition unless they are told otherwise. As such, the writer should identify any non-issues in the analysis and explain why those will not be addressed. We typically end the global roadmap paragraph with a slightly more detailed global prediction of the resolution of the client's claim or charge. In addition to the prediction itself, this sentence will briefly support that prediction with a few supporting facts. The paragraph has introduced the issues in context, preparing the reader for contextual predictions of the resolution of these issues, noting how the client facts support these predictions.

Recall the material from Chapter 13 where we addressed the checklist for the content of a global roadmap.

### Global Roadmap

1. A topic sentence that includes a global prediction as to the client's claim or charge.
2. The global rule of law, with its conditions and the relationship between the conditions clearly set forth, and with proper attribution.
3. An announcement of any non-issues, which are conditions that will not be addressed in the memo, ideally with a brief explanation as to why the conditions will not be addressed.
4. An announcement of the issues that will be addressed in the memo.
5. A global prediction, which is the prediction as to the resolution of the client's claim or charge, supported by key client facts related to that global prediction. A sentence or two should suffice, as this is simply the overall prediction and does not contain the separate issue predictions that will appear at the end of each issue roadmap.

Also, recall the template for drafting a global roadmap paragraph, introduced in Chapter 15.

### Global Roadmap

The client's claim will likely [INSERT GLOBAL PREDICTION]. In order to demonstrate the claim, the client must show [INSERT APPLICABLE GLOBAL RULE OF LAW, INCLUDING CONDITIONS]. [INSERT CITATION.] [INSERT ANY NON-ISSUES.] [INSERT ISSUES ADDRESSED IN THE MEMO]. Because [INSERT RESOLUTION OF ISSUE SUPPORTED BY RELEVANT CLIENT

FACTS] and because [INSERT RESOLUTION OF ISSUE SUPPORTED BY RELEVANT CLIENT FACTS], [INSERT GLOBAL PREDICTION].[1]

Below is an illustration of a global roadmap from The Smell Shoppe hypothetical, concerning the tortious interference with business expectancy example:

| | |
|---|---|
| Mr. Gene Arnold will likely be unsuccessful in his tortious interference with business expectancy claim against Mr. Green. In order to successfully prevail in this claim, Mr. Arnold will need to prove four elements: "(1) [the plaintiff's] reasonable expectancy of entering into a valid business relationship; (2) the defendant's knowledge of the expectancy; (3) the defendant's intentional and unjustified interference that prevents the realization of business expectancy; and (4) damages resulting from the interference." *Chicago's Pizza, Inc. v. Chicago's Pizza Franchise Ltd., USA*, 893 N.E.2d 981, 993 (Ill. App. Ct. 2008). As per the instruction of the senior partner, this memo will not discuss whether Mr. Green knew of Mr. Arnold's expectancy, nor will it discuss whether Mr. Arnold suffered damages as a result of the interference. Instead, this memo will only discuss whether Mr. Arnold possessed a reasonable expectancy of entering into a valid business relationship and whether it was Mr. Green's intentional and unjustified interference that prevented the realization of business expectancy. Notwithstanding the likelihood that Mr. Arnold will be successful in showing that he possessed a reasonable expectancy of entering into a valid business relationship, he will likely fail in his claim. This is because Mr. Green was not dishonest with customers and therefore Mr. Arnold will be unable to show that Mr. Green intentionally and unjustifiably interfered with the realization of business expectancy. | **Global roadmap paragraph.** The writer begins with a global prediction. This is not a mystery, so there is no reason to keep the reader guessing as to the ultimate resolution of the claim or charge.<br><br>The rule of law, with conditions clearly identified and with proper attribution.<br><br>An identification of non-issues, with clarification as to why these will not be addressed.<br><br>An identification of the issues addressed in the memo.<br><br>A reiteration of the global prediction, now situated in predictions as to the resolution of each issue from the rule, justified by facts from the client's situation. |

As noted, the global roadmap begins with a global prediction. Why is that the case? Because the law-trained reader wants to see the "bottom line up front." This is an analytical document, not a mystery. Moreover, the global prediction helps the paragraph serve its essential function—to provide a roadmap for the reader. Including the global prediction in the roadmap provides essential context and direction for the reader.

Also, note that the global rule of law is the currently existing rule of law, not a historical overview of how that existing rule of law developed. Recall the discussion of emergent and existing rules of law in Chapter 6. In preparing a memo involving the assault with a FitBit, attorney Sofía would want to use the emergent rule that develops from *State v. Johnson* and, as a result of that case, becomes the existing rule.

---

1. Note that this template is a loose guide for the different components of the global roadmap. When you are drafting a global roadmap for a client matter you will likely find that some of these components require more than one sentence.

She would not want to include the historical development of the rule as the court processed it first in *State v. Bird* and then in *State v. Johnson*. Why? Because that would be unnecessary for the reader. The reader is interested in the current, applicable law, not in how it developed over time.

What if all the conditions are at issue, such that there are no non-issues? How should you indicate that in the global roadmap? If all the conditions are at issue, the drafting is simplified. After you spell out the global rule of law you can skip the "announcement of any non-issues" and go directly to the "announcement of the issues." And because you just stated the conditions, your announcement of the issues can be brief. Let's assume that all four conditions in the above global road-map are at issue. With no non-issues to dispose of, that portion of the global roadmap would read as:

> In order to successfully prevail in this claim, Mr. Arnold will need to prove four elements: "(1) [the plaintiff's] reasonable expectancy of entering into a valid business relationship; (2) the defendant's knowledge of the expectancy; (3) the defendant's intentional and unjustified interference that prevents the realization of business expectancy; and (4) damages resulting from the interference." *Chicago's Pizza, Inc. v. Chicago's Pizza Franchise Ltd., USA*, 893 N.E.2d 981, 993 (Ill. App. Ct. 2008). This memo will discuss all four issues.

 **CRASH WARNING: Non-Issues Signal a Condition You Will Not Be Addressing**

A non-issue means any part of the global rule you identify as a condition in your global roadmap and yet elect not to address in the remainder of your memo. New legal writers sometimes overuse this concept by identifying "non-issues" even though these had not been established as conditions. Not only is this unnecessary, it can also create confusion. The purpose of identifying conditions as non-issues is so that the reader is not surprised when the memo does not address a condition that you have stated as part of the global rule. If the item has not been identified as a condition and is later identified as a non-issue, the reader may wonder if your statement of the global rule was incomplete.

Put differently, in stating the global rule, you are implicitly telling the reader that the memo will address the listed conditions. Thus, for any conditions the memo will not, in fact, address, you need to alert the reader so she knows not to expect any discussion of that condition. Absent such an alert, the reader would be confused and wonder what happened to the expected issue segment for that condition.

Assume that you are writing a memo about whether the plaintiff has established adverse possession, and that such claim requires proof of three conditions (that the use was hostile, intentional, and without permission). Compare the following examples.

- **Ineffective use of non-issue concept:** The plaintiff must prove that the use was hostile, intentional, and without permission. This memo will not address a claim for trespass.

- **Ineffective use of non-issue concept:** The plaintiff must prove that the use was hostile, intentional, and without permission. This memo will not address the related concepts of ownership and prescriptive easements.
- **Effective use of non-issue concept if permission is a non-issue:** The plaintiff must prove that the use was hostile, intentional, and without permission. Because the defendant admits no permission was given, that element is satisfied and thus will not be addressed in this memo.
- **Effective use of non-issue concept if there are no non-issues; i.e., all three conditions are at issue:** The plaintiff must prove that the use was hostile, intentional, and without permission. All three conditions will be addressed.

Both of the ineffective examples include unnecessary, and potentially confusing, sentences. The reader would not expect that the memo will address a claim for trespass or the concepts of ownership and prescriptive easements, so the writer does not have to alert the reader that these will not be included. In contrast, the first effective example manages readers' expectations by flagging that the issue of "without permission" will not be addressed in the memo. Finally, the last effective example illustrates the way the author should simply and clearly indicate that all conditions are at issue and thus will be addressed.

## II. Issue Roadmaps

An issue roadmap also orients the reader to upcoming analysis, albeit with a more limited scope and thus more specific content than a global roadmap. An issue roadmap begins what we call an "issue segment," which analyzes a particular issue/condition. Thus, following the issue roadmap, the remainder of the issue segment includes rule explanation and rule application. The issue roadmap provides a foundation that helps orient the reader to the explanation and application of an issue.

Recall the material from Chapter 13 where we addressed the checklist for the content of an issue roadmap:

*Issue Roadmaps*

1. A topic sentence that announces the issue/condition that will be addressed in the issue roadmap.
2. The rule of law for the issue/condition: any definitions, standards, or guiding factors that are related to the court's analysis of the issue/condition.
3. The rule proof: the fact-based holding from the precedent, which provides "proof" of the rule.
4. A prediction of the resolution of that issue/condition, supported by key client facts related to that prediction.

Let's look at each of these ingredients in a little more detail. First, the **topic sentence** announces the issue being addressed. Where applicable for subsequent issue roadmaps, the topic sentence should include transition language to reinforce the relationship between issues (e.g., "The second issue the court will consider," or "Also, the court will examine").

Next, the writer sets forth **the rule for that issue/condition**. This includes any definitions, standards, or guiding factors the court will consider as it analyzes the issue. Note that these considerations will frame the rest of the Discussion for this issue/condition, including both the more specific factual material from the precedent that will follow in the rule explanation, and the structure and content of the rule application.

Sometimes part of the rule may not require discussion. How should that be communicated to the reader? Just as a global roadmap can dispose of a condition as a non-issue, so too can an issue roadmap dispose of part of the issue rule as a non-issue. Imagine, for example, that the rule for the element of whether a dog is dangerous is as follows: "A dog is dangerous if it has been used as a fighting dog or if it otherwise exhibits dangerous tendencies." What if in your client's situation the dog unquestionably had not been used as a fighting dog? If so, there would be no need to address that part of the issue rule. Instead, after the sentence setting forth the rule, the writer would dispose of that part of the issue rule as a non-issue, e.g., "Because the parties agree that Fido was never used as a fighting dog, this memo only addresses whether Fido otherwise exhibits dangerous tendencies."

Next, the writer includes the fact-based holding from the precedent, which functions as a *rule proof*. By "rule proof," we mean that the inclusion of the fact-based holding from the precedent shows your skeptical reader that the rule components you identified, typically guiding factors, are indeed what the court considered and applied. For example, imagine you stated "place intended for children" as a guiding factor. You need to "prove" that "place intended for children" is indeed a guiding factor—something the court will consider when evaluating a specific rule condition. You do this by showing that the court's holding in the prior case was based on the fact that the location being discussed, for example a daycare center, served children. In this way, the fact-based holding from the precedent case reinforces the more generalized guiding factors.

Note also that, stylistically, you want to state the fact-based holding, followed by a citation, rather than beginning the sentence with the case name. For example, consider this rule proof from The

Smell Shoppe example: "A plaintiff will be found to have possessed a reasonable expectancy of entering into a valid business relationship when it can be demonstrated that specific customers called the defendant's store with the belief that they were doing business with the plaintiff. *Id.* at 994." Beginning the sentence instead with "In *Chicago's Pizza*..." would be jarring to the reader, introducing unnecessary detail. The issue roadmap is not the place to introduce a specific case to the reader; this happens in the rule explanation that follows.

Finally, your issue roadmap will end with a **prediction as to the resolution of the issue**. The prediction should indicate to the reader how the court likely will rule, including reference to the key client facts that support that prediction. It cannot and should not refer to all facts that support the prediction, as that would be unwieldy. As such, you should aim to keep your issue prediction relatively short. One sentence usually will suffice, and you should never need more than two sentences.

Stylistically, the prediction must actually make a prediction (i.e., it cannot simply say "it is possible" or "the court might"). At the same time, the prediction should not be so definite that it conveys certainty to the reader about what the court will do (i.e., it should not say "the court will" or "the court must"). Instead, an effective prediction indicates your determination of what the court likely will do while allowing for the uncertainty that is inherent in legal decisions. Thus, a fairly confident prediction would read, "It is highly likely that...," and a less confident prediction would read, "It is more likely than not...." Most often, a prediction will fall somewhere between these two extremes and thus might read "It is likely that the court will hold...."

An example of an effective issue prediction is thus as follows: "Because Fido bit two people, one of whom required surgery, it is highly likely the court will hold Fido is dangerous."

Recall the template for drafting an issue roadmap, introduced in Chapter 15:

### Issue Roadmap

> The first issue for the court to consider [INSERT FIRST ISSUE/ CONDITION]. To analyze this issue the court will consider [INSERT ISSUE/ CONDITION RULE, INCLUDING DEFINITIONS, STANDARDS, AND GUIDING FACTORS]. [INSERT CITATION.] [INSERT RULE PROOF.] [INSERT CITATION.] The court will likely [INSERT PREDICTION AS TO THE RESOLUTION OF FIRST ISSUE SUPPORTED BY RELEVANT CLIENT FACTS].

Below is an illustration of an issue roadmap from The Smell Shoppe example:

**First issue roadmap paragraph.** The issue roadmap begins by announcing the issue.

These are the guiding factors for the issue, gleaned from the key facts of the precedent case.

**Rule proof:** A fact-based holding from the precedent case to ground the guiding factors in specific facts from the precedent case.

A prediction as to the resolution of the first issue, supported by facts from the client's situation.

> The court will first consider whether Mr. Arnold possessed a reasonable expectancy of entering into a valid business relationship. *Id.* In assessing whether Mr. Arnold possessed this expectancy, the court will consider the specific contemplation of customers and the customers' belief that they were doing business with Mr. Arnold. *Id.* at 993-94. A plaintiff will be found to have possessed a reasonable expectancy of entering into a valid business relationship when it can be demonstrated that specific customers called the defendant's store with the belief that they were doing business with the plaintiff. *Id.* at 994. Because Mr. Arnold spoke to several people regarding their experiences while shopping at Mr. Green's candle store who expressed the belief that they were shopping at Mr. Arnold's store, he will likely prevail on this element.

---

### ⧉ CHECK IN: Roadmap Paragraphs

There are a few common errors new writers make when drafting roadmap paragraphs. For the global roadmap, a common mistake is to neglect to dispense with non-issues. This is confusing to the law-trained reader, who will have carefully tracked the conditions of the rule and will therefore expect that all conditions will be addressed in the memo.

For issue roadmaps, a common error is not articulating guiding factors with sufficient context. The reader should understand what the guiding factor is, and the relationship between the guiding factor and the condition should be clear. Another common mistake with issue roadmaps is having too many guiding factors. Generally, guiding factors are most effective if you have between two and four for each condition.

Recall the second contested issue in the tortious interference with business expectancy problem: intentional and unjustified interference that prevented the realization of business expectancy. Assume you characterized the guiding factors in the manner below.

> In assessing this element, the court will consider orders, information about customers, information about business owners, truthful or misleading statements, and advertisements.

Can you identify any problems with how you characterized those guiding factors? Consider what might be unclear to the reader in terms of the labels/descriptions of these guiding factors.

Another misstep new writers make is failing to differentiate between the rule of law for the condition and the fact-based holding.

Consider the following issue roadmap for the reasonable expectancy element discussed above. Pay particular attention to the rule proof: the content related to the fact-based holding. Does it actually provide a fact-based holding? Or does its simply repeat, albeit in slightly different words, the rule for that condition?

> The court will first consider whether Mr. Arnold possessed a reasonable expectancy of entering into a valid business relationship. *Id*. In assessing whether Mr. Arnold possessed this expectancy, the court will consider the specific contemplation of customers and the customers' belief that they were doing business with Mr. Arnold. *Id*. 993-94. A plaintiff will need to show the specific contemplation of customers and the customers' belief they were doing business in order to prove that the plaintiff possessed a reasonable expectancy. *Id*. Because Mr. Arnold spoke to several people regarding their experiences while shopping at Mr. Green's candle store who expressed the belief that they were shopping at Mr. Arnold's store, he will likely prevail on this element.

Finally, new writers may struggle with incorporating standards or definitions. What if *Chicago's Pizza* had included the following language: "The reasonableness of the expectancy is judged by an objective standard"? First and foremost, we would want to include that content in the issue roadmap because it is part of the rule for that condition. Sometimes new writers focus on guiding factors to the exclusion of other significant parts of the rule.

In the paragraph below, consider the effectiveness of *where* the writer has included this information about the standard for this condition.

> The court will first consider whether Mr. Arnold possessed a reasonable expectancy of entering into a valid business relationship. *Id*. In assessing whether Mr. Arnold possessed this expectancy, the court will consider the specific contemplation of customers and the customers' belief that they were doing business with Mr. Arnold. *Id*. 993-94. A plaintiff will be found to have possessed a reasonable expectancy of entering into a valid business relationship when it can be demonstrated that specific customers called the defendant's store with the belief that they were doing business with the plaintiff. *Id*. at 994. The reasonableness of the expectancy is judged by an objective standard. *Id*. Because Mr. Arnold spoke to several people regarding their experiences while shopping at Mr. Green's candle store who expressed the belief that they were shopping at Mr. Arnold's store, he will likely prevail on this element.

How does the placement of the standard affect your understanding of the rule? Where might you move it to improve clarity?

### CHAPTER 17

# Drafting the Rule Explanation

In Chapter 16, you learned how to draft global roadmap and issue roadmap paragraphs. You learned that the issue roadmap paragraph orients the reader to the discussion of a particular issue. That discussion first explains how the law has been applied in prior cases. In this chapter, you will learn how to draft the rule explanation paragraph(s) for a single issue memorandum.

## Study Guide Questions for Chapter 17

1. What are the ingredients for a rule explanation paragraph?
2. What does the rule explanation accomplish? How?
3. How should the framing sentence of a rule explanation paragraph be constructed? What is the content of that sentence?
4. What type of material from the precedent case belongs in the rule explanation? What kind of content does not?
5. What kind of material from the client's situation belongs in the rule explanation? What kind does not?
6. What does it mean to have the facts from the precedent case "flow from" the framing sentence?
7. What new terms were introduced in this chapter? How do these terms relate to your existing understanding of predictive memo writing? Did your understanding of any other terms change as a result of reading this chapter?

## I. Rule Explanation in Context: The Bridge Between the Issue Roadmap and the Rule Application Section for an Issue

Rule explanation provides the bridge between the issue roadmap, where the writer has set forth the rule of law for the condition with very limited context, and the application of the rule of law to the client's situation. To further satisfy the skepticism of the law-trained reader, the rule explanation provides a more detailed rule proof, explaining how prior cases have resolved the issue. It also shows how the standards, definitions, and guiding factors influenced prior court rulings. Finally, it provides a foundation for the application that will follow. Specifically, in rule application, the reader will expect to see analogies drawn between client facts and the case facts used in rule explanation.

In the rule explanation paragraphs the reader learns how the law has been applied in prior cases. But that does not mean you will be inserting full case briefs in the rule explanation. As we know from prior chapters, rule explanation is part of an issue segment that addresses only a *single* issue/condition. So, you will be explaining a prior court's analysis of a single issue/condition, rather than addressing how the court analyzed the entire claim or charge.

Because rules of law are rarely straightforward, for most legal issues you will want to include rule explanation showing the reader how the law has been applied in prior cases. There may be instances, however, where a rule is so clear and straightforward that no illustration is necessary. Recall the Chapter 10 rule-based reasoning example involving a name change following a divorce. This type of rule is likely clear enough that rule explanation would be unnecessary. Thus, the entire issue segment, including the identification of the issue, the issue rule, and the application to the client's situation, can be put forth in a single paragraph without case illustrations, as in the following example.

> Ella Ramos almost certainly will be granted the requested name change. The statute expressly allows a person, as part of their divorce, to "have their last name restored to the ... name as it existed before the marriage." Ella thus is clearly entitled to a name change under the statute. She falls under the statute's purview because she seeks the name change as part of her divorce. In addition, the change in name that she requests is expressly allowed under the statute. Specifically, she requests that her name be restored to "Helton," which was her "last name as it existed before the marriage."

Recall the Chapter 13 checklist for drafting rule explanation paragraphs.

### Rule Explanation Paragraphs

1. A framing sentence that illustrates how the guiding factors inform the court's analysis of the issue/condition.
2. Facts from the precedent case that are related to those guiding factors.
3. The court's holding on the issue/condition in light of those facts.
4. The court's reasoning; i.e., why it resolved the issue the way it did.

The placement of the rule explanation section within each issue segment further explains its purpose. Rule explanation appears after the issue roadmap and before rule application. The issue roadmap has provided direction to the reader by announcing generalized, guiding factors that direct courts' analyses of the issue. You also will use those guiding factors as the basis for the comparisons you will make in rule application.

Rule explanation thus bridges the two sections. It provides context for the material provided in the issue roadmap—an explanation of how these guiding factors actually influenced a prior court. It also provides the foundation for the comparisons made in rule application where you will note critical similarities or differences between the facts from your rule explanation cases and the facts of your client's case. The issue segment for each issue/condition therefore should be cohesive, with the guiding factors acting as the thread that weaves together the material throughout the issue segment.

### Diagram 17-1: Rule Explanation

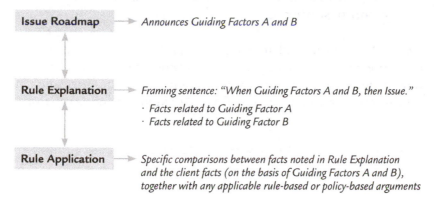

Note the intentional progression of the material in a rule explanation paragraph. The framing sentence provides essential direction for the reader. It introduces relevant case material deductively, moving from the general legal principle to the specific application in prior cases. In this way, the framing sentence previews how the guiding factors informed the court's decision on the issue. Relevant case facts (i.e., those that were relevant to the court's ruling on the specific issue) typically come next, providing the foundation, or context, for the court's holding. The holding itself follows, along with the rationale, collectively setting forth how and why the court reached its decision on the particular issue.

Reorganizing these components of rule explanation would interfere with the logical arrangement of the material and confuse the reader. For example, a statement of the holding and/or rationale that precedes the facts would lack context and be unsupported. Similarly, beginning the rule explanation with the case facts, instead of a framing sentence, would make it more difficult for the reader to understand the importance of the facts.

## II. The Template with Ingredients for a Rule Explanation Paragraph

Recall from Chapter 15 the following template that describes the ingredients for a rule explanation paragraph:

> When [INSERT GUIDING FACTORS BEING ILLUSTRATED], [INSERT RESOLUTION OF ISSUE]. [INSERT CITATION.] [INSERT FACTS FROM PRECEDENT AUTHORITY RELEVANT TO ISSUE.] [INSERT CITATION.] [INSERT COURT'S RESOLUTION OF ISSUE] [INSERT COURT'S REASONING]. [INSERT CITATION.]

### A. Starting the Rule Explanation Paragraph: The Framing Sentence

Notice that the rule explanation paragraph follows a predictable and deductive framework. It begins with a framing sentence that identifies how guiding factors relate to the resolution of the issue. The template for that framing sentence is a useful tool to keep in mind as you draft.

> *Framing Sentence:* "When [insert guiding factors being illustrated], [insert holding for the issue].

As its name suggests, the framing sentence frames the information that follows it. This cues you, the writer—and eventually the reader—as to what comes next: the facts related to the guiding factors identified in the framing sentence. So, in The Smell Shoppe hypothetical, you might use the following as a framing sentence:

> When a defendant allows customers to place orders with its business while being dishonest with them about an affiliation with the plaintiff's store, and uses that false affiliation to advertise its store, the plaintiff will be successful in showing that it was the defendant's intentional and unjustified interference that prevented the realization of business expectancy.

What facts would the reader expect to see? Those facts from the case that reinforce the importance of those generalized guiding factors. Consider the following example from The Smell Shoppe hypothetical. Can you identify any problems with the explanation paragraph?

When a defendant allows unknowing customers to place orders with its business, the plaintiff will be successful in showing that it was the defendant's intentional and unjustified interference that prevented the realization of business expectancy. *Id.* In *Chicago's Pizza*, the court held that that the plaintiff was successful in showing that it was the defendant's intentional and unjustified interference that prevented the realization of business expectancy. *Id.* The court noted that the defendant prevented the plaintiff from realizing business with the testifying customers after permitting the customers to place orders with its store and being dishonest with them about an affiliation. *Id.* Because the plaintiff was able to demonstrate that the defendant allowed the customers to proceed with sales while being dishonest with them regarding its affiliation and listing the plaintiff's locations on its advertisements, the court found in favor of the plaintiff on this element. *Id.*

Recall that you are using the framing sentence to signal to the reader what guiding factors have guided a court's analysis. The reader had the expectation that all guiding factors would be explained by facts from the precedent cases, and that there would be no facts from the precedent case that were not signaled by guiding factors in the framing sentence. So, the reader is likely confused by two aspects of this rule explanation. First, there are no facts in the paragraph to support the guiding factor relating to false advertisements, and second, there is nothing in the framing sentence to suggest the importance of the defendant's dishonesty as to affiliation. Simply referring to the customers as "unknowing" in the framing sentence fails to alert the reader to the importance of the guiding factors and how the facts from the case in the rule explanation paragraph reinforce those guiding factors. Consider the following revision with the new text in bold:

When a defendant allows customers to place orders with its business **while being dishonest with them about an affiliation with the plaintiff's store, and uses that false affiliation to advertise its store,** the plaintiff will be successful in showing that it was the defendant's intentional and unjustified interference that prevented the realization of business expectancy. *Id.* In *Chicago's Pizza*, the defendant prevented the plaintiff from realizing business by permitting customers to place orders with the defendant's store and being dishonest with them about an affiliation with the plaintiff's business. *Id.* **Furthermore, the court specifically rejected an argument presented by the defendant that the customers simply mistook the defendant's store for the plaintiff's.** *Id.* **The court pointed out that defendant's advertisements listed multiple locations when in fact there was only one.** *Id.* **More specifically, the court emphasized the fact that the advertisements listed the corresponding address of the plaintiff's store.** *Id.* Because the plaintiff was able to demonstrate that the defendant allowed the customers to proceed with sales while being dishonest with those customers regarding an affiliation with the plaintiff, and because the defendant listed the plaintiff's locations on its advertisements, the court ruled in favor of the plaintiff on this element. *Id.*

Now you can see that the content of the paragraph matches the guiding factors signaled in the framing sentence. The paragraph below demonstrates the content alignment between the guiding factors in the framing sentence and the facts that support those guiding factors illustrated in the rule explanation.

When a defendant allows customers to place orders with its business while being dishonest with them about an affiliation with the plaintiff's store, and uses that false affiliation to advertise its store, the plaintiff will be successful in showing that it was the defendant's intentional and unjustified interference that prevented the realization of business expectancy. *Id.* In *Chicago's Pizza*, the defendant prevented the plaintiff from realizing business by permitting customers to place orders with the defendant's store and being dishonest with them about an affiliation with the plaintiff's business. *Id.* Furthermore, the court specifically rejected an argument presented by the defendant that the customers simply mistook the defendant's store for the plaintiff's. *Id.* The court pointed out that the defendant's advertisements listed multiple locations when in fact there was only one. *Id.* More specifically, the court emphasized the fact that the advertisements listed the corresponding address of the plaintiff's store. *Id.* Because the plaintiff was able to demonstrate that the defendant allowed the customers to proceed with sales while being dishonest with those customers regarding an affiliation with the plaintiff, and because the defendant listed the plaintiff's locations on its advertisements, the court ruled in favor of the plaintiff on this element. *Id.*

## B. The Other Ingredients of a Rule Explanation Paragraph

What are the other ingredients in the rule explanation paragraph? First, you explicitly state the court's holding for that issue. Returning to our Dangerous Dog hypothetical, an example of a holding could be: "Thus, the court held the dog was not dangerous." Note the holding is just that—the court's holding.

In addition to the holding, we add the final ingredient: the court's reasoning. Why did the court hold as it did for this condition? You may have to infer a court's reasoning, as courts sometimes do not spell out why they held as they did. Even under these circumstances, you will still cite to the case from which you drew that inference. Building on the dangerous dog holding presented above, here's an example of how you might explain the court's reasoning for its "not dangerous" finding: "The court reasoned that although the dog bit someone, the dog did so as a defensive maneuver." Can you see how the reasoning sometimes helps show the relationship between guiding factors? Here, the reasoning explains the relationship between the guiding factors of the dog's history of biting and whether the dog was provoked.

Sometimes the holding and reasoning are blended together into a single sentence. Even so, they remain two distinct components. For example, the last sentence in a rule explanation paragraph might effectively combine these two components as follows: "Because the animal both physically and genetically bore greater similarity to a wolf than a dog, the court held the animal is not a dog under the statute." Generally speaking, this technique works as long as the holding still stands out and the reasoning is relatively straightforward. But if the court's reasoning is relatively complex, you will want to separate these two ingredients.

Finally, notice two other features of the rule explanation. First, notice what is *not* a component in a rule explanation paragraph. There is *nothing* about your client in the rule explanation. All of the content comes from the precedent case. Second, notice that the facts from the precedent case and the court's holding are presented in the past tense. So, while the framing sentence is in the present tense, "When guiding factors are present/not present, courts hold," all of the sentences that follow illustrate facts and decisions that happened in the past and so are stated using the past tense.

---

> ### ⧈ CHECK IN: Rule Explanation Paragraph
>
> For each rule explanation paragraph below, consider whether the writer has included the necessary ingredients. What ingredients are missing? How does that affect the impact of the rule explanation paragraph?
>
> **Example 1:** The *Wilson* court held that no satisfactory explanation existed for the delay in sealing the evidence. *Wilson*, 212 F.3d. 212 (8th Cir. 2009). The court referenced numerous reasons in reaching this conclusion. *Id.* at 215.
>
> **Example 2:** In *U.S. v. Wilson*, 212 F.3d. 212 (8th Cir. 2009), the Eighth Circuit held that there was no satisfactory explanation

for the delay in sealing the wiretap evidence. Specifically, the Court rejected the government's argument that the change in personnel in its regional wiretap unit justified the delay. *Id.* at 215. When Jim Smiley took over for Sally Jamal there was an almost two-day period in which no evidence that came in was sealed. *Id.*

**Example 3:** When the length of the delay is significant, and the cause of delay is within the government's control, courts hold there is no satisfactory explanation. In *U.S. v. Wilson*, 212 F.3d. 212 (8th Cir. 2009), the government failed to seal the wiretap evidence in question for almost two days after it was intercepted. *Id.* at 214. During that two-day period, a new lead technician took over in the regional wire-tap unit to which the evidence was delivered. *Id.* While the change in personnel was planned, it nonetheless led to some delays across the board in sealing evidence. *Id.* The Eighth Circuit held there was no satisfactory explanation for the delay in sealing the evidence. *Id.* at 215. The Court squarely rejected the government's argument that the change in personnel in its regional wiretap unit justified the delay. *Id.* Instead, the Court reasoned that a delay of that length and under those circumstances raises precisely the kind of suspicion that the statute seeks to avoid. *Id.* at 216. The Court pointed out that the change in personnel here was neither unusual nor unanticipated, and it was not grounds for a government unit to cease to perform its criti-cal role. *Id.*

## III. Variations in Rule Explanation: Multiple Rule Explanation Paragraphs Using the Same Authority

Often, if you have only one authority, you will only have one rule expla-nation paragraph for a condition. However, this is not always the case. You may have several rule explanation paragraphs, even when you are using a single authority. When you have substantial material to communicate, you may want to divide it into multiple paragraphs for clarity. In that case, be sure to include a helpful transition between paragraphs so that the reader knows you are continuing the discussion of the case.

Consider the following example, in which the writer used more than one paragraph to illustrate the relevant facts from the precedent case. Assume for purposes of this illustration that the precedent authority gave rise to an additional guiding factor in The Smell Shoppe hypo-thetical: "affirmative attempts by the defendant to mislead custom-ers." Because the rule explanation paragraph would become unwieldy given the additional content, the writer has broken the rule explanation into more than one paragraph.

> When a defendant allows customers to place orders with its business while being dishonest with them about an affiliation with the plaintiff's store, uses that false affiliation to advertise its store, and makes affirmative attempts to mislead customers, the plaintiff will be successful in showing that it was the defendant's intentional and unjustified interference that prevented the realization of business expectancy. *Id.* In *Chicago's Pizza*, the defendant prevented the plaintiff from realizing business by permitting customers to place orders with the defendant's store and being dishonest with them about an affiliation with the plaintiff's business. *Id.* Furthermore, the court specifically rejected an argument presented by the defendant that the customers simply mistook the defendant's store for the plaintiff's. *Id.* The court pointed out that defendant's advertisements listed multiple locations when in fact there was only one. *Id.* More specifically, the court emphasized the fact that the advertisements listed the corresponding address of the plaintiff's store. *Id.*
>
> In addition, the court noted the affirmative attempts by defendant employees to convince customers that they were working with the plaintiff. *Id.* These attempts included the defendant employees wearing the plaintiff's logo. *Id.* Because the plaintiff was able to demonstrate that the defendant allowed the customers to proceed with sales while being dishonest with those customers regarding an affiliation with the plaintiff, and because the defendant listed the plaintiff's locations on its advertisements, while deliberately misleading customers, the court ruled in favor of the plaintiff on this element. *Id.*

You might also elect to use multiple rule explanation paragraphs where you have guiding factors that are distinct or that require additional explanation such that it makes sense for them to be considered in separate explanation paragraphs. So, for example, in the illustration above, the writer could have had two rule explanation paragraphs, each framed by a sentence announcing the guiding factors the paragraph will explain. The illustration below demonstrates this organizational strategy.

> When a defendant allows customers to place orders with its business while being dishonest with them about an affiliation with the plaintiff's store, and uses that false affiliation to advertise its store, the plaintiff will be successful in showing that it was the defendant's intentional and unjustified interference that prevented the realization of business expectancy. *Id.* In *Chicago's Pizza*, the court held that that the plaintiff was successful in showing that it was the defendant's intentional and unjustified interference that prevented the realization of business expectancy. *Id.* The court noted that the

defendant prevented the plaintiff from realizing business with the testifying customers after permitting the customers to place orders with their store and being dishonest with them about their affiliation. *Id.* Furthermore, the court specifically expressed its disagreement with an argument presented by the defendant stating that the customers simply mistook the defendant's store for the plaintiff's. *Id.* The court pointed out that defendant's advertisements listed multiple locations while they only had one. *Id.* More specifically, the court took notice of the fact that the advertisements listed the corresponding address of the plaintiff's store. *Id.*

In addition, when the defendant makes affirmative attempts to mislead the plaintiff's customers, the court will conclude that it was the defendant's intentional and unjustified interference that prevented the realization of business expectancy. In *Chicago's Pizza,* the court noted the defendant employees attempted to convince customers that they were working with the plaintiff. *Id.* These attempts included the defendant employees wearing the plaintiff's logo. *Id.* The court also emphasized that several customers testified that defendant employees would sing the advertising jingle of the plaintiff's business and would engage in misleading conversations about the defendant's business. *Id.* Because the plaintiff was able to demonstrate that the defendant allowed the customers to proceed with sales while being dishonest with them regarding their affiliation and listing the plaintiff's locations on their advertisements, while deliberately misleading customers, the court found in favor of the plaintiff on this element. *Id.*

In both of the examples above showing multiple rule explanation paragraphs, note that the content within the paragraphs is relatively consistent. Each example communicates the same ingredients—the facts that comport with the paragraph's focus as noted in the framing sentence. They also provide the same holding and reasoning, found at the end of the second paragraph in each example.

 **CRASH WARNING: Omit Your Client's Facts from the Rule Explanation and Choose Precedent Facts Carefully**

Because you likely will be drafting the rule explanation section before you draft the rule application section, it sometimes is tempting to try to insert your client's arguments into the rule explanation section. After all, your client's situation is the focal point of the Discussion, and you are rightfully eager to start making analogies and distinctions from the precedent case to your client's situation. As tempting as this is, it is not effective. Your reader needs to fully understand the law's application in the precedent before he is able to see how your client's situation compares. That is why the rule explanation section precedes the rule application section: It is a necessary foundation for the arguments to follow in the rule application section.

To help avoid inserting the client's situation into the rule explanation section, some new legal writers find it helpful to use highlighting. They highlight their client's facts anywhere they appear in the draft of the Discussion. That makes it obvious if such facts have been improperly inserted into the rule explanation section.

Another mistake sometimes made by new writers is to include *all* relevant facts from a precedent case in the rule explanation, rather than just the relevant facts related to the issue being addressed. Remember, a rule explanation appears in an issue segment related to a *single* issue. Therefore, in rule explanation paragraphs, you want to focus the reader's attention on only those facts significant to the issue being addressed. In other words, at this point you will not include facts that are significant to another issue unless they are also relevant to this one. Highlighting can help you avoid this pitfall as well. If you highlighted facts from the precedent case in the rule explanation but do not see those facts revisited in your rule application for that issue, you have likely included facts in your rule explanation that may be relevant to a different issue.

### CHAPTER 18

# Drafting the Rule Application

Having laid a solid framework for our analysis in the issue road-map (Chapter 16) and rule explanation (Chapter 17), we now turn our attention to the application of the rule. In rule application we apply the rule to the client's situation by making arguments for both parties/positions. Many of those arguments employ analogies in which the writer compares the facts of the client's situation to the facts from a precedent case that have been described in the rule explanation.

## Study Guide Questions for Chapter 18

1. What is the basic content of rule application?
2. What is counter-analysis?
3. How is material from the issue roadmap related to rule application?
4. How is the material from the rule explanation related to the rule application?
5. What is "monologuing," and how can the writer avoid this mistake?
6. What is the difference between the "party/position" and "issue-component" organizational approach to rule application?
7. What does it mean for a fact from the precedent case to "make its debut" in rule application? Why is this problematic?
8. What is the relationship between rule explanation and rule application? How does your understanding of this relationship inform the organization of rule explanation and rule application?
9. What new terms were introduced in this chapter? How do these terms relate to your existing understanding of predictive memo writing? Did your understanding of any other terms change as a result of reading this chapter?

We now come to the final section of the Discussion: rule application. This is the section in which you set forth the arguments. Because this is a predictive memo in which we want to show what a court likely will do, we need to provide arguments for both parties, not just our client.

Recall the material from Chapter 13 where we addressed the checklist for rule application.

### Rule Application Paragraphs

1. Broken down by the components of the rule of law for the condition, most typically by guiding factors.
2. For each component:
   a. A topic or thesis sentence: an announcement of the aspect of the rule of law for the condition that will be addressed.
   b. One or more forms of legal reasoning to support arguments:
      i. Analogical arguments and counter-arguments, comparing and contrasting facts from the precedent case to the client's case;
      ii. Rule-based arguments and counter-arguments;
      iii. Policy-based arguments and counter-arguments.
   c. Ideally, each component of the issue rule of law should be addressed by each party's perspective.
3. At the end of rule application, an issue prediction: a prediction as to the court's resolution of that issue/condition.

What are the ingredients, or content, of this section? Think of the rule application section as the place in which you express the parties' likely arguments. You already have begun to generate your arguments. Specifically, during the pre-drafting process (Chapters 13 and 14), after discerning the guiding factors, you then used those guiding factors as a basis to generate arguments. Those arguments are the material that you will use to draft the rule application.

## I. Content of the Arguments

Your rule application comprises arguments, both your client's arguments and the opposing party's arguments. As we have noted, the arguments that will be advanced by the parties can be called either "argument and counter-argument" or "analysis and counter-analysis." Note that it is not essential that you think of the "argument" or "analysis" as that of your client—these terms often refer to the *initial* arguments advanced in the rule application section, followed by responsive arguments ("counter-argument" or "counter-analysis").

### A. What Arguments Are Included in Your Rule Application?

Recall that lawyers use three primary forms of reasoning to make arguments: rule-based reasoning, analogical reasoning, and policy-based reasoning. We suggest you take this opportunity to ensure you can describe, in your own words, these three types of arguments. Review Chapters 9 through 12 to check or refresh your understanding of these forms of legal reasoning.

While analogical reasoning is the most prevalent, rule-based reasoning can be equally important. Thus, your rule application section likely will employ both types of reasoning and, when available, will also include policy arguments.

During the pre-drafting process (Chapters 13 and 14) you should already have generated many potential arguments based on your client's case. That pre-drafting work will greatly assist you as you draft your rule application, as you already will have an idea of what arguments you intend to make.

## B. How Are Arguments Conveyed? The Basic Formula for a Rule Application Paragraph

Recall the template for a rule application paragraph first presented in Chapter 15.

### Rule Application Paragraph

[INSERT TOPIC SENTENCE INDICATING PARAGRAPH'S SCOPE.] [INSERT ARGUMENTS THAT SUPPORT THE TOPIC SENTENCE, INCLUDING RULE-BASED ARGUMENTS, ANALOGICAL ARGUMENTS, AND (WHERE APPLICABLE) POLICY ARGUMENTS.]

As this template suggests, each paragraph in your rule application should begin with a topic sentence. That topic sentence introduces the paragraph's scope. Like all topic sentences, that sentence provides the reader with the context for the remainder of the paragraph. The topic sentence should not be an analogy because a single analogy is one part of the paragraph but not the topic of the entire paragraph.

Ineffective:  Starting with an Analogy Instead of a Topic Sentence
Like the dog in *Carr* who bit one person who required emergency care, Herky bit two people. Thus, both dogs are dangerous.

Effective:  Starting with a Topic Sentence Before Providing Arguments, Such as Analogies
The City will argue that the dog's biting history suggests he is dangerous. Like the dog in *Carr* who bit one person who

required emergency care, Herky also bit someone. Indeed, Herky bit people on two separate occasions, thus showing a stronger propensity toward biting than the dog in *Carr* who was deemed dangerous despite only biting one person. That neither person who was bitten by Herky required emergency care should carry little weight given that Herky bit two people in a mere one-month period. That suggests Herky is likely to bite again, with the possibility of inflicting more harm the next time.

Note that the ineffective example starts with an analogy instead of a topic sentence for the paragraph, makes weak use of the facts, and focuses on the comparison rather than the client. In contrast, the effective example begins with a helpful topic sentence rather than jumping immediately into an analogy, makes good use of the facts, and keeps the focus on the client, while using the comparisons as support. After the topic sentence, the remainder of the paragraph consists of arguments. You almost always will have an analogical argument, and you will often have a rule-based argument. The effective example includes both.

## C.  Weaving Facts with the Rule

Regardless of the types of arguments you make, your rule application should not simply recite facts. Instead, effective rule application requires you to weave case facts with the rule to make an argument. New legal writers often make the mistake of *monologuing*, reciting fact after fact after fact without tethering those facts to the legal rule. This leaves the reader to guess why those facts matter. By tethering the facts to the legal rule, the writer tells the reader not only why those facts matter, but also how the court arguably will view the facts based upon the rule.

### Ineffective: Monologuing
Herky bit two people. Specifically, Herky bit a child when the child wandered into his yard. In addition, three weeks later, Herky bit an adult when he was out for a walk with his owner.

### Effective: Weaving Facts with Rule
Herky's history of biting suggests he is dangerous. Herky not only has bitten people on two separate occasions, the two occasions were within mere weeks of each other. The frequency of the bites suggests that the biting was not simply a situational fluke, but rather that the dog has a propensity to bite and thus poses an ongoing danger. Moreover, that one bite occurred when the dog was outside of his property suggests that Herky poses a risk to the public at large.

The ineffective example is monologuing. Nowhere does the writer tether the facts (all the biting history) to the legal rule (whether the dog is dangerous and, specifically, the guiding factor of the dog's history of biting). The reader thus is left to guess why those facts are significant. In contrast, the effective rule-based argument avoids monologuing by tethering the facts to rule. This makes the argument clear, explaining why these facts matter and how these facts support the particular result for which the writer advocates.

## D. How Many Rule Application Paragraphs?

As you draft your rule application for each issue segment, be mindful that your rule application section for an issue will almost always have multiple paragraphs. The template simply shows the content of a single paragraph. As you can see from the memo excerpt at the end of this chapter and in the sample memos in Appendix A, each issue segment typically will have multiple rule application paragraphs.

# II. Organizing the Arguments

Recall our discussion in Chapter 16 where we examined how the global rule of law forms the large-scale organizational framework of the Discussion section. You announce the global rule of law in the global roadmap, which signals the remaining Discussion content for the reader. If the global rule of law has three arguable issues, the reader will anticipate a discussion of three issue segments (issue roadmap, followed by rule explanation for that issue, followed by rule application for that issue).

The smaller scale organization for the rule application of a particular issue—the issue segment comprised of the issue roadmap, rule explanation, and rule application—will be framed by the components of the rule for that particular issue: its definitions, standards, and guiding factors. You have announced those in the issue roadmap, leading the reader to anticipate that you will address how each side may assess each of those components.

So, in organizing the rule application, we want to keep in mind how each party will argue that the standards, definitions, and guiding factors compel a ruling in their favor. Although there is no definitive template for the *small-scale organization* of the rule application, there are two common approaches. Writers typically either organize the arguments by each *party's position* on all of the components of the rule for that issue, or they organize the rule application by the *issue components* (standards, definitions, and guiding factors). In either case, you want to make sure to address each party's position on all of the components of the rule.

**Party/position approach:** In the first approach, the writer organizes the rule application based upon the party/position it supports, putting together all the arguments that are favorable to one side for the various guiding factors. Under this *party/position approach*, the writer transitions to the arguments that are favorable to the other side (i.e., the counter-arguments) only after he has completed making the arguments for the first party.

Note that under this organizational pattern it does not matter which party's position you start with—your client's or the opposing party's. How do you determine which party's position to address first? It depends. In some cases, it simply doesn't matter. This is true when the arguments are relatively balanced and each party has several arguments to assert. However, when there is considerable material in favor of one party and the opposing party has little to argue, it makes sense to begin with the party with stronger support—the likely prevailing party. Order also matters when one party's argument provides the foundation for the other party's argument; here, you first want to lay out the foundational arguments, followed by the counter-arguments.

**Issue-components approach:** In the alternative approach, the writer organizes the rule application by standards, definitions, and guiding factors, putting together all of the arguments related to that standard, definition, or guiding factor, regardless of which party they support. Under this *issue-components approach*, you include both parties' arguments for that issue-component before proceeding to the next component.

Some considerations that weigh in favor of each organizational pattern follow:

| CONSIDERATIONS THAT WEIGH IN FAVOR OF ORGANIZING BY PARTY/POSITION | CONSIDERATIONS THAT WEIGH IN FAVOR OF ORGANIZING BY ISSUE-COMPONENT |
|---|---|
| Related standards, definitions, guiding factors | Distinct standards, definitions, guiding factors |
| Relatively short and pithy arguments | More complex arguments for some or all of the standards, definitions, guiding factors |

**Whatever organizational scheme you choose, your underlying content remains the same.** You will still present each party's entire position on the issue as framed by the issue-components. However, the order in which you communicate these points will vary.

Note that you will "wrap up" the analysis of each issue with a prediction as to the court's resolution of the issue. For the party/position approach, that prediction will come at the conclusion of the final par-ty's argument (known here as the final counter-arguments). At that point, the reader will have the benefit of the arguments both parties will advance.

In addition, if you use the issue-component organizational struc-ture, you might also elect to include "mini-predictions" at the con-clusion of the analysis of issue components, such as guiding factors. Keep in mind, though, that these mini-predictions are not a substitute for your issue prediction. Also, keep in mind that guiding factors are considerations, not requirements; a court need not actually reach a "conclusion" on each guiding factor individually. Thus, these mini-predictions simply signal to the reader how a court might view the analysis for that guiding factor.

The below examples illustrate each organization scheme. The first example illustrates a rule application organized using the issue-components approach. (Note, too, that we have indicated how the writer might include mini-predictions at the conclusion of rule appli-cation for each issue component if she elected to do so. Even where the writer elects to include these mini-predictions, there must also be an issue prediction, as this concludes the analysis of the issue for the reader.) The second example illustrates a rule application organized using the party-position approach.

## ▓ CONCEPT IN ACTION: Organizing Your Arguments

The following excerpt from the Warrantless Bomb Search hypotheti-cal is organized by the issue-components approach. We have formatted the "topic" sentences in bold to emphasize the organizational approach followed.

> **First, the objective information available to the agents suggested an immediate and severe risk.** A bomb prepared for rigging to a motorcycle presents a serious and immediate danger to the target of the explosion, any person who might be nearby, and law enforcement agents who attempt to defuse it. *Id.* at 961. Further, unlike the situation in *Purcell,* in which the information learned by the agents on site undermined the information contained in the tip, here the information learned by the agents on site corroborated the tip information. *See id.* When they arrived at the site, the agents knew that Van Zanda was previously connected to a mob bombing, and they also had received the informant's tip that the device was prepared for rigging to another gangster's motorcycle. Agents' concerns that a bomb was hidden inside the shipping container were then bolstered by Scooter the bomb-sniffing dog, who "hit" on the container. That corroboration of the tip and prior history is unlike the situation in *Purcell* in which the tip and prior history were not confirmed but instead were contradicted by what agents observed in the hotel room—only drug paraphernalia and the notable absence of any meth lab items. *See id.* Further, the bomb posed an immediate

risk even if the defendant had no intention of activating it—a bomb, especially a civilian one, is inherently unstable and can detonate accidentally. Faced with the credible evidence that there may be a bomb and that such bomb may explode, the risk of danger was high. *See id.* Indeed, this is precisely the type of risk for which the exigent circumstances exception exists: Every minute that the search is delayed due to having to obtain a warrant increases the likelihood that the bomb will detonate.

**Even so, Van Zanda may argue that objective information did not indicate an immediate risk.** While the risk from a bomb can be high and imminent, the information objectively known to the agents at the time of the search did not indicate that the bomb was unstable or likely to be detonated immediately. Instead, the objective evidence—a tip that the defendant planned to rig another gangster's motorcycle with a bomb—suggested it was unlikely that the bomb would be intentionally activated in the container and thus the bomb presented no immediate risk. Thus, just as the agents in *Purcell* lacked any "evidence to suggest that methamphetamine manufacture was ongoing," here the agents lacked evidence that would suggest that the threat from the bomb was imminent. *See id.* at 961.

> The writer could elect to provide additional direction in the form of a mini-prediction, such as: "On balance, the court will likely agree that the objective evidence indicated an immediate risk."

**Second, the agents subjectively believed that there was a risk from a bomb.** The agents' actions of clearing the site and wearing bomb suits indicate that they believed there was a risk. Further, upon information and belief, the agents will testify that they believed there was a strong likelihood of a risk from a bomb in the container. That is decidedly unlike the situation in *Purcell* in which no agent testified "to believing that methamphetamine cooking was ongoing." *See id.* at 961.

**Nonetheless, Van Zanda may contend that the agents did not truly subjectively believe there was a risk from a bomb given the unnecessarily long delay before they searched.** Likewise, Van Zanda may argue that the agents' subjective belief is best discerned from their actions, and here their actions show that they did not truly fear that a bomb might detonate. Thus, like the agents in *Purcell* who did not act immediately, here too the agents revealed a lack of legitimate concern about the claimed threat. *See id.* at 962.

> Potential mini-prediction: "The court likely will agree that the actions of the agents do not support their subjective belief in the risk." Note that this is a prediction as to the court's evaluation of the competing positions on the guiding factor, not a prediction as to the court's resolution of the issue.

**Finally, the agents' actions were consistent with the asserted risk.** The agents demonstrated a belief that there was an immediate risk of danger when they cleared employees out of the Van Zanda headquarters and donned specialized blast suits before the search of the container. These swift actions stand in stark contrast to the actions of the agents in *Purcell*, who took no protective measures that would be consistent with the asserted threat. *See id.* Further, although the agents here talked to The Earl before the search, they did so only to the extent necessary to gain information to assess the credibility of the tip. In contrast, in *Purcell*, the agents engaged in relatively lengthy conversation with the defendant's girlfriend that was not geared toward helping them assess the asserted threat. *Id.*

**In contrast, Van Zanda may argue that the agents' behavior was not consistent with the asserted risk.** Van Zanda will likely argue that the fact that agents spent ten minutes speaking with The Earl outside the shipping container prior to the search was inconsistent with the asserted risk. Moreover, during the period in which the agents spoke with The Earl, the agents took no protective measures, which was also not consistent with the asserted risk. That lack of urgency or protective measures is similar to the situation in *Purcell,* in which agents questioned the fugitive's girlfriend inside their hotel room and failed to evacuate hotel guests. *See id.* Just as the agents' actions in *Purcell* suggested they did not truly fear a meth lab explosion in the hotel room, here it is likely a court would reach the similar conclusion that the agents did not truly fear a bomb explosion. *See id.* at 962.

      **While the court may agree that the agents' actions were not entirely consistent with the claimed threat, it is likely that the court nonetheless will hold that there was an exigent circumstance based upon the risk of danger.** The agents eventually took protective measures, including clearing the area before conducting the search, which shows their level of concern at the time of search. Further evidence of the risk of danger stems from the fact that the information the agents learned on site heightened, rather than lessened, the credible threat.

— Here, the writer already included a mini-prediction on this guiding factor at the end of this paragraph.

    Now note how The Smell Shoppe hypothetical is organized using the party/position approach.

      **It is likely that Mr. Arnold will be able to show that he possessed a reasonable expectancy of entering into a valid business relationship.** Like the plaintiff's customers in *Chicago's Pizza*, the customers in Mr. Arnold's situation contemplated specific business relationships with him. *See id.* Mr. Arnold will argue that, like the testimony of the customers in *Chicago's Pizza*, he also has customers who can testify to their specific contemplation in conducting business with him. *See id.* Namely, Mr. Arnold himself will testify that he began hearing people in the community express concerns about his candles, including telling him that the candles "just weren't what they used to be." This is similar to the testimony of the customers in *Chicago's Pizza* who expressed that they clearly believed they were doing business with the plaintiff. *Id.* Indeed, in Mr. Arnold's case, the customers' contemplation that they were doing business with him is even stronger, insofar as the customers specifically complained that his candles were weak in potency and were burning down too quickly, notwithstanding the fact that he had not made any changes to his candle-making practices. The dissatisfied community members may also be called to testify to their specific contemplation of conducting business with Mr. Arnold's candle shop, similar to the testimony of the customers in *Chicago's Pizza*. *See id.*

      **In addition, Mr. Arnold will assert that customers in fact believed they were doing business with him, not Mr. Green.** As with the convincing testimony of the customers in *Chicago's Pizza*, Mr. Arnold can use the testimony of his customers to illustrate their belief that they were in fact doing business with him when they purchased their candles with the confidence that they would be strongly scented and long-lasting, just as Mr. Arnold's candles had proven to be. *See id.*

      **Alternatively, Mr. Green will argue that Mr. Arnold did not have a reasonable expectancy of a business relationship.** He will argue that unlike the defendant in *Chicago's Pizza*, he did not receive phone calls from customers who directly indicated that they believed they were doing business with Mr. Arnold. *See id.* He may further distinguish his situation from that of *Chicago's Pizza* by showing that he did not process the order from a customer who conveyed that she believed she was purchasing from Mr. Arnold. *See id.* Additionally, Mr. Green may argue that if other customers believed they were conducting business with Mr. Arnold's business, he was not made aware of this misapprehension. Notwithstanding Green's assertions, it is likely that Mr. Arnold will prevail on this element because he will be able to show that his customers specifically contemplated doing business with him and believed that they were in fact doing business with him.

---

Here are examples showing what your rule application section outline would look like for each organizational approach if you have two guiding factors.

### Organization Using Issue-Components Approach

I. Arguments for Guiding Factor 1
   a. Guiding Factor 1 arguments for party 1
   b. Guiding Factor 1 arguments for party 2

II. Arguments for Guiding Factor 2
   a. Guiding Factor 2 arguments for party 1
   b. Guiding Factor 2 arguments for party 2

### Organization Using Parties/Position Approach

I. Arguments for Party 1
   a. Guiding Factor 1 arguments for party 1
   b. Guiding Factor 2 arguments for party 1

II. Arguments for Party 2
   a. Guiding Factor 1 arguments for party 2
   b. Guiding Factor 2 arguments for party 2

As you can see, under both approaches the writer advances arguments for both parties based upon both guiding factors. It is simply the organization that differs; i.e., either all of one party's arguments are presented together before moving on to the other party's arguments, or alternatively, both parties' arguments for one issue-component are presented before moving on to both parties' arguments for the next issue-component.

Note, too, that under either approach your rule application almost certainly will contain more than one paragraph. In the two examples above, each major heading (those designated with Roman numerals) would be its own paragraph. This means that under either approach your rule application would include at least two paragraphs. Indeed, the rule application may end up being more than two paragraphs if the content under the heading warrants it. For example, under the issue-components approach above, imagine that the arguments for guiding factor one for each party were extensive. In this case, each party's arguments for guiding factor one might warrant its own paragraph. You need not decide how many paragraphs to break your rule application into when you are outlining; instead, as you are drafting (or when you are revising), you should consider if a paragraph should be divided for the reader's benefit. In general, any paragraph that is longer than two-thirds of a page should be split into more than one paragraph.

You may be wondering if you have to choose one organizational approach for all of the issues in your Discussion or whether you could, for example, use the party/position approach for one issue and the issue-components approach for another issue. Using varied organizational approaches would be perfectly acceptable. In making this determination, you simply need to decide—for each issue—which approach is most effective using the considerations discussed above. If you do decide to use more than one organizational scheme in the same memo, be mindful that this could create confusion for the reader. Effective topic sentences will help alleviate any potential confusion.

## III. Presenting the Arguments: Stylistic Options

Once you have decided which organizational approach to employ, you have a stylistic choice to make in terms of how you format the arguments in your rule application.

In one format you will *explicitly* announce the party making the argument, such as "Smith will argue that she acted in self-defense." Following that statement, you will have a series of comparisons to cases in which the defendant successfully argued self-defense and distinctions from cases in which the defendant did not prove self-defense. You would then provide a transition to counter-arguments, such as, "In contrast, the prosecution will assert that Smith has not demonstrated self-defense." That statement would be followed by comparisons between the client facts and cases in which the defendant did not prove self-defense and distinctions between cases in which the defendant successfully argued self-defense. In this format, the arguments are specifically labeled as relating to a particular party's position.

Alternatively, you can format the rule application so that the party's position is *implicit*. In this format, you would likely begin with the arguments you believe will ultimately be successful: "The court likely will conclude that Smith acted in self-defense." In this format you are not labeling the argument as the one advanced by Smith, but it is implicit that this is the position Smith would advance. Under this format you can also assert the opposing party's argument implicitly, beginning that part of the application with something like "Alternatively, certain arguments suggest that Smith did not act in self-defense." This assertion implicitly announces the prosecution's position without labeling it as such.

The "argument labeling" format is typically easier to work with for beginning legal writers. Advancing the arguments implicitly is more complicated, and it is more difficult to lead the reader through the application.

## IV. Drafting Effective Analogical Arguments

Recall from Chapter 11 that effective analogical arguments share three features. First, they are based on a particular component of the rule for the condition, most often around a guiding factor. Second, they must be factually detailed, including the pertinent facts from not only your client's case, but also from the precedent case. Third, when comparing facts from a precedent to facts from the client's case, the focus should remain on the client's case. The client's case is, after all, the reason for the memo, and the analogies are arguments in the client's case.

What does it mean to say the argument should be based around part of the test, such as a guiding factor? It means that the writer should not only craft the analogy around a part of the test but should do so explicitly. Consider the following sentence in which the writer makes a comparison: "An apple is like a pear." If the rule is based upon whether the item is a fruit, that argument could, with more detail, be effective; e.g., "Like a pear, an apple also is a fruit." Does that seem excessive and unnecessary? Consider if the rule is not whether the item is a fruit but whether the item is round. If that is the rule, the argument "An apple is like a pear" is dead wrong. The necessary analogy would make its dissimilarity clear: "Unlike a pear that is oblong, an apple's shape is circular." The basis of comparison matters. By making that basis of comparison explicit, your reader can himself evaluate the merits of your argument.

As you keep in mind the features of effective analogical arguments, pay particular attention to ensuring your arguments make specific and explicit comparisons and distinctions. This means that you will refer explicitly to the facts of the precedent as well as to your client's facts. This can seem repetitive, given that the rule application immediately follows the rule explanation, where you have just set forth facts from the precedent cases. Nonetheless, it is essential that you draw the comparisons explicitly so that the reader does not have to infer or backtrack to identify the precedent case facts that are relevant to a particular argument. In addition, it is important that you actually *tether* the client facts to precedent case facts. This means that you explain the relationship between client facts and precedent facts, showing the reader how similarities or differences compel a certain result. It is insufficient to merely place facts side by side, hoping the reader will *reason by proximity*, and infer the relationship merely by your placement of material.

Consider, for example, an argument that reads: "An apple is round. Likewise, a tennis ball is round." We can infer that the reason the writer is putting these facts side by side is so that we can see that these items are similar in shape. But the writer does not actually make that analogy for us. She leaves it to us to connect those dots. Far better would be a sentence that reads, "Like a tennis ball that is round, an apple's shape is similarly round." We avoid making the reader reason by proximity and, instead, clearly state that the shape of the items forms the basis for comparison.

Consider the following ineffective legal example.

> Mr. Arnold will argue that he began hearing people in the community express concerns about his candles, including telling him that they "just weren't what they used to be." In *Chicago's Pizza*, customers said they clearly believed they were doing business with the plaintiff. *Id*.

Here the writer has juxtaposed client facts with facts from the precedent case but has not explained the relationship for the reader. The reader is left to figure out how these facts are similar and, more importantly, why that similarity matters. It's not enough to tee up the ball; you need to hit it square on and follow through on your swing. In other words, do not rely on the reader to make (the right) assumptions.

Instead, the writer needs to explain the relationship between the facts, showing the significance of similarities or distinctions. Consider the following improvement:

> It is likely that Mr. Arnold will be able to show that he possessed a reasonable expectancy of entering into a valid business relationship. Like the plaintiff's customers in *Chicago's Pizza*, the customers in Mr. Arnold's situation contemplated specific business relationships with him. *See id*. Mr. Arnold will argue that, like the testimony of the customers in *Chicago's Pizza*, he also has customers who can testify to their specific contemplation in conducting business with him. *See id*. Namely, Mr. Arnold himself will testify that he began hearing people in the community express concerns about his candles, including telling him that the candles "just weren't what they used to be." This is similar to the testimony of the customers in *Chicago's Pizza*, who expressed that they clearly believed they were doing business with the plaintiff. *Id*. Indeed, in Mr. Arnold's case, the customers' contemplation that they were doing business with him is even stronger, insofar as the customers specifically complained that his candles were weak in potency and were burning down too quickly, notwithstanding the fact that he had not made any changes to his candle-making practices. The dissatisfied community members may also be called to testify to their specific contemplation of conducting business with Mr. Arnold's candle shop, similar to the testimony of the customers in *Chicago's Pizza*. *See id*.

In addition, Mr. Arnold will assert that customers in fact believed they were doing business with him, not Mr. Green. As with the convincing testimony of the customers in *Chicago's Pizza*, Mr. Arnold can use the testimony of his customers to illustrate their belief that they were in fact doing business with him when they purchased their candles with the confidence that they would be strongly scented and long-lasting, just as Mr. Arnold's candles had proven to be. *See id.*

Notice how the writer in this comparison explains the relationship between precedent facts and the client's facts. The writer focuses on the reason that the condition arguably is satisfied; i.e., the customers in both the precedent case and in the client's situation made statements that evidenced their belief that they were doing business with the plaintiff. The writer did not settle for a comparison, saying merely that the client's situation was similar to the precedent case; instead he went one step further by showing how the client's facts are arguably even more compelling.

 **EQUIPPING YOURSELF: Use of Citations and Signals**

Developing the habit of capturing citation information, including page numbers, during legal research can save you considerable time when you start to write. As you are aware, each time you refer directly or indirectly to a legal source in a memo you must provide attribution in the form of a citation. Where the textual sentence refers directly to the source, as in quoting or directly paraphrasing material from the source, you simply provide a citation at the end of the sentence.

Sometimes the cited source *indirectly* supports the textual sentence, or, less often, it may contradict the material in the textual sentence. In that case, you will use a **signal** to introduce the citation. These introductory signals tell your reader how the source supports or contradicts the textual sentence. They are discussed in detail in the citation manuals *The Bluebook* and *The ALWD Guide to Legal Citation*.

The *"See"* signal indicates indirect support; the reader would need to make an inference from the cited authority to understand how it supports the textual sentence. Therefore, you will likely use the *"See"* signal in your rule application where you have textual sentences that blend content from your client's claim or charge with material from a judicial decision. You should have lots of these blended sentences in rule application as you analogize and distinguish client facts from the facts of analogous cases. So, for example, recall our Dangerous Dog hypothetical. When you write the rule application for that example, you might have a sentence like this: "Like the schnauzer at issue in *State v. Jones*, Watkins will argue that her Doberman is not a dangerous dog." Because part of the material in the textual sentence refers to a precedential authority (*Jones*), and part refers to the client's facts, you would include the *"See"* signal in front of your citation to *Jones*, as the reader has to infer the relationship between *Jones* and the client's facts.

---

### ✂ CHECK IN: Identifying and Assessing Discussion Ingredients

For each excerpt below, answer the following questions related to the wiretap hypothetical:

- In what component of the memo (e.g., roadmap, rule explanation, rule application) would you expect to see the following material?
- For that particular memo component, has the writer incorporated sufficient detail and presented the material effectively? Explain the basis for your answer.

#### Excerpt 1:

Like *Liberte*, the delay in sealing the evidence in this case was due to a mistake. *Id*.

#### Excerpt 2:

In *Liberte*, the investigator forgot to submit the evidence right away to be sealed. *Id*. Here, the personnel in the lab changed and caused the delay.

#### Excerpt 3:

Like the delay in *Liberte*, which occurred because of the investigator's forgetfulness, here too the delay was caused simply by human error. *Id*. Specifically, there was miscommunication between intake personnel at the lab and the technical staff. While unfortunate, such miscommunication is not uncommon in a busy work unit and cannot be considered unusual.

#### Excerpt 4:

Like the delay in *Liberte*, which occurred because of the investigator's forgetfulness, the defendant will assert that the delay in this case was similarly caused simply by human error. *Id*. Specifically, the defendant will emphasize that there was miscommunication between intake personnel at the lab and the technical staff, a common and foreseeable error not unlike forgetfulness. *Id*. While unfortunate, such miscommunication is not uncommon in a busy work unit, cannot be considered unusual, and, like the insufficient excuse for delay offered in *Liberte*, should similarly preclude use of the evidence here. *Id*.

#### Excerpt 5:

Like the delay in *Liberte*, which occurred because of the investigator's forgetfulness, the defendant will assert that the delay in this case was similarly caused simply by human error. *Id*. Specifically,

> the defendant will emphasize that there was miscommunica-
> tion between intake personnel at the lab and the technical staff,
> a common and foreseeable error not unlike forgetfulness. *Id.*
> While unfortunate, such miscommunication is not uncommon
> in a busy work unit, cannot be considered unusual and, like the
> insufficient excuse for delay offered in *Liberte*, should similarly
> preclude use of the evidence here. *Id.*
>
> In contrast, the State will assert that the forgetfulness asso-
> ciated with the delay in *Liberte* was entirely inexcusable and a
> failure to demonstrate "reasonable diligence." *Id.* In contrast,
> the miscommunication, while unfortunate, cannot be equated
> with the inattention to detail by the government in *Liberte* and
> should excuse the failure to seal in this case. *Id.*

## V. The Relationship Between Rule Explanation and Rule Application: Impact on Organization

You may be wondering if you must always include all your rule explanation paragraphs for an issue/condition before moving on to your
rule application paragraphs. In other words, is it ever appropriate to
present some of your rule application without first having presented
all of your rule explanation? The short answer is yes. Providing some
rule application before concluding your rule explanation can be appropriate, depending on how conceptually distinct the guiding factors are
from each other.

Recall from Chapter 17 that while there typically will be only one
rule explanation paragraph when using a single authority, it can be
effective to break your rule explanation into separate paragraphs if the
guiding factors are analytically distinct. This same logic applies to the
organization of your rule explanation and rule application sections.

Namely, when the guiding factors for an issue/condition are relatively distinct from each other, it may make sense to organize your
analysis by guiding factor, with rule explanation immediately followed
by rule application. That is, for the first guiding factor (or group of
related guiding factors), you would present rule explanation followed
by rule application. Then you would do the same for the next distinct
guiding factor(s). Breaking up the discussion in this way enables your
reader to focus on these distinct aspects of the issue/condition separately, thus avoiding the confusion that might arise if your reader must
process too much unrelated information at the same time.

Organizationally, this means your outline for an issue segment
might be as follows, where guiding factor three is analytically distinct
from guiding factors one and two:

> **Issue roadmap:**
>
> RE Guiding Factors 1 & 2
>
> RA Guiding Factors 1 & 2
>
> RE Guiding Factor 3
>
> RA Guiding Factor 3

In contrast, when the guiding factors are conceptually similar, it would not be effective to provide some rule application before completely presenting your rule explanation. Rather, with similar guiding factors, it makes sense to include all rule explanation followed by all rule application. Thus, where the guiding factors for an issue/condition are interrelated, your outline for that issue segment would be:

> **Issue roadmap:**
>
> RE Guiding Factors 1, 2 & 3
>
> RA Guiding Factors 1, 2 & 3

Note that if the guiding factors are relatively distinct, you likely will have chosen to organize your rule application by issue-components, not party/position.

## VI. The Role of Rule-Based Arguments in Your Rule Application: Using Rule-Based Arguments in Conjunction with Analogical Arguments

While analogical arguments are the bread-and-butter of your legal analysis, do not overlook the role of rule-based arguments in your rule application section. Recall from Chapter 10 that rule-based reasoning takes the existing legal rule and applies it to the client's facts. Unlike analogical arguments, rule-based reasoning does not rely on drawing similarities or distinctions between the client's facts and the facts from a precedent. Instead, it takes the rule and shows why the facts do or do not satisfy that rule. The fact that it takes the rule itself and applies it directly to the client's situation makes it a powerful tool.

The following excerpt, taken from the Warrantless Bomb Search memo in Appendix A, illustrates a rule application paragraph in which the writer begins with a rule-based argument and then makes an analogical argument. This example demonstrates how including a rule-based argument before making an analogical argument is often a useful technique. Starting with a rule-based argument allows the writer to describe the salient client facts that relate to this guiding factor (i.e., whether the agents' behavior was consistent with the asserted risk), such that the analogical argument that follows is less verbose and thus less cumbersome. Having already described the client facts as part of the rule-based argument simplifies the analogical argument: The writer can immediately move into the comparison to the precedent facts and make a succinct comparison.

Rule-based reasoning (focusing on whether behavior is "consistent with the asserted risk" and, based upon that part of the rule, arguing that client's behavior falls short)

Analogical reasoning (also focusing on whether behavior is "consistent with the asserted risk" but doing so by comparing relevant facts about behavior in precedent case to relevant facts about behavior in client's situation)

In contrast, Van Zanda may argue that the agents' behavior was not consistent with the asserted risk. Van Zanda will likely argue that the fact that agents spent ten minutes speaking with The Earl outside the shipping container prior to the search was inconsistent with the asserted risk. Moreover, during the period in which the agents spoke with The Earl, the agents took no protective measures, which was also not consistent with the asserted risk. That lack of urgency or protective measures is similar to the situation in *Purcell*, in which agents questioned the fugitive's girlfriend inside their hotel room and failed to evacuate hotel guests. *See id.* Just as the agents' actions in *Purcell* suggested they did not truly fear a meth lab explosion in the hotel room, here it is likely a court would reach the similar conclusion that the agents did not truly fear a bomb explosion. *See id.* at 962.

# The Next Level: Legal Analysis and Drafting a Legal Discussion Using Multiple Authorities

Up until this point, you have been using a single authority to analyze your legal question. In this module, the focus shifts to drafting with multiple, synthesized authorities. While using only a single authority can effectively teach the foundations of legal analysis, in practice lawyers typically must analyze multiple authorities to answer a client's legal question. In Part I of this module (Chapters 19 through 22), we focus on pre-drafting analysis using multiple authorities. In Part II of this module (Chapters 23 through 26), we focus on drafting the legal Discussion using multiple authorities.

### PART I

# Legal Analysis and Pre-Drafting Analysis Using Multiple Authorities

**R**ecall the process you engaged in for pre-drafting analysis using a single authority. In a nutshell, you: (1) determined the global rule—its result, conditions, and the way the conditions relate to one another; (2) examined how each condition had been applied in a similar prior opinion—identifying the court's fact-based holding for that condition; and (3) determined the rule for each condition—its definitions, standards, explicit guiding factors, and the implicit guiding factors you discerned from the fact-based holding.

With multiple authorities, the goal is the same: you must determine the global rule and, within that rule, the rule for each issue/condition. You must also examine prior applications of the rule for each condition. However, you will now be using multiple authorities to inform your analysis and will therefore have to *synthesize* the prior authorities to determine the rule. You also will have to determine which cases best illustrate the rule's application for any given issue.

You will discover that having additional authorities that interpret and/or apply the rule increases your understanding of the rule and its application. Specifically, each additional authority may: (1) modify the global rule, such as by adding an exception to it; (2) modify the rule for one or more conditions of the global rule, such as by adding a standard or definition, by narrowing or broadening guiding factors, by adding new guiding factors, and/or by making implicit guiding factors explicit; and (3) show the rule's application to a similar set of facts, enhancing your understanding of how the rule works in practice.

# Making the Transition: The Components of a Multiple Authorities Legal Discussion

Before we explore the process of pre-drafting with multiple authorities, this chapter glimpses ahead to the ultimate product of that pre-drafting analysis: the legal Discussion in a memorandum that uses multiple authorities.

---

### Study Guide Questions for Chapter 19

1. Generally speaking, what are the components of a legal Discussion that incorporates multiple authorities?
2. What role do multiple authorities play in the global roadmap?
3. What role do multiple authorities play in each issue/condition roadmap?
4. How is the rule explanation section affected by the integration of multiple authorities?
5. How is the rule application section affected by the integration of multiple authorities?
6. What new terms were introduced in this chapter? How do these terms relate to your existing understanding of predictive memo writing? Did your understanding of any other terms change as a result of reading this chapter?

---

Up until this point, your legal analysis has consisted of using a single case. That single case fulfilled all purposes of your legal analysis and drafting—understanding the rule of law, showing how the law had been applied to a precedent case, and making analogies to your client's situation. You now have a solid foundation for what lawyers actually do: use multiple authorities to analyze their client's situation. Let's first consider what stays the same and what changes when adding more authorities into the mix.

## I. What Is the Same?

The **large-scale organization** of the Discussion remains unchanged; the Discussion still contains a single global roadmap paragraph that announces the global rule. As always, the conditions announced in the global rule provide a framework for the subsequent analysis. The reader will expect to see each arguable condition (issue) analyzed in its own issue segment. At the end of the Discussion, the reader will expect a Conclusion.

The **small-scale organization** of the Discussion also stays largely the same; each issue/condition still has its own issue segment. In each issue segment the reader still expects a full analysis of that issue, which still includes an issue roadmap followed by the rule explanation and, finally, the rule application for that issue.

Thus, the components of each part of your Discussion remain largely the same. They are outlined below with the changes noted in bold.

### Global Roadmap

1. A topic sentence that includes a global prediction as to the client's claim or charge.
2. The **synthesized** global rule of law, with its conditions and the relationship between the conditions clearly set forth, and with proper attribution.
3. An announcement of any non-issues, which are conditions that will not be addressed in the memo, ideally with a brief explanation as to why the conditions will not be addressed.
4. An announcement of the issues that will be addressed in the memo.
5. A global prediction, which is the prediction as to the resolution of the client's claim or charge, supported by key client facts related to that global prediction. A sentence or two should suffice, as this is simply the overall prediction and does not contain the separate issue predictions that will appear at the end of each issue roadmap.

### Issue Roadmaps

1. A topic sentence that announces the issue/condition that will be addressed in the issue roadmap.
2. The **synthesized** rule of law for the issue/condition: any definitions, standards, or guiding factors related to the court's analysis of the issue/condition.
3. The rule proof: the **synthesized** fact-based **holdings** from the **precedents**, which provides "proof" of the rule.
4. A prediction of the resolution of that issue/condition, supported by key client facts related to that prediction.

### Rule Explanation Paragraphs

1. A framing sentence that illustrates how the guiding factors inform the court's analysis of the issue/condition.

2. Facts from the precedent case that are related to those guiding factors.
3. The court's holding on the issue/condition in light of those facts.
4. The court's reasoning; i.e., why it resolved the issue the way it did.

### Rule Application Paragraphs

1. Broken down by the components of the rule of law for the condition, most typically by guiding factors.
2. For each component:
   a. A topic or thesis sentence: an announcement of the aspect of the issue rule of law for the condition that will be addressed.
   b. One or more forms of legal reasoning to support arguments:
      i. Analogical arguments and counter-arguments, comparing and contrasting facts from the precedent case to the client's case;
      ii. Rule-based arguments and counter-arguments;
      iii. Policy-based arguments and counter-arguments.
   c. Ideally, each component of the issue rule of law should be addressed by each party's perspective.
3. At end of rule application, an issue prediction: a prediction as to the court's resolution of that issue/condition.

### Global Conclusion

1. A global prediction as to the resolution of the client's claim or charge.
2. A reiteration of the issue prediction for each issue/condition.

## II.  What Is Different?

The large-scale and small-scale organization of your Discussion largely remain the same as they were when you used only a single authority. You can see from the list above that the biggest change is that you will now be using the *synthesized* global rule of law and *synthesized* rule of law for the condition proved by *synthesized* fact-based holdings. Chapter 20 discusses in detail the process of discerning the synthesized rule of law, and Chapter 21 provides guidelines for selecting the best cases to both discern the legal rules and make arguments.

Although your Discussion components and organization remain largely the same, the content within the various parts of the Discussion changes when you synthesize and integrate multiple authorities. Each additional authority potentially brings new information about the rule of law and its application. That new information may confirm, enhance, and/or modify your understanding of the existing rule of law. In turn, that new understanding may be reflected in the following components:

- Roadmap paragraphs: Additional authorities likely will modify the roadmap paragraphs. At a minimum, you will be citing additional authorities to support your synthesized rule of law, particularly in issue roadmaps. You also likely will have more detailed rules of law and rule proofs for the various issues. Chapter 24 delves into drafting roadmap paragraphs with multiple authorities, including revised paragraph templates.
- Rule explanation: In order to integrate the additional authorities, you will add content to the rule explanation. Chapter 25 explains how rule explanation changes with multiple authorities, including both techniques to use (framing sentences, transitions, signals), pitfalls to avoid (the parade of cases), and options for organizing this section (by guiding factors or by the cases).
- Rule application: The expanded rule explanation likely will lead you to incorporate additional or more refined arguments. Chapter 26 explains how rule application changes with multiple authorities, including tips for effectively conveying this information and options for organizing this section (by issue-component or by party/position).
- Conclusion: It is possible that the predicted resolution of an issue/condition or the overall resolution of the claim/charge may change as a result of the new understanding of the rule.

With the addition of multiple authorities, more variation exists in the organization and content of your Discussion. As a result, you now will make even more independent choices about organization and content. For instance, the templates introduced in Module III will apply even more loosely.

 **CONCEPT IN ACTION: Integrating Multiple Authorities into a Memo**

Read the following annotated Discussion from the multiple authorities memorandum in The Smell Shoppe hypothetical. (The entire memorandum, including the Heading, Question Presented, etc., is in Appendix B.) As you read, use the annotations to assist you in seeing how the multiple authorities have been integrated into the Discussion. Specifically, consider the large- and small-scale organization of the Discussion; where and how additional authorities are included; and, in general, which parts of the Discussion have been most impacted by the inclusion of additional authorities.

## DISCUSSION

Mr. Arnold will likely be unsuccessful in his tortious interference with business expectancy claim against Mr. Green. In order to successfully prevail in this claim, Mr. Arnold will need to prove four elements: "(1) [the plaintiff's] reasonable expectancy of entering into a valid business relationship; (2) the defendant's knowledge of the expectancy; (3) the defendant's intentional and unjustified interference that prevents the realization of business expectancy; and (4) damages resulting from the interference." *Chicago's Pizza, Inc. v. Chicago's Pizza Franchise Ltd., USA*, 893 N.E.2d 981, 993 (Ill. App. Ct. 2008). *See also RRRR Inc. v. Plaza 440 Private Residences Condo. Assn.*, 2017 IL App. (1st) 160194 at *7 (2017) (citing elements from *Chicago's Pizza*). Per the instruction of the senior associate, this memo will not discuss whether Mr. Green knew of Mr. Arnold's expectancy, nor will it discuss whether Mr. Arnold suffered damages as a result of the interference. Instead, this memo will only discuss whether Mr. Arnold possessed a reasonable expectancy of entering into a valid business relationship and whether it was Mr. Green's intentional and unjustified interference that prevented the realization of Mr. Arnold's business expectancy.

*Notice how this additional, more recent authority, RRRR, simply reinforces that the rule of law announced in Chicago's Pizza remains in effect.*

### 1. Whether Arnold Possessed a Reasonable Expectancy of Entering into a Relationship

The court will first consider whether Mr. Arnold possessed a reasonable expectancy of entering into a valid business relationship. *Chicago's Pizza*, 893 N.E.2d at 993. In assessing this reasonable expectancy, the court will consider the specific contemplation of customers and their belief that they were doing business with the plaintiff. *See, e.g., id.* A plaintiff will be found to have possessed a reasonable expectancy of entering into a valid business relationship when specific customers called the defendant's store with the belief that they were calling and doing business with the plaintiff. *Chicago's Pizza*, 893 N.E.2d at 993-94. In addition, the court will also consider the amount of contact between the plaintiff and prospective customers. *Mannion v. Stallings & Co.*, 561 N.E.2d 1134, 1139 (Ill. App. Ct. 1990). A court will hold that a plaintiff possessed a reasonable expectancy of entering into a valid business relationship when the plaintiff had moved past negotiations with prospective customers and had received a signed agreement providing compensation amounts. *Id.* Because Mr. Arnold had contact with several people regarding their experiences while shopping at Mr. Green's candle store, and the customers expressed the belief that they were shopping at Mr. Arnold's store, Mr. Arnold will likely prevail on this element.

*Mannion provided an additional, implicit, guiding factor.*

*Here, we use the fact-based holding of Mannion as rule proof for our implicit guiding factor.*

When customers demonstrate specific contemplation of doing business with the plaintiff and they express the belief that they are doing business with the plaintiff, the plaintiff will be successful in showing a reasonable expectancy of entering into a valid business relationship. *Chicago's Pizza*, 893 N.E.2d at 994. In *Chicago's Pizza*, the court determined that the testifying customers contemplated a business relationship with the plaintiff. 893 N.E.2d at 993. The court stated that it was clear that the testifying customers contemplated a business relationship with the plaintiff, because one customer stated that he called the defendant's store believing it was one of the plaintiff's four locations and because he also asked for the phone number to another one of the plaintiff's locations so that it could deliver to him. *Id.* This customer then proceeded to place an order with the defendant's store. *Id.* Another customer similarly testified that he did believe that he was ordering from the plaintiff when in fact he was ordering from the defendant. *Id.* at 993-94. Because the plaintiff successfully demonstrated a specific contemplation from the customers and because the customers expressed belief that they were doing business with the plaintiff, the court found in favor of the plaintiff on the element. *Id.*

In contrast, where there is no contemplation by customers that they are doing business with the plaintiff, the court will not find a reasonable expectancy of business relationship. *Euclid Ins. Agencies, Inc. v. Am. Ass'n of Orthodontists*, No. 95 C 3308, 1997 WL 548069, at *4 (N.D. Ill. 1997). In *Euclid Insurance Agencies* the plaintiff had no contact with prospective customers, and the customers therefore had no specific contemplation of doing business with the plaintiff. *Id.* The lack of contemplation by customers therefore contributed to the court's conclusion that the plaintiff did not have a reasonable expectancy of entering into a business relationship with the customers. *Id.*

In addition, when a plaintiff has had significant contact with prospective customers, the court will hold that the plaintiff has established a reasonable expectation of business relationship. *Mannion*, 561 N.E.2d at 1139. In *Mannion* the court noted that several steps had been taken by the plaintiff to secure a particular line of business with a specific customer. *Id.* Because the plaintiff had received written correspondence outlining a particular line of business with a contemplated customer with whom the defendant also interacted, the court ruled in favor of the plaintiff, finding it had a reasonable expectation of a business relationship. *Id.* In contrast, where the plaintiff has never had contact with prospective customers, the court will determine that there is no expectancy of establishing a business relationship. *Euclid Ins. Agencies*, 1997 WL 548069, at *4. In *Euclid Insurance Agencies*, an insurance provider claimed tortious interference with business expectancy against a professional association that provided insurance to its members. *Id.* The court held there was no expectancy of establishing such a relationship, placing particular emphasis on the fact that the plaintiff had never dealt directly with any members of the professional organization regarding insurance. *Id.* Because the plaintiff had never dealt directly with the prospective customers, the court ruled that the plaintiff failed to establish a reasonable expectation of business relationship. *Id.* at *5.

It is likely that Mr. Arnold will be able to show that he possessed a reasonable expectancy of entering into a valid business relationship. Like the plaintiff's customers in *Chicago's Pizza*, the customers in Mr. Arnold's situation contemplated specific business relationships with him. 893 N.E.2d at 993. Mr. Arnold will argue that like the testimony of the customers in *Chicago's Pizza*, he too will be able to call customers to testify to their specific contemplation in conducting business with him. *See id.* Namely, Mr. Arnold himself will testify that he began hearing people in the community express concerns about his candles, as they were telling him that the candles "just weren't what they used to be." This is similar to the testimony of the customers in *Chicago's Pizza* who testified that they clearly believed they were doing business with the plaintiff. *See id.* at 994. His relationship with customers is therefore even stronger than that of the plaintiff in *Mannion* who was able to establish a reasonable expectation of business relationship on the basis of a developing, as opposed to established, relationship. *See* 561 N.E.2d at 1139. It can also be contrasted with the unsuccessful plaintiff in *Euclid Insurance Agencies* that was unable to establish a reasonable expectation of business relationship because it had never been in direct contact with prospective customers. *See* 1997 WL 548069, at *4. As with the convincing testimony of the customers in *Chicago's Pizza*, and the contact between the plaintiff and prospective customer in *Mannion*, Mr. Arnold can use the testimony of his customers to establish their belief that they were in fact doing business with him when they purchased their candles. *See Chicago's Pizza*, 893 N.E.2d at 994; *see also Mannion*, 561 N.E.2d at 1139.

> Here we set up a rule application with *Mannion*, showing that Arnold's facts are even more compelling than those at issue in *Mannion*.

> **Rule application**: Arnold's position that his situation can be distinguished from that of the unsuccessful plaintiff in *Euclid* and is instead more comparable to *Chicago's Pizza* and *Mannion*.

Alternatively, Mr. Green can argue that unlike the defendant in *Chicago's Pizza*, he did not receive phone calls from customers directly indicating that they believed they were doing business with the plaintiff. *See* 893 N.E.2d at 994. He may further distinguish his situation from that of *Chicago's Pizza* by showing that he did not proceed to process an order after learning that the customer believed she was purchasing from the plaintiff. *See id.* Mr. Green may also assert the argument that unlike the plaintiff in *Mannion*, Mr. Arnold was not in any transactional stages with the customers. *See* 561 N.E.2d at 1139. Further, Mr. Green will point out that Mr. Arnold had not taken orders from the customers and did not receive any statements outlining compensation. *See id.* Mr. Green may assert that it is unclear whether the customers ever had contact with Mr. Arnold, similar to the customers in *Euclid Insurance Agencies* who had no direct contact with the plaintiff. *See* 1997 WL 548069, at *4. Notwithstanding, it is likely that Mr. Arnold will prevail on this element because his customers will demonstrate a specific contemplation of doing business with him and a belief that they were in fact doing business with him.

> Green's rule application and attempt to distinguish his position from *Mannion*.

> Green's rule application, attempting to favorably reconcile his position with the ruling in *Euclid*.

### 2. Whether Green's Intentional and Unjustified Interference Prevented the Business Expectancy

Next, the court will consider whether it was Mr. Green's intentional and unjustified interference that prevented Mr. Arnold's realization of a business expectancy. *Chicago's Pizza*, 893 N.E.2d at 993. In assessing this element, the court will consider the defendant's conduct in facilitating a mistaken belief of customers as to an affiliation with the plaintiff's business. *See, e.g., id.* at 994. The court will also consider whether the defendant's challenged conduct was privileged. *Mannion*, 561 N.E.2d at 1140. A plaintiff will successfully demonstrate that it was the defendant's intentional and unjustified interference that prevented the realization of business expectancy when the defendant allows customers to place orders with their business while being dishonest with those customers when they inquire about the defendant's affiliation to the plaintiff's business. *Chicago's Pizza*, 893 N.E.2d at 993. Further, a plaintiff can demonstrate interference with a business expectancy when the defendant diverts business opportunities by representing an affiliation with the plaintiff through advertising materials. *E.J. McKernan Co.*

> Note that we have taken the guiding factors we used in the single authority memo with *Chicago's Pizza* ("the defendant's conduct in allowing customers to place orders under a mistaken belief, the defendant's truthfulness to the customers regarding an affiliation with the plaintiff's business, and the content of any of the defendant's advertisement") and have collapsed them into this guiding factor ("facilitating a mistaken belief of customers"). This enables us to better capture and thus better communicate the guiding factors.

> *Mannion* provides another guiding factor.

> This fact-based holding from *E.J. McKernan* provides additional rule proof for the guiding factor of "facilitating a mistaken belief of customers."

*v. Gregory*, 623 N.E.2d 981, 995 (Ill. App. Ct. 1993). In contrast, where the defendant's challenged actions are privileged, the court will hold that the defendant's actions are not an unjustified interference. *RRRR Inc.*, 2017 IL App. (1st) 160194, at *26. Because Mr. Green was not dishonest about his business's affiliation, did not divert business opportunities, and may be able to assert a privilege, it is unlikely that Mr. Arnold will prevail on this element.

*RRRR* provides a fact-based holding for the new guiding factor related to privilege.

When a defendant facilitates a mistaken belief by customers as to an affiliation with the plaintiff's business, a plaintiff will be successful in showing that it was the defendant's intentional and unjustified interference that prevented the realization of business expectancy. In *Chicago's Pizza*, the defendant prevented the plaintiff from realizing business by permitting customers to place orders with the defendant's store while being dishonest with them about an affiliation with the plaintiff's business. 893 N.E.2d at 993. Furthermore, the court specifically rejected an argument presented by the defendant that the customers simply mistook the defendant's store for the plaintiff's. *Id.* The court pointed to the defendant's advertisements listing multiple locations when in fact there was only one. *Id.* More specifically, the court emphasized the fact that the defendant's advertisements went so far as to list the corresponding address of the plaintiff's store. *Id.* The court thus held that the defendant's interference had prevented the plaintiff's realization of business. *Id.* The court reasoned that because the plaintiff was able to demonstrate that the defendant acted improperly in allowing the customers to proceed with sales while being dishonest with them regarding an affiliation with the plaintiff, and because the defendant listed the plaintiff's locations on its advertisements, the defendant had interfered with the plaintiff's business. *Id.*

*E.J. McKernan* provides additional factual gloss for the more generalized factor of "facilitating a mistaken belief" so we use this case in the rule explanation.

Similarly, in *E.J. McKernan*, the court considered how the defendant's conduct in facilitating customers' mistaken beliefs contributed to its intentional and unjustifiable interference with the plaintiff's realization of business expectancy. 623 N.E.2d at 995. The court noted that the defendant directly diverted business from the plaintiff by using information from the plaintiff's master list, which contained confidential information regarding the plaintiff's buyers and sellers. *Id.* Additionally, the court emphasized the fact that one order was placed directly with the plaintiff company but was then filled and billed in favor of the defendant company. *Id.* Because the defendant directly diverted business and filled an order placed with the plaintiff, the court ruled that it was the defendant's intentional and unjustified interference that prevented the realization of business expectancy. *Id.*

We need a rule explanation for the guiding factor of privilege that came from *RRRR*.

In contrast, where a defendant can assert a privilege for its conduct, a plaintiff will not be able to demonstrate that the defendant intentionally and unjustifiably interfered with a business expectancy. In *RRRR* the court noted that the defendant neighbor was justified in blocking the plaintiff's outdoor seating in his restaurant because the defendant was in the course of making required repairs to its building. 2017 IL App. (1st) 160194 at *7. Thus the court held that the defendant did not intentionally and unjustifiably interfere with the plaintiff's business expectancy. *Id.* The court emphasized that, in order to demonstrate intentional and unjustified interference, the "plaintiff must show that defendant acted intentionally with the purpose of injuring the plaintiff's expectancy [and] [t]o the extent that a party acts to enhance its own business interests, it has a privilege to act in a way that may harm the business expectancy of others." *Id.* Further, the court noted that because the defendant was privileged in its actions, by way of protecting its interests, the plaintiff would be required to prove malicious intent, which the facts did not establish. *Id.* However, because the defendant was justified in its actions by way of privilege and the plaintiff could not prove malicious intent, the court ruled that the plaintiff failed on this element. *Id.*

It is unlikely that Mr. Arnold will be able to show that it was Mr. Green's intentional and unjustified interference that prevented the realization of business expectancy. Mr. Arnold may argue that, like the defendant's conduct in *Chicago's Pizza*, Mr. Green allowed customers to proceed with their purchases after learning that they had believed they were doing business with Mr. Arnold. *See* 893 N.E.2d at 993. Specifically, Mr. Arnold can demonstrate that the defendant permitted customer sales after the customers were misled to believe that they were shopping at the newest location of the stores affiliated with the location of the Elgin and DeKalb stores. Second, Mr. Arnold can argue that like the defendant's advertisements in *Chicago's Pizza*, Mr. Green placed advertisements that led customers to believe there was an affiliation between the two parties. *See id.* Namely, Mr. Arnold will point to the fact that Mr. Green placed advertisements in the form of a website with similar branding and printable coupons that used the phrase "our newest location," implying there was more than one location to shop from. Mr. Arnold may also argue that like the defendants in *McKernan*, Mr. Green diverted business from his company by using a similar logo and subsequently misleading customers. *See* 623 N.E.2d at 995.

> Arnold's rule application for *E.J. McKernan*.

Alternatively, Mr. Green may argue that unlike the defendant in *Chicago's Pizza*, who actively misled customers, when he received a call inquiring about the affiliation with the other stores, he was honest and informed the caller that there was no affiliation with those stores. *See Chicago's Pizza*, 893 N.E.2d at 993. He will further distinguish his advertising situation from the one in *Chicago's Pizza* by stating that his coupons did not expressly provide multiple locations like the misleading material at issue in *Chicago's Pizza*, but rather just identified the one true location of his store. *See id.* Mr. Green may also distinguish himself from the defendant in *McKernan* by stating that he did not directly divert any orders that were given to Mr. Arnold. 623 N.E.2d at 995. Further, Mr. Green may argue that, like the defendant in *RRRR*, he too possesses a privilege to advertise his own business and that as such, Mr. Arnold will need to show malicious intent. 2017 IL App. (1st) 160194 at *7. He will further assert that, like the lack of evidence of malice in *RRRR*, Arnold too will fail to meet that burden. *See id.* It is unlikely that Mr. Arnold will prevail on this element because Mr. Green was not dishonest when he received a phone call regarding the affiliation, and his website's printable coupons only listed one location. Moreover, he did not directly divert business from Arnold, and he may be able to assert privilege.

> Green's rule application for *McKernan*.

> Green's rule application, drawing a similarity to *RRRR* for this element.

Thus, Mr. Arnold likely will not succeed in his tortious interference with business expectancy claim against Mr. Green. Mr. Arnold will likely be able to demonstrate that he possessed a reasonable expectancy of entering into a valid business relationship with customers because customers did indicate they thought they were doing business with him. Notwithstanding, he will likely fail to prove that it was Mr. Green's intentional and unjustified interference that prevented the realization of business expectancy because Mr. Green was not dishonest, did not directly divert business from Mr. Arnold, and may be able to assert a privilege.

Let's look at the ways in which the various authorities have been integrated into the Discussion of the above memorandum.

**First, notice the large-scale and small-scale organization of the Discussion.** Has it changed from the organization employed with only a single authority? No, it has not. That organization reflects the fundamental structure of legal analysis, and thus will not change no matter how much additional authority is considered. A legal Discussion will always contain one global roadmap, followed by a separate issue segment for each issue. Each issue segment will always contain a single-issue roadmap, rule explanation paragraphs, rule application paragraphs, and an issue prediction.

**Second, notice *generally* where and how additional authorities have been included throughout the Discussion.** The citations of the new authorities are annotated to help you see where they are included.

**Third, for each section of the Discussion (i.e., global roadmap, issue roadmaps, rule explanation sections, rule application sections, conclusions), notice *specifically* where and how additional authorities have been integrated.**

- How has the global roadmap incorporated multiple authorities? Is the content different? How so? Are more cases cited?
- How has each issue roadmap incorporated multiple authorities? Is the content different? How so? Are more cases cited?
- How has each issue's rule explanation section incorporated multiple authorities?
- How has each issue's rule application section incorporated multiple authorities?

**Fourth, consider which parts of the Discussion have changed most significantly with the integration of multiple authorities and which have changed the least.** Typically, the use of multiple authorities results in the following changes:

- Almost always, the global roadmap will change the least. Even so, there may be ways in which the global rule is tweaked, and it is possible, although not likely, that your global prediction may change if the global rule and/or a rule for one of the conditions changes significantly.
- Issue roadmaps likely reflect a modified and/or more detailed issue rule of law, such as new standards or definitions, as well

as refinement or addition of guiding factors. Similarly, the rule proof for an issue becomes more detailed, as it now reflects the fact-based holdings from multiple authorities. Along with these changes, your issue prediction may change as well.

- The rule explanation section almost certainly will be greatly expanded; you have more authorities from which you can select the most helpful examples to show the rule's application. As you can see, this section now necessarily has multiple paragraphs within each issue.

- The rule application section almost certainly will contain more arguments. Having more authorities better enables a lawyer to make arguments for each party—a significant advantage. With only a single authority, you may have found making arguments for both parties challenging.

- Sometimes the global conclusion will change. As noted above, if the rule changes significantly, that may result in a change to your issue prediction and even to your global prediction.

In the remainder of this module, we first explore analyzing multiple authorities, focusing on the process of synthesis. Next, we address the pre-drafting process for a multiple authorities Discussion. Finally, we discuss the drafting considerations when using multiple authorities.

### CHAPTER 20

# Integrating Multiple Authorities into the Rule: Synthesized Rules of Law

This chapter focuses on the process by which lawyers integrate multiple authorities into the synthesized rule of law.

---

**Study Guide Questions for Chapter 20**

1. What is a synthesized rule of law?
2. How is it different from an emergent rule of law? How is it similar to an emergent rule of law?
3. What is the relationship between an existing rule of law and a synthesized rule of law? Which type of rule is typically the most detailed?
4. When should a lawyer use a synthesized rule of law?
5. What strategies can you employ when synthesizing seemingly inconsistent cases?
6. What new terms were introduced in this chapter? How do these terms relate to your existing understanding of predictive memo writing? Did your understanding of any other terms change as a result of reading this chapter?

---

Recall from Module II that when a court interprets and applies an existing legal rule, the rule that emerges from that case is referred to as the emergent legal rule. When more than one case in a jurisdiction interprets a legal rule, the emergent rules from those cases are combined into a single rule. This new rule, the *synthesized rule of law*, becomes the new existing rule that the lawyer will use in his legal analysis. This chapter first explains what a synthesized rule of law is and then explores the process by which lawyers arrive at a synthesized rule of law from multiple authorities.

## I. What Is a Synthesized Rule of Law?

A synthesized rule of law can be thought of as a combination of two or more emergent legal rules. As such, it shares certain features of emergent rules. For example, like an emergent rule, a synthesized rule generally is more detailed than the existing legal rule that preceded it. That is because in interpreting and applying the existing rule, the court had to clarify, modify, or otherwise add detail to that rule.

Typically, cases do not explicitly tell us, clearly and unequivocally, the synthesized legal rule. Instead, the lawyer must do the work of reading cases in conjunction with one another and piecing together a coherent, synthesized legal rule that accounts for the law-centered interpretations and fact-based holdings contained in the various cases. This process of piecing together the existing legal rule from the emergent rules is known as *synthesis*. The process of synthesis occurs not only with the global rule but also with the rule for each issue.

## II. The Process of Synthesis: How Lawyers Use Cases to Synthesize the Legal Rule

Because the lawyer ultimately must apply the existing, synthesized legal rule to the client's situation, the lawyer first needs to ascertain what that existing legal rule is. Recall the procedure when we had only a single authority: We took the existing rule of law and processed it within that single authority to arrive at the emergent rule of law. Because we had no additional authorities to process and integrate, the emergent rule of law became the existing legal rule that we then used and applied to our client's situation. With more authorities to integrate, our goal remains the same—to ascertain the legal rule and ultimately apply it to our client's situation—but the process to achieve that goal becomes a bit more complex.

As you read this chapter, keep in mind Judge Learned Hand's apt description of the process of synthesis that occurs within the law over time: "[The law] stands as a monument slowly raised, like a coral reef, from the minute accretions of past individuals, of whom each built upon the relics which his predecessors left, and in his turn left a foundation upon which his successors might work."[1] The synthesized rule reflects this additive and ongoing process.

### A. The Basics of Rule Synthesis

Although a synthesized rule is a combination of two or more emergent rules, lawyers do not typically arrive at the synthesized rule merely

---

1. Learned Hand, Book Review, 35 Harv. L. Rev. 479, 479 (1922) (reviewing Benjamin N. Cardozo's *The Nature of the Judicial Process*).

by combining two or more emergent rules. Instead, you can think of the process as more of a building block approach: Our processing of each additional authority adds to our understanding of the rule of law. Eventually, after processing all the authorities, a new existing rule emerges, reflecting the synthesis of the rule from the various authorities.

 **CONCEPT IN ACTION: Rule Synthesis**

Let's look at the process of synthesis using the Dangerous Dog hypothetical.

> **Existing rule** (statute): "All dangerous dogs must be licensed."
> **New Case:** In Case A, the court held an elderly dog did not have to be licensed even though it previously had posed a threat.

> We process this case to arrive at an emergent rule:
> **Emergent rule** (starts with existing rule and incorporates law from Case A): All dangerous dogs must be licensed **unless they are exempted from the licensing requirements due to age**.

> This is where the process would have stopped if we had only a single authority, Case A. The emergent rule would now be a rule with an exception.

> However, assume we now have located an additional case.
> **New case:** In Case B, the court held the owner did not have to register a dog until the dog was in its current household for at least three months.

> We process this case as well to arrive at a synthesized rule:
> **Synthesized rule** (starts with emergent rule and incorporates Case B): All dangerous dogs must be licensed **within three months of the dog moving into its current household** unless they are exempted from the licensing requirements due to age.

The synthesized rule remains a rule with an exception but now includes additional detail on the point at which a dog must be licensed.

Note the process by which we arrived at the synthesized rule. With each step, we added to our knowledge of the existing rule. For example, when Case B came along, we did not start from scratch with the original existing rule (in this case, the statute) and see how Case B processed that rule. Instead, we took the emergent rule from Case A as our starting point and refined that rule based upon the new interpretation set forth in Case B. That refinement resulted in the synthesized legal rule. If there are no additional authorities, we would use that synthesized legal rule in our legal analysis.

As the court refines the rule of law, it generally is bound by stare decisis, such that each new authority should follow the existing rule. The emergent rule does not disregard the existing rule; instead, the emergent rule generally builds upon that existing rule, creating a synthesized rule that is more detailed and well-developed than the existing rule was. (The only exception is when a court overturns, or dramatically changes, the prior rule. Fortunately, in such cases the court typically acknowledges explicitly the modification to the law.)

Note that synthesis is an ongoing process. With each new authority, the opportunity exists for the existing rule to be modified or refined. Sometimes this modification is drastic, such as a new exception to the global rule; sometimes it is a refinement, such as clarification of the time by which a new dog in a household must be licensed.

Let's take the above example, and assume that yet another authority comes along. In Case C the court holds that a once-threatening dog that now has a debilitating condition is exempted from licensing. How do we reflect this additional authority in the rule? In other words, how do we synthesize this new case with our existing understanding of the rule?

We start by reminding ourselves of the existing rule, which here is the synthesized rule that emerged following Case B, namely: "All dangerous dogs must be licensed within three months of the dog moving into its current household unless they are exempted from the licensing requirements due to age."

Next, we consider how the court's decision in Case C confirms, disconfirms, or adds to our understanding of that existing rule. We immediately note that not only may a dog be exempted due to age (what we already understood to be the rule), but that, in addition, a dog may be exempted due to disability (the new understanding gleaned from Case C). Thus, the synthesized rule that emerges from Case C can be stated as: "All dangerous dogs must be licensed within three months of the dog moving into its current household unless they are exempted from the licensing requirements due to age **or disability**."

 **CRASH WARNING: The Process of Synthesis Is Additive**

The process of synthesis is necessarily additive. Thus, once the rule has been processed, that becomes your starting point when you approach the next case. Rather than starting with the original existing rule, you start where you left off: with the existing synthesized rule. Keeping this in mind will not only save you time, it will also result in a better understanding of the rule as you refine it with each instance.

Graphically, the synthesis looks like this:

Diagram 20-1

> **Existing Synthesized Rule**
>
> All dangerous dogs must be licensed within three months of the dog moving into its current household unless they are exempted from the licensing requirements due to age.

> **Emergent Synthesized Rule**
>
> All dangerous dogs must be licensed within three months of the dog moving into its current household unless they are exempted from the licensing requirements due to age **or disability**.

## B. Different Types of Synthesis: Ways in Which an Additional Authority May Process the Existing Rule

Not every additional authority will modify the existing global rule as in the above examples. Below we consider the different types of synthesis. These types of synthesis should seem familiar because they are the same ways that a single authority could process an existing rule. You may want to review Chapter 8 at this point to remind yourself of the ways in which cases may modify existing rules.

### 1. A Case Can Simply Confirm the Existing Rule and Add Little or No New Information

First, a case can simply confirm the existing rule, adding little or no new information. In such instances, the additional case is still helpful because it provides useful confirmation of our understanding of the existing rule as accurate current law. In addition, even if the rule itself does not change, our understanding of the rule may still be enhanced based upon how the court in this new case applies the existing synthesized rule to the new set of facts.

Take, for instance, the above hypothetical in which the court carved out an exception to the dangerous dog licensing requirement for older dogs. Imagine that the judicial opinion that created that exception was issued in 1984, and that since that case the courts had not issued a more recent decision that addressed licensing an older dog. Imagine further that the court issued a decision today in which it held that, "But, as we have previously stated in *State v. Senior Canine*, older dogs are exempted from these licensing requirements. 11 N.W. 444, 446 (Wisc. 1984). As such, the dog in question in this case, Juniper, at the ripe age of 14 years, is not subject to the licensing requirement."

Would this new case modify the existing global rule? Not really. The rule remains the same. Does that mean this new case is not helpful? No. It confirms that the rule announced back in 1984 is still good law. Such confirmation always helps, especially when it comes from a much more recent case. In Chapter 21, in which we discuss how to select which cases to use and cite in your analysis, one consideration will be whether a case is recent. All other things being equal, a more recent case stating the global rule is preferred to an older case.

## 2.  A Case May Modify the Existing Rule, Most Often by Changing or Refining the Guiding Factors

Second, a case may modify the global rule or the rule for a condition. A global rule could be modified in terms of its conditions. More frequently, however, the global rule remains relatively consistent, but the rule for an issue/condition is modified. Most commonly, this modification comes from new information contained in a case about the issue's definitions, standards, or guiding factors. Indeed, a new case will almost always, at a minimum, help clarify and refine the guiding factors.

Because guiding factors play a critical role in legal analysis, the next section focuses on the process of synthesizing guiding factors. First, we illustrate this process in a non-legal context. Following that, we examine the same process in a legal context.

## C.  Synthesis of Guiding Factors in a Non-Legal Context

### Curfew Hypothetical

Synthesizing guiding factors is something we do in a non-legal context in our everyday lives. Recall the curfew example we considered in Chapter 8 when we first learned about how to discern implicit guiding factors. In that example, the teen's parent told him that he must be home by a "reasonable time" but did not specify exactly what that meant. By looking at multiple past instances, the teen inferred that in deciding what constitutes a "reasonable time," his dad considers (1) whether it is a school night, and (2) whether there is a special occasion. In other words, the teen discerned that these two implicit guiding factors are what his dad considers when determining if a time is reasonable or not.

Although we did not identify the process as such, in Chapter 8 the teen was engaging in synthesis when he considered multiple past instances to understand the rule. By looking at those multiple instances of what his dad deemed a "reasonable time," the teen was able to infer implicit guiding factors that his dad uses in coming to a decision about whether he has arrived home at a reasonable time.

Recall also from Chapter 8 that we often have some flexibility in how we label implicit guiding factors. That window of discretion, however, typically narrows as new decisions are added into the mix; each additional instance teaches us more about what, specifically, the decision maker considers. For instance, in Chapter 8 we saw how the teenager had to adjust the existing guiding factors when a new instance provided further insight into what his dad considered significant.

The process of synthesizing guiding factors can involve considering precedent instance by instance, but it can also involve considering multiple past cases *at the same time*, rather than sequentially as they occur. For instance, let's say that our hypothetical teenager has not routinely tracked the circumstances under which he gets in trouble for being late and those under which he does not. However, he has just purchased tickets to see his favorite band live. He desperately wants to avoid being grounded before the concert and decides to try to make sense of his dad's past decision making on whether he had, indeed, arrived home at a reasonable time.

How does the process of synthesis work when it occurs at the same time, rather than sequentially? As depicted in the chart below, the teen would start by examining relevant facts from past instances.

**Key Facts from Additional Instances**

| FOOTBALL GAME FACTS | FRIEND'S PARTY FACTS | SCHOOL MUSICAL FACTS |
|---|---|---|
| Arrived home at 1 a.m. after school football game | Arrived home at 1 a.m. after bonfire at a friend's house celebrating the last day of school | Arrived home at 11 p.m. after attending the annual school musical on a Thursday night |
| Game held on Friday night | | |
| Dad furious | Dad livid | Dad angry |

After identifying these facts, the teen begins the *process of synthesis* by evaluating how these facts may (or may not) modify the existing implicit guiding factors.

> **Existing Implicit Guiding Factors**
> GF 1: Whether it is a school night
> GF 2: Whether there is a special occasion

And what does that evaluation reveal? The teen quickly notes that the guiding factor of "whether there is a special occasion" needs to change. Why? The end-of-the-year celebration was no doubt a special occasion, yet his dad had been angry that he got home at an "unreasonable time." He considers modifying that guiding factor to be "whether there is a school-sponsored event." He realizes, however, that this would still be too broad, because the football game was a "school-sponsored event," yet his dad was still unhappy. He decides to identify that guiding factor even more narrowly by labeling it as "whether there is a school-sponsored special occasion." This modified guiding factor fits both the football game and the friend's party.

But there still is the nagging issue of what his dad is considering when he gets mad that the son got home at 11 p.m. after a school musical. The school musical, which only occurs once a year, is not only school-sponsored but, unlike the football game, it is also a special occasion. Yet, he still got in trouble. Why? The teen notes a significant difference between the musical and any of the other cases: It occurred on a school night. This does not modify the guiding factors—he already has an existing guiding factor of "whether it is a school night." However, it provides the teen with insight into the relationship between the two guiding factors; his dad will weigh whether it is a school night more heavily than whether it is a school-sponsored special occasion.

Thus, after evaluating these additional instances, the teen's synthesized guiding factors would now be stated as follows:

> **Synthesized Implicit Guiding Factors (New Existing Implicit Guiding Factors)**
>
> GF 1: Whether it is a school night
>
> GF 2: Whether there is a **school-sponsored** special occasion

The new rule derived by following the process of synthesis now is "In determining what constitutes a 'reasonable time,' the dad considers (1) whether it is a school night as the most important consideration, and (2) whether there is a school-sponsored special occasion as another consideration."

## D. Synthesis of Guiding Factors in the Legal Context

The process for synthesizing guiding factors is no different in the legal context. As lawyers, we conduct research and, we hope, find multiple cases that address our legal issue. Thus, we might have a stack of cases, each of which interprets and applies the rule of law for a certain claim

**GEARING UP: You Can't Find What Doesn't Exist**

While having more decisions is almost always more helpful, you cannot control the number of past decisions on your issue. In this non-legal hypothetical, you can imagine that this boy's younger siblings would have multiple examples of precedent upon which they could draw, without having to rely on their own actions to test their father's conception of "reasonable time." Similarly, in a legal context, the number of relevant prior cases is dictated by the frequency with which your legal issue has been litigated, as well as by the uniqueness of your legal question.

or charge. We do not look at each case in isolation but rather look at the cases as a group to determine the synthesized guiding factors.

### Warrantless Bomb Search Hypothetical

Take, for example, the Warrantless Bomb Search hypothetical. Recall that one condition was whether the threat posed a risk of danger to the police or others. Using only *Purcell*, we examined the relevant case facts to discern three guiding factors for that condition, as shown in Diagram 20-2.

Diagram 20-2: Implicit Guiding Factors from a Single Authority

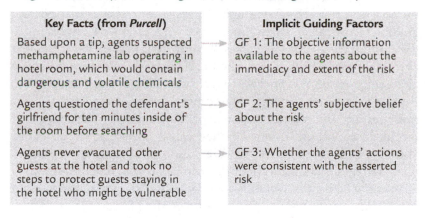

| Key Facts (from *Purcell*) | Implicit Guiding Factors |
| --- | --- |
| Based upon a tip, agents suspected methamphetamine lab operating in hotel room, which would contain dangerous and volatile chemicals | GF 1: The objective information available to the agents about the immediacy and extent of the risk |
| Agents questioned the defendant's girlfriend for ten minutes inside of the room before searching | GF 2: The agents' subjective belief about the risk |
| Agents never evacuated other guests at the hotel and took no steps to protect guests staying in the hotel who might be vulnerable | GF 3: Whether the agents' actions were consistent with the asserted risk |

Now, however, we have additional authorities that address this condition. So, just as we did in the non-legal context, we must discern the synthesized implicit guiding factors. As our first step, we identify and list the key facts from the additional authorities, as shown in the following chart.

## Key Facts from Additional Authorities

| *HENRY* FACTS | *JOHNSON* FACTS |
|---|---|
| Complaint that two men were inside selling drugs | Report that a missing girl was being held against her will |
| Stolen car outside motel room | Found the missing girl there by herself behind a locked gate |
| When one man walked out of room and was detained, another person inside the motel room immediately slammed the door shut | Though defendant had threatened violence against the victim if she ever escaped, neither the defendant nor anyone other than the girl was in the apartment at the time of the search |
| After an officer knocked on the door for approximately two minutes, a second man inside the room stepped out and was detained | Search was done after police had removed the victim from danger |
| From open doorway, one officer spotted what he believed to be a black revolver under a bed inside the room | |
| Officer could not see the entire room from the doorway, so he entered the room immediately to retrieve the firearm | |

Having extracted the facts the courts considered in these two cases, we now do the work of synthesis. Namely, we consider our existing guiding factors (from *Purcell*) in light of what facts were important to the court in these additional cases. We note that in these new cases, the agents' subjective belief about whether there was a risk is not noted, let alone emphasized. We conclude that although it is mentioned in *Purcell*, the fact that it is not mentioned in other, later cases suggests that it is unimportant. If it were an important consideration by the court, that fact likely would be mentioned in these cases—one way or the other. We also note that, to the extent they are important, the facts from *Purcell* related to the agents' subjective belief can be situated under the guiding factor of "whether the agents' actions were consistent with the asserted risk." Thus, we omit our original second guiding factor.

In addition, we see that these additional authorities confirm the other two guiding factors (what we originally called the first and third). So, we keep those guiding factors without modification. This makes our synthesized guiding factors as follows:

> **Synthesized Implicit Guiding Factors**
>
> GF 1: The objective information available to the agents about the immediacy and extent of the risk
>
> ~~GF 2: The agents' subjective belief about the risk~~
>
> GF 3̶2: Whether the agents' actions were consistent with the asserted risk

**CRASH WARNING: Multiple Cases May Limit Your Discretion in Labeling Synthesized Guiding Factors**

As discussed in Chapter 8, when guiding factors are implicit, you have discretion in terms of how you articulate them, and lawyers can use that discretion to benefit their clients. Although this discretion still exists when inferring guiding factors from multiple authorities, it often becomes more constrained. The additional authorities provide more information about what facts are guiding the courts' decisions and why, often leading to a more precise understanding of each implicit guiding factor. Because our articulation of guiding factors must conform to prior case interpretations, the more precise "the zone of interpretation" becomes, the fewer reasonable labels we can assign.

Note that additional experiences do not necessarily narrow a guiding factor. Instead, they may broaden it. In the curfew example discussed earlier in this chapter, imagine we learned that the father took no issue with his son arriving home at 1 a.m. following an annual family gathering of the cousins. Based on that decision, the teen would broaden his existing guiding factor of "whether I'm attending a school-sponsored special event" to now include special family gatherings as well. He could label this guiding factor as "whether I'm attending a special event among family or sponsored by the school."

Thus, we can see that more cases do not always make a rule stricter. Instead, more cases almost always clarify the contours of a rule, whether making it stricter or broader. Indeed, sometimes an additional authority can eliminate a guiding factor, by making clear, either implicitly or explicitly, that it is not, in fact, something the decision maker considers.

The same principles apply with synthesizing guiding factors from legal cases. The more cases you have, the better your understanding of the court's rule, including its implicit guiding factors. The Warrantless Bomb Search hypothetical illustrates this phenomenon. With only a single authority, the writer discerned three guiding factors, one of which was "the agents' subjective belief about the risk." Once additional authorities were considered, it became clear that the agents' subjective belief was not, in fact, a guiding factor that the court separately considered. Rather, it was considered part of one of the other guiding factors of "whether the agents' actions were consistent with the asserted risk." As such, the rule for the condition was modified to remove that as a guiding factor.

This process is exactly what Learned Hand described: with each new decision, we took "the relics" of the existing law and added to it, building a new "foundation upon which... successors might work."

Note that in discerning the synthesized guiding factors, we took the existing guiding factors as our starting point. From there we "tested" those guiding factors against the additional authorities in order to discern if those were, in fact, truly what the court considers. Based on this test, we then would either remove the guiding factor altogether, retain it as stated, or retain it with modification. In a nutshell, we found that one guiding factor was not something the court truly considered and that the other two guiding factors were sound without modification.

Our rule for that issue now reflects this synthesis; i.e., it indicates only two guiding factors for this issue:

> In determining whether there is a risk of danger, courts consider the objective information available to the agents about the immediacy and extent of the risk and whether the agents' actions were consistent with the asserted risk. *See, e.g.*, *U.S. v. Johnson*, 22 F.3d 674, 680 (6th Cir. 1994).

## E. Synthesis When Cases Seem Inconsistent

It may sometimes seem as though the cases you are attempting to synthesize are inconsistent. For example, it may appear that the cases apply a different rule to the same legal question or that the cases reach inconsistent results despite similarities in the fact patterns. What should you do when the cases that you are trying to synthesize seem inconsistent? Remember that under our system of stare decisis, courts must follow binding precedent. That means that only rarely are cases within a jurisdiction truly inconsistent. So, here are some specific things to look for when attempting to reconcile and synthesize seemingly inconsistent cases.

1. **Are the cases from different jurisdictions?** It is not uncommon for different jurisdictions to have different legal rules. That such cases are inconsistent may well be true, but it is not cause for concern. There is no need for those cases to be synthesized, and they simply reflect variations of legal rules across jurisdictions.
2. If the cases are indeed within the same jurisdiction, consider the following, remembering that it is unlikely that the cases are truly inconsistent.
   - **Has the court simply used different language to describe the same rule of law?** If so, that is not an inconsistency but rather a confusing use of language. It is your job in drafting the memo to make the rule clear and consistent for your reader, despite the courts' language variations.
   - **Are there factual differences between the cases that explain the courts' holdings?** When courts reach a different result despite seemingly similar facts, it almost always is because there was a legally significant factual difference. It is your job to look for that factual difference and find out why it mattered to the court. Doing so will not only make clear that the rule is not inconsistent, it also will help you truly understand the underlying rule and its application.
   - **Might one case be the rule and the other case the exception to the rule?** Sometimes a court will carve out an exception to the legal rule based upon facts presented in a case. Again, that

does not mean that those courts are using inconsistent rules; it means that the court has modified the rule by adding an exception to it.

3. If all else fails, consider:
   - **What are the levels of courts?** When there is seeming inconsistency between cases, the case from the higher-ranking court in that jurisdiction governs.
   - **What are the dates of the decisions?** Legal rules evolve over time, such that a more recent case likely will more accurately convey the existing legal rule than does an older, seemingly inconsistent, decision. It may well be that the underlying rule of law changed. Perhaps, for example, a statute was enacted that supplanted the old common-law rule. Or perhaps policy considerations changed as society evolved. Whatever the reasons, a more recent case likely reflects the prevailing rule.

### CHAPTER 21

# Sorting and Selecting Authorities

This chapter addresses one of the biggest challenges when working with multiple authorities: how to select the specific cases to use in the various parts of your Discussion.

## Study Guide Questions for Chapter 21

1. What are the ways in which cases can be useful in legal analysis?
2. What types of cases are most useful in discerning the overall rule of law? Why?
3. What types of cases are most useful in discerning the rule of law for any given condition? Why?
4. In selecting cases to use to make analogical arguments, what types of cases are most useful? Why?
5. What new terms were introduced in this chapter? How do these terms relate to your existing understanding of predictive memo writing? Did your understanding of any other terms change as a result of reading this chapter?

## I. For What Purposes Do Lawyers Select Cases?

In Chapter 20, we explored how we use multiple authorities to process the existing legal rule, resulting in a synthesized rule. But how do we select those authorities? In other words, among a stack of relevant cases, how does the lawyer determine which authorities to use to discern the synthesized rule? As you may have inferred from Chapter 20, when a case provides new information about the rule of law, you will likely want to use it. Yet, you also need to remember that discerning the synthesized rule of law is not the only purpose for which you select authorities. You will also select cases to include in your rule explanation. Ultimately, those are the cases you will also use in your rule application to make analogical arguments.

Assume that your research has identified a series of cases that addresses your legal question in the pertinent jurisdiction. At first you might be tempted to incorporate every case that you have located into your legal analysis, lest you ignore relevant authority. However, part of your job as a lawyer is to sort through the myriad authorities and select the most useful ones.

So how do you decide which cases are useful? This is not a singular question, because cases can be useful in different ways. Some cases may provide information about the global legal rule; some may provide information about the rule for one or more of the conditions/issues; and some may best illustrate the application of the rule for one or more conditions. Therefore, when deciding whether a case is useful, you want to ask yourself the following questions:

- Does this case provide any law-centered interpretations (i.e., standards, definitions, or explicit parts of the rule, including explicit guiding factors) for either the global rule of law or for the rule of law for one or more of the conditions (i.e., the issue rule of law for each condition)?
- Does this case help discern what guiding factors courts implicitly use for one or more of the conditions?
- Does this case show how the rule of law has been applied to similar facts for one or more of the conditions?

A case need not be useful in all of the above ways. For example, a case may be useful simply because it provides the global rule. It may not be useful for any other purpose, perhaps because it does not contain similar facts to your client's situation.

At the other extreme, a case may be useful in all of the above described ways: it may contain express information about the global rule, as well as the rule for each condition that is at issue, it may contain implicit guiding factors for each condition at issue, and it may contain similar facts to your client's situation for each condition at issue, making it a helpful rule explanation case in each issue segment of your Discussion.

While we wish all cases were so useful, in reality, cases rarely are useful in every way possible. Instead, a single case likely will be helpful only in a couple ways. Thus, a large part of working with multiple cases is determining which cases to use for various purposes and parts of your memo, recognizing that case selection and synthesis are critical skills in drafting an effective memo.

Below we consider in detail how lawyers select which cases are most useful for understanding the rule of law and how they select which cases are most factually similar.

## A. Selecting Cases That Provide the Rule of Law

One purpose for which we select cases is to discern the rule of law, both the global rule of law and the rule of law for each condition. Recall that the rule of law consists of the global rule of law (the conditions, the relationships between such conditions, and the result) and the rule of law for each condition (the definitions, standards, and/or guiding factors that help us better understand each condition). Collectively, this comprises the rule of law for the claim or charge.

### Burglary Statute Hypothetical

Before we consider how we select which additional authorities to use to discern the rule of law, let's revisit the burglary example first discussed in Chapter 8 and, in particular, the existing legal rule that emerged from a single authority that processed the burglary statute. (Recall that we only focused on the first element/condition and treated the other elements as non-issues. For simplicity's sake, we will do the same below.)

> **Global Rule for Burglary (Note that the language of the global rule is explicitly provided by statute.)**
>
> "A person commits burglary if he:
> 1. Unlawfully enters;
> 2. A building or structure;
> 3. With the intent to commit a crime while inside the building or structure."
>
> **Rule for Issue/Condition of "Unlawfully Enters" (Note that the language of the rule for the condition was discerned by analyzing a single authority's processing of the rule.)**
>
> Unlawful entry does not require the use of physical force, and it is judged under the objective, not subjective, standard of what a "reasonable person" would think. Whether entry is unlawful depends upon: (1) the history, if any, between the defendant and the homeowner; and (2) any visual indications regarding whether the home was open to the public.

When we only had a single authority, we did not have a lot to go on, particularly in discerning the guiding factors for the issue/condition of "unlawfully enters." Now that we have multiple authorities available, we will likely be able to further refine this rule of law. Depending on what the additional cases indicate, we might change our statement of either the global rule of law or, more likely, the issue rule of law. Below we consider how additional authorities might modify the burglary rule based only on a single authority, as stated above.

## 1.   Selecting Cases to Discern the Global Rule of Law

When selecting cases to discern the global rule of law, keep in mind that most of the time the addition of multiple authorities will not drastically alter the global rule of law. The conditions almost always will remain the same. While stare decisis means that the rule of law generally remains consistent over time, as courts must follow their precedents, that principle is not absolute. On occasion, a new opinion may overrule a precedent, such that the global rule of law changes. This happened, for example, in *Brown v. Board of Education*, in which the Supreme Court of the United States, holding that "separate but equal" is "inherently unequal," effectively overruled its precedent from *Plessy v. Ferguson*. From that day on, the global rule of law for the Equal Protection Clause under the Fourteenth Amendment changed.

Even when the conditions for the synthesized global rule of law remain unchanged, additional authorities may still modify other aspects of the global rule. For instance, an additional authority might suggest the relative importance of each condition. Or it might provide additional information about the rule's overall purpose or some global aspect of the rule, such as a standard or definition. An additional authority sometimes creates an exception to the general rule. And, finally, an additional authority may simply confirm the existing rule of law, which itself is useful, particularly when that additional authority is recent or from a court high in the judicial hierarchy. If a case does one, some, or all of these things, we want to select it and use it to fulfill that specific function.

Let's consider some ways a case may refine the *global* rule of law in the context of the burglary statute example.

Assume that in **Case A** the court announces, "Because the penalties for burglary are serious, courts must apply exacting standards for each of these elements, ensuring that entry that falls short of burglary is not so penalized." Would we want to select and use Case A in a memo discussing the burglary rule? Yes; it provides useful information about how the court will analyze all of the conditions. We would include a sentence in our global roadmap laying out this standard.

Next, assume that in **Case B** the court states, "While all elements must be proven, whether requisite intent existed is almost invariably the most critical element." We would use Case B to let the reader know more about the relative weight and significance of the elements. Among other things, we will use this case in our global roadmap to signal to the reader that intent is not only the most important element, it is also likely to be the more detailed and contested part of the memo's Discussion.

Finally, assume that in **Case C** the court held, based upon a newly enacted statute, that there is a five-year statute of limitations for burglary, meaning that a person must be charged within five years of the alleged criminal acts. That, too, would be information we would want to include in our global roadmap to understand the global rule of law.

While these cases do not alter the outline for the global rule of law—the conditions are still the same—each provides additional "gloss" that helps the reader understand the global rule of law. Thus, having selected the cases for those particular uses, we annotate our rule outline, including the information gleaned from those cases, as set forth below.

> **Synthesized Global Rule of Law Emerging from Cases A, B, and C**
>
> "A person commits burglary if he:          —— The basic outline of rule
>    1. Unlawfully enters;          elements remains the same.
>    2. A building or structure;
>    3. With the intent to commit a crime while inside the building or structure."
>
> • Because the penalties for burglary are serious, courts —— We continue to describe
> must apply exacting standards for each of these elements,          the rule, incorporating the
> ensuring that entry that falls short of burglary is not so          information from **Case A**,
> penalized. [Full Case A citation.]          **Case B**, and **Case C** into our
> • While all elements must be proven, whether requisite          rule outline so we can include
> intent existed is almost invariably the most critical ele-          it in our memo outline and
> ment. [Full Case B citation.]          later in our global roadmap.
> • The statute of limitations for burglary is five years. [Full
> Case C citation.]

## 2. Selecting Cases to Discern the Rule of Law for a Condition

Just as we select cases to discern the global rule of law, we engage in a similar process in selecting cases to use in discerning the rule of law for a condition. As discussed in Chapter 20, the addition of multiple authorities will almost always significantly impact the rule of law for each of the conditions at issue. Additional cases may refine the rule for a condition by modifying, describing, making explicit, adding, or subtracting a guiding factor; by adding a definition for the condition; or by adding a standard to the condition. We want to identify and select those cases that help convey the synthesized rule of law for each condition at issue. Ultimately, those are the cases we will use in our issue roadmap for that condition.

 **CONCEPT IN ACTION: Using Cases to Refine the Rule for the Condition**

Let's consider case selection for the condition of "unlawfully enters," which is at issue in the burglary example. Our current understanding of the rule for this condition from a single authority is reflected below.

Rule of law for condition of "unlawfully enters":

> Unlawful entry must be proven beyond a reasonable doubt. Unlawful entry does not require the use of physical force, and it is judged under the objective, not subjective, standard of what a "reasonable person" would think. Whether entry is unlawful depends upon: (1) the history, if any, between the defendant and the homeowner; and (2) any visual indications regarding whether the home is open to public.

Assume that **Case C**, in addition to refining the global rule, also addressed the condition of whether the defendant "unlawfully entered," noting that the defendant's history of access to the *home* was relevant, even in the absence of a history with that particular *homeowner*. This expands our understanding of this guiding factor. Thus, Case C would be an example of a case that helps in more than one way. We can use it for the purpose of stating the synthesized global rule and also for the purpose of describing the synthesized rule for the "unlawfully enters" issue, particularly the first guiding factor.

In **Case D** the court states, "While physical force is not required, it almost always is sufficient to show the entry was unlawful." Why would we want to select and use that case? Because it provides us with a standard that gives guidance on how the condition can be evaluated.

In **Case E** the court notes that it considers any visual indications regarding whether the home is open to the public. Do we want to select and use this case? Yes, we do. While it does not modify any factors or change our understanding of the law, it confirms that understanding. Moreover, this particular case makes an otherwise implicit guiding factor explicit. What we previously inferred to be one of the court's implicit considerations has been confirmed, solidifying our understanding of the rule.

Finally, in **Case F** the court addresses whether the defendant unlawfully entered but simply states, "That the defendant's entry was lawful can hardly be disputed. The defendant had a key, given to him by the home's owner, who had asked him to check on the house while he was away. We see no basis to disturb the trial court's ruling on this issue." Do we want to select and use this case for the purpose of synthesizing the rule? Probably not. Although it addresses the condition at issue, it does not offer any additional refinement of our existing guiding factors. If it was the only case we located for this condition, we would have no choice but to use it. However, as described above, we already have cases that provide us with the same—and, in fact, more—information about the rule for this condition.

Taking these authorities together, the synthesized rule of law for the issue of "unlawfully enters" using the selected cases becomes:

### Synthesized Rule of Law for Condition of "Unlawfully Enters" That Emerges from Cases C, D, and E

Unlawful entry must be proven beyond a reasonable doubt; —— We incorporate the new standard we learned from **Case D** and other information from **Case C** and **Case E** into our synthesized rule for this condition, so we can include it in our memo outline and our issue roadmap.

Unlawful entry must be proven beyond a reasonable doubt; it is judged under the objective, not subjective, standard of what a "reasonable person" would think. Unlawful entry does not require the use of physical force, **although such physical force will "almost always" satisfy this element.** [Cite Case D.] Whether entry is unlawful depends upon: (1) ~~the history, if any, between the defendant and the homeowner~~ the defendant's history of access to the home, if any; and (2) any visual indications regarding whether the home is open to public. [Cite Case C]; [Cite Case E].

## B. Selecting Factually Similar Cases

The above section discussed selecting cases in order to discern the rule of law, both the global rule of law and the rule of law for each issue/condition. This case selection will affect the roadmap paragraphs, which set forth the rule. In addition to selecting cases for that purpose, we also select cases factually similar to our client matter and use those in our rule explanation section. In this section, we will look more closely at this latter type of case selection.

When you only had a single authority, you did not have the ability to "select" a case. You were forced to use that single case in your rule explanation section for each issue/condition and, relatedly, to make analogical arguments for both sides based only on that single authority. Sometimes that was a strain, such as when the authority more clearly aligned with one side.

The good news is that you are no longer "stuck" with a single authority. The downside is that you have to review many potential cases and decide which ones to use in your rule explanation section. Lawyers select cases that will be used in making analogical arguments by identifying the most factually similar cases for each issue/condition. Note that in selecting cases that helped you discern implicit guiding factors (when working on the synthesized rule of law) you already likely identified factually analogous cases that will be among those you use in your rule explanation section.

At first it might seem like the "best" cases are only those that have outcomes that support your client. And, of course, it is helpful to have authorities that support your client's position. But because thorough legal analysis must first be performed objectively, not persuasively, a lawyer needs to select the cases that are the most predictive. That means that the lawyer wants to make analogical arguments—for both sides—using the cases with facts most similar to their client's case. It is those cases that will be most impactful with the court.

Indeed, one important rule of thumb is to include, when possible, a factually similar case that supports each side's position for a given issue. Therefore, in the burglary example above, the lawyer would ideally want a factually similar case in which the court held the entry was lawful and another in which the court held the entry was unlawful.

### 1.   How Do Lawyers Determine Which Cases Are Factually Similar?

Let's look specifically at how lawyers determine which cases are factually similar. We do this by going through the case selection process in the context of another dangerous dog hypothetical.

 **CONCEPT IN ACTION: Selecting Cases for Analogical Arguments**

Imagine that the city has notified your client that her dog may potentially be classified as dangerous and thus be required to be licensed as such. You talk to your client and learn the following facts about her dog. Her dog was on a tether in his family's front yard, sleeping on a sunny day. When approaching the front door of the client's house, the mail carrier did not notice the dog and stumbled over it. That startled not only the mail carrier but also the dog, who awakened and bit the mail carrier's ankle. The mail carrier said the bite did not break the skin, so she did not seek medical attention.

You research and locate the following four cases.

**Case A:** A dog bit a guest who was visiting his owner's home. The dog was eating from his dinner bowl when the guest approached and put her hand directly in the dog's bowl. The court held the dog was not dangerous.

**Case B:** While out for a walk with her owner, a dog bit a small child who approached her. The dog had not bitten anyone before, and her owner explained that the dog was surprised when the child approached suddenly. The child was taken to an urgent care clinic, which cleaned up the wound and prescribed an antibiotic. The court held the dog was dangerous.

**Case C:** A dog got loose in the neighborhood. While loose, she approached and bit five different people, two of whom required emergency care. She had previously gotten loose and bitten one person. The court held the dog was dangerous.

**Case D:** A dog in a fenced-in backyard was known to bark furiously at people who passed by. The dog never bit anyone or made physical contact of any kind, but did bare her teeth and growl at the passersby. The court held the dog was not dangerous.

Which of these cases do you think would be the most useful for making analogical arguments? Why?

Let's go through this case selection process together:

1. **First, because we want to find the most factually similar case** *for each position*, **we sort the cases by their holding.** Namely, we note that Cases B and C are ones in which the court held the dog was dangerous, whereas in Cases A and D the court held the dog was not dangerous.

2. **Next, we consider the two cases in which the court held that the dog was dangerous, Case B and Case C, to determine which one is most factually analogous.** Case B is the most analogous case that supports the position that the client's dog is dangerous. Case C is simply too extreme in terms of the facts (and thus unlike our client's situation) to help us meaningfully predict what a court will do with our case. Case B, though, depicts facts that are somewhat similar to our client's facts.

3. **Lastly, we go through the same process for the two cases, Cases A and D, in which the court held that the dog was not dangerous, to determine which one is most factually analogous to our client's case.** Case A is the most analogous case that supports the position that the client's dog is not dangerous. Its facts are less extreme than the facts of Case D. Because they are closer factually to our client's situation, they are more predictive of how a court may rule in our case.

Note that as you select cases, it can be helpful to graphically depict, or map out, where the cases fit in relation to each other and to your client's situation. This helps you to visualize which cases are indeed closest factually to your client's case and helps you ensure that you focus on selecting a case for each position. In Diagram 21-1 you can see where each of these four cases falls on the spectrum from "dangerous" to "not dangerous" and also see where our client's situation falls on this spectrum. As this diagram shows, our client's facts are not nearly as extreme as those in Cases C and D; rather they fall somewhere between the facts of Cases A and B.

Diagram 21-1

 **GEARING UP: Case Selection Is Key to Both Rule Explanation and Application**

Later in this module, when we examine drafting the Discussion with multiple authorities, we will learn that the cases we select as factually analogous will be the bread-and-butter of our rule explanation section. By extension, these cases will also provide the foundation for our rule application arguments. This highlights the importance of carefully selecting which cases are most factually similar.

 **CHECK IN: Selecting Cases for Analogical Arguments**

Recall the Warrantless Bomb Search hypothetical where you represent the federal government, which wants to show that its search and seizure of drugs did not violate the Fourth Amendment. The federal agent found the drugs when searching a shipping container, after the government received a tip indicating that this container contained a bomb inside. Further, the federal agent's bomb-sniffing dog confirmed that tip when the dog "hit" on the container (meaning the dog believed it contained bomb materials).

You have researched and located four potential cases that address the condition of whether the officer reasonably believed that there was a risk of danger to the public.

Case A: The court held there was a risk of danger to the public when an officer arrived at a home in response to a 911 call in which a man claimed he was suicidal and planned to detonate a bomb to blow up himself, his house, and anything else nearby. Before entering the home, the officer observed through the window that the man was wearing a bomb and holding a device that would trigger the bomb.

Case B: The court held there was no risk of danger to the public when the police questioned a man sitting on a park bench with a backpack beside him. When the man refused to open the bag or tell the police what was in it, the police searched the bag, which contained illegal drugs and a knife.

**Case C:** The court held there was a risk of danger to the public when the police searched the trunk of the defendant's car when he arrived at work. The police were on site in the workplace parking lot to question the defendant because he had made threats in his workplace. Among these threats, the man had told co-workers the day before that "he always 'packed heat' in his car" and that "people were going to be sorry." When questioning the defendant, the police noticed that the defendant was acting erratically, being evasive, and kept shifting to look at the trunk when asked if he had any weapons on him or in the vehicle.

**Case D:** The court held there was no risk of danger to the public when the police searched a defendant's duffel bag, based solely on a tip from the defendant's friend that the defendant frequently carried illegal assault weapons, but with no confirmation on site of what may have been inside the duffel bag.

Which of these cases do you think would be the most useful for making analogical arguments? Why?

## 2. Selecting at Least One "Factually Similar" Case for Each Position

As noted above, when selecting factually analogous cases, a lawyer wants to include at least one case that supports each position. As you might imagine, that can be challenging when the most analogous cases primarily support one position over the other. A lawyer faced with that situation does the best with what she has, selecting the most factually similar case for that position, even if that case is not all that factually similar.

Why is it important to have a case whose holding supports each party's position for all conditions at issue? To answer this question, think about the purpose of the rule explanation section. The writer is illustrating how courts have previously analyzed the rule for a condition. Ultimately (in rule application), the writer wants to compare the court's prior application of the rule to the client's situation, making analogies and drawing distinctions. The more completely we understand the admittedly gray line between what facts are sufficient to satisfy the condition and what facts are insufficient, the better able we will be to make arguments for both parties as well as to make a meaningful prediction.

Here's another way to think about the importance of identifying at least one case supporting each party's position for each given condition. Recall the challenges you may have faced in making arguments for both positions when you only had a single authority. You likely found it much easier to make arguments for the party/position that matched the holding of the precedent case. If, for example, the precedent case that you used for your rule explanation held that the dog was dangerous, it may well have been easier to make arguments for the city, as opposed to your client. If, on the other hand, the precedent case held the dog was not dangerous, you likely found it easier to make arguments that showed the dog was not dangerous.

In predictive analysis, you don't merely need to make arguments for each side, you want to identify the *best possible* arguments for each side. Only by considering the strongest possible arguments can you realistically predict the outcome. Looking at multiple authorities provides more potential arguments for each party/position.

### 3.  Plugging Gaps When Selecting Factually Similar Cases

Yet another consideration when selecting factually analogous cases is to select cases that show all aspects of the rule's application for that condition. This means making sure that, to the extent possible, you select cases that collectively show how the rule for that condition—including the guiding factors—has been applied in similar cases.

Let's consider an example. For the condition/issue of "unlawful entry," assume you have selected the two most similar cases: Case A, which held the entry was unlawful, and Case B, which held the entry was lawful. Further assume that while Case A discussed both of this condition's guiding factors (history of access to the home and visual indications), Case B only discussed one guiding factor (the visual indications). What should you do? If there was a case that was factually similar, held the entry was lawful, and discussed both factors, you likely would have already selected that instead of Case B. But there was not. Instead, you are left to "plug the gap," meaning find a case that shows a court's exploration of the part of the test for the condition that Case B does not address; i.e., find a case that addresses the defendant's history of access to the home.

The existence of any gaps, and the importance of filling them, will become more apparent when you outline and draft your Discussion. For now, however, keep in mind that we are selecting cases so we can eventually make analogical arguments with them in our rule application section. If we have cases that either individually or collectively address the guiding factors from both parties' perspectives, our rule application section will be stronger.

## 4.  Takeaways for Selecting Factually Similar Cases

It can be difficult to decide which factually similar cases to select. Below we recap the principal considerations discussed and demonstrated above.

**Remember the Overall Purpose of Rule Explanation and Rule Application.** Your rule explanation focuses on how the law has been applied in prior cases in order to help the reader understand the rule of law. Your rule application presents arguments about how the court will likely apply that law in your client's case. In so doing, you will compare the precedent cases introduced in your rule explanation section to your client's situation, explaining how those comparisons will compel a particular holding. Thus, your rule explanation section provides the foundation for the cases you will use in your rule application section. Put differently, you will not introduce new cases as part of rule application. Because rule application builds on rule explanation, both are important to keep in mind when selecting factually similar cases.

**Select Cases That Are the Most Factually Similar to Your Case.** This is the most important consideration. Without factually similar cases, your ability to make meaningful, predictive arguments in your rule application section is constrained.

**When Selecting Factually Similar Cases, Try to Do So for Each Particular Condition.** Remember that when you evaluate a case's usefulness, you must separately consider its usefulness for each condition. A case may be factually similar, and thus useful, for one condition but not for another condition. Thus, you would only include that case in the rule explanation section for the condition for which it is useful.

**Ideally Select at Least One Case That Supports Your Side as Well as the Other Side.** Finding cases that support each side will help you identify the tension in the rule's application, such as we saw above in our Dangerous Dog hypothetical. It will also help you develop the strongest possible arguments for each side, improving your ability to predict the likely outcome of the client matter under consideration.

**Ideally Select an Assortment of Cases That Collectively Will Cover All Aspects of the Rule for the Given Condition.** Ensure that the cases you've selected illustrate the application of each condition's rule, including each condition's guiding factors. Doing so will help ensure that in each issue segment of your Discussion you have thoroughly explained prior applications of the rule for that condition.

**Do the Best with What You Have.** As you might imagine, sometimes it is difficult to heed all of these guidelines given the cases available. For example, maybe the only cases that support one side's position are not all that factually similar. Even so, predictive analysis still requires us to select the best—even if highly imperfect—cases for each side for each issue.

**CRASH WARNING: Case Selection Is Not All or Nothing**

A case may be factually similar, and thus helpful, for one condition but not for other conditions. That is not a problem; it simply means you will select and use that case for one particular issue segment of your Discussion and not for the others.

The flip side is also true: a case may be factually similar for several, or even all, of the rule's conditions. You are not limited to using such a case for only one condition.

Instead, you should independently evaluate its usefulness for each condition. If, after doing so, you determine the case is useful for all conditions, then you will select and use it for all conditions. Looking ahead, that means that in each condition's issue segment of the Discussion, you will consider that case in your rule explanation and also make comparisons and distinctions between its facts and the client facts in rule application.

## II. Other General Considerations When Selecting Cases

The discussion above shows the specific considerations that lawyers employ when selecting cases to use to state the rule of law or to show the rule's application in cases that are factually similar to our client's. We now take a step back and look at some overarching considerations that lawyers also take into account as they make these case selection decisions.

### A. The Date of the Authority

All other things being equal, it is helpful to select more recent authorities for use in your Discussion. This is especially true in your roadmap paragraphs, in which you are conveying the global rule of law to your reader. More recent authorities assure your reader that the rule of law you present is indeed the current law.

As long as the law has not changed, having more recent authorities in your rule explanation section is less important than having them in your roadmaps. You likely will not have an abundance of factually similar cases from which to choose, and it is more important to select factually similar cases on the basis of their usefulness rather than their date of decision.

### B. The Level of Court of the Authority

Generally, the higher the court is in the relevant legal hierarchy, the more authoritative and thus the more useful its opinions. When possible, select and use cases from the highest court in which that information is available. Again, this rule of thumb is especially important in your roadmap paragraphs, where both recent decisions and decisions from a higher court reassure your reader that you are conveying the current rule of law.

## C. The Thoroughness of the Authority's Decision and Reasoning

When selecting factually similar cases (as opposed to cases that provide information about the global rule of law), look for cases in which the court thoroughly explains its decision. A well-written legal opinion provides the procedural background, the facts, the holding, and the reasoning. Some opinions may clearly state the holding and the facts that formed the basis for the holding but not explain the legal significance of those facts. Without such an explanation, we lack insight into why the court reached its conclusion, making it more difficult to use that case for predictive purposes.

 **EQUIPPING YOURSELF: Using Case Headnotes to Help You Select Cases**

Wise use of *headnotes* can help you select cases. Headnotes are editorial enhancements added to the start of a legal opinion by private publishers like West and Lexis. Because each headnote summarizes a legal issue discussed in the case, headnotes can be used to help you (1) find cases that discuss the legal question at issue, and (2) flag the portions of the decision that discuss that particular issue. Using headnotes as a research aid will save you considerable time; however, it is imperative to remember that they are no substitute for carefully reading each case yourself.

 **CHECK IN: More Practice with Selecting Cases for Analogical Arguments**

Assume your client has been sued for misappropriation of its competitor's trade secret. Your client's sales manager acknowledges using the competitor's unique marketing approach after learning about it at the competitor's annual stockholders' meeting. You have located the following cases:

> Case A: A company is sued for using its competitor's "secret" ingredient of anise seasoning in its pizza sauce. The company's top chef discovered the anise seasoning in the competitor's sauce by tasting the sauce and noting the distinct anise flavor. The company had not ever released the information but would

share it with curious customers who specifically requested it. The court held the sauce recipe with anise was not a secret.

**Case B**: A company is sued for using its competitor's "secret" formula for identifying lucrative businesses to purchase. The company acknowledges using the formula but says that it learned the formula from its competitor's website on the page entitled "What Sets Us Apart." The court held the formula at issue was not a secret.

**Case C**: A company is sued for using its competitor's "secret" recipe for a house salad dressing. The company found a copy of the recipe posted anonymously on the Internet. The competitor explains that the recipe is only made known to employees of the company. The court held the recipe was secret.

**Case D**: A company is sued for using its competitor's unique manufacturing process. The company learned about the process through its employee who formerly worked as an engineer for the competitor. The competitor says the process is only known by select employees, who sign agreements acknowledging it is proprietary. The court held the manufacturing process was secret.

Which cases would be most predictive for purposes of making analogical arguments? Why?

 **CRASH WARNING: Avoiding Authority Overload While Selecting the "Best" Cases**

You likely will find many cases that provide similar information, whether that is an implicit guiding factor, a definition, a similar application of the law, or something else. Not only do you not *need* to select and use all of those authorities in your Discussion, you should avoid doing so. Instead, you should carefully select the "best" cases based on the case selection principles discussed in this chapter.

Note that this selection is an impartial process because we are writing an objective memorandum with the goal of being predictive, not persuasive. Thus, we cannot cherry-pick those cases that support our client's position and ignore those cases that undercut our client's position. Instead, you need to select cases that lay the foundation for you to make your client's best arguments, as well as those that lay the foundation for you to anticipate and articulate the opposing party/position's best arguments. Note, too, as we will discuss in Chapter 32, that persuasive writing builds on objective analysis. Thus, even when we write to persuade, we still cannot ignore cases that do not favor our client, although we will change the way we address these authorities.

## III.  Looking Ahead

Where and how do you think you will incorporate the cases you have selected into your legal analysis? The short answer is that you will incorporate multiple cases in much the same way that you did a single authority. Namely, you will incorporate cases that provide the rule of law into your roadmap paragraphs. Your global roadmap paragraph will incorporate the cases you have selected to help explain the global rule of law. Similarly, your issue roadmap paragraphs will incorporate the cases you have selected to help explain that issue/condition's rule of law, including cases that enable you to discern the guiding factors.

You will incorporate cases that show the rule for a given condition's application into your rule explanation section. For example, having selected two cases with divergent holdings that are the most similar to your client's situation and thus the most predictive, each case will be included in your rule explanation section. You likely will include other cases as well in order to provide the fullest possible illustration of the role that the guiding factors played in previous cases. Eventually, the cases described in your rule explanation section become the basis for the analogical arguments in your rule application section.

### CHAPTER 22

# The Process of Pre-Drafting with Multiple Authorities

**B**uilding upon the lessons of the previous chapters in this module, this chapter looks holistically at the pre-drafting process for multiple authorities.

---

### Study Guide Questions for Chapter 22

1. How is the pre-drafting analysis process for multiple authorities the same as it was when using only a single authority?

2. How does the process of discerning the synthesized rule of law, discussed in Chapter 20, relate to the pre-drafting process?

3. How does the process of selecting cases, discussed in Chapter 21, affect the pre-drafting process?

4. What does it mean to describe the pre-drafting analysis process as cumulative?

5. What does it mean to describe the pre-drafting analysis as being taken issue-by-issue? Why is this critical?

6. What new terms were introduced in this chapter? How do these terms relate to your existing understanding of predictive memo writing? Did your understanding of any other terms change as a result of reading this chapter?

---

The pre-drafting process remains important when moving from a single authority to multiple authorities. In fact, pre-drafting your Discussion becomes even more consequential because of the complexities and choices of integrating multiple authorities. You have already learned how to synthesize rules of law from multiple authorities (Chapter 20) and how to select which cases to use in various parts of your Discussion (Chapter 21). In this chapter we will combine that information into a pre-drafting process.

## I. How Is Pre-Drafting Generally Different with Multiple Authorities?

Recall from Chapter 13 that, when you had a single authority, the pre-drafting process entailed analyzing that authority in terms of how it informed the global rule of law, the rule of law for each condition, and the potential arguments for each party/position. Because there was only a single authority, you didn't have to select which authorities to use in that process. And, of course, you also didn't have to synthesize authorities. These two additional steps—the need to select and synthesize authorities—alter the process. Namely, instead of analyzing each new authority in relation to the existing rule, you will now consider each new authority in light of your cumulative understanding of the rule. Diagram 22-1 depicts the process.

The process of synthesis is additive, meaning that each additional authority builds on our current understanding of the legal rule. The following "effective" flowchart shows that Case A provides a new understanding of the rule. This emergent rule from Case A "becomes" the new existing rule. We then take that new existing rule as our starting point when considering how Case B may modify it.

**Diagram 22-1: The Process of Rule Synthesis with Multiple Authorities**

**Effective**

Existing Rule → *Case A modifies the existing rule* → **Emergent Rule (from Case A)** *becomes new Existing Rule* → *Case B modifies the "new" existing rule, i.e., the emergent rule from Case A* → **Emergent Rule (from Case B)** *becomes new Existing Rule*

Note that in the effective example, when we process Case B, we start from our understanding of the rule, as enhanced by the additional authority we have already considered (Case A). In contrast, in the "ineffective" flowchart, the writer attempts to "turn back the clock," returning to the previously existing rule of law rather than starting with the "new" existing rule of law.

**Ineffective**

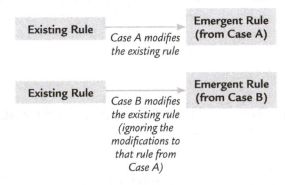

## II. Reconsidering the Foundational Checklist for Pre-Drafting

Before we look at the particulars of pre-drafting with multiple authorities, let's review the general process of pre-drafting, which we first encountered in Chapter 13. Pay attention in particular to the comments, which show a lawyer's thoughts on how using multiple authorities will influence the pre-drafting process.

1. Identify the global rule of law that guides your client's claim or charge.
2. Break the global rule of law down into its result, conditions, and a structure for how the conditions relate to one another. *Comment:* With multiple authorities, I will need to first discern the synthesized global rule of law and then break it into its result, conditions, and structure for how the conditions relate to one another.
3. From those conditions, identify the issues and non-issues. Recall that non-issues are simply conditions that will not be addressed in the predictive memorandum because they have been satisfied on the basis of the facts, the parties have stipulated they have been satisfied, or you have been instructed to ignore them.
4. For each issue:
   a. Identify judicial decisions that apply the pertinent rule of law in an analogous factual situation.
      *Comment:* With multiple authorities, I not only will need to select the most predictive cases, I also will need to then process each selected case in terms of its key facts, generalizing those facts to inform the guiding factors, etc. I will need to do this cumulatively, considering the existing guiding factors as I look at each additional authority.
   b. Identify the key facts from the judicial decision that guided the court's analysis of that issue.
   c. Discern the rule of law. (This will be the rule of law for the particular condition at issue.)
      i. Identify any standards or definitions for that condition.
      ii. Generalize the key facts from the judicial decision into guiding factors; these guiding factors will form the basis of analogical comparisons to your client's facts.
      *Comment:* With multiple authorities, I will need to create a synthesized rule for each condition that takes into account what I learned from each selected case. This synthesized rule will include synthesized conditions, synthesized definitions, and synthesized guiding factors.

    **d.** On the basis of the guiding factors for that condition, compare the key facts of the judicial decision with the facts of your client's situation, making analogies and distinctions from both parties' perspectives.

    *Comment:* With multiple authorities, I am going to be making a lot more analogies and distinctions. The guiding factors that form the basis for these comparisons will likely change. Moreover, for each guiding factor, I will more likely be able to make arguments for both parties/positions by comparing and contrasting the client's situation to various cases.

    **e.** Consider any additional rule-based and policy arguments and counter-arguments for that issue based on the rule of law and your client's situation.

    *Comment:* With additional authorities there is potential for additional arguments of these varieties. Additional authorities might also enhance or undermine existing rule-based or policy-based arguments.

## III. Worksheet Approach to Gathering Content with Multiple Authorities

As the revised checklist above indicates, the big picture of your legal analysis and pre-drafting process does not fundamentally change when you move from working with only a single authority to working with multiple authorities. However, you will be working with considerably more material, so it is essential that you employ a process to organize this material.

### The Smell Shoppe Hypothetical

Similar to the worksheet you used when working with a single authority in Chapter 13, here we provide a worksheet to help you gather, analyze, and organize your content when working with multiple authorities. We have completed the worksheet using a familiar context: The Smell Shoppe hypothetical. As you review this worksheet, pay attention to both the information sought and the answers provided.

## WORKSHEET: Pre-Drafting Using Multiple Authorities

### THE GLOBAL RULE, INCLUDING CONDITIONS/ISSUES

1. **Based only upon a single authority, what is the existing global rule of law? Outline it here.** *Note*: If you have not already undertaken your analysis with only a single authority, your first step is to identify a recent authority for the global rule. That will serve as your starting point; i.e., your existing global rule of law.

   Starting authority: *Chicago's Pizza, Inc. v. Chicago's Pizza Franchise Ltd.*, USA, 893 N.E.2d 981 (Ill. App. Ct. 2008)

   The elements of the tort of intentional interference with a business expectancy include:

   "(1) [the plaintiff's] reasonable expectancy of entering into a valid business relationship;

   (2) the defendant's knowledge of the expectancy;

   (3) the defendant's intentional and unjustified interference that prevents the realization of business expectancy; and

   (4) damages resulting from the interference."

2. **Identify and select those cases that are most helpful in processing the *global* rule of law.** List the case(s) below and briefly note why each listed case is helpful. In selecting cases, remember the principles discussed in Chapter 21.

   *Chicago's Pizza.* Helpful in processing the global rule, clearly listed in full. Appears to be landmark case that other cases mention when describing the elements of tortious interference.

   *RRRR Inc. v. Plaza 440 Private Residences Condo. Assn.*, 2017 IL App. (1st) 160194 (2017). Unpublished and from a lower court than *Chicago's Pizza*, but more recent by almost ten years. Cites to *Chicago's Pizza* for the elements of this claim, confirming that *Chicago's Pizza* still is good law. Cite in global roadmap to show the continuing validity of the four elements set forth in *Chicago's Pizza*.

   *Note:* Because this answer is only intended to help us select cases, we can record information in rough notes; e.g., using incomplete sentences. Note, too, we can just use the short case name for *Chicago's Pizza* because we have already recorded the full cite elsewhere on the worksheet. Record information on the worksheet in a manner that makes sense to you, trying to be efficient while completing the worksheet but also ensuring you have the information you need when you begin drafting.

3. **Using the cases you have selected, outline the *synthesized* global rule of law, modifying it from the existing global rule from a single authority, as needed.**

   No modification needed; the synthesized global rule is the same as the existing global rule:

   The elements of the tort of intentional interference with a business expectancy include:

   "1. [the plaintiff's] reasonable expectancy of entering into a valid business relationship;

   2. the defendant's knowledge of the expectancy;

   3. the defendant's intentional and unjustified interference that prevents the realization of business expectancy; and

   4. damages resulting from the interference."

4. **Determine which of these conditions are at issue.** For each condition listed in the synthesized rule of law, determine if it is an issue or non-issue and why. Include that information in the table below. Depending on how many conditions you have, you may not need all of the rows below.

| CONDITION | ISSUE OR NON-ISSUE | WHY? |
|---|---|---|
| 1. Reasonable expectancy | Issue | Facts are contested |
| 2. Defendant's knowledge | Non-issue | Asked to ignore |
| 3. Intentional and unjustified interference | Issue | Facts are contested |
| 4. Damages | Non-issue | Asked to ignore |

### ANALYSIS OF ISSUE SEGMENT FOR ISSUE ONE

1. List the first issue/condition here.

   Issue One: Whether the plaintiff had a reasonable expectancy of entering into a valid business relationship. '

2. Discern the synthesized rule of law for this issue/condition, using the following steps.

   a. To begin, what is the existing legal rule for that condition? Outline it here.

   *Note:* Here we start with the existing rule, which we discerned from *Chicago's Pizza*. We know that is the existing rule because we already undertook our analysis with that single authority. In practice, you likely will not have already undertaken your analysis with only a single authority, and thus at this step you will need to identify what, at least initially, appears to be the most helpful authority for this condition. You will use that authority to discern the starting point for the existing rule.

   Existing rule for this issue from *Chicago's Pizza*: In assessing whether the plaintiff possessed a reasonable expectancy of entering into a valid business relationship, the court will consider the specific contemplation of customers and the customers' belief that they were doing business with the plaintiff.

   b. Identify those cases that are helpful in providing law-centered interpretations (definitions, standards, and/or explicit guiding factors). For each case identified, include how specifically it is helpful.

   *Note:* If you started with an existing case (such as, in this example, *Chicago's Pizza*), you should include that below.

   There are no explicit standards, definitions, or guiding factors related to this issue in our authorities.

   c. Identify those cases that are factually analogous, and from those cases discern the implicit guiding factors. For each case, consider the facts that were significant to the court's holding on this issue. From there go through the process of synthesizing the implicit guiding factors. Refer to Chapter 20 for a refresher on noting key case facts and using them to discern guiding factors.

   *Chicago's Pizza, Inc.* at 993-94: A plaintiff will show a reasonable expectancy of entering into a valid business relationship when specific customers called the defendant's store and the customers expressed belief that they were doing business with the plaintiff.

   *Mannion v. Stallings & Co.*, 561 N.E.2d 1134 (Ill. App. Ct. 1990). A plaintiff will show a reasonable expectancy of entering into a valid business relationship when the plaintiff had moved past negotiations and received a signed agreement providing compensation amounts.

*Euclid Ins. Agencies, Inc. v. Am. Ass'n of Orthodontists*, No. 95 C 3308, 1997 WL 548069 (N.D. Ill. 1997). Plaintiff will not be successful in showing a reasonable expectancy of entering into a valid business relationship where the plaintiff has never had contact with prospective customers.

*Note:* Pinpoint cites are included here, along with full citations for all new cases. Although it might take an extra second to record the pinpoint information, it will save you time in the long run.

d. Using the information gathered from the above selected cases, provide the emergent rule of law for this condition, including standards, definitions, and/or guiding factors. This is your synthesized issue rule of law.

In determining whether the plaintiff has a reasonable expectancy, the court will consider the specific contemplation of customers and their belief that they were doing business with the plaintiff. *Chicago's Pizza, Inc.* 893 N.E.2d at 993-94. Additionally, the court will examine the amount of contact between the plaintiff and prospective customers. *Mannion v. Stallings & Co.*, 561 N.E.2d 1134, 1139 (1990).

3. **Select and further analyze the cases for your rule explanation section.** List those cases that are factually analogous and thus will be useful in your rule explanation section. Note that these cases likely will be ones that helped provide guiding factors above. For each case listed, complete the information in the chart below.

| CASE NAME | CONDITION SATISFIED (+ OR –) | WHICH GUIDING FACTORS ARE ADDRESSED IN THIS CASE? | FACT-BASED HOLDING FOR THIS CASE |
|---|---|---|---|
| *Chicago's Pizza* | + | Specific contemplation of customers; the customers' belief that they were doing business with the plaintiff | A plaintiff will be found to have possessed a reasonable expectancy of entering into a valid business relationship when it can be demonstrated that specific customers called the defendant's store with the belief that they were calling and doing business with the plaintiff |
| *Mannion v. Stallings & Co.* | + | The amount of contact between the plaintiff and prospective customers in order to establish a business relationship | A plaintiff will show a reasonable expectancy of entering into a valid business relationship when the plaintiff has moved past bidding stages and negotiations and received a signed agreement providing compensation amounts |
| *Euclid Ins. Agencies, Inc. v. Am. Ass'n of Orthodontists* | – | Specific contemplation of customers; the amount of contact between the plaintiff and prospective customers in order to establish a business relationship | A plaintiff will not be successful in showing a reasonable expectancy of entering into a valid business relationship where the plaintiff has had no contact with prospective customers |

4. Using the fact-based holdings from the cases selected above, formulate a synthesized rule proof for this condition. Remember that your *synthesized rule proof* should encompass fact-based holdings that demonstrate all of the guiding factors. In other words, you want to include sufficient detail from your array of cases to "prove" to your reader that your guiding factors have a factual basis in the cases. Beyond the need to cover all guiding factors, you have considerable latitude in how you convey your synthesized rule proof. In deciding the most effective approach, let readability guide you.

*A plaintiff will be found to have possessed a reasonable expectancy of entering into a valid business relationship when specific customers called the defendant's store with the belief that they were calling and doing business with the plaintiff. The court will also determine that a plaintiff possessed a reasonable expectancy of entering into a valid business relationship when the plaintiff has moved past negotiations with prospective customers and had received a signed agreement providing compensation amounts.*

5. **Determine what potential arguments are available for this condition.** For each guiding factor for this condition, compare the facts of your client's case to the facts of the authorities you selected as factually similar. Based on that comparison, you will make analogies and distinctions from the perspective of each party/position. Complete the table below. Note that it is largely a continuation of your existing table, with the deletion of the original final column (fact-based holding) and the addition of two new columns.

| CASE NAME | CONDITION SATISFIED (+ OR –) | WHICH GUIDING FACTORS ARE ADDRESSED IN THIS CASE? | HOW IS THIS CASE SIMILAR TO CLIENT'S SITUATION? | HOW IS THIS CASE DISTINGUISHABLE FROM CLIENT'S SITUATION? |
|---|---|---|---|---|
| *Chicago's Pizza* | + | Specific contemplation of customers; the customers' belief that they were doing business with the plaintiff | Arnold similarly had conversations with customers that indicated the customers believed they were doing business with Arnold, rather than Green | Unlike the defendant in Chicago's Pizza, Green did not hear directly from customers that they thought they were dealing with Arnold, and Green did not allow customers to process orders after he learned they were mistaken |
| *Mannion v. Stallings & Co.* | + | The amount of contact between the plaintiff and prospective customers in order to establish a business relationship | Mr. Arnold's relationship with his customers was strong, arguably even stronger than that of the plaintiff in Mannion, who was able to establish a reasonable expectation of business relationship on the basis of a developing, as opposed to established, relationship | Unlike the plaintiff in Mannion, Mr. Arnold was not in any transactional stages with the customers |

| CASE NAME | CONDITION SATISFIED (+ OR –) | WHICH GUIDING FACTORS ARE ADDRESSED IN THIS CASE? | HOW IS THIS CASE SIMILAR TO CLIENT'S SITUATION? | HOW IS THIS CASE DISTINGUISHABLE FROM CLIENT'S SITUATION? |
|---|---|---|---|---|
| *Euclid Ins. Agencies, Inc. v. Am. Ass'n of Orthodontists* | – | The specific contemplation of customers; the amount of contact between the plaintiff and prospective customers in order to establish a business relationship | | Unlike customers who had the contemplation of doing business with Mr. Arnold, the customers in this case were not even aware of the plaintiff; the plaintiff in this case had no direct contact with customers, unlike Mr. Arnold |

**ANALYSIS OF ISSUE SEGMENT FOR ISSUE TWO**

1. List the second issue/condition here.

   Issue Two: Whether the defendant's intentional and unjustified interference prevented the realization of business expectancy.

2. Discern the synthesized rule of law for this issue/condition, using the following steps.

   a. To begin, what is the existing legal rule for that condition? Outline it here.

   *Note:* Here we start with the existing rule, which we discerned from *Chicago's Pizza.* We know that is the existing rule because we already undertook our analysis with that single authority. In practice, you likely will not have already undertaken your analysis with only a single authority, and thus at this step you will need to identify what, at least initially, appears to be the most helpful authority for this condition. You will use that authority to discern the starting point for the existing rule.

   Existing issue rule from *Chicago's Pizza:* A plaintiff will be successful in demonstrating that it was the defendant's intentional and unjustified interference that prevented the realization of business expectancy when the defendant allows customers to place orders with its business while being dishonest with the customers when they inquire about an affiliation with the plaintiff's store. Further, a plaintiff can demonstrate interference with an expectation of a business relationship when the defendant represents an affiliation with the plaintiff through advertising materials.

   b. Identify those cases that are helpful in providing law-centered interpretations (definitions, standards, and/or explicit guiding factors). For each case identified, include how specifically it is helpful.

   *Note:* If you started with an existing case (such as, in this example, *Chicago's Pizza*), you should include that below.

   There are no explicit standards, definitions, or guiding factors related to this issue in our authorities.

c. **Identify those cases that are factually analogous, and from those cases discern the implicit guiding factors.** For each case, consider the facts that were significant to the court's holding on this issue. From there go through the process of synthesizing the implicit guiding factors. Refer to Chapter 20 for a refresher on noting key case facts and using them to discern guiding factors.

*Chicago's Pizza at 993:* A plaintiff will be successful when the defendant allows customers to place orders with its business while being dishonest with them when they inquire about an affiliation to the plaintiff's store.

*E.J. McKernan Co. v. Gregory,* 623 N.E.2d 981 (Ill. App. Ct. 1993). A plaintiff will be successful in showing that it was the defendant's intentional and unjustified interference that prevented the realization of business expectancy when the defendant diverts business opportunities by representing an affiliation with the plaintiff through advertising materials.

*RRRR Inc. v. Plaza 440 Private Residences Condo. Assn.,* 2017 IL App. (1st) 160194 (2017). The plaintiff will not be successful in showing intentional and unjustified interference when the defendant's actions are privileged.

d. **Using the information gathered from the above selected cases, provide the emergent rule of law for this condition, including standards, definitions, and/or guiding factors. This is your synthesized issue rule of law.**

In assessing whether the defendant's intentional and unjustifiable interference prevented the realization of the plaintiff's business expectancy, the court will consider: (1) the defendant's conduct in facilitating a mistaken belief of customers as to an affiliation with the plaintiff's business, and (2) whether the defendant's challenged conduct was privileged.

*Note:* Consider what has happened. The three guiding factors from *Chicago's Pizza* with which we started (e.g., the existing rule listed above) now have been collapsed into a single guiding factor. In addition, we have added a new guiding factor. This consolidation allowed us to limit the total number of guiding factors to two, while retaining the important considerations. We could have left the three guiding factors as is and simply added in a fourth. Either choice would be acceptable.

Note also that the "collapsed" guiding factor of "the defendant's conduct in facilitating a mistaken belief of customers as to an affiliation with the plaintiff's business" can be supported by both *Chicago's Pizza* and *E.J. McKernan Co.*

When we draft the rule of law for this issue in our Discussion, we therefore will have a few options for how we provide attribution for this guiding factor in the memo. We could cite to both cases, which would require us to craft explanatory parentheticals for the reader to show how each case supports the guiding factor. Alternatively, we could use the *See, e.g.,* signal and cite to one of the cases, signaling to the reader that this is but one from a number of cases that support this guiding factor. You can see in our sample memo in Appendix B (also excerpted in Chapter 19) that we have taken the latter approach.

3. **Select and further analyze the cases for your rule explanation section.** List those cases that are factually analogous and thus will be useful in your rule explanation section. Note that these cases likely will be ones that helped provide guiding factors above. For each case listed, complete the information in the chart below.

| CASE NAME | CONDITION SATISFIED (+ OR –) | WHICH GUIDING FACTORS ARE ADDRESSED IN THIS CASE? | FACT-BASED HOLDING FOR THIS CASE |
|---|---|---|---|
| *Chicago's Pizza* | + | The defendant's conduct in facilitating a mistaken belief of customers as to an affiliation with the plaintiff's business | A plaintiff will be successful when the defendant allows customers to place orders with its business while being dishonest with them when they inquire about an affiliation to the plaintiff's store |
| *E.J. McKernan Co. v. Gregory* | + | The defendant's conduct in facilitating a mistaken belief of customers as to an affiliation with the plaintiff's business | A plaintiff will be successful in showing that it was the defendant's intentional and unjustified interference that prevented the realization of business expectancy when the defendant diverts business opportunities by representing an affiliation with the plaintiff through advertising materials |
| *RRRR Inc. v. Plaza 440 Private Residences Condo. Assn.* | – | Whether the defendant's actions are privileged | The plaintiff will not be successful in showing intentional and unjustified interference when the defendant's actions are privileged |

4. **Using the fact-based holdings from the cases selected above, formulate a synthesized rule proof for this condition.** Remember that your synthesized rule proof should encompass fact-based holdings that demonstrate all of the guiding factors. In other words, you want to include sufficient detail from your array of cases to "prove" to your reader that your guiding factors have a factual basis in the cases. Beyond the need to cover all guiding factors, you have considerable latitude in how you convey your synthesized rule proof. In deciding the most effective approach, let readability guide you.

*A plaintiff will be successful in demonstrating that it was the defendant's intentional and unjustified interference that prevented the realization of business expectancy when the defendant allows customers to place orders with its business while being dishonest with them when they inquire about an affiliation to the plaintiff's store or when the defendant diverts business opportunities by representing an affiliation with the plaintiff through advertising materials. However, the plaintiff will not be successful where the defendant's actions are privileged.*

*Note:* Our synthesized rule proof relating to the first guiding factor results in a long textual sentence. The sentence also would require attribution to two cases (*Chicago's Pizza* and *E.J. McKernan*), together with an explanatory parenthetical for each. We know that we want to avoid unnecessarily long sentences in legal writing. Where possible, we might also like to avoid unnecessarily complicated citation. So, when drafting the synthesized rule proof in our Discussion, the option we chose in our sample memo was to break the rule proof into more than one sentence, citing a single case for each sentence. You can see this in Appendix B.

5. **Determine what potential arguments are available for this condition.** For each guiding factor for this condition, compare the facts of your client's case to the facts of the authorities you selected as factually similar. Based on that comparison, you will make analogies and distinctions from the perspective of each party/position. Complete the table below. Note that it is largely a continuation of your existing table, with the deletion of the original final column (fact-based holding) and the addition of two new columns.

| CASE NAME | CONDITION SATISFIED (+ OR –) | WHICH GUIDING FACTORS ARE ADDRESSED IN THIS CASE? | HOW IS THIS CASE SIMILAR TO CLIENT'S SITUATION? | HOW IS THIS CASE DISTINGUISHABLE FROM CLIENT'S SITUATION? |
|---|---|---|---|---|
| *Chicago's Pizza* | + | The defendant's conduct in facilitating a mistaken belief of customers as to an affiliation with the plaintiff's business | Mr. Green allowed customers to proceed with their purchases after learning that they had believed they were doing business with Mr. Arnold | Mr. Green received a call inquiring about the affiliation with the other stores; he was honest and informed them that there was no affiliation with those stores |
| *E.J. McKernan Co. v. Gregory* | + | The defendant's conduct in facilitating a mistaken belief of customers as to an affiliation with the plaintiff's business | Like the defendants in *McKernan*, Mr. Green diverted business from Mr. Arnold's company by using a similar logo and subsequently misleading customers | Mr. Green may distinguish himself from the defendant in *McKernan* by stating that he did directly divert any orders that were given to Mr. Arnold |
| *RRRR Inc. v. Plaza 440 Private Residences Condo. Assn.* | – | Whether the defendant's actions are privileged | | Like the defendant in *RRRR, Inc.*, Mr. Green too possesses a privilege to advertise his own business and as such, Mr. Arnold will need to show malicious intent |

### PART II

# Drafting the Discussion Using Multiple Authorities

In Part II, we address drafting the Discussion using multiple authorities. In doing so, we will heavily utilize the pre-drafting analysis we undertook in Part I.

### CHAPTER 23

# Organizing and Outlining a Discussion with Multiple Authorities

In this chapter, we begin drafting the multiple authority memo by organizing and outlining the Discussion.

### Study Guide Questions for Chapter 23

1. How is the large-scale organization of a Discussion that uses multiple authorities similar to the large-scale organization of a single authority memo?
2. How does the pre-drafting process inform our ability to draft the large-scale organization for the Discussion?
3. How does the pre-drafting process inform our small-scale organization for the Discussion?
4. How is the rule explanation section different when you have multiple cases?
5. How is the rule application section different when you have multiple cases?
6. What new terms were introduced in this chapter? How do these terms relate to your existing understanding of predictive memo writing? Did your understanding of any other terms change as a result of reading this chapter?

After you have completed the pre-drafting process described in Chapter 22, you are ready to begin drafting your Discussion. As always, the first draft is an annotated outline.

## I. In General: How Multiple Authorities Affect the Outline of Your Discussion

How will using multiple authorities affect the outline of your Discussion? In other words, if you start with an outline of your Discussion based only on a single authority, how will you modify that outline to integrate additional authorities? The organization of your Discussion may change in two general ways.

First, the large-scale organization could change. This uncommon possibility will occur only if additional authorities alter the global rule of law.

Second, the small-scale organization—namely, the organization of each issue segment—may change. Notably:

- The issue roadmap will likely change. Any changes in the rule of law for a condition, such as modification of guiding factors or addition of a standard or definition, will alter the issue roadmap for that condition.
- The rule explanation section will definitely change as you use additional, factually similar cases to clarify the legal rule. These additional cases will also help you identify the strongest arguments available for each side. As discussed in Chapter 21, we try to select at least one case in which each condition was satisfied and one case in which each condition was not—an impossibility when using only a single case. With multiple authorities, you can often, but not always, achieve this goal.
- The rule application section will change to reflect the changes in the rule of law for the condition (e.g., a modification to the guiding factors) as well as to integrate arguments using the additional authorities highlighted in the rule explanation.

In the next section we look at each of these changes in greater depth.

## II. The Large-Scale Organization of a Discussion Using Multiple Authorities

Just as when we had only a single authority, the initial stage of drafting is mapping out your large-scale organization. This large-scale organization provides an outline of your Discussion. In this section, we will first review how lawyers use the global rule of law to structure the large-scale organization of their Discussion. Then we will explore how using multiple authorities may affect a Discussion's large-scale organization.

### A. Review: Large-Scale Organization with a Single Authority

#### Burglary Statute Hypothetical

Let's review how in Chapter 14 we mapped out the large-scale organization with a single authority using the burglary statute example.

We started, as always, with the global rule of law, as we had discerned it from the pre-drafting analysis process. Because this rule comes from a statute and we want to ensure we use the exact same language, we put the rule in quotation marks.

"A person commits burglary if he:
  a. Unlawfully enters;
  b. A building or structure;
  c. With the intent to commit a crime while inside the building or structure."

We then detailed what the large-scale organization would look like if all conditions were at issue. We noted we would have three issue segments, one for each contested issue. Had we decided that the second condition, whether what was entered was "a building or structure," was not at issue, we would have disposed of it as a non-issue in our global roadmap. A streamlined version of that outline would look like this:

*Global Roadmap:* Predicts the likely resolution of the client's claim or charge and sets forth the global rule of law, noting any non-issues. The reader will understand that burglary requires the satisfaction of three elements, two of which are at issue.

*Issue/Condition 1:* Unlawful Entry
  • Issue 1 Roadmap
  • Issue 1 Rule Explanation Section
  • Issue 1 Rule Application Section, including a prediction as to resolution of issue

*Issue/Condition 2:* Intent to Commit Crime
  • Issue 2 Roadmap
  • Issue 2 Rule Explanation Section
  • Issue 2 Rule Application Section, including a prediction as to resolution of issue

*Global Conclusion:* A prediction as to the court's likely resolution of the client's burglary charge and a reiteration of the court's likely resolution of each contested condition.

We would have then annotated the outline, as we did in Chapter 15 with The Smell Shoppe hypothetical. We would have used the templates for each paragraph type and added specific case content, ingredients, to support our analysis.

As you will see below, the use of multiple authorities does not change this process; we still will outline the large-scale organization of our Discussion based upon the global rule of law. The global rule of law is, after all, the framework for all of the legal analysis in the Discussion. The only difference is that with multiple authorities we use the synthesized global rule of law as that framework. Below we examine how that may (or may not) affect the large-scale organization.

## B.  Large-Scale Organization with Multiple Authorities

Usually your large-scale organization will remain the same as you add additional authorities. Those additional authorities are unlikely to alter the existing global rule of law, so your Discussion will likely still have the same conditions/issues. But if an authority does alter your global rule of law, your large-scale organization will be similarly affected.

Imagine that the legislature amended the burglary statute by adding a definition for the condition of a "building or a structure."[1] Under this new definition, it becomes questionable whether the entry in your client's situation was, in fact, entry into a "building or a structure." Accordingly, that condition can no longer be treated as a non-issue. Instead, it must be addressed in the Discussion through its own issue segment. The resulting change to the large-scale organization would look like this:

> *Global Roadmap:* Predicts the likely resolution of the client's claim or charge and sets forth the global rule of law, noting any non-issues. The reader will understand that burglary requires the satisfaction of three elements, all of which are at issue.
>
> *Issue/Condition 1:* Unlawful Entry
> * Issue 1 Roadmap
> * Issue 1 Rule Explanation Section
> * Issue 1 Rule Application Section, including a prediction as to resolution of issue 1
>
> *Issue/Condition 2:* Building or Structure
> * Issue 2 Roadmap
> * Issue 2 Rule Explanation Section
> * Issue 2 Rule Application Section, including a prediction as to resolution of issue 2
>
> *Issue/Condition 3:* Intent to Commit a Crime
> * Issue 3 Roadmap
> * Issue 3 Rule Explanation Section

---

1. For purposes of showing how the global rule may change, we are assuming that the new law applies retroactively. As you may already be aware from your criminal law class, a criminal law's retroactive effect is not a foregone conclusion and may, in fact, have constitutional *ex post facto* implications.

- Issue 3 Rule Application Section, including a prediction as to resolution of issue 3 .

*Global Conclusion:* A prediction as to the court's likely resolution of the client's burglary charge and a reiteration of the court's likely resolution of each contested condition.

Because of the change in the law, there is now another issue to be analyzed, which obviously must be reflected in the large-scale organization. When a change to the global rule of law occurs, it drastically affects your Discussion's large-scale organization. However, such changes are rare. The synthesized global rule usually remains basically the same as the global rule, and you will integrate additional authorities without needing to make changes to the large-scale organization of your Discussion.

## III. Small-Scale Organization: Focusing on the Organization of Each Issue Segment of Your Discussion

The use of multiple authorities will almost always change the small-scale organization of your Discussion, in contrast to the effect on the synthesized global rule. New authorities usually modify our understanding of the rule of law for a given condition, whether through law-centered interpretations or fact-based holdings that give rise to new guiding factors or that cause us to refine guiding factors. In turn, our expanded understanding affects the entire Discussion issue segment.

### A. Issue Roadmap Changes

Any changes in the rule of law for a condition, such as a modification of guiding factors or the addition of a standard or definition, will alter the issue roadmap for that condition. Such changes are common. Because the issue roadmap includes the issue rule of law, that paragraph will change to reflect the synthesized rule of law and a synthesized rule proof. Additional cases may also impact the analysis of the issue and therefore change the issue prediction that appears in the issue roadmap.

Let's return to the burglary statute example, focusing on the issue rule of law for "unlawfully enters" based upon a single authority.

### Rule of Law for Condition of "Unlawfully Enters"

> Unlawful entry must be proven beyond a reasonable doubt. Unlawful entry does not require the use of physical force, and it is judged under the objective, not subjective, standard of what a "reasonable person" would think. In determining whether entry is unlawful, the court considers: (1) the history, if any, between the defendant and the homeowner and (2) any visual indications regarding whether the home was open to the public.

### Synthesized Rule of Law for Condition of "Unlawfully Enters"

Assume that, based upon your synthesis of that issue rule, your rule of law changes.

> Unlawful entry must be proven beyond a reasonable doubt. Unlawful entry does not require the use of physical force, and it is judged under the objective, not subjective, standard of what a "reasonable person" would think. Whether entry is unlawful depends upon: (1) the defendant's history **of access to the home**; (2) any **written** indications regarding whether the home is open to the public; and (3) **whether the structure was locked or otherwise physically secured.**

As you can see, the synthesized rule of law for this condition differs from the existing rule of law. The additional authorities broadened the first guiding factor; rather than the defendant's history with the *homeowner*, that guiding factor is now expanded to include the defendant's history *of access to the home*. In contrast, the second guiding factor appears narrowed; rather than *any* visual indications, it now references only *written* indications. Finally, we have a new guiding factor: whether the structure was locked or secured. Your issue roadmap will now include the synthesized rule, rather than the rule that existed with only a single authority.

Diagram 23-1 visualizes how you combine the rule from multiple cases to form the synthesized rule of law, which, in turn, you apply to the client's facts.

 **CRASH WARNING: Apply One Synthesized Rule**

Remember that in conducting synthesis you combine the rule of law for a given condition from multiple authorities. It is that synthesized rule of law that you set forth in your issue roadmap and apply to your client's situation. You do not separately apply the rule from each authority to your client's situation.

Diagram 23-1

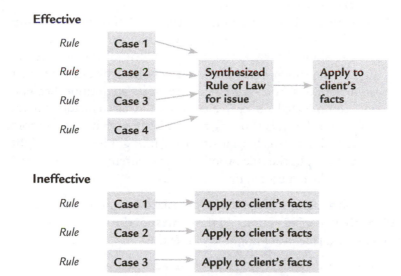

In addition, the rule proof content of your issue roadmap is now synthesized as well. What does this mean? Recall that your rule proof is simply the fact-based holding of the precedent case that applied the law to that condition. You now have multiple precedent cases, so you have multiple fact-based holdings to present together in a synthesized rule proof. This synthesized rule proof will convey the various fact-based holdings in conjunction with one another.

How do you combine those myriad fact-based holdings into a synthesized rule proof? The only hard-and-fast rule is that your rule proof should encompass fact-based holdings that demonstrate all of the guiding factors. In other words, you want to include sufficient detail from your array of cases to "prove" to your reader that your guiding factors have a factual basis in the cases.

Beyond the need to cover all guiding factors, you have considerable latitude in how you convey your synthesized rule proof. In deciding the most effective approach, let readability guide you. In particular, consider the following:

- What level of detail seems appropriate for the rule proof, given the precision or breadth of the guiding factors? Where the guiding factors are relatively narrow, we need not be as specific in our rule proof. In contrast, where the guiding factors are relatively broad, additional factual detail in the rule proof might help the reader understand the guiding factor. You want to strike a balance between providing the necessary information and avoiding information overload.

- Are sentences clear and concise? In general, you want to avoid unnecessarily long sentences.
- Will your attribution become too complex? If one case can support all of the facts in the rule proof, you can use the *See, e.g.,* signal to show the reader that this is but one of several cases that support the rule proof. If, however, you have blended two fact-based holdings in a single sentence, your attribution becomes more complicated. For each cite, you will need to include explanatory parentheticals showing the reader how that case supports the textual sentence. In that situation, it might be more straightforward to split the rule proof into two sentences, each of which need only be supported by a single case.

Let's look at some examples of synthesized rule proofs, keeping in mind the above considerations. In the context of the burglary example, the synthesized rule proof might look like this:

> When the defendant frequently has accessed a home with the previous or current owner's knowledge and there are no indications of a change in ownership or that he now is unwelcome, courts hold that that the entry is lawful. [CITE CASES 1 AND 3.] In contrast, when the entry was previously allowed, but now circumstances are changed, such as a locked door to alert the defendant he is no longer welcome, courts hold the entry is unlawful. [CITE CASE 2.]

Notice that the synthesized rule proof contains two sentences. One sentence combines the fact-based holdings for the guiding factors in which the result was favorable to the defendant, and the other sentence combines the fact-based holdings for the same guiding factors in which the result was favorable to the State. This approach works in this instance because all of the guiding factors are addressed, and the synthesized rule proof is readable.

Let's look at a different example in which the synthesized rule proof includes more detail.

> A plaintiff will be found to have possessed a reasonable expectancy of entering into a valid business relationship when specific customers called the defendant's store with the belief that they were calling and doing business with the plaintiff. *Chicago's Pizza*, 893 N.E.2d at 993-94. In addition, the court will also consider the amount of contact between the plaintiff and prospective customers. *Mannion v. Stallings & Co.*, 561 N.E.2d 1134, 1139 (Ill. App. Ct. 1990). A court will hold that a plaintiff possessed a reasonable expectancy of entering into a valid business relationship when the plaintiff had moved past negotiations with prospective customers and had received a signed agreement providing compensation amounts. *Id.*

**CRASH WARNING: Rule Proof Only Needs to Prove Your Guiding Factors, Not Address Every Fact**

Keep in mind that your synthesized rule proof will not include *every* fact that was considered by the court in a precedent case. You are starting with your fact-based holdings, in which you already have determined the legally significant facts. Your rule explanation section, which will immediately follow your issue roadmap with your rule proof, will include additional factual detail that provides more context for the synthesized rule proof.

In this case, the guiding factors are relatively broad, warranting this more detailed, but still clear, approach.

## B. Rule Explanation Changes

Your rule explanation will include the additional cases that you selected as most factually similar. When you outlined your rule explanation using only a single authority, the process was relatively straightforward. Because you were working from only one authority, your rule explanation section for each issue was relatively short—often only a single paragraph—and simply included the facts and reasoning from that single authority. This process becomes more complex with multiple authorities.

### 1. Organizing Your Rule Explanation Section with Multiple Authorities: Two Approaches

When deciding how best to organize these multiple authorities, the writer typically chooses between two primary approaches. The rule explanation section can be organized around the cases (*case approach*) or organized around the guiding factors (*guiding factors approach*).

In the case approach to organizing rule explanation, the writer provides each case's information, case by case. That means that the writer takes a particular case, and, typically in one paragraph, discusses all of its information relating to the entire rule of law for the issue/condition, including any guiding factors addressed in that case. The rule explanation is separate for each case.

The opposite is true when the writer uses the guiding factors approach to organizing rule explanation. There, the writer's rule explanation section is drafted so that all of the discussion of a particular guiding factor is in one place. This means that the writer focuses on the guiding factor, including all information from the selected cases that address that particular guiding factor. As such, when a case considers more than one guiding factor, the discussion of the case may be scattered throughout the rule explanation section, although the discussion of any given guiding factor will all be in one place. Under this approach, a rule explanation paragraph may focus on just one guiding factor or may consider more than one guiding factor. The latter typically occurs when two guiding factors are interrelated, such that discussing them in tandem is helpful.

Both approaches can be effective, and neither approach is necessarily preferable to the other. Even so, both approaches have advantages and disadvantages, which we briefly discuss below and then consider in more detail in Chapter 25. Remember that regardless of the particular approach, the same information from the cases will be conveyed, just presented in a different order. Looking ahead, you can see the importance of framing sentences, which signal to the reader the content and organization of each paragraph.

 **CONCEPT IN ACTION: Rule Explanation Organizational Options**

Let's look at how a writer might organize a rule explanation section using each of these approaches.

Assume you have selected four cases for your rule explanation section for a given condition that has three guiding factors:

- Case A (favorable to prosecution—includes guiding factors 1 and 2)
- Case B (favorable to defendant—includes guiding factor 1)
- Case C (favorable to defendant—includes guiding factors 1 and 2)
- Case D (favorable to prosecution—includes guiding factor 3)

How might the rule explanation section look under the case organizational approach?

- RE paragraph for Case B (will reference guiding factor 1)
- RE paragraph for Case C (will reference guiding factors 1 and 2)
- RE paragraph for Case A (will reference guiding factors 1 and 2)
- RE paragraph for Case D (will reference guiding factor 3)

Alternatively, how might the rule explanation section look under the guiding factors organizational approach?

- RE paragraph(s) for guiding factor 1 (will reference Case A, Case B, and Case C)
- RE paragraph(s) for guiding factor 2 (will reference Case A and Case C)
- RE paragraph(s) for guiding factor 3 (will reference Case D)

Under either approach, the writer provides all of the pertinent information from all four cases she has selected. The difference is simply in the way the writer presents the information. Note that we indicated this was an example of how the writer "might" organize the section using these approaches. That is because even once you have chosen a general organizational approach, there is no single way to further organize that section. For example, in the outline above in which the rule explanation is organized around the cases, the writer could have chosen to put the cases in a different order, starting with the cases supporting the prosecution's position for certain guiding factors, followed by cases supporting the defense's position for those same guiding factors, and concluding with the case that supports the prosecution's position for the final guiding factor:

- RE paragraph for Case A (will reference guiding factors 1 and 2)
- RE paragraph for Case C (will reference guiding factors 1 and 2)
- RE paragraph for Case B (will reference guiding factor 1)
- RE paragraph for Case D (will reference guiding factor 3)

Similarly, in the outline organized around the guiding factors, the writer could have chosen to put the rule explanation paragraphs for guiding factors 1 and 2 together, such that the outline would only have two points:

- RE paragraph(s) for guiding factors 1 and 2 (will reference Case A, Case B, and Case C)
- RE paragraph(s) for guiding factor 3 (will reference Case D)

Thus, in outlining your rule explanation, you should keep in mind that you have several decisions to make. You can choose to organize by the cases or by the guiding factors. In addition, within either of these frameworks, you have discretion in how you organize the information from the cases.

## 2. Deciding Which Approach to Use

As noted above, either organizational scheme can work, and neither is perfect. So, you may wonder when a writer might prefer one approach over the other. Although there is no definitive rule, it can be effective to organize around the cases when the guiding factors are highly related, making it hard to explain the court's holding and reasoning without looking at those guiding factors together. When guiding factors addressed in a single case are discussed in separate paragraphs in the rule explanation, it is not possible to convey to the reader how those guiding factors relate to one another and, taken together, resulted in the court's holding.

On the other hand, when the guiding factors are relatively distinct from one another, it can be useful to organize around the guiding factors. This approach allows the reader to get a better feel for each guiding factor, because it pulls together the myriad facts relevant to that guiding factor, regardless of which case they came from.

In addition, sometimes a writer simply prefers one approach over the other because it seems more intuitive to him. So, unless your professor has a different preference, use the approach that works best for you, taking into consideration the nature of the rule of law you need to explain.

## C. Rule Application Changes

Your rule application section will change to reflect any modifications to the rule of law for that condition and to include arguments that use the additional authorities. These changes will affect both the organization and the content of that section.

### 1. Changes to the Organization of the Rule Application Section

As discussed in Part III A above, the issue roadmap will incorporate a synthesized rule that likely will have been modified as a result of using additional authorities. The aptly named issue roadmap previews the "route" that will be taken in the rest of the issue segment of your Discussion. Therefore, the rule application's organization will also change to reflect the changes in the synthesized rule.

 **CONCEPT IN ACTION: How Does the Outline for a Rule Application Section Change to Reflect Changes in the Rule for the Condition?**

Within the context of the burglary hypothetical, assume the rule application section for the condition of "unlawful entry" in a single authority memo was organized using the issue-components approach as follows:

Guiding Factor 1: History with Homeowner
- Defendant's arguments for guiding factor 1
- Prosecution's arguments for guiding factor 1

Guiding Factor 2: Visual Indications
- Defendant's arguments for guiding factor 2
- Prosecution's arguments for guiding factor 2

However, as noted in Part III A above, the additional authorities modified the rule for this condition, as shown below. Still using the issue-components approach, how does this change in the rule affect the rule application outline for this issue? The writer might now organize the rule application for that issue as follows:

### Guiding Factor 1: History of Access to the Home
- Defendant's arguments for guiding factor 1
- Prosecution's arguments for guiding factor 1

### Guiding Factor 2: Written Indications
- Defendant's arguments for guiding factor 2
- Prosecution's arguments for guiding factor 2

### Guiding Factor 3: Locked/Secured
- Defendant's arguments for guiding factor 3
- Prosecution's arguments for guiding factor 3

A similar change would occur to the rule application if the writer instead had chosen to organize the section using the party/position approach. (Recall that the primary difference between these approaches is whether you address all arguments for a single guiding factor together or whether you instead address together all arguments of one party related to the entire issue/condition rule. For a more detailed reminder of the difference between the party/position and issue-components approach, refer to Chapter 18, which introduced these organizational schemes.) Under the party/position approach, the rule application section integrating multiple authorities might look like this:

### Defendant's Arguments
- Def's arguments guiding factor 1: History of Access to the Home
- Def's arguments guiding factor 2: Written Indications
- Def's arguments guiding factor 3: Locked/Secured

### Prosecution's Argument(s)
- Pros's arguments guiding factor 1: History of Access to the Home
- Pros's arguments guiding factor 2: Written Indications
- Pros's arguments guiding factor 3: Locked/Secured

## 2. Changes to the Content of the Rule Application Section

The content of the rule application section almost always will change when you add multiple authorities. With a single authority, your rule application could only make analogical arguments by comparing and contrasting your client's situation with one precedent case. When you include multiple authorities for your rule explanation, you now have a pool of cases to use to make analogical arguments in your rule application section.

In Chapter 26, we will discuss in detail the specific content of the new arguments based upon multiple authorities, but for now simply notice how the outline from above changes to include analogies to multiple cases, expanding the content of those arguments. With only a single case, every part of this outline would be limited to comparing or distinguishing Case A.

### Guiding Factor 1: History of Access to Home
- Defendant's arguments for guiding factor 1 (comparing Cases B and C and distinguishing Case A)
- Prosecution's arguments for guiding factor 1 (comparing Case A and distinguishing Case B and C)

### Guiding Factor 2: Written Indications
- Defendant's arguments for guiding factor 2 (comparing Case C and distinguishing Case A)
- Prosecution's arguments for guiding factor 2 (comparing Case A and distinguishing Case C)

### Guiding Factor 3: Locked/Secured
- Defendant's arguments for guiding factor 3 (distinguishing Case D)
- Prosecution's arguments for guiding factor 3 (comparing Case D)

## IV. Putting It Together: A Sample Outline for a Discussion with Multiple Authorities

Below we have included a sample outline for the large-scale organization of a Discussion section using multiple authorities. Keep in mind that this is an example, not a template. Thus, this is simply one way that a Discussion with multiple authorities could be organized; it is not the only way. As discussed in detail above, the writer has choices about which organizational approach to use in the rule explanation section as well as in the rule application section. The parenthetical notes indicate the changes to each section as you move from a single authority to multiple authorities. For additional detail on all of the components to include in each part of the Discussion, review Chapter 19.

Global Roadmap (uses synthesized global rule of law)
Segment for Issue/Condition 1:
- Issue 1 Roadmap (includes synthesized rule of law for issue 1)

- Issue 1 Rule Explanation Section
  - RE paragraph for Case B (will reference guiding factors 1 and 2)
  - RE paragraph for Case C (will reference guiding factor 1)
  - RE paragraph for Case A (will reference guiding factor 2)
- Issue 1 Rule Application Section
  - Defendant's Arguments (comparisons and distinctions to guiding factors 1, 2, and 3 using Cases A, B, and C)
  - Prosecution's Arguments (comparisons and distinctions to guiding factors 1, 2, and 3 using Cases A, B, and C)

Segment for Issue/Condition 2:
- Issue 2 Roadmap (includes synthesized rule of law for issue 2)
- Issue 2 Rule Explanation Section
  - RE paragraph for Case E (will reference guiding factor 1 and 2)
  - RE paragraph for Case B (will reference guiding factors 2 and 3)
  - RE paragraph for Case D (will reference guiding factor 2 and 3)
- Issue 2 Rule Application Section
  - Defendant's Arguments (comparisons and distinctions to guiding factors 1, 2, and 3 using Cases B, D, and E)
  - Prosecution's Arguments (comparisons and distinctions to guiding factors 1, 2, and 3 using Cases B, D, and E)

Global Conclusion

 **CHECK IN: Rule Explanation and Rule Application Organization**

In the above outline of a Discussion, what organizational approach has the writer used for the rule explanation section? How can you tell?

What organizational approach has the writer used for the rule application section? How can you tell?

## V. Using Visual Maps to Assist with Organization of Your Discussion

Outlines are an essential tool to help you adhere to the expected format and content of a legal memo Discussion. In addition to outlining, sometimes it can be helpful to map out your Discussion visually, either before or while you draft your outline. This can be a useful technique to see how the information fits together and where you may have gaps. Two examples of such visual maps follow in Diagram 23-2 and Diagram 23-3.

### Dangerous Dog Hypothetical

Diagram 23-2

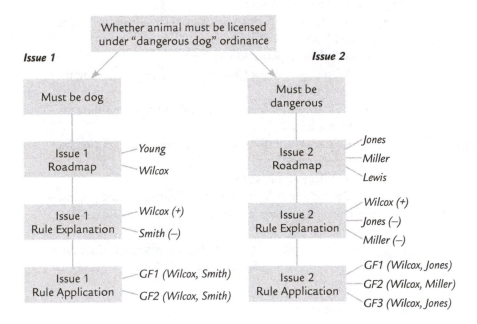

Diagram 23-3

| ISSUE | KEY CASES SYNTHE-SIZED RULE | KEY ANALOGICAL CASES |
|---|---|---|
| Issue 1: must be dog | *Young* *Wilcox* | *Wilcox* (+) *Smith* (−) |
| Issue 2: must be dangerous | *Jones* *Miller* *Lewis* | *Wilcox* (+) *Jones* (−) *Miller* (−) |

### CHAPTER 24

# Drafting the Roadmaps with Multiple Authorities

I n this chapter, we move from the annotated outline of the Discussion using multiple authorities and draft the global and issue roadmaps.

---

### Study Guide Questions for Chapter 24

1. In what ways do your multiple authority roadmap paragraphs remain the same as they were with only a single authority?

2. In what ways do your multiple authority roadmap paragraphs differ from the ones you created using only a single authority? What is the biggest change?

3. What changes to the structure and content might you see in your global roadmap?

4. What changes to the structure and content might you see in your issue roadmaps?

5. When integrating multiple authorities, why are the issue roadmaps more likely to change than the global roadmap?

6. What new terms were introduced in this chapter? How do these terms relate to your existing understanding of predictive memo writing? Did your understanding of any other terms change as a result of reading this chapter?

---

At this point, you have a working annotated outline of your Discussion that integrates multiple authorities. It is now time to draft your Discussion. Just as we did with only a single authority, we consider each part of the Discussion separately, starting with the roadmap paragraphs.

## I. In General: What's the Same and What's Different in Roadmap Paragraphs for Memos with Multiple Authorities?

Much of your roadmap paragraphs will remain the same when you integrate additional authorities. Namely:

- The purpose of your roadmap paragraphs is still to orient the reader to the information that follows, and you will still organize your analysis around the rule of law.

- The components of your roadmap paragraphs largely remain the same.
- Your global roadmap still is generally only a single paragraph, as are each of your issue roadmaps.
- You still will have an issue roadmap for each issue/condition in your Discussion.

Although the structure and purpose remain the same, the content of your roadmap paragraphs will change when you integrate additional authorities. The biggest changes will occur when your rule of law has changed. Specifically, your global roadmap will reflect any changes to the synthesized global rule of law. Your global roadmap will also reflect any changes to what conditions are at issue. Finally, your global prediction might change with the introduction of additional authorities.

In addition, your issue roadmaps will almost certainly change. As you learned in Chapter 19 when synthesizing the legal rule using multiple authorities, such synthesis typically results in a more detailed and modified understanding of the rule for each issue/condition. Often, additional authorities may have provided a clearer understanding of the guiding factors or added a helpful definition. Because your issue roadmap will provide the synthesized rule of law for an issue/condition, the rest of the paragraph will change as well—including your rule proof and issue prediction—to reflect this more nuanced rule.

Below we look first at the global roadmap and then at the issue roadmap, both in the context of multiple authorities.

## II. Global Roadmap Integrating Multiple Authorities

As noted above, the structure and basic ingredients for your global roadmap remain largely the same when you integrate additional authorities. It will contain:

1. A topic sentence that includes a global prediction as to the client's claim or charge.
2. The *synthesized* global rule of law, with its conditions and the relationship between the conditions clearly set forth, and with proper attribution.
3. An announcement of any non-issues, which are conditions that will not be addressed in the memo, ideally with a brief explanation as to why the conditions will not be addressed.
4. An announcement of the issues that will be addressed in the memo.

5. A global prediction, which is the prediction as to the resolution of the client's claim or charge, supported by key client facts related to that global prediction. A sentence or two should suffice, as this is simply the overall prediction and does not contain the separate issue predictions that will appear at the end of each issue roadmap.

Notice that the only change in terms of the components is that the rule of law included is now the *synthesized* rule of law.

Likewise, the template for your global roadmap is largely the same as when you only had a single authority:

> The client's claim will likely [INSERT GLOBAL PREDICTION]. In order to demonstrate the claim, the client must show [INSERT APPLICABLE SYNTHESIZED GLOBAL RULE OF LAW, INCLUDING CONDITIONS]. [INSERT CITATION.] [INSERT ANY NON-ISSUES.] [INSERT ISSUES ADDRESSED IN THE MEMO.] Because [INSERT RESOLUTION OF ISSUE SUPPORTED BY RELEVANT CLIENT FACTS] and because [INSERT RESOLUTION OF ISSUE SUPPORTED BY RELEVANT CLIENT FACTS], [INSERT GLOBAL PREDICTION].[1]

Given that the basic structure and components typically remain the same, what changes might you need to reflect in your global roadmap? Your pre-drafting analysis answers this question. In this process, detailed in Chapter 22, you considered whether and how the synthesized rule changed with the integration of multiple authorities. You also considered whether the same conditions were still at issue.

For example, you may have to alter the global roadmap to reflect which conditions are at issue, even if the conditions themselves do not change. Recall that in Chapter 23 we hypothesized how a legislative amendment changed the definition of the condition of what constitutes a "building or a structure." In our hypothetical, that substantive change in the law changed this condition of "must be a building or a structure" from a non-issue to an issue. In turn, the global roadmap would no longer identify the condition of "building or structure" as a non-issue, but rather would include it as an issue to be addressed in the memo.

While it's uncommon for the synthesized global rule to change substantively from the existing rule, when such a change occurs, it is critical to reflect that change in the global roadmap. Because the global rule provides the direction and scope for the rest of the Discussion, any changes to that rule will have a cascading effect on your Discussion.

---

1. Note that this template is a loose guide for the different components of the global roadmap. When you are drafting a global roadmap for a client matter you will likely find that some of these components require more than one sentence.

In the typical situation in which the synthesized global rule of law is no different from the existing one, your global roadmap using multiple authorities will be largely the same as it was with only a single authority. Indeed, often the only change to your global roadmap is the inclusion of additional citations to authority to support and confirm your announcement of the global rule of law. Of course, the analysis of additional authorities might also alter your global prediction.

The following example illustrates the minor changes to the global roadmap in the Warrantless Bomb Search hypothetical. We have noted the changes that have occurred based on the use of additional authorities.

*Watson* is a new authority; we cite it (and the SCOTUS case to which it cites) to show the strength of support for this foundation global rule of law.

Similarly, we cite to *Henry* to show additional authority for the exigency exception.

The global prediction remains the same; although the additional authorities help us better understand the contours of the global rule, they do not change the likely result we get when we apply that rule to the client facts.

> The government wants to know whether the items seized in the warrantless search of the container must be suppressed. While the Fourth Amendment "generally requires officers to possess a warrant before conducting a search," "[t]here are, however, exceptions to the warrant requirement." *United States v. Purcell*, 526 F.3d 953, 960 (6th Cir. 2008); *see also United States v. Watson*, 483 F.3d 1382, 1387 (6th Cir. 2007) (citing *Illinois v. Rodriguez*, 497 U.S. 177, 181 (1990)). One exception to the warrant requirement is "the existence of exigent circumstances." *Purcell*, 526 F.3d. at 960 (citing *Mincey v. Arizona*, 437 U.S. 385, 392-93 (1978)); *see also Henry v. Newland*, 263 F.3d 1384, 1395 (6th Cir. 2001). The other "well-delineated" exception to the warrant requirement is consent to search. *Id.* The government bears the burden of proving either exception. *Id.* (citing *United States v. Atchley*, 474 F.3d 840, 851 (6th Cir. 2007)). This memo addresses both exceptions—namely, whether an exigent circumstance existed to justify the search and whether the officers obtained consent to search. Because of the pending threat of a bomb as well as the permission granted by someone with a key to the container, it is likely the court will conclude the search was constitutional.

## III. Issue Roadmap with Multiple Authorities

Like your global roadmap, your issue roadmaps using multiple authorities will retain the same general structure and components as they had when using only a single authority. The issue rule of law included is now the *synthesized* issue rule of law, and the rule proof is now a *synthesized* rule proof. The rest of the components remain the same.

### Issue Roadmaps

1. *A* topic sentence that announces the issue/condition that will be addressed in the issue roadmap.
2. The *synthesized* rule of law for the issue/condition: any definitions, standards, or guiding factors related to the court's analysis of the issue/condition.

3. The rule proof: This is the *synthesized* fact-based holdings from the precedents, which provides "proof" of the rule.

4. A prediction of the resolution of that issue/condition, supported by key client facts related to that prediction.

In addition, the template for drafting an issue roadmap basically remains the same regardless of how many authorities are integrated. The rule and rule proof both reflect the synthesized rule.

> The first issue for the court to consider [INSERT FIRST ISSUE/ CONDITION]. To analyze this issue the court will consider [INSERT SYNTHESIZED ISSUE/CONDITION RULE, INCLUDING DEFINITIONS, STANDARDS, AND GUIDING FACTORS]. [INSERT CITATION.] [INSERT SYNTHESIZED RULE PROOF.] [INSERT CITATION.] The court will likely [INSERT PREDICTION AS TO THE RESOLUTION OF FIRST ISSUE SUPPORTED BY RELEVANT CLIENT FACTS].

But while the components and structure largely remain the same, the specific content of each issue roadmap is likely to change significantly when integrating multiple authorities. Most notably, as discussed in detail in Chapter 21, the synthesized rule of law for an issue/ condition frequently is modified due to the additional understanding that arises from using multiple authorities. That change in the issue rule, in turn, affects the substantive content of the now-synthesized rule proof, as well as the issue prediction.

Specifically, consider the issue roadmap for the element of whether exigent circumstances justified the warrantless search from the Warrantless Bomb Search memorandum. As you review this excerpt, notice how the integration of multiple authorities has altered the content as compared to the roadmap when there was only a single authority used (Appendix A). We have noted these changes in the annotated version below.

This is a law-centered interpretation (a standard) from a new authority. This standard was not included in our initial authority (*Purcell*).

> The government will first argue that exigent circumstances justified the warrantless search. *See id.* (quoting *United States v. Rohrig*, 98 F.3d 1506, 1515 (6th Cir. 1996)). "The government bears the burden of showing the existence of exigent circumstances by particularized evidence," and this burden is not satisfied by mere speculation that the exigency exists. *Henry*, 263 F.3d at 1395 (quoting *United States v. Tarazon*, 989 F.2d 1045, 1049 (9th Cir.1993)). This memo focuses only on whether the search was justified based on a "risk of danger to police or to others." *Purcell*, 526 F.3d. at 960 (quoting *Rohrig*, 98 F.3d at 1515). In determining whether such risk exists, courts consider the objective information available to the agents about the immediacy and extent of the risk and whether the agents' actions were consistent with the asserted risk. *See, e.g., United States v. Johnson*, 22 F.3d 674, 680 (6th Cir. 1994).

Our synthesized guiding factors are modified with the inclusion of additional authorities. When using only a single authority, we understood that there were three guiding factors. Now with two additional authorities on this issue, we understand that there actually are only two. We could have cited to *Johnson* and *Henry*, both of which support these guiding factors, but we opted to use *"see, e.g.,"* instead to shorten the citation.

The synthesized rule proof is much more detailed than when we had only a single authority. Now that we have three authorities we are using to show the application of this rule in precedent cases, we have all three fact-based holdings to synthesize into the rule proof. We provide enough detail from these fact-based holdings to sufficiently prove the rule. As discussed in Chapter 23, that synthesized rule proof gives the reader a preview of what courts have held and why, which the writer will more fully discuss in the rule explanation section.

While the presence of a firearm or other weapon at a scene alone does not constitute a danger justifying a search, such a risk of danger does exist when police have evidence that a weapon is present and poses an immediate threat from being unsecured or otherwise in a volatile state. *Johnson*, 22 F.3d at 680-81; *Henry*, 263 F.3d at 1395. On the other hand, when agents observe evidence of drug use, but not drug manufacturing, which is the danger purported to exist, and agents do not take immediate protective actions, courts hold no exigent circumstance exists. *Purcell*, 526 F.3d at 960. Because the agents received a tip that a bomb was ready to be planted, Scooter the police dog "hit" on the container, and agents took precautions such as clearing the area, a court will likely find an exigent circumstance existed. *See id.*

Note that there can be flexibility in the order in which the synthesized rule and rule proof are presented. A writer will always start by stating at least part of the synthesized rule because, without that, there is nothing to "prove." However, the writer may opt not to provide the entire rule all at once. Instead, the writer may elect to present part of the rule first, then the rule proof for that part, and then present the rest of the rule, followed by its rule proof. Splitting the rule may make more sense when the two parts of the rule are relatively distinct, making it clearer to address the rule and rule proof for each part, as opposed to presenting the entire rule and then the entire rule proof. Whatever variation a writer employs should fulfill the purposes of an issue roadmap: (1) to clearly and accurately convey information about the rule for that issue/condition, and (2) to provide direction for the issue segment that is to come.

### CHAPTER 25

# Drafting the Rule Explanation with Multiple Authorities

In this chapter, we continue drafting the Discussion of a memo using multiple authorities, focusing now on the rule explanation section.

**Study Guide Questions for Chapter 25**

1. How does the structure of the rule explanation section change when additional authorities are included?

2. When are transitions and/or framing sentences necessary in a rule explanation paragraph?

3. How does the rule explanation section differ when organizing the information using the case approach versus the guiding factors approach?

4. How can a writer include additional authority using the *see also* signal to enhance her rule explanation section?

5. What new terms were introduced in this chapter? How do these terms relate to your existing understanding of predictive memo writing? Did your understanding of any other terms change as a result of reading this chapter?

The last chapter considered how roadmap paragraphs change when your Discussion uses multiple authorities. This chapter shows how using multiple authorities also has a large impact on your rule explanation section. This is not surprising, given that rule explanation is all about the precedent cases, and you now have multiple precedent cases with which to work.

## I. In General: What's the Same and What's Different in Rule Explanation Paragraphs for Memos with Multiple Authorities?

Regardless of how many authorities you use, the purpose of your rule explanation section remains the same; rule explanation illustrates

**CRASH WARNING: Draft the Rule Explanation Section Separately for Each Issue**

Remember that the rule explanation section for each issue is analytically distinct from the rule explanation section for the other issues. To help maintain your focus on one issue at a time, we recommend drafting each issue's rule explanation section separately.

to your reader how courts have applied the rule for an issue/condition in factually similar cases. The large-scale organization, too, remains the same; each issue segment of the Discussion still must have its own rule explanation section.

Even so, because integrating additional authorities results in an expanded rule explanation section for each issue, you will encounter new challenges (and opportunities) in drafting the rule explanation. You have already tackled many of these challenges in earlier chapters in which you determined which cases to use (Chapter 21) and decided how to organize the information from those cases into an outline for your rule explanation section (Chapter 23). In this chapter, we consider several unique aspects of drafting the rule explanation section when using multiple authorities, including the use of framing sentences, transitions, and signals. We also highlight some challenges that arise when using multiple authorities and address ways to respond to those challenges.

## II. Drafting a Rule Explanation Using Multiple Authorities

Recall that a single-authority rule explanation paragraph contains the following ingredients:

1. A framing sentence that illustrates how the guiding factors inform the court's analysis of the issue/condition.
2. Facts from the precedent case that are related to those guiding factors.
3. The court's holding on the issue/condition in light of those facts.
4. The court's reasoning; i.e., why it resolved the issue the way it did.

Because you are integrating multiple cases, you will have multiple rule explanation paragraphs for each issue. This makes the selection of which cases to use paramount. Fortunately, at the pre-drafting and outlining stages, you already selected the cases you planned to use in each issue segment. Recall that those decisions were based in large part on which cases best addressed various guiding factors. Ideally, you wanted to select cases that, collectively, illustrated the application of each of the rule's guiding factors for each party's position.

Recall, too, that how you organize the information from those selected cases is somewhat flexible. When using the case approach to organize your rule explanation, the ingredients for each rule explanation paragraph largely will remain the same. You typically will start each paragraph with a framing sentence identifying the guiding factors the particular case illustrates, followed by the facts, holding, and reasoning from that case. In contrast, when using the guiding factors approach to organize your rule explanation, the ingredients for each rule explanation paragraph will contain facts, sometimes from several cases, relating to the specific guiding factor(s) around which that paragraph is organized. It will show how and why those facts were important to the court.

## A. The Importance of Framing Sentences with Multiple Authorities

The framing sentence signals the content of the rest of the paragraph, just as it did when there was only a single authority. A well-crafted framing sentence can greatly aid your reader in understanding how you have organized the information from the cases and in digesting that information. Your framing sentence also will still generally follow the "When [insert guiding factors being illustrated], [insert holding for the issue]" approach.

Typically, each rule explanation paragraph needs its own framing sentence because each additional paragraph generally has a different scope than the preceding paragraph. For example, using the case approach to organization, the framing sentences for consecutive paragraphs might read as in the following examples. (Notice how each successive paragraph has not only its own framing sentence, but also a transition.)

- "When [guiding factors 1 and 2], courts hold [condition satisfied]."
- "Moreover, when [guiding factor 3], courts more likely hold [condition satisfied]."
- "In contrast, when [no guiding factors 1 and 2], courts hold [condition not satisfied]."

In certain instances, you may deviate from the guideline that each rule explanation paragraph starts with its own framing sentence. This is appropriate when the successive paragraph simply expands on the prior paragraph's focus or provides an illustration highly related to the prior paragraph. In such cases, you can choose to forgo a framing sentence and instead simply provide a transition.

Look at the multiple authority memo for The Smell Shoppe (Appendix B) to see an example of the use of a transition without a separate framing sentence. The paragraph regarding the second issue begins, "Similarly, in *E.J. McKernan*, the court considered how the defendant's conduct in facilitating customers' mistaken beliefs...." The writer did not include a separate framing sentence here because the topic of the successive paragraph was covered by the framing sentence from the preceding paragraph: "When a defendant facilitates a mistaken belief by customers as to an affiliation with the plaintiff's business, a plaintiff will be successful in showing that it was the defendant's intentional and unjustified interference that prevented the realization of business expectancy." Given that, a transition adequately signaled the topic of this paragraph to your reader.

## B. Using Transitions Between Rule Explanation Paragraphs

As discussed above, you will use transitions at the start of successive rule explanation paragraphs. Transitions are critical when an issue segment in the Discussion has more than two rule explanation paragraphs. Without a transition leading into a subsequent paragraph, the reader does not understand the relationship between the paragraphs. The following chart provides commonly used transitions.

Diagram 25-1

| TRANSITIONS INDICATING SIMILAR CASE | TRANSITIONS INDICATING CONTRASTING CASE |
|---|---|
| Similarly | In contrast |
| Moreover | On the other hand |
| In addition | Nonetheless |
| Likewise | Even so |
| Furthermore | But |

 **CONCEPT IN ACTION: Use of Transitions**

Consider the following framing sentences taken from the sample, multi-authority Warrantless Bomb Search memo. These sentences were at the start of two consecutive rule explanation paragraphs in the segment of the Discussion that analyzed whether there was a "risk of danger." As you review these sentences, notice how the simple inclusion of the transition phrase "on the contrary," immediately signals to the reader that you are about to explain information about the same topic as the preceding paragraph, but that factually supports the opposite position.

> When agents possess objective information that demonstrates an immediate and significant risk and agents' actions are consistent with the asserted risk, courts hold there is a risk of danger demonstrating an exigent circumstance. [Rest of rule explanation paragraphs.]
>
> On the contrary, when the objective information available to the agents suggests the risk is not immediate, courts hold there is no risk of danger that demonstrates exigent circumstances. [Rest of rule explanation paragraphs.]

## C. Using Signals to Include Additional Supporting Cases in the Rule Explanation Section

As discussed in Chapter 21, selecting cases for each issue of your Discussion's rule explanation section is a challenging process. First and foremost, you have to consider which cases are most factually similar and thus serve as the most useful predictors of what a court will likely do in your client's case. In addition, for each issue segment of your Discussion, you must strive to find a case in which that issue was satisfied and another in which it was not. And, finally, you must consider how well reasoned the various cases are. A case that is factually similar, yet lacks any reasoning and meaningful analysis, has less predictive value because we are not sure why the court held as it did for that issue.

Ultimately, you will take all of these considerations into account and select the most useful cases to include in your rule explanation section for each issue. These selected cases will be extensively discussed in your rule explanation section, as well as being used extensively in your rule application section.

Sometimes, however, a case may be helpful simply to show your reader that there is another case that supports the same proposition you just discussed. Rather than including an extensive discussion of that cumulative case, the *see also* signal provides a shorthand way to include that additional authority. Why would you want to do this? Sometimes it is helpful for your reader to know that while you may not be discussing other cases, they do exist and stand for the same proposition. Thus, the *see also* signal allows you to show your reader the existence of additional authority without consuming too much of your reader's time and attention with largely cumulative material.

Note that when you use the *see also* signal, you should include a parenthetical after your citation. That parenthetical will explain to the reader the relevance of that case by briefly indicating the circumstances under which another court has similarly applied the law.

## 🞧 CONCEPT IN ACTION: Using the *See Also* Signal

Imagine that in the Warrantless Bomb Search example above, you found two cases that, while largely cumulative, together provided a deeper understanding of the law's application than either would have alone. A good option is to pick the marginally better case to include fully in your rule explanation section and then to reference the additional case via a *see also* signal, which itself is followed by a citation and parenthetical explanation. Notice in the excerpt below how using the *see also* signal with an additional authority enhances the rule explanation paragraph.

> When agents possess objective information that demonstrates an immediate and significant risk and agents' actions are consistent with the asserted risk, courts hold there is a risk of danger demonstrating an exigent circumstance. *Henry*, 263 F.3d at 1395. In *Henry*, police officers searched a motel room following a complaint that two men were inside selling drugs. *Id.* at 1388. The officers identified a stolen car parked outside the suspect's motel room. *Id.* When the officers knocked on the motel room door, they detained one man from the suspect's room when he stepped onto an outside porch, but another person inside the motel room immediately slammed the door shut. *Id.* After an officer knocked on the door for approximately two minutes, a second man inside the room stepped out and was detained. *Id.* From the open doorway, one officer spotted what he believed to be a black revolver under a bed inside the room. *Id.* The officer could not see the entire room from the doorway, so he entered the room immediately to retrieve the firearm. *Id.*
>
> Based on these facts, the court found that there was a risk of danger to the officers or other people in the proximity of the motel. *Id.* at 1395. The court noted that even though the officers already detained two men at the time of the warrantless search, there could have been other occupants inside who had access to the gun but who were not visible from the doorway. *Id.* The officers would have reason to believe that any hidden person inside the motel room was also involved with drug activity and the stolen car. *Id.* The court also highlighted the fact that someone inside the room slammed the door shut to keep law enforcement out of the room, heightening the concern about the risk of danger. *Id.*; *see also United States v. Allimaster*, 205 F.3d 101, 107 (12th Cir. 2011) (holding risk of danger existed when, after arresting one person at the location, officers saw a shadow in the kitchen that they believed to be a person where large knives were visible on the kitchen counter).

## III. Challenges in Drafting Rule Explanation Sections Using Multiple Authorities

Whether you use the cases approach or guiding factors approach, it is important to stay focused on the purpose of your rule explanation section: to illustrate how the law for that issue has been applied in similar cases. This overall purpose serves two functions. First, it helps both the writer and the reader better understand the legal rule we described in the issue roadmap. Second, it provides the foundation for the analogical arguments we will make in the rule application section.

Yet staying focused can be challenging when you have multiple cases to weave into your rule explanation section. Two tips can help. First, cull the critical facts from each case, in order to help "prove" that the guiding factors you identified in the framing sentence are indeed what the court considered. Second, make sure your rule explanation includes any case facts from the precedent that you intend to reference in your rule application.

## A. Avoiding the Parade of Cases

Some novice legal writers make the mistake of adding too many cases to their rule explanation section and presenting them without the necessary transitions and/or framing sentences. This is colloquially known as a *parade of cases*, something the writer should take pains to avoid. How can you avoid having your rule explanation section read like an unhelpful parade of cases?

**First, carefully select the cases that best illustrate the rule's application.** Your work selecting which cases demonstrate which guiding factors will help you avoid a parade of cases. You will already have considered which cases you are using and for what particular purpose. This thoughtful selection will help you avoid including too many cases.

Note, too, that your determination of how many cases are appropriate for a rule explanation section hinges not on a hard-and-fast rule but on how you are using the cases. The optimal number may vary considerably depending on the complexity of the issue, as well as how many cases are necessary to adequately cover the guiding factors. At one end of the spectrum, it would be hard to imagine a rule explanation section having fewer than two cases; at the other end of the spectrum, a rule explanation section with a double-digit number of cases likely would overwhelm the reader.

**Second, include transitions, typically with framing sentences, at the start of each rule explanation paragraph.** Your framing sentences indirectly convey to your reader the purpose for which you are using the case(s) described in that paragraph. Likewise, the use of transitions for successive rule explanation paragraphs shows your reader how these paragraphs fit together and helps him digest the information within. Especially when using the cases approach to rule explanation organization, the framing sentences help the writer focus on the guiding factors that will be addressed in the case that follows. This, in turn, helps the reader understand the way in which the writer has organized the cases coherently and logically.

## B. Unique Challenges When Using the Guiding Factors Approach

When using the guiding factors approach, the writer should be mindful of several challenges.

- First, the writer must be careful that he specifies which case he is discussing. Because the guiding factors approach often discusses the facts from more than one case within a single paragraph, it can be confusing to the reader if the writer does not clearly indicate which case provides which facts.
- Second, the writer needs to be sure to only include the part of that case that pertains to the guiding factor(s) discussed in that paragraph. This becomes an issue when a case addresses multiple guiding factors and the writer must discuss different case facts in different places in the rule explanation section, based on which guiding factor applies.
- Finally, the writer must be careful not to overstate the basis for the court's holding. It is tempting to say that because of a particular guiding factor, the court held the condition was satisfied. We are, after all, trying to tell the reader not only the pertinent facts but also what the court ultimately did with those facts. Still, only rarely will a single guiding factor determine the court's holding. More often, the court bases its decision on all of the guiding factors discussed in that case.

Take the following example, which is a paragraph from a rule explanation section organized around the guiding factors.

> When the aggressor has a weapon, courts are far more likely to hold that the defendant reasonably believed she faced imminent death or great bodily harm. In *State v. Alford*, the aggressor charged the defendant with a machete knife. [Cite *Alford*.] Likewise, in both *State v. Brown* and *State v. Cliff*, the aggressor exposed his loaded handgun to the defendant. [Cite *Brown*; cite *Cliff*.] In all of these cases, the court held that the defendant reasonably believed she faced imminent death or great bodily harm. [Cite each case.] The court emphasized in each instance the severity of the threat posed by such weapons, due to their ability to easily inflict deadly harm. [Cite one case, possibly using *e.g.* signal and explanatory parenthetical.]

This paragraph helpfully identifies the possession of a weapon as a critical guiding factor. Yet, these truncated case discussions leave questions about the extent to which the presence of weapons influenced the court's determination in each case. Did the court interpret this guiding factor in tandem with another guiding factor, such as verbal threats regarding how the aggressor planned to use the weapons? Based on the information provided, we do not know. The court might have reached a different holding, notwithstanding the possession of weapons, were it not also for the existence of verbal threats or some other guiding factor.

Indeed, when we organize rule explanation around guiding factors, any one part of the Discussion typically provides only a partial view of the facts that contributed to the court's ultimate holding on that issue. Therefore, we must take care to avoid misleading our reader about why the court held as it did. For example, it likely would not be accurate to say, "When the aggressor has a weapon, courts hold that the defendant reasonably believed she faced imminent death or great bodily harm." That framing sentence overstates the significance of that particular guiding factor and tells the reader that it was "because" of that guiding factor, and only that guiding factor, that the court held as it did in the cases that follow. That is almost never the case, given that courts consider various guiding factors in conjunction with one another.

In contrast, if we use the cases approach, we can definitively explain why the court held as it did. Our case discussion will include all guiding factors and related facts that the court addressed for that issue. Thus, we can be more precise in describing why the court held as it did because we are presenting the reader with a complete view of the contributing facts.

 **CRASH WARNING: Organizing Your Rule Explanations Within Different Issue Segments**

Up until this point, we have been considering what the rule explanation section entails for one issue/condition. If your Discussion contains two or more issues, you will have two or more rule explanation sections, i.e., a rule explanation within each issue segment. Given that, you may be wondering if each rule explanation section must employ the same organizational strategy. Put differently, could you organize the rule explanation section around the cases for issue one and then switch gears for issue two and organize that rule explanation section around the guiding factors? In theory, yes, you could; as noted above, the organizational approach you choose depends, in part, on the way the cases illustrate the guiding factors for a given issue. Thus, it would make sense that the optimal organizational approach might vary by the issue. Even so, keep in mind that this may be more challenging to write, and that kind of variation in the different rule explanation sections of a memo also easily could confuse the reader.

## C. Unique Challenges When Using the Organizing by the Cases Approach

Although the cases approach makes it easier to explain the court's holding, that precision comes at a price. Specifically, the facts from different cases that relate to a given guiding factor are never considered alongside each other, but instead are scattered throughout different rule explanation paragraphs. Thus, the reader is not able to see how various facts play out under a particular guiding factor. Moreover, in the rule application section, the writer will have to gather facts from various case precedents in order to make analogical arguments related to a particular guiding factor.

In addition, using the cases approach makes it far easier to fall into the "parade of cases" trap. When you elect to organize the section around the cases, you may start to think of this section as merely a series of case descriptions, with little rhyme or reason as to the significance of those cases and the particular purpose that each case serves. To avoid this, keep your purpose in mind, carefully select cases, and use effective transitions and framing sentences.

You may be discouraged to learn that each organizational approach has significant drawbacks. However, simply being aware of the drawbacks of each approach will help you to minimize them. Further, knowing that no approach is perfect should prepare you for the reality that writing the rule explanation section is not easy; you should anticipate some struggle. A legal writer has no choice but to employ a principled organizational strategy, so pick the one that makes the most sense to you for the rule of law you are discussing, but remain aware of potential obstacles so that you can avoid them as best you can.

---

 **CHECK IN: Reviewing Rule Explanation Sections**

Review the multiple authority memos in Appendix B. The Smell Shoppe memo organizes the rule explanation section using the guiding factors approach, whereas the Warrantless Bomb Search memo uses the cases approach. For each memo:
- First, create an outline of the rule explanation section.
- Next, review the framing sentences and transitions. How do these features assist the reader in digesting the information that follows?

## IV. Putting It Together: A Checklist for Your Rule Explanation Section When Using Multiple Authorities

While a rule explanation section that includes multiple authorities does not lend itself to a template due to inherent variations, the following checklist will help you draft effective rule explanation sections.

1. Have I selected the cases using the case selection principles in Chapter 21? Namely, have I selected factually similar cases? Do I have a case in which the condition was satisfied and one in which it was not? Do I have cases that demonstrate the guiding factors I identified in my issue roadmap?
2. Have I presented the case facts logically and clearly, organizing with either the cases approach or the guiding factors approach?
3. Does each paragraph have a framing sentence and/or a transition, such that my reader knows the scope of that paragraph?
4. Have I included only those facts that tie to my framing sentence for that paragraph? If I have organized using the cases approach, have I included all facts from that case that are relevant to the condition? If I have organized using the guiding factors approach, have I included all facts from any cases I have selected that tie to the guiding factor(s) identified in my framing sentence?

### CHAPTER 26

# Drafting the Rule Application with Multiple Authorities

In this chapter, we continue drafting the Discussion for a multiple-authority memo, focusing on the rule application section.

---

### Study Guide Questions for Chapter 26

1. In what ways does the multiple authority rule application section remain the same as the single authority rule application section?

2. In what ways does the multiple authority rule application section change from the single authority rule application section?

3. When using multiple authorities, is it effective to compare those cases to one another? Why or why not?

4. Are topic sentences necessary for each rule application paragraph? Why or why not? What makes an effective topic sentence?

5. What new terms were introduced in this chapter? How do these terms relate to your existing understanding of predictive memo writing? Did your understanding of any other terms change as a result of reading this chapter?

---

## I. In General: What's the Same and What's Different in Rule Application Paragraphs for Memos with Multiple Authorities?

Much about the structure and content of your rule application paragraphs will remain the same when you integrate additional authorities:

- Each issue segment will still have its own rule application section.
- The purpose of your rule application paragraphs remains the same: to make arguments for both parties/positions.
- The components of the rule application paragraphs largely remain the same. You still will make arguments for each party/position, consisting of rule-based reasoning, analogical reasoning, and policy-based reasoning.

**CRASH WARNING: Draft Each Rule Application Separately**

Like your rule explanation section, each issue has its own rule application section that must be analyzed separately. For that reason, we recommend that you draft each issue segment of your Discussion (issue roadmap, rule explanation section, and rule application section) separately from other issue segments. This will help you keep the analysis for each issue distinct, as well as help ensure each segment of your Discussion is internally cohesive.

- You will still integrate the facts of your client's position into your argument, rather than reciting facts without explicitly tying them to the rule.
- In making analogies, you still will focus on explicit and detailed comparisons rather than reasoning by proximity.
- Your arguments still are based on the components of the rule for that issue/condition, most notably the guiding factors.

Recognize, however, that your rule application section will be greatly expanded based upon the use of multiple authorities. These extra cases will not only enable you to craft more arguments, they will also help you make more sophisticated arguments.

## II. Drafting a Rule Application Section Using Multiple Authorities

When using multiple authorities, the rule application section for each issue continues to include arguments for both parties/positions. Those arguments continue to be based on the components of the rule of law for that condition. In addition, those arguments still include analogies.

Similarities notwithstanding, when using multiple authorities, the specific content of your rule application section will likely change in several ways. Let's first look at changes to the rule application section as a whole.

### A. Changes in the Organization and Overall Content of the Rule Application Section

#### Burglary Statute Hypothetical

As you learned in Chapter 23, the organization of your rule application section likely will change in order to reflect any changes in the synthesized rule of law for that issue. Recall, for example, how the organization of the rule application section in the burglary hypothetical for the condition of "unlawful entry" evolved as a result of changes to the rule stemming from the consideration of additional authorities. Specifically, because the guiding factors changed, so did the outline of the rule application section.

### Unlawful Entry Outline Based Upon the Single Authority Rule for That Condition Using Issue-Components Approach (from Chapter 23)

**Guiding Factor 1: History with Homeowner**
- Defendant's arguments for guiding factor 1
- Prosecution's arguments for guiding factor 1

**Guiding Factor 2: Visual Indications**
- Defendant's arguments for guiding factor 2
- Prosecution's arguments for guiding factor 2

### Unlawful Entry Outline Based Upon the Synthesized Rule for That Condition

**Guiding Factor 1: History of Access to the Home**
- Defendant's arguments for guiding factor 1
- Prosecution's arguments for guiding factor 1

**Guiding Factor 2: Written Indications**
- Defendant's arguments for guiding factor 2
- Prosecution's arguments for guiding factor 2

**Guiding Factor 3: Locked/Secured**
- Defendant's arguments for guiding factor 3
- Prosecution's arguments for guiding factor 3

In addition to the outline changing, the use of additional authorities means that the arguments in the rule application section will change. No longer will analogical arguments be based upon a single authority. Instead, you will draw from multiple authorities to craft comparisons and distinctions. This will result in more arguments and a greatly expanded and enriched rule application section.

Consider, for example, the annotated version of the outline for the condition of unlawful entry. In particular, note how many new arguments are available given the addition of three cases: Cases B, C, and D.

#### Guiding Factor 1: History of Access to the Home
- Defendant's arguments for guiding factor 1 (comparing Cases B and C and distinguishing Case A)
- Prosecution's arguments for guiding factor 1 (comparing Case A and distinguishing Cases B and C)

#### Guiding Factor 2: Written Indications
- Defendant's arguments for guiding factor 2 (comparing Case C and distinguishing Case A)
- Prosecution's arguments for guiding factor 2 (comparing Case A and distinguishing Case C)

#### Guiding Factor 3: Locked/Secured
- Defendant's arguments for guiding factor 3 (distinguishing Case D)
- Prosecution's arguments for guiding factor 3 (comparing Case D)

## B. Components of a Rule Application Section Using Multiple Authorities

Now let's look specifically at the components of a rule application paragraph when using multiple authorities.

**The topic sentence:** You will start with a topic sentence, which can be framed neutrally or conclusively. The topic sentence must indicate to the reader the topic of that paragraph. Direct, short topic sentences are most effective for rule application paragraphs. That means your topic sentences generally should not contain arguments or even relevant facts. You will include those items in the remainder of the paragraph. Under the deductive approach that your law-trained reader expects, the paragraph should start broadly (i.e., identify the topic) and then provide supporting detail (i.e., the arguments).

Your topic sentences will vary based upon whether you have elected to organize your arguments using the issue-components approach or the party/position approach. (See Chapter 23 to review these options.)

For example, if you are using the issue-components approach, each paragraph in your rule application focuses on a particular issue-component, most typically a guiding factor. Thus, in the above outline for the burglary hypothetical, the topic sentence for guiding factor 1 (history of access to the home) could read either:

- First, the Defendant will argue he has a history of access to the home. *[Framed explicitly.]*
  OR

- First, the court will likely conclude that the Defendant has a meaningful history of accessing the home. *[Framed implicitly.]*

If you are instead using the party/position organizational approach, each paragraph will focus on the arguments of a particular party/position. Thus, your topic sentence might read:

- The Defendant will argue that his entry was not unlawful. *[Framed explicitly.]*
  OR
- The court will likely conclude that the Defendant's entry was not unlawful. *[Framed implicitly.]*

As you can see, when using the party/position approach, the paragraphs are focused on the various arguments of a party taken together; as such, the topic sentences typically reflect that level of generality.

**The arguments:** After your topic sentence, you reach the heart of your legal analysis: the supporting arguments. The preceding parts of your Discussion culminate here, as you use the information you already have conveyed in the roadmap paragraphs and rule explanation paragraphs to develop arguments. Because of the groundwork you have laid, the arguments in your rule application should make sense to your reader. For example, because your reader understands the legal rule for the issue from your issue roadmap and understands the rule's prior application from your rule explanation section, he is well-prepared to understand your rule application arguments as to how the court will apply the rule in your client's case.

Generally speaking, the types of arguments you will make when using multiple authorities are no different than those you can make when using only a single authority. Your arguments applying the rule to your client's facts will now be grounded in whatever components (standards, definitions, and guiding factors) you identified in the synthesized rule for that issue/condition. You will continue to make analogical arguments, comparing and distinguishing the facts and reasoning from precedent cases to your client's situation. These arguments will stem from the cases that you included in your expanded rule explanation section. Finally, you will continue to make policy arguments, where available. These arguments, too, will be based in content that you already have communicated in your roadmaps and/or rule explanation paragraphs.

*Burglary Example Revisited*: Continuing with the burglary illustration, let's look at the argument that follows a neutrally framed topic sentence that uses the issue-components approach, as described above. Note that, as is usually the case with the addition of multiple authorities, the analogical arguments reference more than one case, creating a more detailed, and thus predictive, argument.

**CRASH WARNING: No Authorities Make Their Debut in the Rule Application Section**

You may wonder if it is ever appropriate to introduce a new case in your rule application section or to make an analogy to a case not yet discussed. The answer to both queries is an emphatic *"No."* Cases do not debut in rule application. Every case used in your rule application section should first be introduced in your rule explanation section. Even more specifically, every fact or reasoning from a precedent case used in your rule application section should first be introduced in your rule explanation section. While this may seem unnecessary or redundant, consider how confusing it would be to first hear about a case in the rule application section. Having no context for that case and no understanding of its facts, the reader would not appreciate the analogy.

---

**Topic sentence for guiding factor one, history of access to the home.**

**After topic sentences, we make the defendant's arguments for this guiding factor.**

**Argument using rule-based reasoning.**

**Analogical argument favorably comparing client's case to Case B and Case C.**

**Analogical argument distinguishing client's case from Case A.**

**We use the transition "even so" to signal that we are switching gears to the other party/position. We remain, as set forth in our outline, focused on the first factor, but now we are making the arguments for the other party/position.**

**Analogical argument distinguishing client's case from Case B and Case C.**

**Analogical argument favorably comparing client's case to Case A.**

First, the Defendant will argue he has a meaningful history of accessing the home. The Defendant's connection to the home was based on a sincere belief that he was permitted to enter the home because his longtime friend lived there. Much like the defendants in both Case B and Case C, whose close relatives lived in the home, here the Defendant's longtime friend lived in the home. *See* cite to Case B and Case C. Thus, just as in those cases, the Defendant here believed he was permitted to enter the home. *See* cite to Case B and Case C. The Defendant's longstanding relationship with the home's occupant distinguishes this case from Case A. *See* cite to Case A. There, the defendant had dated the home's occupant for a few weeks and did not enjoy a familial-like relationship with the occupant. Cite to Case A.

Even so, the State will argue that the Defendant's relationship with the home is not meaningful enough to suggest permission to enter. Indeed, the Defendant's relationship with the home is based solely on a longtime friend living there, which is far less meaningful than the relationships that existed in Case B and Case C. *See* cite Case B and Case C. In those cases, the defendants had close relatives in the homes, creating an expectation of familiarity and access to the home not enjoyed by someone who is merely a longtime friend. Cite to Case B and Case C. Thus, this case is more similar to Case A, in which the defendant was dating the home's occupant, yet the court noted the lack of a meaningful history of access to the home. Cite Case A. In fact, this case presents weaker facts than Case A, given that dating is more intimate than even a longtime friendship, and thus arguably provides a greater sense of familiarity and access. *See* cite to Case A.

### 1. Breaking It Down: Why Are These Arguments Effective?

Let's focus on what makes these arguments effective. As we review these points, remember that the rule application section follows our rule explanation section for this issue/condition. The three cases from which we make analogical arguments all would have been introduced as part of the rule explanation.

**The argument structure and content follow the outline we previously drafted.** Recall our outline for the rule application section addressing this guiding factor:

> Guiding Factor 1: History of Access to the Home
> - Defendant's arguments for guiding factor 1 (comparing Cases B and C and distinguishing Case A)
> - Prosecution's arguments for guiding factor 1 (comparing Case A and distinguishing Cases B and C)

We have followed that outline in terms of both the organization and the content.

**The analogies are specific, explicitly comparing facts from the prior case to the facts of the client's case.** In other words, the writer has avoided reasoning by proximity. Consider how much less useful the argument would have been to the reader if the writer had simply put the facts side by side:

> The Defendant here had a longtime friend who lived in the home. The defendants in both Case A and Case C have close relatives who lived in the home. Cite Cases A and C. [*Ineffective analogy—reasoning by proximity.*]

The raw information is there, but the argument is not. The writer assumes the reader will identify the similarity and its implication, which may or may not occur. Instead, the writer should directly provide this information to ensure the reader arrives at the desired logical outcome. For example:

> Much like the defendants in both Case B and Case C, whose close relatives lived in the home, here the Defendant's longtime friend lived in the home. *See* cite Cases B and C. Thus, just as in those cases, the Defendant here believed he was permitted to enter the home. *See* cite to Case B and Case C. [*Effective analogy.*]

**The writer has told us why the analogy matters.** In the following example, we know that the comparison matters because it helps show that a sense of familiarity may, in turn, suggest access.

> In fact, this case presents weaker facts than Case A, given that dating is more intimate than even a longtime friendship, and thus arguably provides a greater sense of familiarity and access. *See* cite to Case A. [*Effective analogy because it tells why the analogy matters.*]

Had the writer instead conveyed that information as follows, the argument would not be as effective:

> In fact, this case presents weaker facts than Case A, given that dating is more intimate than even a longtime friendship. *See* cite to Case A. *[Ineffective analogy because it compares the facts without explaining why the analogy matters.]*

Legal writers can compare lots of things, but those comparisons only matter if they are legally significant. Again, you do not want to leave it to your reader to identify that legal significance; you want your writing to clearly convey it. When you re-read your analogy, is the meaning of the analogy stated or merely implied? If the latter, you need to re-work your comparison.

**The writer has kept the focus on the client's case when comparing the prior cases to the client's case.** As you read the rule application paragraph above, there is no question that the focus is on the client's case. The precedent cases are used to *support* arguments in the client's case. In the simple example below, you can see that the client's case is the focal point, and Case A is simply being used to support the client's argument.

> The Defendant's longstanding relationship with the home's occupant distinguishes this case from Case A. *See* cite to Case A. *[Effective.]*

How much less effective would this sentence be if the focus were instead on Case A rather than the defendant's situation?

> In Case A the defendant did not have a longstanding relationship with the home's occupant, which distinguishes it from the Defendant's situation. *See* cite to Case A. *[Ineffective.]*

**The writer has not recited facts in a vacuum, but instead has integrated the rule into the discussion of the facts in order to make arguments.**

> First, the Defendant will argue he has a meaningful history of accessing the home. The Defendant's connection to the home was based on a sincere belief that he was permitted to enter the home because his longtime friend lived there.

Consider if the writer instead had included a sentence that simply read, "The Defendant's longtime friend lived in the home." Why does that fact matter? We do not know. Only by connecting the fact to a component of the rule (e.g., referring to the history/connection to the home) does the significance of that fact become clear.

### 2. Organizing Arguments Under the Party/Position Approach

Note that the above burglary example uses the issue-components organizational approach. If you were using the party/position approach instead, remember that the underlying content of your arguments would be the same. However, because the rule application would be organized around the parties/positions rather than around the issue-components, the organization of those arguments would differ. Thus, if your topic sentence was "The Defendant will argue that his entry was not unlawful," that paragraph would include all the Defendant's arguments about why the entry was lawful. That necessarily would mean making arguments based upon the guiding factors, including "the defendant's history of access to the home." Depending on the quantity and depth of a Defendant's arguments, this may require more than one paragraph.

In addition, you would not address the other party/position's arguments until after you had completed your discussion of the Defendant's arguments. At that point, you might begin with a topic sentence indicating this transition to new content, such as "Even so, the State will argue that the Defendant's entry was unlawful."

 **CONCEPT IN ACTION: Rule Application Using the Party/Position Approach**

Below is an excerpt of a rule application paragraph from The Smell Shoppe hypothetical in Appendix B. Notice that the topic sentence announces that the paragraph is about Mr. Arnold's various arguments relating to the reasonable expectancy issue/condition. Then, within the paragraph itself you can see that the writer has included arguments relating to each of the three guiding factors for that element.

> It is likely that Mr. Arnold will be able to show that he possessed a reasonable expectancy of entering into a valid business relationship. Like the plaintiff's customers in *Chicago's Pizza,* the customers in Mr. Arnold's situation contemplated specific business relationships with him. 893 N.E.2d at 993. Mr. Arnold will argue that like the testimony of the customers in *Chicago's Pizza,* he too will be able to call customers to testify to their specific contemplation in conducting business with him. *See id.* Namely, Mr. Arnold himself will testify that he began hearing people in the community express concerns about his candles, as they were telling him that the candles "just weren't what they used to be." This is similar to the testimony of the customers in *Chicago's Pizza* who testified that they clearly believed they were doing business with the plaintiff. *See id.* at 994. His relationship with customers is therefore even stronger than that of the plaintiff in *Mannion* who was able to establish a reasonable expectation of business relationship on the basis of a developing, as opposed to established, relationship. *See* 561 N.E.2d at 1139. It can also be contrasted with the unsuccessful plaintiff in *Euclid Insurance Agencies* that was unable to establish a reasonable expectation of business relationship because it had never been in direct contact with prospective customers. *See* 1997

WL 548069, at *4. As with the convincing testimony of the customers in *Chicago's Pizza,* and the contact between the plaintiff and prospective customer in *Mannion,* Mr. Arnold can use the testimony of his customers to establish their belief that they were in fact doing business with him when they purchased their candles. *See Chicago's Pizza,* 893 N.E.2d at 994; *see also Mannion,* 561 N.E.2d at 1139.

Whatever organizational approach you use, keep in mind that the way the rule application section is organized does not impact the underlying arguments you make. It is simply a matter of packaging. In the party/position approach, you will make all of one party/position's arguments first, for each component of the rule, before moving on to the other party/position's arguments for each component of the rule. In the issue-components approach, your rule application proceeds by addressing each component, first making one party's arguments and then the other party's arguments, and so on, for each issue-component.

---

 **CHECK IN: Comparing Rule Application Paragraphs**

Read the following two examples of rule application paragraphs. Consider:

- Which has a stronger topic statement? Why is it stronger?
- Which has a stronger argument? What makes it more effective?
- How are the multiple authorities used in the examples? Which is more effective, and why?
- Did you notice any other features that made one version more effective than the others?

*Example 1*

Jazz has bitten at least one person who needed emergency medical attention. In *Wilcox,* the dog had bitten two children, whereas in *Feisty Schnauzer Owner,* the dog had no bite history. Jazz is more like the dog in *Wilcox.*

*Example 2*

First, Jazz has a demonstrated history of biting. Just as the *Wilcox* dog had bitten two children on two separate occasions, Jazz is known to have bitten at least one person. *See* 300 N.W.2d at 334. Indeed, the person bitten by Jazz required emergency medical attention, suggesting a perhaps even greater danger than that posed by the dog in *Wilcox,* who was deemed dangerous despite the fact that his bite victims did not require any kind of medical care. *See id.* at 335. Jazz is unlike the dog in *Feisty Schnauzer Owner*, who was not deemed dangerous because it had no bite history. *See* 402 N.W.2d at 122.

## C. Other Considerations When Drafting Rule Application Paragraphs

### 1. Use Transitions Between Your Rule Application Paragraphs

Just as when you were using only a single authority, using transitions between your rule application paragraphs will assist your reader in digesting the information. These transitions have the added benefit of keeping you on track by reinforcing the small-scale organization of your rule application section.

Examples of useful transitions include phrases such as "in addition," "likewise," "finally," "even so," "in contrast," and "on the other hand." You may also use other suitable transitions, as you prefer. Sometimes simply enumerating the successive rule application paragraphs provides the most useful transition; e.g., "First," "Second," "Third," and "Finally."

### 2. Provide the Foundation for Your Rule Application Section with an Effective Rule Explanation Section

An effective rule application section starts with an effective rule explanation section. Specifically, make sure your rule explanation provides sufficient detail about the facts and reasoning from the precedent cases so that you can support your comparisons in your rule application paragraphs. Without this foundation, your reader will not be able to follow the comparison or understand its significance. Remember, every fact from the precedent that you use in the rule application paragraph must first be introduced in your rule explanation paragraph.

As discussed in Chapter 18, when the guiding factors for an issue/condition are analytically distinct from one another, you might choose to provide both rule explanation and rule application for one guiding factor (or set of related guiding factors) before doing the same for the next guiding factor. You will choose whether to present your entire rule explanation together or split it up with the associated rule application, based upon which approach will allow you to communicate with the reader most clearly. You may wish to review the considerations from Chapter 18 as you make this determination.

Recall from Chapter 17 that while there typically will be only one rule explanation paragraph when using a single authority, it can be effective to break your rule explanation into separate paragraphs if the guiding factors are analytically distinct. This same logic applies to the organization of your rule explanation and rule application sections.

Namely, when the guiding factors for an issue/condition are analytically distinct from one another, it may make sense to organize your analysis by guiding factor, with rule explanation immediately followed by rule application. That is, for the first guiding factor (or group of related guiding factors) you would present rule explanation followed by rule application. Then you would do the same for the next distinct guiding factor(s). Breaking up the discussion in this way enables your reader to focus on these distinct aspects of the issue/condition separately, thus avoiding the confusion that might arise if your reader must process too much unrelated information at the same time. (Note that if the guiding factors are relatively distinct, you likely will have chosen to organize your rule application by issue-components not party/position.)

### 3. Explain the Relevance of the Analogy or Distinction

It is not enough to compare facts; you need to explain *why* that comparison matters. Compare the following snippets from rule application paragraphs.

> *Less effective:*
> Like *Wilcox*, where the dog bit two children, here the dog bit one person.

> *More effective:*
> Just as the *Wilcox* dog had bitten two children on two separate occasions, Jazz is known to have bitten at least one person. *See* 300 N.W.2d at 334. Indeed, the person bitten by Jazz required emergency medical attention, suggesting a perhaps even greater danger than that posed by the dog in *Wilcox*, who was deemed dangerous despite the fact that his bite victims did not require any kind of medical care. *See id.* at 335.

The first example may leave the reader wondering, "So what?" In contrast, the second example shows *why* the biting comparison matters— because that history indicates the danger the dog now poses. Moreover, the second example extends the analogy to explain why the facts of the client's case are even more compelling than the facts that were deemed sufficient in the prior case.

### 4. Consider Starting with a Rule-Based Argument Before Making Analogical Arguments

Why can it be helpful to start with a rule-based argument before making analogical arguments? To be effective, analogical arguments must be specific in comparing the facts of the prior case to the facts of the present case. That specificity means that the writer often needs to convey many facts to complete the analogy. Often this results in a long, cumbersome sentence, bogged down in factual details. When you first apply the rule to the facts, you avoid the need for such a detail-laden sentence when you get to the analogical argument. You convey the facts of the client's case first in conjunction with the rule itself. Then, when you move on to the analogy, you need only reference the facts of the prior case.

Compare the following examples.

**Less effective:**
*Bailey* is dissimilar in that the court found the defendant could not recover under the statute because there was no action on the part of the dog that caused the fall and subsequent injuries. In the present case, an overt act was committed by the dog, which caused Rush to be injured. *Bailey,* 2 A.2d at 19.

**More effective:**
Fluffy's actions likely will be classified as overt and provoking. Fluffy engaged in overt and provoking acts when he ran and barked alongside Rush. Fluffy's behaviors are thus distinguishable from the dog in *Bailey,* who was lying motionless on a step. *See Bailey,* 2 A.2d at 19. Fluffy was far more active than a sleeping dog. He also was right next to Rush and not behind a locked gate as was the dog in *Bailey. See id.* at 19-20. Indeed, he was so close to Rush that he could have touched him.

The second sentence—"Fluffy engaged in overt and provoking acts when he ran and barked alongside Rush."—applies the rule to the facts. It does not rely on a comparison to another case; it relies only on the legal rule (here, the guiding factor of whether the actions were overt and provoking) and the facts of the present case.

Notice, too, in addition to applying the rule to the fact before making the comparison, this example begins with a helpful topic/thesis statement. We know the paragraph focuses on the guiding factor of whether the act was overt and provoking.

### 🔳 CONCEPT IN ACTION: Effective Rule Application

Below is an excerpt of an effective rule application paragraph from a memo. As you read, note how the writer uses the technique of making rule-based arguments first and how that facilitates the subsequent analogical arguments. Notice, too, how the topic sentence immediately alerts you to the paragraph's focus; whether you have read any other part of the memo, you know from that topic sentence that every argument in that paragraph revolves around "whether the Jacksons honestly believed they owned the disputed property."

The topic sentence tells the reader the scope of this paragraph—the reader could jump in at this point and understand this paragraph's purpose.

Immediately after the topic sentence, the writer makes a rule-based argument. Notice how having made this argument, and thus describing the facts of the client's situation in the context of this argument, facilitates the subsequent analogical arguments.

The paragraph ends with analogical arguments. The writer makes two arguments—one compares the client's situation to *Jones,* and the other distinguishes the client's situation from *Meyers.*

The Jacksons will show that they honestly believed they owned the disputed property. Specifically, the Jacksons believed their realtor's unambiguous statements regarding the location of the property line, which they learned before purchasing the property. Further, the evidence shows that the Jacksons had no doubt about the property line until well after their purchase. Ms. Jackson's reaction—"You have got to be kidding me! That's our property!"—to the city official who told her she was wrong about the property line underscores the sincerity of her belief. Thus, like the plaintiff in *Jones* who relied upon a fence as showing the property line, here the Jacksons similarly, and sincerely, relied upon their realtor's assertion. *See Jones,* 23 N.W.2d at 330. This is unlike the plaintiff's belief about the property line in *Meyers,* which was not based upon any objective measure and instead fluctuated over time. *Meyers,* 70 N.W.2d at 21.

# Completing the Legal Memorandum: Additional Components, Finishing Touches, and Variations

You have learned how to write the most critical component of your memo—the Discussion section—by applying the foundational concepts addressed in the prior four modules. In this Module, we first cover the remaining sections of the memo. We then examine polishing your work, including editing and revising both large-scale and small-scale organization, checking for errors in grammar and other writing mechanics, and refining to meet audience expectations. Next, we consider how to draft emails and craft talking points that effectively communicate your legal analysis. The book concludes by considering the transition from predictive to persuasive writing.

# Additional Memo Considerations: Question Presented, Short Answer, Statement of Facts, Internal Discussion Headings, and Conclusion

In this chapter, we start by addressing the memo's expected heading, then move into the three remaining sections of the memo: the Question Presented, the Short Answer, and the Statement of Facts. We conclude by considering two additional aspects of the Discussion section: first, why you may choose to include headings within your Discussion to facilitate the reader's understanding of your analysis, and second, the conclusions you need to provide within the Discussion.

---

### Study Guide Questions for Chapter 27

1. How do lawyers use predictive memoranda in the present and future?
2. What is the content of a Question Presented?
3. How do we refer to the parties in the Question Presented?
4. What three things does the Short Answer accomplish?
5. How are the parties referred to in the Short Answer?
6. What does it mean to "allude" to the law in the Short Answer?
7. What is the purpose of the Statement of Facts in a predictive memorandum?
8. What new terms were introduced in this chapter? How do these terms relate to your existing understanding of predictive memo writing? Did your understanding of any other terms change as a result of reading this chapter?

# I. Memo Heading

The memo always begins with a heading. This section identifies the document as a Memorandum and contains the following clauses:

| | |
|---|---|
| To: | (The attorney to whom the memo is directed) |
| From: | (The author of the memo) |
| Re: | (The "about" clause, indicating the client and legal matter addressed in the memorandum) |
| Date: | (The date the memo is delivered) |

# II. Substantive Memo Sections Beyond the Discussion

## A. Question Presented

The Question Presented, also known as the Statement of the Issue, is the first substantive section of the memo. Here, the writer poses the legal question that arises out of the client's situation.

Understanding how lawyers use predictive memoranda in practice illuminates the necessary content of the Question Presented. The primary use of the inter-office memorandum is to memorialize the predictive, or objective, analysis of the client's claim or charge. Typically, a junior associate is tasked with the responsibility of researching and analyzing all or a portion of a client's claim or charge. When the lawyer completes this analysis, she memorializes it in the predictive memorandum.

She then gives the memo to the assigning lawyer. That lawyer may decide to share it with others within the firm, such as lawyers working on related matters on behalf of the client. Depending on the situation, the lawyer may also decide to share the memo with the client.

Predictive memoranda are also sometimes used in the future, for example when a lawyer faces a question that may be related to analysis completed for a prior claim or charge. Because of this potential later use, lawyers tend to write the Question Presented so that it is easy to quickly determine whether the memo contains analysis sufficiently analogous to later cases that reviewing the memo in full might be beneficial to the analysis of the later claim or charge.

To accommodate both current and possible later uses, it is helpful to include the following in the Question Presented: the jurisdiction of the law analyzed in the memo; the client's claim or charge; and the significant facts from the client's case that give rise to the legal issue.

Identifying the jurisdiction under which the legal question is being analyzed establishes an important parameter for the reader. Because the rules of law vary from state to state and between the state and federal levels of government, the legal analysis in the memo cannot be assumed to apply to a similar legal question in a different jurisdiction. As such, the source of law, including its jurisdiction, will be a critical consideration for possible future use of the memo. For instance, a lawyer who later has a legal issue regarding underground storage tanks arising under Montana law may not be interested in your memo on underground storage tanks if it analyzed the issue under South Carolina law.

Clearly, yet succinctly, identifying the client's claim or charge—the legal question being considered—will help prepare the original reader for the scope of the rest of the memo. In addition, it will help other firm lawyers later identify whether the memo may be potentially useful in their cases.

When presenting key facts related to the client's claim or charge, you should include those that are both favorable and unfavorable. These contrasting facts frame the question and signal the legal tension that the Discussion section of the memorandum addresses.

Finally, in the Question Presented lawyers refer to the parties descriptively, rather than by their names. So, we might refer to a landlord and tenant, or an owner of an underground storage tank, rather than using proper names. We do this because these descriptive labels provide the uninitiated reader with more information and context about the memo's scope than proper names do. A lawyer later looking for underground storage tank analysis might not know that "Ms. Nguyen" owned an underground storage tank. Introducing her, instead, as the owner of an underground storage tank clearly defines her role.

Therefore, one helpful way to approach a Question Presented is to use a template known as the "Under/Does/When" formula. The "under" clause introduces the Question Presented and enables the lawyer to identify the jurisdiction of law consulted in the legal memo; it sometimes also denotes the substantive area of law (tax, environmental, etc.). The second clause introduces the client's legal question. The writer can use "does," "is," or "can" as the verb to announce the legal question. The final clause begins with "when" and announces the key facts that give rise to the legal tension.

- Under [insert jurisdiction and possibly substantive area of law]
- Does/Is/Can [insert client's claim or charge]
- When [insert key facts giving rise to legal tension]

Note that the Question Presented will necessarily be influenced by the controlling rule of law and the conditions at issue in the legal memo. However, those conditions are not expressly stated in the Question

Presented, but rather guide the writer's choice of what facts are legally significant and thus important to include in the "when" clause.

Take, for example, the dangerous dog statute. You are aware that the rule of law is that "all dangerous dogs must be licensed." You have read a case in which the court concluded that a 14-year-old dog did not need to be licensed as dangerous because of his age. Your client owns a Great Dane named Sophie. The life expectancy of a Great Dane is eight to ten years. Sophie is seven. The owner has questioned whether Sophie needs to be licensed as a dangerous dog. You are aware that the issue in this case will be whether Sophie is exempted from the rule due to her age and the life expectancy of her breed. You might therefore pose the question as follows:

> Under Idaho law, is a dog exempted from the licensing requirement for dangerous dogs when she is seven years old and a Great Dane, whose life expectancy is eight to ten years?

You can see that the legal tension arises from Sophie's breed and her actual age. You have therefore incorporated the facts that give rise to the legal tension.

Let's take another example in the context of the burglary statute example.

> Under Ohio law, does a defendant commit burglary when he entered a house while it was unlocked and retrieved a video game system that belonged to him, but when he also took video games that did not belong to him?

## B.  Short Answer

In the Short Answer section, the lawyer briefly identifies the prediction as to the resolution of the client's claim or charge. Because it is an initial section of the memo, a lawyer reading the memo would not have substantial context for the law governing the claim. The legal reader will therefore not know what conditions are at issue and/or what facts will be most important for the resolution of those contested issues.

The Short Answer therefore should accomplish three things. First, it should actually answer the question. While it is sometimes difficult to make a prediction, particularly as a law student or new lawyer, remember that you are not guaranteeing the results. Nonetheless, you still need to present a bottom-line answer based on your research and analysis and should avoid "waffling" in your prediction. That means that words such as "maybe" or "possibly" are not terribly helpful in the Short Answer. However, because we are not guaranteeing a result, lawyers typically use the term "likely" to frame their prediction.

Second, the Short Answer should *allude* to the law. We use the term "allude" to reinforce that, although we will not be citing cases or statutes in the Short Answer, we do want to signal to the reader what conditions are at issue. These, obviously, come from the law. Nonetheless, by convention, and to ensure ease of reading for this section, we will not be citing the applicable legal source.

Third, the Short Answer should justify the prediction of the resolution of each contested issue by tying it to the underlying client facts. The relationship between the prediction of the resolution of the issue and the facts that support that prediction should be clear to the reader. As with rule application, we do not want to reason by proximity.

In contrast to the Question Presented, in the Short Answer we refer to the parties by name. The Question Presented is the *only* section of the memo where we refer to the parties descriptively, rather than by their name. Do you recall why?

So, an example of the Short Answer for the dangerous dog example might read as follows:

> Short Answer: Yes, it is likely that Sophie the Great Dane will be exempted from the licensing requirement. Dogs may be exempted for old age, and Sophie, while only seven, has a life expectancy of eight to ten years, so that a court will likely conclude she is exempted from the licensing requirement due to age. Ms. Patel will therefore not need to apply for a license.

Here the writer has answered the legal question: whether Sophie will be exempted from the licensing requirement.

Here the writer is alluding to the law/legal condition of the age exemption.

Here the writer has tethered key facts—the life expectancy of the breed—to the prediction as to the application of the exemption.

Note that we refer to the parties by name in the Short Answer.

Let's look at another Short Answer example in the context of a burglary charge.

> No, it is not likely that Tony Smith will be convicted of burglary. Because Smith had access to the home, as it was not locked or physically secured upon his entry, the State will be unlikely to show that the entry was unlawful. In addition, because Smith entered the home with the intent to retrieve his own items, it is not likely that the State will be able to show that he entered with intent to commit a crime.

## C. Statement of Facts

The Statement of Facts provides the context for the legal review set forth in the memo. Because the resolution of the legal question turns on the facts, the facts will form the basis for the predictions you make in the memo. The purpose of the Statement of Facts is therefore to explain to the reader the factual basis for the predictions made in the memo. The Statement of Facts includes both legally significant facts and contextual facts.

## What Facts?

**Legally significant facts:** Legally significant facts are those that a court would consider relevant in evaluating a claim or charge. In our dangerous dog example, we know that one issue the court must consider is whether the dog is dangerous. So, any facts that could be related to the dangerous nature of the dog, including breed, history of biting, strength of the dog, sharpness of teeth or claws, and the like would be legally significant to the court. The name of the dog would not likely be legally significant. Note that legally significant facts may be unfavorable to your client's position. Notwithstanding, you need to include all of the facts that influence the court's analysis, both those that assist your arguments and those that you will have to overcome when you transition to persuasion.

Some legally significant facts might be unknown at the time of writing the memo. Imagine, for instance, that when the client was interviewed, the lawyer had not yet researched the law and therefore did not ask questions regarding all legally significant facts. Ideally, you can obtain those facts prior to producing the final version of the memo. However, when you are aware that a court would want to consider a fact that is unknown at the time the memo is prepared, you still want to include that information. You would likely include this uncertainty both in the Statement of Facts and in the Discussion where the absence of that fact influences your analysis. In our dangerous dog context, an example might be to state that the dog's history of biting or aggressive behavior is currently unknown.

**Contextual facts:** Contextual facts are not legally significant but may help the reader understand the client's situation. In our dangerous dog example, although a dog's name will not impact how the court considers whether he is dangerous, it may provide helpful context for the memo, especially if the dog is referred to by name in the Discussion. Often contextual facts need not be included with as much detail as legally significant facts.

---

 **CRASH WARNING: "Checking" Your Statement of Facts**

Although you may well write a first draft of your Statement of Facts before you write the Discussion, your work on the Discussion often prompts you to revise the Statement of Facts. As you present your analysis in the Discussion, the legal significance of certain facts becomes clearer. So, you will want to go back and check your Statement of Facts after you have drafted your Discussion. Every fact mentioned in your Discussion should also be included in your Statement of Facts.

Note that the flip side is not true: You may include facts, particularly contextual facts, in your Statement of Facts that you do not include in your Discussion.

## Organizational Strategies

We generally begin the Statement of Facts with an introduction to the parties and an identification of the legal issue. We then have a few organizational options. We can organize the facts chronologically or by the legal issues presented. We can also use a combination of these two organizational frameworks, organizing the facts first by the legal issues and then presenting those facts chronologically within each issue.

## Stylistic Considerations

Generally, present the facts as clearly and concisely as possible, while providing context where necessary. Think carefully about the amount of detail you include, avoiding unnecessary detail.

You also want to present the facts neutrally and objectively, avoiding editorial commentary. Related to this, you should describe the facts objectively, being careful not to characterize those facts or draw inferences from them.

Likewise, keep in mind that your Statement of Facts is not a list of bullet points, nor should it read that way. Instead, you are presenting the facts to your reader as a narrative, making the story flow and connecting the information throughout.

Finally, the Statement of Facts typically describes something that already has happened, so you will be writing using the past tense.

 **CRASH WARNING: Legal Arguments and Citations Do Not Belong in Your Statement of Facts**

Just as it is not appropriate to include "spin" in your Statement of the Facts in a memorandum, it also is not appropriate to include legal arguments. Because you will avoid making legal arguments in your Statement of Facts, you should not need to cite to any legal authority. If you think you need a citation to a case, it probably means that you have veered beyond a Statement of Facts and moved into material that belongs in your Discussion.

 **CONCEPT IN ACTION: Sample Statement of Facts**

Below is the statement of facts from the Warrantless Bomb Search hypothetical. As you review it, note the ways in which the writer has organized the material and adhered to the features described above.

### STATEMENT OF FACTS

This case involves the search of a shipping container owned by "Double T" Van Zanda that was conducted by FBI agents without a search warrant. On December 30, 2018, agents from the Cincinnati FBI field office conducted a warrantless search of a shipping container on the lot of Van Zanda Trucking, located in Woodlawn, Kentucky. The search unfolded after agents received a tip from an informant that Double T Van Zanda a Woodlawn mobster and owner of the trucking company, was using the shipping container to store a bomb. The informant told agents that the bomb was intended for use in the attempted murder of another gangster.

The FBI agents immediately dispatched to the reported location. When the agents arrived at Van Zanda Trucking, their bomb-sniffing dog "hit" on the shipping container in question, indicating the dog's probable detection of a bomb. At that point, FBI agents also were aware that Van Zanda had previously been tied to a mob bombing.

Before searching the container, FBI agents also spoke with and received permission from a man named "The Earl" to search the container. The Earl, who was at the scene of the container when the FBI agents arrived, told the agents that he had rented the container to store a guitar collection. He explained, however, that because of an argument with Van Zanda, he had moved a majority of his guitar collection out one month earlier. When the agents asked if they could look inside the container, The Earl replied, "OK." He then opened the shipping container for the agents using his own key.

The agents did not find a bomb inside the container. However, along with a few guitars that belonged to The Earl, agents discovered cocaine and marijuana—leading to a federal indictment of Van Zanda. Van Zanda's defense attorneys are preparing to file a motion to suppress the evidence gleaned from the warrantless search.

## D.  Headings

Each section of the memo has its own heading, or label. As illustrated in the sample memos in the appendices, the Question Presented, Short Answer, Statement of Facts, and Discussion are clearly labeled with a heading. In addition, headings can be useful within the Discussion section of the memo in a few situations. The first is the situation in which your memo addresses a number of different legal topics, in other words, multiple claims or charges. The second is when the writer determines that headings will be useful to alert the reader to the discussion of each analytical issue in a memo involving a single legal question (claim or charge). For the former situation—multiple topic memos—headings are almost always a good idea. In the second situation—single topic memos—the writer should consider the complexity of the memo and whether the use of headings would assist the reader in navigating the Discussion.

**Multiple legal topic memoranda:** When the memo addresses more than one legal topic, using headings in the Discussion section will help your reader navigate the section. For example, consider a situation in which you represent a client who is dissolving a relationship with her partner. There are two claims you have been asked to address. The first is whether the client has a legally binding relationship, and the second is the extent to which the client may be entitled to an arguably joint asset. The answers to these questions will be governed by different tests, each of which will likely have several conditions and therefore several arguable issues. You will therefore have two analytical sections of the memo tied to the two claims, each of which will likely involve the analysis of multiple, arguable issues.

In this situation, you will want not only to include headings in the Discussion, but also to include a Discussion roadmap that alerts the reader to the legal topics that will be addressed. You will then include headings for each claim or charge addressed in the memo, and you may also guide the reader through the analysis by including subheadings for each issue addressed in the claim or charge. Note that, because your headings are designed to provide direction for the reader, they should not simply be topical but should indicate how the claim, charge, or issue will be resolved. Consider the following example.

### DISCUSSION

Joe Abebe and Sarah Walker will likely be deemed to have a common-law marriage. They have indicated an agreement to be married, have lived together continuously, and have held themselves out as a married couple. However, it is less clear whether Sarah will be entitled to an equitable distribution of the monetary value of the restored Ford pickup. While the couple purchased the pickup together early in their relationship, the title has been held by Joe since he restored it to operating condition. This memo will address both the issue of the validity of the marriage and Sarah's entitlement to a portion of the value of the Ford.

— This is a *Discussion* roadmap. It is necessary where the memo addresses more than one legal topic. Note that, like all roadmaps, it provides direction for the reader as to the content that follows, and it alerts the reader to the resolution of the topics that follow.

#### I. Sarah and Joe Have a Common-Law Marriage

The court will likely conclude that Sarah and Joe have established a common-law marriage. In Iowa, a party claiming common-law marriage must demonstrate the following: "The couple had an agreement that the parties were/are married; The couple lived together continuously as spouses; The couple presented themselves publicly as a married couple." *Burns v. Felker*, 633 N.W.2d 564 (Iowa 1992). Because Joe is challenging the validity of the marriage, all of these elements are at issue. Because friends of the couple will testify as to Joe and Sarah's stated intention to be treated as a married couple and their actions evidencing this intent, and because Joe and Sarah have lived together for eleven years, Sarah will demonstrate that they have a common-law marriage.

— Note that the heading not only alerts the reader to the first issue, but also provides direction by indicating the prediction of the issue.

—A global roadmap that identifies the prediction of the claim or charge, identifies the issues, and reinforces the prediction on the basis of relevant facts.

Again, note that the a. Joe and Sarah Evidenced Their Agreement to Be a Married Couple
headings that alert the reader      • Issue Roadmap for this issue
to the discussion of each           • Rule Explanation for this issue
issue are not neutral, but          • Rule Application for this issue
rather state the prediction    b. Joe and Sarah Lived Together as Spouses Continuously for Eleven Years
of the issue. In this way the       • Issue Roadmap for this issue
headings provide direction for      • Rule Explanation for this issue
the reader.                         • Rule Application for this issue
                               c. Joe and Sarah Presented Themselves Publicly as a Married Couple
                                    • Issue Roadmap for this issue
                                    • Rule Explanation for this issue
                                    • Rule Application for this issue

### II. Sarah Will Not Likely Demonstrate Entitlement to the Monetary Value of the Ford

• Global Roadmap for this Claim/Charge
• Headings for Each Disputed Issue

**Single Legal Topic Memoranda:** In a single legal topic memorandum, you may also elect to include headings to guide the reader through the analysis of the claim or charge. In this instance, you would follow the format above, using headings for each arguable issue in the Discussion. As in the above example, your heading should identify the resolution of the issue, rather than simply announcing it.

## E.  Conclusion

You will want to include conclusions for your reader in your memorandum. For a conclusion regarding the analysis of a claim or charge, you will follow a deductive pattern. You should first identify the prediction as to the resolution of the claim or charge, and then reiterate your predictions as to the resolution of each arguable issue related to the claim or charge. Your conclusion is at the end of the analysis of the claim or charge. Below is the example of the conclusion for The Smell Shoppe multiple authority memo:

A prediction as to the resolution of the claim/charge.

Thus, Mr. Arnold likely will not succeed in his tortious interference with business expectancy claim against Mr. Green. Mr. Arnold will likely be able to demonstrate that he possessed a reasonable expectancy of entering into a valid business relationship with customers because customers did indicate they thought they were doing business with him. Notwithstanding, he will likely fail to prove that it was Mr. Green's intentional and unjustified

A reiteration of the prediction as to the resolution of each arguable issue.

interference that prevented the realization of business expectancy because Mr. Green was not dishonest, did not directly divert business from Mr. Arnold, and may be able to assert a privilege.

If your memorandum includes more than one claim or charge (i.e., a multiple topic memorandum), in addition to a conclusion at the end of the analysis of each claim or charge, you also need an overall conclusion. This final conclusion simply reiterates the prediction of each topic addressed in the memo. Below is an example of an overall conclusion for a multiple issue memo:

Because Sarah and Joe have lived together and held themselves out as — A reiteration as to the prediction of the first claim.
husband and wife, Sarah will be able to demonstrate that she and Joe have a valid common-law marriage. However, because Joe took responsibility for restoring the Ford and, when it became operational, placed the title to — A reiteration as to the prediction of the second claim.
the Ford in his name, Sarah will not likely be entitled to a portion of the monetary value of the Ford.

### CHAPTER 28

# Revising, Editing, and Proofreading Your Legal Memorandum

After you have a complete draft of your memorandum (or at least of your Discussion), it is time to work on improving that draft. This chapter covers techniques for revising, editing, and proofreading, each of which is a separate step in the legal writing process.

---

### Study Guide Questions for Chapter 28

1. How are revising, editing, and proofreading different?
2. What is the purpose of revising?
3. What are some revising focal points and techniques?
4. What is the purpose of editing?
5. What are some editing focal points and techniques?
6. What is the purpose of proofreading?
7. What are some proofreading focal points and techniques?
8. What new terms were introduced in this chapter? How do these terms relate to your existing understanding of predictive memo writing? Did your understanding of any other terms change as a result of reading this chapter?

---

So, you have a complete draft of your entire legal memorandum. You now need to revise, edit, and proofread your work. These three separate, critical steps generally take longer than new legal writers expect, so allow plenty of time to complete these tasks.

First, you will undertake the intensive revision process in which you critically review the big picture. You will consider the overall structure and clarity of your draft. Focusing on the large-scale organization of your memo, you might reorganize content and add new material to ensure your arguments clearly follow the deductive progression expected by the law-trained reader. In short, revision can include big changes.

Second, you will edit your memo. In this process you will also review your writing for substantive changes, but on a smaller scale than revision. You will review the style, coherence, clarity, and flow of your memo, making sure you have laid out clear, well-supported, logical arguments.

Finally, you will complete your writing process by thoroughly proofreading your work. You will conduct a final review of your work—fixing errors, ensuring correct formatting, and putting the final polish on your memo. Thorough editing helps you protect the effort you invested in the entire writing process, ensuring you do not undermine your credibility with easily avoidable mistakes in grammar, spelling, and the like.

# I.  Revising Your Legal Memorandum

Legal writing is a recursive process, so good legal writers expect to re-visit and modify parts of their draft based upon their subsequent work. Once you have a complete, or nearly complete, draft of your memorandum, it is time to revise. Revision means you "re-vision" your memo from an outside reader's perspective, making sure you have done everything possible to help the reader follow your legal analysis. Because you want to evaluate your memo with fresh eyes, if possible, give yourself ample time to set aside your draft for at least a few hours before revising it. During the revision process, your focus is on the most important part of your memo—the Discussion section.

## A.  Revision Checklist Questions

At the revision stage you will ask big-picture questions to identify any problems likely to affect the Discussion as a whole. Large-scale organization questions loom large at the revising stage. Consider the following questions as you revise your draft:

- *Have I answered the legal question posed?*

Re-read the assignment, especially the assignment prompt, to make sure your memorandum responds to the question posed.

- *Have I accurately and clearly stated the global legal rule?*

The rest of the Discussion flows from the global legal rule, so any inaccuracy or lack of clarity here will have a significant, negative impact.

- *Have I accurately identified what conditions are at issue in my global roadmap?*

Because any condition that you identify as a non-issue will not be discussed in the rest of the memo, you want to double-check that you have gotten this right. That might mean reconsidering whether the satisfaction of the condition is as one-sided and undisputed as you first concluded. Or it might mean re-reading the prompt for the memo assignment to make sure you correctly understood any conditions that should not be considered.

- *Does my large-scale organization flow predictably from the global road-map, including a segment of discussion for each issue identified?*

For each issue/condition, your law-trained reader expects to see a predictable and self-contained segment of discussion. It should be apparent where the discussion for one issue ends and another one begins.

- *Are there transitions between the issue segments of my discussion to assist my reader in understanding the relationship between these sections? Did I include headings, if needed? Have I used a consistent and parallel sentence structure when identifying each issue?*

A law-trained reader should be able to glance at your memo and get an understanding of the different issues it addresses. Using headings helps accomplish this goal, as does using transitions and consistent and parallel sentence structure. Compare the following three topic sentences, each of which introduces an issue/condition in a memo. These sentences would not be consecutive; they would be separated by the related segments of discussion. Note that the parallel construction and transitions in the effective version signal to the reader that a new segment is starting.

**Ineffective:**
- The State must show Smith's entry was unlawful.
- The court will consider if Smith entered a building or structure.
- The next question is whether the Defendant intended to commit a crime while inside the building or structure.

**Effective:**
- First, the State must show Smith's entry was unlawful.
- Second, the State must show Smith entered a building or structure.
- Finally, the State must show that Smith intended to commit a crime while inside the building or structure.

- *Does my memorandum provide a global conclusion at the end?*

Your reader expects you to come full circle in your analysis. You will begin with your global prediction, and you must complete the circle by ending with that global prediction. Your global conclusion should be short and to the point. It will state your global prediction, supported with succinct predictions for each issue/condition.

For example, an effective global conclusion for the burglary example might read:

> In sum, the State likely will be unable to show that Smith committed burglary. The State likely can show that Smith's entry was unlawful because he entered the building without permission and through a window. The State also can easily show that Smith entered a building because the entry occurred at a vacant middle school. Even so, the State likely will not be able to show that Smith possessed the requisite intent to commit a crime given that he was highly inebriated and will maintain he was entering the building only to seek shelter from the sub-zero temperatures.

## B. Techniques for Revising

To answer these questions, you may find it helpful to use one, or both, of the following, time-tested revising techniques. These techniques are not mutually exclusive, and neither is necessarily better than the other. Thus, we recommend that you use whichever technique(s) resonates with you.

### Revising by Labeling Paragraphs

Recall the annotated memos presented in Chapters 4, 14, and 16. The annotations labeled different memo components to help you identify them. As a writer, you can use similar notes to evaluate your Discussion section. For instance, you might write labels in the margins to indicate the content of the paragraph, such as "global roadmap" or, later in your rule application, "RA F1" to indicate the part of the Discussion where you provide the rule application for the first factor. This will help you determine whether you have included all necessary content and whether you have organized it logically. For instance, if your margin notes place RA F2 before RA F1, you would know you need to rearrange content.

Similarly, if it is not clear to you what specific content a given paragraph covers, that likely means that paragraph's scope needs to be better defined in a topic sentence or by adding/removing content.

### Revising Using a Reverse Outline Technique

In the reverse outline technique, the writer "reverse engineers" an outline based upon the completed draft. Sometimes the writer literally creates an outline, but more often the writer simply writes the information that she would have included in an outline in the margins of the memo. In this way, a reverse outline is similar to the revising by labeling paragraphs technique. However, in this approach, the writer typically also indicates the hierarchy between the parts of the memo, using the type of numbering found in a formal outline. For instance, the margin notes might include "I. Global roadmap" and "II.B. Issue 1 RE Case 1."

## II. Editing Your Memo

After you have revised your memo, you should be satisfied that the Discussion contains the information needed to address your legal question. Editing is the next step in the process. When you edit, you still focus on fixing substantive problems with your draft. However, having already addressed the more significant substantive problems during revision, your changes should now be less substantial. That is, they likely will not completely alter the Discussion. In addition, when you edit, you consider all parts of the memo, not just the Discussion.

### A. Editing Checklist Questions

Consider the following questions as you edit your draft:

- *With each issue segment of my discussion, have I followed the expected deductive structure, progressing from an issue roadmap, to rule explanation, to rule application, and ending with an issue prediction?*

Each issue segment should include one issue roadmap paragraph (or, in rare instances, one additional paragraph if the law is exceptionally complex and involved), a rule explanation section, and a rule application section that concludes with an issue prediction—all in that order. Remember the lasagna analogy? Any gaps in this expected structure and content will confuse your reader and leave her dissatisfied with your analysis.

- *Does my rule explanation section provide a bridge between my issue roadmap and my rule application? More broadly, do the parts of my issue segment generally align?*

Remembering the purpose of the different paragraph types provides a helpful lens for reviewing your memo. The rule explanation discusses one case (in a single authority memo) or multiple cases (in a multiple authority memo) with the goal of demonstrating that the rule you set forth in the issue roadmap was indeed what the court previously applied. You also included your rule explanation discussion because you wanted to show specifically how that rule applied in a factually similar situation, to prepare the reader for the next section—rule application—where you will use the facts and reasoning from the prior case (or cases) to make analogical arguments.

So, all of these parts of your issue segment should align; the guiding factors you identify in your issue roadmap should be the guiding factors the court applied, as illustrated in your rule explanation case(s). Further, your rule application should be based on the relevant guiding factors you have identified. You should have adequate material from your rule explanation discussion to develop specific and meaningful analytical arguments.

- *Is my rule application organized around either the party/position approach or the issue-components approach? Is this organization clear from the topic sentences in my rule application section?*

It bears repeating that your rule application needs to be organized. Whether you use the party/position approach or the issue-components approach, your rule application should be organized in such a way that your reader can easily track the organization.

Also keep in mind that once you have focused on what is important to the court by discerning guiding factors, it only makes sense that you would build arguments around these considerations, no matter which organizational approach you use. In other words, as you organize the arguments, whether by party/position or issue-components, you should clearly show the importance of the guiding factors as the basis for the arguments you make. This should certainly be evident when using the issue-components organizational framework. However, if you employ the party/position approach, the reader should still be able to see how the arguments revolve around those legally significant bases of comparison—the guiding factors.

In order to check your work, highlight references to guiding factors. This will help you verify you have conveyed the guiding factors in a clear and well-organized manner that strengthens your arguments.

- *Do my rule application paragraphs sufficiently and clearly make arguments, or do they instead make the mistake of either reasoning by proximity (i.e., putting similar facts side by side without explaining their connection and legal significance) or monologuing (reciting multiple facts without tethering those to the legal rule)?*

You should not have sentences in your rule application that simply recite the facts of your client's case or that simply reiterate the facts and reasoning from a prior case. In your rule application, facts and reasoning from a prior case must be connected explicitly to the facts of your client's situation and tethered to the legal rule. Do not leave your reader to decide for himself why something matters. Put differently, the reader should not be left asking, "So what?"

- *Does each paragraph have a main idea? Is that main idea communicated through a topic or thesis statement at the beginning of the paragraph?*

If you find a paragraph without a main idea, that paragraph needs to be re-worked. Ask yourself what you intended that paragraph to cover and adjust accordingly. On the other hand, if a single paragraph contains multiple main ideas, you likely will need to separate that content into more than one paragraph. Finally, you may find that a paragraph has a main idea, but rather than being properly situated at the start of the paragraph, that idea is buried in the middle or tagged on to the end. In that case, you will reorder sentences and also reword as necessary.

- *Are there one or more paragraphs in my Discussion that I cannot easily label as either a roadmap paragraph, a rule explanation paragraph, a rule application paragraph, or a global conclusion paragraph?*

In other words, ask yourself if you have included anything that should not be part of your Discussion. Have you editorialized? Included information not directly tethered to the particular legal rule? Blended different parts of your Discussion together, obscuring the purpose a given paragraph serves? Ensure that your Discussion contains the content that your law-trained reader expects and nothing extraneous.

- *Do my paragraphs and sentences progress logically?*

Because memo writing follows a deductive approach, the logical progression requires that you provide general information before more specific, supporting information. In addition, check to make sure the paragraphs flow logically and that the sentences within each paragraph also flow logically. This consideration is often particularly important in your rule application section, which has a less rigid structure.

Remember to consider your work through the eyes of the reader, who may be encountering this information for the first time. Often certain information has to be presented first in order to lay the foundation for other information. For example, if you are making an argument about a dog's physical characteristics, it would not make sense to jump into detailed descriptions of those characteristics before you have identified the guiding factor you are examining. Compare:

**Ineffective:**
- While small in stature, Fido has sharp claws, including dew-claws. He also has a strong jaw. He has strong legs and does not hesitate to jump up on people. These facts demonstrate he possesses physical characteristics that suggest he could pose a threat.

*Effective:*

- Fido possesses physical characteristics that suggest he could pose a threat. While small in stature, Fido has sharp claws, including dewclaws. He also has a strong jaw. He has strong legs and does not hesitate to jump up on people.

Note, too, that in the effective example, the first sentence provides a strong topic statement for the main point of the paragraph.

- *Does my memo contain all the expected sections in addition to the Discussion, i.e., the Header, the Question Presented, the Short Answer, and the Statement of Facts?*

In addition to ensuring you have included all the expected sections, review each section of your memo against the appropriate memo checklist in Appendix C. Also make sure your Question Presented and Short Answer align with your Discussion in terms of scope and content. Finally, ensure that any facts that you included in your Discussion are also included in your Statement of Facts section. Then reverse the process and see if all the facts in your Statement of Facts section are included in your Discussion. You may find you have included facts that provide helpful context in your Statement of Facts section that you do not mention in your Discussion; that is okay. However, if you find legally significant facts that only appear in the Statement of Facts section, you need to edit your Discussion to incorporate those facts.

## B. Editing Techniques

Consider using some of the following editing techniques. Just as with revising techniques, you likely will find certain editing techniques to be most useful or intuitive to you.

### The Read-Aloud Method

One way to edit is by reading your memo aloud. As you are reading, make note of any lack of transitions, material that does not flow logically, and awkward sentences. Also make note of the rhythm of your memo. Are most of your sentences long and verbose? Try to vary the length and complexity of your sentences.

### Editing by Reviewing Topic Sentences

Reviewing just the topic/thesis sentences without also reading the rest of each paragraph shows whether the argument flows in a logical, coherent fashion. Because a memorandum has an expected structure in which the various paragraphs should predictably and cohesively fit, cutting and pasting your topic sentences should also help you identify deficiencies in both your large-scale and small-scale organization.

In addition, reviewing the topic sentences in isolation should reveal any weak topic sentences. For example, you may note that your topic sentence for a rule application paragraph is overly broad, such as "The Defendant has many arguments." On the other hand, you may notice that your topic sentence is too narrow and thus does not truly capture the full scope of that paragraph. For instance, in our curfew hypothetical, a topic sentence focusing on summer vacation would not fully encompass the discussion of the guiding factor of whether it was a school night.

### Editing by Highlighting

Because a legal Discussion follows a conventional structure and progression, you can also check your structure through strategic highlighting. We suggest first highlighting all of the places that mention the facts of your client's situation. Then, use a different color to highlight all of the places that mention facts from a precedent case. Finally, with yet another color, highlight all the places in which you set forth a legal rule without making an argument.

With the highlighting completed, you can check your work. Does your memo reference the facts of your client's situation in a rule explanation paragraph? It should not, so make the appropriate edits to correct that. Also note where your memo references the facts of precedent cases. Such references should primarily occur in the rule explanation section. Later references in the rule application should reference only those precedent facts already described in a rule explanation paragraph.

Last, notice places in which you have set forth the legal rule without making an argument. Those places should be limited to your global and issue roadmaps. The components of the rule will be referenced elsewhere but only in the context of making an argument. The following excerpt from a rule application shows this common mistake and the fix for it: making specific arguments.

> **Ineffective:**
> Next, the court considers any visual indications as to whether the home was open to the public. Such indications may include signs and barriers to entry. The trailer Smith entered had a sign that read "Holdt Construction—Authorized Persons Only." It also was locked.

> **Effective:**
> Next, the court considers any visual indications as to whether the home was open to the public. The trailer Smith entered

had a sign posted that read "Holdt Construction—Authorized Persons Only," thus, unambiguously indicating that unauthorized persons were prohibited from entry. In addition, the door to the trailer was locked, albeit with a flimsy padlock, which posed a barrier to entry and thus further indicated that Smith was not permitted to enter.

Notice that the ineffective rule application excerpt simply states the law and then the facts of the client's situation. In contrast, the effective excerpt explicitly connects both pieces in order to make an argument.

## III.  Proofreading Your Memo

Proofreading is the final step in the legal writing process. The purpose of proofreading is not to make seismic changes to your document but instead to polish it. This polishing includes checking for errors in punctuation, grammar, sentence structure, and verb tense. It also includes looking for spelling errors and typos. You will also want to review your citations to ensure they are correct. Finally, this is your last chance to make sure the formatting correctly adheres to the specifications for your assignment, which may be very particular. You will find that courts have strict formatting requirements, including margin sizes, word/page limits, pagination, line spacing, and more. You must take care to comply with these requirements.

Although you already have been reviewing your memo for readability, clarity, and coherence while revising and editing, the proofreading stage provides a final opportunity to check these things. By the time you reach this last stage of the writing process, you will likely be eager to be finished with your memo. Keep in mind, though, that attentive proofreading will help build your reader's confidence in the memo by showing your commitment to and care regarding your work product.

What items should you look for at the proofreading stage? Chapter 29 contains many of the stylistic and language-related items that you should integrate into both drafting and proofreading. Further, the specific writing tips, such as common punctuation and usage errors described in the latter part of that chapter, also should help focus your proofreading efforts. Sometimes it is helpful when proofreading to go through your memo several times, each time with one or two specific points in mind, such as punctuation and sentence structure.

As noted, it also can be very useful to read your memo aloud. You may already have done this at the editing stage, but now the focus is on each word, each punctuation mark, etc. Because reading aloud forces you not to skip over anything, it makes it likely you will notice errors in spelling, punctuation, and the like. It also increases the chances that you will notice awkward, verbose, or grammatically incorrect sentences. When you find yourself stumbling over a sentence or re-reading it, you know you need to make it more readable. When one of the authors clerked for a federal court of appeals judge, a final "read aloud" was a required step before the judicial opinion was released for publication. While time consuming, the read-aloud method almost always helped identify errors.

### CHAPTER 29

# Writing Using a Lawyer's Language and Style

Legal writing follows certain conventions with respect to nomenclature and style. This chapter first highlights a few fundamental practices unique to legal writing, then ends with some tips for effective professional writing in general.

## Study Guide Questions for Chapter 29

1. What are some differences in the ways that lawyers refer to courts' actions as opposed to lawyers' actions?
2. When might you want to paraphrase and when might you want to quote information from another source? In which instances do you need to cite the source?
3. What are some ways in which you can familiarize yourself with legal writing conventions?
4. What new terms were introduced in this chapter? How do these terms relate to your existing understanding of predictive memo writing? Did your understanding of any other terms change as a result of reading this chapter?

This chapter highlights a few fundamental practices regarding how lawyers use terminology and the particular styles often utilized in legal writing. As you read cases in your classes, notice the language and style that courts use. Similarly, as you read sample memos, pay attention to the language and style choices made by the writer. By actively reading examples of legal writing, you will discern and start to assimilate many of these conventions.

This chapter concludes with some pointers for effective writing in general. While not unique to legal writing, these tips will help you focus on some of the basic features of good writing that will improve your legal writing as well.

## I. Introduction to the Language of the Law

- Courts can "apply" the law but never "apply" the facts.

  *Incorrect:* The Court applied the facts of the case and held that the warning was insufficient.

*Correct:* The Court applied the test from *McDonalds* and held that the warning was insufficient.

- Courts decide, hold, determine, find, consider, etc., but never feel or believe.

*Incorrect:* The Court felt that the manager improperly considered the employee's race when he failed to promote him.

*Correct:* The Court determined that the manager improperly considered the employee's race when he failed to promote him.

- Different terms apply in the criminal context versus the civil context.

| Criminal Cases | Civil Cases |
|---|---|
| accused | sued |
| charged | action filed against |
| found guilty | found liable |
| not guilty | not liable |
| the State | the plaintiff |
| prosecutor | plaintiff's counsel |
| illegal | unlawful |

- Lawyers don't tell judges what to do; instead, lawyers generally make requests.

*Ineffective:* This Court must find that the firing occurred after the Plaintiff filed her internal complaint.

*Effective:* The Plaintiff requests that this Court find that the firing occurred after the plaintiff filed her internal complaint.

- Generally, lawyers capitalize "Defendant," "Plaintiffs," the "State," etc., when referencing a specific party in the claim or charge currently being analyzed.

*Ineffective:* The defendant contends that this rule should not apply retroactively.
*Effective:* The Defendant contends that this rule should not apply retroactively.

## II. Introduction to Legal Writing Style

- Avoid first and second person pronouns, and instead use the third person.

*Ineffective:*
Our client contends that the firing was illegal.
I believe we can show that the firing was illegal.

*Effective:*
Plaintiff Smith contends that the firing was illegal.

*Ineffective:*
Below, I assert three arguments in support of the trade secrets claim.

*Effective:*
Three arguments support the trade secrets claim. (Or, "This memo outlines three arguments in support of the trade secrets claim.")

- **Be concise.**

*Ineffective:*
The action has several requirements for removal. Some of these requirements are more important than others, but all are required before removal may occur. To understand these requirements, it is easiest to break down 28 U.S.C. Sec. 1441(a) into its component parts and discuss each part separately.

*Note:* The first sentence tells us that requirements exist. The second sentence primarily just underscores what we already generally know to be true. Similarly, the last sentence adds nothing a law-trained reader does not already know: that each requirement should be analyzed.

*Effective:*
The plaintiff bears the burden of demonstrating that the action meets the requirements for removal under 28 U.S.C. Sec. 1441(a).

- **Include "the" before nouns: Write like a lawyer, not a police report.**

*Ineffective:* Defendant denies she hit victim.
*Effective:* The Defendant denies she hit the victim.

- **Use gender-neutral language; e.g., avoid generic use of "he" and sexist modifiers.**

*Ineffective:* The law must not be used as a vehicle to oppress men.

*Effective:* The law must not be used as a vehicle of oppression.

*Ineffective:* The case was assigned to Judge Walters, a female judge appointed by President Nixon.

*Effective:* The case was assigned to Judge Walters, an appointee of President Nixon.

- Use bias-free language; e.g., avoid irrelevant minority status references and use preferred terminology.

  *Ineffective:* The Latino lawyer representing the city council said council members are "pleased by the verdict and hopeful that this matter finally will be put to rest."

  *Effective:* The lawyer representing the city council said council members are "pleased by the verdict and hopeful that this matter finally will be put to rest."

  *Ineffective:* The policy protects handicapped persons.

  *Effective:* The policy protects persons with disabilities.

- Do not use contractions.

  *Ineffective:* The Plaintiff can't show good cause.

  *Effective:* The Plaintiff cannot show good cause.

  *Ineffective:* Without proof of intent, the claim isn't satisfied.

  *Effective:* Without proof of intent, the claim is not satisfied.

- Be consistent in using key words and phrases rather than switching to a new word or phrase for variety's sake.

  *Ineffective:*
  The prosecutor abused his discretion in bringing the kidnapping charge. Here, the prosecutor exercised improper judgment when he charged the Defendant with kidnapping in addition to assault.

  *Effective:*
  Prosecutorial discretion is critical to a fair and impartial legal system. Here, the prosecutor abused that discretion when he charged the Defendant with kidnapping in addition to assault.

## III. Quoting and Paraphrasing in Legal Writing

Legal writers frequently use quotations in their memoranda and other writing. Legal writing requires careful attribution of sentences, and even phrases, taken from another source. Your reader expects that you will identify your information source through both proper citation and appropriate use of quotation marks.

Proper attribution is not only required, it is beneficial. Ideas carry more weight when they come from an authoritative, or even persuasive, source of law, rather than originating from the writer herself. Imagine the difference between a court stating that Title VII is not a "general civility code for the American workplace" versus those words originating with the lawyer who wrote the memorandum. The words originating with the court carry a lot more weight.

Beyond the absolute requirement to cite your sources, you have some latitude in how you incorporate information from other sources into your writing. Let's look specifically at guidelines for the use of quotation marks as well as the strategic use of quotations in legal writing.

## A. When Must You Use Quotation Marks?

Quotation marks are necessary to show that the writer is using the words of another. In legal writing, you frequently will quote judicial opinions in order to show the words originated with a court. Unfortunately, there is no agreed-upon, bright-line rule explaining when you must use quotation marks. However, many legal writers rely on a five-word rule of thumb. Under that benchmark, when you use five consecutive words from another source, you must use quotation marks.

But this rule of thumb is not absolute. Sometimes, as discussed below, a writer will use a short, but unique and notable, phrase from another source. In such situations, the writer should use quotation marks not only to give credit to the original author but also to enhance the credibility of those particular words.

## B. When Is Paraphrasing Better than Quoting?

Effective legal writing requires the writer to be judicious in the use of quotes, reserving quotes for those occasions in which the writer wants to draw special attention to the words themselves, such as when the exact words matter.

Often, the exact words matter when those words originate from a statute or other established rule of law. In such instances, it is useful to quote those words even if they are fewer than five consecutive words. The use of quotation marks signals to the reader that these are indeed the exact words of the statute or other rule of law and, further, that these words originate from a source of law. Recall our Chapter 6 discussion about how exact wording can be critical to interpreting the law, particularly for enacted law.

The exact words also matter when using a "phrase that pays."[1] A phrase that pays is a short phrase taken from an outside source that succinctly, and uniquely, communicates a concept. Take the example of the phrase "breathing space" used in First Amendment jurisprudence. That phrase was first used in 1964 by Justice William Brennan in *New York Times v. Sullivan*. Since then, the Supreme Court itself has treated it as a phrase that pays, repeatedly quoting it. For example, more than two decades later, in 1988, Chief Justice William Rehnquist borrowed and quoted that phrase to emphasize a point in *Hustler Magazine v. Falwell*, writing: "[I]t reflects our considered judgment that such a standard is necessary to give adequate 'breathing space' to the freedoms protected by the First Amendment." While only two words long, that phrase's significance and credibility is bolstered by the use of quotation marks. Thus, like the Court itself, a legal writer would want to treat this as a phrase that pays and quote it when initially introducing the concept.

Most of the time, however, it is the concept—not the actual words—that needs to be communicated. In that case, the writer should paraphrase rather than quote the original source. Compare your reaction to the following excerpts. Do you agree that the second example better spotlights the point that Title VII is not a "general civility code for the American workplace"?

### Less Effective:
While there is little question that Parker's behavior was offensive, and even that Maybury was the target of many of his most vulgar behaviors, the evidence does not establish a claim of discrimination in violation of Title VII. "When evidence does not show that there was an objectively hostile environment, the claim must be rejected." *Smith v. Jones,* 1111 F.3d 10, 12 (12th Cir. 2012). Title VII is not "a general civility code for the American workplace." *Oncale v. Sundowner Offshore Servs., Inc.,* 523 U.S. 75, 80 (1998). "Courts overstep their bounds when they attempt to police the workplace of vulgar language." *Smith,* 1111 F.3d at 13 (12th Cir. 2012).

### More Effective:
While there is little question that Parker's behavior was offensive, and even that Maybury was the target of many of his most vulgar behaviors, the evidence does not establish a claim of discrimination in violation of Title VII. Title VII is not "a general civility code for the American workplace." *Oncale v.*

---

1. Professsor Mary Beth Beazley is credited with coining this term. *See* Terrill Pollman & Judith M. Stinson, *Irlafarc! Surveying the Language of Legal Writing*, 56 ME. L. REV. 239, 289 (2004).

*Sundowner Offshore Servs., Inc.*, 523 U.S. 75, 80 (1998). Courts cannot police foul and vulgar language in the workplace that does not rise to the standard of creating an objectively hostile work environment. *Smith v. Jones,* 1111 F.3d 10, 12 (12th Cir. 2012).

## IV. Tips for Effective Writing in General

Below are some tips for writing more effectively. While not unique to legal writing, these suggestions can help you improve your legal writing. You can find many additional useful resources online that specifically address grammar, punctuation, and sentence structure. For instance, many colleges and universities have writing centers that offer online collections of writing resources.

1. Avoid beginning sentences with "It is" or "There is/are."
2. Write "because" when giving a reason; write "since" when referring to a time sequence.
3. Shorten sentences that take three or more lines; break a page-long paragraph into two or more paragraphs.
4. Vary sentence length. A short sentence that follows a longer one can be effective.
5. Be consistent with names and use of titles. Start with the full name and then use only the last name or a title with last name, depending on your professor's preference.
6. Match nouns with the suitable pronoun and verb. Singular nouns have singular pronouns and verbs; plural nouns have plural pronouns and verbs. Pay particular attention to collective nouns—words used to refer to an entire group. When the group is acting as a unit, use a singular pronoun and verb. When the group is acting individually, use the plural.

   *Incorrect:* The <u>Court</u> stated that <u>they</u> could not accept the city's interpretation of Michelangelo's *David* as obscene.

   *Correct:* The <u>Court</u> stated that <u>it</u> could not accept the city's interpretation of Michelangelo's *David* as obscene.

   *Incorrect:* The <u>legislature vote</u> on the issue today.

   *Correct:* The <u>legislature votes</u> on the issue today.

7. Avoid colloquial language.

   *Incorrect:* The Court treated the Defendant's wealth as <u>a big deal</u>.

   *Correct:* The Court <u>emphasized</u> the Defendant's wealth.

8. Use active instead of passive verbs by making the subject do whatever action you discuss. Also, avoid mixing active and passive verbs in the same sentence.

   *Passive:* The gun <u>was fired by Smith</u> when Jones called him "a politician so sleazy even his own mother wouldn't claim him."

   *Active:* <u>Smith fired</u> the gun when Jones called him . . . .

9. Beware of beginning sentences with *–ing* words (gerunds), which can create ambiguity as to how the clause applies.

   *Incorrect:* <u>Claiming</u> to have been in Paris when the burglary occurred, the <u>jury</u> acquitted <u>the defendant</u> based on dated photographs of her at the Rodin Museum. [Oops—the jury did not claim to have been in Paris.]

   *Correct:* The jury acquitted the defendant because she had produced dated photographs of herself at the Rodin Museum in Paris when the burglary occurred.

10. Read your writing aloud to reveal omitted words and awkward sentences. Rework an awkward sentence by any or all of the following methods:
    • Answer the question: "What am I trying to say?"
    • Make the sentence into two or more simple sentences.
    • Shorten long clauses or make a long clause into a stand-alone sentence.
    • Change pronouns into nouns, even if you repeat the noun.
    • Use an active instead of a passive verb.

11. Brush up on common punctuation rules, as necessary, to be able to identify and fix errors, like the following mistakes:

    • Run-on or comma-splice sentences

      *Incorrect:* The burden lies with the prosecution, it must show proof beyond a reasonable doubt.

      *Correct:* The burden lies with the prosecution. It must show proof beyond a reasonable doubt.

    • Semicolon and colon confusion

      *Incorrect:*
      The court considers two factors; (1) the likelihood of success on the merits, and (2) the irreparable harm if no injunction is issued.

      *Correct:*
      The court considers two factors: (1) the likelihood of success on the merits, and (2) the irreparable harm if no injunction is issued.

*Incorrect:*

A hostile work environment claim is a subset of Title VII; rather than a separate statute.

*Correct:*

A hostile work environment claim is a subset of Title VII, rather than a separate statute. [This is correct because a complete sentence must come before and after the semicolon when used in this manner. Here, the second clause is only a sentence fragment, making the comma the appropriate punctuation.]

- Inaccurate placement of quotation marks

*Incorrect:* Title VII is not a "general civility code".

*Correct:* Title VII is not a "general civility code."

*Incorrect:* Title VII is not a "general civility code", nor is its purpose to remedy poor management decisions.

*Correct:* Title VII is not a "general civility code," nor is its purpose to remedy poor management decisions.

### CHAPTER 30

# Email Communication

Lawyers send many types of work-related email messages to solicit and share information with various parties. This chapter first addresses the unique challenges of professional email and then discusses one specific type of email lawyers write: an email relaying legal analysis to a supervisor. The chapter concludes with general email tips.

---

### Study Guide Questions for Chapter 30

1. What are some of the considerations for sharing written legal analysis that are the same regardless of whether it is shared in an email or a formal memo? What are some considerations that are different?

2. Which, if any, of the potential email pitfalls do you think might be the biggest hazards for you?

3. What strategies for ensuring you write effective email messages best resonate with you? What others can you think of that were not suggested in this chapter?

4. What new terms were introduced in this chapter? How do these terms relate to your existing understanding of predictive memo writing? Did your understanding of any other terms change as a result of reading this chapter?

---

Most of us, for better or worse, write personal email with ease. As a lawyer, writing email requires additional attention.

## I. Unique Challenges of Professional Email Communication

The nature of email can present some unique communication challenges for both the writer and the reader. An awareness of these issues will help you avoid the potential pitfalls associated with writing a professional email and will help you adapt your communication to suit your reader and facilitate her understanding of your message.

### A. Challenges of Email as a Medium

In a professional context, unless you mindfully approach the task of writing an email, two key advantages of this communication medium can easily become disadvantages: (1) the ease of sending email—shooting off a quick message—and (2) the wide range of uses for email. These aspects of email communication may lead writers to treat email more informally than they should. Many of our personal email communications tend to reflect a stream-of-consciousness writing style, replete with asides and casual personal touches. We might quickly send a message, only to immediately send a follow-up with additional information we neglected to include in the initial email. (Does "Oops! Forgot the attachment!" seem at all familiar?) We also expect friends to forgive the occasional typo.

By and large, we want to avoid these practices with workplace email messages. Luckily, we can, by establishing a professional mindset when composing work-related emails and by incorporating the kinds of effective writing habits for legal communication discussed throughout this book. In the next section, we consider specific strategies for accomplishing both.

In addition to recognizing how email may influence our writing style, we also need to contemplate our reader's situation. Several aspects of email may affect the way your message is received and read. First, consider that many people check their email on a phone. What might seem a relatively short message on a computer monitor can easily appear voluminous on a small screen. Second, realize that many of us struggle to keep our inboxes in check. This can adversely affect the attention we give to an email or how carefully we read our messages. Many people scan email rather than reading it slowly and deliberately, word for word. They may also perceive email as something of a nuisance. Even when your message was solicited and anticipated, it might still arrive in a sea of spam, affecting the mindset of the person receiving it.

Some of these obstacles might not apply to our specific context, in which someone has expressly asked you to analyze a legal issue and, likely, is eagerly awaiting your response. In this case, your recipient might very well read your message extremely carefully, looking at it on a computer. However, you have no control over whether that happens. Moreover, under any circumstances, you want to employ email composition strategies that can help your reader understand your message quickly and accurately.

## B. Strategies to Address These Challenges

### 1. Pay Attention to Tone

You need to consider the tone of your email to assure it meets the expectations of your particular workplace. If you are new to an organization and have not yet identified its norms, consider that in American business and legal culture, it is safer to err on the side of being overly formal than overly casual. For instance, you should begin your email message with a salutation, just as you would do with a print letter, and unless you are positive that your supervisor wants you to address him by his first name, use his title and last name instead.

Also, consider that social "niceties," like a message salutation ("Hi, Sam,…"), help set a friendly, yet professional, tone for your message. Written communication lacks cues like vocal inflection and facial expressions. In personal messages, we might overcome this barrier with emoticons. Because we want to avoid that level of informality in a work email, it is particularly important to ensure we are phrasing and packaging our message in a way that might seem crisp, but that is not rudely abrupt.

Maintaining a distinct separation between work and personal email can help ensure you approach work email professionally. It is easier to stay in a professional mindset when you are not switching between responding to a client's email message and setting up weekend plans with friends. The principle is similar to the recommendation to limit distractions when working from home by setting up a dedicated work space or by simply shutting the door of the room. These kinds of environmental cues help put you in "work mode." Adopting a policy of only using your work email account for work matters and only accessing personal email accounts on personally owned devices can also protect the privacy of your personal communications.

## 2. Craft a Helpful Subject Line

Including a descriptive, yet brief, subject in the email header is your first line of defense against a reader's tendency to quickly scan her inbox. Often likened to newspaper headlines, email subject lines alert your reader to the topic she will find addressed in the body of the message. In the same way that you include a descriptive *re:* clause in a formal legal memorandum, you want to be specific in your email subject line. In fact, this may be even more important with email because you want to make it easy for your supervisor to find the message again in the future.

Recall that in The Smell Shoppe hypothetical, our memo heading included "Re: Arnold Matter: Whether Mr. Arnold Can Prove Tortious Interference with Business Expectancy." In the email context, we might shorten this to "Arnold—Tortious Interference with Business Expectancy," but we would not want to shorten it to something like "Client Matter" or even just "Arnold." These latter two subject lines would be insufficiently descriptive. Of course, you would also want to follow established law firm standards for email headings. For instance, you might be asked to begin each heading with the case file number rather than the client name.

Typically, if you are replying to an email, you won't change the subject line. Keeping the same subject enables people to sort by subject and easily find the initial message and all of the responses to it. However, if you are significantly altering the focus of your email, you may choose to create a new subject.

Finally, in the event that you need to send a lengthy email, it may be helpful to cue the recipient to that fact in the subject line. You can signal this with something like "(Long)" at the end of the subject line.

## 3. Include a Signature Line and Legal Disclaimer

You want to set a standard email signature that includes, at minimum, your full name, title, and contact information. This reminds the reader who completed the work in the email and makes it easy for her to respond to you, not just via reply email, but also by phone. Some lawyers treat their signatures as business cards, including branding information like the firm colors and logo, as well as other personal marketing details, like a link to your bio page on the firm website, a photo, and professional social media links. Others find this excessive.

It is also critical to remember that many lawyer communications are privileged and/or confidential attorney work product. While such privileges are largely beyond the scope of this chapter, we note that these protections should attach to emails and that the lawyer has a duty to give notice of such protections through a legal disclaimer attached to the end of every work email. Your particular state's rules governing lawyers determine the requirements of such a disclaimer. We provide the below merely as an example of the type of disclaimer that should be considered:

> This email and any attached documents contain information from the law firm of García, Bengston & Locke, which may be confidential and/or legally privileged. These materials are intended only for the personal and confidential use of the addressee identified above. If you are not the intended recipient or an agent responsible for delivering these materials to the intended recipient, you are hereby notified that any review, disclosure, copying, distribution or the taking of any action in reliance on the contents of this transmitted information is strictly prohibited. If you have received this email in error, please immediately notify the sender of this message.

## 4. Consider Content and Organization

Your biggest challenge will likely be determining how to compose the body of your email to keep it as brief as possible while not losing essential content. Fortunately, many of the same legal writing strategies already discussed will help with this task. In Section II below we address this challenge, focusing in particular on drafting emails that convey legal analysis.

## 5. Ensure Readability

You can also facilitate the reader's understanding of your email through formatting. Particularly because many readers scan email, using bold headings, such as Question, Answer, and Analysis, can facilitate reader comprehension. Similarly, bulleted or numbered lists can make it easier to digest an email message.

If you have a long paragraph (and have already determined all those words are truly necessary), break it into shorter paragraphs and leave a blank line between each. Especially for readers viewing your message on a phone screen, long blocks of text can quickly become overwhelming, decreasing the odds of comprehension.

## 6. Review Before Hitting "Send"

Be sure to review your message, revising and editing it to ensure your communication is as concise as possible while still being clear and accurate. Take this opportunity to review the matter you were asked to address and make sure your response is on point, provides the requested amount of depth, and does not veer into unnecessary tangential matters. Ensure you have a descriptive subject line and an appropriate tone. The read-aloud technique for editing, discussed in Chapter 28, can be particularly effective for evaluating both the clarity and tone of email messages. Carefully proofread your message, correcting any spelling, grammar, or usage errors.

Think through the message one more time before you hit send. Did you include any referenced attachments, and are they the correct item and latest version? Is there anything else important to convey in this message? Did you include all necessary recipients and exclude those who do not need to receive the message?

## II. Drafting Emails That Convey Legal Analysis

The body of an email message is not the ideal medium for conveying lengthy, complex analysis. Therefore, you need to carefully consider what information is essential and what can be eliminated. Whatever the particular purpose of your message, the legal analysis and writing techniques discussed throughout this book should continue to inform how you draft your email. In other words, while the email may not be structured like a predictive memo, it nonetheless conveys legal analysis. As such, the same principles apply.

First, pre-writing analysis remains critical. If you are summarizing a legal memorandum you have already written, you have completed this work. You may, however, be starting from scratch, having just been asked to investigate a legal issue and provide your analysis via email. Of course, before starting any work project, it is always essential to have clarity about the task. How you approach the work and deliver the results will depend, in part, upon the level of detail the assigning attorney needs, how much time they would like you to spend on it, when it is due, the ultimate use for the information, and the like. Even with a very narrow question, you will likely still have to complete at least some of the work of identifying and understanding the legal rule, considering the arguments that each side can make in the case at hand, and analyzing which arguments are most likely to be successful.

Next, once you have a clear grasp on the question you are addressing and what you need to say about it, you will outline your message. You still want to employ a deductive framework to deliver your legal analysis; however, you may not include all of the sections that would be included in a formal memo.

Start the email with a clear indication of the legal question you investigated. This may not be quite as in-depth as the Question Presented section of a formal memo, but by summarizing the specific legal issue you are addressing you will clarify your scope and provide vital context for the rest of the message. Even if you are responding to an email that contains the research request, you should still lead with this information to show your understanding of the issue and to prevent your reader from having to look down the thread to the original message to find the question asked. This saves your reader time, particularly when a multiple message email chain exists (e.g., perhaps you originally responded to the request for research by asking some clarifying questions). Even in the absence of a lengthy chain, you want your email to stand alone, not to make sense only if read alongside other messages. This will also facilitate understanding if your message is forwarded to a third party.

Then, depending on the request, you might provide an abbreviated Statement of Facts. If the facts are not separately recounted, they still need to be integrated into your analysis.

Next, you will provide an abbreviated Short Answer. This will include your global prediction as to the resolution of the client's claim or charge.

Finally, you will communicate your analysis. The level of supporting detail you provide in the rest of the email depends on the exact parameters of the request. If your supervisor wanted you to produce a formal memo and submit it to her via email, most of the analysis may appear in the attachment; the body of the email might simply summarize the main point.

On the other hand, if you were asked to provide an informal analysis of an issue in lieu of a formal memo, you still need to provide many of the elements that would otherwise be in the Discussion section of the memo. You need to be ruthless in determining the essential information and only including that. You also will likely need to combine information, such as addressing rule explanation material and rule application arguments in tandem. Even so, the same tools that facilitate understanding in a formal memo, such as topic sentences and transitions, can still provide useful reader cues in an abbreviated email analysis. Keep the words that enhance understanding and eliminate any fluff.

After conveying your legal analysis, you need a closing. Invite the reader to contact you with any additional questions, or, if the matter is truly complex, suggest setting up a follow-up meeting. If there are specific areas outside of the original request for which additional research seems valuable, provide those specific suggestions.

In almost all cases you want to avoid simply referring the reader to an attachment in order to address her question. Provide all the critical information in the body of the email and refer to the attachment for additional detail. If you include an attachment, name it descriptively. Both practices will save your reader time and will also ensure she feels secure opening the attachment. With phishing schemes becoming increasingly sophisticated, including the ability to spoof email addresses, an email that simply says, "Here is the memo you requested," with an attachment called "Memo," is not only unhelpful, it could appear to be a hazard.

## CONCEPT IN ACTION: Example of an Effective Email Conveying Informal Legal Analysis

Assume that Louise Jasper has come to the García, Bengston, & Locke law firm because she wants to end her relationship with Larry Wilmer, her live-in partner. However, she is concerned a court will find they were in a common-law marriage, thus subjecting her to undesirable financial consequences as the partner with more assets and income.

The firm's senior partner has asked the law clerk to conduct research and analyze whether Ms. Jasper likely fulfills the requirements for common-law marriage in New Jersey. The partner has stated that she needs the analysis by the end of the day and does not want a long memo. She said, "Just send me an email with your analysis, so I can give it a quick read before I meet with Ms. Jasper at 4:00 today." Below is an example of an effective email in response to that request.

Ms. Senior Partner:

You asked whether a court would likely conclude that our client, Ms. Jasper, is in a common-law marriage with Mr. Wilmer. A court will probably find that Ms. Jasper and Mr. Wilmer have a common-law marriage.

Specifically, under New Jersey state law, Mr. Wilmer should be able to demonstrate that the parties assumed a marital relationship by mutual consent and agreement because numerous symbols of marriage exist (wedding-like rings, engravings indicating they both share the last name of "Wilmer") and the parties' conduct and testimony reveals they felt married. They addressed each other as "my wife," "my husband," and "my better half." They also confirmed their marriage by cohabitation and public repute because they lived together for nine years (with a brief interruption) and, in fact, most of their friends believe they are married.

However, Ms. Jasper could argue that their conduct shows that they did not intend to be married. Ms. Jasper stated that she did not want a formal marriage and has never stated she felt married. These facts distinguish her case from similar ones where a common-law marriage was found. Additionally, Ms. Jasper could point to their brief separation as interrupting their cohabitation and thus suggesting no marital relationship. Further, Ms. Jasper could argue that the public did not perceive them as married, but rather only a select group of friends did. This is unlike many cases in which a common-law marriage was found to exist, in which friends, family, co-workers, and other community members uniformly perceived the couple as married.

Please let me know if you need further research or more detailed information regarding my research and analysis.

Sincerely,
Aliyah

Aliyah Alexander
Law Clerk, García, Bengston, & Locke
555-555-5555

This email and any attached documents contain information from the law firm of García, Bengston & Locke, which may be confidential and/or legally privileged. These materials are intended only for the personal and confidential use of the addressee identified above. If you are not the intended recipient or an agent responsible for delivering these materials to the intended recipient, you are hereby notified that any review, disclosure, copying, distribution or the taking of any action in reliance on the contents of this transmitted information is strictly prohibited. If you have received this email in error, please immediately notify the sender of this message.

## III. Additional Email Tips

In addition to the specific considerations discussed above for professional emails, including emails that provide legal analysis, below we share some additional email tips.

### A. Professionalism

We should all know that electronic communications are not necessarily assured to be private. As you review your message, make sure you are not committing to writing (in an easily shared format) anything you would be embarrassed to have broadcast to the world. Also, make sure to follow any organizational policies on encryption or disclaimers that must be included in email communications.

### B. Style

As discussed earlier, you will generally want to avoid emoticons in professional emails. In addition, you should typically avoid other overly casual aspects of electronic communication, such as texting acronyms. For some forms of email communication, such as soliciting participants for a social or charitable event or a team-building newsletter, it might be acceptable to include a meme, but generally you would not do so in a professional setting.

Keep in mind that you might have email readers who have low vision, dyslexia, are color blind, or use a screen reader. Fortunately, many accessible design practices are easy to adopt and tend to help all readers. In addition to the formatting tips above, select a sans-serif font that is easy to read and avoid fonts with a light line weight. Make sure you have distinct color contrast between your font and your background. In addition, avoid the use of all caps, which not only can be difficult to read, but also comes across to your reader as if you are shouting.[1]

---

1. To read more about accessibility issues related to e-mail, see the Web Accessibility Initiative's Web Content Accessibility Guidelines at https://www.w3.org/WAI/standards-guidelines/wcag/ or the checklist the Department of Health and Human Services developed based on these guidelines, available at https://www.hhs.gov/web/section-508/making-files-accessible/checklist/email-508-checklist/index.html. In addition, if you search the help information for your email program, you might find information about its accessibility settings.

## C. Recipients

It is common advice to input the email address of the recipient only after you have thoroughly reviewed your email. In this way, you can ensure you do not inadvertently send the message before you intend to do so.

Also, think strategically about who needs to receive a message. In part, this might depend on workplace culture. Some organizations place a greater emphasis on making sure everyone who might possibly need to know something has had that information shared with them, while others prioritize limiting communications so as to not overwhelm employees with information only tangentially related to them. Individual employees may also have strong preferences and become upset either when information is not shared with them or when too much information is shared with them. Directly asking your supervisor and other key colleagues about their preferences for being copied on email messages can be the easiest way to avoid problems. Remember that even someone who would like to be informed at certain checkpoints might not necessarily want to receive every email discussion along the way.

Be very careful with "reply" versus "reply all." A fairly common method of committing an email faux pas (or worse) involves replying to an entire discussion list when you only intended to reply to the sender.

Finally, use caution when forwarding messages. Consider, in part, whether the original sender intended that the information be kept confidential. Email etiquette may require that you ask for permission to share the message beyond the initial audience. Note, too, that a string of messages may be attached to the forwarded message. Even if it is appropriate to forward the latest message, you want to be certain that the earlier messages do not contain information that perhaps should not be shared.

## D. Automated Features

Explore the features of your email program that can help you review your messages. These commonly include spelling and grammar checks or alerts if it appears you neglected to include an intended attachment. You may also be able to set a delay to schedule delivery of your message for a future time, or, as a standard, provide a brief window to cancel delivery of a message you just sent.

Most email programs also let you set some level of automatic reply. The most common type is the auto reply stating you are out of the office. When composing an out-of-office message, you might want to include information about when you are likely to return the incoming message and who can be contacted in the meantime in case of emergency. While it is beyond the scope of this chapter to suggest effective management practices for incoming email, note that most programs also enable you to establish a variety of other rules for processing received messages that can help ensure you see your most important emails.

## E.  Other Forms of Communication

Finally, remember that, although extremely convenient, email is not the best form of communication for all needs. For instance, if you have many questions about an assignment from a supervisor, it might be easier to try to schedule a meeting and discuss those questions face-to-face or over the telephone. Should this be impractical, try to make sure that, to the extent possible, you ask all of your questions in a single email and number them to facilitate response.

Avoid sending email when you are extremely emotional. Someone might have sent you something that made you angry. Instantly firing back a brutally honest response ("I'm right—you're wrong!") may be tempting, but it rarely yields good long-term results.

---

**✂ CHECK IN: Effective Emails**

Consider the following email message. In what ways does it comport with the principles above? In what ways does it fall short? Revise the message to improve its effectiveness.

From:    Aliyah.Alexander@LawFirm.Com
To:      Michael.Zachary@LawFirm.Com
Cc:      EveryOtherAttorney@LawFirm.Com
Subject: As Discussed

Hey man,

So glad we bumped into each other yesterday—always nice to see you and happy to get an interesting research project. So, I took a quick look into that matter you asked about, and I've got some top notch stuff for you!!

Unfortunately, sweet little Bootsie will probably be found to be dangerous.

These are the cases I looked at: Davenport v. Dearfield. Court held that a Great Dane that startled a neighbor who approached the house

---

when the dog was sleeping on a front porch did not engage in threatening behavior. Arco v. Anderson. A dog bit a guest who was visiting her owner's home. The dog was eating from her dinner bowl when the guest approached and put his hand directly in the dog's bowl. The court held the dog was not dangerous. Bustillo v. Baxter. A mini dachshund left his porch to chase a jogger. He bared his teeth and growled at the runner but did not bite her. The court held the dog was dangerous. Cantwell v. Chen. A dog got loose in the neighborhood. While loose, she approached and bit five different people, two of whom required emergency care. She had previously gotten loose and bitten one person. The court held the dog was dangerous. Davis v. Donaghey. A dog in a fenced-in backyard was known to bark furiously at people who passed by. The dog never bit anyone or made physical contact of any kind, but did bare her teeth and growl at the passersby. The court held the dog was not dangerous.

Like we discussed, the opposing party will have to prove by clear and convincing evidence that our client's dog, Bootsie, has engaged in threatening behavior. For that, courts consider the dog's overt actions and physical characteristics. Bootsie ran into the neighbor's yard, barking and growling at the plaintiff's child, who was sitting in the grass. The court will likely find these overt and provoking acts, as they did with Bustillo and Cantwell, rather than finding it not dangerous, like they did with Davenport, Arco and Davis. Just check the attached memo for complete details.

Hit me up if you need anything else! Or if you "need" someone to catch the next Pirates game with you—I've heard you have some sweet season tickets!!

### CHAPTER 31

# Drafting Talking Points for Your Legal Memorandum

Often your written analysis will lead to follow-up oral communication. This chapter focuses on how to create *talking points* that convey the main points of your legal memorandum.

---

**Study Guide Questions for Chapter 31**

1. What is the purpose of talking points for your memorandum?
2. What are the common features of effective talking points?
3. How detailed should talking points be? Why?
4. Are talking points inductive or deductive? Why is that important?
5. What new terms were introduced in this chapter? How do these terms relate to your existing understanding of predictive memo writing? Did your understanding of any other terms change as a result of reading this chapter?

---

After writing a legal memorandum, you often will be asked to share the high points of your analysis in person. This in-person communication is typically informal, meaning that you are called upon to convey information in the course of a meeting, rather than through a planned presentation. Usually the assigning lawyer wants an oral recap of the legal analysis reflected in your memo. You may also be meeting with the client and need to provide her with an oral summary of your legal analysis.

With both contexts in mind, this chapter discusses developing talking points in order to organize your thoughts before you present them. These talking points function as informal notes for you; you probably will not share your written talking points with your audience. They serve to keep you on track so that you share the most important information in an organized and deductive way.

## I. Guidelines for Developing Talking Points

Your talking points will depend on the particular situation, including your audience, as well as your personal preferences. Although there is no formal structure that you must employ for your talking points, you should address the following content areas.

- *What legal question (claim or charge) did you explore?*

It is important to start with the big picture—identifying what are you discussing—before you proceed to the details. Many of us have experienced confusion when someone starts to explain something to us without first providing context. This leaves us struggling to figure out that context while simultaneously trying to digest the new information.

- *What is the global rule of law for that claim or charge?*

Just as the global rule of law provides the framework for your written Discussion, it also provides the necessary framework for the rest of your talking points.

- *What is your main takeaway?*

You will want to share your global prediction as well as your issue predictions.

- *What is your support for your main predictions?*

Your talking points will not provide the detailed support that your memo contains. For example, you will not exhaustively consider the rule explanation cases or provide all of the arguments contained in your rule application sections. Instead, you will provide a summary that highlights the most important information. You might note a key case or two, as well as indicating its similarity to your client's situation, but that is not always necessary.

- *Were there any gaps in your analysis?*

If you were missing key information (whether it is now knowable or not), you likely will want to point that out. For example, your research may have indicated that certain facts—which you do not have—may be relevant to your prediction. You therefore should point out the follow-up factual investigation that is needed to fully consider the client's claim or charge.

- *What challenges do you see going forward?*

You will want to take the opportunity to alert your colleagues—and appropriately set expectations for your client—to any anticipated obstacles. For example, is there an argument that will be especially challenging for your client? Is there factual information that currently is unknown that may significantly affect your analysis and prediction? Is the rule of law unsettled, such that your analysis depends on predictions about which rule of law the court will apply (as opposed to how the court will apply a settled rule of law)?

Just as your legal memorandum follows a deductive approach (going from general to more specific information), so, too, should your talking points. As emphasized throughout this book, deductive analysis is the cornerstone of all legal analysis and communication, whether written or oral. Your audience wants to first hear the general issue (the big question) and the general prediction before you provide any supporting detail.

Stylistically, talking points are usually most effective when they are not complete sentences. Noting a few words or a phrase is usually ideal. You don't need to spell out everything you wish to communicate; rather, just note enough to trigger your thoughts for that point. Using bullet points or a basic outline is usually the most effective way to lay out your talking points, making it easy to glance down at them and keep yourself on track.

## II. Talking Points in Action: Talking Points for the Warrantless Bomb Search Fourth Amendment Memorandum

Let's develop talking points for the Warrantless Bomb Search hypothetical. Assume you will be using these talking points in an upcoming meeting with the lawyer who assigned you the memorandum. She has not had an opportunity to review your memorandum yet.

> Before you look at the information below, please review the complete memo using multiple authorities, contained in Appendix B. Your task is to take the voluminous information contained in that memo and streamline it into effective talking points. Below, we reprint each of the prompt questions, followed by the written talking points the attorney might use to prepare for the meeting.

1. *What legal question (claim or charge) did you explore?*
   * *Question is whether the federal agents' search of Van Zanda's storage container violated the Fourth Amendment*
   * *No warrant → so memo focuses on two exceptions to the rule against warrantless searches*

2. *What is the global rule of law for that claim or charge?*
   * *Fourth Amendment requires warrant unless exception*
   * *Exception 1: exigent circumstances*
   * *Exception 2: consent to search*
   * *Only need one exception*

3. *What are the main takeaways?*

- Conclusion: no violation; both exceptions exist
- Exception 1: exigent circumstance due to "risk of danger" from bomb
- Exception 2: consent existed from The Earl's "apparent authority"

4. *What is your support for the main takeaways?*

- Exigent circumstance:

  - *Credible risk* of harm to themselves or others—credible belief of volatile bomb from tip; Van Zanda's prior involvement in bombing; and "hit" by bomb-sniffing dog; Agents acted consistent with bomb threat—wore bomb suits (unlike precedents with inconsistent behavior, such as didn't clear a building)
  - Consent: The Earl did not have actual authority, but apparent authority is enough. Why apparent authority? He said so; he had a key to container; his guitars were in container. No reason for agents not to believe him, given this confirmation (which is unlike cases with no apparent authority)
  - Must only prove one exception: here either way provides exception

5. *Were there any gaps in your analysis?*

- No gaps
- Need to confirm, though, agents will testify truly believed bomb

6. *What challenges do you see going forward?*

- Defendant likely will dispute volatility of bomb—if not believed to be volatile/unstable, Government had time to get a warrant
- Defendant likely will argue "unnecessary delay" by Government so no true threat
- Defendant likely will argue that The Earl created ambiguity about his authority when he mentioned falling out with Van Zanda → contend that Government should have asked more questions to confirm authority

---

### ✂ CHECK IN: Creating Talking Points

Create talking points for The Smell Shoppe multiple authorities memorandum in Appendix B. After you have done so, use these talking points to give an oral recap of your analysis as if you were at a meeting with the assigning attorney. This is a simulation you can do on your own, simply for practice.

### CHAPTER 32

# From Predictive to Persuasive Writing

In this chapter, we discuss the transition from predictive to persuasive writing. Our goal is to help show some of the similarities and differences of these two types of legal writing.

## Study Guide Questions for Chapter 32

1. What features are shared by both predictive and persuasive legal writing?
2. What are the main differences between predictive and persuasive writing?
3. What strategies can you employ to address binding authority that appears to undercut your position? What strategy must you avoid in this situation?
4. What new terms were introduced in this chapter? How do these terms relate to your existing understanding of predictive memo writing? Did your understanding of any other terms change as a result of reading this chapter?

Now that you have learned about and practiced objective, also known as predictive, legal writing, your next challenge will be to write persuasively. You may be looking forward to this endeavor, especially if a desire to advocate brought you to law school. Or, you may be somewhat deflated by the proposition of tackling a new type of legal writing when you are just getting the hang of predictive legal writing.

Whatever your level of enthusiasm may be, the good news is that effective persuasive legal writing bears many similarities to predictive legal writing. Moreover, persuasive legal writing is less formulaic; you no longer will employ the rigid structure to which you have grown accustomed in writing a legal memorandum (roadmaps, rule explanation, and rule application). Some students lament this lack of structure, but most come to enjoy the creativity inherent in persuasive writing.

Persuasive legal writing comes in various forms. We use the example of a legal brief in order to compare its general purpose and features to a legal memorandum.

## I. What Is the Same?

Much remains the same. Predictive writing was the vehicle by which you learned about the fundamentals of legal analysis, i.e., identifying the issue, discerning the law, and applying the law to your facts. These fundamentals remain critical to all types of legal writing. Thus, you still will be explaining the law using cases and making arguments about the law's application to your client's situation. You still will be communicating using a deductive approach, in which you go from general to specific, starting with the rule and its prior application before moving on to your client's arguments.

## II. What Is Different?

Overall, you will work with the same material (cases, facts, etc.) when writing persuasively as you did when writing a memo. That does not mean, though, that you will use those materials in the same way. The main difference between predictive and persuasive writing is your audience and, thus, your purpose. Because your goal is now to persuade someone who may or may not be inclined to agree with your client's position, you will learn to use persuasive writing techniques. Let's look specifically at some differences to keep in mind when writing persuasively.

*Your audience is not part of your team.*

With predictive writing you were writing to an ally—someone who was aligned with your client, whether the assigning attorney or perhaps your client himself. Your purpose was to give them an informed and objective analysis so that they, in turn, could make sound decisions. In persuasive writing your audience is very different. You now are writing to an "outsider," whether that is the court, the opposing party, or someone else who is not part of your team/side. It makes sense that you will need to adjust the content and style of your writing to suit your new audience.

*You will address counter-arguments strategically rather than neutrally.*

Because you are not tasked with providing an objective analysis, you should not *make* the other party/position's arguments in your brief. However, this does not mean that you will ignore the counter-arguments. For strategic reasons, you most likely will acknowledge the other side's arguments, but rather than objectively detailing those arguments, trying to make them as strong as possible, you will instead minimize them by showing they are poorly reasoned, factually distinct, etc. And you will do so in a way that reinforces your position rather than coming from a purely defensive posture.

Thus, rather than making the other side's argument as you did in predictive writing, you will stake out your position on the other side's argument. Consider the following example. The first sentence exemplifies the kind of objectivity that we expect in predictive writing, whereas the second sentence illustrates how the same information can be conveyed persuasively.

**Objective:** The Prosecution will argue that Smith's entry was unlawful because he entered without express permission.

**Persuasive:** While Smith entered without express permission, he had implicit permission to enter due to his relationship with the home's owner.

*Your purpose is to convince your audience to adopt your position over another position.*

Your purpose is not to present balanced information or "be the expert" and explain the intricacies of the law. Instead, you are striving to get your audience, usually a court, to agree with your position. If doing so requires you to explain the intricacies of the law, then so be it. But the question you should ask yourself when you are drafting a persuasive document is, "How can I get the court to agree that my client's position on the legal question is the right one?"

*Every part of the brief, indeed every sentence, is an opportunity to persuade.*

This means you will phrase the Question Presented persuasively, the Table of Contents persuasively, the Statement of Facts persuasively, the law persuasively, and your client's arguments persuasively. Every sentence provides an opportunity to persuade in terms of what information you choose to include, what information you emphasize, and how you advance your position.

Consider the following topic sentences. The first one is an example of objective writing, in which the writer introduces the topic in a neutral fashion. The second example introduces the topic persuasively. By taking a position on the topic, it suggests to the reader how the topic should be viewed.

**Objective:** First, the court will consider whether the entry was unlawful.

**Persuasive:** First, Smith's entry was lawful.

Note, too, that we would not want to frame this sentence in reference to what the other side plans to argue, e.g., "First, the Prosecution will argue that Smith's entry was unlawful." That would both create a defensive tone and result in a missed opportunity to persuade.

**RULES OF THE ROAD: Ethical Limits to Persuasion**

Lawyers must follow ethical rules that limit the bounds of persuasion. For example, one ethical rule is that lawyers must disclose binding, adverse authority. That means even if a case is decidedly not favorable to your client's position, if it is a binding authority, the lawyer is required to disclose it. Similarly, another ethical rule is that the lawyer must state the facts accurately and not misleadingly. That means a lawyer can neither "make up" facts nor fail to disclose material facts.

Although these ethical rules appropriately limit the bounds of persuasion, they don't mean a lawyer has to throw in the towel. The lawyer must cite to an adverse authority but can still attempt to minimize that authority's application in his client's case, such as by arguing it is factually distinct or implicitly overruled by another authority. Likewise, a lawyer must disclose the facts and accurately convey them but can do this while emphasizing helpful facts and de-emphasizing unhelpful facts.

 **CONCEPT IN ACTION: Comparing Objective Discussion of a Rule of Law to a Persuasive Discussion of That Rule from the Warrantless Bomb Search Hypothetical**

Let's compare how the rule for the issue/condition of "whether there was consent to search" is described in a predictive memo Discussion versus how that same rule might be described in a persuasive brief. When you finish reading this example, can you tell whether the persuasive example was written by counsel for the Government or for the Defendant?

### RULE FROM PREDICTIVE MEMORANDUM

The government also can justify the warrantless search by showing that the agents had consent to search the container. "In order to consent to a search, the person purporting to consent must possess either actual or apparent authority over the item or place to be searched." *Id.* at 962. The government concedes that The Earl lacked actual authority, so the only question is whether he had apparent authority. Apparent authority is judged by an objective standard based on the information known to the agent at the moment of search. *Id.* In the third-party context, the agent must have reasonably believed the person giving consent possessed joint access or control over the property searched. *Id.* In determining whether such apparent authority over the property searched existed, courts consider: (1) whether the person reasonably asserted access and control over the property and (2) whether the context confirmed or created ambiguity regarding the spoken assertion. *Id.*

### SAME RULE FROM PERSUASIVE BRIEF

Although a warrantless search may be justified by showing that the agents had consent to search, such consent must come from a person who "possess[es] either actual or apparent authority over the item or place to be searched." *Id.* at 962. It is not enough that the government agent subjectively believed the person giving consent possessed such authority; the government must instead show that such a belief was objectively reasonable at the time of the search. *Id.* When the question of consent arises in the third-party context, apparent authority is valid only if the agent reasonably believed the person giving consent possessed joint access or control over the property searched. *Id.* In making this determination, the court first examines whether the person expressing consent reasonably asserted access and control over the property. Even if so, the court next scrutinizes whether the context in which the consent was given created ambiguity regarding the spoken assertion rather than confirmed it. *Id.*

Did you discern that the second example is from a persuasive brief of the Defendant, not the Government? How could you tell? Because it employs various persuasive strategies that suggest the rule is too rigorous to satisfy. It also uses exclusionary language (e.g., "only if" and "even if") to suggest that the rule is not all-encompassing but rather must be fulfilled in specific and limited ways. Also, the verb "considers" as used in the objective version is replaced by the words "examines" and "scrutinizes," which further signals to the reader the rigor of the test.

# Sample Memos Using Single Case Authority

## MEMORANDUM

To:     Senior Partner
From:  Junior Associate
Re:     Arnold Matter: Whether Mr. Arnold Can Prove Tortious Interference
         with Business Expectancy
Date:   August 17, 2020

---

### QUESTION PRESENTED

Under Illinois law, is a defendant liable for tortious interference with business expectancy when it created a competing business with a logo similar to that of the plaintiff's business, yet indicated that it was not affiliated with the plaintiff's business during a phone call inquiry, and when it created an online website with printed coupons stating, "Come See Us at Our New Location," but when that coupon only listed the defendant's one true business location?

### SHORT ANSWER

No, it is not likely that Mr. Green will be liable for tortious interference with business expectancy. Because Mr. Arnold can demonstrate a specific contemplation from his customers and can demonstrate that the customers expressed their belief that they were doing business with his store, it is likely that the court will find that he possessed a reasonable expectancy of entering into a valid business relationship. However, because Mr. Green was not dishonest with customers when he received a phone call regarding the affiliation, it is unlikely that the court will find that it was Mr. Green's intentional and unjustified interference that prevented the realization of business expectancy.

### STATEMENT OF FACTS

This is a case involving an allegation of tortious interference with business expectancy on behalf of Gene Arnold against Carl Green. Both parties operate candle businesses in the Chicago area.

1

Gene Arnold opened his first candle and scents store, called The Smell Shoppe, in 2010 in Chicago, Illinois. He incorporated in 2011. His candles and wax scents became popular and well known for the variety of scents offered, the potency of scents, and how long they lasted. He also offers his candles at reasonable prices and is kind to his customers. He was so successful that by 2015 he had opened two additional shops, one in Elgin, Illinois, and another in DeKalb, Illinois. They both bore the name "The Smell Shoppe" with a corresponding logo, which was an outline of an orange candlestick with a red fire on top. Mr. Arnold has had a steady rise in sales since the birth of The Smell Shoppe and has contributed to two competitors going out of business during his eight years of scent making. His sales are especially high during the winter holiday season, when customers buy candles for gift giving. One of Mr. Arnold's competitors that was forced out of business was "Candles, Etc.," a shop that was owned by Carl Green. That business closed in 2014.

Mr. Green later decided to try his hand at a candle business again. On January 1, 2016, he opened his store that he called "Smell Shop" in Chicago, Illinois. He created a business logo of an outline of a blue, unlit candle sitting in a candleholder. Mr. Green's candles were cheaply made, as he was probably still suffering from the effects of his first closed business. In effort to quickly rebuild capital, he charged double the price and posted "buy one, get one half off" coupons for Smell Shop to make the prices seem like a good deal. He created a website at smellshop.com where people could access these coupons as well as view the candle options.

Meanwhile, Mr. Arnold started to notice a significant decline in his sales in the Chicago store towards the middle of 2017. He became extremely concerned when he noticed a marked decline in his holiday sales. This was particularly unusual for Mr. Arnold, as this was the most profitable time of the year. He began hearing from people in the community that his candles "just weren't what they used to be." He would hear complaints that the potency was weak and that the candles were burning down too quickly. Customers also did not appreciate the increase in price, especially considering the decrease in quality coupled with a notable decline in customer service. They complained that the owner "didn't seem to know anything about the candles he was selling." They also complained that he acted "put off by having to answer their questions." They informed Mr. Arnold that they would not be coming back. All of this came as a shock to Mr. Arnold, and he struggled to make sense of these complaints. Nothing in his business practices had changed—he was still offering the same high-quality candles and still providing great customer service.

Desperate to win back customers, he therefore tried to offer better deals in an attempt to lure in more customers over the holiday season. Mr. Arnold also informed these complaining customers that he hadn't opened a new store and that he was not sure what they were referencing. In response, at least four customers replied that they were, of course, talking about the new location in Chicago. They said that the owner of that location told them the Chicago shop was the newest location and was affiliated with the Elgin and DeKalb stores. Mr. Arnold remained perplexed about what these angry customers meant and simply tried to pacify them with better deals and great customer service.

In early 2018, things got stranger: Mr. Arnold's staff started receiving customers arriving with "buy one, get one half off" coupons that he had never seen before. His staff noticed the coupons had been printed from a website called smellshop.com. The coupons further read, "Come See Us at Our Newest Location," with only Mr. Green's shop's address listed. Mr. Arnold was puzzled by this, as he didn't have an online presence, nor had he opened a new location at the address listed. Mr. Arnold instructed one of his employees to investigate this website. The employee did so and found the brand to be very similar to what Mr. Arnold had been using all these years, with a similar name and logo. After doing some digging, Mr. Arnold found out that the owner was Mr. Green. Mr. Arnold recognized him as the former owner of Candles, Etc., one of the businesses that shut down back in 2014 after Mr. Arnold started seeing great success in his candle-making business. Curious, Mr. Arnold's wife called the number listed on the website. She inquired of the person answering whether the shop was connected to "The Smell Shoppe" locations in Elgin, Illinois, and DeKalb, Illinois. The person answering hesitated and then replied, "No, ma'am, we just have the one location in Chicago," and then abruptly hung up.

Mr. Arnold now understands the true source of his customers' confusion and unhappiness. He is concerned about the impact this has had on his business. On the basis of these facts, Mr. Arnold would like to file a claim of tortious interference with business expectancy against Mr. Green.

## DISCUSSION

Mr. Gene Arnold will likely be unsuccessful in his tortious interference with business expectancy claim against Mr. Green. In order to successfully prevail in this claim, Mr. Arnold will need to prove four elements: "(1) [the plaintiff's] reasonable expectancy of entering into a valid business relationship; (2) the defendant's knowledge of the expectancy; (3) the defendant's intentional and unjustified interference that prevents the realization of business expectancy; and (4) damages resulting from the interference." *Chicago's Pizza, Inc. v. Chicago's Pizza Franchise Ltd., USA*, 893 N.E.2d 981, 993 (Ill. App. Ct. 2008). As per the instruction of the senior partner, this memo will not discuss whether Mr. Green knew of Mr. Arnold's expectancy, nor will it discuss whether Mr. Arnold suffered damages as a result of the interference. Instead, this memo will only discuss whether Mr. Arnold possessed a reasonable expectancy of entering into a valid business relationship and whether it was Mr. Green's intentional and unjustified interference that prevented the realization of business expectancy. Notwithstanding the likelihood that Mr. Arnold will be successful in showing that he possessed a reasonable expectancy of entering into a valid business relationship, he will likely fail in his claim. This is because Mr. Green was not dishonest with customers and therefore Mr. Arnold will be unable to show that Mr. Green intentionally and unjustifiably interfered with the realization of business expectancy.

### 1. Whether Arnold Possessed a Reasonable Expectancy of Entering into a Business Relationship

The court will first consider whether Mr. Arnold possessed a reasonable expectancy of entering into a valid business relationship. *Id.* In assessing whether Mr. Arnold possessed this expectancy, the court will consider the specific contemplation of customers and the customers' belief that they were doing business with Mr. Arnold. *Id.* at 993-94. A plaintiff will be found to have possessed a reasonable expectancy of entering into a valid business relationship when it can be demonstrated that specific customers called the defendant's store with the belief that they were doing business with the plaintiff. *Id.* at 994. Because Mr. Arnold spoke to several people regarding their experiences while shopping at Mr. Green's candle store who expressed the belief that they were shopping at Mr. Arnold's store, he will likely prevail on this element.

When customers demonstrate specific contemplation of doing business with the plaintiff and they express the belief that they are doing business with the plaintiff, the plaintiff will be successful in showing a reasonable expectancy of entering into a valid business relationship. *Id.* at 993-94. In *Chicago's Pizza*, the court stated that it was clear that the testifying customers contemplated a business relationship with the plaintiff. *Id.* at 993. In particular, one customer stated he had called the defendant's store believing it was one of the plaintiff's four locations and he asked for the phone number to another location of the plaintiff's restaurant so that it could deliver to him. *Id.* Another customer testified that he did believe that he was ordering from the plaintiff when in fact he was ordering from the defendant. *Id.* at 993-94. Moreover, the court noted the fact that the first testifying customer proceeded to then order from the defendant after being told that the location he had called was able to deliver to him. *Id.* Because the plaintiff successfully demonstrated a specific contemplation from the customers and because the customers expressed belief that they were doing business with the plaintiff, the court found the plaintiff had established a reasonable expectancy of business relationship. *Id.*

It is likely that Mr. Arnold will be able to show that he possessed a reasonable expectancy of entering into a valid business relationship. Like the plaintiff's customers in *Chicago's Pizza*, the customers in Mr. Arnold's situation contemplated specific business relationships with him. *See id.* Mr. Arnold will argue that, like the testimony of the customers in *Chicago's Pizza*, he also has customers who can testify to their specific contemplation in conducting business with him. *See id.* Namely, Mr. Arnold himself will testify that he began hearing people in the community express concerns about his candles, including telling him that the candles "just weren't what they used to be." This is similar to the testimony of the customers in *Chicago's Pizza* who expressed that they clearly believed they were doing business with the plaintiff. *Id.* Indeed, in Mr. Arnold's case, the customers' contemplation that they were doing business with him is even stronger, insofar as the customers specifically complained that his candles were weak in potency and were burning down too quickly, notwithstanding the fact that he had not made any changes to his candle-making practices. The dissatisfied community members may also be called to testify to their specific contemplation of conducting business with Mr. Arnold's candle shop, similar to the testimony of the customers in *Chicago's Pizza. See id.*

In addition, Mr. Arnold will assert that customers in fact believed they were doing business with him, not Mr. Green. As with the convincing testimony of the customers in *Chicago's Pizza*, Mr. Arnold can use the testimony of his customers to illustrate their belief that they were in fact doing business with him when they purchased their candles with the confidence that they would be strongly scented and long-lasting, just as Mr. Arnold's candles had proven to be. *See id.*

Alternatively, Mr. Green will argue that Mr. Arnold did not have a reasonable expectancy of a business relationship. He will argue that unlike the defendant in *Chicago's Pizza*, he did not receive phone calls from customers who directly indicated that they believed they were doing business with Mr. Arnold. *See id.* He may further distinguish his situation from that of *Chicago's Pizza* by showing that he did not process the order from a customer who conveyed that she believed she was purchasing from Mr. Arnold. *See id.* Additionally, Mr. Green may argue that if other customers believed they were conducting business with Mr. Arnold's business, he was not made aware of this misapprehension. Notwithstanding Green's assertions, it is likely that Mr. Arnold will prevail on this element because he will be able to show that his customers specifically contemplated doing business with him and believed that they were in fact doing business with him.

### 2. Whether Green's Intentional and Unjustified Interference Prevented the Business Expectancy

Next, the court will consider whether it was Mr. Green's intentional and unjustified interference that prevented Arnold's realization of a business expectancy. *Id.* at 994. In assessing this element, the court will consider the defendant's conduct in allowing customers to place orders under a mistaken belief, the defendant's truthfulness to the customers regarding an affiliation with the plaintiff's business, and the content of any of the defendant's advertisements. *Id.* at 994. A plaintiff will be successful in demonstrating that it was the defendant's intentional and unjustified interference that prevented the realization of business expectancy when the defendant allows customers to place orders with its business while being dishonest with the customers when they inquire about an affiliation with the plaintiff's store. *Id.* Further, a plaintiff can demonstrate interference with an expectation of a business relationship when the defendant represents an affiliation with the plaintiff through advertising materials. *Id.* Because Mr. Green was not dishonest when he received a phone call regarding an affiliation with Arnold's business, and because his website's printable coupons only listed one location to shop from, it is unlikely that Mr. Arnold will prevail on this element.

When a defendant allows customers to place orders with its business while being dishonest with them about an affiliation with the plaintiff's store, and uses that false affiliation to advertise its store, the plaintiff will be successful in showing that it was the defendant's intentional and unjustified interference that prevented the realization of business expectancy. *Id.* In *Chicago's Pizza*, the defendant prevented the plaintiff from realizing business by permitting customers to place orders with the defendant's store and being dishonest with them about an affiliation with the plaintiff's business. *Id*. Furthermore, the court specifically rejected an argument presented by the defendant that the customers simply mistook the defendant's store for the plaintiff's. *Id*. The court pointed out that the defendant's advertisements listed multiple locations when in fact there was only one. *Id*. More specifically, the court emphasized the fact that the advertisements listed the corresponding address of the plaintiff's store. *Id*. Because the plaintiff was able to demonstrate that the defendant allowed the customers to proceed with sales while being dishonest with those customers regarding an affiliation with the plaintiff, and because the defendant listed the plaintiff's locations on its advertisements, the court ruled in favor of the plaintiff on this element. *Id*.

It is unlikely that Mr. Arnold will be able to show that it was Mr. Green's intentional and unjustified interference that prevented the realization of business expectancy. Mr. Arnold may argue that, like the defendant's conduct in *Chicago's Pizza*, Mr. Green allowed customers to proceed with their purchases after learning that the customers believed they were doing business with Mr. Arnold. *See id*. Specifically, Mr. Arnold can demonstrate that Mr. Green permitted customers' sales after those customers were misled to believe that they were shopping at the newest location of the stores affiliated with Arnold's existing stores. Second, Mr. Arnold can argue that like the defendants in *Chicago's Pizza*, Mr. Green proceeded to place advertisements that further cemented customers' belief that there was an affiliation between the two parties. *See id*. Namely, Mr. Arnold will point to the fact that Mr. Green placed advertisements in the form of a website with similar branding and printable coupons that used the phrase "our newest location," strongly implying there was more than one location.

In contrast, Mr. Green will assert that he did not intentionally or unjustifiably interfere with Mr. Arnold's business. He will argue that, unlike the defendant in *Chicago's Pizza* who actively misled customers, Mr. Green was not dishonest. *See id*. In fact, when someone called Green's store inquiring about the affiliation with the other stores, he was honest and informed the caller that there was no affiliation with Arnold's stores. *See id*. He will further distinguish his advertising situation from that of the one in *Chicago's Pizza* by stating that his coupons did not expressly provide multiple locations like the misleading material at issue in *Chicago's Pizza*, and instead identified only the one true location of his store. *See id*. Green may also argue that the court should narrowly construe what actions are "unlawful and unjustifiable interference," particularly when the defendant's actions are commercial speech. A defendant's right to advertise in the way it deems most effective would be stifled if the plaintiff's argument were accepted. Notwithstanding Mr. Arnold's arguments, it is unlikely that he will prevail on this element because Mr. Green was not dishonest when he received a phone call regarding the affiliation and the website's printable coupons only listed one location.

Thus, Mr. Arnold likely will not succeed in his tortious interference with business expectancy claim against Mr. Green. Despite Mr. Arnold's success in proving that he possessed a reasonable expectancy of entering into a valid business relationship, he will likely fail to prove that it was Mr. Green's intentional and unjustified interference that prevented the realization of business expectancy.

# MEMORANDUM

To:      Assistant U.S. Attorney
From:   Law Clerk
Re:      Van Zanda (V0112-1): Whether Warrantless Search of Container
         Was Permitted
Date:    August 17, 2020

## QUESTION PRESENTED

Under Sixth Circuit Fourth Amendment law, is a warrantless search permitted when the FBI received a tip from an informant that an explosive device is located inside the area searched, when a bomb-sniffing dog "hit" on the container identified by the informant, and when consent to search came from a person who did not own the container searched and had removed most of his property from the container a month prior, yet who had access to it?

## SHORT ANSWER

Yes, it is likely the FBI's warrantless search of Van Zanda's shipping container was permitted under the Fourth Amendment. First, an exigent circumstance justified the warrantless search because the FBI agents received a tip concerning potential explosives that posed a credible and immediate threat. Second, the FBI agents received proper consent for the warrantless search because they received permission from a person whose use and access to the space gave him authority to consent to the search.

## STATEMENT OF FACTS

This case involves the search of a shipping container owned by "Double T" Van Zanda that was conducted by FBI agents without a search warrant. On December 30, 2018, agents from the Cincinnati FBI field office conducted a warrantless search of a shipping container on the lot of Van Zanda Trucking, located in Woodlawn, Kentucky. The search unfolded after agents received a tip from an informant that Double T Van Zanda, a Woodlawn mobster and owner of the trucking company, was using the shipping container to store a bomb. The informant told agents that the bomb was intended for use in the attempted murder of another gangster.

The FBI agents immediately dispatched to the reported location. When the agents arrived at Van Zanda Trucking, their bomb-sniffing dog "hit" on the shipping container in question, indicating the dog's probable detection of a bomb. At that point, FBI agents also were aware that Van Zanda had previously been tied to a mob bombing.

Before searching the container, FBI agents also spoke with and received permission from a man named "The Earl" to search the container. The Earl, who was at the scene of the container when the FBI agents arrived, told the agents that he had rented the container to store a guitar collection. He explained, however, that because of an argument with Van Zanda, he had moved a majority of his guitar collection out one month earlier. When the agents asked if they could look inside the container, The Earl replied, "OK." He then opened the shipping container for the agents using his own key.

The agents did not find a bomb inside the container. However, along with a few guitars that belonged to The Earl, agents discovered cocaine and marijuana—leading to a federal indictment of Van Zanda. Van Zanda's defense attorneys are preparing to file a motion to suppress the evidence gleaned from the warrantless search.

## DISCUSSION

The government wants to know whether the items seized in the warrantless search of the container must be suppressed. While the Fourth Amendment "generally requires officers to possess a warrant before conducting a search," "[t]here are, however, exceptions to the warrant requirement." *United States v. Purcell*, 526 F.3d 953, 960 (6th Cir. 2008). One exception to the warrant requirement is "the existence of exigent circumstances." *Id.* (citing *Mincey v. Arizona*, 437 U.S. 385, 392-93 (1978)). The other "well-delineated" exception to the warrant requirement is consent to search. *Id.* The government bears the burden of proving either exception. *Id.* (citing *United States v. Atchley*, 474 F.3d 840, 851 (6th Cir. 2007)). This memo addresses both exceptions—namely, whether an exigent circumstance existed to justify the search and whether the agents obtained consent to search. Because of the pending threat of a bomb as well as the permission granted by someone with a key to the container, it is likely the court will conclude the search was constitutional.

### 1. Exigent Circumstances

First, the government can argue that exigent circumstances justified the warrantless search. "Qualification for the exigent circumstances exception is not easy, for '[w]hen there is neither a warrant nor consent, courts will only permit a search or seizure to stand under extraordinary circumstances.'" *Id.* at 960 (quoting *United States v. Chambers*, 395 F.3d 563, 565 (6th Cir. 2005)). Further, "[i]t is the government's burden to prove the existence of exigency." *Id.* (quoting *Atchley*, 474 F.3d at 851). While there are various categories of exigent circumstances, per the assigning attorney's instructions, this memo focuses only on whether the search could be justified based on a "risk of danger to police or to others." *Id.* at 960 (quoting *United States v. Rohrig*, 98 F.3d 1506, 1515 (6th Cir. 1996)). In determining whether there is such a risk of danger, courts consider the objective information available to the agents about the immediacy and extent of the risk, the agents' subjective belief about the risk, and whether the agents' actions were consistent with the asserted risk. *Id.* at 962. When agents observe evidence of drug use, but not drug manufacturing, which is the purported danger, and agents do not attempt to clear the area to protect others nearby, courts hold no exigent circumstance exists. *Id.* Because the police dog "hit" on the container following a police tip and agents took meaningful precautions, a court will likely find an exigent circumstance existed.

When agents do not articulate a subjective belief of immediate risk and fail to take quick action and precautionary measures, and where no objective evidence suggests an immediate risk, courts hold no exigent circumstance exists. In *United States v. Purcell*, the defendant sought to suppress evidence of a firearm found during a search of a backpack located in a hotel room in which the defendant was staying. *Id*. Although the agents had information that the defendant had previously run a meth lab, there were no items in the hotel room suggesting an active meth lab. *Id*. Instead the items in the room, drug paraphernalia, suggested only drug use. *Id*. In addition, for ten minutes before searching the room, agents questioned the defendant's girlfriend inside the room that allegedly contained a meth lab. *Id*. The agents took no steps to protect guests staying in the hotel. *Id*. at 962. Finally, none of the agents testified "to believing that methamphetamine cooking was ongoing" when they arrived at the hotel. *Id*. at 961. The court held that there was no exigent circumstance. *Id*. The court noted that while an active methamphetamine lab generally would pose a risk of danger because of flammable chemicals used in the cooking process, there was "no evidence to suggest that methamphetamine manufacture was ongoing, thus there was no exigency to justify the search." *Id*. The court also noted that the agents' own behaviors, which included questioning the defendant's girlfriend inside the hotel room for ten minutes, showed little concern for a possible explosion. *Id*. at 962.

First, the objective information available to the agents suggested an immediate and severe risk. A bomb prepared for rigging to a motorcycle presents a serious and immediate danger to the target of the explosion, any person who might be nearby, and law enforcement agents who attempt to defuse it. *Id*. at 961. Further, unlike the situation in *Purcell*, in which the information learned by the agents on site undermined the information contained in the tip, here the information learned by the agents on site corroborated the tip information. *See id*. When they arrived at the site, the agents knew that Van Zanda was previously connected to a mob bombing, and they also had received the informant's tip that the device was prepared for rigging to another gangster's motorcycle. Agents' concerns that a bomb was hidden inside the shipping container were then bolstered by Scooter the bomb-sniffing dog, who "hit" on the container. That corroboration of the tip and prior history is unlike the situation in *Purcell* in which the tip and prior history were not confirmed but instead were contradicted by what agents observed in the hotel room—only drug paraphernalia and the notable absence of any meth lab items. *See id*. Further, the bomb posed an immediate risk even if the defendant had no intention of activating it—a bomb, especially a civilian one, is inherently unstable and can detonate accidentally. Faced with the credible evidence that there may be a bomb and that such bomb may explode, the risk of danger was high. *See id*. Indeed, this is precisely the type of risk for which the exigent circumstances exception exists: Every minute that the search is delayed due to having to obtain a warrant increases the likelihood that the bomb will detonate.

Even so, Van Zanda may argue that objective information did not indicate an immediate risk. While the risk from a bomb can be high and imminent, the information objectively known to the agents at the time of the search did not indicate that the bomb was unstable or likely to be detonated immediately. Instead, the objective evidence—a tip that the defendant planned to rig another gangster's motorcycle with a bomb—suggested it was unlikely that the bomb would be intentionally activated in the container and thus the bomb presented no immediate risk. Thus, just as the agents in *Purcell* lacked any "evidence to suggest that methamphetamine manufacture was ongoing," here the agents lacked evidence that would suggest that the threat from the bomb was imminent. *See id.* at 961.

Second, the agents subjectively believed that there was a risk from a bomb. The agents' actions of clearing the site and wearing bomb suits indicate that they believed there was a risk. Further, upon information and belief, the agents will testify that they believed there was a strong likelihood of a risk from a bomb in the container. That is decidedly unlike the situation in *Purcell* in which no agent testified "to believing that methamphetamine cooking was ongoing." *See id.* at 961.

Nonetheless, Van Zanda may contend that the agents did not truly subjectively believe there was a risk from a bomb given the unnecessarily long delay before they searched. Likewise, Van Zanda may argue that the agents' subjective belief is best discerned from their actions, and here their actions show that they did not truly fear that a bomb might detonate. Thus, like the agents in *Purcell* who did not act immediately, here too the agents revealed a lack of legitimate concern about the claimed threat. *See id.* at 962.

Finally, the agents' actions were consistent with the asserted risk. The agents demonstrated a belief that there was an immediate risk of danger when they cleared employees out of the Van Zanda headquarters and donned specialized blast suits before the search of the container. These swift actions stand in stark contrast to the actions of the agents in *Purcell*, who took no protective measures that would be consistent with the asserted threat. *See id.* Further, although the agents here talked to The Earl before the search, they did so only to the extent necessary to gain information to assess the credibility of the tip. In contrast, in *Purcell*, the agents engaged in relatively lengthy conversation with the defendant's girlfriend that was not geared toward helping them assess the asserted threat. *Id.*

In contrast, Van Zanda may argue that the agents' behavior was not consistent with the asserted risk. Van Zanda will likely argue that the fact that agents spent ten minutes speaking with The Earl outside the shipping container prior to the search was inconsistent with the asserted risk. Moreover, during the period in which the agents spoke with The Earl, the agents took no protective measures, which was also not consistent with the asserted risk. That lack of urgency or protective measures is similar to the situation in *Purcell,* in which agents questioned the fugitive's girlfriend inside their hotel room and failed to evacuate hotel guests. *See id.* Just as the agents' actions in *Purcell* suggested they did not truly fear a meth lab explosion in the hotel room, here it is likely a court would reach the similar conclusion that the agents did not truly fear a bomb explosion. *See id.* at 962.

While the court may agree that the agents' actions were not entirely consistent with the claimed threat, it is likely that the court nonetheless will hold that there was an exigent circumstance based upon the risk of danger. The agents eventually took protective measures, including clearing the area before conducting the search, which shows their level of concern at the time of search. Further evidence of the risk of danger stems from the fact that the information the agents learned on site heightened, rather than lessened, the credible threat.

### 2. Consent to Search

Even if there was no exigency, the government also can justify the warrantless search by showing that the agents had consent to search the container. "In order to consent to a search, the person purporting to consent must possess either actual or apparent authority over the item or place to be searched." *Id.* at 962. The government concedes that The Earl lacked actual authority, so the only question is whether he had apparent authority. Apparent authority is judged by an objective standard based on the information known to the agent at the moment of search. *Id.* In the third-party context, the agent must have reasonably believed the person giving consent possessed joint access or control over the property searched. *Id.* In determining whether such apparent authority over the property searched existed, courts consider: (1) whether the person reasonably asserted access and control over the property and (2) whether the context confirmed or created ambiguity regarding the spoken assertion. *Id.* When a person asserts control and authority over the searched bags, yet shortly thereafter the agents have reason to doubt the bags belong to her, courts hold that the apparent authority does not exist. *Id.* A court will likely find that The Earl had ongoing apparent authority to consent to the search because he had a key to the container searched, his guitars were inside the container, and no doubt arose regarding his authority or control of the container.

When a person asserts control and authority over property, yet the context suggests that assertion is inaccurate, courts hold that the apparent authority does not exist. In *Purcell,* agents discovered a firearm in a bag they searched in a hotel room. *Id.* at 958. When the agents arrived at the hotel room, they questioned the defendant's girlfriend, who was sharing the hotel room with the defendant. *Id.* She gave the agents permission to search the hotel room, including the bags in it. *Id.* at 957. The agents found only the defendant's personal belongings in the first bag they searched, even though the girlfriend had asserted the bags belonged to her. *Id.* at 958. The agents did not clarify the girlfriend's authority over any other bags in the room at that point, even though the girlfriend was standing outside the hotel room. *Id.* Instead, the agents searched an additional bag, which was where they found the firearm at issue. *Id.* The court held that there was no consent to search the second bag because the girlfriend did not have apparent authority over it. *Id.* at 964. The court reasoned that the girlfriend's "apparent authority, which justified the search of the first bag, dissipated upon the discovery" of only the defendant's personal effects in that bag "and was not reestablished." *Id.* Rather, "ambiguity clouded" the girlfriend's authority to consent to the search of any additional bags. *Id.*

The Earl reasonably asserted access and control over the shipping container. The Earl expressly asserted access and control when he told the agents he had a rental agreement to use the shipping container and that he stored various pieces from his guitar collection there. *See id.* Further, The Earl demonstrated that access and control over that shared space when he opened the shipping container for agents with his own key. *See id.* Thus, similar to the situation in *Purcell* in which the defendant's girlfriend had access to the bags, claimed the bags were hers, and had her purse on top of one of the bags, here too the agent was reasonable to believe, at least based upon the assertion alone, that authority existed. *Id.* at 957. The Earl's assertion of authority is even stronger than the girlfriend's in *Purcell* because The Earl's key leaves no doubt about his access to the property. *See id.*

Alternatively, Van Zanda will likely argue that The Earl failed to reasonably assert control. Notably, The Earl's statement of control was undermined by his statement that he had moved most of his property out of the shipping container following an argument with Van Zanda a month prior. Unlike the situation in *Purcell*, in which the defendant's girlfriend expressed no limitations on her asserted control, here The Earl implicitly qualified his own assertion of control and authority. *See id.*

In addition, the context surrounding The Earl's assertion of control confirmed that he was, in fact, in control. Unlike the doubt created in *Purcell* when the agents discovered only the defendant's personal belongings in a bag that his girlfriend had claimed was hers, here no uncertainty arose. *See id.* To the contrary, all of the evidence—The Earl's possession of a key to the container and, after the fact, the storage of his guitars found in the container—provided confirming information that The Earl possessed access and control over the container.

Van Zanda may argue that the doubt about The Earl's asserted control arose when The Earl told the police that he had moved most of his guitar collection out of the shipping container a month earlier. Like the ambiguity created in *Purcell* when the search of the first bag indicated it likely did not belong to the person asserting control, here The Earl's admission that he had moved most of his collection out of the shipping container at least casts some doubt on his continuing authority and control. *See id.* Typically, a person who retained control over a storage space would continue to use it for its intended purpose. The fact that The Earl had only a few items left there suggests he was in limbo, such that he may or may not truly have control over the container. Nonetheless, given the consistent and undisputed indicators of The Earl's apparent authority, the court is likely to hold that the consent by The Earl was valid because apparent authority existed.

## CONCLUSION

Taken together, the FBI agents likely had justification for the warrantless search of the container, such that the motion to suppress should be denied. First, the warrantless search was justified by an exigent circumstance in the form of a present danger. Alternately, the warrantless search was justified because the FBI obtained consent to search the container from a person with apparent authority.

# Sample Memos Using Multiple Case Authorities

---

**MEMORANDUM**

To:     Senior Partner
From:   Junior Associate
Re:     Arnold Matter: Whether Mr. Arnold Can Prove Tortious Interference
        with Business Expectancy
Date:   August 17, 2020

---

### QUESTION PRESENTED

Under Illinois law, is a defendant liable for tortious interference with business expectancy when it created a competing business with a logo similar to that of the plaintiff's business, yet indicated that it was not affiliated with the plaintiff's business during a phone call inquiry, and when it created an online website with printed coupons stating, "Come See Us at Our New Location," and when that coupon only listed the defendant's one true business location?

### SHORT ANSWER

No, it is not likely that Mr. Green will be liable for tortious interference with business expectancy. Because Mr. Arnold can demonstrate a specific contemplation from his customers and can demonstrate that the customers expressed their belief that they were doing business with his store, it is likely that the court will find that he possessed a reasonable expectancy of entering into a valid business relationship. However, because Mr. Green was not dishonest with customers when he received a phone call regarding the affiliation and because his website's printable coupons only listed the one true location, he did not directly divert the plaintiff's business, and because he may be able to assert privilege, it is unlikely that the court will find that it was Mr. Green's intentional and unjustified interference that prevented the realization of business expectancy.

### STATEMENT OF FACTS

This is a case involving an allegation of tortious interference with business expectancy on behalf of Gene Arnold against Carl Green. Both parties operate candle businesses in the Chicago area.

1

415

Gene Arnold opened his first candle and scents store, called The Smell Shoppe, in 2010 in Chicago, Illinois. He incorporated in 2011. His candles and wax scents became popular and well known for the variety of scents offered, the potency of scents, and how long they lasted. He also offers his candles at reasonable prices and is kind to his customers. He was so successful that by 2015 he had opened two additional shops, one in Elgin, Illinois, and another in DeKalb, Illinois. They both bore the name "The Smell Shoppe" with a corresponding logo, which was an outline of an orange candlestick with a red fire on top. Mr. Arnold has had a steady rise in sales since the birth of The Smell Shoppe and has contributed to two competitors going out of business during his eight years of scent making. His sales are especially high during the winter holiday season when customers buy candles for gift giving. One of Mr. Arnold's competitors that was forced out of business was "Candles, Etc.," a shop that was owned by Carl Green. That business closed in 2014.

Mr. Green later decided to try his hand at a candle business again. On January 1, 2016, he opened his store that he called "Smell Shop" in Chicago, Illinois. He created a business logo of an outline of a blue, unlit candle sitting in a candleholder. Mr. Green's candles were cheaply made, as he was probably still suffering from the effects of his first closed business. In effort to quickly rebuild capital, he charged double the price and posted "buy one, get one half off" coupons for Smell Shop to make the prices seem like a good deal. He created a website at smellshop.com where people could access these coupons as well as view the candle options.

Meanwhile, Mr. Arnold started to notice a significant decline in his sales in the Chicago store towards the middle of 2017. He became extremely concerned when he noticed a marked decline in his holiday sales. This was particularly unusual for Mr. Arnold, as this was the most profitable time of the year. He began hearing from people in the community that his candles "just weren't what they used to be." He would hear complaints that the potency was weak and that the candles were burning down too quickly. Customers also did not appreciate the increase in price, especially considering the decrease in quality coupled with a notable decline in customer service. They complained that the owner "didn't seem to know anything about the candles he was selling." They also complained that he acted "put off by having to answer their questions." They informed Mr. Arnold that they would not be coming back. All of this came as a shock to Mr. Arnold, and he struggled to make sense of these complaints. Nothing in his business practices had changed—he was still offering the same high-quality candles and still providing great customer service.

Desperate to win back customers, he therefore tried to offer better deals in an attempt to lure in more customers over the holiday season. Mr. Arnold also informed these complaining customers that he hadn't opened a new store and that he was not sure what they were referencing. In response, at least four customers replied that they were, of course, talking about the new location in Chicago. They said that the owner of that location told them the Chicago shop was the newest location and was affiliated with the Elgin and DeKalb stores. Mr. Arnold remained perplexed about what these angry customers meant, and simply tried to pacify them with better deals and great customer service.

In early 2018, things got stranger: Mr. Arnold's staff started receiving customers arriving with "buy one, get one half off" coupons that he had never seen before. His staff noticed the coupons had been printed from a website called smellshop.com. The coupons further read, "Come See Us at Our Newest Location," with only Mr. Green's shop's address listed. Mr. Arnold was puzzled by this, as he didn't have an online presence, nor had he opened a new location at the address listed. Mr. Arnold instructed one of his employees to investigate this website. The employee did so and found the brand to be very similar to what Mr. Arnold had been using all these years, with a similar name and logo. After doing some digging, Mr. Arnold found out that the owner was Mr. Green. Mr. Arnold recognized him as the former owner of Candles, Etc., one of the businesses that shut down back in 2014 after Mr. Arnold started seeing great success in his candle-making business. Curious, Mr. Arnold's wife called the number listed on the website. She inquired of the person answering whether the shop was connected to "The Smell Shoppe" locations in Elgin, Illinois, and DeKalb, Illinois. The person answering hesitated and then replied, "No, ma'am, we just have the one location in Chicago," and then abruptly hung up.

Mr. Arnold now understands the true source of his customers' confusion and unhappiness. He is concerned about the impact this has had on his business. On the basis of these facts, Mr. Arnold would like to file a claim of tortious interference with business expectancy against Mr. Green.

## DISCUSSION

Mr. Arnold will likely be unsuccessful in his tortious interference with business expectancy claim against Mr. Green. In order to successfully prevail in this claim, Mr. Arnold will need to prove four elements: "(1) [the plaintiff's] reasonable expectancy of entering into a valid business relationship; (2) the defendant's knowledge of the expectancy; (3) the defendant's intentional and unjustified interference that prevents the realization of business expectancy; and (4) damages resulting from the interference." *Chicago's Pizza, Inc. v. Chicago's Pizza Franchise Ltd., USA*, 893 N.E.2d 981, 993 (Ill. App. Ct. 2008). *See also RRRR Inc. v. Plaza 440 Private Residences Condo. Assn.*, 2017 IL App. (1st) 160194, at *7 (2017) (citing elements from *Chicago's Pizza*). Per the instruction of the senior associate, this memo will not discuss whether Mr. Green knew of Mr. Arnold's expectancy, nor will it discuss whether Mr. Arnold suffered damages as a result of the interference. Instead, this memo will only discuss whether Mr. Arnold possessed a reasonable expectancy of entering into a valid business relationship and whether it was Mr. Green's intentional and unjustified interference that prevented the realization of Mr. Arnold's business expectancy.

### 1. Whether Arnold Possessed a Reasonable Expectancy of Entering into a Business Relationship

The court will first consider whether Mr. Arnold possessed a reasonable expectancy of entering into a valid business relationship. *Chicago's Pizza*, 893 N.E.2d at 993. In assessing this reasonable expectancy, the court will consider the specific contemplation of customers and their belief that they were doing business with the plaintiff. *See, e.g., id.* A plaintiff will be found to have possessed a reasonable expectancy of entering into a valid business relationship when specific customers called the defendant's store with the belief that they were calling and doing business with the plaintiff. *Chicago's Pizza*, 893 N.E.2d at 993-94. In addition, the court will also consider the amount of contact between the plaintiff and prospective customers. *Mannion v. Stallings & Co.*, 561 N.E.2d 1134, 1139 (Ill. App. Ct. 1990). A court will hold that a plaintiff possessed a reasonable expectancy of entering into a valid business relationship when the plaintiff had moved past negotiations with prospective customers and had received a signed agreement providing compensation amounts. *Id.* Because Mr. Arnold had contact with several people regarding their experiences while shopping at Mr. Green's candle store, and the customers expressed the belief that they were shopping at Mr. Arnold's store, Mr. Arnold will likely prevail on this element.

When customers demonstrate specific contemplation of doing business with the plaintiff and they express the belief that they are doing business with the plaintiff, the plaintiff will be successful in showing a reasonable expectancy of entering into a valid business relationship. *Chicago's Pizza*, 893 N.E.2d at 994. In *Chicago's Pizza,* the court determined that the testifying customers contemplated a business relationship with the plaintiff. 893 N.E.2d at 993. The court stated that it was clear that the testifying customers contemplated a business relationship with the plaintiff, because one customer stated that he called the defendant's store believing it was one of the plaintiff's four locations and because he also asked for the phone number to another one of the plaintiff's locations so that it could deliver to him. *Id.* This customer then proceeded to place an order with the defendant's store. *Id.* Another customer similarly testified that he did believe that he was ordering from the plaintiff when in fact he was ordering from the defendant. *Id.* at 993-94. Because the plaintiff successfully demonstrated a specific contemplation from the customers and because the customers expressed belief that they were doing business with the plaintiff, the court found in favor of the plaintiff on the element. *Id.*

In contrast, where there is no contemplation by customers that they are doing business with the plaintiff, the court will not find a reasonable expectancy of business relationship. *Euclid Ins. Agencies, Inc. v. Am. Ass'n of Orthodontists*, No. 95 C 3308, 1997 WL 548069, at *4 (N.D. Ill. 1997). In *Euclid Insurance Agencies,* the plaintiff had no contact with prospective customers, and the customers therefore had no specific contemplation of doing business with the plaintiff. *Id.* The lack of contemplation by customers therefore contributed to the court's conclusion that the plaintiff did not have a reasonable expectancy of entering into a business relationship with the customers. *Id.*

In addition, when a plaintiff has had significant contact with prospective customers, the court will hold that the plaintiff has established a reasonable expectation of business relationship. *Mannion,* 561 N.E.2d at 1139. In *Mannion,* the court noted that several steps had been taken by the plaintiff to secure a particular line of business with a specific customer. *Id.* Because the plaintiff had received written correspondence outlining a particular line of business with a contemplated customer with whom the defendant also interacted, the court ruled in favor of the plaintiff, finding it had a reasonable expectation of a business relationship. *Id.* In contrast, where the plaintiff has never had contact with prospective customers, the court will determine that there is no expectancy of establishing a business relationship. *Euclid Ins. Agencies,* 1997 WL 548069, at *4. In *Euclid Insurance Agencies,* an insurance provider claimed tortious interference with business expectancy against a professional association that provided insurance to its members. *Id.* The court held there was no expectancy of establishing such a relationship, placing particular emphasis on the fact that the plaintiff had never dealt directly with any members of the professional organization regarding insurance. *Id.* Because the plaintiff had never dealt directly with the prospective customers, the court ruled that the plaintiff failed to establish a reasonable expectation of business relationship. *Id.* at *5.

It is likely that Mr. Arnold will be able to show that he possessed a reasonable expectancy of entering into a valid business relationship. Like the plaintiff's customers in *Chicago's Pizza,* the customers in Mr. Arnold's situation contemplated specific business relationships with him. 893 N.E.2d at 993. Mr. Arnold will argue that like the testimony of the customers in *Chicago's Pizza,* he too will be able to call customers to testify to their specific contemplation in conducting business with him. *See id.* Namely, Mr. Arnold himself will testify that he began hearing people in the community express concerns about his candles, as they were telling him that the candles "just weren't what they used to be." This is similar to the testimony of the customers in *Chicago's Pizza* who testified that they clearly believed they were doing business with the plaintiff. *See id.* at 994. His relationship with customers is therefore even stronger than that of the plaintiff in *Mannion* who was able to establish a reasonable expectation of business relationship on the basis of a developing, as opposed to established, relationship. *See* 561 N.E.2d at 1139. It can also be contrasted with the unsuccessful plaintiff in *Euclid Insurance Agencies* that was unable to establish a reasonable expectation of business relationship because it had never been in direct contact with prospective customers. *See* 1997 WL 548069, at *4. As with the convincing testimony of the customers in *Chicago's Pizza,* and the contact between the plaintiff and prospective customer in *Mannion,* Mr. Arnold can use the testimony of his customers to establish their belief that they were in fact doing business with him when they purchased their candles. *See Chicago's Pizza,* 893 N.E.2d at 994; *see also Mannion,* 561 N.E.2d at 1139.

Alternatively, Mr. Green can argue that unlike the defendant in *Chicago's Pizza,* he did not receive phone calls from customers directly indicating that they believed they were doing business with the plaintiff. *See* 893 N.E.2d at

994. He may further distinguish his situation from that of *Chicago's Pizza* by showing that he did not proceed to process an order after learning that the customer believed she was purchasing from the plaintiff. *See id.* Mr. Green may also assert the argument that unlike the plaintiff in *Mannion*, Mr. Arnold was not in any transactional stages with the customers. *See* 561 N.E.2d at 1139. Further, Mr. Green will point out that Mr. Arnold had not taken orders from the customers and did not receive any statements outlining compensation. *See id.* Mr. Green may assert that it is unclear whether the customers ever had contact with Mr. Arnold, similar to the customers in *Euclid Insurance Agencies* who had no direct contact with the plaintiff. *See* 1997 WL 548069, at *4. Notwithstanding, it is likely that Mr. Arnold will prevail on this element because his customers will demonstrate a specific contemplation of doing business with him and a belief that they were in fact doing business with him.

### 2. Whether Green's Intentional and Unjustified Interference Prevented the Business Expectancy

Next, the court will consider whether it was Mr. Green's intentional and unjustified interference that prevented Mr. Arnold's realization of a business expectancy. *Chicago's Pizza,* 893 N.E.2d at 993. In assessing this element, the court will consider the defendant's conduct in facilitating a mistaken belief of customers as to an affiliation with the plaintiff's business. *See, e.g., id.* at 994. The court will also consider whether the defendant's challenged conduct was privileged. *Mannion,* 561 N.E.2d at 1140. A plaintiff will successfully demonstrate that it was the defendant's intentional and unjustified interference that prevented the realization of business expectancy when the defendant allows customers to place orders with its business while being dishonest with those customers when they inquire about the defendant's affiliation to the plaintiff's business. *Chicago's Pizza,* 893 N.E.2d at 993. Further, a plaintiff can demonstrate interference with a business expectancy when the defendant diverts business opportunities by representing an affiliation with the plaintiff through advertising materials. *E.J. McKernan Co. v. Gregory,* 623 N.E.2d 981, 995 (Ill. App. Ct. 1993). In contrast, where the defendant's challenged actions are privileged, the court will hold that the defendant's actions are not an unjustified interference. *RRRR Inc.,* 2017 IL App. (1st) 160194, at *26. Because Mr. Green was not dishonest about his business's affiliation, did not divert business opportunities, and may be able to assert a privilege, it is unlikely that Mr. Arnold will prevail on this element.

When a defendant facilitates a mistaken belief by customers as to an affiliation with the plaintiff's business, a plaintiff will be successful in showing that it was the defendant's intentional and unjustified interference that prevented the realization of business expectancy. In *Chicago's Pizza,* the defendant prevented the plaintiff from realizing business by permitting customers to place orders with the defendant's store while being dishonest with them about an affiliation with the plaintiff's business. 893 N.E.2d at 993. Furthermore, the court specifically rejected an argument presented by the defendant that the customers simply mistook the defendant's store for

6

the plaintiff's. *Id*. The court pointed to the defendant's advertisements listing multiple locations when in fact there was only one. *Id*. More specifically, the court emphasized the fact that the defendant's advertisements went so far as to list the corresponding address of the plaintiff's store. *Id*. The court thus held that the defendant's interference had prevented the plaintiff's realization of business. *Id*. The court reasoned that because the plaintiff was able to demonstrate that the defendant acted improperly in allowing the customers to proceed with sales while being dishonest with them regarding an affiliation with the plaintiff, and because the defendant listed the plaintiff's locations on its advertisements, the defendant had interfered with the plaintiff's business. *Id*.

Similarly, in *E.J. McKernan*, the court considered how the defendant's conduct in facilitating customers' mistaken beliefs contributed to its intentional and unjustifiable interference with the plaintiff's realization of business expectancy. 623 N.E.2d at 995. The court noted that the defendant directly diverted business from the plaintiff by using information from the plaintiff's master list, which contained confidential information regarding the plaintiff's buyers and sellers. *Id*. Additionally, the court emphasized the fact that one order was placed directly with the plaintiff company but was then filled and billed in favor of the defendant company. *Id*. Because the defendant directly diverted business and filled an order placed with the plaintiff, the court ruled that it was the defendant's intentional and unjustified interference that prevented the realization of business expectancy. *Id*.

In contrast, where a defendant can assert a privilege for its conduct, a plaintiff will not be able to demonstrate that the defendant intentionally and unjustifiably interfered with a business expectancy. In *RRRR*, the court noted that the defendant neighbor was justified in blocking the plaintiff's outdoor seating in his restaurant because the defendant was in the course of making required repairs to its building. 2017 IL App. (1st) 160194, at *7. Thus, the court held that the defendant did not intentionally and unjustifiably interfere with the plaintiff's business expectancy. *Id*. The court emphasized that, in order to demonstrate intentional and unjustified interference, the "plaintiff must show that defendant acted intentionally with the purpose of injuring the plaintiff's expectancy [and] [t]o the extent that a party acts to enhance its own business interests, it has a privilege to act in a way that may harm the business expectancy of others." *Id*. Further, the court noted that because the defendant was privileged in its actions, by way of protecting its interests, the plaintiff would be required to prove malicious intent, which the facts did not establish. *Id*. However, because the defendant was justified in its actions by way of privilege and the plaintiff could not prove malicious intent, the court ruled that the plaintiff failed on this element. *Id*.

It is unlikely that Mr. Arnold will be able to show that it was Mr. Green's intentional and unjustified interference that prevented the realization of business expectancy. Mr. Arnold may argue that, like the defendant's conduct in *Chicago's Pizza*, Mr. Green allowed customers to proceed with their purchases after learning that they had believed they were doing business with Mr. Arnold. *See* 893 N.E.2d at 993. Specifically, Mr. Arnold can demonstrate that the defendant permitted customer sales after the customers were misled to believe that they were shopping at the newest location of the stores affiliated with the location of the Elgin and DeKalb stores. Second, Mr. Arnold can argue that like the defendant's advertisements in *Chicago's Pizza,* Mr. Green placed advertisements that led customers to believe there was an affiliation between the two parties. *See id.* Namely, Mr. Arnold will point to the fact that Mr. Green placed advertisements in the form of a website with similar branding and printable coupons that used the phrase "our newest location," implying there was more than one location to shop from. Mr. Arnold may also argue that like the defendants in *McKernan,* Mr. Green diverted business from his company by using a similar logo and subsequently misleading customers. *See* 623 N.E.2d at 995.

Alternatively, Mr. Green may argue that unlike the defendant in *Chicago's Pizza,* who actively misled customers, when he received a call inquiring about the affiliation with the other stores, he was honest and informed the caller that there was no affiliation with those stores. *See Chicago's Pizza,* 893 N.E.2d at 993. He will further distinguish his advertising situation from the one in *Chicago's Pizza* by stating that his coupons did not expressly provide multiple locations like the misleading material at issue in *Chicago's Pizza,* but rather just identified the one true location of his store. *See id.* Mr. Green may also distinguish himself from the defendant in *McKernan* by stating that he did not directly divert any orders that were given to Mr. Arnold. 623 N.E.2d at 995. Further, Mr. Green may argue that, like the defendant in *RRRR,* he too possesses a privilege to advertise his own business and that as such, Mr. Arnold will need to show malicious intent. 2017 IL App. (1st) 160194, at *7. He will further assert that, like the lack of evidence of malice in *RRRR,* Arnold too will fail to meet that burden. *See id.* It is unlikely that Mr. Arnold will prevail on this element because Mr. Green was not dishonest when he received a phone call regarding the affiliation, and his website's printable coupons only listed one location. Moreover, he did not directly divert business from Arnold, and he may be able to assert privilege.

Thus, Mr. Arnold likely will not succeed in his tortious interference with business expectancy claim against Mr. Green. Mr. Arnold will likely be able to demonstrate that he possessed a reasonable expectancy of entering into a valid business relationship with customers because customers did indicate they thought they were doing business with him. Notwithstanding, he will likely fail to prove that it was Mr. Green's intentional and unjustified interference that prevented the realization of business expectancy because Mr. Green was not dishonest, did not directly divert business from Mr. Arnold, and may be able to assert a privilege.

## MEMORANDUM

To:      Assistant U.S. Attorney
From:   Law Clerk
Re:      Van Zanda (V0112-1): Whether Warrantless Search of Container
          Was Permitted
Date:    August 17, 2020

### QUESTION PRESENTED

Under Sixth Circuit Fourth Amendment law, is a warrantless search permitted when the FBI received a tip from an informant that an explosive device is located inside the area searched, when a bomb-sniffing dog "hit" on the container identified by the informant, and when consent to search came from a person who did not own the container searched and had removed most of his property from the container a month prior, yet who had access to it?

### SHORT ANSWER

Yes, it is likely the FBI's warrantless search of Van Zanda's shipping container was permitted under the Fourth Amendment. First, an exigent circumstance justified the warrantless search because the FBI agents received a tip concerning potential explosives that posed a credible and immediate threat. Second, the FBI agents received proper consent for the warrantless search because they received permission from a person whose use and access to the space gave him authority to consent to the search.

### STATEMENT OF FACTS

This case involves the search of a shipping container owned by "Double T" Van Zanda that was conducted by FBI agents without a search warrant. On December 30, 2018, agents from the Cincinnati FBI field office conducted a warrantless search of a shipping container on the lot of Van Zanda Trucking, located in Woodlawn, Kentucky. The search unfolded after agents received a tip from an informant that Double T Van Zanda a Woodlawn mobster and owner of the trucking company, was using the shipping container to store a bomb. The informant told agents that the bomb was intended for use in the attempted murder of another gangster.

The FBI agents immediately dispatched to the reported location. When the agents arrived at Van Zanda Trucking, their bomb-sniffing dog "hit" on the shipping container in question, indicating the dog's probable detection of a bomb. At that point, FBI agents also were aware that Van Zanda had previously been tied to a mob bombing.

Before searching the container, FBI agents also spoke with and received permission from a man named "The Earl" to search the container. The Earl, who was at the scene of the container when the FBI agents arrived, told the agents that he had rented the container to store a guitar collection. He

1

explained, however, that because of an argument with Van Zanda, he had moved a majority of his guitar collection out one month earlier. When the agents asked if they could look inside the container, The Earl replied, "OK." He then opened the shipping container for the agents using his own key.

The agents did not find a bomb inside the container. However, along with a few guitars that belonged to The Earl, agents discovered cocaine and marijuana—leading to a federal indictment of Van Zanda. Van Zanda's defense attorneys are preparing to file a motion to suppress the evidence gleaned from the warrantless search.

## DISCUSSION

The government wants to know whether the items seized in the warrantless search of the container must be suppressed. While the Fourth Amendment "generally requires officers to possess a warrant before conducting a search," "[t]here are, however, exceptions to the warrant requirement." *United States v. Purcell*, 526 F.3d 953, 960 (6th Cir. 2008); *see also United States v. Watson*, 483 F.3d 1382, 1387 (6th Cir. 2007) (citing *Illinois v. Rodriguez*, 497 U.S. 177, 181 (1990)). One exception to the warrant requirement is "the existence of exigent circumstances." *Purcell*, 526 F.3d at 960 (citing *Mincey v. Arizona*, 437 U.S. 385, 392–93 (1978)); *see also Henry v. Newland*, 263 F.3d 1384, 1395 (6th Cir. 2001). The other "well-delineated" exception to the warrant requirement is consent to search. *Id.* The government bears the burden of proving either exception. *Id.* (citing *United States v. Atchley*, 474 F.3d 840, 851 (6th Cir. 2007)). This memo addresses both exceptions—namely, whether an exigent circumstance existed to justify the search and whether the officers obtained consent to search. Because of the pending threat of a bomb as well as the permission granted by someone with a key to the container, it is likely the court will conclude the search was constitutional.

### 1. Exigent Circumstances Exception to Search Warrant Requirement

The government will first argue that exigent circumstances justified the warrantless search. *See id.* (quoting *United States v. Rohrig*, 98 F.3d 1506, 1515 (6th Cir. 1996)). "The government bears the burden of showing the existence of exigent circumstances by particularized evidence," and this burden is not satisfied by mere speculation that the exigency exists. *Henry*, 263 F.3d at 1395 (quoting *United States v. Tarazon*, 989 F.2d 1045, 1049 (9th Cir. 1993)). This memo focuses only on whether the search was justified based on a "risk of danger to police or to others." *Purcell*, 526 F.3d at 960 (quoting *Rohrig*, 98 F.3d at 1515). In determining whether such risk exists, courts consider the objective information available to the agents about the immediacy and extent of the risk and whether the agents' actions were consistent with the asserted risk. *See, e.g., United States v. Johnson*, 22 F.3d 674, 680 (6th Cir. 1994). While the presence of a firearm or other weapon at a scene alone does not constitute a danger justifying a search, such a risk of danger does exist when police have evidence that a weapon is present and poses an immediate threat from being unsecured or otherwise in a volatile state.

*Johnson*, 22 F.3d at 680–81; *Henry*, 263 F.3d at 1395. On the other hand, when agents observe evidence of drug use, but not drug manufacturing, which is the danger purported to exist, and agents do not take immediate protective actions, courts hold no exigent circumstance exists. *Purcell*, 526 F.3d at 960. Because the agents received a tip that a bomb was ready to be planted, Scooter the police dog "hit" on the container, and agents took precautions such as clearing the area, a court will likely find an exigent circumstance existed. *See id.*

When agents possess objective information that demonstrates an immediate and significant risk and agents' actions are consistent with the asserted risk, courts hold there is a risk of danger demonstrating an exigent circumstance. *Henry*, 263 F.3d at 1395. In *Henry*, police officers searched a motel room following a complaint that two men were inside selling drugs. *Id.* at 1388. The officers identified a stolen car parked outside the suspect's motel room. *Id.* When the officers knocked on the motel room door, they detained one man from the suspect's room when he stepped onto an outside porch, but another person inside the motel room immediately slammed the door shut. *Id.* After an officer knocked on the door for approximately two minutes, a second man inside the room stepped out and was detained. *Id.* From the open doorway, one officer spotted what he believed to be a black revolver under a bed inside the room. *Id.* The officer could not see the entire room from the doorway, so he entered the room immediately to retrieve the firearm. *Id.*

Based on these facts, the court found that there was a risk of danger to the officers or other people in the proximity of the motel. *Id.* at 1395. The court noted that even though the officers already detained two men at the time of the warrantless search, there could have been other occupants inside who had access to the gun but who were not visible from the doorway. *Id.* The officers would have reason to believe that any hidden person inside the motel room was also involved with drug activity and the stolen car. *Id.* The court also highlighted the fact that someone inside the room slammed the door shut to keep law enforcement out of the room, heightening the concern about the risk of danger. *Id.*; *see also United States v. Allimaster*, 205 F.3d 101, 107 (12th Cir. 2011) (holding risk of danger existed when, after arresting one person at the location, officers saw a shadow in the kitchen that they believed to be a person where large knives were visible on the kitchen counter).

On the contrary, when the objective information available to the agents suggests the risk is not immediate, courts hold there is no risk of danger that demonstrates exigent circumstances. *Johnson*, 22 F.3d at 680. In *Johnson*, police officers searched the defendant's apartment without a warrant and seized firearms after receiving a report that a missing girl was being held there against her will. *Id.* at 676. When the officers arrived at the apartment, they found the missing girl there by herself behind a locked gate. *Id.* Though he had threatened violence against the victim if she ever escaped, neither the defendant nor anyone other than the girl was in the apartment at the time of the search. *Id.* at 677. The court held that there was not a risk of danger

3

justifying a warrantless search of the closet. *Id.* at 680. The court noted that by the time of the search the police had removed the victim from danger and had "ample time to secure the premises and to obtain a search warrant." *Id.*

Similarly, when officers' actions are not consistent with the asserted risk, courts hold no exigent circumstances exist. *Purcell*, 526 F.3d at 965. In *Purcell*, agents conducted a warrantless search of a defendant's backpack and located a firearm. *Id.* at 961. Though the agents attempted to justify their search based on a suspicion that the defendant might be operating a dangerous methamphetamine lab, the court held that no risk of danger existed. *Id.* The court noted that agents questioned the defendant's girlfriend for ten minutes inside the room, even though they supposedly feared dangerous and volatile chemicals might be present in the room. *Id.* The court also highlighted the fact that the agents took no steps to protect guests staying in the hotel who might be vulnerable. *Id.* None of these actions demonstrated a subjective belief on the part of the agents that a danger was present. *Id.*

Here, the objective information available to the FBI agents suggested the risk was both immediate and severe. The agents knew that a bomb was present inside the shipping container and that it was in a volatile state, both facts which underscore the belief that there was an immediate and severe risk. *See id.* Like the officer in *Henry* who spotted what he believed to be a handgun while standing at the door of a motel room, the FBI agents received credible evidence that an explosive device was in the shipping container when a trusted informant offered the tip about a planned hit. *See* 263 F.3d at 1395. The agents' suspicions that a bomb was present were also bolstered when Scooter "hit" on the container immediately. Further, because an unstable bomb can detonate on its own, the objective evidence indicated an even greater threat than the handgun, a device that must be deliberately triggered by a person. *See id.* at 1396. This makes the risk posed in this case more credible that that deemed to pose an exigency in *Henry*. *Id.* Thus, the objective evidence regarding the bomb, including its potential volatility, suggests a greater threat than that which existed in *Johnson*, in which the officer knew no one was in the apartment who could trigger the firearm. *See* 22 F.3d at 680.

Even so, Van Zanda might argue that the objective evidence did not suggest that any bomb inside the shipping container was so volatile as to threaten the safety of the agents or others nearby. Like the firearms found in a closet in *Johnson* with no one around to use them, here the alleged bomb did not truly pose an immediate threat. *See id.* Even if there was a bomb in the shipping container, the agents had little reason to think it was so volatile that it might detonate on its own. Further, given the specialized blast suits the agents wore as well as the fact that agents had cleared the area of bystanders, a bomb posed little actual threat at that point. *See id.*

In addition, the FBI agents acted consistent with their belief that there was a bomb in a volatile state. Unlike the agents in *Purcell*, who "did not seem particularly concerned for their own safety," the agents at Van Zanda Trucking both cleared the site and wore bomb suits that would protect them

4

from a blast, revealing a sincere concern about a bomb detonating. *See* 526 F.3d at 961. Although the agents did talk to The Earl briefly before clearing the site, they acted swiftly after speaking with The Earl. In contrast, the officers in *Purcell* did not act swiftly or with purpose, but instead engaged in relatively lengthy conversation with the defendant's girlfriend that was not geared toward helping them assess the asserted threat. *See id.* The agents' actions thus were like those of the officers in *Henry* who acted consistent with the asserted threat by immediately retrieving the firearm that posed the threat. *See* 263 F.3d at 1396. While the agents did not act as quickly as the officers in *Henry* did to remove the threat, the agents had good reason for the delay as they had to gather confirming information. *See id.* Once the threat was confirmed, they acted with the swiftness and immediacy that one would expect given the threat.

In contrast, Van Zanda may contend the FBI agents' acts were inconsistent with the threat being asserted. Notably, the agents did not immediately conduct the search but instead spent ten minutes speaking with The Earl outside the shipping container, suggesting that they were not truly concerned about the bomb detonating. Thus, Van Zanda may argue that the agents' actions are similar to those of the officers in *Purcell*, who, by standing and talking to the defendant's girlfriend before conducting the search, did not act with "particular concern for their own safety." *See* 526 F.3d at 963. Further highlighting this lack of any true concern is the fact that while questioning The Earl, the agents did nothing to secure the area, such as clearing the area of people. That lack of concern is similar to the officers in *Purcell* who, while questioning the defendant's girlfriend, took no protective measures, such as evacuating hotel guests, which one would expect if they believed there was a meth lab in the hotel room. *See id.* Had the agents truly been concerned about a bomb detonating, they would surely have acted much more urgently and swiftly, like the officers in *Henry*, who took immediate and swift action to remove the threat of the firearm. *See* 263 F.3d at 1395-96.

While the court may agree that the agents' actions were not entirely consistent with the claimed threat, it is likely that the court nonetheless will hold that there was an exigent circumstance based upon the risk of danger. The agents eventually took protective measures, including clearing the area before conducting the search, which shows their level of concern at the time of search. Further evidence of the risk of danger stems from the fact that the information the agents learned on site heightened, rather than lessened, the credible threat.

### 2. Consent to Search Exception to the Search Warrant Requirement

Even if there was no exigency, the government also can justify the warrantless search by showing that the agents had consent to search the container. "In order to consent to a search, the person purporting to consent must possess either actual or apparent authority over the item or place to be searched." *Purcell*, 526 F.3d at 962. The government concedes that The Earl lacked actual authority, so the only question is whether he had apparent authority. *See id.* Apparent authority is judged by an objective standard based on the information known to the agent at the moment of search. *Id.* In the third-party context, the agent must have reasonably believed the person giving consent possessed joint access or control over the property searched. *Id.* In determining whether such apparent authority over the property searched existed, courts consider: (1) whether the person reasonably asserted access and control over the property, and (2) whether the context confirmed or created ambiguity regarding the spoken assertion, particularly in light of any indication by the owner of the intent to exclude third parties from using or exerting control over the object. *Id.*; *Watson*, 483 F.3d at 1388. When a person asserts control and authority over searched bags, yet shortly thereafter agents have reason to doubt the bags belong to that person, courts hold that the apparent authority does not exist. *Purcell*, 526 F.3d at 962-63. In contrast, when a person asserts control and authority over a joint shared space, and agents are not made aware of attempts by the owner to keep others out, courts hold that apparent authority exists. *Watson*, 483 F.3d at 1393. A court will likely find that The Earl had ongoing apparent authority to consent to the search because he had a key to the container searched, his guitars were inside the container, and no ambiguity existed regarding his authority or control of the container.

When a person asserts control and authority over a shared space and nothing in the context creates ambiguity regarding the assertion's accuracy, courts hold that apparent authority exists. *Watson*, 483 F.3d at 1392. In *Watson*, agents conducting a child pornography investigation searched a defendant's computer after his father, with whom he lived, authorized the search. *Id.* Though the computer was located in the defendant's bedroom, his father owned the home and had "unlimited access" to the bedroom. *Id.* at 1384. The father told the agents that he always felt free to enter the room as long as the door was open. *Id.* To conduct an initial search of the computer, a forensic computer expert with the agents used software that allowed him to access the computer's hard drive without first determining whether the computer was password protected. *Id.* The court held that the defendant's father had apparent authority to consent to the search of the computer. *Id.* at 1401. The court emphasized that the father owned the house, paid the Internet and cable bill, and had access to the room whenever he pleased. *Id.* at 1402. Further, the court noted that the computer was "in plain view on the desk in [defendant's] room and it appeared available for use by other household members." *Id.* Additionally, because their software allowed them to search the hard drive without a password, the court noted that the agents had no indications that the computer was password protected. *Id.* at 1393.

Alternately, when a person asserts control and authority over property, yet the context suggests that assertion is inaccurate, courts hold that the apparent authority does not exist. *Purcell*, 526 F.3d at 956. In *Purcell*, officers discovered a firearm in a bag they searched in a hotel room. *Id.* at 958. When the officers arrived at the hotel room, they questioned the defendant's girlfriend, who was sharing the hotel room with the defendant. *Id.* She gave the officers permission to search the hotel room, including the bags in it. *Id.* at 957. The agents found only the defendant's personal belongings in the first bag they searched, even though the girlfriend had asserted that the bags belonged to her. *Id.* at 958. The agents did not clarify the girlfriend's authority over any other bags in the room at that point, even though the girlfriend was standing outside the hotel room. *Id.* Instead, the agents searched an additional bag, which was where they found the firearm at issue. *Id.* The court held that there was no consent to search the second bag because the girlfriend did not have apparent authority over it. *Id.* at 964. The court reasoned that the girlfriend's "apparent authority, which justified the search of the first bag, dissipated upon the discovery" of only the defendant's personal effects in that bag "and was not reestablished." *Id.* Rather "ambiguity clouded" the girlfriend's authority to consent to the search of any additional bags. *Id.*

The government will argue that The Earl reasonably asserted access and control over the shipping container. The Earl expressly asserted access and control when he told the agents he had a rental agreement to use the shipping container and that he stored various pieces from his guitar collection there. *See id.* Further, The Earl demonstrated that access and control over that shared space when he opened the shipping container for agents with his own key. *See id.* Thus, similar to the situation in *Purcell* in which the defendant's girlfriend had access to the bags, claimed the bags were hers, and had her purse on top of one of the bags, here too the agent was reasonable to believe, at least based upon the assertion alone, that authority existed. *See id.* at 957. The Earl's assertion of authority is even stronger than the girlfriend's in *Purcell* because the Earl's key leaves no doubt about his access to the property. *See id.*

Alternatively, Van Zanda will likely argue that The Earl failed to reasonably assert control. Notably, The Earl's statement of control was undermined by his statement that he had moved most of his property out of the shipping container following an argument with Van Zanda a month prior. Unlike the situation in *Purcell*, in which the defendant's girlfriend expressed no limitations on her asserted control, here The Earl implicitly qualified his own assertion of control and authority. *See id.*

Moreover, the government will argue that the context of the asserted control confirmed, rather than disconfirmed, The Earl's assertion of control and authority. Unlike the doubt created in *Purcell* when the agents discovered only the defendant's personal belongings in a bag that his girlfriend had claimed was hers, here no uncertainty arose. *See id.* at 958. To the contrary, the context here—namely, The Earl's possession of a key to the container and, after the fact, the storage of his guitars found in the container—confirmed the belief that The Earl possessed access and control over the container. That is similar to the confirming context that existed in *Watson*, where the father giving consent to search his son's computer was able to let agents into his son's room so that they could access the computer. *See* 483 F.3d at 1384-85. In fact, because The Earl had a key to the container, the context supports his authority to consent even more strongly than in

*Watson*, where the father qualified his authority to enter the room to times when the door was open. *Id*. at 1384. Although the fact that The Earl had moved most of his items out of the shipping container may suggest that in the future he would not have control and authority, the fact that he still had some of his property in the container and still had a key to the container shows his continuing control at that point.

In contrast, Van Zanda will argue that even if The Earl reasonably asserted control, the context surrounding The Earl's assertion of control disconfirmed that he was, in fact, in control. Namely, The Earl admitted that, following a fight with Van Zanda a month earlier, The Earl had moved most of his collection out of the storage container, suggesting that he was in limbo, such that he may or may not truly have control over the container. While not conclusive, like the ambiguity created in *Purcell* when the search of the first bag indicated it likely did not belong to the person asserting control, here the fact that The Earl had moved most of his property casts doubt on his authority and control. *See* 526 F.3d. at 957.

The context surrounding The Earl's assertion of authority failed to cast doubt on that authority. Given the consistent indicators of The Earl's apparent authority, the court is likely to hold that the consent by The Earl was valid because apparent authority existed.

## CONCLUSION

Taken together, the FBI agents likely had justification for the warrantless search of the container, such that the motion to suppress should be denied. First, the warrantless search was justified by an exigent circumstance in the form of a present danger. Alternately, the warrantless search was justified because the FBI obtained consent to search the container from a person with apparent authority.

8

# Checklists for Memo Writing

## Checklist for a Single Case Memo

### Global Roadmap

1. A topic sentence that includes a global prediction as to the client's claim or charge.
2. The global rule of law, with its conditions and the relationship between the conditions clearly set forth, and with proper attribution.
3. An announcement of any non-issues, which are conditions that will not be addressed in the memo, ideally with a brief explanation as to why the conditions will not be addressed.
4. An announcement of the issues that will be addressed in the memo.
5. A global prediction, which is the prediction as to the resolution of the client's claim or charge, supported by key client facts related to that global prediction. A sentence or two should suffice, as this is simply the overall prediction and does not contain the separate issue predictions that will appear at the end of each issue roadmap.

### Issue Roadmaps

1. A topic sentence that announces the issue/condition that will be addressed in the issue roadmap.
2. The rule of law for the issue/condition: any definitions, standards, or guiding factors that are related to the court's analysis of the issue/condition.
3. The rule proof: the fact-based holding from the precedent, which provides "proof" of the rule.
4. A prediction of the resolution of that issue/condition, supported by key client facts related to that prediction.

### Rule Explanation Paragraphs

1. A framing sentence that illustrates how the guiding factors inform the court's analysis of the issue/condition.

2. Facts from the precedent case that are related to those guiding factors.
3. The court's holding on the issue/condition in light of those facts.
4. The court's reasoning; i.e., why it resolved the issue the way it did.

### Rule Application Paragraphs

1. Broken down by the components of the rule of law for the condition, most typically by guiding factors.
2. For each component:
   a. A topic or thesis sentence: an announcement of the aspect of the rule of law for the condition that will be addressed.
   b. One or more forms of legal reasoning to support arguments:
      i. Analogical arguments and counter-arguments, comparing and contrasting facts from the precedent case to the client's case;
      ii. Rule-based arguments and counter-arguments;
      iii. Policy-based arguments and counter-arguments.
   c. Ideally, each component of the issue rule of law should be addressed from each party's perspective.
3. At the end of rule application, an issue prediction: a prediction as to the court's resolution of that issue/condition.

### Global Conclusion

1. A global prediction as to the resolution of the client's claim or charge.
2. A reiteration of the issue prediction for each issue/condition.

# Checklist for Multiple Authorities Memo

## *Global Roadmap*

1. A topic sentence that includes a global prediction as to the client's claim or charge.
2. The **synthesized** global rule of law, with its conditions and the relationship between the conditions clearly set forth, and with proper attribution.
3. An announcement of any non-issues, which are conditions that will not be addressed in the memo, ideally with a brief explanation as to why the conditions will not be addressed.
4. An announcement of the issues that will be addressed in the memo.
5. A global prediction, which is the prediction as to the resolution of the client's claim or charge, supported by key client facts related to that global prediction. A sentence or two should suffice, as this is simply the overall prediction and does not contain the separate issue predictions that will appear at the end of each issue roadmap.

## *Issue Roadmaps*

1. A topic sentence that announces the issue/condition that will be addressed in the issue roadmap.
2. The **synthesized** rule of law for the issue/condition: any definitions, standards, or guiding factors related to the court's analysis of the issue/condition.
3. The rule proof: the **synthesized** fact-based **holdings** from the **precedents**, which provides "proof" of the rule.
4. A prediction of the resolution of that issue/condition, supported by key client facts related to that prediction.

## *Rule Explanation Paragraphs*

1. A framing sentence that illustrates how the guiding factors inform the court's analysis of the issue/condition. *Note*: Consecutive rule explanation paragraphs should contain a transition that bridges that paragraph to the preceding one.
2. Facts from the precedent case that are related to those guiding factors.
3. The court's holding on the issue/condition in light of those facts.
4. The court's reasoning; i.e., why it resolved the issue the way it did.
   *Note:* Additional, secondary cases that illustrate a similar application may be included using a "*see also*" case signal.

### Rule Application Paragraphs

1. Broken down by the components of the rule of law for the condition, most typically by guiding factors.
2. For each component:
   a. A topic or thesis sentence: an announcement of the aspect of the issue rule of law for the condition that will be addressed.
   b. One or more forms of legal reasoning to support arguments:
      i. Analogical arguments and counter-arguments, comparing and contrasting facts from the precedent case to the client's case;
      ii. Rule-based arguments and counter-arguments;
      iii. Policy-based arguments and counter-arguments.
   c. Ideally, each component of the issue rule of law should be addressed by each party's perspective.
3. At end of rule application, an issue prediction: a prediction as to the court's resolution of that issue/condition.

### Global Conclusion

1. A global prediction as to the resolution of the client's claim or charge.
2. A reiteration of the issue prediction for each issue/condition.

## Revision Checklist Questions

At the revision stage you will ask big-picture questions to identify any problems likely to affect the Discussion as a whole. Large-scale organization questions loom large at the revising stage. Consider the following questions as you revise your draft:

☐ *Have I answered the legal question posed?*

Re-read the assignment, especially the assignment prompt, to make sure your memorandum responds to the question posed.

☐ *Have I accurately and clearly stated the global legal rule?*

The rest of the Discussion flows from the global legal rule, so any inaccuracy or lack of clarity here will have a significant, negative impact.

☐ *Have I accurately identified what conditions are at issue in my global roadmap?*

Because any condition that you identify as a non-issue will not be discussed in the rest of the memo, you want to double-check that you have gotten this right. That might mean reconsidering whether the satisfaction of the condition is as one-sided and undisputed as you first concluded. Or it might mean re-reading the prompt for the memo assignment to make sure you correctly understood any conditions that should not be considered.

☐ *Does my large-scale organization flow predictably from the global roadmap, including a segment of discussion for each issue identified?*

For each issue/condition, your law-trained reader expects to see a predictable and self-contained segment of discussion. It should be apparent where the discussion for one issue ends and another one begins.

☐ *Are there transitions between the segments of my discussion to assist my reader in understanding the relationship between these sections? Did I include headings, if needed? Have I used a consistent and parallel sentence structure when identifying each issue?*

A law-trained reader should be able to glance at your memo and get an understanding of the different issues it addresses. Using headings helps accomplish this goal, as does using transitions and consistent and parallel sentence structure. Compare the following three topic sentences, each of which introduces an issue/condition in a memo. These sentences would not be consecutive; they would be separated by the related segments of discussion. Note that the parallel construction and transitions in the effective version signal to the reader that a new segment is starting.

*Ineffective:*
- The State must show Smith's entry was unlawful.
- The court will consider if Smith entered a building or structure.
- The next question is whether the Defendant intended to commit a crime while inside the building or structure.

*Effective:*
- First, the State must show Smith's entry was unlawful.
- Second, the State must show Smith entered a building or structure.
- Finally, the State must show that Smith intended to commit a crime while inside the building or structure.

☐ *Does my memorandum provide a global conclusion at the end?*

Your reader expects you to come full circle in your analysis. You will begin with your global prediction, and you must complete the circle by ending with that global prediction. Your global conclusion should be short and to the point. It will state your global prediction, supported with succinct predictions for each issue/condition.

For example, an effective global conclusion for the burglary example might read:

> In sum, the State likely will be unable to show that Smith committed burglary. The State likely can show that Smith's entry was unlawful because he entered the building without permission and through a window. The State also can easily show that Smith entered a building because the entry occurred at a vacant middle school. Even so, the State likely will not be able to show that Smith possessed the requisite intent to commit a crime given that he was highly inebriated and will maintain he was entering the building only to seek shelter from the sub-zero temperatures.

## Editing Checklist Questions

Consider the following questions as you edit your draft:

☐ *With each issue segment of my discussion, have I followed the expected deductive structure, progressing from an issue roadmap, to rule explanation, to rule application, and ending with an issue prediction?*

Each issue segment should include one issue roadmap paragraph (or, in rare instances, one additional paragraph if the law is exceptionally complex and involved), a rule explanation section, and a rule application section that concludes with an issue prediction—all in that order. Remember the lasagna analogy? Any gaps in this expected structure and content will confuse your reader and leave her dissatisfied with your analysis.

☐ *Does my rule explanation section provide a bridge between my issue roadmap and my rule application? More broadly, do the parts of my issue segment generally align?*

Remembering the purpose of the different paragraph types provides a helpful lens for reviewing your memo. The rule explanation discusses one case (in a single authority memo) or multiple cases (in a multiple authority memo) with the goal of demonstrating that the rule you set forth in the issue roadmap was indeed what the court previously applied. You also included your rule explanation discussion because you wanted to show specifically how that rule applied in a factually similar situation, to prepare the reader for the next section—rule application—where you will use the facts and reasoning from the prior case (or cases) to make analogical arguments.

So, all of these parts of your issue segment should align; the guiding factors you identify in your issue roadmap should be the guiding factors the court applied, as illustrated in your rule explanation case(s). Further, your rule application should be based on the relevant guiding factors you have identified. You should have adequate material from your rule explanation discussion to develop specific and meaningful analytical arguments.

☐ *Is my rule application organized around either the party/position approach or the issue-components approach? Is this organization clear from the topic sentences in my rule application section?*

It bears repeating that your rule application needs to be organized. Whether you use the party/position approach or the issue-components approach, your rule application should be organized in such a way that your reader can easily track the organization.

Also keep in mind that once you have focused on what is important to the court by discerning guiding factors, it only makes sense that you would build arguments around these considerations, no matter which organizational approach you use. In other words, as you organize the arguments, whether by party/position or issue-components, you should clearly show the importance of the guiding factors as the basis for the arguments you make. This should certainly be evident when using the issue-components organizational framework. However, if you employ the party/position approach, the reader should still be able to see how the arguments revolve around those legally significant bases of comparison—the guiding factors.

In order to check your work, highlight references to guiding factors. This will help you verify you have conveyed the guiding factors in a clear and well-organized manner that strengthens your arguments.

☐ *Do my rule application paragraphs sufficiently and clearly make arguments, or do they instead make the mistake of either reasoning by proximity (i.e., putting similar facts side by side without explaining their connection and legal significance) or monologuing (reciting multiple facts without tethering those to the legal rule)?*

You should not have sentences in your rule application that simply recite the facts of your client's case, or that simply reiterate the facts and reasoning from a prior case. In your rule application, facts and reasoning from a prior case must be connected explicitly to the facts of your client's situation and tethered to the legal rule. Do not leave your reader to decide for himself why something matters. Put differently, the reader should not be left asking, "So what?"

☐ *Does each paragraph have a main idea? Is that main idea communicated through a topic or thesis statement at the beginning of the paragraph?*

If you find a paragraph without a main idea, that paragraph needs to be reworked. Ask yourself what you intended that paragraph to cover and adjust accordingly. On the other hand, if a single paragraph contains multiple main ideas, you likely will need to separate that content into more than one paragraph. Finally, you may find that a paragraph has a main idea, but rather than being properly situated at the start of the paragraph, that idea is buried in the middle or tagged on to the end. In that case, you will reorder sentences and also reword as necessary.

☐ *Are there one or more paragraphs in my Discussion that I cannot easily label as either a roadmap paragraph, a rule explanation paragraph, a rule application paragraph, or a global conclusion paragraph?*

In other words, ask yourself if you have included anything that should not be part of your Discussion. Have you editorialized? Included information not directly tethered to the particular legal rule? Blended different parts of your Discussion together, obscuring the purpose a given paragraph serves? Ensure that your Discussion contains the content that your law-trained reader expects and nothing extraneous.

☐ *Do my paragraphs and sentences progress logically?*

Because memo writing follows a deductive approach, the logical progression requires that you provide general information before more specific, supporting information. In addition, check to make sure the paragraphs flow logically and that the sentences within each paragraph also flow logically. This consideration is often particularly important in your rule application section, which has a less rigid structure. Remember to consider your work through the eyes of the reader, who may be encountering this information for the first time. Often certain information has to be presented first in order to lay the foundation for other information. For example, if you are making an argument about a dog's physical characteristics, it would not make sense to jump into detailed descriptions of those characteristics before you have identified the guiding factor you are examining. Compare:

*Ineffective:*

While small in stature, Fido has sharp claws, including dewclaws. He also has a strong jaw. He has strong legs and does not hesitate to jump up on people. These facts demonstrate he possesses physical characteristics that suggest he could pose a threat.

*Effective:*

Fido possesses physical characteristics that suggest he could pose a threat. While small in stature, Fido has sharp claws, including dewclaws. He also has a strong jaw. He has strong legs and does not hesitate to jump up on people.

Note, too, that in the effective example, the first sentence provides a strong topic statement for the main point of the paragraph.

☐ *Does my memo contain all the expected sections in addition to the Discussion, i.e., the Header, the Question Presented, the Short Answer, and the Statement of Facts?*

In addition to ensuring you have included all the expected sections, review each section of your memo against the appropriate memo checklist here. Also make sure your Question Presented and Short Answer align with your Discussion in terms of scope and content. Finally, ensure that any facts that you included in your Discussion are also included in your Statement of Facts section. Then reverse the process and see if all the facts in your Statement of Facts section are included in your Discussion. You may find you have included facts that provide helpful context in your Statement of Facts section that you do not mention in your Discussion; that is okay. However, if you find legally significant facts that only appear in the Statement of Facts section, you need to edit your Discussion to incorporate those facts

# Answers to Check In Exercises

## Module I, Chapter 4 Check In

### Assessing the Features of a Predictive Memo

Read through the following memo. (See page 62.) When you have finished, go through the checklist of Key Features of a Predictive Memo (embedded in answer below). With which of these features does it comply? On which features does it fall short? (Hint: It does fall short.) When it falls short, how did that affect your understanding of and/or confidence in the memo?

### Answer

- It covers a precise, client-centered topic. The memo is based around the client's particular legal situation. Note that the memo did not set out to explain any and all aspects of tortious interference with business; it set out to provide a prediction for one particular client. So, it is client-focused.

  The memo is client-focused. It does seem to focus on Mr. Arnold's tortious interference with business expectancy claim.

- The information moves from general principles to specific application of those principles: As discussed in Chapter 3, this is a deductive framework (general to specific). In a predictive memo, the Discussion starts with a statement of the applicable legal rule; it then gives an example of how the rule has been used by courts before and follows with an application of that rule to the client's situation.

  The Discussion section was somewhat difficult to follow, particularly right at the beginning. This is because the first paragraph addresses one of the issues of the claim—reasonable expectancy of business relationship. However, the subsequent paragraph is then directed at the entire claim—how to demonstrate interference with business expectancy. In order to move deductively and allow the reader to have a general understanding of the claim, the information about the entire claim should have been the first paragraph. By reorganizing and proceeding from more general information about the claim or charge, and then moving to specific issues related to that general claim or charge, the reader has more context and direction.

- The law is applied from both the perspective of the client and the perspective of the opposing party. In other words, it presents both analysis and counter-analysis. To thoroughly assess the strength of the client's argument, you also need to evaluate the strength of the opposition's argument. As in a game of chess, the best players think through their opponent's moves just as carefully as they think through their own.

  The writer has not given the opposing party's argument ample consideration. This undermines the reader's confidence in the analysis and in the prediction.

- It comes full circle. It both starts and ends with the big picture: the overall legal question and the overall prediction.

  The global prediction is in the second paragraph, rather than the first, so the organization is difficult to follow. Moreover, the final paragraph of the memo makes a prediction about the second issue—whether it was the defendant's intentional and unjustified interference that prevented the realization of business expectancy—but not a prediction about the global resolution of the entire claim—whether the defendant tortiously interfered with business expectancy.

## Module I, Chapter 5 Check In

*Identifying Memo-Writing Steps and Categorizing Legal Problems*

### Part 1

Below is a list of work you might conduct if tasked with writing a predictive memo related to the Warrantless Bomb Search hypothetical. Assign the appropriate writing process step number to each of the lettered actions listed below. Note any actions that should not be included as part of the writing process, as well as any steps that are missing.

- A. Develop likely arguments that our client, the U.S. government, will make.
- B. Identify the emergent legal rule related to the permissibility of evidence acquired through a warrantless search.

C. Find cases from the Sixth Circuit that are factually similar.

D. Find cases from neighboring circuits that are factually similar.

E. Create an outline of the memo from which you can then identify the emergent legal rule.

F. Develop a keen understanding of the factual situation.

G. Develop arguments that the potential defendant, Van Zanda, may make.

## Part 1 Answer

| THE STEPS IN THE WRITING PROCESS (IN ORDER AND AS LISTED IN TEXT) | CHECK-IN ANSWER: ALIGNMENT OF THE LISTED ACTIONS WITH THE EXPECTED WRITING PROCESS STEPS/IDENTIFICATION OF MISSING STEPS |
|---|---|
| 1. Understand your client's factual situation. | F: Develop a keen understanding of the factual situation. |
| 2. Determine the legal question. | This entire step is missing from the action list. |
| 3. Determine the applicable global rule of law. | B: Identify the emergent legal rule related to the permissibility of evidence acquired through a warrantless search. |
| 4. Determine the conditions for the rule and assess which conditions are at issue. | B—possibly: Identify the emergent legal rule related to the permissibility of evidence obtained through a warrantless search. |
| 5. Select cases that are analogous. | C: Find cases from the Sixth Circuit that are factually similar. |
| 6. Analyze and develop arguments as to the likely application of the rule of law to your client's situation. | A: Develop likely arguments that our client, the U.S. government, will make. *and* G: Develop arguments that the potential defendant, Van Zanda, may make. Note: These are one step. |
| 7. Determine whether additional research is necessary to further develop the analysis of an element or factor. | This entire step is missing from the action list. |
| 8. Outline the Discussion section of your memo. | This entire step is missing from the action list. |
| 9. Draft the Discussion section of your memo. | This entire step is missing from the action list. |
| 10. Revise and edit the Discussion section of your memo. | This entire step is missing from the action list. |
| 11. Draft and edit the remaining sections of your memo. | This entire step is missing from the action list. |
| 12. Proofread your entire memo. | This entire step is missing from the action list. |

| THE STEPS IN THE WRITING PROCESS (IN ORDER AND AS LISTED IN TEXT) | CHECK-IN ANSWER: ALIGNMENT OF THE LISTED ACTIONS WITH THE EXPECTED WRITING PROCESS STEPS/IDENTIFICATION OF MISSING STEPS |
|---|---|
| Not a step—should not be included. | D: Find cases from neighboring circuits that are factually similar. <br><br> —As we will discuss more in Chapter 6, the law of neighboring jurisdictions is not binding on the court (mandatory), although it might be persuasive and thus useful in limited instances. Thus, this is not a typical step in the writing process. <br><br> E: Create an outline of the memo from which you can then identify the emergent legal rule. <br><br> —You need to find the rule before you outline the memo. In fact, as discussed more in Chapter 7, you create an outline of the rule, which, among other things, will help you create an outline of your memo. |

### Part 2

Try to answer the questions listed in the Equipping Yourself: **Categorizing a Legal Problem** box on page 77 in relation to the Warrantless Bomb Search hypothetical.

### Part 2 Answer

☐ How can you categorize this research need? Does it involve civil or criminal law? Is it substantive or procedural? What specific topical area is involved (e.g., torts, labor and employment, environmental law)?
Criminal, Constitutional Law. Has both substantive and procedural aspects. Search and seizure, Fourth Amendment.

☐ Is this likely to be a matter of federal, state, or local law?
Federal.

☐ How much do you already know about the area of law?
If it is new to you, you might want to start with a descriptive secondary source rather than jumping straight into the law itself.

☐ What type of legal authority is likely to apply? Common law? A specific type of enacted law (constitution, statute, regulation, e.g.)?
U.S. Constitution (Fourth Amendment) and interpretive case law.

## Module II, Chapter 6 Check Ins

### *Sources of Law*

While visiting a friend in West Dakota, David has been arrested for operating a vehicle while intoxicated. What sources of law do you likely need to consult and why?

### *Answer*

I will start with enacted laws because criminal laws generally are enacted laws.

### *Existing and Emergent Legal Rules*

Recall from Chapter 2 Sofía's client, Jeffers Peterson, who was charged with assault with a dangerous weapon when, after a sporting match, he slapped someone across the face while wearing a Fitbit. The discussion in Chapter 2 pertained to the element of what constitutes a "dangerous weapon."

Now assume that Sofía wants to know if her client may be able to successfully defend himself by showing that the person he allegedly assaulted gave "implied consent" to the assault. Sofía found a Massachusetts case on point, *State v. Bird*, that discusses the implied consent defense in relation to assaults that occur in the context of sporting events. The case states:

> It is well-established that consent may operate as a defense to many crimes, and in the context of consensual sporting events, the doctrine of implied consent has particular application. Participants in sporting events are deemed to have consented to the physical contact and even possibly bodily harm that is part of their sport.

In an effort to better understand the implied consent defense, Sofía looks for additional authority. She finds the case of *State v. Johnson* in which the court held that the defendant did not commit assault because the alleged victim, who was his opponent in a racquetball game, gave "implied consent" to the alleged assault. In so holding, the court stated:

> Here, the defendant indisputably injured Mr. Jabar when the ball the defendant hit slammed into Mr. Jabar's cheek, crushing his cheekbone. While Mr. Jabar contends that in order to inflict such a serious injury the defendant must have hit the ball harder than was reasonable in the context of the racquetball match, we think that is precisely the point of racquetball—to hit the ball hard and fast. That it hit Mr. Jabar's face is truly unfortunate but that is contact that Mr. Jabar implicitly agreed to when he participated in the racquetball game.

### Answer

☐ **What was the existing legal rule of law based upon *State v. Bird*?**

The existing rule from *State v. Bird* is that "Implied consent is a defense to assault. In sporting events, participants are deemed to have consented to the physical contact and even possibly bodily harm that is part of their sport."

☐ **What is the emergent legal rule of law that comes out of *State v. Johnson*?**

The emergent rule from *State v. Johnson* adds to the existing rule from *Bird*. Implied consent is a defense to assault. In sporting events, participants are deemed to have consented to the physical contact and even possibly bodily harm that is part of their sport. In determining what contact and harm is deemed "part of the sport," a court will consider whether the contact arose from an essential and/or expected part of the sport and whether the contact occurred during the sporting match.

☐ **Which rule would Sofía use to make arguments and predictions on behalf of her client? Why?**

Sofía would use the emergent rule, because it is the current rule and provides the most complete understanding of the components of the rule. Note that the emergent rule is not particularly helpful to her client, as the injury did not occur during the game, but she will still use the current and most detailed rule.

## Module II, Chapter 7 Check Ins

### Elements and Factors

Do you think rules in criminal law are likely to contain elements or factors? Why? What about laws governing contracts? What about laws governing child custody and other family law matters? Why?

### Answer

I think criminal laws are likely to contain elements because criminal laws should be specific about precisely what is required in order to be convicted of a crime, and whatever is required should be something that is either satisfied or not, rather than a sliding scale. I think this also is true for contracts. A court would not want to recognize a contract between parties unless it is sure the parties intended that contract. Elements, rather than factors, provide this assurance.

Child custody and other family law matters are likely to be factors. Those laws likely are not amenable to have specific requirements and instead are likely matters of degree and things to consider rather than satisfy.

### Rule Type and Outline

Consider the following legal rule that governs on-street parking: "Unless deemed safe or a parking turn-out is provided, on-street parking is prohibited."

### Answer

☐ **What type of rule is this?**

It is of the "rule with an exception" type, with an either/or exception.

☐ **How would you outline this rule?**

On-street parking shall be prohibited *unless*
1. deemed safe or
2. parking turn-outs are provided.

☐ **Looking ahead, how do you think you would organize a memo that applies this rule to a client's situation?**

In terms of the memo organization, it likely will be:

I.   Describe global rule with two exceptions
II.  Analysis of exception one (element of whether "deemed safe")
III. Analysis of exception two (element of whether "parking turn-outs provided")
IV.  Conclusion

Note that this is just the overall outline. As you may be thinking, Parts II and III in particular need to be further broken down themselves because the analysis for those elements entails an IRAC discussion. Specifically, as we discuss in Module III, each element will have its own segment of discussion, including an issue roadmap paragraph, rule explanation paragraphs, and then rule application paragraphs, providing arguments for both sides. For now, though, we simply would know from outlining the rule that there will be two separate analyses in our discussion—one for each element.

## Module II, Chapter 8 Check Ins

### How a Case Processes a Rule

Recall the local ordinance that stated: "All dangerous dogs must be licensed." Recall further that that the rule broke down into two elements: (1) that the animal must be a dog; and (2) that the animal must be dangerous.

Read the following fictitious case in which this ordinance is at issue. (See page 119.) As you read, consider how this case interprets and applies the "dangerous dog" ordinance.

### *Answer*

☐ **Specifically, what law-centered interpretations emerge from this case?**

- Two-part test for global rule with elements of "dog" and "dangerous" (law-centered interpretation that confirms the two-part test we understood from the ordinance).
- For element of dangerous, must prove dog is dangerous by "clear and convincing evidence" (law-centered interpretation that provides a standard).
- To be dangerous, the dog must "pose a significant threat to the public" (law-centered interpretation that defines "dangerous").
- The breed of the dog, at least when not a stereotypically dangerous breed, does not matter (law-centered interpretation that provides a standard for "dangerous" by telling us what does not matter, that might otherwise think would matter).

☐ **What is the fact-based holding for the element at issue?**

- First ask, what is the holding? *Wilcox* held that dog is dangerous.

- Next ask, why did the court reach that holding? Because of the dog's sharp teeth and because the dog has bitten people two times, despite no need for medical attention.
- For fact-based holding you put these two together, thus telling the reader what the court held and why it so held: "When a dog has sharp teeth and has bitten people twice, even though medical care was not required either time, courts hold the dog is dangerous."
- The writer could also include that breed doesn't matter in this fact-based holding, in which case the fact-based holding would read: "When a dog not of a dangerous breed has sharp teeth and has bitten people twice, even though medical care was not required either time, courts hold the dog is dangerous."

☐ **What are the implicit guiding factors for that element?**

- The fact-based holding tells us what facts were significant to the court, namely, that the dog has sharp teeth and had bitten two people.
- From these legally significant facts, we can discern guiding factors:

| FACT | GUIDING FACTOR |
|---|---|
| Razor-sharp teeth | Dog's physical characteristics capable of causing harm |
| Bit two children | Dog's history of biting |
| No medical care required | Whether medical care required for previous bites |

☐ **Outline the rule that emerges from this case, including the global rule and the rule for the element/condition at issue.**

An animal must be licensed if:

1. The animal is a dog; and
2. The dog is dangerous. A dog is dangerous if it "poses a significant threat to the public." The breed of the dog, at least when not a stereotypically dangerous breed, does not matter. Instead, in determining the threat posed by the dog, the court considers (1) whether the dog possesses physical characteristics that are capable of causing harm; (2) the dog's history of biting; and (3) whether medical care was necessary for any previous bites.

### Framing Fact-Based Holdings

Recall that there is flexibility in how a fact-based holding is framed.

Above we noted the fact-based holding for *Purcell* could be stated as:

> Apparent authority does not exist when a person asserts control and authority over the searched bags, yet shortly thereafter the officers have reason to doubt the bags belong to her.

Yet that is not the only possible way to frame that fact-based holding. For example, it could be framed more narrowly, such as:

> Apparent authority does not exist when a person asserts control and authority over property to which she has access, yet it becomes clear that the assertion is false.

This holding is narrower in the sense that it suggests the surrounding context needs to be directly disconfirming, not merely casting doubt. Why would a lawyer want to use this narrower version of the fact-based holding? Which party/position would that narrower characterization favor?

### Answer

A lawyer would want to use the narrower version in her memorandum when she wanted to portray *Purcell* as more extreme factually and thus distinct from the client's situation, i.e., emphasizing that it is not enough to merely cast doubt on the apparent authority but rather it must directly disconfirm. That characterization would favor the prosecution, who wants to argue that *Purcell* is distinguishable because there the evidence directly disconfirmed the apparent authority whereas in this case it merely cast doubt.

## Module II, Chapter 9 Check In

### *Legal Reasoning*

Now that you have labels for the three types of legal reasoning, can you find examples in your other courses of these types of legal reasoning used either in cases or during in-class discussions?

   Why is it important to discern the legal rule before applying that rule? Put differently, would it be possible to reason by analogy without having a grasp of the legal rule? Why not?

### *Answer*

Without the legal rule, you do not have any law to apply. At most, you would just be guessing about what the law is in terms of making arguments. Reasoning by analogy requires me to compare specific facts from a precedent case to my client's situation. I would have no idea what facts were important to compare without knowing the components of the rule; e.g., the guiding factors.

## Module II, Chapter 10 Check In

### *Rule Mastery and Rule-Based Reasoning*

Imagine that your client, Sandra, has been sued by a neighbor who tripped and fell on her sidewalk. In his lawsuit, the neighbor claims that he sustained injuries caused by Sandra's dog. Specifically, the neighbor alleges he was walking on the sidewalk past Sandra's fenced yard, when Sandra's large Mastiff dog began barking wildly and lunging at the fence. The neighbor claims he was so startled by the dog's behavior that he tripped and fell on the sidewalk.

   You have found the rule that addresses the owner's potential liability, and one condition of that rule is that the plaintiff *must prove* by clear and convincing evidence that the dog has engaged in threatening behavior. You also found a case that interprets that rule that says that in determining whether a dog has engaged in threatening behavior, courts consider the dog's overt actions and physical characteristics.

*Answer*

☐ **First, describe what type of global rule this is. Is the condition of whether a dog has engaged in threatening behavior an element or a factor? How do you know this?**

We know this global rule contains elements because it says "must prove," which tells me that this is a requirement without which the result (here, owner liability) will not occur.

☐ **Second, state the rule for the condition at issue. What are its components: definitions/standards/guiding factors?**

Rule for condition/element of "the dog engaged in threatening behavior":

The plaintiff must prove by **clear and convincing evidence** (this is a standard) that the defendant's dog engaged in threatening behavior. In determining whether a dog has engaged in threatening behavior, courts consider **the dog's overt actions directed at the plaintiff and the dog's physical characteristics** (these are guiding factors).

☐ **Finally, using the rule for the condition that you have discerned, make one or more rule-based reasoning arguments. For example, what rule-based reasoning argument could the plaintiff/neighbor make regarding the dog's overt actions? What rule-based reasoning argument could the defendant/owner make about the dog's overt actions? Similarly, what rule-based reasoning arguments could each party make regarding the dog's physical characteristics?**

Defendant's rule-based argument about GF of overt action: Here, the dog's overt actions do not suggest a threat because they were not directed at the plaintiff. The dog did what dogs do when people pass by—barked and lunged at the fence—and, given the barrier of the fence, the dog could not possibly have taken any overt action directed at the plaintiff.

Plaintiff's rule-based argument about GF of overt action: Nonetheless, the plaintiff will contend the dog took overt actions directed at him. Namely, the dog's barking and lunging at the fence were in direct response to the plaintiff passing by and thus were directly aimed at the plaintiff, showing those actions were overtly directed at the plaintiff.

Defendant's rule-based argument about GF of physical characteristics: The dog's physical characteristics do not suggest any threat to the plaintiff. Again, because there was a fence that separated the plaintiff and the dog, no physical characteristic of the dog could have posed any threat.

Plaintiff's rule-based argument about GF of physical characteristics: Even so, the plaintiff will argue that the dog's physical characteristics did pose a threat. As a Mastiff, the dog was very large and imposing, and thus its physical characteristics were imposing and threatening to the plaintiff, notwithstanding the fence between them.

## Module II, Chapter 11 Check In

*Making Analogical Arguments*

Recall the check-in problem from Chapter 10 in which Sandra was being sued by a neighbor for injuries he claims to have sustained when Sandra's dog barked and lunged at the fence. Further recall that one condition of the rule is that the plaintiff must prove by clear and convincing evidence the dog has engaged in threatening behavior and that in determining whether a dog has engaged in threatening behavior, courts consider the dog's overt actions toward the plaintiff and the dog's physical characteristics.

You have now located an additional case, *Davenport v. Dearfield*, in which the court held that a Great Dane that startled a neighbor who approached the house when the dog was sleeping on a front porch did not engage in threatening behavior.

What analogical arguments can you make on behalf of the client? What analogical arguments can you make on behalf of the neighbor? Which argument do you find most compelling, and why?

*Answer*

Client's analogical arguments for two guiding factors: Like the dog in *Davenport v. Dearfield* that merely laid on the porch, here the dog did not overtly act toward the plaintiff but instead was acting entirely toward the fence, not a person. Indeed because of that fence between the dog and the plaintiff, there existed a barrier that made harm even less likely than the situation in *Dearfield*.

Also, just as the Great Dane's physical characteristics did not pose a threat in *Dearfield*, neither did the Mastiff's physical characteristics in the present case. The Mastiff, while large and strong like the Great Dane, had no specific characteristic that enhanced the threat from any overt actions.

Plaintiff's analogical arguments for two guiding factors: Unlike the dog in *Dearfield* that was simply laying on a porch fast asleep and thus engaged in no act, here the dog engaged in the overt act of lunging and barking directly toward and in response to the plaintiff. Also, unlike the Great Dane whose physical characteristics posed no threat in *Dearfield*, here the dog in question possessed physical characteristics that posed a threat because of the dog's behaviors. While in *Dearfield* the size and strength of the Great Dane was not significant because the dog was sleeping, in the present case the dog was wide awake and aggressively lunging toward the fence. Thus, the dog's size and strength greatly increased the threat posed to the plaintiff because of what harm the dog could have inflicted if it got through or over the fence.

## Module II, Chapter 12 Check In

### *Making Policy-Based Arguments*

Recall the check-in problem from Chapters 10 and 11 in which a neighbor sued a dog's owner for injuries he sustained when the dog barked and lunged at him. Further recall that one condition of the rule is that the plaintiff must prove the dog has engaged in threatening behavior and that in determining whether a dog has engaged in threatening behavior, courts consider the dog's overt actions toward the plaintiff and the dog's physical characteristics.

Now assume you have found a case that discusses the policy behind this rule of owner's liability. In that case, the court explains, "Dog owners must be held responsible for the aggressive acts of their dogs in order to provide an incentive for owners to control their dogs. At the same time, a dog's owner cannot control the reactions of other people to their dog, and as such should not be held responsible for a person's overreaction to natural dog behavior."

Using the policies set forth above: (1) What policy-based arguments might the owner make? (2) What policy-based arguments might the neighbor-plaintiff make?

### *Answer*

Defendant dog owner's policy-based argument: Holding the defendant dog owner liable in this case would contravene this ordinance's purpose. That purpose of the ordinance is to hold owners liable for aggressive acts but not for "a person's overreaction to natural dog behavior." CITE CASE. That purpose squarely applies in the present case, in which the plaintiff had an "overreaction to a natural dog behavior," namely, an overreaction to a dog barking and lunging at the fence.

Plaintiff's policy-based argument: Holding the defendant dog owner liable for her dog's actions would serve the ordinance's purpose, which is to "hold owners liable for their dog's aggressive acts" that are under their "control." CITE. The aggressive acts of a Mastiff lunging and barking merely because a person is passing by is something the owner could have, but did not, control.

## Module III, Chapter 14 Check In

### *Large-Scale Organization*

Map out the large-scale organization for the Discussion of a memo that involves the following global rule of law for the crime of grand larceny. Assume all conditions are issues.

To prove a defendant committed grand larceny, the State must prove: (1) The wrongful taking, obtaining, or withholding; (2) Of someone else's property; (3) With the intent to either deprive the owner of the property or enrich someone else.

### Answer

Global Roadmap: Lay out global rule for grand larceny: three conditions/all issues

Segment 1: Wrongful taking, obtaining, or withholding
> Issue Roadmap (wrongful taking, obtaining, or withholding)
> Rule Explanation (wrongful taking, obtaining, or withholding)
> Rule Application (wrongful taking, obtaining, or withholding)

Segment 2: Of someone else's property
> Issue Roadmap (of someone else's property)
> Rule Explanation (of someone else's property)
> Rule Application (of someone else's property)

Segment 3: With the intent to either deprive the owner of the property or enrich someone else
> Issue Roadmap (intent)
> Rule Explanation (intent)
> Rule Application (intent)

Global Conclusion

## Module III, Chapter 15 Check In

### Creating an Annotated Outline

Using material from the worksheet above (see page 189), create an annotated outline for the second issue in The Smell Shoppe hypothetical.

### Outline for Issue 2

ISSUE ROADMAP: Issue 2
Issue/Condition to Note in Topic Sentence: The defendant's intentional and unjustified interference that prevents the realization of the business expectancy.

Issue/Condition Rule of Law: In assessing Mr. Green's intentional and unjustified interference that prevents the realization of the business expectancy, the court will consider the defendant's conduct in allowing customers to place orders under a mistaken belief, the defendant's truthfulness to the customers regarding an affiliation with the plaintiff's business, and the content of any of the defendant's advertisement.

Rule Proof: A plaintiff will be successful in demonstrating that it was the defendant's intentional and unjustified interference that prevented the realization of business expectancy when the defendant allows customers to place orders at its business while being dishonest with the customers when they inquire about an affiliation with the plaintiff's store, and the defendant represented that affiliation through advertising.

Prediction: Arnold will not prevail on this issue.

RULE EXPLANATION

Case facts from *Chicago's Pizza*, including the following: Customers calling/order from the defendant store, intending to do business with the plaintiff store; defendant lied to customers regarding its affiliation with the plaintiff stores; defendant's advertisements represented that it had several locations, when in fact it just had the one. Holding and Rationale from *Chicago's Pizza*: Held in favor of plaintiff because defendant was knowingly dishonest in its engagement with customers.

RULE APPLICATION

Comparisons of the following facts on the basis of the identified guiding factors:

| GUIDING FACTOR (INCLUDE WHY THIS GUIDING FACTOR IS IMPORTANT) | *CHICAGO'S PIZZA* FACTS | THE SMELL SHOPPE FACTS | COMPARISON |
|---|---|---|---|
| The defendant allowing customers to place orders under a mistaken belief. | Customers calling/ordering from the defendant's store, intending to do business with the plaintiff's store | Customers came to shop at Green's store possibly believing it was the "newest location;" Green allowed them to place orders | The plaintiff in *Chicago's Pizza* has a clearer argument for this guiding factor. It might be a stretch to infer that Green allowed the customers to place orders after knowing for certain that the customers believed they were doing business with Arnold |

| GUIDING FACTOR (INCLUDE WHY THIS GUIDING FACTOR IS IMPORTANT) | *CHICAGO'S PIZZA* FACTS | THE SMELL SHOPPE FACTS | COMPARISON |
|---|---|---|---|
| The defendant's truthfulness to the customers regarding an affiliation with the plaintiff's business | Defendant lied to customers regarding its affiliation with the plaintiff's stores | Green was honest about his affiliation when he received the phone call inquiring | The defendant in *Chicago's Pizza* was explicitly untruthful, whereas Green was honest |
| The content of the defendant's advertisements | Defendant's advertisements represented that it had several locations, when it fact it just had the one | Green created coupons stating "Our Newest Location," even though he just had one location | The defendant's advertisements in *Chicago's Pizza* were arguably more misleading |

## Module III, Chapter 16 Check In

### *Roadmap Paragraphs*

Recall the second contested issue in the tortious interference with business expectancy problem: intentional and unjustified interference that prevented the realization of business expectancy. Assume you characterized the guiding factors in the manner below:

> In assessing this element, the court will consider orders, information about customers, information about business owners, truthful or misleading statements, and advertisements.

Can you identify any problems with how you characterized those guiding factors? Consider what might be unclear to the reader in terms of the labels/descriptions of these guiding factors.

### *Answer*

> The guiding factors lack clarity. For example, it is not clear who made orders or what type of information about customers is important. It is also unclear who must make misleading statements or whose advertisements might be the basis of the court's analysis. It is also unclear how these generalized, guiding factors relate to the issue of intentional and unjustified interference.

> Consider the following issue roadmap for the reasonable expectancy element discussed above. Pay particular attention to the fact-based holding content. Does it actually provide a fact-based holding?

Or does its simply repeat, albeit in slightly different words, the rule for that condition?

> The court will first consider whether Mr. Arnold possessed a reasonable expectancy of entering into a valid business relationship. *Id.* In assessing whether Mr. Arnold possessed this expectancy, the court will consider the specific contemplation of customers and the customers' belief that they were doing business with the Mr. Arnold. *Id.* 993-94. **A plaintiff will need to show the specific contemplation of customers and the customers' belief they were doing business in order to prove that the plaintiff possessed a reasonable expectancy.** *Id.* Because Mr. Arnold spoke to several people regarding their experiences while shopping at Mr. Green's candle store who expressed the belief that they were shopping at Mr. Arnold's store, he will likely prevail on this element.

### Answer

Here, the rule proof, in bold above, remains at the generalized level of the guiding factors. It would be improved by using a fact-based holding that grounds the generalized guiding factors in specific facts from the case. So, recall what happened in *Chicago's Pizza*—customers called the defendant's store and expressed the belief that they were doing business with the plaintiff. Use those specific facts for rule proof: A plaintiff will be found to have possessed a reasonable expectancy of entering into a valid business relationship when it can be demonstrated that specific customers called the defendant's store with the belief that they were doing business with the plaintiff.

In the paragraph below, consider the effectiveness of *where* the writer has included this information about the standard for this condition.

> The court will first consider whether Mr. Arnold possessed a reasonable expectancy of entering into a valid business relationship. *Id.* In assessing whether Mr. Arnold possessed this expectancy, the court will consider the specific contemplation of customers and the customers' belief that they were doing business with the Mr. Arnold. *Id.* 993-94. A plaintiff will be found to have possessed a reasonable expectancy of entering into a valid business relationship when it can be demonstrated that specific customers called the defendant's store with the belief that they were doing business with the plaintiff. *Id.* at 994. **The reasonableness of the expectancy is judged by an objective standard.** *Id.* Because Mr. Arnold spoke to several people regarding their experiences while shopping at Mr. Green's candle store who expressed the belief that they were shopping at Mr. Arnold's store, he will likely prevail on this element.

How does the placement of the standard affect your understanding of the rule? Where might you move it to improve clarity?

### Answer

This location, in bold above, is out of place. This is part of the rule, so it should appear before the fact-based holding. In addition, it is a more general part of the rule than the sentence that provides the guiding factors and should therefore precede that sentence. Thus, we would want to move the sentence from its above location to the second sentence in the paragraph.

## Module III, Chapter 17 Check In

### Rule Explanation Paragraph

For each rule explanation paragraph below, consider whether the writer has included the necessary ingredients. What ingredients are missing ingredients? How does that affect the impact of the rule explanation paragraph?

### Answer

- Example 1: The *Wilson* court held that no satisfactory explanation existed for the delay in sealing the evidence. *Wilson*, 212 F.3d. 212 (8th Cir. 2009). The court referenced numerous reasons in reaching this conclusion. *Id.* at 215.

  Has the holding but that's it. Needs a framing sentence, detailed discussion of the facts (not simply a vague reference to "the numerous reasons"), and court's reasoning.

  Impact: The reader does not have sufficient information to understand why the court held as it did; reader has no basis to make analogical arguments; and, in general, the reader does not have any information other than what the court held.

- Example 2: In *U.S. v. Wilson*, 212 F.3d. 212 (8th Cir. 2009), the Eighth Circuit held that there was no satisfactory explanation for the delay in sealing the wiretap evidence. Specifically, the Court rejected the government's argument that the change in personnel in its regional wiretap unit justified the delay. *Id.* at 215. When Jim Smiley took over for Sally Jamal there was an almost two-day period in which no evidence that came in was sealed. *Id.*

  This paragraph is better because it has the facts as well as the holding. But it still lacks a framing sentence and it does not include the court's reasoning.

  Impact: Without a framing sentence, the reader does not know what the case stands for and thus lacks a framework for how the case is important and why it is included; without reasoning the reader also does not fully understand why these facts mattered to the court. There is a difference between knowing which facts were significant to the court and knowing *why* those facts were significant.

- Example 3: When the length of the delay is significant, and the cause of delay is within the government's control, courts hold there is no satisfactory explanation. In *U.S. v. Wilson*, 212 F.3d. 212 (8th Cir. 2009), the government failed to seal wiretap evidence in question for almost two days after it was intercepted. *Id.* at 214. During that two-day period, a new lead technician took over in the regional wiretap unit to which the evidence was delivered. *Id.* While the change in personnel was planned, it nonetheless led to some delays across the board in sealing evidence. *Id.* The Eighth Circuit held there was no satisfactory explanation for the delay in sealing the evidence. *Id.* at 215. The Court squarely rejected the government's argument that the change in personnel in its regional wiretap unit justified the delay. *Id.* Instead, the Court reasoned that a delay of that length and under those circumstances raises precisely the kind of suspicion that the statute seeks to avoid. *Id.* at 216. The Court pointed out that the change in personnel here was neither unusual nor unanticipated, and it was not grounds for a government unit to cease to perform its critical role. *Id.*

Ah, this RE paragraph is effective and includes all of the checklist items. Starts with a framing statement, provides relevant facts, provides the explicit holding for this issue, and provides helpful reasoning.

Impact: The reader starts with a solid framework from the framing sentence, followed by the information needed in the expected order. This rule explanation paragraph thus provides an effective bridge between the issue roadmap and the rule application. It reinforces the rule and the rule proof from the issue roadmap by showing the rule's prior application. And it provides a solid foundation for the writer to make detailed and meaningful analogical arguments in the rule application.

## Module III, Chapter 18 Check In

### Identifying and Assessing Discussion Ingredients

For each excerpt below, answer the following questions related to the wiretap hypothetical:

### Answer

☐ In what component of the memo (e.g., issue roadmap, rule explanation, rule application) would you expect to see the following material?

All of these paragraphs are RA paragraphs. We know that because they are making arguments about our client's case.

☐ **For that particular memo component, has the writer incorporated sufficient detail and presented the material effectively? Why?**

> **Excerpt 1:** Like *Liberte*, the delay in sealing the evidence in this case was due to a mistake. *Id.*

**Excerpt 1:** Whoa – how is this "like *Liberte*"? Need to make an explicit comparison.

Also, vague reference to "due to a mistake" is unclear. Is this an argument? If so, need to make it an argument by stating why this matters; be explicit about why it is significant that the delay is "due to a mistake."

> **Excerpt 2:** In *Liberte*, the investigator forgot to submit the evidence right away to be sealed. *Id.* Here, the personnel in the lab changed and caused the delay.

**Excerpt 2:** Better than Excerpt 1 because at least it includes the significant facts from *Liberte*, which helps advance the argument. But this is classic (and undesirable) "reasoning by proximity"—rather than explicitly comparing the facts, the writer has simply put them side by side, expecting the reader to not only connect the dots but also to understand the legal significance once she does so.

> **Excerpt 3:** Like the delay in *Liberte* which occurred because of the investigator's forgetfulness, here too the delay was caused simply by human error. *Id.* Specifically, there was miscommunication between intake personnel at the lab and the technical staff. While unfortunate, such miscommunication is not uncommon in a busy work unit and cannot be considered unusual.

**Excerpt 3:** This is better because it provides more detail about how our client's case is similar to the precedent. But it still isn't explicit about why this comparison is legally significant (i.e., unlike Excerpt 4 doesn't say significant because it is a "common and foreseeable error" not unlike forgetfulness). Without that tether, the argument is incomplete because it is not expressly tied to the legal rule

> **Excerpt 4:** Like the delay in *Liberte*, which occurred because of the investigator's forgetfulness, the defendant will assert that the delay in this case was similarly caused simply by human error. *Id.* Specifically, the defendant will emphasize that there was miscommunication between intake personnel at the lab and the technical staff, a common and foreseeable error not unlike forgetfulness. *Id.* While unfortunate, such miscommunication is not uncommon in a busy work unit, cannot be considered unusual, and, like the insufficient excuse for delay offered in *Liberte*, should similarly preclude use of the evidence here. *Id.*

**Excerpt 4:** This is even better yet. Not only is there a detailed comparison, the significance of that comparison is explicit—namely, the commonality is that they both are foreseeable. So, this excerpt makes clear that it is legally significant if the cause of the delay is an issue that was foreseeable.

> **Excerpt 5:** Like the delay in *Liberte*, which occurred because of the investigator's forgetfulness, the defendant will assert that the delay in this case was similarly caused simply by human error. *Id.* Specifically, the defendant will emphasize that there was miscommunication between intake personnel at the lab and the technical staff, a common and foreseeable error not unlike forgetfulness. *Id.* While unfortunate, such miscommunication is not uncommon in a busy work unit, cannot be considered unusual and, like the insufficient excuse for delay offered in *Liberte*, should similarly preclude use of the evidence here. *Id.*
>
> In contrast, the State will assert that the forgetfulness associated with the delay in *Liberte* was entirely inexcusable and a failure to demonstrate "reasonable diligence." *Id.* In contrast, the miscommunication, while unfortunate, cannot be equated with the inattention to detail by the government in *Liberte* and should excuse the failure to seal in this case. *Id.*

**Excerpt 5:** This example is the best of the excerpts and is highly effective. Not only does it make a strong argument (see above), it also includes a counterargument.

## Module IV, Chapter 21 Check Ins

### Selecting Cases for Analogical Arguments

Recall the Warrantless Bomb Search hypothetical where you represent the federal government, which wants to show that its search and seizure of drugs did not violate the Fourth Amendment. The federal agent found the drugs when searching a shipping container, after the government received a tip that this container contained a bomb inside. Further, the federal agent's bomb-sniffing dog confirmed that tip when the dog "hit" on the container as well (meaning the dog believed it contained bomb materials).

You have researched and located four potential cases that address the condition of "whether there is a risk of danger to the public."

Case A: The court held there was a risk of danger to the public when an officer arrived at a home in response to a 911 call in which a man claimed he was suicidal and planned to detonate a bomb to blow up himself, his house, and anything else nearby. Before entering the home, the officer observed through the window that the man was wearing a bomb and holding a device that would trigger the bomb.

Case B: The court held there was no risk of danger to the public when the police questioned a man sitting on a park bench with a backpack beside him. When the man refused to open the bag or tell the police what was in it, the police searched the bag, which contained illegal drugs and a knife.

Case C: The court held there was a risk of danger to the public when the police searched the trunk of the defendant's car when he arrived at work. The police were on site in the workplace parking lot to question the defendant because he had made threats in his workplace. Among these threats, the man had told co-workers the day before that "he always 'packed heat' in his car" and that "people were going to be sorry." When questioning the defendant, the police noticed that the defendant was acting erratically, being evasive, and kept shifting to look at the trunk when asked if he had any weapons on him or in the vehicle.

Case D: The court held there was no risk of danger to the public when the police searched a defendant's duffel bag, based solely on a tip from the defendant's friend that the defendant frequently carried illegal assault weapons, but with no confirmation on site of what may have been inside the duffel bag.

### Answer

☐ *Which cases do you think would be the most useful for making analogical arguments? Why?*

Least useful cases: Case A and B—both extreme facts, where very clearly the condition either was or was not satisfied.

Most useful cases: Cases C and D.

C is the closest case factually in which the court held there was a risk.

D is the closest case factually in which the court held there was not a risk. These cases are not as extreme as the fact patterns in Cases A and B, and thus will be most useful for helping us predict what the court will do given the facts of our client's situation.

### More Practice with Selecting Cases for Analogical Arguments

Assume your client has been sued for misappropriation of its competitor's trade secret. Your client's sales manager acknowledges using the competitor's unique marketing approach after learning about it at the competitor's annual stockholders' meeting. You have located the following cases:

Case A: A company is sued for using its competitor's "secret" ingredient of anise seasoning in its pizza sauce. The company's top chef discovered the anise seasoning in the competitor's sauce by tasting the sauce and noting the distinct anise flavor. The company had not ever released the information but would share it with curious customers who specifically requested it. The court held the sauce recipe with anise was not a secret.

Case B: A company is sued for using its competitor's "secret" formula for identifying lucrative businesses to purchase. The company acknowledges using the formula but says that it learned the formula from its competitor's website on the page entitled "What Sets Us Apart." The court held the formula at issue was not a secret.

Case C: A company is sued for using its competitor's "secret" recipe for a house salad dressing. The company found a copy of the recipe posted anonymously on the Internet. The competitor explains that the recipe is only made known to employees of the company. The court held the recipe was secret.

Case D: A company is sued for using its competitor's unique manufacturing process. The company learned about the process through its employee who formerly worked as an engineer for the competitor. The competitor says the process is only known by select employees, who sign agreements acknowledging it is proprietary. The court held the manufacturing process was secret.

*Answer*

☐ **Which cases would be most predictive for purposes of making analogical arguments? Why?**

Secret ←- Case D ---  Case C ------| | | |--- Case A----Case B ---→ Not Secret

**Case D** is very extreme. The competitor guarded the information, and the only way it was obtained by the company was by hiring the competitor's former employee. It would be a stretch for either party in our case to argue that the current case is similar to Case D.

**Case C** is closer factually. There the facts are mixed with some suggesting secrecy and others suggesting a lack of protection for the information as secret. Thus, this case would serve a helpful predictive function; the competitor could argue that the level of secrecy here is similar to that deemed to be protected as secret in Case C.

At the other end of the spectrum, **Case B** is also extreme and not as similar factually as other cases. The competitor was very public with the information, including publishing it on its web page for the world to access. It would be a stretch to argue that the information provided only to stockholders is non-secretive in the same way.

**Case A** is closer factually to the present case. There the company did share the information, albeit to a limited audience. Thus, Case A is a good case to use to make analogical arguments about why the information at issue in this case is not secret.

Note that we selected the cases that were *most predictive* for purposes of making analogical arguments. That means we want the cases that are closer to our client's situation as these similar cases will help us make a useful prediction as to how a court may rule. Thus, while Case D would be more easily distinguishable from our client's situation than Case C (and thus superficially seems helpful to our client), Case D is not helpful because it is not the case on which the opposing party will rely in making a counterargument. The opposing party will rely on Case C. Therefore, because our memo is objective and predictive, we need to include that likely argument, as well as our prediction on how a court will rule on the parties' likely arguments on the issue of secrecy.

Now that you have selected the most useful cases, let's get more practice with discerning guiding factors. Based upon the facts of these four cases, what do you think are the implicit guiding factors for the element of whether the confinement was secret? While we know from Chapter 8 that the labels and breakdown of implicit guiding factors is flexible, the following breakdown provides an effective example of the implicit guiding factors a lawyer might discern based upon the facts of the selected cases.

GF 1: Availability of the information to persons outside the company

GF 2: Whether the information was independently discoverable without improper actions

GF 3: Steps taken to protect the information alleged to be secret

## Module IV, Chapter 23 Check In

*Rule Explanation and Rule Application Organization*

*Answer*

☐ In the outline of a Discussion (partially reprinted here), what organizational approach has the writer used for the rule explanation section? How can you tell?

- Issue 1 Roadmap (includes synthesized rule of law for issue 1)
- Issue 1 Rule Explanation Section
  - RE paragraph for Case B (will reference guiding factors 1 and 2)
  - RE paragraph for Case C (will reference guiding factor 1)
  - RE paragraph for Case A (will reference guiding factor 2)

- Issue 2 Rule Application Section
  - Defendant's Arguments (comparisons and distinctions to guiding factors 1, 2, and 3 using Cases A, B, and C)
  - Prosecution's Arguments (comparisons and distinctions to guiding factors 1, 2, and 3 using Cases A, B, and C)

The writer has used the organizing by the cases approach. We know this because the rule explanation section discusses the cases separately and successively rather than blending them together by guiding factors.

☐ **What organizational approach has the writer used for the rule application section? How can you tell?**

The writer has used the party/position approach. We know this because the rule application is organized around the parties' arguments, not around the guiding factors.

## Module IV, Chapter 25 Check In

### Reviewing Rule Explanation Sections

Review the multiple authority memos in Appendix B. The Smell Shoppe memo organizes the rule explanation section using the guiding factors approach, whereas the Warrantless Bomb Search memo uses the cases approach. For each memo:

- First, create an outline of the rule explanation section.
- Next, review the framing sentences and transitions. How do these features assist the reader in digesting the information that follows?

### Answer

The Smell Shoppe Memo

Outline of RE Section for First Issue (Smell Shoppe):

RE (GF 1 & 2, mult cases) +
RE (GF 2, mult cases) –
RE (GF 3, mult cases) +

The transition at the start of the second RE paragraph ("in contrast") tells me that this paragraph is discussing a case or cases in which a result was reached that was opposite to that discussed immediately above. Likewise, the transition at the start of the third RE paragraph ("in addition") tells me that paragraph discusses results along the same lines as in the immediately preceding paragraph.

The Warrantless Bomb Search Memo

Outline of RE section:

> RE (Henry) (GF 1 & 2) +
> RE (Johnson (GF 1) –
> RE (Purcell (GF 2) –

The transition at the start of the second RE paragraph ("on the contrary") tells me that this holding is going to be the opposite of that which was discussed immediately above. The transition at the start of the third paragraph ("similarly") tells me that this holding is going to be the same as that which was discussed immediately above. These transitions help me create boxes in my brain for each of these cases consistent with the above outline.

In addition to the transitions, for both sample memos, each of the framing sentences indicates the scope of that paragraph, i.e., which guiding factors are addressed in that paragraph.

## Module IV, Chapter 26 Check In

### *Comparing Rule Application Paragraphs*

Read the following two examples of rule application paragraphs. Consider:

- Which has a stronger topic statement? Why is it stronger?
- Which has a stronger argument? What makes it more effective?
- How are the multiple authorities used in the examples? Which is more effective and why?
- Did you notice any other features that made one version more effective than the others?

#### Example 1
Jazz has bitten at least one person who needed emergency medical attention. In *Wilcox*, the dog had bitten two children, whereas in *Feisty Schnauzer Owner*, the dog had no bite history. Jazz is more like the dog in *Wilcox*.

#### Example 2
First, Jazz has a demonstrated history of biting. Just as the *Wilcox* dog had bitten two children on two separate occasions, Jazz is known to have bitten at least one person. *See* 300 N.W.2d at 334. Indeed, the person bitten by Jazz required emergency medical attention, suggesting a perhaps even greater danger than that posed by the dog in *Wilcox*, who was deemed dangerous despite the fact that his bite victims did not require any kind of medical care. *See id.* at 335. Jazz is unlike the dog

in *Feisty Schnauzer Owner*, who was not deemed dangerous because it had no bite history. *See* 402 N.W.2d at 122.

### Answer

☐ **Which has a stronger topic statement? Why is it stronger?**

Example 2 has a stronger topic sentence. It identifies the topic (history of biting). It also accurately conveys the scope of the paragraph, whereas the narrow recitation of the facts in Example 1 does not.

☐ **Which has a stronger argument? What makes it more effective?**

Example 2 has a stronger argument. In addition to the better topic sentence, it keeps the focus on the client's situation, by comparing the precedents to the client's case, not to each other. Also, the analogical arguments make detailed comparisons of the facts rather than "reasoning by proximity." Overall these things make it more compelling and effective in making the writer's point.

☐ **How are the multiple authorities used in the examples? Which is more effective and why?**

As noted above, rather than comparing the multiple authorities to each other, the writer in the second example compares them to the client's situation. Because the rule application is where we make arguments about the client's situation that, by definition, means that all arguments should focus on the client.

In addition, in the second example the writer uses analogical reasoning to suggest that the facts of the client's case are even more compelling than those of the precedent. That can be an effective technique because it shows that if the facts of the precedent were "enough," then the even stronger facts in the client's situation make this a no-brainer. In this instance, that may not be what the clients wants to hear, but whether it makes the other side's argument or the client's argument, a predictive memo should provide objective advice to the client.

☐ **What other improvements did you notice?**

It includes citations. Also, the facts are tied to the reasoning; i.e., the need for medical attention is tied back to the threat posed.

## Module V, Chapter 30 Check In

### Effective Emails

Consider the following email message. In what ways does it comport with the principles above? In what ways does it fall short? Revise the message to improve its effectiveness.

From:       Aliyah.Alexander@LawFirm.Com
To:         Michael.Zachary@LawFirm.Com
Cc:         EveryOtherAttorney@LawFirm.Com
Subject:    As Discussed

Hey Man,

So glad we bumped into each other yesterday—always nice to see you and happy to get an interesting research project. So, I took a quick look into that matter you asked about, and I've got some top notch stuff for you!!

Unfortunately, sweet little Bootsie will probably be found to be dangerous.

These are the cases I looked at: Davenport v. Dearfield. Court held that a Great Dane that startled a neighbor who approached the house when the dog was sleeping on a front porch did not engage in threatening behavior. Arco v. Anderson. A dog bit a guest who was visiting her owner's home. The dog was eating from her dinner bowl when the guest approached and put his hand directly in the dog's bowl. The court held the dog was not dangerous. Bustillo v. Baxter. A mini dachshund left his porch to chase a jogger. He bared his teeth and growled at the runner but did not bite her. The court held the dog was dangerous. Cantwell v. Chen. A dog got loose in the neighborhood. While loose, she approached and bit five different people, two of whom required emergency care. She had previously gotten loose and bitten one person. The court held the dog was dangerous. Davis v. Donaghey. A dog in a fenced-in backyard was known to bark furiously at people who passed by. The dog never bit anyone or made physical contact of any kind, but did bare her teeth and growl at the passersby. The court held the dog was not dangerous.

Like we discussed, the opposing party will have to prove by clear and convincing evidence that our client's dog, Bootsie, has engaged in threatening behavior. For that, courts consider the dog's overt actions and physical characteristics. Bootsie ran into the neighbor's yard, barking and growling at the plaintiff's child, who was sitting in the grass. The court will likely find these overt and provoking acts, as they did with Bustillo and Cantwell, rather than finding it not dangerous, like they did with Davenport, Arco and Davis. Just check the attached memo for complete details.

Hit me up if you need anything else! Or if you "need" someone to catch the next Pirates game with you—I've heard you have some sweet season tickets!!

### Answer

The above email provides an answer up front. It also closes with an invitation to conduct further research as necessary, albeit an inappropriately informal close. It uses a sans serif font and has some white space for readability, but also includes some very dense paragraphs. In most other ways, it could be improved. Below is a sample revised version, together with notes on what make the revisions more effective.

From:     Aliyah.Alexander@LawFirm.Com
To:       Michael.Zachary@LawFirm.Com
Cc:

Subject: Hurley – Dangerous Dog – Threatening Overt Actions

Hi, Michael:

**Request:** In the Hurley matter, you asked whether the overt actions of our client's dog, Bootsie, will likely lead the court to determine that she engaged in threatening behavior.

Yes, the court will likely find Bootsie's overt actions threatening and declare her dangerous. As requested, this analysis focuses on the element of whether Bootsie engaged in threatening behavior, as evidenced by her overt actions.

**Analysis:** The court will most likely follow the ruling in *Bustillo v. Baxter* 26 H.3d 274 (Hyp. App. Ct. 2011), where a mini dachshund who chased, bared his teeth, and growled at a jogger, was found dangerous. Bootsie exhibited similar overt and threatening actions by running directly up to the plaintiff's child and loudly barking and growling at her. Bootsie's behavior is arguably more threatening because she approached the child who was sitting in the grass in her own yard, rather than chasing someone who was running on a public street.

In contrast, the facts in the closest ruling where the court found the dog not dangerous, *Davis v. Donaghey* 56 H.3d 312 (Hyp. App. Ct. 2017), can still be easily distinguished. Although the dog in that case did exhibit the overt action of baring her teeth, growling, and barking furiously at passersby, the dog did not directly run up to anyone. Moreover, the dog was in a fenced-in backyard, and, as such, considerably less threatening.

I have attached the complete memo for your review.

Please let me know if you can help further on this or any other matter.

---

The cc line is now blank, as there is likely no need to copy all other attorneys in the firm on this message.

A much more specific subject line will help the recipient know what your message will discuss and find the email again in the future.

The salutation is more formal.

The brief recap of the matter investigated provides context to the supervising attorney, rather than forcing him to remember how he presented the legal issue to investigate. Providing this information up front also makes it easier for others to understand the message if it is later shared with them.

The use of bold headings to distinguish different parts of the email make it easier to navigate. In addition, the paragraphs are kept fairly short with white space in between to aid readability.)

Aliyah gives her bottom-line prediction up front. She explicitly acknowledges the aspect of the rule of law the supervising attorney asked her to explore.

Rather than recapping the facts of four cases, the email now focuses only on the two most relevant cases, briefly explaining why, in this instance, the court is more likely to follow one than the other.

It is customary and appropriate to offer further assistance.

Sincerely,

Aliyah Alexander
Law Clerk, García, Bengston, & Locke
555-555-5555

The referral to the ——— This email and any attached documents contains informa-
attachment and request to tion from the law firm of García, Bengston & Locke, which may be
indicate whether further confidential and/or legally privileged. These materials are intended
assistance is needed are only for the personal and confidential use of the addressee identi-
phrased vmore professionally. fied above. If you are not the intended recipient or an agent respon-
A signature is provided with sible for delivering these materials to the intended recipient, you are
name, title, contact and the hereby notified that any review, disclosure, copying, distribution or
firm's legal disclaimer. the taking of any action in reliance on the contents of this transmitted information is strictly prohibited. If you have received this email
in error, please immediately notify the sender of this message.

## Module V, Chapter 31 Check In

### *Creating Talking Points*

Create talking points for The Smell Shoppe multiple authorities memorandum in Appendix B. After you have done so, use these talking
points to give an oral recap of your analysis as if you were at a meeting
with the assigning attorney. This is a simulation you can do on your
own, simply for practice.

### *Answer*

☐ *What legal question (claim or charge) did you explore?*

Q is whether Arnold can show tortious interference with business
expectancy against Mr. Green

☐ *What is the global rule of law for that claim or charge?*

To prove tortious interference with business expectancy, the plaintiff
must show:

"(1) [the plaintiff's] reasonable expectancy of entering into a valid
business relationship;
(2) the defendant's knowledge of the expectancy;
(3) the defendant's intentional and unjustified interference that prevents the realization of business expectancy; and
(4) damages resulting from the interference."

☐ *What are the main takeaways?*

- Mr. Arnold likely cannot prove tortious interference.
- Why?

  - Can show that he possessed a reasonable expectancy of entering into a valid business relationship
  - But cannot show Mr. Green's "intentional and unjustified interference" caused him to lose customers

☐ *What is your support for the main takeaways?*

- Can prove reasonable expectancy—testimony of his usual customers will show
- But cannot prove "intentional and unjustified interference" because likely cannot show Mr. Green was dishonest—he was not clearly untruthful

☐ *Were there any gaps in your analysis?*

- Need to get more information from customers
- Also need to determine what Mr. Green will say is his legitimate reason for his advertising

☐ *What challenges do you see going forward?*
Unless we can find facts that prove Mr. Green was deliberately being misleading (simultaneous emails? Testimony from others even if not Mr. Green about his intentions?) it will be hard to show he was "unjustified" in his advertisement.

# U.S. v. Purcell (modified)

Note: This is not the published opinion; the textbook authors have modified the opinion for purposes of illustrating key concepts. Please use this modified version for all exercises in this textbook.

526 F.3d 953

United States Court of Appeals,

Sixth Circuit.

UNITED STATES of America, Plaintiff-

Appellant,

v.

Frederick PURCELL, Jr., Defendant-Appellee.

No. 07-5517.

|

Argued: March 13, 2008.

|

Decided and Filed: May 29, 2008.

Sutton, Circuit Judge, filed a separate opinion concurring in part and dissenting in part.

**\*956**

Before: MOORE, GILMAN, and SUTTON, Circuit Judges.

MOORE, J., delivered the opinion of the court, in which GILMAN, J., joined. SUTTON, J. (pp. 965-68), delivered a separate opinion concurring in part and dissenting in part.

**OPINION**

**KAREN NELSON MOORE, Circuit Judge.**

In this case we are asked whether the discovery of men's clothing in a bag that a female claimed to own erases for future bags the apparent authority that justified the officers' warrantless search of the first bag, thereby making a subsequent search illegal. We hold that the discovery of men's clothing eviscerated any apparent authority, but that the officers could have reestablished apparent authority by asking the supposed bag owner to verify her control over the other bags to be searched. Furthermore, we hold that exigent circumstances did not justify the illegal search. Because the officers in the instant case did not reestablish apparent authority and could not justify proceeding with a warrantless search by claiming an exigency, we hold that district court did not err when it suppressed the firearm that officers discovered after any apparent authority dissipated, and we **AFFIRM** the district court's partial grant of the defendant's motion to suppress.

## I. BACKGROUND

### A. Factual Background

On June 28, 2006, Special Agent John Scott ("Scott") and the Southern Ohio Fugitive Apprehension Strike Team ("SOFAST")[1] received a tip that Frederick Purcell, Jr. ("Purcell"), an escapee from prison, was staying at a hotel in Kentucky. The tip indicated that Purcell was residing at the hotel with his girlfriend, Yolande Crist ("Crist").

---

1. The U.S. Marshal Service runs SOFAST, which employs members of various state and federal law-enforcement agencies.

As Scott and the other members of SOFAST drove to the hotel, they received information that Purcell "was a meth manufacturer and that Blue *957 Ash[, Ohio police] had arrested him for manufacturing meth." Joint Appendix ("J.A.") at 64 (Hr'g Tr., John Scott Test. at 6:23-24).

Upon arrival at the hotel, the SOFAST agents quickly identified Purcell standing outside and arrested him without incident. After arresting Purcell, Scott and the other SOFAST agents went to Purcell's hotel room. The agents were concerned that, given what they knew of his history, Purcell may have been manufacturing methamphetamine in the room. As Agent Scott noted, "I'm basically an ATF agent so my knowledge of meth manufacturing is basically the explosive potential of it. So we were concerned about endangerment of the hotel guests." J.A. at 65 (Scott at 7:15-17).

The officers knocked on the door to Purcell's room and could hear the shower running as well as a fan blowing. After about three minutes, Crist opened the door and assured the officers that there was no methamphetamine manufacturing occurring in the room. Crist then gave her consent for the officers to take a quick look around the room. Although Crist would later authorize a full search of the room, during this first search the agents did only what Crist authorized them to do: perform a cursory sweep of the room.

During this initial sweep of the room, the agents observed "two duffel type bag suitcases near the door" and a backpack located between the bed and window at some distance from the two duffel bags. (Omitted from J.A., Scott at 16:19-20); J.A. at 95 (Dec. 14, 2006, Hr'g Tr., M. Duane Rolfsen Test. at 58:21-24). Clothes covered most of the rest of the floor, but despite the mess, the agents noticed several suspicious items, such as possible marijuana leaves, steel wool, a butane torch, the shower operating at full strength, and a box fan blowing air out from the shower. Having observed these suspicious items, the agents called for assistance from officers with experience identifying and handling methamphetamine labs.

Agent Matthew Duane Rolfsen ("Rolfsen") of the Northern Kentucky Drug Strike Force was called to the scene because he was certified to process methamphetamine labs and had dealt with Purcell on a prior occasion. Agent Rolfsen, like the first agents to arrive on the scene, was also concerned about the hazards that a methamphetamine lab in a hotel room might pose:

> Our immediate concern, due to his past history and what he was actually serving time on when he escaped, was the meth lab itself, was for the community safety and the hotel safety and the patrons' safety that were in the hotel. If there is a meth lab, there is a lot of chemical hazards. There's a lot of safety hazards. It's a possibility of dying from the fumes and the chemicals involved in making methamphetamine.

**J.A. at 81 (Rolfsen at 33:9-15).**

Upon arriving at the hotel, Agent Rolfsen talked to Agent Scott and then conducted his own cursory sweep of the hotel room. Agent Rolfsen observed the same suspicious items as Agent Scott, but Agent Rolfsen also noticed cookware "consistent with manufacturing methamphetamine," cutting agent, "a metal spoon with burnt material," a torch, "brass material consistent with use for making pipes to smoke" drugs, and "plastic tubes, which is consistent with snorting various drugs." J.A. at 83 (Rolfsen at 35:2-13). Although the agents identified some evidence, such as the cookware, that was consistent with methamphetamine production, it is notable that Agent Rolfsen did not smell any of the telltale chemical odors that often accompany methamphetamine labs. Agent Rolfsen noted, however, that the lack of smell was not conclusive: "once you've *958 done the cook, there's not always a smell. Depends how much material is still there." J.A. at 89 (Rolfsen at 49:10-14).

After making his initial sweep of the room, Agent Rolfsen asked Crist for and received permission to conduct a more complete search. As Agent Rolfsen and other officers began the search, they asked Crist whether there was anything in the room that could be dangerous, and "[s]he indicated there was a firearm in the room." J.A. at 84 (Rolfsen at 36:20-24). Crist did not mention any methamphetamine-related dangers, but she did state that a firearm was in one of the bags in the room, although she was not sure which one. Agent Rolfsen moved toward the duffel bags by the door and pointed to "a green brown bag" and asked Crist "[i]s it this bag?" Crist responded that "it might be." J.A. at 85 (Rolfsen at 37:1-3). Agent Rolfsen opened that first duffel bag near the door, and as he was searching it Crist "said that was her bag because she set her purse on top of it." J.A. at 94 (Rolfsen at 56:6-7). Upon opening the bag, Agent Rolfsen discovered marijuana but no firearm. In addition to the marijuana, Agent Rolfsen discovered that the bag did not contain Crist's personal effects, as one might expect, but instead contained only men's clothing.

The discovery of the men's clothing inside the bag indicated that it was actually Purcell's bag, not Crist's, as she had claimed. This was not a complete surprise for the agents because they knew that Purcell owned some of the items in the room even though they did not know initially which bags were his; "[Crist] definitely said there was [sic] items in that room that belonged to Fred Purcell." J.A. at 92 (Rolfsen at 53:15-16). Although Agent Rolfsen realized that Crist had misstated her ownership of the bag, he did not ask her to verify whether she owned any of the other bags in the room. Shortly thereafter, another agent found the firearm in a brown-green backpack that was not sitting near the other closed bags by the door but was instead sitting "on the floor by the bed and between the bed and the window." J.A. at 95 (Rolfsen at 58:21-24). After discovering the firearm, the agents asked Crist who owned the backpack, and Crist noted that she owned the backpack itself, but she had given it to Purcell for his use.

As it turned out, Purcell was the sole user of both the bag containing the firearm and the bag containing the marijuana. None of Crist's effects were in Purcell's bags, he did not give her permission to go through his bags, and she never went through them. Crist did own the backpack

itself, but at the time of the search, Purcell had exclusive use of the backpack that contained the firearm.

## B. Procedural Background

On August 9, 2006, a grand jury indicted Purcell for being a felon in possession of a firearm in violation of 18 U.S.C. § 922(g)(1), a fugitive from justice knowingly possessing a firearm in violation of 18 U.S.C. § 922(g)(2), an unlawful user of marijuana in possession of a firearm in violation of 18 U.S.C. § 922(g)(3), and for possession of marijuana in violation of 21 U.S.C. § 844(a).[2]

Prior to trial, on November 21, 2006, Purcell filed a motion to suppress both the firearm and the marijuana that the agents discovered in the search of his luggage. On March 23, 2007, the district court granted Purcell's request to suppress the firearm and denied Purcell's request to suppress the marijuana.

In reaching its conclusion, the district court rejected the government's assertion **\*959** that the search was justified under the exigent-circumstances exception to the Fourth Amendment. The district court did not believe that the agents were legitimately concerned about the dangers of a methamphetamine lab after completing their cursory sweeps of the room; the agents' "actions in asking a second time for consent, that time to search the room, strongly suggests that the immediate danger was no longer present." J.A. at 21 (Mem. Op. & Order at 9). The district court went on to say that "[t]here is nothing to suggest that a search of the luggage was necessary as part of the exigency of ensuring there was no meth lab in the room, nor would it be objectively reasonable to find that such a search was within the scope of Crist's initial consent to look around to verify the area was safe." J.A. at 22 (Mem. Op. & Order at 10).

The district court also rejected the government's assertion that Crist had either actual or apparent authority to consent to the search of

---

2. The indictment also included a count seeking forfeiture of the firearm.

the bag that held the firearm. First, the district court concluded that Crist did not have actual authority to consent to the search of either bag: "Ms. Crist gave no testimony that would suggest she enjoyed any mutual use, access, or control of the duffel bag or backpack or the items within it, and the Government has provided no evidence to refute this claim." J.A. at 28 (Mem. Op. & Order at 16). Second, according to the district court, there was apparent authority for the officers to search the first bag because at the time of the search of the first bag "there was no evidence offered to suggest reason to doubt the accuracy or truthfulness of her response that the duffel bag was hers." J.A. at 31 (Mem. Op. & Order at 19). In contrast, the district court found that Crist's apparent authority was "extinguished with the search of that first bag" after the officers found it was filled with men's clothing, leaving Crist with no apparent authority to consent to the search of the second bag. J.A. at 32 (Mem. Op. & Order at 20).

On April 3, 2007, the government filed a motion for reconsideration, asking the district court to use *United States v. Atchley,* 474 F.3d 840 (6th Cir.), *cert. denied,* --- U.S. ----, 127 S.Ct. 2447, 167 L.Ed.2d 1145 (2007), to hold that the search of all of the luggage in Purcell's hotel room was valid under the exigency exception to the Fourth Amendment. On April 18, 2007, the district denied the government's motion for reconsideration of the district court's suppression order, concluding that *Atchley* did not justify a warrantless search in this case. The district court believed that, in contrast to *Atchley,* "further search was not driven by any objectively reasonable urgency for fear of a hidden lab or dangerous chemicals, but rather for the firearm specifically, or perhaps maybe some other weapon or item that might pose a danger generally to those searching." J.A. at 45 (Apr. 18, 2007, Mem. Order at 9).

On April 20, 2007, the government filed an interlocutory appeal challenging the district court's suppression of the firearm. We have authority to hear this case under 18 U.S.C. § 3731, authorizing the court of appeals to hear interlocutory appeals brought by the United States following a district court's suppression of evidence that "is a substantial proof of a fact material in the proceeding." 18 U.S.C. § 3731.

## II. ANALYSIS

"In assessing a challenge to the district court's ruling on a motion to suppress, we review the district court's factual findings for clear error, and its legal conclusions *de novo." United States v. Waller,* 426 F.3d 838, 843 (6th Cir. 2005); *accord Atchley,* 474 F.3d at 847.

*960 Our search jurisprudence typically requires officers to possess a warrant before conducting a search. There are, however, exceptions to the warrant requirement. "One of those 'well-delineated' exceptions is the consent of the person searched. An officer with consent needs neither a warrant nor probable cause to conduct a constitutional search." *United States v. Jenkins,* 92 F.3d 430, 436 (6th Cir. 1996), *cert. denied,* 520 U.S. 1170, 117 S.Ct. 1436, 137 L.Ed.2d 543 (1997). And one of the other exceptions is the existence of exigent circumstances. *Mincey v. Arizona,* 437 U.S. 385, 392-393, 98 S.Ct. 2408, 57 L.Ed.2d 290 (1978). On appeal, the government has presented alternative arguments attempting to justify the agents' warrantless search under one of these two exceptions, providing no other justifications for the warrantless search other than arguing that (1) exigent circumstances justified the search, and (2) Crist had apparent authority to consent to the search of the backpack. We conclude that there was neither any exigent circumstance nor apparent authority to justify the search of the backpack.

### A. Exigent Circumstances

The government claims that the warrantless search that led to the discovery of the firearm was justified by exigent circumstances. Although the Fourth Amendment makes a warrant or obtaining consent a prerequisite for a legal search, "'[t]he need to protect or preserve life or avoid serious injury is justification for what would be otherwise illegal absent an exigency or emergency.'" *Id.* (quoting *Wayne v. United States,* 318 F.2d 205, 212 (D.C. Cir. 1963)). Qualification for this exception is not easy, for "[w]hen there is neither a warrant nor consent, courts will only permit a search or seizure to stand under extraordinary circumstances." *United States v. Chambers,* 395 F.3d 563, 565 (6th Cir. 2005).

In order to establish the applicability of this exception to the Fourth Amendment's requirements, "[i]t is the government's burden to prove the existence of exigency." *Atchley,* 474 F.3d at 851. "While it is not possible to articulate a succinct yet exhaustive list of circumstances that qualify as 'exigent,' we have previously characterized the situations in which warrantless entries are justified as lying within one of four general categories: (1) hot pursuit of a fleeing felon, (2) imminent destruction of evidence, (3) the need to prevent a suspect's escape, and (4) a risk of danger to the police or others." *United States v. Rohrig,* 98 F.3d 1506, 1515 (6th Cir. 1996). Courts that have found that exigent circumstances existed "uniformly cite the need for prompt action by government personnel, and conclude that delay to secure a warrant would be unacceptable under the circumstances." *Id.* at 1517. The case at hand presents a question of whether the circumstances indicated a risk of danger that made it unacceptable for the agents to delay their search in order to procure a warrant.

Methamphetamine labs are rightly regarded as highly dangerous. "Certain of the chemicals used in this process are toxic and inherently dangerous. During the manufacturing process, some of these chemicals, which are highly flammable, present a threat of explosion. These chemicals pose an additional risk should anything go wrong during the manufacturing process. The process produces toxic gases, which pose a serious risk to those who inhale them, and other dangerous byproducts." *United States v. Layne,* 324 F.3d 464, 470 (6th Cir.), *cert. denied,* 540 U.S. 888, 124 S.Ct. 270, 157 L.Ed.2d 160 (2003). "Many of these chemicals emit dangerous fumes and vapors. The byproduct of the process includes highly flammable and explosive phosphine gas." *Id.* Although methamphetamine labs are *961 dangerous, the danger is primarily tied to the heating process and the resulting fumes or explosiveness; on their own, the ingredients

are safe enough that they are common, easily accessible products. *See* Drug Enforcement Administration, *Fact Sheet: Fast Facts About Meth,* http://www.usdoj.gov/dea/pubs/pressrel/methfact03.html (last visited Apr. 28, 2008).

In the instant case, the government claims that the possibility that Purcell was manufacturing methamphetamine in his hotel room created a danger to the agents and hotel guests that justified the warrantless search of Purcell's luggage. According to the government, our holding in *Atchley* compels the conclusion that an exigency existed, but we disagree.

In the case at hand, the only reasons why the officers suspected that there was a methamphetamine lab in Purcell's room were that he had previously operated methamphetamine labs and they noticed some drug-related items in his hotel room. However, not one agent testified to believing that methamphetamine cooking was ongoing when the agents arrived. This is in sharp contrast to *Atchley.* In that case, there was a significant amount of evidence indicating that the dangerous manufacture of methamphetamine was ongoing: "Officer Engle stated that he smelled a chemical which he associated with methamphetamine manufacturing. When the officers entered, they observed in plain view two large glass jars appearing to contain a solvent, a large bottle of gas line anti-freeze, rubbing alcohol, and a police radio scanner." *Atchley,* 474 F.3d at 845. Given that the manufacture of methamphetamine is so dangerous, the *Atchley* court found the warrantless search justified because the officers had significant evidence of methamphetamine manufacture; in contrast, we observed that evidence of simply drug use or possession "would not establish the exigency necessary to validate a warrantless search." *Id.* at 851.

In Purcell's case, there was no evidence to suggest that methamphetamine manufacture was ongoing, thus there was no exigency to justify searching Purcell's luggage. In the absence of an exigency, *Atchley* simply does not control this case. Had there been evidence of an ongoing methamphetamine lab, *Atchley* would have entitled the agents to search small containers, such as small pieces of luggage, even though an operational laboratory could not have fit in Purcell's baggage. *See id.* at 846 ("The district court found that although Cobb and Engle's search of the refrigerator, ice chest, ammunition can, and drawer was not justified as part of the protective sweep, it was nonetheless lawful because the items that were in plain view gave the officers probable cause to suspect that the motel room served as a methamphetamine laboratory."). In this case, however, the predicate that would justify the search of small places such as luggage— evidence of a methamphetamine lab that creates an exigency—was simply not present.

Furthermore, evidence of a methamphetamine laboratory by itself is not always sufficient to create an exigency. *Id.* at 851 n. 6 ("We do not intend to say that there should be a *per se* rule that whenever evidence of a methamphetamine laboratory is apparent, there is always exigency."). In this case, however, not only was there no evidence of an operating methamphetamine laboratory, but also the government's claims of exigency appear to be only a post hoc justification for the warrantless search because the agents searching Purcell's room did not seem particularly concerned for their own safety or the safety of other hotel guests after they had conducted their sweep of Purcell's room. If the officers were truly concerned about **\*962** a dangerous condition, why did the agents twice ask Crist for permission to search the room? And if the agents were worried about a methamphetamine laboratory, why were they searching in the luggage for a firearm? The answers to these questions belie the government's assertion that the agents were concerned about a possible methamphetamine lab in Purcell's hotel room. We therefore hold that exigent circumstances did not justify the warrantless search of Purcell's backpack.

## B. Consent

The government's only other argument is that Crist's consent justified the warrantless search of Purcell's luggage. In order to consent to a search, the person purporting to consent must possess either actual or apparent authority over the item or place to be searched. *United States*

*v. Caldwell,* 518 F.3d 426, 429 (6th Cir. 2008). Once an individual with actual or apparent authority consents to the search, "[t]he standard for measuring the scope of a suspect's consent under the Fourth Amendment is that of 'objective' reasonableness—what would the typical reasonable person have understood by the exchange between the officer and the suspect?" *Florida v. Jimeno,* 500 U.S. 248, 251, 111 S.Ct. 1801, 114 L.Ed.2d 297 (1991). Thus, when an officer receives consent, he is allowed to search only what is reasonably covered by the consent given; "[i]t is very likely unreasonable to think that a suspect, by consenting to the search of his trunk [of his car], has agreed to the breaking open of a locked briefcase within the trunk, but it is otherwise with respect to a closed paper bag." *Id.* at 251-52, 111 S.Ct. 1801.

Purcell did not and was not entitled to bring an interlocutory appeal challenging the district court's denial of his motion to suppress the marijuana. *United States v. Shameizadeh,* 41 F.3d 266, 267 (6th Cir. 1994) (Order) ("Although 18 U.S.C. § 3731 permits the government to take an immediate appeal from an order *granting* a pretrial motion to suppress, that statute does not provide for a cross-appeal by a defendant.... Thus, while the defendants may raise as part of the government's appeal any alternative arguments which would have supported the order of suppression, they may not... raise any arguments as to evidence not ordered suppressed by the district court."). When defending the grant of the motion suppressing the firearm, Purcell acknowledges that apparent authority justified the search of the first duffel bag, which yielded the marijuana. Appellee Br. at 12 ("Thus, as the district court properly concluded, '[the officers'] reliance upon Crist's response [regarding the first bag] was reasonable, as there was no evidence offered to suggest reason to doubt the accuracy or truthfulness of her response that the duffel bag was hers.'" (quoting Mem. & Op. at 19)). We therefore assume that the district court was correct in holding that apparent authority justified the search of the first bag. We do, however, hold that neither actual nor apparent authority justified the search of the second bag, which yielded the firearm.

## C. Actual Authority

Actual authority in third-party consent cases "rests... on mutual use of the property by persons generally having joint access or control for most purposes, so that it is reasonable to recognize that any of the co-inhabitants has the right to permit the inspection in his own right and that the others have assumed the risk that one of their number might permit the [property] to be searched." *United States v. Matlock*, 415 U.S. 164, 171 n. 7, 94 S.Ct. 988, 39 L.Ed.2d 242 (1974). Crist offered uncontroverted testimony establishing that her personal effects were not in Purcell's *963 bags, Purcell exercised exclusive control over his bags, and Purcell never gave Crist permission to open his bags. These factors would all tend to establish that Crist lacked actual authority to consent to the search of the bag containing Purcell's clothing and the firearm. On appeal, however, the government does not claim that Crist had actual authority to consent to the search of Purcell's bags; therefore, we do not address whether Crist had actual authority to consent to the search, and we simply assume that she did not possess actual authority.

## D. Apparent Authority

"We have held that even where third-party consent comes from an individual without actual authority over the property searched, there is no Fourth Amendment violation if the police conducted the search in good faith reliance on the third-party's *apparent authority* to authorize the search through her consent." *Morgan*, 435 F.3d 660, 663 (6th Cir. 2006)(finding apparent authority where a wife claimed to have authority to access to her husband's computer). In investigating whether officers reasonably concluded an individual possessed apparent authority, the "determination of consent... must 'be judged against an objective standard: would the facts available to the officer at the moment... warrant a man of reasonable caution in the belief' that the consenting party had authority over the [property]?" *Illinois v. Rodriguez*, 497 U.S. 177, 188, 110 S.Ct. 2793, 111 L.Ed.2d 148 (1990) (second omission in original) (quoting *Terry v. Ohio*, 392 U.S. 1, 21-22, 88 S.Ct. 1868, 20 L.Ed.2d 889

(1968)). In the third-party consent context, this means the officer must have reasonably believed the person giving consent possessed joint access or control over the property searched.

In the case at hand, when the agents began their search of the luggage in the hotel room, they had a good-faith basis to believe that Crist had joint access or control over the bags. Crist asserted control over the duffel bag that yielded the marijuana and gave consent to search. She said the bag was hers. Her words, standing alone, indicate that she had the requisite access and control. Her statement made sense in light of the circumstances as she was able to access the bags and her purse was sitting on top of the duffel bag.

However, further context was revealed during the search of this first bag that called into question Crist's asserted control over the bags. During the search of the first bag, the officer learned that it contained only men's clothing and no personal effects of Crist. A reasonable officer cannot ignore that information and must consider the assertion of control in light of the context that evolves. Here, that context created ambiguity and doubt regarding Crist's asserted control. Any otherwise apparent authority evaporated. *See Rodriguez*, 497 U.S. at 188, 110 S.Ct. 2793 ("Even when the invitation is accompanied by an explicit assertion that the person lives there, the surrounding circumstances could conceivably be such that a reasonable person would doubt its truth and not act upon it without further inquiry."); *Jenkins*, 92 F.3d at 437 ("Of course, if the consenter provides additional information, the context may change in such a manner that no reasonable officer would maintain the default assumption.").

The government attempts to argue that even if Crist's initial assertions of control over the bags are not enough to sustain her apparent authority after the discovery of the men's clothing, the fact that Crist was in an intimate relationship with Purcell provided another basis for her apparent authority. Being in an intimate relationship, however, does not endow a would-be-consenter with any additional sheen of apparent authority that would survive the discovery of evidence that contradicts the consenter's asserted authority. *See Morgan*, 435 F.3d at 663 (finding apparent authority from a wife's assertion of common authority, but not from the fact that the party granting consent was the defendant's wife); *Waller*, 426 F.3d at 848 (approvingly citing *United States v. Salinas-Cano*, 959 F.2d 861 (10th Cir. 1992), where the Tenth Circuit did not automatically find consent where a girlfriend attempted to consent to a search of her boyfriend's briefcase). Thus, the facts **\*965** surrounding any particular intimate relationship might contribute to the officers' good-faith basis for initially believing a would-be-consenter's assertion of authority, but that good-faith belief is still subject to the same constraints that apply whenever new information comes to light that creates ambiguity as to apparent authority.[3]

Thus, we conclude that the discovery of the men's clothing in the duffel bag that Crist claimed was hers created ambiguity sufficient to erase any initial apparent authority. Thus, at the point the firearm was discovered, there was no valid consent. The firearm was discovered as part of an illegal search, and the district court did not err when it suppressed the firearm.

## III. CONCLUSION

For the foregoing reasons, we conclude that exigent circumstances did not justify the search of the hotel room and that Crist did not have apparent authority to consent to the search of the second bag. Accordingly, the district court did not err when it suppressed the firearm, and we **AFFIRM** the district court's partial grant of the motion to suppress.

SUTTON, Circuit Judge, concurring in part and dissenting in part.

---

3. The dissent urges this court to create a new default assumption that "itinerant, intimate couples sharing close quarters have joint use of indistinguishable containers within the space they occupy." Dissenting Op. at 967. Although there are no doubt many couples who do share luggage when they travel, the possible travel habits of some is hardly a sound basis for an unprecedented expansion of police authority.

The question at hand is whether the officers' search of the backpack was "[ ]reasonable." U.S. Const. amend. IV. In answering that question, we know (1) that searches based solely upon consent are reasonable, *Schneckloth v. Bustamonte*, 412 U.S. 218, 222, 93 S.Ct. 2041, 36 L.Ed.2d 854 (1973), (2) that each joint user of a container "clearly ha[s] authority to consent to its search" because one user "assume[s] the risk that [the other] would allow someone else to look inside," *Frazier v. Cupp*, 394 U.S. 731, 740, 89 S.Ct. 1420, 22 L.Ed.2d 684 (1969), and (3) that officers need not be "correct" that an individual has authority to consent to a search but must only "reasonably believe[ ]" that the individual has common authority over the premises and items to be searched, *Illinois v. Rodriguez*, 497 U.S. 177, 185, 189, 110 S.Ct. 2793, 111 L.Ed.2d 148 (1990).

The officers reasonably relied on Crist's consent to search the backpack for several reasons. Crist, to start, had unquestioned authority over the hotel room: She rented the room in her name; she opened the door to the officers; and her personal effects were in the room. No one thus contests Crist's authority to permit the officers to enter the hotel room and to search it.

Once Crist permitted the officers to enter the hotel room, the only spaces not already in plain view—and therefore potentially covered by her further consent to search the room—would have been the closet, the bathroom, the dresser and the luggage. Crist's consent to search the room necessarily would seem to cover the closet, the bathroom and the dresser. And if it covered these areas, why wouldn't it cover the luggage of this non-platonic couple—particularly after what Crist told the officers and after what the officers saw? Crist told the officers that she and Purcell were in an intimate relationship and that they had stayed together in the hotel room for several days. And she confirmed that the first bag the officers opened was her **\*966** own. What the officers saw confirmed Crist's authority to permit the officers to search the two bags or at least confirmed the absence of any exclusivity between Crist's luggage and Purcell's. Crist's possessions were scattered about the room. None of the bags in the hotel room was locked, individually marked or otherwise naturally affiliated with one or the other of them. And no clear arrangement of the containers indicated that some were more private than others. On these facts alone, it would seem reasonable for officers to infer that a couple sharing a bed would share access to unmarked, unlocked and androgynous-looking luggage.

But there is more. Crist authorized a targeted search, and she also knew the general contents of the two bags she gave the officers permission to search. After allowing a protective sweep of the hotel room, Crist specifically consented to the officers' search for a "firearm" when they asked if there was "anything in the room that could hurt" them. JA 84. She "direct[ed] [the officers] to look in certain bags because she believed that was where the gun" might be, JA 76, which itself confirmed mutual access to the bags. And when the officers found orange peels in a bag of marijuana in the first duffel bag, Crist told them that the orange peels "help[ ] keep [the marijuana] fresh," JA 88, further suggesting mutual access to the bag. An individual's "knowledge of the contents" of a searched space bolsters the reasonableness of an officer's reliance on that individual's authority to consent to the search. *United States v. Grayer,* 232 Fed.Appx. 446, 449 (6th Cir. Apr. 5, 2007).

Most strikingly, however, Purcell was not an everyday traveler; he was a fugitive. As the officers well knew in arresting Purcell before they entered the hotel room, he was a prison escapee, a member of a group that generally travels lightly and that is more likely to rely on the generosity of others than on its own possessions in getting by from day to day. What then was unreasonable about believing that Crist had authority to consent to the search of the luggage when she had rented the room, knew the contents of both bags that were searched and had stayed there for several days—and not just with any companion but with a fugitive companion?

One might wonder, indeed, whether fugitives have *any* legitimate expectation of privacy in their belongings. Individuals released from prison on parole, with the government's consent, have substantially diminished privacy rights, making reasonable searches unaccompanied by a warrant and without individualized suspicion. *See Samson v. California,* 547 U.S. 843, 856, 126 S.Ct. 2193, 165 L.Ed.2d 250 (2006). Why reward a fugitive, who necessarily left prison without the government's consent, by giving him more constitutional privacy than he had before he escaped from prison? *See United States v. Roy,* 734 F.2d 108, 112 (2d Cir. 1984) (holding that a fugitive has no more Fourth Amendment rights than when he was in prison in part because "[a] contrary determination would offer judicial encouragement to the act of escape and would reward an escapee for his illegal conduct").

But we need not climb that wall now. Purcell's known status as a fugitive at a minimum contributed to the reasonableness of the officers' judgment that Crist had authority to consent to the search of the luggage. The officers could reasonably infer that Purcell did not bring the duffel bag and backpack with him when he escaped from prison. And while it is possible that he purchased the bags after his escape, that is not the question; the issue is whether an officer could reasonably conclude that an individual living on the lam was sharing luggage with an intimate traveling *967 companion—as indeed turned out to be the case. The officers' reliance on all of these circumstances in the end turns on precisely the kinds of "factual and practical considerations of everyday life on which reasonable and prudent" officers may act, *Brinegar v. United States,* 338 U.S. 160, 175, 69 S.Ct. 1302, 93 L.Ed. 1879 (1949), and on this record an officer "of reasonable caution" would be "warrant[ed] ... in the belief" that this couple shared access to luggage, *Rodriguez,* 497 U.S. at 188, 110 S.Ct. 2793 (internal quotation marks omitted).

*United States v. Waller,* 426 F.3d 838 (6th Cir. 2005), does not hold (or even say) otherwise. It merely observes that in some circumstances it may become "unclear whether the property about to be searched"—there a suitcase—"is subject to 'mutual use' by the person giving consent." *Id.* at 846 (internal quotation marks omitted). But the circumstances of Waller's case are not the circumstances of Purcell's. Waller was not a fugitive; his suitcase was found in a house he did not occupy; and there was no evidence that any of Waller's possessions were "mutual[ly] use[d]" by anyone else. *Id.* at 845-47, 849.

The presence of male clothing in one bag also did not invalidate the search. Crist told the officers, it is well to remember, that the first container searched was "her bag." JA 94. If the officers perceived Crist's asserted authority over the bag as truthful, as they reasonably could have, then the presence of Purcell's clothes *confirmed* that the couple shared luggage. And if Crist was merely confused about which bag contained her possessions, that confusion would buttress a reasonable belief that no clear boundaries existed between the possessions of the pair, which is hardly an improbable scenario when it comes to a traveling couple. Why the varied contents of one bag, which plainly included jointly used items (marijuana), *must* be viewed to undermine rather than reinforce the inference of mutual use escapes me. It is no more unusual for a fugitive to keep his clothes in a companion's luggage than it is unusual for a fugitive to stay in a hotel rented in a companion's name. The circumstances made it a virtual certainty that some male clothes would be in the luggage, indeed perhaps even a male, prison-issue, orange jump suit. There is nothing surprising (or authority diminishing) about finding Purcell's clothes in a bag that Crist owned and understandably shared with her fugitive companion.

It is true that "[b]eing in an intimate relationship... does not endow a would-be-consenter with any additional sheen of apparent authority that would survive the discovery of evidence that *contradicts* the consenter's asserted authority." Maj. Op. at 964 (emphasis added). But that is beside the point. The intimate relationship helps to explain the presence of male clothing in Crist's bag and therefore shows that nothing "contradict[ed]" Crist's authority to permit inspection of the room's containers. If the officers started with the reasonable premise that itinerant, intimate couples sharing close quarters

have joint use of indistinguishable containers within the space they occupy (especially when one of the pair is a fugitive), their discovery of male clothing did more to reaffirm that premise than to refute it. The question after all is not whether the officers were *certain* that Crist exercised "joint access or control for most purposes," *United States v. Matlock,* 415 U.S. 164, 171 n. 7, 94 S.Ct. 988, 39 L.Ed.2d 242 (1974); it is whether there was enough *uncertainty* to undermine the officers' "reasonable... belief that [she] had authority to consent," *Rodriguez,* 497 U.S. at 187, 110 S.Ct. 2793 (internal quotation marks omitted).

**\*968** In *United States v. Melgar,* 227 F.3d 1038 (7th Cir. 2000), the Seventh Circuit faced a similar situation. In upholding the search of a floral purse, it held that apparent authority exists over containers in a jointly occupied living space unless "the police ... have reliable information that the container is *not* under the authorizer's control." *Id.* at 1041. "[T]he real question for closed container searches," Judge Wood recognized, "is which way the risk of uncertainty should run." *Id.* The court resolved this question by rejecting a comparable rule to the one the majority embraces today—that uncertainty should be resolved by making consent searches "permissible only if the police have positive knowledge that the closed container is also under the authority of the person who originally consented"—because such a rule "would impose an impossible burden on the police. It would mean that they could *never* search closed containers within a dwelling *(including hotel rooms)* without asking the person whose consent is being given *ex ante* about every item they might encounter." *Id.* at 1041-42 (second emphasis added). At least one other circuit has embraced this view. *See United States v. Navarro,* 169 F.3d 228, 232 (5th Cir. 1999) (holding that apparent authority existed where there was no evidence that the consenter "advised that the luggage in the vehicle was not his"). We should do the same here. The majority seeing it differently, I respectfully dissent from this part of its opinion.

# Sources of Law

The United States has multiple sources of law. The U.S. Constitution serves as the "supreme law of the land," providing the framework for the federal government, defining the scope of its powers, and establishing basic rights for U.S. citizens. Law can be created by governmental bodies from each branch, *acting in their official capacity*. (Think: a judge writing a majority court opinion, not a judge sharing opinions in a law review article.)

### Where Does Law Come from and Which Law Applies?

| LEVEL OF GOVERNMENT |
| --- |
| Each level of government (federal, state, and local)[1] has its own sources of law. For instance, the U.S. Constitution governs the entire United States. States have their own constitutions, applicable just to that state. Local governmental units (e.g., counties or municipalities) often have similar foundational documents, such as a charter. |
| Some areas of law are more likely to be covered at one level than another (e.g., intellectual property-federal, family law-state, and zoning law-local). For some topics, multiple governmental levels apply (e.g., employment law). |

| PRIMARY LEGAL MATERIALS | |
| --- | --- |
| Primary legal materials are the actual sources of law. There are two broad types: enacted law and common law. | |
| ENACTED LAW | COMMON LAW |
| The most common sources are listed below in hierarchical order, from highest to lowest:<br><br>**Constitutions**<br><br>**Statutes**<br><br>• Published separately as slip laws, chronologically by legislative session as session laws, and organized by topic into statutory codes.<br><br>• Typically called ordinances at the local level.<br><br>**Regulations / Executive Orders** | Judicial opinions interpret enacted law, often clarifying how it should be applied, and also address conflicts not governed by enacted law. Common law does not overturn enacted law unless the enacting governmental body acted beyond its authorized scope. This might mean that the law is judged unconstitutional, or the enacting governmental body otherwise surpassed its legal authority.<br><br>Judicial branch courts<br><br>• Hierarchical within both federal and state systems, typically with lowest courts considered trial courts, an intermediate appellate level, and a final appellate level.<br><br>• *Stare decisis* is the doctrine by which courts follow precedent set by prior court decisions.<br><br>**Administrative courts** also issue quasi-judicial opinions with decisions guided, in part, by past decisions. Typically, if parties to a dispute exhaust their administrative remedies, they can appeal to a judicial branch court. |

---

1. While outside the scope of this chart, international law can also be mandatory authority, and foreign law can be persuasive authority.

| SECONDARY LEGAL MATERIALS | |
|---|---|
| Secondary sources are not the law themselves, but discuss, analyze, and help shape the law. Common types: | |
| • Restatements of the Law<br>• Treatises<br>• Journal articles, e.g., law reviews<br>• Encyclopedias and dictionaries | • Annotations (e.g., A.L.R.)<br>• Study aids and practice aids<br>• Model or uniform laws or codes<br>• Finding aids (e.g., digests, research guides, citators) |
| MANDATORY AND PERSUASIVE AUTHORITY (LAW) | |
| Courts resolving conflicts must follow *mandatory authority*, which includes (1) enacted law from the same jurisdiction, and (2) common law from a higher court in the same jurisdiction. Courts can consider, but are not bound by, *persuasive authority*, which includes laws from other jurisdictions and all secondary legal materials. | |

# Glossary of Terms and Concepts

This glossary provides simple definitions of concepts that can be quite complex. It is intended as a starting reference to assist you as you learn these new ideas. The chapters provide more detailed information on these concepts. You may choose to annotate this glossary as you delve more deeply into particular concepts, adding detail that you find useful and framing ideas in ways that make sense to you.

**Analogical reasoning**   **Argument** based on analogy between a situation that has already been resolved by a court and a new situation posed by a client.

**Appellant**   Complaining party on appeal; lost in lower court.

**Appellee**   Respondent on appeal; prevailed in lower court.

**Argument/analysis**   One side's (likely) explanation of how the legal rule should be applied to the facts of the case. Compare with **counter-argument/ counter-analysis.**

**Bright-line rule**   Rule that leaves little, if any, room for competing interpretations.

**Case approach (to rule explanation organization)** Strategy for **small-scale organization** of **rule explanation** in a multiple authority memo that first addresses all the ways that a single precedent case illustrates the application of the legal rule and then moves on to the next case. Contrast with **guiding factors approach.**

**Claim or charge (legal claim or charge)**   The legal filing that triggers and defines the scope of the dispute. In a civil matter the claim is the legal right the lawyer wants the court to address; in a criminal matter, the charge is the statement of a criminal offense.

**Common law**   Rules developed by a court that typically evolve over time; compare with **enacted law.**

**Conclusion (global)**   Global prediction of the resolution of the **claim or charge** and reiteration of the issue **predictions** for each **issue/condition**; appears at the end of the **Discussion** in a legal memorandum.

**Concurring opinion**   Separate opinion in a case that agrees with the court's ruling but often expresses different reasons for arriving at that result.

**Conditions (of a rule)**   What is assessed to determine whether the rule's result will be triggered; may be **elements** or **factors**.

**Contested condition**   Condition for which each side has a viable argument as to whether it is satisfied. If a condition is contested, it is at **issue**.

**Counter-argument/Counter-analysis**   Other side's (likely) explanation of how the legal rule should be applied to the facts of the case. Compare with **argument/analysis.**

**CREAC**   Acronym for way of organizing a legal argument: conclusion, rule, explanation, application, conclusion. Compare with **IRAC.**

**Deductive framework**   Framework that starts from general principles and moves to specific examples; used in the memo **Discussion** section. Compare with **inductive reasoning**.

**Definitions**   One way of explaining the meaning of the **condition** at **issue**; specifies the meaning of a word or phrase.

**Discretionary conditions**   **Factors** that do not all need to be satisfied for the overall rule to be satisfied.

**Discussion**   Most important legal memorandum section, where the writer identifies the key law and applies it to the client's situation; written in a **deductive** manner, proceeding from a more general explanation of the law to a more specific application.

**Disjunctive conditions**   Mutually exclusive **conditions** requiring a choice as to which applies.

**Disposition (of a case)**   The court's final determination in a case.

**Dissenting opinion**   Separate opinion in a case that disagrees with the court's ruling.

**Elements**   Type of rule **condition** required to satisfy the rule. Compare with **factors.**

**Elements test**   Test to assess **elements**; most typically, elements work like a checklist, and all must be satisfied (deemed "true") for the condition to be satisfied.

**Emergent legal rule**   The new legal rule that emerges when a court **processes** the **existing legal rule** by ruling on a new dispute.

**Enacted law** Rules passed by a governmental body to apply broadly to all citizens in future. Examples: statutes, ordinances, regulations, constitutional provisions. Compare with **common law.**

**Existing legal rule (of law)** Starting point for **predictive analysis**; may be explicitly or implicitly stated and found in **enacted law** or **common law.**

**Fact-based holdings** Court rulings that applied the rule to the facts of the case, revealing what facts are important to the court for a particular **issue.**

**Factors** Type of rule **condition** that is considered but not required. Compare with **elements.**

**Factors test** Test to assess **factors**; typically these are weighed against each other, and the test can be likened to a scale.

**Global roadmap** Broad **roadmap paragraph** at the beginning of the **Discussion** that orients the reader to that entire section.

**Global rule** Overall legal rule with three components: **result, conditions**, and relationship between conditions.

**Gloss** Detail that more fully explains what is important to a court in interpreting or applying the rule.

**Guiding factor** Something the court will consider when evaluating a specific rule **condition**; may be explicitly stated by the court, but is more typically implicitly inferred by the lawyer by looking at courts' past **fact-based holdings.**

**Guiding factors approach (to rule explanation organization)** Strategy for **small-scale organization** of **rule explanation** in a multiple authority memo that completely discusses a particular **guiding factor**, explaining how the facts from multiple precedent cases illustrate it, before moving on to the next guiding factor. Note that when closely related, more than one guiding factor may be considered together. Note, too, that the same case may be included in the discussion of more than one guiding factor. Contrast with **case approach.**

**Heading** Legal memorandum section that includes subject of memo, date, author, and recipient.

**Headnote** Editorial enhancements added to a judicial opinion that identify the legal **issues** the case discusses and flag the locations in the opinion where this discussion occurs.

**Hierarchy (of judicial authority)** Levels of the court system; typically, the higher the court in a jurisdiction, the more authoritative its opinions.

**Holdings** Court's answers to the **issues** presented.

**Inductive reasoning** Using specific examples to derive general principles; basis of **pre-drafting predictive analysis**. Compare with **deductive framework.**

**IRAC** Acronym for way of organizing a legal argument: issue, rule, application, conclusion. Compare with **CREAC.**

**Issue** Contested **condition** of a rule. Because the parties do not agree as to whether this part of the rule has been satisfied, each will make arguments about why it does or does not apply. Contrast with **non-issue.**

**Issue-components approach** Small-scale organization of **rule application** that presents all of the **arguments** and **counter-arguments** for a particular component of a **rule for a condition**, e.g., a single **guiding factor**, before moving on to the next component. Contrast with **party/position approach.**

**Issue roadmap** **Roadmap paragraph** at the beginning of an **issue segment** to introduce the reader to the analysis of a **condition** that will follow.

**Issue segment** Part of the memo's **Discussion** that analyzes one of the contested **conditions**; includes an **issue roadmap, rule explanation**, and **rule application** for the **rule for the condition.**

**Large-scale organization** Expected deductive progression of information in a **Discussion** section of a legal memorandum, framed by the **global rule** of law.

**Law-centered interpretations** Explicit explanation of the rule that does not rely on the case facts.

**Legal reasoning** Form of argument that applies legal rules to case facts; three main types: **analogical, rule-based**, and **policy-based.**

**Mandatory/binding law** Law that must be followed in a particular jurisdiction.

**Mandatory/cumulative conditions** Condition that must be satisfied for the rule to be satisfied.

**Monologuing** Mistake of merely reciting facts without tethering them to the legal rule.

**Non-issue** Condition not necessary to address in a memo **Discussion** because it is either uncontested or because instructions indicate it should be omitted from the analysis. The omitted issue should simply be noted as a non-issue and a reason briefly stated. Contrast with **issue.**

**Parade of cases** Mistake of presenting too many cases in **rule explanation** without providing the necessary transitions or framing sentences that help illustrate the purpose of including each particular case.

**Party/position approach** Small-scale organization of **rule application** that starts by presenting all of one party's **arguments** related to the **rule for the condition**, followed by all of the other side's **counter-arguments**. Contrast with **issue-components approach.**

**Persuasive law** Law from another jurisdiction that may be considered but does not have to be followed.

**Persuasive writing** Written communication of persuasive analysis that includes strategically presented **counter-analysis**; the purpose is to convince someone, typically the court, to adopt a particular client's position. Contrast with **predictive writing.**

**Policy-based reasoning** Argument that invokes the justification for the law when it was created to show that the same justification compels a particular result in a client's case.

**Policy behind the rule**   Purpose or reason for the rule of law.

**Precedent**   Decided legal case that can be used to determine how future cases should be similarly resolved.

**Prediction**   Determination of how the court is likely to rule based on legal analysis; may be a global (overall) prediction or an **issue** prediction.

**Predictive analysis**   Neutral analysis of law from both parties' perspectives.

**Predictive/objective memorandum**   Common form of **predictive writing**, created for the law-trained reader and consisting of five sections: **Heading, Question Presented, Short Answer, Statement of Facts,** and **Discussion.**

**Predictive writing**   Written communication of **predictive analysis** that sets forth an objective analysis of the law, including the likely **arguments** of both sides in a dispute. Contrast with **persuasive writing.**

**Pre-drafting process**   **Inductive** process of ensuring a clear understanding of the client's situation and the applicable legal rule(s) before starting to draft the analysis.

**Procedural law**   Rules related to the process of applying and enforcing the law.

**Process a rule (of law)**   Court's interpretation of a legal rule and application to the case before it, which deepens the understanding of the rule's meaning. Two primary types: **law-centered interpretations** and **fact-based holdings.**

**Question Presented**   Legal memorandum section that presents the **issue**(s) discussed in the memo; i.e., the legal question that arises out of the client facts.

**Reason by proximity (reasoning by proximity)**   Mistake of not clearly making an **argument,** but instead putting similar facts side by side and leaving it to the reader to connect the facts and determine their legal significance.

**Reasoning (of the court)**   Court's rationale explaining why it reached its **holding.**

**Result (of a rule)**   What follows if the court concludes the client's **claim** or **charge** is established in accordance with the rule's **conditions.**

**Roadmap paragraphs**   Paragraphs intended to orient the reader to material that follows.

**Rule application**   Applying the law to the legally significant facts using one or more forms of **legal reasoning.** Key components include: (1) **analysis** and **counter-analysis** relevant to the **issue**/condition, and (2) **prediction** as to the court's determination of the issue/condition.

**Rule-based reasoning**   **Argument** that relies upon the language and principles of the rule; logical syllogism.

**Rule explanation**   Provides meaning of legal rule by showing how the court has previously analyzed a

**condition**; discusses key facts from the prior cases and shows how the court reached a **fact-based holding** by applying the rule to these facts.

**Rule for the condition (Issue rule)**   Rule for one of the **conditions** of the **global rule**; provides **guiding factors, definitions,** and/or **standards** that provide additional insight into the meaning of the rule.

**Rule proof**   Using the **fact-based holding** from the **precedent** to demonstrate that the court applied the components (most commonly **guiding factors**) identified for the **rule for the condition.**

**Short Answer**   Legal memorandum section with three objectives: (1) answer the legal question, (2) allude to the law applicable to the client's situation, and (3) justify the prediction with key facts from the client's situation.

**Small-scale organization**   Organization of content within a smaller portion of a memo, such as an **issue segment** or one of its subsets, such as the **rule application** paragraphs.

**Standards**   Some type of additional information about how a court does—or does not—evaluate a **condition**; often appear as an articulation of a weight, or measurement, that guides the court's analysis.

**Stare decisis**   Latin for "to stand by things decided," legal doctrine that says courts must follow existing binding **precedent**; i.e., similar situations result in similar decisions.

**Statement of Facts**   Legal memorandum section that memorializes the facts that the author of the memo relied on to frame the analysis; demonstrates what the writer knew at the time the **prediction** was made, which is significant because if a fact later comes to light, it may change the prediction.

**Substantive law**   Rules that define and regulate legal rights and duties; common categories include contracts, real property, and torts.

**Synthesis**   Process of piecing together a new legal rule from multiple **emergent rules**, with each new emergent rule building upon the prior **existing legal rule.**

**Synthesized legal rule**   The new legal rule, a combination of two or more **emergent legal rules,** typically determined implicitly by looking at the **fact-based holdings** and **law-centered interpretations** of multiple **precedent** cases.

**Synthesized rule proof**   Using the **fact-based holdings** from multiple **precedent** cases to demonstrate that the court applied the components (most commonly **guiding factors**) identified for the **rule for the condition.**

**Talking points**   Personal notes to help organize the memo writer's thoughts when information must be communicated orally and informally.

**Topic/thesis sentence**   First sentence of the paragraph; indicates the purpose of the paragraph.

# Index

Active reading, 16-40, 44, 371
*ALWD Guide to Legal Citation*, 230
American Bar Association, 13, 45, 80
Analogical reasoning. *See also* Reasoning
    generally, 48-49, 110, 135, 147-153
    cases, selection of, 74, 76, 271-281
    citations, use of, 230
    combining different types of reasoning, 143, 152-153
    comparisons in, 147-151
    defined, 12, 136-138
    distinction, drawing of, 137, 342, 344
    distinguishing facts from precedent, 148-149
    effective arguments, 151-152, 228-229, 337-338, 342-343
    examples, 137, 143, 151, 229, 234, 272-275, 336-338, 342, 344
    ineffective analogical argument, 229, 337-338, 342-343
    key features, 151-152
    overview, 136-138
    policy-based vs., 158
    prevalence of, 138, 147
    relevance of analogy or distinction, 342, 344
    rule application section, use in. *See* Rule application
    rule-based in conjunction with, 233-234, 342-344
    signals, use of, 230
    single authority, 271
Appellant, defined, 41
Appellate standard of review, 29
Appellee, defined, 41
Arguments
    generally, 10, 133, 135, 149, 186, 286
    analogical. *See* Analogical reasoning
    counter-arguments. *See* Counter-arguments
    editing, 364-368
    effective arguments, 151-152, 228-229, 336-338, 342-343, 365-368
    email communications, 386-387
    examples, 18, 112, 137, 143, 151, 173, 191-194, 209-210, 212-214, 223-227, 229, 234, 245-246, 272-275, 333-334, 336-340, 342, 344
    global roadmap and, 177
    guiding factors and, 113-114, 121, 207, 308-311, 333-334, 337
    "labeling" format, 227-228
    multiple authorities, 284, 286, 298, 325, 328, 331-341

    organization of, 221-227, 334-335, 338-341
    persuasive writing, 47-48, 398-399
    policy based. *See* Policy-based reasoning
    predictive analysis, 1, 4, 8-9, 48, 62, 65, 81
    presentation of, 227-228
    revision process, 359-360
    rule application section. *See* Rule application: arguments in
    rule based. *See* Rule-based reasoning
    standards and, 111
    statement of facts, 352-353
    stylistic options, 227-228
    talking points and, 394
    templates, 186-187, 219
    worksheets, 170, 172, 290, 294
Attorney work product, 384
Authority
    adverse, 138, 400
    binding, 87-89, 131, 262, 400, 483
    cases. *See* Cases
    codes, 87, 483-484
    common law. *See* Common law
    constitutions, 74, 77, 86, 483
    court systems, 88-89
    enacted law. *See* Enacted law
    federal, 87-88, 483
    hierarchy of, 4, 88-89, 268, 278-279, 483
    local, 87, 483
    mandatory, 87-89, 131, 262, 400, 483-484
    persuasive, 87, 131, 483-484
    primary, 483. *See also* Common law; Enacted law
    regulations, 86, 483
    rules, 86
    secondary, 77, 484
    selection of. *See* Cases, selection of
    state, 87-88, 483
    statutes. *See* Statutes

Bias-free language, 374
*The Bluebook*, 230
Briefing cases. *See* Cases: briefing of
Bright-line rule, 106, 111, 375

Capitalization, 372
Case law. *See* Cases; Common law

Cases
    binding authority, 87-89, 131, 262, 400, 483
    briefing of, 41-44, 168, 206
    casebooks, 16
    citation, 41
    editorial enhancements, 17, 21, 279
    emergent rule, outline of, 128-129
    existing rule, interpretation of, 122-124
    fact-based holdings. *See* Fact-based holdings
    factors, interaction between, 122-123
    guiding factors, interaction of, 123
    law-centered interpretation, 107-109, 119, 124-129
    in multiple authority memorandum. *See* Cases,
        selection of
    other jurisdictions, 131
    persuasive authority, 131
    precedent. *See* Precedent
    prior cases used to make predictions, 48-49
    reading full cases vs. excerpts, 16-17
    rule of law, discerning, 89-94, 107-131, 266-271
    skimming, 20-22, 29-30, 35, 39-40, 44
    unedited, 17, 21
Cases, selection of
    analogical arguments, 74, 76, 272-275, 279-280
    avoiding overload, 280
    "best" cases, 272, 280
    court, level of, 278-279
    date of the authority, 278
    deductive framework and, 65
    discerning the rule of law. *See* Cases: rule of law,
        discerning
    factually similar cases, 271-278
    gaps, filling of, 276
    global rule of law, 267-269
    guidelines, 277-278
    headnotes, use of, 279. *See also* Headnotes
    opposing party/position, 280
    plugging gaps, 276
    purposes for, 265-278
    questions to ask regarding usefulness, 266
    recency of authority, 278
    rule explanation paragraphs, 320-321
    rule of law provided, 266-271
    thoroughness of decision and reasoning, 279
    worksheet, pre-drafting, 287, 289-294
Checklists
    discussion section, 166-167, 431-439
    editing, 363-366, 437-439
    elements as, 10, 96, 114
    features of predictive memo, 62, 431-439
    global conclusion, 432, 434, 436
    global roadmap, 431, 433
    issue roadmaps, 431, 433
    multiple authority memo, 433-434
    pre-drafting process, 285-286
    revising, 360-362, 435-436
    rule application, 432, 434
    rule explanation, 329, 431-433

    single authority memo, 431-432
    writing memo, 62, 431-439
Citations
    case briefs, in, 41
    examples, 41, 52, 58, 63, 68, 119-120, 123, 125-127,
        169, 191, 197-198, 211-212, 243-248, 252,
        255, 262, 287-294, 304, 316-318, 324, 355,
        376-377, 405-408, 410-414, 417-422, 424-430,
        473-482
    for fact-based holding, 200
    full, 289
    global roadmap, 316
    manuals, 230
    parenthetical explanation, 323, 324
    pinpoint, 289
    proofreading, 368
    quotations, 374-375
    signals, 230, 317, 323-324
    statement of facts, inappropriateness in, 353
    templates, 186-187, 196, 201, 208, 269, 315, 317
    worksheets, 169, 287-294
Client-centered reading, 16-40
Common law, 9, 74, 86-87, 90, 104, 114, 122, 138, 263,
        483. *See also* Cases.
Communication, forms of
    email. *See* Email communication
    oral, 391, 393-396
    talking points, 393-396
    written. *See* Checklists; Drafting process; Editing;
        Email communication; Framing sentences;
        Outlines; Persuasive writing; Predictive
        memorandum; Style of legal
        writing; Template; Transitions
Conclusion. *See also* Global prediction
    CREAC/IRAC, 181
    examples, 40, 71, 356-357, 414, 430
    global. *See* Global conclusion
    multiple authority memorandum, 242, 356-357,
        414, 430
    multiple claims or charges, 357
    single authority memorandum, 40, 356
Concurring opinion, 43
Conditions. *See also* Issues
    contested, 51, 299, 301
    cumulative, 98
    diagram, 114
    defined, 10
    discretionary, 50, 98
    disjunctive, 10
    elements. *See* Elements
    exceptions, rule with, 99, 102
    factors. *See* Factors
    gloss, 114
    issue segment. *See* Issue segment of discussion
    mandatory, 98
    relationship to one another, 98-99, 104, 105,
        122-124
    result, 10-12, 50, 74, 91, 95, 98-100, 105-106, 114, 163

rule of law and. *See* Rule of law for the condition
  types, 10, 114. *See also* Elements; Factors
  words used, guidance from, 99, 105
Consistency, 49, 118, 122, 147, 214, 256, 262-263, 361,
  374, 377
Constitutions, 74, 77, 86, 483
Contested condition, 51, 299, 301
Counter-arguments. *See also* Arguments
  defined, 8-9, 149
  examples, 151, 192
  persuasive writing, 48, 149, 398
  predictive analysis, 8-9, 48, 62, 65, 69, 75, 149
  pre-drafting checklist, 286
  rule application section. *See* Rule application:
    counter-arguments in
Court system
  cases, selection of, 268, 278-279
  diagram, 88
  federal courts, 88-89, 483
  hierarchy of courts, 88-89, 268, 278-279, 483
  state courts, 88, 483
  structure of U.S. system, 88-89, 483
CREAC framework, 13, 175, 177, 181
Criminal vs. civil cases, terms used in, 372

Deductive framework
  cases, selection of, 65
  conclusion, 356
  defined, 47, 53, 62, 68, 177, 207, 334, 398
  editing process, 363, 365
  email communications, 386
  global roadmap, 177
  inductive vs., 47, 53
  IRAC/CREAC, 177
  revision process, 359
  roadmap paragraphs, 177, 195
  rule application, 334
  rule-based reasoning, 136, 141
  rule explanation, 208
  talking points, 393, 395
  writing the memo, 45, 47, 53, 62, 164, 166, 365, 386,
    395, 398
Definitions. *See also* Standards
  cases, selection of, 266
  examples, 19, 111-112, 129
  global rule of law, 167, 169, 268
  incorporation of, 203
  interpretation of rules through, 110-114, 118
  issue components, 221-222
  issue roadmap, 165, 178-179, 186-187, 199, 201, 240,
    248, 316-317
  law-centered interpretations, 11, 125, 170, 172, 266,
    288, 291
  modification of rule, 256
  rule application, 221-222
  rule explanation, 205
  rule of law for the condition, 161, 165-166, 199-201,
    237, 240, 267, 269, 285, 335
  standards vs., 11, 112

  in statutes, 87
  synthesized, 285
  worksheets, 169-170, 172, 288-292
Disclaimer in email communications, 384, 388
Discretionary conditions, 50, 98
Discussion section of legal memorandum
  annotated, 191-194, 242-248
  authorities, selection of. *See* Cases, selection of
  components, 164-166, 239-242, 248
  conclusion, 40, 71, 242, 356-357, 414, 430
  deductive framework. *See* Deductive framework
  drafting process. *See* Drafting process
  editing. *See* Editing
  examples, 58-61, 63-65, 68-71, 243-248, 355-356,
    405-408, 410-414, 417-422, 424-430
  first draft, 188-190, 297
  gathering content, 167-173, 286-294
  global conclusion. *See* Global conclusion
  global roadmap. *See* Global roadmap
  headings, 354-356
  integrating multiple authorities, 242-248, 251-263
  internal discussion headings, 354
  issue roadmap. *See* Issue roadmap
  issue segment. *See* Issue segment
  large-scale organization, 175-181, 239, 241, 298-301,
    310-311
  multiple authority memorandum, 243-248, 297-344
  outline, sample, 310-311. *See also* Outlines:
    discussion section
  outlining the components, 75, 185-194, 297-298,
    310-311
  pre-drafting, 163-173, 185-194, 237-294. *See also*
    Pre-drafting analysis
  revision of. *See* Revising
  roadmaps. *See* Roadmaps
  rule application paragraphs. *See* Rule application
  rule explanation paragraphs. *See* Rule explanation
  selecting authorities, 265-280. *See also* Cases,
    selection of
  single authority memorandum, 159-234
  small-scale organization, 221, 240-241, 298, 301-310
  sorting authorities, 265-280
  synthesis in multiple authority memo. *See*
    Synthesizing rules of law
  templates, 185-190, 315-317, 349
  visual maps, use of, 312
  worksheets, 167-173, 189-190, 286-294
Disjunctive conditions, 10
Dissenting opinion, 43
Drafting process
  discussion section. *See* Discussion section of legal
    memorandum
  editing. *See* Editing
  flowchart summary of steps, 76
  multiple authority memorandum, 295-344
  proofreading. *See* Proofreading
  revising. *See* Revising
  roadmaps. *See* Roadmaps
  rule application paragraphs. *See* Rule application

rule explanation paragraphs. *See* Rule explanation
single authority memorandum, 185-194
steps for writing memo, 73-80

Editing. *See also* Proofreading; Revising
    checklist questions, 363-366
    email communication, 385
    highlighting, 367-368
    read-aloud method, 366, 385
    steps for writing memo, 75-76, 359-360, 363
    techniques, 366-368
    topic/thesis sentences, review of, 366-367
Editorial enhancements, 17, 21, 279. *See also* Headnotes
Elements. *See also* Conditions; Factors
    defined, 95-96, 114
    factors vs., 50, 95-98, 105-106
Elements test
    defined, 10, 50
    either/or test, 99, 101
    examples, 90-91, 96, 98-99, 100
    guiding factors, use of, 106, 114
    mandatory elements test, 98-100, 106
    outlines, 100-101
Email communication
    generally, 381-392
    automated features, 390-391
    content, 382, 384-385, 387
    disclaimer, 384
    examples, 384, 387-388, 391-392
    legal analysis in, 385-388
    organization, 384-385
    professionalism, 389
    readability, 385
    recipients, 385, 390
    reviewing before hitting "send," 385
    signature line, 384
    style, 389
    subject line, 383-384
    tips, 389-392
    tone, attention to, 382-383
Emergent legal rule. *See also* Existing legal rule
    analogical reasoning, 138
    defined, 10, 90-91, 107, 109, 118, 133, 251
    diagrams, 90, 93
    examples, 86, 90-93, 118
    global rule of law vs., 197
    inductive analysis, 53
    outlining, 118, 128-129
    sources, 74, 90-91, 107, 133
    synthesizing rules of law, 251-255, 284, 289, 292
    worksheets, 169-172, 251-252, 289, 292
Enacted law. *See also* Constitutions; Statutes
    binding authority, 87, 483
    criminal laws, 86
    defined, 9
    examples, 89-90, 104, 268
    existing legal rule, source of, 74, 86, 91, 93, 104, 263
    importance of reading text of, 89

policy-based reasoning, 138
    predictive analysis based on, 9
    quoting exact wording vs. paraphrasing, 375
Ethical rules
    client's legal issue, determination of, 80
    judgmental immunity, 52
    jurisdictional variations, 80
    legal arguments, framing of, 138
    Model Rules of Professional Conduct, 13, 45, 80
    persuasion, limits to, 400
    preparation of memo, 45
    reasonable interpretation of judicial opinions, 124
    uncertainty in the law, 52
Existing legal rule. *See also* Emergent legal rule
    changes in law, 107, 263
    date of decision, 263
    defined, 9-10
    definitions, interpretation with, 110-112
    diagrams, 90, 93, 109
    examples, 86, 91-93, 104, 109, 267
    global rule of law, 74, 197
    guiding factors, interpretation with, 113-122. *See also*
        Guiding factors
    interpretation of, 110-124, 131, 133, 251. *See also*
        Interpretation of legal rule
    persuasive authority, 131
    processing of, 90, 93, 107, 125, 242, 268, 284
    rule-based reasoning. *See* Rule-based reasoning
    showing how conditions fit together, 122-124
    sources of, 74, 86, 93, 104, 109
    standards and definitions, interpretation with, 110-112
    synthesis, process of. *See* Synthesizing rules of law
    synthesized rule of law vs., 252, 302
    worksheets, 169, 288, 291
Explicit guiding factors. *See also* Guiding factors; Implicit
        guiding factors
    case processing of rule, 110
    cases, selection of, 266
    defined, 113, 120
    examples, 50, 107-108, 123
    implicit vs., 11, 106, 113, 115-120
    law-centered interpretations, 125, 170, 172, 266,
        288, 291
    making implicit factors explicit, 237, 270
    rule of law for the condition, 237, 266, 269
    worksheets, 170, 172, 288, 291

Fact-based holding. *See also* Holding; Rule proof
    analogical reasoning, 138, 161
    case used to discern fact-based holding, 124-129, 138,
        161, 170-171, 237
    common errors, 202-203
    defined, 11, 108
    examples, 108-109, 126-127, 129, 191, 193, 202, 243,
        245-246, 289-290, 318
    framing of, 128
    guiding factors, 11, 113-118, 125, 129, 249, 301,
        303-305

interpretation of rules, 110
issue roadmaps, 240
rule proof. *See* Rule proof
synthesized, 240-241, 252, 289-290, 293-294, 303-305, 317-318
Factors. *See also* Conditions; Elements
defined, 96, 106, 114
elements vs., 50, 95-98, 105-106
guiding. *See* Guiding factors
relative weight and relationship between factors, 101, 122-123
relevance of factor, 101
test. *See* Factors test
Factors test
balancing test, 99, 101
defined, 10, 50, 96
discretionary, 99, 101
elements test vs., 106
examples, 96-97, 122-123
outlines, 101
Facts. *See also* Fact-based holdings
case briefs, tips for, 41
contextual facts, 351-352
ethical rule regarding accuracy, 400
key facts from additional authorities, 259-260
legally significant facts, 351-352
material facts, failure to disclose, 400
misleading facts, 124, 138, 400
precedent, distinguishing from, 148-149
rule application, weaving facts to the rule in, 220-221
rule-based reasoning, tethering facts to the rule in, 143-144, 221
statement of. *See* Statement of facts
Forms
legal, 188
templates. *See* Templates
worksheets. *See* Worksheets
Framing sentences
checklists, 329, 431, 433
defined, 165, 206-210, 240, 306
examples, 192-193, 207-211, 214, 322-323, 327
importance of, 306, 321-322
rule explanation. *See* Rule explanation: framing sentences
template, 208
transitions, 322-323, 325

Gender-neutrality, 373
Global conclusion
changes in, 249
checklists, 432, 434, 436
contents, 166, 188, 241, 361, 432, 434
defined, 166, 180, 194, 241, 299, 301, 432, 434
examples, 71, 194, 299, 301, 362, 436
multiple authority memo, 241, 249, 299, 301, 311
revision checklist questions, 361-362
template, 188

Global prediction
changes in, with use of multiple authorities, 248-249, 314-316
defined, 165, 177, 196, 240, 315
email communication, 386
examples, 68, 71, 189, 191-192, 197, 316
global conclusion, 166, 241, 249
global roadmap, 164, 196, 240, 248
organization of memo, 65, 361, 386
short answer, 386
steps for writing memo, 75
talking points, 394
templates, 186, 188, 196-197, 315
Global roadmap
cases, incorporation of, 281
changes in, with use of multiple authorities, 248, 314-316
common error, 202
content, 75, 164-165, 196, 248, 314-316
defined, 13, 300
drafting process, 195-199, 314-316
examples, 65, 68, 189, 191, 197, 300, 355
framework, 177, 178-181
global prediction. *See* Global prediction
global rule of law. *See* Global rule of law
issues, 165, 196-198
large-scale organization from. *See* Large-scale organization
multiple authority memorandum, 248, 300-301, 310-311, 314-316
non-issues, 68, 165, 169, 178, 186, 196-200, 202, 240, 299, 314-315
outlines, 189, 300-301, 310-311
single authority memorandum, 195-199
structure, 314
templates, 186, 196-197, 315
topic sentence, 164, 196
worksheet, 189
Global rule of law
cases, selection of, 266-269, 271, 279, 281
changes in, with use of multiple authorities, 300-301, 315
components, 166, 196, 240, 267
date of authority, 278
defined, 10, 91-92, 197, 267
diagram, 114
examples, 68, 167, 189, 191, 267, 269, 287, 316
importance of, 178-180
interpretation of, 110, 266
large-scale organization of discussion, 181, 221, 298, 300-301, 394
modification of, 110
non-issues, 169, 178, 198
outline, 269
pre-drafting process, 164-168, 283-287, 299
recent authorities, 278
single authority, 169
steps for writing memo, 74-76

synthesizing, 240-241, 269, 285-287, 300-301, 310,
     314-316
talking points, 394-395
templates, 185-186, 196
worksheets, 169, 189, 287
Gloss, 10-11, 19, 114, 246, 269
Glossary, 485-487
Grammar, 360, 368-369, 377, 385, 390
Guiding factors. *See also* Rule of law for the condition
analogical reasoning, 49-51, 149, 166, 228, 286
defined, 11, 49, 106, 112-114, 206-207
discretion in labeling implicit factors, 51, 118,
     121-122, 202, 261
element, satisfaction of, 106
examples, 11-12, 19-20, 49-50, 52-53, 68, 70, 113-118,
     121-123, 127, 129-130, 142-144, 150, 170-173,
     190, 191, 193, 200, 202, 211-212, 221, 224-225,
     234, 243-246, 256-262, 267, 270, 276, 288-294,
     302, 308-310, 317, 326, 333-334, 336-339,
     343, 367
existing legal rule, interpretation of, 110, 113-122
expert tips for working with, 129-131
explicit. *See* Explicit guiding factors
fact-based holding, discerning from, 117, 118
identification of, 49-51, 166-167, 170, 172, 237, 285
implicit. *See* Implicit guiding factors
importance of, 121
interpretation of rules, 110, 113-122
labeling of, 121-122, 129-131, 167, 257-258, 261
number of, 121
role in road maps, 121, 164-165, 178, 179, 186, 187,
     199-202, 240, 248-249, 298, 301, 314, 316-317,
     364
role in rule application, 121, 165, 190, 218, 221,
     232-233, 241, 298, 310, 332-335, 341-342,
     364. *See also* Issue-components approach to
     organization
role in rule explanation, 165, 187, 205, 206-210, 211,
     213, 232-233, 240-241, 320-321, 329, 341-342,
     364. *See also* Rule explanation: guiding factors
     approach to organization
rule proof. *See* Rule proof
synthesized, legal context, 258-262, 285, 317
synthesized, non-legal context, 256-258
testing of, 130
tips, 129-131

Header for legal memorandum
clauses to include, 348
date completed, 66, 71
examples, 56, 62, 66, 383
Headings
discussion section, 354-356
email communication, 383
examples, 56, 62, 65, 66, 355-356, 383
internal, 354-356
memo. *See* Header for legal memorandum
multiple topic memorandum, 355-356

sections in memo, 354-356
single topic memorandum, 356
Headnotes, 17, 279
Holding
analogical reasoning from, 138
cases, selection of, 273-277, 279, 281, 288, 292
defined, 43
editorial enhancements, 17
examples, 19-21, 43, 69, 189, 192, 243, 245-246, 268,
     289-290, 293-294, 318, 324
fact-based. *See* Fact-based holding
guiding factors, 115-119, 122, 321, 326
inconsistent cases, 262
rule explanation paragraphs, 13, 69, 206-207, 210-211,
     241, 307, 320-321, 326-328
rule proof. *See* Rule proof

Implicit guiding factors. *See also* Explicit guiding factors;
     Guiding factors
case processing of rule, 110, 119-120
cases, selection of, 271, 288, 292
challenges, 118
defined, 115-120
discretion in labeling, 121-122, 202, 257
examples, 115-118, 125, 127, 129-130, 244,
     256-258, 261
explicit vs., 11, 106, 113, 115-120
generalizations from specific facts, 50
identifying and articulating, 50, 167, 256
labeling, 118, 121-122, 129, 130-131, 167, 257
making implicit factors explicit, 237, 270
multiple authorities, 131, 258-260, 288, 292
rule of law for the condition, 237, 266
single authority, 259
synthesized, 258-260, 288, 292
worksheet, 288, 292
Inductive reasoning
analytical process, 47, 50, 53, 177
inferring guiding factors, 118
pre-drafting analysis, 53, 177
Interoffice memorandum. *See* Predictive memorandum
Interpretation of legal rule
definitions, 110-112
guiding factors. *See* Guiding factors
policy behind rule, 111
standards, 110-112
IRAC framework, 13, 177, 180-181
Issue. *See also* Question presented
case briefs, 42-43
defined, 10, 51
ethical obligation of lawyer, 80
examples, 6, 12, 21, 29, 32-35, 39-42, 52, 66, 68-71,
     105, 169-172, 178-180, 189, 191-194, 197-199,
     202-203, 206, 262, 267-271, 276, 287-294,
     299-301, 312, 332-335, 339, 350, 352, 355-356
non-issue. *See* Non-issue
roadmap. *See* Issue roadmap
worksheet, 287-294

Issue-components approach to organization
  defined, 222, 340
  editing checklist, 364
  examples, 223-225, 308-309, 333-336
  multiple authority memorandum, 308-309, 333-336, 340
  party/position approach vs., 222
  single authority memorandum, 221-227
  rule application section, 221-227, 308-309, 333-336, 340, 364
  varied approaches, use of, 227
Issue prediction
  changes in, with use of multiple authorities, 248-249, 301, 314, 317
  CREAC/IRAC framework, 177
  defined, 166, 218, 241
  effective example, 201
  examples, 71, 201
  global prediction vs., 165, 196, 240, 315
  length, 201
  mini-predictions, 223-225
  takeaway, 394
  talking points, 394
Issue roadmap
  changes in, with use of multiple authorities, 298, 301-305
  common error, 202
  components, 68-69, 165, 178, 199-200, 316-317
  defined, 13
  diagram, 207
  drafting process, 199-203, 316-318
  examples, 65, 68-71, 178, 189, 191, 193, 202
  guiding factors. *See* Guiding factors
  issue rule. *See* Rule of law for the condition
  key components. *See* components, *this heading*
  multiple authority memorandum, 248, 298, 301-305, 308, 316-318
  outline, 189
  prediction, 165, 199, 201
  purposes, 318
  resolution of issue, prediction as to, 165, 199, 201
  rule of law, 165, 199, 316
  rule proof. *See* Rule proof
  single authority memorandum, 199-203
  synthesized rule of law, 316-317
  synthesized rule proof, 316-318
  templates, 186-187, 201, 317
  topic sentence, 165, 199-200, 316
  worksheet, 189
Issue rule of law. *See* Rule of law for the condition
Issue segment
  generally, 69, 105, 198, 318
  analysis of, 170-173, 288-294
  cases, selection of, 278
  components, 75, 164, 178-179, 199, 206-207, 221, 240, 248, 301-310, 332, 364
  CREAC/IRAC framework, 177

  defined, 75, 164, 199, 363-364
  diagram, 181
  editing questions, 363-364, 437
  examples, 178-181, 206-207
  global roadmap framework, 178-180
  guiding factors, 232-233
  issue roadmaps. *See* Issue roadmaps
  issue rule. *See* Rule of law for the condition
  large-scale organization, 300, 320
  multiple authority memorandum, 298, 301-310
  order of contents, 363
  organization of, 298
  outline, 232-233, 299, 310-311
  rule application paragraphs. *See* Rule application
  rule explanation paragraphs. *See* Rule explanation
  separate drafting, 332
  small-scale organization, 298, 301-310
  transitions, 322-323, 361
  worksheet, pre-drafting, 288-294

Judicial decisions. *See* Cases; Common law

Language of the law, 9, 12, 100-102, 107-108, 143, 157, 371-372, 377-379. *See also* Definitions; Law-centered interpretations
Large-scale organization
  defined, 13
  discussion section, 13, 175-181, 221, 239-242, 248, 297-298, 301, 310-311, 320
  editing and revising, 345, 359-361, 367
  issue segment, 320
  multiple authority memorandum, 239, 241, 248, 297-298, 300-301, 310-311
  outline of discussion with multiple authorities, 310-311
  outline of rule, 103
  revision stage, 359-361
  single authority memorandum, 175-181, 298-300, 301
Law-centered interpretations
  generally, 301
  defined, 11, 107, 110
  definitions, 11, 125, 170, 172, 266, 288, 291
  examples, 11, 107-108, 108-109, 124-127, 317
  explicit guiding factors, 113, 115, 170, 172, 266, 288, 291
  outlining the emergent rule, 128
  standards, 11, 170, 172, 266, 288, 291, 317
  synthesized legal rule, 252
  worksheets, 170, 172, 288, 291
Learning strategies, 4-8. *See also* Active reading; Cases: briefing of
Legal analysis. *See* Arguments; Conditions; Counter-arguments; Emergent legal rule; Existing legal rule; Guiding Factors; Reasoning; Predictive analysis; Pre-drafting analysis; Synthesizing rules of law; Worksheets
Legal claim, defined, 41-42
Legal forms, 188

Legal memorandum. *See* Predictive memorandum
Legal reasoning. *See* Reasoning
Legal research. *See* Research
Legal rules. *See* Rule of law
Legal writing style. *See* Style of legal writing
Legislative history, 157
Looping, 7, 8

Maps, visual, 312. *See also* Outlines
Model Rules of Professional Conduct, 13, 45, 80. *See also*
     Ethical rules
Monologuing, 220-221, 364
Multiple authority memorandum
     conclusion, 242, 356-357
     discussion section, 243-248, 297-344. *See also*
         Discussion section
     drafting process, 295-344
     global conclusion, 241, 249, 299, 301, 311. *See also*
         Global conclusion
     global roadmap, 248, 300-301, 310-311, 314-316. *See*
         *also* Global roadmap
     issue roadmap, 248, 298, 301-305, 308, 316-318. *See*
         *also* Issue roadmap
     issue segment, 298, 301-310. *See also* Issue segment
     large-scale organization, 300-301
     legal analysis, 237-294
     outline of discussion section, 310-311
     pre-drafting analysis, 237, 283-294
     roadmaps, 242, 313-318. *See also*
         Roadmaps
     rule application, 242, 249, 298, 308-310, 331-344. *See*
         *also* Rule application
     rule explanation, 242, 249, 298, 305-308, 319-329. *See*
         *also* Rule explanation
     rule of law for the condition, 302. *See also* Rule of law
         for the condition
     rule proof, 249, 303-305. *See also* Rule proof
     sample memos, 415-430
     selection of authorities. *See* Cases, selection of
     small-scale organization, 298, 301-310
     synthesis in. *See* Synthesizing rules of law
Multiple topic memorandum, 354-357

Non-issue
     cautions, 105, 198-199, 202
     defined, 10, 51, 166, 314
     effective use of, 199
     examples, 129, 189, 191, 197, 267
     global roadmap, 68, 165, 169, 178, 186, 196-200, 202,
         240, 299, 314-315
     ineffective use of, 198-199
     pre-drafting, 285, 287-288
     revision checklist question, 360
     worksheets, 169, 189, 287-288

Objective analysis. *See* Predictive analysis
Objective memorandum. *See* Predictive memorandum
Objective standard, 125-126

Opinions, 9, 17, 22. *See also* Cases
Organization of memorandum
     issue-components approach. *See* Issue-components
         approach to organization
     large-scale. *See* Large-scale organization
     party/position approach. *See* Party/position
         approach to organization
     small-scale. *See* Small-scale organization
Outlines
     annotated discussion section, 191-194
     discussion section, 75-76, 188-194, 310-311
     elements test, 100-101
     emergent rule, 128-129
     factors test, 101
     global roadmap, 189, 300-301, 310-311
     global rule of law, 269
     issue roadmap, 189
     issue segment, 232-233, 299, 310-311
     multiple authority memorandum
         discussion section, 310-311
     reverse outline technique, 362-363
     rule application, 226, 308-311
     rule explanation, 311
     rule of law, 105, 269
     sample outline for multiple authority memorandum,
         310-311
     talking points, 395

Parade of cases, 325, 328
Paraphrasing, 375-377
Party/position approach to organization
     defined, 222, 340
     editing checklist, 364
     examples, 225-226, 309, 335-336, 338-341
     issue-components approach vs., 222
     multiple authority memorandum, 309, 331-332,
         334-336
     rule application section, 221-227, 309, 331-332,
         334-336, 364
     single authority memorandum, 221-222, 225-227
     varied approaches, use of, 227
Persuasive authority. *See* Authority
Persuasive writing. *See also* Predictive writing
     audience, 398
     counter-arguments in, 149, 398-399
     defined, 9
     ethical rules, 400
     examples, 399-401
     objective analysis, 280
     predictive writing vs., 47-48, 398-401
     purpose of, 48, 399
Policy-based reasoning
     additional authorities, effect of, 286
     analogical reasoning vs., 158
     examples, 139, 156-157
     how to develop arguments, 157-158
     identification of policy, 157-158
     introduction, 155-157

overview, 12, 135, 138-139
rule application, 165, 179-180, 207, 218, 241, 331,
   432, 434
rule-based vs., 158
Polishing, 368-369
Precedent
generally, 4, 40-42, 173, 239, 259
analogical reasoning, 47, 53, 136-138, 143, 147-152,
   179, 214, 217-218, 228-230, 234, 241, 276, 335
binding, 262, 268
citation information, 41
editing by highlighting, 367
ethical rules, 80
examples, 112, 259, 396
facts, distinguishing from, 148-149
guiding factors, 116, 118, 191, 202, 209, 212, 241,
   257, 320
multiple, 303
policy-based reasoning, 139
rule application, 69, 179, 192, 309, 318, 328, 336, 338,
   341, 367
rule-based reasoning and non-reference to, 136, 141,
   143, 233
rule explanation, 165, 187, 192, 200, 206, 208, 211,
   214-215, 276-277, 319, 325, 341
rule proof, 165, 191, 193, 199-200, 202, 240, 303,
   305, 317
stare decisis. See Stare decisis
Prediction
examples, 189, 191-193, 201, 202
importance of, 48
predictive legal analysis. See Predictive analysis
style, 201
Predictive analysis
analogical reasoning, 47-49
deductive. See Deductive framework
defined, 8-9, 47, 81
guiding factors to reason by analogy, 49-51
inductive, 47, 50, 53, 177
persuasive writing, 280, 398
predictive memorandum, relationship with, 1. See also
   Predictive memorandum
prior cases used to make predictions, 48-49
question presented, 348
solving client problems, 51-53
understanding of, 47-48
Predictive memorandum
analogical reasoning. See Analogical reasoning
analysis and counter-analysis. See Arguments;
   Counter-arguments
annotated, 65-71
application of rule. See Rule application
checklists. See Checklists
client-focus, 62, 65
conclusion. See Conclusion
defined, 1, 4, 12, 45, 280
discussion. See Discussion section of legal
   memorandum
drafting process. See Drafting process

editing. See Editing
ethical rules regarding memo preparation, 45. See also
   Ethical rules
examples, 55-71, 403-430
explanation of rule. See Rule explanation
facts, statement of. See Statement of facts
global roadmap. See Global roadmap
header. See Header
issue. See Question presented
key features, 62-65
language and style, 371-379
large-scale organization. See Large-scale organization
multiple authorities, use of. See Multiple authority
   memorandum
multiple topic, 354-357
organization, 65-71
other names for, 4, 45
persuasive writing vs., 397-401
policy-based reasoning. See Policy-based reasoning
pre-drafting. See Pre-drafting analysis
proofreading, 368-369
question presented. See Question presented
revising. See Revising
roadmaps. See Roadmaps
rule application paragraphs. See Rule application
rule-based reasoning. See Rule-based reasoning
rule explanation paragraphs. See Rule explanation
sample memos, 56-71, 403-430
sections of, overview, 12
short answer. See Short answer
single authority, use of. See Single authority
   memorandum
single topic, 356
small-scale organization. See Small-scale organization
sorting and selecting authorities, 265-281. See also
   Cases, selection of
statement of facts. See Statement of facts
steps for writing, 73-76
structure, 55-71
style, 372-374
talking points. See Talking points
Predictive writing. See also Persuasive writing; Predictive
   memorandum
defined, 9, 47-48
persuasive writing vs., 47-48, 398, 399
Pre-drafting analysis
email communication, 386
foundational checklist, 285-286
gathering content, 163-173, 286-294
importance of, 44, 76-80
legal research, 77
multiple authority memorandum, 237, 283-294
multiple vs. single authority, 283-284
selection of authorities. See Cases, selection of
single authority memorandum, 163-173, 237, 283-284
steps, 74-77, 166-167, 237
synthesizing authorities. See Synthesizing rules of law
worksheet approach to gathering content, 167-173,
   286-294

Procedure in case brief, what to include, 41-42
Processing of legal rule, 4, 10, 169, 253, 267, 287
Proofreading, 75-76, 360, 368-369
Proximity, reasoning by, 332, 337, 364
Punctuation, 368-369, 377-378

Question presented
   generally, 348-350
   components, 348
   descriptive labels for parties, 349
   editing checklist, 366
   email communication, 386
   examples, 56, 63, 65-66, 350, 403, 409, 415, 423
   jurisdiction, 348-349
   persuasive writing, 399
   steps for writing memo, 75, 348-350
   substantive area of law, 349
   under/does/when format, 66, 349
Quoting
   attribution, 374-375
   citations, 374-375
   examples, 376-377
   paraphrasing vs., 375-377
   "phrase that pays," 376
   quotation marks, 374-376

Read-aloud method
   editing, 366, 378, 385
   proofreading, 368-369
Reasoning
   generally, 133-140
   analogical. See Analogical reasoning
   combining different types, 152-153
   of court, 43, 165, 187, 206, 208, 210-211, 241, 279,
      320
   deductive. See Deductive framework
   defined, 12, 135
   inductive. See Inductive reasoning
   overview of types, 12, 135-139
   policy based. See Policy-based reasoning
   by proximity, 332, 337, 364
   rule based. See Rule-based reasoning
Research
   analysis of research needs, 77
   cases, 17, 89-90, 258-259. See also Cases: rule of law,
      discerning; Cases, selection of
   citation information, 230
   currency in, 71
   email requests, 386-388, 391
   ethical rules, 52
   gaps in analysis, 394
   headnotes, use of, 17, 279
   legal forms, 188
   pre-drafting process, 44, 77
   primary vs. secondary legal materials, 77, 483-484
   questions to ask and answer, 77
   sources of law, 85-86, 89, 483-484
   statutes, 87, 483

steps for writing predictive memo, 48, 75-76, 348,
   350, 394
strategies, 5
Result
   analogical reasoning, 136-137, 228
   conditions met/satisfied, 10-12, 50, 74, 91, 95, 98-100,
      105-106, 114, 163
   defined, 10
   global rule of law, 161, 166, 237, 267, 285
   legal rule, 9-10, 51, 100, 103-105
   not guaranteeing, 350
   predictive legal analysis, 8, 47, 149
   rule-based reasoning, 135
   synthesized rule proof, 304
Revising
   checklist questions, 360-362
   discussion section of memo, 75-76, 359-363
   email communication, 385
   labeling paragraphs, 362
   reverse outline technique, 362-363
   techniques, 362-363
Roadmaps
   cases, selection of, 278-279, 281
   common errors, 202-203
   date of decisions, 278-279
   discussion roadmap, 355
   drafting process, 195-203, 313-318
   global. See Global roadmaps
   headings in discussion, 355
   higher court decisions, 278-279
   issue. See Issue roadmaps
   multiple authority memorandum, 242, 313-318
   multiple vs. single authority memorandum, 313-314
   purpose of, 195
   single authority memorandum, 195-203, 313-314
Rule application
   analogical arguments in, 217-220, 228-234, 265,
      331-332, 335, 342-343
   "argument labeling" format, 227-228
   arguments in, 62, 65, 69, 74-76, 164-165, 167, 179-
      180, 187, 192, 207, 214, 217-223, 227-234, 241-
      242, 249, 265, 298, 308-311, 325, 328, 331-344
   cases, selection of, 274, 277, 281, 336
   changes in, with use of multiple
      authorities, 308-310, 332-334
   checklist, 165-166, 218
   citations, use of, 230
   components, 13, 69, 165-166, 179-180, 192, 218-221,
      309-310, 334-341
   content changes, 309-310
   conveying arguments, 219-220
   counter-arguments in, 69, 164-165, 167, 179-180, 192,
      218, 222-223, 227, 241, 286
   diagram, 207
   distinction, relevance of, 342
   drafting of, 217-234, 331-344
   editing, 364-365
   effective examples, 219-221, 342

effectiveness of arguments, 336-338
examples, 69, 71, 108-109, 190, 192-193, 219-220,
    223-226, 245, 247, 308-309, 339-344, 367-368
explaining relevance of analogy or distinction, 342
formatting the arguments, 227-228
formula for, 219-220
foundation for, 341-342
guiding factors, 121
implicit party/position format, 227-228
ineffective examples, 219-221, 342
issue-components approach. *See*
    Issue-components approach to organization
issue segment, 221, 331, 332
key components. *See* components, *this heading*
mini-predictions, 223-225
multiple authority memorandum, 242, 249, 298,
    308-310, 331-344
multiple paragraphs, 221, 226-227
no case debut in, 336
number of paragraphs to include, 221, 226-227
organization, 308-310, 338-342, 364
organization changes with use of multiple authorities,
    308-309, 332-334
outlines for organizational approaches, 226, 308-311,
    333-335, 337
overview, 65
party/position approach. *See* Party/position approach
    to organization
policy arguments, 219, 331, 335
prediction, 222-223
presenting arguments, 227-228
proximity, reasoning by, 229
purpose, 331
roadmap paragraphs, 13
rule-based arguments, 219-220, 233-234, 331, 335,
    342-343
rule-based vs. analogical arguments, 342-343
rule explanation, relationship to, 232-233
rule of law for the condition. *See* Rule of law for the
    condition
separate drafting of issue segments, 332
signals, use of, 230
single authority memorandum, 217-234, 308, 341
smaller scale organization, 221
starting with rule-based argument, 342-344
steps for writing predictive memo, 74-75
stylistic options, 227-228
synthesized rule, 333
templates, 165-166, 187, 219
topic sentences, 219-220, 227, 334-336, 339, 344
transitions, 227, 336, 339, 341
weaving facts to the rule, 220-221
Rule-based reasoning
    analogical reasoning combined, 143, 152-153,
        233-234
    examples, 136, 143, 151, 156, 219-220, 234, 336, 344
    key features, 143-145
    key language from rule, integration of, 143

overview, 12, 135-136, 141-143
policy-based vs., 158
in rule application section, 187, 207, 233-234, 241, 331
tethering facts to the rule, 143-144, 221
Rule explanation
    bridge between issue roadmap and rule application,
        205-207
    cases approach to organization, 305-308, 321, 324,
        327-328
    cases, selection of, 274, 277, 281, 320-321, 325, 328
    cautions, 214-215
    challenges in multiple authority memorandum,
        324-328
    changes in, with use of multiple authorities, 305-308
    checklist, 165, 206, 329
    components, 13, 69, 165, 178-180, 207, 210-212,
        320, 321
    context, 205-207
    diagram, 207
    drafting, 205-215, 319-329
    editing, 363-364
    examples, 69, 70, 189, 192-193, 206, 211-214, 244,
        246, 306-307, 321, 326
    framing sentences, 69, 165, 206-210, 242, 320-322,
        325, 328. *See also* Framing sentences
    guiding factors approach to organization, 305-308,
        324, 326-327
    holding, 165, 206, 210-211, 320
    issue roadmap, 205-207
    issue segments, 75, 206-207, 215, 266, 327
    mistakes made, 214-215
    multiple authority memorandum, 242, 249, 298,
        305-308, 319-329
    multiple paragraphs for each issue, 320
    multiple paragraphs using same authority, 212-214
    number of cases, 325
    organization using multiple authorities, 305-308, 321,
        324, 326-328
    other ingredients, 210-212
    outline, 311
    parade of cases, avoiding, 325, 328
    past tense, 211
    placement, 206-207
    purpose, 65, 319-320, 324-325, 328, 363-364
    reasoning, 165, 206, 211, 320
    rule application, relationship to, 232-233
    separate section for each issue, 320
    signals, use of, to include additional supporting cases,
        323-324
    single authority but multiple paragraphs, 212-214
    single authority memorandum, 205-215
    templates, 165, 187, 208-212
    tips, 325
    transitions, 212, 321-323, 325, 328
    variations, 212-214
    what it does, 205-206
Rule of law
    approach of lawyers to, 104-105

case briefs, 42
cases, role of, 89-93, 107-131
changes in, 90, 107
components, 95-100
conditions. See Conditions; Rule of law for the condition
elements vs. factors, 95-99, 105-106
emergent. See Emergent legal rule
examples, 11, 32, 104-105, 189, 191, 197, 400-401
exceptions, rule with, 99, 102
existing. See Existing legal rule
global. See Global rule of law
implicit vs. explicit guiding factors, 115-122. See also
     Guiding factors
incomplete rule of law, 89
interpretation of. See Interpretation of legal rule
issue. See Rule of law for the condition
key features, 95-100
layers, 91
multiple cases, emergent rules from, 93-94
outlining, 100-105
overview, 85-94
persuasive brief, 400-401
predictive memorandum, 400
processing by cases, 89-93, 107-109
result of rule. See Result
rule of law for the condition. See Rule of law for
     the condition
sources of law. See Sources of law
stare decisis, and changes in, 90, 107
synthesized. See Synthesizing rules of law
words used, guidance from, 99, 105
working with rules, 95-106
Rule of law for the condition
  analogical arguments, 149, 228
  cases, selection of, 266-271
  changes in, with use of multiple authorities, 298,
       308-309
  defined, 11, 74, 267
  definitions. See Definitions
  discerning, 269-271
  each condition, 91-92
  examples, 19, 144-145, 206, 267, 269-271, 289,
       291-292, 301-302, 308-309, 400-401
  fact-based holding vs., 202
  global rule vs., 10
  gloss, 19
  guiding factors. See Guiding factors
  issue roadmaps, 165, 205, 298
  multiple authority memorandum, 248, 302
  non-issue, 200
  refining, 269-271
  rule application section, 166, 218, 241, 308-309
  standards. See Standards
  synthesized. See Synthesizing rules of law
Rule proof
  defined, 165, 191, 193, 199-200, 202, 240
  examples, 69, 189, 191, 193, 200-202, 243, 245,
       304, 318

issue roadmap, 178-179, 186-187, 189, 199, 201, 240,
     242, 314. See also Issue roadmap
multiple authority memorandum, 249, 303-305
rule explanation, 205
synthesized, 290, 293, 301, 303-305, 316-318
templates, 186-187, 201
Rule synthesis. See Synthesizing rules of law
Ruling. See Holding

Sample memos
  annotated memo, 66-71
  multiple authority memos, 415-430
  single authority memos, 56-71, 403-414
Selecting authorities. See Cases, selection of
Sentence structure, 368, 377
Short answer
  editing checklist, 366
  examples, 56, 63, 65, 351, 403, 409, 415, 423
  objectives, 66, 350-351
  steps for writing predictive memo, 75
Signals. See also Citations
  examples, 292, 304, 317, 324, 326
  use of, 230, 242, 292, 304, 320, 323-324
Single authority memorandum
  checklist of ingredients, 166-167
  conclusion, 356
  content as appeared in discussion, 164-166
  content gathering, 163-168
  discussion section, 159-234. See also Discussion
       section
  drafting process, 183-234
  global roadmap, 195-199. See also Global roadmap
  issue roadmap, 199-203. See also Issue roadmap
  large-scale organization, 175-181, 298-300, 301
  pre-drafting analysis, 163-173, 237, 283-284. See also
       Pre-drafting analysis
  pre-drafting to drafting, 185-194
  roadmaps, 195-203, 313-314
  rule application, 217-234, 308, 341. See also Rule
       application
  rule explanation, 205-215
  sample memos, 56-71, 403-414
  worksheet approach to gathering content, 167-173
Skimming cases, 20-22, 29-30, 35, 39-40, 44
Small-scale organization. See also Issue-components
       approach to organization; Party/position
       approach to organization
  discussion section, 240-242, 248, 297, 345
  editing and revising, 345, 367
  issue segment, 298, 301-310
  multiple authority memorandum, 298, 301-310
  rule application paragraphs, 221, 341
Sources of law. See Authority
Spelling, 360, 368-369, 385, 390
Standard of review, 29
Standards. See also Definitions; Explicit guiding factors;
       Guiding factors

case modification of rule, 256
cases, selection of, 266
defined, 11, 110-112
definitions vs., 11, 110-112
examples, 19, 111-112, 116, 203, 268-269
gloss, 114
interpretation of existing legal rule, 110-112
issue components, 221-222
issue roadmaps, 68-69, 165, 178-179, 186-187, 192,
    199, 201, 240, 248, 316-317
law-centered interpretations, 125, 170, 172, 266,
    288, 291
objective, 111, 116
rule application, 221-222
rule explanation, 205
rule of law for the condition, 110-114, 129, 161,
    165-166, 172, 200-222, 237, 240, 248, 267, 285,
    289, 292, 335
subjective, 111
worksheets, 169-170, 172, 288-289, 291-292
Stare decisis
  generally, 4
  analogical reasoning, 147, 153
  binding/mandatory law, 87, 262
  changes in rule of law, 83, 90, 107, 110, 268
  defined, 48, 254
  policy-based reasoning and, 139
Statement of facts
  checking statement, 352
  citations, inappropriateness of, 353
  contextual facts, 351, 352
  editing checklist, 366
  email communication, 386
  examples, 56-58, 63, 65-68, 353-354, 403-405,
    409-410, 415-417, 423-424
  inappropriate items to include, 353
  legal arguments, inappropriateness of, 353
  legally significant facts, 351, 352
  organizational frameworks, 353
  past tense, 353
  persuasive writing, 399
  steps for writing predictive memo, 75
  stylistic considerations, 353
Statement of the issue, 348. See also Question presented
Statutes. See also Enacted law
  codes, 87, 483-484
  enacted law, 9, 77, 263
  examples, 108-109, 253, 263
  existing legal rule, 74, 253
  legislative history, 157
  policy-based reasoning, 155, 157
  primary authority, 483
  quotations, 375
  short answer, not cited in, 351
  sources of law, 86-87
Style of legal writing, 227-228, 371-374
Substantive law, 41
Synthesizing rules of law

additive process, 254
basics of rule synthesis, 252-255
cases, use of, 93-94, 252-263
confirmation of existing rule, 255-256
defined, 12, 251-252, 316
diagram of synthesis, 255
examples, 253-255, 269, 271, 289, 292, 302
existing legal rule vs., 252, 302
guiding factors, synthesis of, 256-262
inconsistent cases, 262-263
key facts from additional authorities, 259-260
legal context, 258-262
modification of existing rule, 256
non-legal context, 256-258
process of synthesis, 252-263
simultaneous vs. sequential synthesis, 257
steps for writing predictive memo, 74
template, 317
types of synthesis, 255-256
ways in which additional authority processes existing
    rule, 255-256
worksheets, 288-289, 291-292

Talking points
  content areas, 394-396
  deductive analysis, 395
  drafting of, 8, 393-396
  example, 395-396
  global rule of law, 394-395
  guidelines for development of, 393-395
  style, 395
  takeaways, 394, 396
Templates
  discussion section, 185-190, 242
  forms, 188
  global conclusion, 188
  global roadmap, 186, 196-197, 315
  issue roadmap, 186-187
  legal forms, 188
  rule application, 165-166, 187, 219
  rule explanation, 187
"Thinking like a lawyer," 15, 40-41
Topic sentences. See also Rule application
  editing by reviewing, 366-367
  email communication, 387
  examples, 219-220, 336, 344, 361, 366, 399
  objective, 399
  persuasive, 399
Topic/thesis statement, 343, 366. See also Topic sentences
Transitions
  commonly used, 322
  counter-arguments, 227
  editing lack of, 366
  email communications, 387
  examples, 126, 194, 322-323, 336, 339, 341
  issue roadmap, 179
  issue segment, 179, 322-323, 361
  rule application paragraphs, 222, 227, 339, 341

rule explanation paragraphs, 212, 242, 320-323, 325, 328-329
  topic sentence, 200

Under/does/when format, 66, 349. *See also* Question presented

Visual maps, 312

Work product, 384
Worksheets
  discussion section, 189-190
  pre-drafting using multiple authorities, 286-294
  pre-drafting using single authority, 167-173